Brittany & Normandy

THE ROUGH GUIDE

There are more than eighty Rough Guide titles covering
destinations from Amsterdam to Zimbabwe

Forthcoming titles include
China • Corfu • Jamaica • New Zealand • South Africa
Southwest USA • Vienna • Washington DC

Rough Guide Reference Series
Classical Music • Jazz • The Internet • World Music

Rough Guide Phrasebooks
Czech • French • German • Greek • Italian • Mexican Spanish
Polish • Portuguese • Spanish • Thai • Turkish • Vietnamese

Rough Guides on the Internet
http://www.roughguides.com/
http://www.hotwired.com.rough

Rough Guide Credits

Series editor:	Mark Ellingham
Text editor & typesetter:	Greg Ward
Editorial:	Martin Dunford, Jonathan Buckley, Jo Mead, Alison Cowan, Samantha Cook, Amanda Tomlin, Annie Shaw, Lemisse Al-Hafidh, Catherine McHale, Paul Gray, Vivienne Heller, Alan Spicer (Online UK), Andrew Rosenberg (Online US)
Production:	Susanne Hillen, Andy Hilliard, Melissa Flack, Judy Pang, Link Hall, Nicola Williamson, David Callier, Helen Ostick
Marketing & Publicity:	Richard Trillo, Simon Carloss (UK), Jean-Marie Kelly, Jeff Kaye (US)
Finance:	John Fisher, Celia Crowley, Catherine Gillespie
Administration:	Tania Hummel, Margo Daly

Thanks on this fourth edition go above all to Samantha Cook, for her company, support, and incisive wit.

I owe a great deal to the many people who have worked on this book over the years – Kate Baillie, who made extensive contributions to the original manuscript back in 1986; Don Grisbrook, who put in a lot of legwork to improve it all last time around; Raymond Travers, who has kept his finger on the pulse of Breton music; Susanne Hillen, who has been masterminding production since the old days; Deborah Jones, who provided some great illustrations (which I'm sure will return); Sam Kirby, who has drawn some excellent new maps and Pat Yale for proofreading this new edition; Toby Oliver of *Brittany Ferries*, who has given much-appreciated help; and Mark Ellingham, who has been providing constructive input and advice for ten years now.

Many thanks also to former colleagues at Rough Guides, including Jules Brown and Gail Jammy, and to the friends and family who have travelled with me or been kind enough to point out my deficiencies.
Four editions' worth of readers' letters have helped to make the book what it is, too; among those who sent much-valued suggestions and comments this time around were Judith and Damien Burke, Catherine C Delahay, Jim Dominy, Rebecca Ferguson, William Galloway and Susan Freedman, Sally MacLennan, Matt Parton, Graham Rhind, Andy Ryan, Lance Salway, NJ Shaw, Sue Starbury, and Ben Taylor. Thanks to all.

This fourth edition published 1995 by Rough Guides Ltd, 1 Mercer Street, London WC2H 9QJ.
Reprinted in June 1996.

Distributed by the Penguin Group:

Penguin Books, 27 Wrights Lane, London W8 5TZ
Penguin Books USA Inc, 375 Hudson Street, New York 10014, USA
Penguin Books Australia Ltd, 487 Maroondah Highway, PO Box 257, Ringwood, Victoria 3134, Australia
Penguin Books Canada Ltd, 10 Alcorn Avenue, Toronto, Ontario, Camada M4V 1E4
Penguin Books (NZ) Ltd, 182–190 Wairau Road, Auckland 10, New Zealand

Previous editions published by Harrap Columbus in 1987 and 1990, and by Rough Guides Ltd in 1992.
Rough Guides were formerly published as Real Guides in the United States and Canada.

Typeset in Linotron Univers and Century Old Style to an orginal design by Andrew Oliver.
Printed by Cox and Wyman, Reading, Berks.
Illustrations on p.1 and p.315 by Deborah Jones.
Incidental illustrations in Part One and Part Four by Ed Briant.

368pp includes index

A catalogue record for this book is available from the British Library.

ISBN -85828-126-1

Brittany & Normandy

THE ROUGH GUIDE

by

Greg Ward

THE ROUGH GUIDES

UPDATES: YOU CAN HELP

Each new edition of this book is based on thorough first-hand research of the entire region. However, if you do spot any detail which may have changed since publication – for example, restaurants and hotels come and go, opening hours change, and so on – or find anything which you feel should be included, we would be extremely glad to hear from you.

All future contributions will also be credited in print, and a copy of the next edition (or any other *Rough Guide* if you prefer) is the reward for the best letters. Please mark all letters "Rough Guide Brittany & Normandy update", and send to:

Rough Guides, 1 Mercer Street, London WC2H 9QJ
or Rough Guides, 375 Hudson Street, 3rd Floor, New York NY10014

CONTENTS

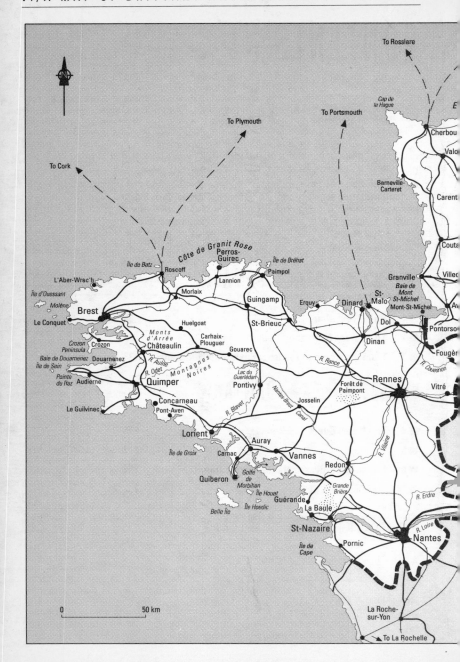

To Poole & Portsmouth

To Portsmouth

To Portsmouth, Rosslare & Cork

To Newhaven

To Boulogne

English Channel

Côte d'Albâtre

Le Tréport

St-Valéry-en-Caux

Dieppe

Barfleur

Fécamp

St-Vaast

Etretat

Le Havre

Caudebec

Rouen

Beauvais

D Day Beaches

Trouville
Deauville

Honfleur

Arromanches

Bayeux

Ouistreham

Cabourg

Pont Audemer

Les Andelys

BESSIN

St-Lô

Caen

Lisieux

Giverny

SUISSE NORMANDE

PAYS D'AUGE

Vernon

Evreux

River Seine

Paris

Vire

Falaise

Vimoutiers

Conches

Pont D'Ouilly

Argentan

River Orne

River Risle

Flers

Verneuil-sur-Avre

Dreux

Domfront

Bagnoles

Alençon

Mortagne

Chartres

Mayenne

Bellême

Laval

Le Mans

Orléans

Forêt de Berié

R. Loir

Angers

Blois

R. Loire

Tours

Poitiers

INTRODUCTION

The French nation is made up of strongly individual regions, but both **Brittany** and **Normandy** are among the most distinct. This sense of a separate identity – in cultures and peoples, landscapes and histories – is undoubtedly a major aspect of their appeal to visitors. A journey through the two regions enables you to experience much of the best that France has to offer: wild coast and sheltered white sand beaches; sparse heathland and dense forests; medieval ports and evidence of the prehistoric past; and, every bit as important, abundant seafood and (especially in Normandy) a compelling and exuberant cuisine.

Brittany

Brittany is the more popular of the two regions, with both French and foreign tourists. Its attractions lie most obviously along the **coast**, which, speckled with offshore islands and islets, makes up over a third of France's seaboard. In parts of the north, and in the western region of Finistère, it can be nothing but rocks and cliffs, its exposed headlands buffeted by the full force of the Atlantic and swept by dangerous currents. But elsewhere, especially in the southern resorts around the Morbihan and La Baule, it is the gentlest, most sheltered of seas, the sands rambling for miles or broken into coves between steep cliff headlands.

The sheer extent of the Breton coastline means that it's always possible to find a spot where you can walk alone with the elements. Although in high season it can be hard to find solitude on the sandy beaches or in the small bays with their sun-struck swimmers, there could never be enough visitors to cover all the twists of Finistère's coast. As well as exploring the mainland resorts and seaside villages – each of which, from ports the size of **St-Malo** or **Vannes** down to little-known harbour communities such as Erquy, Le Pouldu, L'Aber-W'rach or Piriac-sur-mer can be relied upon to offer at least one welcoming, characterful little hotel or restaurant – it's worth making the time to take in at least one of **the islands**. Boat trips out to these sea-encircled microcosms can be among the most enjoyable highlights of a trip to Brittany. The magical Île de Bréhat is just a ten-minute crossing from the north coast near Paimpol, while historic Belle-Île to the south is under an hour from Quiberon. Certain other islands are set aside as bird sanctuaries, while, off Finistère, the Îles d'Ouessant and Molène are as remote and strange as Orkney or the Shetland Isles.

The **Celtic** elements in Brittany are inextricably linked with its seafaring past. Anciently the land was known as *Armorica* (from the Breton for "the land of the sea", *ar-mor*), and it was from fishing and shipbuilding, along with occasional bouts of piracy and smuggling, that its people made their living. The harshness of the Breton coast and the poor communications with its interior and with "mainland" France enforced isolation. Christianity took time to establish itself, strongly but idiosyncratically, in a region where Druids survived on the Île de Sein until Roman times, and it was only in 1532 that the territory lost its independence and became a province of France. Even then it was a reluctant partner, treated virtually as a colony by the national government, who until well into this century felt it necessary to suppress the Breton language and traditions. Today, there is something of a reversal, with the **language** and **culture** being rediscovered and reasserted. If you are a Celt – Welsh, Scots or Irish – you will find shared words, and great appreciation in their use. For everyone, though, the traditions are active, accessible and enjoyable at the various Inter-Celtic **festivals**, the biggest of which takes place at Lorient in early August.

Times even before the Celts are evoked by the vast wealth of **megalithic remains** scattered across Brittany. The single most famous site is Carnac, where the spectacular alignments of menhirs are thought to have been erected as part of a prehistoric observatory. Lesser known but equally compelling remains include the extraordinary burial tumuli on the island of Gavrinis, in the gulf of Morbihan, and at Barnenez outside Morlaix in the north. Not all such relics are found near the sea; the moors and woodlands of **inland Brittany**, too, conceal unexpected ancient treasures. This is the realm of legend, with the **forests** of Huelgoat and Paimpont in particular, left-overs from Brittany's mythic dark ages, identified with the tales of Merlin, the Fisher King and the Holy Grail. In the Little Britain of King Arthur's domain, an other-worldly element still seems entrenched in the land and people.

Normandy

NORMANDY has a less harsh appearance and a more mainstream – and more prosperous – history. It too is a seaboard province, colonized by Norsemen from Scandinavia and colonizing in turn; first of all, in the eleventh and twelfth centuries, England, Sicily and parts of the Near East, and later on Canada. It has always had large-scale **ports**: Rouen, on the Seine, is as near as ships can get to Paris; Dieppe and Le Havre have important transatlantic trade. **Inland**, it is overwhelmingly agricultural – a wonderfully fertile belt of tranquil pastureland, where most visitors head straight for the restaurants of towns such as Vire and Conches.

The pleasures of Normandy are perhaps less intense and unique than those of Brittany. Many of its better-known areas of **seaside** are a little overdeveloped. The last of the Napoleons created towards the end of the last century a "Norman Riviera" around Trouville and Deauville, and a somewhat pretentious air still hangs about their elegant promenades. However, the ancient ports – **Honfleur** and **Barfleur** especially – are visual delights, and numerous seaside villages can still be found that remain unspoiled by crowds or affectations. Even if you just plan to visit for a weekend break from England, delightful little towns are tucked away within a dozen miles of each of the major Channel ports – the Cotentin peninsula around Cherbourg is one of the best, and least explored, areas – while along the Seine, too, there are several idyllic resorts.

Normandy also boasts extraordinary **architectural** treasures, although only the much-restored capital, **Rouen**, has preserved a complete medieval centre. The attractions are more often single buildings than entire towns. Most famous of all is the spectacular *merveille* on the island of **Mont-St-Michel**, but there are also the monasteries at Jumièges and Caen; the cathedrals of Bayeux and Coutances; and Richard the Lionheart's castle above the Seine at Les Andelys. Bayeux can in addition offer its vivid and astonishing **Tapestry**. Many other great Norman buildings survived into this century, only to be destroyed during the Allied landings in 1944 and the subsequent **Battle of Normandy**, which has its own legacy in a series of war museums, memorials and cemeteries. These are hardly conventional sights, though as part of the fabric of the province they are moving and enlightening.

Routes

Individual **highlights** are detailed in introductions to each of the specific chapter regions. Dictatorial itineraries aren't given – much of the fun in both provinces is in rambling off on side roads – but the text is structured as logically as possible in continuous routes or definable areas.

Ways to get around are set out on p.26. If you read this before deciding how to travel, think about **cycling**; both provinces are ideal, with short distances between each town and the next. Otherwise, a car is probably the best alternative. Unless you plan to stay within a limited area, public transport can be frustrating.

Climate and time of year

Every French town or district eagerly promotes a *"micro-climat"*, maintaining that some meteorological freak makes it milder or drier or more balmy than its neighbours. On the whole, however, the bulk of Normandy and Brittany follows a fairly set pattern. A genuine **summer**, more reliable than in Britain, begins around mid-June and lasts, in a good year, through to mid-October. **Spring** and **autumn** are mild but sporadically wet. If you come for a week in April or November, it could be spoilt by rain; a fortnight, however, should yield better luck – the rainy spells rarely last more than a couple of days. **Winter** is not too severe, though in western Brittany, especially, it can be damp and very misty on the coast.

Sea temperatures are not Mediterranean, and any greater warmth felt in the Channel waters off the Norman coast as opposed to the south of England is probably more psychological than real. The south coast of Brittany is a different matter – consistently warm through the summer months, with no need for you to brace yourself before going into the sea.

The other factor that may affect planning is the **tourist season**. On the coast, this gets going properly around July, reaches a peak during the first two weeks of August and then fades quite swiftly – but try to avoid the great *rentrée* at the end of the month, when the roads are jammed with cars returning to Paris. Inland, the season is less defined; highlights such as Monet's gardens at Giverny and parts of the Nantes–Brest canal can be crowded out in midsummer, but, in August at any rate, some smaller hotels close to enable their owners to take their own holidays at the seaside. Conversely, those seaside resorts that have grown up without really being attached to a genuine town take on a distinctly ghost-like appearance during the winter months – and are often entirely without facilities.

	April		May		June		July		August		Sept		Oct	
	Max °C	Hrs Sun	Max °C	Hrs Sun	Max °C	Hrs Sun	Max °C	Hrs Sun	Max °C	Hrs Sun	Max °C	Hrs Sun	Max °C	Hrs Sun
Brittany														
Brest	13	6.3	16	6.9	19	7.0	20	7.0	21	6.7	19	5.2	16	3.9
Carnac	13	7.3	15	7.8	18	8.5	19	8.5	20	8.1	18	6.6	15	4.7
St Brieuc	13	6.7	15	7.2	18	7.2	20	7.3	20	7.2	19	5.8	16	4.0
Normandy														
Caen	13	6.1	17	7.4	20	7.5	22	7.4	22	7.5	20	5.7	15	4.2
Cherbourg	12	6.0	15	7.3	18	7.1	19	7.2	20	7.2	18	5.5	15	3.7

CLIMATE CHART

PART ONE

THE

BASICS

GETTING THERE FROM BRITAIN

With the Channel Tunnel and the long-established ferry companies engaged in an all-out price war, there can never have been a better time for British holiday-makers to visit Brittany and Normandy.

The tunnel itself crosses the Channel well to the east of Normandy – at the Pas de Calais, the narrowest point – but its opening will no doubt transform tourism in the region. The ferry operators, *Brittany Ferries* in particular, are confident of maintaining their level of business; it simply seems likely that there will be more English travellers in northern France than ever before, especially in such accessible Norman cities as Rouen, and perhaps more long-distance commuters too.

FERRIES

The most direct route to Normandy or Brittany, for motorists, cyclists and pedestrians, is still to take a cross-Channel ferry to any of four Norman and two Breton ports; it is however slightly cheaper to go via Calais, Boulogne or Dunkerque. All these services are detailed in the box on p.5.

As the tunnel lurched towards full operation, ferry **fares** have come down enormously, with the various operators moving away from their emphasis on one-way fares to suggest all sorts of bargain return deals. So many special offers, seasonal and off-peak discounts and all-inclusive packages are now on offer that it is all but impossible to predict what you will actually be asked to pay; each specific sailing has its own price code. All the ferry companies carry **children** under four – and (*Irish Continental* excepted) **cycles** – free; children up to thirteen are normally charged half the adult fare. **Booking ahead** is strongly recommended for motorists, certainly in high season; passengers/cyclists can normally just turn up and board at any time of year.

Return fares for a car and two adults on *Brittany Ferries* sailings to Caen, Cherbourg, Roscoff or St-Malo range from £61 for three days in low season up to £310 for a month-long trip in midsummer; a pedestrian or cyclist can pay anything between £18 and £62 return. Flexibility is all, and there's no pressure to cross to and back from the same French port.

Any **travel agent** will have a variety of fares and brochures on offer. *AA* members who buy ferry tickets through a high-street *AA Shop* can get extra discounts on brochure prices.

THE CHANNEL TUNNEL

The **Channel Tunnel** has slashed travelling time by train from London to Lille and Paris, with *Eurostar* high-speed trains running from London Waterloo to Lille in two hours and Paris Gare du Nord in three hours. At the time of publication the service was limited to four or five trains a day to Paris and two to Lille, but the frequency can be expected to increase. Eventually there should be direct trains to cities such as Rouen, and through trains from other parts of the United Kingdom.

Tickets from London to Paris cost £155 return (standard), £195 (first class), or a non-refundable £95 (APEX fare) if booked 14 days in advance. Bookings can be made through high-street travel agents, by calling *Eurostar* direct (Mon–Sat 8am–8pm, Sun 8am–5pm; ☎01233/617575), or through *SNCF (French Railways)* in London, Glasgow or Manchester.

It's also possible to take your **car** across to France on the *Le Shuttle* service, which whisks through the Channel Tunnel in 35 minutes, to emerge at Sangatte, just outside Calais. The tunnel entrance is off the M20 at Junction 11A, just outside Folkestone. At the time of going to press, *Le Shuttle* were running one service every hour, day and night. You don't have to buy a

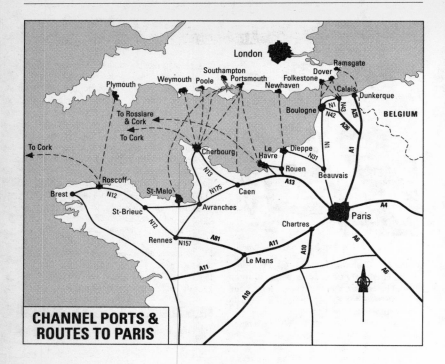

CHANNEL PORTS & ROUTES TO PARIS

ticket in advance. Inside the carriages, you can get out of your car to stretch your legs during the crossing. **Tickets** are available through *Le Shuttle*'s Customer Service Centre (☎01303/271100) or travel agents; fares are calculated per car, regardless of the number of passengers, with prices ranging from £49 for a day return, to £68 for a single, £75 for a 5-day return, and £136 for a standard return.

COMBINED TRAIN/FERRY ROUTES

Rail travellers can buy **connecting tickets** from any British station to any French station, via any of the ferry routes. Details and prices (again with special and seasonal offers) are obtainable from any *British Rail* travel centre. In London, the main booking office is at Victoria Station (see p.7).

For details of **rail passes** valid in Brittany and Normandy, including *EuroDomino*, *InterRail* and *Eurail* passes, see p.26 onwards.

To take advantage of combined **discount rail/ferry tickets**, you have a more limited choice. The main options are the under-26 *BIGE* tickets, marketed in Britain by *Eurotrain* which are valid for two months and can be used (along pre-specified routes) with unlimited stopovers. The routes, however, are geared to long-distance European travel and use only the main ferry crossings. To get to Brittany on a *BIGE* ticket you'd have to travel via Paris to Nantes or Rennes.

Incidentally, rail passengers catching ferries from **Portsmouth** should be warned that "Portsmouth Harbour" station is nowhere near the cross-Channel ferry terminals; there is a connecting bus service, but allow plenty of time.

BY COACH

You can get a *Eurolines* coach from any British town, via London, to **Caen**, **Cherbourg**, **Le Havre**, **Roscoff**, **Rouen** or **St-Malo**. Services are marketed by the *National Express* company, and tickets sold at regional coach terminals.

FERRIES FROM BRITAIN: ROUTES AND FREQUENCIES

	Operator	Crossing	Frequency
BRITTANY			
Portsmouth–St-Malo	*Brittany Ferries*	8hr 45min	mid-March to mid-Nov 1 nightly at 8.30pm; mid-Nov to mid-March Wed & Fri 8.30pm
Plymouth–Roscoff	*Brittany Ferries*	6hr	mid-April to mid-Sept 1–3 daily; mid-March to mid-April & mid-Sept to mid-Nov 1–2 daily; mid-Nov to mid-March Mon, Fri & Sun
NORMANDY			
Southampton–Cherbourg	*Stena Sealink*	6–10hr	1–2 daily all year
Portsmouth–Cherbourg	*P&O European Ferries*	4hr 45min	1–3 daily all year
Poole–Cherbourg	*Brittany Ferries*	4hr 15min	1–2 daily all year
Portsmouth–Caen	*Brittany Ferries*	6hr	2–3 daily all year
Portsmouth–Le Havre	*P&O European Ferries*	5hr 45min	2–3 daily all year
Newhaven–Dieppe	*Stena Sealink*	4hr	4 daily all year
PAS-DE-CALAIS			
Folkestone–Boulogne	*Hoverspeed*	55min	5 daily all year (*Seacat catamaran*)
Dover–Calais	*Stena Sealink*	1hr 30min	25 daily all year
Dover–Calais	*P&O European Ferries*	1hr 15min	20–25 daily all year
Dover–Calais	*Hoverspeed*	35–50min	20–24 daily all year (*Hovercraft and Seacat*)
Ramsgate–Dunkerque	*Sally Ferries*	2hr 30min	5 daily all year

Brittany Ferries
Wharf Rd, Portsmouth PO2 8RU ☎01705/827701
Millbay Docks, Plymouth PL1 3EW ☎01752/221321
Poole ☎01202/666466
24-hour brochure service ☎01752/269926

Hoverspeed
Maybrook House, Queen's Gardens,
Dover CT17 9UQ ☎01304/240101

P&O European Ferries
Channel House, Channel View Rd,
Dover CT17 9TJ ☎01304/203388

Continental Ferry Port, Mile End,
Portsmouth PO2 8QW ☎01705/827677
London ☎0181/575 8555

Sally Line
Argyle Centre, York St, Ramsgate,
Kent CT11 9DS ☎01843/595522
81 Piccadilly, London W1V 9HF ☎0181/858 1127

Stena Sealink Line
Charter House, Park St,
Ashford, Kent TN24 8EX ☎01233/647047
24-hour information, Dover ☎01304/240028

The **routes** are:

#112 London–Le Havre (2 daily, April–Dec only, 9hr, £37 return).

#113 London–Caen (1–2 daily, April to mid-Nov only, 11hr, £39 return).

#114 London–Cherbourg via Poole (1 daily mid-July to mid-Sept, 3–6 weekly mid-April to mid-July & mid-Sept to mid-Nov, 10hr, £41 return).

#115 London–Cherbourg via Portsmouth (1 daily, April–Dec only, 10hr overnight, £37 return).

#116 London–St-Malo (1 daily, April–Oct only, 13hr overnight, £45 return).

#118 London–Roscoff (1 daily April to mid-Sept, 2 weekly mid-Sept to mid-Nov, 13hr overnight, £59 return). In July & August, a connecting bus, #118A, leaves Roscoff each morning to Morlaix, Huelgoat, Quimper, Benodet, Lorient, Auray and Vannes.

#127 London–Rouen via Le Havre (1–2 daily, 13hr overnight, £59 return).

#127 Bristol–Rouen via Bath, Poole, Bournemouth,

Southampton, Portsmouth and Le Havre (1 daily mid-June to mid-Sept, otherwise 2–4 weekly, 18hr overnight, £71 return). Continuing service to Paris.

#179 London–Nantes via Calais, Tours and Angers (2 weekly, 15hr overnight, £87 return).

Discounts are available for young people; some fares are, however, subject to a surcharge during peak seasons.

BY AIR

There are flights from **London** to four Breton and four Norman airports. While they remain more expensive than the train/ferry or coach/ferry deals, for speed and convenience they make an attractive option for short breaks.

The **routes** are:

London (Gatwick)–Brest (Guipavas). 1hr 15min flight. 1–2 daily, all year. £170 APEX return, £145 weekend. *Brit Air.*

London (Gatwick)–Caen. 45min (direct), or 1hr 45min via Le Havre. Daily, all year. £135 APEX return, £120 weekend. *Brit Air.*

London (Gatwick)–Deauville. 45min. Daily, July–Aug; 2 weekly, rest of the year. £125 single fare only. *Lucas Aigle-Azur (Air France).*

London (Gatwick)–Le Havre. 45min. Daily, Mon–Fri only, all year. £135 APEX return, £120 weekend. *Brit Air.*

London (Gatwick)–Nantes. 1hr. Daily except Sat, all year. £185 return July–Sept, £158 Oct–June; max stay one month. *Air France.*

London (Gatwick)–Nantes. 1hr 25min. 1–2 daily, all year. £161 APEX return, £148 weekend. *Brit Air.*

London (Gatwick)–Nantes (via Rouen). 2hr. Daily, April–Oct; Mon–Fri only rest of the year. £190 single, youth standby £95 single, discount returns £185–210. *Air Vendée.* Also summer service (marketed by *Nouvelles Frontières*: see box) on *Corse Air.* Friday only, £140 return.

London (Gatwick)–Rennes. 1hr 40min (indirect, via Le Havre or Caen). 1–3 daily, March–Oct; 3 flights weekly in winter. £170 return, £145 weekend. *Brit Air.*

London (Gatwick)–Rouen. 45min. Daily, April–Oct. £145 for a single or discount return. *Air Vendée.*

Tickets and details for all the above can be obtained from *Air France* in London, from *Brit Air* or *Air Vendée* in Brittany, or major travel agents.

Cheaper flights are always available to Paris – an alternative point to fly to en route to Brittany or Normandy – and you might well want to consider the combined **air and rail** deals detailed in the box below.

Flying **from other parts of Britain**, several regional airports, including Glasgow, Manchester and Belfast, offer direct scheduled (and expen-

AIR AND RAIL

Air France, in conjunction with *SNCF*, the French state railway, offers very good-value deals whereby you can **fly direct to Paris** from any one of sixteen UK or Irish airports and then take a **train** on. You can buy a return ticket to any specific destination, or get a *EuroDomino* pass (see p.28), which entitles you either to three, five or ten days unlimited train travel within a one-month period.

The table below shows the cost of round-trip travel, including a return flight to Paris, to selected French cities, and of *EuroDomino* passes, from various UK and Irish airports. All prices are in sterling, and are for second-class rail travel. For further details contact any *Air France* or *SNCF* office.

	London	Birmingham	Edinburgh	Glasgow	Manchester
Brest	£161	£195	£243	£243	£210
Caen	£127	£161	£209	£209	£176
Granville	£140	£174	£222	£222	£189
Lisieux	£122	£156	£204	£204	£171
Nantes	£145	£179	£227	£227	£194
Quimper	£161	£195	£243	£243	£210
Rennes	£143	£177	£225	£225	£192
Rouen	£117	£157	£199	£199	£166
3-day pass	£209	£143	£291	£291	£258
5-day pass	£251	£285	£333	£333	£300
10-day pass	£323	£257	£405	£405	£372

USEFUL ADDRESSES IN BRITAIN

AIRLINES

Brit Air
239 Longbridge House, Gatwick North Terminal,
West Sussex RH6 0NP   ☎01293/502044
BP 156, Morlaix, Brittany 29204 ☎98.62.10.22
Rennes Airport, Brittany 35136 ☎99.29.60.11
Nantes Airport, Loire-At 44340 ☎40.84.82.59

Air France   ☎0181/742 6600
177 Piccadilly, London W1V OLX

Air Vendée   ☎51.62.31.65
Aéroport, La Roche-sur-Yon, Brittany 85000

British Airways   ☎0181/897 4000
156 Regent St, London W1R 5TA

British Midland   ☎0171/589 5599
Donington Hall, Castle Donington,
Derby DE4 2SB   or ☎01345/554554

RAIL AND COACH

British Rail   ☎0171/834 2345
Victoria Station, European Rail Enquiries

Eurolines, *National Express*,
Victoria Coach Station, 164 Buckingham Palace
Rd, London SW1W 97P   ☎0171/730 0202
23 Crawley Rd, Luton LU1 1HX   ☎01582/404511

Eurostar   ☎01233/617575
Waterloo Station, London SE1 8SE

Eurotrain   ☎0171/730 3402
52 Grosvenor Gardens, London SW1W 0AG

Le Shuttle   ☎01303/271100
PO Box 300, Folkestone, Kent CT19 4QW

SNCF (French Railways) and Eurostar
179 Piccadilly, London W1V 0VA
enquiries   ☎01891/515477
bookings   ☎0345/300003

Thomas Cook   ☎0171/499 4000
Head office: 45 Berkeley St, London W1A 1EB

Wasteels   ☎0171/834 7066
Platform 2, Victoria Station, London SW1V 1JT

SPECIALIST AGENCIES FOR INDEPENDENT TRAVEL

Campus Travel
52 Grosvenor Gdns,
London SW1W 0AG   ☎0171/730 8832
541 Bristol Rd, Bournbrook, Selly Oak,
Birmingham B29 6AU   ☎0121/414 1848
39 Queens Rd, Bristol BS8 1QE ☎0117/929 2494
5 Emmanuel St,
Cambridge CB1 1NE   ☎01223/324283
53 Forrest Rd, Edinburgh EH1 2QP ☎0131/225 6111
13 High St, Oxford OX1 4DB   ☎01865/242067
Branches at YHA shops and university campuses.

Council Travel   ☎0171/287 3337
28a Poland St, London W1V 3DB

Masterfare   ☎0171/259 2000
269 Old Brompton Rd, London SW5 9JA

Nouvelles Frontières   ☎0171/629 7772
11 Blenheim St, London W1Y 9LE

STA Travel
86 Old Brompton Rd, London SW7 3LH
117 Euston Rd, London NW1 2SX
   tele-sales ☎0171/937 9921
75 Deansgate, Manchester M3 2BW
   tele-sales ☎0161/834 0668
88 Vicar Lane, Leeds LS1 7JH
25 Queens Rd, Bristol BS8 1QE
38 Sidney St, Cambridge CB2 3HX
   tele-sales ☎01223/66966
36 George St, Oxford OX1 2BJ
Also on various university campuses.

South Coast Student Travel ☎01273/570226
61 Ditchling Rd, Brighton, E Sussex BN1 4SD

Trailfinders   ☎0171/937 5400
42–50 Earls Court Rd, London W8 6EJ

Note that addresses and telephone numbers may not be in the same location:
some airlines and agents use a single telephone-sales number for several offices.

sive) flights to Nantes. There are also **flights to Cherbourg** from **Bournemouth**, **Bristol** and **Exeter**, operated by *Air Camelot*: again contact the London *Air France* office for schedules.

If you don't mind stopping off in Jersey, you can also fly on *Jersey European Airways* to Dinard/St-Malo from **Bournemouth**, **Birmingham** or **Exeter**.

SPECIALIST TOURS AND PACKAGES FROM THE UK

Any travel agent can provide details of **package holidays** in Brittany and/or Normandy. Some are straightforward travel-plus-beach-hotel affairs, which, with a fixed base, can be frustrating. Others, such as the French Tourist Board *Gîtes de France* scheme (still the best for renting a cottage; see p.33), offer more flexibility, allowing you a combination of bases. Most packages include ferry crossings, or occasionally flights, in the deal, which means they can work out very good value.

In addition to this (necessarily abbreviated) listing of some of the main operators, most of the ferry companies (see p.5) offer their own accommodation packages. More complete lists are available from the **French Government Tourist Office**, 178 Piccadilly, London W1V OAL (☎0171/491 7622).

Access Travel   ☎01942/888844
16 Haweswater Ave, Astley M29 7BL
Specialists in holidays for people in wheelchairs; self-catering in *gîtes* from £165 per person per week, including ferry crossing.

Belle France   ☎0892/890885
Bayham Abbey, Lamberhurst, Kent TN3 8BG
Individually-tailored bicycle tours of Normandy, especially the region around Domfront. Prices start at £300 per person for a six-night trip, including ferry travel and accommodation in a succession of hotels around 15–20 miles apart; luggage is carried by van.

Blakes Boating Abroad   ☎01603/784131
Wroxham, Norwich NR12 8DH
Self-catering canal trips in Brittany, starting from Messac, between Rennes and Redon. High season rental rates range from £616 per week for a two-berth boat up to £1888 for a twelve-berth vessel, and there are plenty of extra costs on top of that.

Brittany Direct Holidays   ☎0181/641 6060
362–364 Sutton Common Rd, Sutton, Surrey SM3 9PL
A wide variety of holidays throughout Brittany and Normandy. *Chambre d'hôte* holidays cost from £210 per adult for a 9-night trip; self-catering accommodation, mostly in large houses, costs from £150 up to almost £400 each for two weeks in a group of four adults. They also have their own campsite at Île-Tudy in southern Finistère; a 12-night package for a family of four in June costs around £470. Specialist golfing holidays from £119 per person (in a party of four) for a two-night break in Caen.

Cycling for Softies   ☎0161/248 5131
2–4 Birch Polygon, Rusholme, Manchester M14 5HX
Easy-going cycle holiday operator. 7-day tours, including flight and accommodation, bicycle and back-up (but not luggage transfer) for around £700 per person.

French Country Cruises   ☎01572/821330
54 High St East, Uppingham LE1 9PZ
Self-drive canal-boat rental from Redon, April–Oct only. In summer the boats alone cost from just over £1000 for two people up to £2226 for eight.

Guide Dogs Adventure Group   ☎01734/835555
Hillfields, Burghfield, Reading RG7 3YG
Specialists in activity holidays for the visually impaired and unsighted. A week's tandem touring in Normandy for £339 per person with full-board.

Holt's Battlefield Tours   ☎01304/612248
15 Market St, Sandwich, Kent CT13 9DA
Definitive guided tours to famous battlefields, including 5- or 6-day tours of the D-Day Landing Beaches and associated sites for £429 or £535 respectively, and 3-day Dieppe trips for £255.

La France des Villages   ☎01449/737664
Model Farm, Rattlesden, Suffolk IP30 0SY
Off-the-beaten-track specialists, with a variety of villas and farmhouses and some very attractive *chambres d'hôte* in châteaux and farmhouses. Also golf, horse-riding, skiing and boating holidays.

Martin Randall Travel   ☎0181/742 3355
10 Barley Mow Passage, London W4 4PH
Art history tours from £690 for a 5-day Monet tour, including flights to Paris and accommodation.

Normandie Vacances   ☎01922/725705
113 Sutton Rd, Walsall, West Midlands WS5 3AG
Self-catering accommodation in 120 rural *gîtes* all over Normandy, costing up to £516 per adult for two weeks in high season, including ferry. Children free.

Vacances en Campagne   ☎01798/869411
Bignor, nr Pulborough, West Sussex RH20 1QD
A wide selection of properties for rent, up to and including positively luxurious (and expensive) châteaux. High standards, careful information and not cheap, but good value for money.

Vacances Franco-Brittaniques   ☎01242/240310
Normandy House, High St, Cheltenham, Glos GL50 3FB
Cottages all over Brittany and Normandy, especially southern Finistère. Prices, including ferry travel, for a two-week holiday for two range from £170–240 per person in the low season up to £250–320 in summer.

Velo Vacances   ☎0766/770167
ar Dy Feic, Blwch Post 6, Aberteifi, Dyfed SA43 1LN
Very enthusiastically organized cycle tours in West Brittany, including mountain-biking in the Monts d'Arrée. Prices vary from £325 for 10 days to £575 for 12 days in a hotel, and include travel, half-board accommodation, courier service and a baggage van.

Other operators you might wish to try, specializing in camping holidays, include:

Eurocamp   ☎01565/626262
Canvas Holidays   ☎0800/592895
Sunsites   ☎01565/625555

GETTING THERE FROM IRELAND

around IR£55–60 in low season and IR£80 in high season, while for two adults to cross one way with a small car costs between IR£210 and IR£290. In high season, motorists are strongly recommended to book in advance. Buying a return ticket brings significant savings; *Irish Ferries* offer 13-night excursion returns (10-night in July and Aug), while *Brittany Ferries* sell 3-, 7- and 11-day returns, and also offer all-inclusive deals on crossings from Cork to Swansea (daily service; 6hr) and then on to France on any of their Channel routes from England.

Both ferry companies also organize all-in **packages**, with a choice of accommodation in hotels, campsites or self-catering *gîtes*.

You can either contact the companies direct to reserve space in advance (essential at peak season if you're driving), or any competent travel agent at home or France can do it for you. Among those worth trying are *Joe Walsh Tours* (Dublin ☎01/678 9555, Belfast ☎01232/241144), *Thomas Cook* (Dublin ☎01/677 1721, Belfast ☎01232/240 833) and *USIT* (Dublin ☎01/778 117, Cork ☎021/270 900, Belfast ☎01232/242 562).

Much the cheapest way to get to Brittany or Normandy from Ireland – although unfortunately not available in winter – is by ferry from Cork or Rosslare (outside Wexford) to any of five ports along the northern French coast.

Ferry routes and operators are detailed in the box below. Although the exact **prices** vary according to the season and, for motorists, the size of car, not surprisingly *Irish Ferries* and *Brittany Ferries* charge very similar rates to each other. A one-way passenger fare is typically

BY AIR

Brit Air operate two – summer only – direct flights between Ireland and Brittany:

FERRIES FROM IRELAND: ROUTES AND FREQUENCIES

	Operator	Crossing Time	Frequency
Cork–Brest	*Irish Ferries*	15hr 30min	May–Sept 2 wkly
Cork–Cherbourg	*Irish Ferries*	17hr 30min	July–Sept 1 wkly
Cork–Le Havre	*Irish Ferries*	21hr 30min	May–Sept 2 wkly
Cork–Roscoff	*Brittany Ferries*	13–17hr	April–Oct 1–2 wkly
Cork–St-Malo	*Brittany Ferries*	18hr	April–Oct 1 wkly
Rosslare–Brest	*Irish Ferries*	15hr	May–Sept 2 wkly
Rosslare–Cherbourg	*Irish Ferries*	18hr	May–Sept 1–2 wkly
Rosslare–Le Havre	*Irish Ferries*	21hr	July–Sept 2–3 wkly

Brittany Ferries		**Irish Ferries**	
42 Grand Parade, Cork	☎021/277801	2–4 Merrion Row, Dublin 2	☎01/661 0511
		Cork	☎021/504333
		Rosslare	☎053/33158

Cork–Morlaix 2hr 15min flight. Weekly, June–Sept (Sat or Sun). IR£300 return. *Brit Air.*

Cork–Nantes (via Morlaix). 3hr 30min. Weekly, June–Sept (Sat or Sun). IR£330 return. *Brit Air.*

Details from *Brit Air* agents in Cork (☎021/961277) or Morlaix (☎98.62.10.22).

Otherwise, ***Air Inter*** (☎01/677 8899) and ***Aer Lingus*** (☎01/637 0011 or 01232/245151) fly direct from **Dublin** and **Cork** to Paris, with a return Apex fare of £182. Super Apex tickets on *Aer Lingus*, which have to be booked 7 days in advance for a stay including a Saturday night, can cost as little as IR£149 return. Alternatives via Britain are unlikely to be attractive, considering the additional time factor and the cost of a flight from Ireland to Britain. For up-to-date details on the situation, try contacting *USIT*, specialists in student/youth travel (see p.9).

There are no direct flights from **Belfast** to Paris, which makes a routing through London or Amsterdam the best option – special deals on airlines such as *British Airways* can bring the price as low as £75.

GETTING THERE FROM NORTH AMERICA

Getting to France from the US or Canada is straightforward. Paris, the only French transatlantic gateway, has direct flights from over thirty major North American cities. From there, it's simple to continue to Brittany or Normandy by air – a connecting flight to Brest for example, the remotest Breton city, costs an extra US$100 on *Air Inter*, *Air France*'s domestic arm – or by rail. Rouen is just over an hour away from Paris by train, while the new super-fast *TGV* service gets to either Rennes or Nantes in little more than two hours.

Nearly a dozen different scheduled airlines fly to Paris, making it one of the cheapest destinations in Europe – especially in these days of cut-throat inter-airline competition. In fact, only London can offer more discounted flights; and while a visit to England may appeal, the price difference is rarely sufficient to make a stopover in London a money-saving idea.

The least expensive way to take any of these scheduled flights is with a non-refundable **Apex** fare, which normally entails booking 21 days in advance of flying, travelling midweek, and staying for at least seven days. Apart from special offers, this is likely to be the best deal you'll get direct from an airline ticket counter.

The best guarantee of a cheap flight, however, is to contact a travel agent specializing in **discounted fares** (see p.12). The travel sections of the *New York Times, Washington Post,* and *Los Angeles Times* advertise them. Restrictions on such tickets are often not all that stringent; you need not assume that youth or student fares are the best bargain, nor worry if you're not eligible for them. The independent specialists *STA Travel* and *Council Travel* are reliable, but not surprisingly the French group *Nouvelles Frontières* has some good offers. These firms, together with several others, act as "consolidators" for particular airlines with which they maintain contracts to sell seats on specific terms, invariably below the airlines' own fares, though sometimes less conveniently.

Estimating the cost of **round-trip economy class fares** to Paris is tricky, especially as routes, carriers, and the state of the market are in a constant state of flux. The round-trip fares shown in the box below are a general guide to

SAMPLE ROUND-TRIP FARES TO PARIS

Typical lowest discounted fares in low season/high season, flying midweek. All prices are in US$ unless otherwise specified.

Atlanta: $600/$670	**Montréal**: CDN$680/$820
Boston: $570/$680	**New York**: $400/$520
Chicago: $590/$720	**Raleigh-Durham**: $600/$700
Cincinnati: $590/$730	**St Louis**: $650/$780
Dallas: $660/$780	**San Francisco**: $620/$840
Houston: $640/$760	**Toronto**: CDN$680/$820
Los Angeles: $500/$720	**Vancouver**: CDN$800/$1000
Miami: $600/$700	**Washington DC**: $520/$670

USEFUL ADDRESSES IN NORTH AMERICA

AIRLINES

Unless otherwise indicated, all the flights listed below are to Paris.

Air Canada call ☎1-800/555-1212
for local toll-free number
From Montréal, Toronto and Vancouver.

Air France ☎1-800/237-2747
From New York, Washington, Miami, Montréal, Toronto, Chicago, Houston, San Francisco and LA.

American Airlines ☎1-800/433-7300
From New York, Miami, Dallas-Fort Worth, Chicago and Raleigh-Durham.

British Airways US ☎1-800/247-9297
Canada ☎1-800/668-1080
Many North American cities to London, with connections to Paris.

Canadian Airlines ☎1-800/665-1177
From Montréal, Toronto and Vancouver.

Continental Airlines ☎1-800/231-0856
From Newark and Houston.

Delta Airlines ☎1-800/241-4141
From Atlanta, Cincinnati and New York.

Iceland Air ☎1-800/223-5500
From New York, Baltimore and Orlando, via Reykjavik.

KLM ☎1-800/374-7747
From many North American cities, via Amsterdam.

Northwest Airlines ☎1-800/225-2525
From Boston and Detroit .

PIA ☎1-800/221-2552
From New York.

Tower Air ☎1-800/221-2500
From New York.

TWA ☎1-800/892-4141
From New York, Boston, St Louis and Washington.

United Airlines ☎1-800/538-2929
From Washington, Chicago, LA and San Francisco.

US Air ☎1-800/428-4322
From Philadelphia.

Virgin Atlantic Airways ☎1-800/862-8621
New York, Boston, Miami and Orlando to London.

DISCOUNT AGENTS, CONSOLIDATORS AND TRAVEL CLUBS

Council Travel ☎1-800/743-1823
Main office: 205 E 42nd St, New York, NY 10017
US student travel organization with branches (among many others) in San Francisco, Washington DC, Boston, Austin, Seattle, Chicago and Minneapolis.

New Frontiers/Nouvelles Frontières
12 E 33rd St, ☎1-800/366-6387
New York, NY 10016
1001 Sherbrook East, ☎514/526-8444
Suite 720, Montréal, H2L 1L3
French discount travel firm, which also markets charters to Paris and Lyons. Other branches in LA, San Francisco and Québec City.

STA Travel ☎1-800/777-0112
Main office: 48 East 11th St, New York, NY 10003
Worldwide specialist in independent travel with branches in the LA, San Francisco and Boston areas, as well as French branches in Paris and Grénoble.

Travel Cuts ☎416/979-2406
Main office: 187 College St, Toronto, ON M5T 1P7
Canadian student travel organization with branches all over the country.

Interworld Travel ☎305/443-4929
800 Douglass Rd, Miami, FL 33134
Consolidator.

Travac ☎1-800/872-8800
Main office: 989 6th Ave, New York NY 10018
Consolidator; branch in Orlando.

Unitravel ☎1-800/325-2222
1177 N Warson Rd, St Louis, MO 63132
Consolidator.

Discount Travel Int'l ☎1-800/334-9294
Ives Bldg, 114 Forrest Ave,
Suite 205, Narberth, PA 19072
Discount travel club.

Encore Travel Club ☎1-800/444-9800
4501 Forbes Blvd, Lanham, MD 20706
Discount travel club.

Moment's Notice ☎212/486-0503
425 Madison Ave, New York, NY 10017
Discount travel club.

Travelers Advantage ☎1-800/548-1116
3033 S Parker Rd, Suite 900, Aurora, CO 80014
Discount travel club.

Worldwide Discount ☎305/534-2082
1674 Meridian Ave, Miami Beach, FL 33139
Discount travel club.

what you might expect to pay; startling variations are due to specific airlines engaging in price wars on specific routes. Fares are dependent on **season**, and are highest from around early June to the end of August, when everyone wants to travel; they drop during the "shoulder" seasons, September to October and April to May, and you'll get the best deals during the low season, November through March (excluding Christmas). Note that Friday, Saturday and Sunday travel tends to carry a premium. One-way fares are generally slightly more than half the round-trip.

Charter flights (a flight chartered by a tour operator from an airline to ferry tourists) can be even cheaper than these prices for scheduled services. But while discounted scheduled services sometimes carry eligibility restrictions, charter flights hedge you in with restricted dates and major financial penalties if you cancel. They're worth considering if you're very organized and know exactly what you plan to do. Most agents sell them.

If you're prepared to travel light at short notice and for a short duration it might be worth getting a **courier flight**. Now Voyager (☎212/431 1616) arranges such flights to Europe from JFK, Newark, and Houston. Flights (from about $400 round trip) are issued on a first-come, first-served basis, and there's no guarantee that the Paris route will be available at the specific time you want.

FLIGHTS FROM THE US

The most comprehensive range of flights from the US is offered by **Air France**, the French national carrier, which flies non-stop to Charles de Gaulle airport from Anchorage, Boston, Chicago, Houston, Los Angeles, Miami, New York (JFK and Newark), and Washington DC – in most instances daily. Air France tends to be expensive, however.

The **major American competitors** tend to be cheaper, but offer fewer non-stop routes. American and TWA have the biggest range of "direct" routes. The former flies to Paris Orly non-stop from Chicago, Dallas, and New York (JFK and Raleigh-Durham), or with a stop from LA (via Dallas), San Francisco (via Chicago), and San Diego (via JFK) and has good or guaranteed connections from 14 cities in the south and west. TWA flies non-stop to Paris Charles de Gaulle from Boston, New York, St Louis, and Washington DC, and has one-stop flights from Chicago and LA and guaranteed connections (same flight number)

from Atlanta, Kansas City, Portland, San Francisco, and Seattle.

Delta flies non-stop to Paris Orly from Atlanta and Cincinnatti with good or guaranteed connections from over a dozen southern and western cities.

United flies daily non-stop to Paris Charles de Gaulle from Chicago and Washington DC.

Tower Air has direct flights from New York to Paris.

US Air features a direct Philadelphia–Paris routing.

Continental flies daily non-stop from New York (Newark) to Paris Orly and also has direct flights (with a stop or same-number flight change) from Boston, Denver, Houston, LA, and Washington.

Northwest flies daily, direct LA–Detroit–Paris Charles de Gaulle.

Lastly, there are twice-weekly direct flights (often cheap) with **PIA Pakistan International** from New York to Paris Orly.

FLIGHTS FROM CANADA

The strong links between France and Québec's Francophone community ensure regular air services from Canada to Paris. The main route is Vancouver–Toronto–Montréal–Paris Charles de Gaulle. Most departures originate in Toronto, however, with **Air France** flying almost daily from Toronto to Charles de Gaulle, either non-stop or via Montréal. **Air Canada** and **Canadian Airlines** fly direct to Paris from Toronto and Montréal, again pretty well daily, and Canadian Airlines flies in from Vancouver twice weekly to guarantee the connection to Paris.

Travel Cuts and **Nouvelles Frontières** are the most likely sources of good-value discounted seats; call for details as flights vary from season to season.

FLYING VIA THE UK

Although **flying to London** is usually the cheapest way of reaching Europe, price differences these days are minimal enough for there to be little point travelling to France via London unless you've specifically chosen to visit the UK as well. Having said that, you may well be able to pick up a flight to London at an advantageous rate.

In recent years, **Virgin Atlantic** has offered some of the best fares from New York and Newark; and has now added flights from Miami,

Orlando, and Boston to its schedules (all into London Gatwick).

British Airways has entered the fray with a series of rival offers. In summer, the savings are bound to be less, but shop around as there may yet be some European bargains. As well as from JFK and Newark, *British Airways* has regular non-stop flights from Philadelphia, Boston, San Francisco, and Los Angeles – and Detroit via Montréal.

PACKAGE TOURS

Dozens of tour operators specialize in travel to France. Many can put together very **flexible** **deals**, sometimes amounting to no more than a flight and accommodation; if you're planning to travel in moderate or luxury style, or if your trip is geared around special interests, such packages can work out cheaper than the same arrangements made on arrival.

Although a tour is almost certainly more confining than independent travel, it can help you make the most of your time if you're on a tight schedule.

The accompanying box mentions a few of the possibilities, and a travel agent will be able to point out others (remember, bookings made through a travel agent cost no more than going through the tour operator).

TOUR OPERATORS IN NORTH AMERICA

Abercrombie & Kent   ☎1-800/323-7308
1520 Kensington Rd, Oak Brook, IL
De luxe hiking, biking, rail, and canal journeys.

Backroads   ☎1-800/462-2848
1516 Fifth St, Suite L101, Berkeley, CA 94710
Trendy bike tours.

CBT Bicycle Tours   ☎1-800/736-BIKE
415 W Fullerton, #1003, Chicago, IL 60614
European bike tours.

Contiki Tours   ☎1-800/CONTIKI
300 Plaza Alicante, #900, Garden Grove, CA 92640
European vacations for under-35s.

ETT Tours   ☎1-800/551-2085
198 Boston Post Rd, Mamaroneck, NY 10543
Independent tours.

Euro-Bike Tours   ☎1-800/321-6060
PO Box 990, DeKalb, IL 60115
Luxury bike tours.

The French Experience   ☎1-800/28-FRANCE
370 Lexington Ave, Suite 812,
New York, NY 10017
Self-drive tours, and apartment and cottage rentals.

Interhome   ☎201/882-6864
124 Little Falls Rd, Fairfield, NJ 07004
Short-term villa and château rentals.

International Study Tours   ☎1-800/833-2111
225 W 34th St, New York, NY 10122
Culture/art tours.

Nouvelles Frontières   ☎1-800/366-6387
12 E 33rd St, New York, NY 10016
À la carte accommodations.

Vacances en Campagne   ☎1-800/327-6097
PO Box 299, Elkton, VA 22827
Short-term rentals of châteaux and country houses.

GETTING THERE FROM AUSTRALASIA

Fares to major French cities **from Australia** are "common rated" to the same price. The **discount agents** listed below should be able to get you at least ten percent off the following low-season published fares: *Garuda International* (via Bali, Jakarta, Singapore or Bangkok, Abu Dhabi, with two stopovers allowed each way) $1685 to Paris; *Air France* (to 87 destinations within France, including Rouen, Rennes, Nantes and Brest); *British Airways* (via London); *KLM* (Amsterdam); *Lufthansa/Lauda* (Frankfurt); *Alltalia/Qantas* (Rome); *JAL* (overnight in Tokyo), $2199; *Aeroflot* (via Moscow to Paris), $1700; *Thai International*

(Bangkok), $2055; or *Malaysia* (via Kuala Lumpur), $2099.

Airpasses, coupons, and discounts on further flights within Europe vary with airlines, but the basic rules are that they must be pre-booked with the main ticket, are valid for three months, and are available only with a return fare with the one airline – for example, you have to fly to France with *British Airways* alone to be eligible for their airpass deals. *Air France* offers a **Euroflyer** for use in France and Europe at $100 each flight; *British Airways* have a zone system, charging $103 for each flight within France. Both airlines also arrange **fly-drive packages**; check with an agent for current deals as prices are very variable. *KLM*'s **Passport to Europe** uses coupons for single flights: 3 coupons for US$405, up to 6 for US$710; *Lufthansa* start at US$375 for three coupons, with extra flights US$105 each, to a maximum of nine.

The best deals to France **from New Zealand** are (discounted): *Japanese Airlines* (NZ$2200, overnight stop in Tokyo), *Garuda* (NZ$2249), and *Thai International* and *Malaysian Airlines* (NZ$2295). For **stopovers** in Europe, *British Airways* charge NZ$2399 via London; *Qantas-Al Italia* are slightly less at NZ$2295 via Rome and London. If you want to make **side trips** within Europe, *Qantas-Lufthansa* have a 4-coupon deal on a six-month fare for NZ$2600.

AIRLINES IN AUSTRALIA AND NEW ZEALAND			
Aeroflot		**JAL** (New Zealand)	
388 George St, Sydney	☎02/233 7911	120 Albert St, Auckland	☎09/379 9906
Air France		**KLM**	
12 Castlereagh St, Sydney	☎02/233 3277	5 Elizabeth St, Sydney	☎ 0800/222 747
57 Fort St, Auckland	☎09/303 1229	**Lufthansa/Air Lauda**	
Alitalia		143 Macquarie St, Sydney	☎02/367 3800
32 Bridge St, Sydney	☎02/247 1308	109 Queen St, Auckland	☎09/303 1520
Floor 6, 229 Queen St, Auckland	☎09/379 4457	**Malaysian Airlines**	
British Airways		388 George St, Sydney	☎0800/269 998
64 Castlereagh St, Sydney	☎02/258 3300	12–26 Swanson St, Auckland	☎09/373 2741
cnr Queen and Customs, Auckland	☎09/367 7500	**Qantas**	
Garuda		Jamison St, Sydney	☎02/957 0111
175 Clarence St, Sydney	☎02/334 9900	154 Queen St, Auckland	☎09/303 2506
120 Albert St, Auckland	☎09/366 1855	**Thai International**	
JAL (Australia)		75–77 Pitt St, Sydney	☎0800/422 020
201 Sussex St, Sydney	☎02/283 1111	22 Fanshawe St, Auckland	☎09/377 0268

SPECIALIST AGENTS IN AUSTRALASIA

AUSTRALIA

Anywhere Travel ☎02/663 0411
345 Anzac Parade, Kingsford, Sydney

Brisbane Discount Travel ☎07/229 9211
360 Queen St, Brisbane

Discount Travel Specialists ☎09/221 1400
Shop 53, Forrest Chase, Perth

Flight Centres
Circular Quay, Sydney ☎02/241 2422
Bourke St, Melbourne ☎03/650 2899
plus other branches nationwide

France Accommodation ☎03/877 6066
47 North Blackburn Square, Blackburn, Melbourne

France and Travel ☎03/670 7253
55 Hardware St, Melbourne

France Unlimited ☎03/650 9892
232 Flinders St, Melbourne

French and International Travel ☎02/299 8696
383 George St, Sydney

French Bike Tours ☎03/531 8787
16 Goldsmith St, Elwood, Melbourne

French Cottages and Travel ☎03/859 4944
674 High St, East Kew, Melbourne

French Tourist Bureau ☎02/231 5244
12 Castlereagh St, Sydney

French Travel Connection ☎02/956 5884
90 Mount St, Sydney

Passport Travel ☎03/824 7183
320b Glenferrie Rd, Malvern, Melbourne

Renault Eurodrive
cnr Jamieson and York, Sydney ☎02/299 3344
branches in other state capitals

STA Travel
732 Harris St, Ultimo, Sydney ☎02/212 1255
256 Flinders St, Melbourne ☎03/347 4711
other offices in Townsville and state capitals

Topdeck Travel ☎08/410 1110
45 Grenfell St, Adelaide

Tymtro Travel ☎02/411 1222
Suite G12, Wallaceway Shopping Centre,
Chatswood, Sydney

NEW ZEALAND

Budget Travel ☎09/309 4313
PO Box 505, Auckland

Flight Centres
205–225 Queen St, Auckland ☎09/309 6171
152 Hereford St, Christchurch ☎09/379 7145
50–52 Willis St, Wellington ☎04/472 8101
other branches countrywide

STA Travel
10 High St, Auckland ☎09/309 9995
233 Cuba St, Wellington ☎04/385 0561
223 High St, Christchurch ☎03/379 9098
*other offices in Dunedin, Palmerston North and
Hamilton*

RED TAPE AND VISAS

All other passport holders (including British Travel Document holders, Australians and New Zealanders) must obtain a visa **before arrival in France**. Obtaining a visa from your nearest French consulate is fairly automatic, but check their hours before turning up, and leave plenty of time, since there are often queues (which can get particularly long in London in the summer).

Three types of **visa** are issued: a transit visa, valid for two months; a short-stay (*court séjour*) visa, valid for ninety days after the date of issue and good for multiple entries; and a long-stay (*long séjour*) visa, which allows for multiple stays of ninety days over three years, but is issued only after an examination of an individual's circumstances. EU citizens (or other non-visa citizens) who stay **longer than three months** are officially supposed to apply for a *Carte de Séjour*, for which you'll have to show proof of income at least equal to the minimum wage. However, EU passports are rarely stamped, so there is no evidence of how long you've been in the country. If your passport does get stamped, you can cross the border to a neighbouring country, and re-enter for another ninety days legitimately.

Citizens of EU countries, Japan, Canada and the United States do not need any sort of visa to enter France for a tourist stay of up to ninety days. British citizens can for the moment use the British Visitor's Passport and the Excursion Pass (for day trips), both obtainable over the counter at post offices, as well as ordinary passports.

FRENCH EMBASSIES AND CONSULATES OVERSEAS

AUSTRALIA
492 St Kilda Rd, Melbourne, Vic 3001 ☎03/820 0921
31 Market St, Sydney, NSW 2000 ☎02/261 5779

CANADA
Embassy: 2 Elysée, pl Bonaventure,
Montréal, QUE H5A 1B1 ☎514/878 4381– 87
Consulates:
130 Bloor St W, Suite 400,
Toronto, ONT M5S 1N5 ☎416/925 80441
1201-736 Granville St,
Vancouver, BC V6Z 1H9 ☎604/681 2301

IRELAND
36 Ailesbury Rd, Dublin 4 ☎01/694777

NETHERLANDS
Vijzelgracht 2, Amsterdam ☎20/624 8346

NEW ZEALAND
1 Willeston St, PO Box 1695, Wellington ☎04/720200

SWEDEN
Narvavägen 28, Stockholm 115–23 ☎08/63685

UK
French Consulate General (Visas Section),
1 Cromwell Pl, London SW7 ☎0171/581 5292
7–11 Randolph Crescent, Edinburgh ☎0131/ 225 7954

USA
Embassy: 4101/Reservoir Rd NW,
Washington DC 20007 ☎202/944-6000
Consulates:
3 Commonwealth Ave,
Boston MA 02116 ☎617/266 1680
737 North Michigan Ave, Olympia Centre,
Suite 2020, Chicago, IL 60611 ☎312/787 5359
10990 Wilshire Blvd, Suite 300,
Los Angeles, CA 90024 ☎310/479 4426
934 Fifth Ave, New York, NY 10021 ☎212/606 3621
540 Bush St, San Francisco, CA 94108 ☎415/397-4330

CUSTOMS

Customs and duty-free restrictions vary throughout Europe, with subtle variations even within the European Union.

However, since the inauguration of the EU Single Market, travellers entering Britain from another EU country do not have to make a declaration to Customs at their place of entry. You can effectively bring in as much duty-paid wine or beer as you can carry (the legal limits being 90 litres of wine or 110 of beer, which has to be for your own use and not for resale), though there are still restrictions on the volume of tax- or duty-free goods you can bring into the country. The current duty-free allowance for EU citizens is 200 cigarettes, one litre of spirits and five litres of wine; for non-EU residents the allowances are usually 200 cigarettes, one litre of spirits and two litres of wine.

Residents of the USA and Canada can take up to 200 cigarettes and one litre of alcohol home, as can **Australian** citizens, while **New Zealanders** can take 200 cigarettes, 4.5 litres of beer or wine, and just over one litre of spirits.

HEALTH AND INSURANCE

No visitor to France requires vaccinations of any kind, and general health care in the country is of the highest standard. Citizens of all EU and Scandinavian countries are entitled to take advantage of French health services under the same terms as residents, if they have the correct documentation. British citizens need form E111, available from post offices, or in France from offices of the health authorities, the Caisse Primaire d'Assurance Maladie (CPAM). North American and other non-EU citizens have to pay for most medical attention and are strongly advised to take out some form of travel insurance.

MEDICAL TREATMENT

Under the French Social Security system, every hospital visit, doctor's consultation and prescribed medicine is charged (though not upfront in an emergency). Although all employed French people are entitled to a refund of 75–80 percent of their medical expenses, this can still leave a hefty shortfall, especially after a stay in hospital (accident victims have to pay even for the ambulance that takes them there).

To find a **doctor**, stop at any *pharmacie* and ask for an address. Consultation fees for a visit should be around 75–85F, and in any case you'll be given a *Feuille de Soins* (Statement of Treatment) for later documentation of insurance claims. Prescriptions should be taken to a *pharmacie* which is also equipped – and obliged – to

give first aid (for a fee). The medicines you buy will have little stickers (*vignettes*) attached to them, which EU travellers should remove and stick to their *Feuille de Soins* together with the prescription itself. A refund of 40–80 percent, depending on the kind of medicines, is payable in due course.

As getting a refund entails a complicated bureaucratic procedure, a better idea is to take out ordinary **travel insurance**, which generally allows full reimbursement, less the first few pounds of every claim.

In serious **emergencies** you will always be admitted to the **local hospital** (*Centre Hospitalier*), whether under your own power or by ambulance.

TRAVEL INSURANCE

Travel insurance policies usually cover such expenses as the consequences of charter companies going bankrupt, or delayed or lost baggage, as well as sundry illnesses and accidents. The major difference between the standard policies sold in Britain and in North America is that British ones usually include a significant element of protection against theft or damage, while North American policies apply only to items lost from, or damaged in, the custody of an identifiable, responsible third party – hotel porter, airline, luggage consignment, etc. Note that very few insurers will arrange on-the-spot payments in the event of a major expense or loss; you will usually be reimbursed only after going home.

Remember that claims can only be dealt with if a report is made to the local police within 24 hours and a copy of the report (*constat de vol*) sent with the claim; addresses of the Commisariat de police are given in the main towns and cities).

BRITISH AND IRISH INSURANCE

In **Britain** and **Ireland**, travel insurance schemes to cover medical expenses and theft or loss are sold by all travel agents and banks, from around £45 a month: *ISIS* policies, from *STA Travel* or

For more details of what to do in a medical or other emergency, see p.48.

branches of *Endsleigh Insurance*, are usually good value (see p.7). Read the small print before signing up to see what is covered, although most are broadly similar. It is common for money and credit cards to be covered only if they are stolen from your person. If you have any other insurance policies – house and contents insurance, for example – you'll find some of the optional extra cover in travel insurance only duplicates what you already have at home.

NORTH AMERICAN INSURANCE

In the **US and Canada**, insurance tends to be much more expensive, and may be medical cover only. Before buying a policy, check that you're not already covered by existing insurance plans. **Canadians** are usually covered by their provincial health plans; holders of **ISIC cards** and some other student/teacher/youth cards are entitled to accident coverage and hospital in-patient benefits for the period during which the card is valid. **Students** will often find that their student health coverage extends during the vacations and for one term beyond the date of last enrolment. Bank and charge **accounts** (particularly *American Express*) often include some insurance cover on items paid for with the card – travel facilities, accommodation, tours. **Homeowners' or renters'** insurance often covers theft or loss of documents, money and vaulables while overseas, though exact conditions vary from company to company.

TRAVEL INSURANCE IN AUSTRALIA

In **Australia**, *CIC Insurance*, offered by *Cover-More Insurance Services*, Level 9, 32 Walker St, North Sydney (☎02/202 8000) – with some branches also in Victoria and Queensland – has some of the widest cover available and can be arranged through most travel agents. It costs from AUS$140 for 31 days. As with all policies, make sure that you are covered for any activities you might be planning, especially if you are hiking or skiing.

DISABLED TRAVELLERS

France has no exceptional record for providing facilities for disabled travellers, but information is available. In the major cities and coastal resorts there are accessible hotels, and ramps or other forms of access are gradually being added to museums and other sites. The French minister appointed to oversee disability issues is himself disabled, and a number of national organizations provide a national information network: APF, the French paraplegic organization, has regional branches in most *départements*.

Public transport is certainly not wheelchair-friendly, and although many train stations now have ramps to enable wheelchair-users to board and descend from carriages, at others it is still up to the guards to carry the chair. At the time of writing, much your best chance of renting a car with hand controls is through **ITS** in Paris, at 11 bd Auguste-Blanqui, 13e (☎45.88.52.37).

An extensive English-language survey of facilities in Brittany, the *Access Guide to Brittany*, is still available from the *Pauline Hephaistos Survey Project* (39 Bradley Gardens, London W13). Most of the specific information in the guide is very out of date, though the accounts of the ease of movement around individual towns remain valid.

In Britain, both the *Holiday Care Service* and *RADAR* have lists of accessible **accommodation**; most of the cross-Channel ferry companies offer good facilities, though up-to-date information about access is difficult to get hold of. In France, the tourist offices in most big towns have a free booklet *Touristes quand même!*, which provides useful information on accommodation, transport, accessibility of public places and aids such as buzzer signals on pedestrian crossings.

As far as **airlines** go, *British Airways* has a better-than-average record for treatment of disabled passengers, and from North America, *Virgin* and *Air Canada* come out tops in terms of disability awareness (and seating arrangements) and might be worth contacting first for any information they can provide.

For more information, plus first-hand accounts by disabled travellers to France, see the *Rough Guide* special *Able to Travel/Nothing Ventured*, and contact the organizations below. Two British-based tour operators specializing in travel for the disabled are listed in the box on p.8.

TRAVEL WITH A DISABILITY: USEFUL CONTACTS

APF ☎44.16.83.83
(*Association des Paralysés de France*)
22 rue Père-Guerain, Paris 13e
A national organization with regional offices all over France; useful information and lists of new and accessible accommodation. Their guide Où ferons-nous étape *is available at the office for 70F or by post to a French address for 100F.*

CNFLRH ☎45.48.90.13
(*Comité National Français de Liaison pour la Réadaptation des Handicapés*)
38 bd Raspail, 75009 Paris
Information service for disabled travellers; details of accessible accommodation, holiday centres etc, and various useful guides.

Holiday Care Service ☎01293/774535
2 Old Bank Chambers, Station Rd,
Horley, Surrey RH6 9HW
Information on all aspects of travel.

Kéroul ☎514/2523104
4545 av Pierre de Coubertin,
CP 1000, Montréal, PQ H1V 3R2
Specializes in travel for mobility-impaired people.

Mobility International USA ☎503/343 1248
PO Box 3551, Eugene, OR 97403
Information, access guides, tours and exchanges.

RADAR ☎0171/250 3222
12 City Forum, 250 City Road,
London EC1V 8AF   Minicom ☎0171/637 5315
Information on travelling with a disability.

Travel Information Center ☎215/329 5715
Moss Rehabilitation Hospital,
1200 W Tabor Rd, Philadelphia, PA 19141
Write for access information.

TRIPSCOPE ☎0181/994 9294
63 Esmond Rd, London W4 1JE
Phone-in travel information and advice service.

INFORMATION AND MAPS

In France itself you'll find a tourist information centre – *Syndicat d'Initiative* (**SI**), or *Office du Tourisme* as it is sometimes called – in practically every town and many villages (SI addresses, and in more important cases their opening hours, are detailed in the guide). From the SIs you can get free town plans, and specific local information such as listings of hotels, restaurants, leisure activities, bike rental, launderettes and countless other things. Many SIs also publish car and walking itineraries for their areas. They are often also willing to give advice about the best places to go in addition to just handing out paper. They may even conduct free town tours. The regional tourist offices are administrative overseers rather than purveyors of useful practical information.

French Government Tourist Offices in various major cities of the world give away large quantities of maps and glossy brochures covering Brittany and Normandy, including lists of hotels and campsites. Some of these, such as the maps of the inland waterways, and lists of festivals and campsites, can be quite useful; others use a lot of space to say very little.

MAPS

Though their town maps are often very good, the SI handouts very rarely contain usable regional maps. To supplement them – and the maps in this guide – you will probably want a reasonable **road map**. For most purposes, certainly for driving, the *Michelin* 1:200,000 area maps of Brittany (230) and Normandy (231) are more than adequate. Virtually every road they show is pass-

FRENCH GOVERNMENT TOURIST OFFICES

Australia   ☎612/231 5244
BNP Building 12th floor
12 Castlereagh St, Sydney NSW 2000

Canada
1981 av McGill College, Suite 490 ☎514/288 4264
Montréal, QUE H3A 2W9   fax 514/845 4868
30 St Patrick St, Suite 700   ☎416/593 6427
Toronto ONT M5T 3A3   fax 416/979 7587

Denmark   ☎33/11 49 12
NY Ostergade 3.3, DK – 1101 Copenhagen

Ireland   ☎1/703 4046
35 Lower Abbey St   fax 01/874 7324
Dublin 1

Netherlands   ☎020/627 33 18
Prinsengr. 670   fax 020/620 33 39
1017 KX Amsterdam

Norway   ☎22/42 33 87
Storgaten 10A, 0155 Oslo 1   fax 22/42 33 87

Sweden   ☎08/679 79 75
Norrmalmstorg 1 Av, S11146 Stockholm

UK   ☎0171/491 7622*
178 Piccadilly, London W1V 0AL

USA
610 Fifth Ave, Suite 222
New York, NY 10020-2452   ☎212/757 1125
645 North Michigan Ave
Chicago, IL 60611-2836   ☎312/337 6301
9454 Wilshire Blvd
Beverly Hills, CA 90212-2967   ☎213/271 7838
Cedar Maple Plaza
2305 Cedar Springs Blvd   ☎214/720 4010
Dallas, TX 75201   fax 214/720 0250

*In Britain, the FGTO operates an information service, EuropAssistance, on 0891/244123 (Mon–Fri 9am–10pm, Sat 9am–5pm; 49p peak rate, 39p cheap rate). This is much easier to use; brochures will be sent without postage charge, and specific queries are quickly referred to the relevant organization.

MAP AND GUIDE SUPPLIERS

BRITAIN

London
National Map Centre   ☎0171/222 4945
22–24 Caxton St, SW1E 6PO
Stanfords   ☎0171/836 1321
12–14 Long Acre, WC2E 9LP
The Travellers Bookshop   ☎0171/836 9132
25 Cecil Court, WC2

Edinburgh
Thomas Nelson and Sons Ltd   ☎0131/557 3011
51 York Place, EH1 3JD

Glasgow
John Smith and Sons   ☎0141/221 7472
57–61 St Vincent St

Maps by **mail or phone order** are available from *Stanfords* in London.

NORTH AMERICA

Chicago
Rand McNally   ☎312/321-1751
444 N Michigan Ave, IL 60611

Montréal
Ulysses Travel Bookshop   ☎514/289-0993
4176 St-Denis

New York
British Travel Bookshop   ☎1-800/448-3039
551 5th Ave, NY 10176   or 212/490-6688
The Complete Traveler Bookstore   ☎212/685-9007
199 Madison Ave, NY 10016
Rand McNally   ☎212/758-7488
150 East 52nd St, NY 10022
Traveler's Bookstore   ☎212/664-0995
22 West 52nd St, NY 10019

San Francisco
The Complete Traveler Bookstore   ☎415/923-1511
3207 Fillmore St, CA 92123

Rand McNally   ☎415/777-3131
595 Market St, CA 94105

Santa Barbara
Map Link, Inc   ☎805/965-4402
25 East Mason St, CA 9310

Seattle
Elliot Bay Book Company   ☎206/624-6600
101 South Main St, WA 98104

Toronto
Open Air Books and Maps   ☎416/363-0719
25 Toronto St, M5R 2C1

Vancouver
World Wide Books and Maps   ☎604/687-3320
1247 Granville St

Washington DC
Rand McNally   ☎202/223-6751
1201 Connecticut Ave NW, 20036

Note: *Rand McNally* now has 24 stores across the US; call ☎1-800/333-0136 (ext 2111) for the address of your nearest store, or for **direct mail** maps.

AUSTRALIA AND NEW ZEALAND

Adelaide
The Map Shop   ☎08/231 2033
16a Peel St, SA 5000

Melbourne
Bowyangs   ☎03/670 4383
372 Little Bourke St, VIC 3000

Sydney
Travel Bookshop   ☎02/241 3554
20 Bridge St, NSW 2000

Perth
Perth Map Centre   ☎09/322 5733
891 Hay St, WA 6000

able by any car, and those that are tinged in green are usually reliable as "scenic routes". A useful free map for cardrivers, obtainable from filling stations and traffic information kiosks in France, is the **Bison Futé**, showing alternative back routes to avoid the congested main roads, which are clearly signposted on the ground by special green *Bison Futé* road signs.

If you're planning to **walk or cycle,** check the **IGN** maps – their green (1:100,000 and 1:50,000) and purple (1:25,000) series. The *IGN* 1:100,000 is the smallest scale available with contours marked, though the bizarre colour scheme makes it hard to read. *Michelin* maps have little arrows to indicate steep slopes, which is all the information most cyclists will need. For walkers, the **Footpaths of Europe** series (translated by *Robertson McCarta*, 122 King's Cross Rd, London WC1X 9DS) covers the long-distance GR trails (see p.30) in exhaustive detail.

COSTS, MONEY AND BANKS

Brittany and Normandy are not, on the whole, expensive places to visit. Distances (and transport costs) are relatively small; the price of food and accommodation consistently lower than in Britain and much of Northern Europe; and access, at least just across the Channel, straightforward.

On a **shoestring level**, camping and eating at least one picnic meal a day, taking buses or cycling, you could get by easily enough on 170F (£20/US$32) a day. Moving slightly **more upmarket**, staying in modest hotels, spending a bit on restaurants and driving, you should reckon on around 350F (£42/US$65) a day and up.

Accommodation is likely to represent the bulk of your expenditure. Hotels average around 180F for a double room, in the simpler places (note that in this book all hotel prices are coded with symbols, which are explained on p.31). If you're sharing, that works out at little more per person than the 45–66F per person charged by hostels. Camping, of course, can cut costs dramatically, so long as you avoid the plusher private sites; the local *Camping Municipal* rarely asks for more than 20F a head.

Eating out is the real bargain. You should always be able to find a good three-course meal for 70–90F, or a takeaway for a lot less (though *crêperies* seldom work out as cheap as they might appear). Fresh food from shops and markets is surprisingly dear in relation to low restaurant prices, although it's always possible to save money with a basic picnic of bread, cheese and fruit (maybe enhanced by a bottle of wine – cheapest in supermarkets). More sophisticated meals – takeaway salads and ready-to-heat dishes – can be put together for reasonable prices if you shop at *charcuteries* (delis) and the equivalent counters of many supermarkets. As everywhere, **drinks** in cafés and bars are what really make a hole in your pocket – you have to accept that you're paying for somewhere to sit.

Transport costs obviously depend entirely on how (and how much) you travel. Bikes cost nothing if you bring them and around 50F per day (more like 80F for a mountain bike) if you rent from the network of bikeshops and *SNCF* station outlets (see p.29). Trains and buses normally operate on a fixed tariff of 50 centimes (half a franc) per kilometre. If you're driving, petrol prices are amongst the highest in Europe, at something between 5F and 6F for a litre of leaded and slightly less than 5F for unleaded (that's about 26F/imperial gallon, 21F/US gallon), and most motorways have tolls, which mount up at about 20 centimes per kilometre.

As for **sites and museums**, you may find that regular charges make you quite selective about what you visit – even with an **ISIC** student card to soften the blow (many museums have reduced admission for all under-26s, and not just students). But this is no special hardship: the region's attractions lie as much in its towns and landscapes as in anything fenced-off or put in a showcase.

MONEY

French currency is the *franc* (abbreviated as F or sometimes FF), divided into 100 centimes. Francs come in notes of 500, 100, 50, and 20F, and there are coins of 10, 5, 2, and 1F, and 50, 20, 10 and 5 centimes. The exchange rate in recent years has hovered at just over 8F to the pound sterling – traditionally it used to be higher, in the region of 10F, until the collapse of the Exchange Rate Mechanism – or around 5.50F to the dollar.

Standard **banking hours** are 9.30am–noon and 2–4pm; closed Sunday and either Monday or, less usually, Saturday. **Rates of exchange** and **commissions** vary from bank to bank; the *Banque de France*, which has offices in St-Malo, Caen, Quimper and other large towns, usually offers the best rates and takes the least commission. There are **money-exchange counters** at the railway stations of all big cities, and usually one or two in the town centre as well. However, it would be a sensible precaution to buy some French francs before leaving.

The best way to **carry money** depends on your bank, and what facilities it offers. **Travellers' cheques**, generally considered the safest option, are available from almost any major bank (whether you have an account there or not), usually for a service charge of one percent on the amount purchased. Some banks may take 1.25 percent or even 1.5 percent, and your own bank may offer cheques free of charge provided you meet certain conditions – ask first, as you may easily save £10 to £15. *Thomas Cook*, *Visa* and *American Express* are the most widely recognized brands. Obtaining **French franc travellers' cheques** can be worthwhile: they can often be used as cash, and French banks are obliged by law to give you the face value of the cheques when you change them, so commission is only paid on purchase.

Alternatively, Europeans can use **Eurocheques**, now offered by most British banks. In theory, these can be better value with just one percent commission on each cheque (though French banks do occasionally – and wrongly – charge you to cash Eurocheques). However, if you only use the card on one European holiday per year, the annual fee for the service (normally in the region of £15), means that effectively you're paying a much higher rate of commission. On the

> To report a **lost or stolen credit card**, call one of the hotlines listed on p.48.

positive side, you can specify the exact amount you want and use the cheques in shops and restaurants, as well as certain cash-dispensers, and it takes up to six weeks for the money to be deducted from your account.

A similar delay in debiting usually comes with **credit cards**, too, which also charge a lower overall commission. They are widely accepted; just watch for the window stickers. It would be very unusual to come across a hotel that didn't take the best-known names. *Visa/Barclaycard* – known as the *Carte Bleue* – is almost universally recognized, and cash advances can be had at all banks; you can also ask for a PIN number, enabling you to use most cash-dispensing machines in France. *American Express* and *Access* (*Eurocard/Mastercard* in France) rank considerably lower – only the *Crédit Agricole* and the *Crédit Mutuelle* banks provide facilities for the latter.

Finally, if you don't have a bank account, or if you're looking for a simple, cheap alternative, there are **International Giro Cheques**, which can be bought and cashed at any main post office. Post offices are open for longer hours and charge a very low commission, and these cheques help you to avoid queues at busy resort banks; but they have yet to catch on in any significant way.

GETTING AROUND

The best way to travel around Brittany and Normandy is with a car or a bike. Public transport is not very impressive. *SNCF* trains are efficient, as ever in France, and the *Atlantique TGV* has reduced the Paris–Rennes journey to a mere two hours. However, the network here circles the coast and, especially in Brittany, barely serves the inland areas. Where the train stops, an *SNCF* bus may continue the route, and local buses can eventually get you anywhere, so long as you're prepared to fit in with timetables geared principally to market, school or working hours.

Approximate journey times and frequencies can be found in the "Travel Details" at the end of each chapter and local peculiarities are also pointed out in the text of the guide.

If you come without your own transport, the ideal solution is to make longer journeys by train or bus, then to **rent a bike** (never a problem) to explore a particular locality.

DRIVING

Travelling by car has its disadvantages: the expense, most obviously, but also the strong likelihood of reducing your contact with people. However, you do gain freedom of movement and, especially if you're camping, can be a lot more self-sufficient. **Car rental** outlets in the various Channel ports and major cities are listed throughout this book, though few British travellers consider **car rental** – at upwards of £170/US$250 per week – to be an economic alternative to bringing their own car across the Channel.

British, EU and North American **driving licences** are valid, though an *International Driver's Licence* makes life easier if you get a police officer unwilling to peruse a document in English. The vehicle registration document and the **insurance** papers must be carried. Motorists from other EU countries may also need or want to get a **Green Card**, which serves as an extension to your usual insurance. As a rule of thumb, if you have insurance at home then you have the minimum legal coverage in France, and it's up to you whether you want to pay an extra premium to have fully comprehensive cover; this can only be arranged through your own insurance company, so check to see what they recommend.

If your car is right-hand drive, you must have your headlight dip adjusted to the right before you go – it's a legal requirement – and as a courtesy change or paint them to yellow or stick on black glare deflectors. Shops at the ferry terminals sell special headlight deflectors which achieve both aims – you basically pay £6 for two small pieces of sticky yellow plastic, but they do the job.

All the major car manufacturers have garage/service stations in France – get their lists of addresses before you go. If you have an accident or break-in, make a report to the local police (and keep a copy) in order to make an insurance claim.

Petrol/gas (*essence*) or diesel fuel (*gasoil*) is least expensive at out-of-town superstores, and most expensive on the *autoroutes*; reckon on it costing fifteen percent more than in Britain (which makes it worth filling up in the UK if you have the option), or around double the US price. 4-star is *super*; unleaded is *sans plomb*.

RULES OF THE ROAD

The main **rule of the road** to remember in France is that the French drive on the right. The law of *priorité à droite* – which says you have to give way to traffic coming from your right, even when it is coming from a minor road – is being phased out, having long been a major cause of accidents. It still applies in built-up areas, so you still have to be vigilant in towns, keeping a look out along the roadside for the yellow diamond on a white background that gives you right of way – until you see the same sign with an oblique black slash, which indicates vehicles emerging from the right have right of way. "*STOP*" signs mean stop completely: "*CÉDEZ LE PASSAGE*" means "Give Way".

Fines for driving violations are exacted on the spot, and only cash or a French bank account cheque are accepted. Exceeding the speed limit

A MOTORING VOCABULARY

car	*la voiture*	air line	*ligne à air*
garage	*garage*	inflate the tyres	*gonfler les pneus*
service	*service*	battery	*batterie*
to park the car	*garer la voiture*	the battery is dead	*la batterie est morte*
car park/parking lot	*un parking*	plugs	*bougies*
free parking	*parking gratuit*	to break down	*tomber en panne*
paid parking	*parking payant*	insurance	*assurance*
no parking	*défense de stationner/*	green card	*carte verte*
	stationnement interdit	traffic lights	*feux*
petrol/gas (unleaded)	*essence (sans plomb)*	red light	*feu rouge*
petrol/gas station	*poste d'essence*	green light	*feu vert*
diesel fuel	*gasoil*	slow down	*ralentir*
petrol/gas can	*bidon*	give way	*cédez le passage*
fill the tank	*faire le plein*	give way to	*priorité aux piétons*
oil	*huile*	pedestrians	

by 1–30kph can cost as much as 5000F. Speed limits are: 130km/hr (80mph) on the tolled *autoroutes*; 110km/hr (68mph) on two-lane highways; 90km/hr (56mph) on other roads; and 60km/hr (37mph) in towns.

Autoroute driving, if fast, is boring when it's not hair-raising, and the tolls in Normandy are expensive. (It's also rather irrelevant to this book, as if you stay on the autoroute for any length of time you won't be in Brittany or Normandy any more.) For information on road conditions call *Inter Service Route* on ☎48.58.33.33 (24hr). The helpful *Bison Futé* map, free from service stations, details lesser-known routes to steer clear of the crowds – invaluable if you're trying to avoid the endless traffic jams over the weekends between July 15 and August 15. For full French driving regulations, see the "AA Traveller's Guide to Europe" (AA Publications, £6.95).

TRAINS

French **trains**, operated by the nationally owned **SNCF** (Société National des Chemins de Fer), are by and large clean, fast and frequent, and their staff both courteous and helpful. All but the smallest stations (**gares SNCF**) have an information desk and *consignes automatiques* – coin-operated lockers big enough to take a rucksack. Many (indicated in the text of the guide) also rent out bicycles. **Fares** are reasonable, at an average – off-peak – of a little over 50 centimes per kilometre. The ultra-fast *TGV*s (*Trains à Grande Vitesse*) require a supplement at peak times and compulsory reservation costing around 20F. The slowest trains are those marked *Autotrain* in the timetable, stopping at all stations.

Try to use the counter service for buying tickets, rather than the complicated computerized system; the latter changes the price of *TGV* tickets depending on the demand, and you may find you've bought an expensive ticket without realizing that a later train is cheaper.

All **tickets** – but not passes – must be date-stamped in the orange machines at station platform entrances. It is an offence not to "*Compostez votre billet*". Rail journeys may be broken any time, anywhere, but after a break of 24 hours you must "compost" your ticket again when you resume your journey. On night trains an extra 85F or so will buy you a **couchette** – well worth it if you're making a long haul and don't want to waste a day recovering from a sleepless night.

Regional **rail maps** and complete **timetables** are on sale at tobacconist shops. Leaflet timetables for a particular line are available free at stations. *Autocar* at the top of a column means it's an *SNCF* bus service, on which rail tickets and passes are valid.

For details on taking your bicycle by train – or renting one at an *SNCF* station – see p.29.

RAIL PASSES

Details of the various Europe-wide **rail passes** valid in France are given on p.28. Within France, *SNCF* itself offers a whole range of **discount fares** on *Période Bleue* (blue period) and *Période Blanche* (white period) days – in effect, most of the year. A leaflet showing the blue, white (smaller discount) and red (peak) periods is given out at *gares SNCF*.

Couples can have a free **Carte Couple**, entitling them to a 25 discount on *TGV*s or on other trains if they start their journey on a blue period day. Over-60s can get the **Carte Vermeille**, which comes in two versions: the **Quatre Temps**, which costs 140F and covers 4 journeys, and the **Plein Temps** which costs 250F for unlimited travel. Both are valid for one year and offer up to 50 percent off tickets on *TGV*s as well as other journeys starting in blue or white periods. The same percentage reductions are available for under-26s with a **Carissimo** pass, which costs 200F for 4 journeys and 350F for 8, and is valid for one year. This pass also entitles the cardholder to secure the same ticket reductions for up to 3 travelling companions also aged between 12 and 25. Under-16s can obtain the same advantages for themselves and up to 4 travelling companions of any age by purchasing a **Carte Kiwi** (275F for 4 journeys, 425F for unlimited travel for a year).

BUSES

Buses cover far more Breton and Norman routes than the trains – and, even when two towns do have a rail link, they're often quicker, cheaper and more direct. They are almost always short distance, however, so you'll need to change if you're going further than from one town to the next. And, as stressed, **timetables** tend to be constructed to suit working, market and school hours – all often dauntingly early.

Larger towns usually have a central **gare routière** (bus station), most often found next to the *gare SNCF*. However, the private bus companies (who provide most of the Breton services) don't always work together and you'll frequently find them leaving from an array of different points. The most convenient lines are those run as an extension of rail links by *SNCF*; these always run to/from the *SNCF* station (assuming there is one).

CYCLING

Bicycles have high status in France. All the car ferries carry them for nothing; *SNCF* makes minimal charges; and the French (Parisians excepted) respect cyclists – both as traffic, and, when you stop off at a restaurant or hotel, as customers. French drivers normally go out of their way to make room for you – it's the great British caravan you might have to watch out for.

Most importantly, however, **distances** in Brittany and Normandy are not great, the hills sporadic and not too steep, and the scenery nearly always a delight. Even if you're quite unused to it, cycling forty miles per day soon becomes very easy – and it's a good way of keeping yourself fit enough to enjoy the rich regional food.

These days more and more cyclists use **mountain bikes**, which the French call *VTT*s (*Vélos Touts Terrains*), for touring holidays, although if you've ever made a direct comparison you'll know it's much less effort, and much quicker, to cycle long distances and carry luggage on a traditional

---

RAIL PASSES FOR FOREIGN TRAVELLERS

Anyone intending simply to visit Brittany and Normandy – or even to explore all of France – is unlikely to make enough train journeys for it to be worth purchasing a **rail pass**.

The **InterRail** pass, available to anyone under 26 who has been resident in Europe for at least six months, gives one month's unlimited use of all European train services for £249, or 15 days travel in France, Belgium, the Netherlands and Luxembourg for £179. A better alternative for Europeans is a **EuroDomino** pass, which can be bought from the International Rail Centre at London Victoria, or from *SNCF* in France, and offers unlimited rail travel through France for any three (£118), five (£154) or ten (£235) days within a calendar month; passengers under 26 pay £96, £125 and £200 respectively. The pass also entitles holders to fifty percent reductions on certain train/ferry links to France, and can be bought in conjunction with *Air France* flights (see p.6).

Eurail passes, the equivalent for North American travellers and anyone else not normally resident in Europe or North Africa, are on the whole considerably more expensive, with the cheapest 15-day *Eurail Consecutive* pass costing around US$625 if you're over 26 or US$500 for anyone younger. If you can work out exactly how much travelling you're likely to do, you may do better with a 5-, 10-, or 15-day *Flexipass*, only valid in France, which costs from US$440 for over-26s or US$330 for under-26s.

None of the above passes is valid for the Channel Tunnel.

touring or racing bike. Whichever you prefer, do use cycle panniers; a backpack in the sun is unbearable.

One word of warning: most cyclists have a habit of lifting their bicycles by gripping the saddle. If you keep on doing that when you're using panniers, even just to get over kerbs, the entire saddle will eventually snap off when you least expect it, to leave you to ride off in search of a bike shop, sitting on a long sharp spike.

Restaurants and hotels along the way are nearly always obliging about looking after your bike, even to the point of allowing it into your room. Most large towns have well-stocked retail and **repair shops**, where parts are normally cheaper than in Britain or the US. However, if you're using a foreign-made bike, it's a good idea to carry spare tyres, as French sizes are different; neither is it easy to find parts for mountain bikes, the French enthusiasm being directed towards racers instead. Inner tubes are not a problem, as they adapt to either size, though you should always be sure that you get the right valves. The best places to find foreign parts are in *Raleigh* stockists – at Rouen, Rennes and scattered around both provinces.

SNCF run various schemes for cyclists, all of them covered by the free leaflet *Train et Vélo*, available from most stations. *Autotrains* (when marked with a bicycle in the timetable) are usually the only ones on which you can travel with a bike as free accompanied luggage. Otherwise, you have to send your bike as registered luggage (135F parcelled up, 180F unparcelled; 15F for packaging). Although it may

well arrive in less time, the *SNCF* won't guarantee delivery in under five days; and you do hear stories of bicycles disappearing altogether.

You can normally load your bike straight on to the train at the **ferry** port – as on the boat train at Dieppe – but remember that you must first go to the ticket office of the station to register it (there is time). Don't just try to climb on the train with it, as both you and your bike will end up left behind. In addition to the ferries, both *British Airways* and *Air France* take bikes free. You may have to box them though, and you should contact the airlines first. You will also be required to leave a deposit of 1000–1500F (credit cards accepted).

At most *SNCF* stations bikes are also available for **rental** from 44–55F, depending on the type of bike. You can also rent bikes from some tourist offices and a fair number of bike shops (which are much more likely to offer you a mountain bike), and, on islands such as Belle-Île and Ouessant, from numerous seasonal **stalls**. The bikes are often not insured, however, and you will be presented with the bill for its replacement if it's stolen or damaged. Check whether your travel insurance policy covers you for this if you intend to rent a bike.

MOPEDS AND SCOOTERS

Mopeds and **scooters** are relatively easy to find: everyone in France, from young kids to grandmas, rides one of these, and although they're not built for any kind of long-distance travel, they're ideal for shooting around town and nearby. Places which rent out bicycles will often also rent out mopeds; you can expect to pay 160F

A CYCLING VOCABULARY					
to adjust	*ajuster*	to deflate	*dégonfler*	rack	*le porte-*
axle	*l'axe*	dérailleur	*le dérailleur*		*bagages*
ball-bearing	*le roulement à*	frame	*le cadre*	to raise	*relever*
	billes	gears	*les vitesses*	to repair	*réparer*
battery	*la pile*	grease	*la graisse*	saddle	*la selle*
bent	*tordu*	handlebars	*le guidon*	to screw	*visser*
bicycle	*le vélo*	to inflate	*gonfler*	spanner	*la clef*
bottom bracket	*le logement du*	inner tube	*la chambre à air*		*(mécanique)*
	pédalier	loose	*dévissé*	spoke	*le rayon*
brake cable	*le cable*	to lower	*baisser*	to straighten	*rédresser*
brakes	*les freins*	mudguard	*le garde-boue*	stuck	*coincé*
broken	*cassé*	pannier	*le pannier*	tight	*serré*
bulb	*l'ampoule*	pedal	*le pédale*	toe clips	*les cale-pieds*
chain	*la chaîne*	pump	*la pompe*	tyre	*le pneu*
cotter pin	*la clavette*	puncture	*la crevaison*	wheel	*la roue*

a day for a 50cc Suzuki, for example, or 200F for an 80cc motorbike. Crash helmets are compulsory only on machines over 125cc, but you'd be a fool not to wear one even on a moped.

AIDS TO TWO-WHEEL TOURING

For advice on which **maps** to take, see the "Maps" section on p.22. In the UK, the **Cyclists' Touring Club**, Cotterell House, 68 Meadrow, Godalming, Surrey GU7 3HS (☎01483/417217) will suggest routes and supply advice for a small fee, and they run a good insurance scheme.

The *Youth Hostels Association* also sells combined bike-rental and hostel packages; details from Trevelyan House, St Stephen's Hill, St Albans, Herts (☎01727/55215); a number of other operators are included in the box on p.8. Also contact *Bike Events* (PO Box 75, Bath, Avon BA1 1BX, ☎01225/480130) who run trips every year all over the place.

BOAT TRIPS AND INLAND WATERWAYS

Boat trips on many of Brittany and Normandy's rivers, as well as out to the islands, are detailed throughout this book. More excitingly, you can **rent a canoe**, **boat** or even **houseboat** and make your own way along sections of the **Nantes–Brest canal**. The route along the canal is the core of Chapter Six, *Inland Brittany*; the various towns where you can rent vessels are detailed on pages 211 and 281, and some British operators are listed on p.8.

French Government Tourist Offices can also provide lists of French and foreign operators who arrange boat rental, or for a full list write to the *Syndicat National des Loueurs de Bateaux de Plaisance*, Port de la Bourdonnais, 75007 Paris (☎45.55.10.49). Specifically for Brittany, contact the **Comité de Promotion Touristique des**

Canaux Bretons, Office du Tourisme, place du Parlement, 35600 Rennes (☎99.71.06.04).

If you are adventurous enough to take your own boat, there is no charge for use of the waterways in Brittany or Normandy, and you can travel without a permit for up to six months in a year. For information on maximum dimensions, documentation, regulations and so forth, ask at a French Government Tourist Office for the booklet *Boating on the Waterways*.

WALKING

Neither Brittany nor Normandy is serious hiking country. There are no mountains – or extensive areas of wilderness – and casual rambling along the clifftops and beside the waterways is the limit of most people's aims. However, if you're into **long-distance walking**, 21 of the French **GR trails** – the *sentiers de grande randonnée* – run through the area. The GRs are fully signposted and equipped with campsites and rest huts along the way. The most interesting are the *GR 2* (*Sentier de la Seine*) which runs from Le Havre to Les Andelys, the *GR 341* (*Sentier de Bretagne*) along the Granit-Rose coast between Lannion and St-Brieuc, and the *GR 347* (*Val d'Oust au pays Gallo*) between Josselin and Redon.

Each GR path is described in a **Topoguide**, which gives a detailed account of the route (in French), including maps, campsites, sources of provisions and so on. These are produced by the principal French walkers' organization, the *Comité National des Sentiers de Grande Randonnée*, 8 av Marceau, 75008 Paris (☎47.23.62.32), and can be ordered through good map shops overseas, such as those listed on p.23. In addition, many SIs provide guides to their local footpaths.

ACCOMMODATION

Most of the year, accommodation is plentiful in both Brittany and Normandy, and visitors can just turn up at a town and find a room or a place in a campsite. Booking a couple of nights in advance can, however, be reassuring; it saves the effort of trudging round and ensures that you know what you'll be paying.

Phone numbers as well as addresses are given in the guide, and the "Language" section at the back should help you make the call if you're uncertain of your French, though many hoteliers and campsite managers, and almost all youth hostel managers, will speak some English.

Problems arise mainly **between July 15 and August 15**, when the French take their own vacations *en masse*. The first weekend of August is the busiest time of all. During this period, hotel and hostel accommodation can be hard to come

by – particularly in the coastal resorts – and you may find yourself falling back on local SIs for help and ideas. With campsites, you can be more relaxed, unless you're touring with a caravan or camper van.

The **tourist season** in Brittany and Normandy runs roughly from Easter until the end of September; while hotels in the cities remain open all year, those in smaller towns and, especially, seaside resorts often close for several months during the winter. It's quite possible to turn up somewhere in January or February to find that every hotel is closed; in addition, many family-run places close each year for two or three weeks some time between May and September, and some hotels in smaller towns and villages close for one or two nights a week, usually Sunday or Monday. The usual opening dates for each establishment are indicated in the text of the *Guide*, but it's worth checking ahead if you're in any doubt.

HOTELS

Hotels tend to be consistently better value than they are in Britain and much of northern Europe. Recommendations are given in the guide for almost every town or village mentioned, with their prices indicated by the symbols ①, ②, ③, etc, as explained in the box below. In most towns, you'll be able to get a double for around 140–200F (£17–25/US$28–40) and a single for around 110–150F (£13–18/US$20–30), though often if you're prepared to pay a little extra you can get something really special.

ACCOMMODATION PRICE CODES

All **hotel prices** in this book have been coded using the symbols below. The price shown is for the least expensive double room in high season, which for categories ① and ② usually means a room without private bath, shower, or toilet, though there's usually a washbasin. Most hotels in those categories also have a number of rooms with en-suite facilities, which typically cost 30–50F extra. In the ③ category and above, all rooms tend to be equipped with private facilities.

Although many hotels offer rooms at differing prices, ranges (such as ②–⑦) are only indicated when the spectrum is especially broad, or where there are relatively few rooms in the lowest category.

①	up to 120 F	④	220–300F	⑦	500–600F
②	120–160F	⑤	300–400F	⑧	600–700F
③	160–220F	⑥	400–500F	⑨	700F and over

Full **accommodation lists** are available from any French Government Tourist Office (see p.22) or local SIs. Travelling in peak season, especially, it is worth getting hold of these, together with a handbook or free leaflet for the *Logis et Auberges de France*. The latter are independent hotels, promoted together for their consistently good food and reasonably priced rooms; they're recognisable on the spot by a green and yellow logo of a hearth.

One of the great pleasures of travelling in France is the sheer quality of **village hotels**. Not always in terms of fixtures and fittings – at the bottom of the range, you'll find corduroy carpets creeping up the walls, blotchy lino curling from buckled wooden floors, and clanking great brass keys that won't quite turn in the ill-fitting doors – but the standards of service are consistently high, and it's rare indeed to stay in a place that doesn't take pride in maintaining a well-appointed and good-value restaurant serving traditional local food.

All French hotels are **graded** with from zero to three stars. The price more or less corresponds to the number of stars, though the system is a little haphazard, having more to do with ratios of bathrooms per guest than genuine quality; ungraded and single-star hotels are often very good.

At the cheapest level, what makes a difference in **cost** is whether a room contains a shower: if it does, the bill will be around 30–50F more. **Breakfast**, too, can add 20–35F per person to a bill – though there is no obligation to take it and you will nearly always do better at a café. The cost of eating **dinner** in a hotel's restaurant can be a more important factor to bear in mind when picking a place to stay. Officially hotels are not supposed to insist that you take meals, but they often do, and in busy resorts you may not find a room unless you agree to *démi-pension* (half-board). If you are unsure, ask to see the menu before checking in; cheap rooms aren't so cheap if you have to eat a hundred-franc meal.

Genuine **single rooms** are rare; lone travellers normally end up in an ordinary double let at a slightly reduced rate. On the other hand most hotels willingly equip rooms with **extra beds**, for three or more people, at good discount.

In country areas, in addition to standard hotels, you will come across *chambres d'hôte*, bed-and-breakfast accommodation in someone's house or farm. These vary in standard but are rarely an especially cheap option – usually costing the equivalent of a two-star hotel. However, if you strike lucky, they may be good sources of traditional home cooking. Brown leaflets available in SIs list most of them.

HOSTELS, *FOYERS* AND *GÎTES D'ETAPE*

At between 42F and 70F per night for a dormitory bed, *Auberges des Jeunesses* – youth hostels – are invaluable for single budget travellers. For couples, however, and certainly for groups of three or more people (see above), they'll not necessarily save money on the cheaper hotels – particularly if you've had to pay a bus fare out to the edge of town to reach them. However, many

YOUTH HOSTEL ASSOCIATIONS

Australia
Australian Youth Hostels Association
Level 3, 10 Mallett St,
Camperdown, NSW   ☎02/565-1325

Canada
Canadian Hostelling Association
Room 400, 205 Catherine St,   ☎613/237-7884
Ottawa, ON K2P 1C3   or 1-800/663-5777

England and Wales
Youth Hostel Association (YHA)
Trevelyan House, 8 St Stephen's Hill,
St Alban's, Herts AL1   ☎017278/45047
14 Southampton St,
London WC2   ☎0171/836 1036

Ireland
An Oige
39 Mountjoy Square, Dublin 1   ☎01/363111
56 Bradbury Place, Belfast BT7   ☎01232/324733

New Zealand
Youth Hostels Association of New Zealand
PO Box 436, Christchurch 1   ☎03/799-970

Scotland
Scottish Youth Hostel Association
7 Glebe Cres, Stirling FK8 2JA   ☎01786/51181

USA
Hostelling International-American Youth Hostels
733 15th St NW, Suite 840, PO Box 37613,
Washington, DC 20005   ☎202/783-6161

of the hostels in Normandy and Brittany are beautifully sited, and they do allow you to cut costs by preparing your own food in their kitchens, or eating in cheap canteens.

To stay at many of the hostels you're meant to be a member of the *International Youth Hostel Federation* (*IYHF*), which currently costs £9/US$15 for over 18s and £3/US$5 for under 18s. Head offices are listed opposite; you can also join on the spot at most French hostels. A confusion is that there are two rival French youth hostel associations: the *Fédération Unie des Auberges de Jeunesse*, 27 rue Pajol, 75018 Paris (☎44.89.87.27), which has its hostels detailed in the *International Handbook*, and the *Ligue Française pour les Auberges de Jeunesse*, 83 rue de Rennes, 75007 Paris (☎45.48.69.84). *IYHF* membership covers both organizations – and you'll find all their hostels detailed in the text.

A few large towns also provide a more luxurious standard of hostel accommodation in **Foyers des Jeunes Travailleurs/euses**. These are residential hostels for young workers and students, in which for around 65F you can usually get a private room. They normally have a good cafeteria canteen.

A third hostel-type alternative exists in the countryside, especially in hiking or cycling areas, in the **gîtes d'étape**. These are less formal than the youth hostels, often run by the local village or municipality (whose mayor will probably hold the key), and provide basic hospital-style beds and simple kitchen facilities. They are marked on the large-scale *IGN* walkers' maps and listed in the individual GR *Topoguides*. A complete list of all French *gîtes*, *refuges* and hostels is included in the publication *Gîtes et Refuges en France* (65F plus postage from Editions Créer, rue Jean Amariton, Nonette, 63340 St-Germain Lembron); selections are also included in the Tourist Office booklet, *Accueil à la Campagne* (available from most SIs for around 40F).

RENTED ACCOMMODATION: GÎTES DE FRANCE

If you are planning to stay a week or more in any one place it might be worth considering **renting a house**. British travellers can do this by checking the adverts from private and foreign owners in Sunday newspapers (*The Observer* and *The Sunday Times*, mainly); the boxes on pages 8, 14 and 16 of this book contain a selection of

holiday firms across the world that market accommodation/travel packages.

The easiest and most reliable option, however, is to use the official French Government service, the **Gîtes de France**, based in Britain at 178 Piccadilly, London W1V 9DB (☎0171/493 3480). Membership (£3) gets you a copy of their handbook, which contains properties all over France, listed by *département*. The houses vary in size and comfort, but all are acceptable holiday homes. There is a photograph and description of each one, and the computerized booking service means that you can instantly reserve one for any number of full weeks. The cost varies with the season from around £90–160 per person per week – and may include concessionary ferry rates.

CAMPING

Practically every village and town in the country has at least one **campsite**, to cater for the thousands of French people who spend their holiday under canvas.

The cheapest – at around 10–15F per person per night – is usually the **Camping Municipal**, run by the local municipality. In season or when they are officially open, they are always clean with plenty of hot water, and often situated in the prime local position. Out of season, many of them don't even bother to have someone around to collect the overnight charge.

On the coast especially, there are **superior categories** of campsite, where you'll pay prices similar to those of a hotel for the facilities – bars, restaurants, sometimes swimming pools. These have a rather less transitory population than the *Camping Municipals*, with people often spending a whole holiday in the one base. If you plan to do the same – particularly if you've a caravan, camper van or substantial tent – book ahead.

Inland, **camping à la ferme** – on somebody's farm – is another (generally facility-less) possibility. Lists of sites are detailed in the Tourist Board's *Accueil à la Campagne* booklet.

Lastly, a **word of caution**: never camp rough (*camping sauvage*, as the French call it) on anyone's land without first asking permission. If the dogs don't get you, the guns might – farmers have been known to shoot before asking any questions. In many parts of France *camping sauvage* on public land is not tolerated – Brittany is the notable exception. On beaches it's best to camp out where there are other people doing so.

EATING AND DRINKING

The superb range of food available in Brittany and Normandy has to be one of the principal reasons for visiting the area covered in this book; if anything especially so in Normandy. Restaurant quality is consistently high, prices well below British counterparts, and, to be honest, there are towns and villages where just about the only excitement is the gastronomic output.

With no wine production in Normandy (and only the *Muscadet*-style whites coming from the southeast of Brittany), the most interesting local **alcohol** is that derived from the region's orchards. **Cider** is made everywhere, along with its pear equivalent, *poiré*; and there is of course Norman **calvados** (apple brandy), as well as numerous local firewaters.

BRETON FOOD

Brittany's proudest addition to the great cuisines of the world has to be the (white-flour) *crêpe*, and its savoury (buckwheat) equivalent the *galette*; *crêperies* throughout the region attempt to pass them off as satisfying meals, serving them with every imaginable filling. However, there can be few people who plan their holidays specifically around eating pancakes, and gourmets are far more likely to be enticed to Brittany by its magnificent array of **seafood**, shellfish above all – mussels, oysters, clams, scallops. Restaurants in resorts such as **St-Malo** and **Quiberon** jostle for the attention of fish fanatics, while some smaller towns – such as **Cancale**, which specializes in

oysters (*huîtres*), and **Erquy**, with its scallops (*Coquilles St-Jacques*) – go so far as to depend on one specific mollusc for their livelihood.

Although they can't quite claim to be uniquely Breton, two appetizers feature on every self-respecting menu. These are *moules marinières*, giant bowls of succulent orange mussels steamed open in some combination of white wine, shallots and parsley (and perhaps enriched by the addition of cream or *crème fraiche* to become *moules à la creme*), and *soupe de poissons*, traditionally served with a little pot of the garlicky mayonnaise known as *rouille* (coloured with pulverized sweet red pepper) and a bowl of *croutons*. Jars of freshly-made *soupe de poissons* – or crab, or lobster – are always on sale in seaside *poissonneries*, and make an ideal way to take a taste of France home with you. Paying a bit more in a restaurant – typically on menus costing 140F or more – brings you into the realm of the *assiette de fruits de mer*, a mountainous heap of langoustines, crabs, oysters, mussels, clams, whelks and cockles, most of them raw and all (with certain obvious exceptions) delicious. **Main courses** tend to be plainer than in Normandy, for example, with fresh local fish being prepared with relatively simple sauces. Skate served with capers, or salmon baked with a mustard or cheese sauce, are typical dishes, while even the *cotriade*, a stew containing such fish as sole, turbot, or bass, as well as shellfish, is distinctly less rich than the Mediterranean *bouillabaisse*.

Brittany is also better than much of France in maintaining its respect for fresh green **vegetables**, thanks to the extensive local production of peas, cauliflowers, artichokes and the like. Only with the **desserts** can things get rather too heavy; *far Breton*, considered a great delicacy, is a stodgy baked concoction of sponge and custard which owes its gravitas to the addition of such ingredients as pig's blood, while *îles flottantes* are meringue icebergs adrift in a sea of *crème brulée* or custard.

NORMAN FOOD

The food of **Normandy** owes its most distinctive characteristic – its gut-bursting, heart-pounding richness – to the lush orchards and dairy herds of its agricultural heartland, and most especially the area southeast of Caen known as the Pays d'Auge. Menus abound in meat such as veal (*veau*) cooked in *vallée d'Auge* style, which consists largely of the profligate addition of cream and butter. Many dishes also feature orchard fruit, either in its natural state or in successively more alcoholic forms – either as apple or pear cider, or perhaps further distilled to produce brandies (*Calvados* in the case of apples, *poiré* for pears).

Normans have a great propensity for blood and guts. In addition to gamier meat and fowl such as rabbit and duck (a speciality in Rouen, where the birds are strangled to ensure that all their blood gets into the sauce), they enjoy such intestinal preparations as *andouilles*, the blood sausages known in English as chitterlings, and *tripes*, stewed for hours *à la mode de Caen*, but rendered no less palatable.

A full blow-out at country restaurants in the small towns of inland Normandy – places like Conches, Vire and the Suisse Normande – will also traditionally entail one or two pauses between courses for the *trou normand*; a glass of *Calvados* while you catch your breath before struggling on with the feast.

Normandy's long coastline ensures that it too is a great place for **seafood**, serving up much the same range of shellfish as detailed for Brittany, above. Many of the larger ports and resorts have long waterfront lines of restaurants competing for attention, each with its "*copieuse*" *assiette de fruits de mer*. **Honfleur** is probably the most enjoyable of these, but **Dieppe**, **Cherbourg** and **Granville** also spring to mind as offering endless eating opportunities. The menus tend to be much the same as those on offer in Brittany, if perhaps slightly more expensive.

The most famous products of Normandy's meadow-munching cows are of course its **cheeses**; you'll find a history and overview of cheese-making in the Pays d'Auge on p.145.

WEEKLY MARKETS IN BRITTANY AND NORMANDY

The list below features the biggest and best of the **markets** of Brittany and Normandy, with a particular emphasis on those specializing in **fresh food** and local produce.

Bear in mind that in addition to the specific days listed here, most large cities – **Rennes**, **Rouen** and **Caen** for example – tend to have markets every day (with the occasional exception of Mondays).

	NORMANDY	BRITTANY
Monday	Coutances, Pont-Audemer, Pont l'Evêque, St Pierre-sur-Dives	Auray, Concarneau, Lesneven, Ploërmel, Redon, Vitré
Tuesday	Argentan, Deauville, Dieppe, St-Lô, Valognes, Villedieu-les-Poêles	Le Conquet, Locmariaquer, Paimpol, Pont-Aven, St-Malo, La Trinité
Wednesday	Bayeux, Falaise, Yvetot	Carnac, Tréguier, Vannes
Thursday	Brionne, Conches-en-Ouche, Coutances, Deauville, Dieppe, Forges-les-Eaux, Putanges, Ste-Mère-Église	Binic, Hennebont, Lannion
Friday	Alençon, Argentan, Cormeilles, Eu, Pont-Audemer, St-Valéry, Valognes, Vire	Concarneau, Guingamp, Jugon-les-Lacs, Quimperlé, St-Malo, La Trinité
Saturday	Avranches, Bagnoles de l'Orne, Bayeux, Caudebec, Dieppe, Domfront, Falaise, Honfleur, Lisieux, Mortagne-au-Perche, Neufchatel, Orbec, St-Lô	Fougères, Guingamp, Josselin, Locmariaquer, Quimper, St-Brieuc, Vannes
Sunday	Alençon, Brionne, St-Valéry (summer only)	Cancale, Carnac

CAFÉS AND SNACKS

A croissant, *pain au chocolat* (a chocolate-filled croissant) or a sandwich in a bar or café, with hot chocolate or coffee, is generally the best way to eat **breakfast** – at a fraction of the cost charged by most hotels. (The days when hotels gave you mounds of croissants or *brioches* for breakfast seem to be long gone; now it's virtually always bread, jam and a jug of coffee or tea for about 30F.) Croissants and sometimes hard-boiled eggs are displayed on bar counters until around 9.30am or 10am. If you stand – cheaper than sitting down – you just help yourself to these with your coffee. The waiter will keep an eye on how many you've eaten and bill you accordingly.

For **midday meals and light snacks**, most bars and cafés – there's no real difference – advertise *les snacks*, or *un casse-croûte* (a bite), with pictures of omelettes, fried eggs, hot dogs or various sandwiches. Even when they don't, they'll usually make you a half or third of a *baguette* (French bread stick), buttered (*tartine*) and filled. Likely ingredients include *jambon* (ham), *fromage* (cheese), *thon* (tuna), *saucisson* (sausage) or *poulet* (chicken). Toasted sandwiches – most commonly *croques-monsieur* (cheese and ham) or *croques-madame* (cheese and bacon or sausage) – are also invariably on offer. Especially in rural areas, small bars may serve a moderate-priced *plat du jour* (chef's daily special) or *formule* (a limited or no-choice menu).

Many people also recommend **crêpes** for lunch. However, they may taste nice enough, but unless you buy from a market stall *crêpes* are extraordinarily poor value compared to a restaurant meal; you need to eat at least three, normally at over twenty francs each, to feel even slightly full. That they seem to excite children – presumably because they can drench them in chocolate syrup – shouldn't fool parents into thinking of a *crêperie* as a cheap alternative.

For **picnic and takeaway food**, there's nothing to beat buying fresh ingredients in one of the numerous local **markets**, details of which are given in the box on p.35. If there isn't a market around on the day you need it, you'll find *charcuteries* (delicatessens) everywhere – even in small villages. These sell cooked meats, prepared snacks such as *bouchées de la reine* (seafood vol-au-vents), ready-made dishes and assorted salads. You can buy by weight or ask for *une tranche* (a slice), *une barquette* (a carton) or *une part* (a portion). The cheapest, in towns, are the supermarkets' *charcuterie* counters.

Salons de thé, which open from mid-morning to late evening, serve brunches, salads, quiches, etc, as well as cake and ice cream and a wide selection of teas. They tend to be a good deal pricier than cafés or brasseries – you're paying for the ritzy surroundings.

Patisseries, of course, have impressive arrays of cakes and pastries, often using local cream to excess. In addition to standard French pastries, the Bretons specialize in heavy, pudding-like affairs, dripping with butter, such as *kouïgn-anann*, and in *gaufres*, cream-drenched waffles.

RESTAURANTS

There is no shortage of **restaurants** in Brittany or Normandy, and in the towns the choice is added to by numbers of **brasseries**. There's no distinction between the two in terms of quality or price range, though brasseries, which resemble cafés, serve quicker meals at most hours of the day; restaurants tend to stick to the traditional meal times of noon until 2pm and 7pm to 9.30pm. After 9pm or so, restaurants often serve only *à la carte* meals – invariably more expensive than eating the set *menu fixe*. For the more upmarket places it's wise to make reservations – easily done on the same day. In small towns it may be impossible to get anything other than a bar sandwich after 10pm; in major cities, central brasseries will serve until 11pm or midnight and one or two may stay open all night. When hunting, avoid places that are half-empty at peak time, and treat the business of sizing up different menus as an enjoyable appetizer in itself. Don't forget that hotel restaurants are open to non-residents, and are often very good value; the green and yellow *logis de France* symbol is always worth looking out for. On the road, keep an eye open too for the red and blue sign of the *Relais Routiers* – always reasonably priced and gastronomically sound.

Prices and what you get for them are posted outside. Normally there is a choice between one or more *menus fixes* (set menus), where the number of courses has already been determined and choice is limited, and the *carte*, the full menu. At the bottom price-range, say below 70F, *menus fixes* revolve around standard dishes, such as steak and chips (*steack frites*), chicken and chips (*poulet frites*), or various offal concoctions, though it's always worth looking out for the *plat du jour*, which may be more appealing. For 70–130F, virtually any of the restaurants recommended in this guide will serve you a good three-course meal, while four-course blow-outs, including a starter as well as separate meat and fish courses, cost from 130–200F. Most expensive of the lot are the special seafood menus, offering giant platters of assorted crustaceans; away from the big centres such as Cancale and St-Malo, you should be wary of these, as the stuff may have been waiting around for several days for someone foolhardy enough to order it.

Going *á la carte* offers greater flexibility and, in the better restaurants, access to the chef's specialities – though you can expect to pay heavily for the privilege. A simple and perfectly legitimate ploy is to have just one course instead of the expected three or four. You can share dishes or just have several starters – a useful strategy for vegetarians. There's no minimum charge.

In the French sequence of courses, any salad (sometimes vegetables, too) comes separate from the main dish, and cheese precedes a dessert. You will be offered coffee, which is always extra, to finish off the meal.

Service compris (*s.c.*) means the **service charge** is included, which is usually the case on all set menus; *service non compris* (*s.n.c.*), or *service en sus*, means that it isn't, and you need to calculate an additional fifteen percent. **Wine** (*vin*) or a **drink** (*boisson*) is unlikely to be included, although a glass is occasionally thrown in with cheaper menus. When ordering wine, ask for *un quart* (quarter-litre), *un demi-litre* (half) or *une carafe* (a litre). You'll normally be given the house wine unless you specify otherwise; if you're worried about the cost ask for *vin ordinaire*.

The French follow the north American rather than the British line in their attitude towards **children** in restaurants, not simply by offering reduced-price children's menus but in creating an atmosphere, even in otherwise fairly snooty establishments, that positively welcomes kids. It is regarded as self-evident that large family groups should be able to eat out together. A rather murkier area is that of **dogs** in the dining room; it can be quite a shock in a provincial hotel to realize that the majority of your fellow diners are attempting to keep dogs concealed beneath their tables.

DRINKING

Where you can eat you can invariably **drink**, and vice versa. Drinking is done at a leisurely pace, whether as a prelude to food (*apéritif*), a sequel (*digestif*) or the accompaniment, and **cafés** are the standard venue. Every bar or café is obliged to display a full **price list**, usually with progressively increasing prices for drinks at the bar (*au comptoir*), sitting down (*la salle*), and on the terrace (*la terrasse*).

Wine (*vin*) is the regular drink. Red is *rouge*, white *blanc*, or there's *rosé*. *Vin de table* – plonk – is generally drinkable and always cheap; it may be disguised (and priced up) as the house wine, or *cuvée*. Restaurant mark-ups for quality wines can be outrageous, in a country where wine is so cheap in the shops. In bars, you normally buy by the glass, and just ask for *un rouge* or *un blanc*; *un pichet* gets you a quarter-litre jug.

Strictly speaking, no wine is produced in Brittany or Normandy. However, along the lower Loire Valley, the *département* of Loire-Atlantique, centred on Nantes, is still generally regarded as "belonging" to Brittany – and is treated as such in this book. Vineyards here are responsible for the dry white Muscadet – which is what normally goes into *moules marinières* – and the even drier Gros-Plant. You'll find a brief account of how to visit some of the vineyards where they are made on p.280.

Cider (*cidre*) is extremely popular. In Brittany it's a standard accompaniment to a meal of *crêpes* and may be offered on restaurant *menus fixes*.

A LIST OF FOODS AND DISHES

Basics

Pain	Bread	*Poivre*	Pepper	*Fourchette*	Fork
Beurre	Butter	*Sel*	Salt	*Couteau*	Knife
Oeufs	Eggs	*Sucre*	Sugar	*Cuillère*	Spoon
Lait	Milk	*Bouteille*	Bottle	*Table*	Table
Huile	Oil	*Verre*	Glass	*L'addition*	Bill

Snacks

Crêpe	Pancake (sweet)	*Omelette . . .*	Omelette . . .
au sucre	with sugar	*nature*	plain
au citron	with lemon	*aux fines herbes*	with herbs
au miel	with honey	*au fromage*	with cheese
à la confiture	with jam	*Salade de . . .*	Salad of . . .
aux oeufs	with eggs	*tomates*	tomatoes
à la crème de	with chestnut purée	*betteraves*	beetroot
marrons		*concombres*	cucumber
Galette	Buckwheat (savoury)	*carottes râpées*	grated carrots
	pancake	**Other fillings/salads:**	
Un sandwich/ une	A sandwich	*Anchois*	Anchovy
baguette . . .		*Andouillette*	Tripe sausage
jambon	with ham	*Boudin*	Black pudding
fromage	with cheese	*Coeurs de palmiers*	Palm hearts
saucisson	with sausage	*Fonds d'artichauts*	Artichoke hearts
à l'ail	with garlic	*Hareng*	Herring
au poivre	with pepper	*Langue*	Tongue
pâté (de	with pâté (country-style)	*Poulet*	Chicken
campagne)		*Thon*	Tuna fish
croque-monsieur	Grilled cheese and ham	**And some terms:**	
	sandwich	*Chauffé*	Heated
croque-madame	Grilled cheese and bacon,	*Cuit*	Cooked
	sausage, chicken or an egg	*Cru*	Raw
Oeufs	Eggs	*Emballé*	Wrapped
au plat	Fried eggs	*À emporter*	Takeaway
à la coque	Boiled eggs	*Fumé*	Smoked
durs	Hard-boiled eggs	*Salé*	Salted/spicy
brouillés	Scrambled eggs	*Sucré*	Sweet

Soups *(Soupes)* and Starters *(Hors d'Oeuvres)*

Bisque	Shellfish soup	*Velouté*	Thick soup, usually fish or
Bouillabaisse	Marseillais fish soup		poultry
Bouillon	Broth or stock		
Bourride	Thick fish soup	**Starters**	
Consommé	Clear soup	*Assiette*	Plate of cold meats
Pistou	Parmesan, basil and garlic	*anglaise*	
	paste added to soup	*Crudités*	Raw vegetables with
Potage	Thick vegetable soup		dressings
Rouille	Red pepper, garlic and	*Hors d'oeuvres*	Combination of the above
	saffron mayonnaise served	*variés*	plus smoked or marinated
	with fish soup		fish

Fish *(Poisson)*, Seafood *(Fruits de mer)* and Shellfish *(Crustaces* or *Coquillages)*

Anchois	Anchovies	*Daurade*	Sea bream	*Louvine,*	Similar to sea
Anguilles	Eels	*Eperlan*	Smelt or	*loubine*	bass
Barbue	Brill		whitebait	*Maquereau*	Mackerel
Bigourneau	Periwinkle	*Escargots*	Snails	*Merlan*	Whiting
Brème	Bream	*Flétan*	Halibut	*Moules*	Mussels (with
Cabillaud	Cod	*Friture*	Assorted fried fish	*(marinière)*	shallots in white
Calmar	Squid	*Gambas*	King prawns		wine sauce)
Carrelet	Plaice	*Hareng*	Herring	*Oursin*	Sea urchin
Claire	Type of oyster	*Homard*	Lobster	*Palourdes*	Clams
Colin	Hake	*Huîtres*	Oysters	*Praires*	Small clams
Congre	Conger eel	*Langouste*	Spiny lobster	*Raie*	Skate
Coques	Cockles	*Langoustines*	Saltwater crayfish	*Rouget*	Red mullet
Coquilles St-	Scallops		(scampi)	*Saumon*	Salmon
Jacques		*Limande*	Lemon sole	*Sole*	Sole
Crabe	Crab	*Lotte*	Burbot	*Thon*	Tuna
Crevettes grises	Shrimp	*Lotte de mer*	Monkfish	*Truite*	Trout
Crevettes roses	Prawns	*Loup de mer*	Sea bass	*Turbot*	Turbot

Terms: (Fish)

Aïoli	Garlic mayonnaise served with salt cod and other fish	*Fumé*	Smoked
		Fumet	Fish stock
Béarnaise	Sauce made with egg yolks, white wine, shallots and vinegar	*Gigot de Mer*	Large fish baked whole
		Grillé	Grilled
		Hollandaise	Butter and vinegar sauce
Beignets	Fritters	*A la meunière*	In a butter, lemon and parsley sauce
Darne	Fillet or steak		
La douzaine	A dozen	*Mousse/*	Mousse
Frit	Fried	*mousseline*	
Friture	Deep fried small fish	*Quenelles*	Light dumplings

Meat *(Viande)* and Poultry *(Volaille)*

Agneau (de pré-salé)	Lamb (grazed on salt marshes)	*Langue*	Tongue
		Lapin, lapereau	Rabbit, young rabbit
Andouille, andouillette	Tripe sausage	*Lard, lardons*	Bacon, diced bacon
		Lièvre	Hare
Boeuf	Beef	*Merguez*	Spicy, red sausage
Bifteck	Steak	*Mouton*	Mutton
Boudin blanc	Sausage of white meats	*Museau de veau*	Calf's muzzle
Boudin noir	Black pudding	*Oie*	Goose
Caille	Quail	*Os*	Bone
Canard	Duck	*Porc*	Pork
Caneton	Duckling	*Poulet*	Chicken
Contrefilet	Sirloin roast	*Poussin*	Baby chicken
Coquelet	Cockerel	*Ris*	Sweetbreads
Dinde, dindon	Turkey	*Rognons*	Kidneys
Entrecôte	Ribsteak	*Rognons blancs*	Testicles
Faux filet	Sirloin steak	*Sanglier*	Wild boar
Foie	Liver	*Steack*	Steak
Foie gras	Fattened (duck/ goose) liver	*Tête de veau*	Calf's head (in jelly)
Gigot (d'agneau)	Leg (of lamb)	*Tournedos*	Thick slices of fillet
Grillade	Grilled meat	*Tripes*	Tripe
Hâchis	Chopped meat or mince hamburger	*Veau*	Veal
		Venaison	Venison

Meat and Poultry – Dishes and Terms

Boeuf bourguignon	Beef stew with burgundy, onions and mushrooms	Au four	Baked
		Garni	With vegetables
Canard à l'orange	Roast duck with an orange-and-wine sauce	Gésier	Gizzard
		Grillé	Grilled
Cassoulet	A casserole of beans and meat	Magret de canard	Duck breast
		Marmite	Casserole
Coq au vin	Chicken cooked until it falls off the bone with wine, onions and mushrooms	Mijoté	Stewed
		Museau	Muzzle
		Rôti	Roast
Steack au poivre (vert/rouge)	Steak in a black (green/red) peppercorn sauce	Sauté	Lightly cooked in butter
Steack tartare	Raw chopped beef, topped with a raw egg yolk		

Terms:

For steaks:

Blanquette, daube, estouffade, hochepôt, navarin and ragoût	All are types of stews	Bleu	Almost raw
		Saignant	Rare
		À point	Medium
		Bien cuit	Well done
		Très bien cuit	Very well cooked
Aile	Wing	Brochette	Kebab
Carré	Best end of neck, chop or cutlet		

Garnishes and sauces:

Civit	Game stew	Beurre blanc	Sauce of white wine and shallots, with butter
Confit	Meat preserve	Chasseur	White wine, mushrooms and shallots
Côte	Chop, cutlet or rib		
Cou	Neck	Diable	Strong mustard seasoning
Cuisse	Thigh or leg	Forestière	With bacon and mushroom
Epaule	Shoulder	Fricassée	Rich, creamy sauce
Médaillon	Round piece	Mornay	Cheese sauce
Pavé	Thick slice	Pays d'Auge	Cream and cider
En croûte	In pastry	Piquante	Gherkins or capers, vinegar and shallots
Farci	Stuffed		
Au feu de bois	Cooked over wood fire	Provençale	Tomatoes, garlic, olive oil and herbs

Vegetables (légumes), herbs (herbes) and spices (épices), etc.

Ail	Garlic	Endive	Chicory	Piment	Pimento
Algue	Seaweed	Épinards	Spinach	Pois chiche	Chick peas
Anis	Aniseed	Estragon	Tarragon	Pois mange-tout	Snow peas
Artichaut	Artichoke	Fenouil	Fennel		
Asperges	Asparagus	Flageolet	White beans	Pignons	Pine nuts
Avocat	Avocado	Gingembre	Ginger	Poireau	Leek
Basilic	Basil	Haricots	Beans	Poivron	Sweet pepper
Betterave	Beetroot	Verts	String (French)	(vert, rouge)	(green, red)
Carotte	Carrot	Rouges	Kidney	Pommes (de	Potatoes
Céleri	Celery	Beurres	Butter	terre)	
Champignons, cèpes, chanterelles	Mushrooms of various kinds	Laurier	Bay leaf	Primeurs	Spring vegetables
		Lentilles	Lentils		
Chou (rouge)	(Red) cabbage	Maïs	Corn	Radis	Radishes
Choufleur	Cauliflower	Menthe	Mint	Riz	Rice
Ciboulettes	Chives	Moutarde	Mustard	Safran	Saffron
Concombre	Cucumber	Oignon	Onion	Salade verte	Green salad
Cornichon	Gherkin	Pâte	Pasta or pastry	Sarrasin	Buckwheat
Echalotes	Shallots	Persil	Parsley	Tomate	Tomato
		Petits pois	Peas	Truffes	Truffles

Vegetables – Dishes and Terms

Beignet	Fritter	*Parmentier*	With potatoes
Farci	Stuffed	*Sauté*	Lightly fried in butter
Gratiné	Browned with cheese or butter	*À la vapeur*	Steamed
Jardinière	With mixed diced vegetables	*Je suis végétarien*	I'm a vegetarian. Are
À la parisienne	Sautéed in butter (potatoes); with	*(ne). Il y a quelques*	there any non-meat
	white wine sauce and shallots	*plats sans viande?*	dishes?

Fruits *(Fruits)* and nuts *(noix)*

Abricot	Apricot	*Framboises*	Raspberries	*Pistache*	Pistachio
Amandes	Almonds	*Fruit de la*	Passion fruit	*Poire*	Pear
Ananas	Pineapple	*passion*		*Pomme*	Apple
Banane	Banana	*Groseilles*	Redcurrants and	*Prune*	Plum
Brugnon,	Nectarine		gooseberries	*Pruneau*	Prune
nectarine		*Mangue*	Mango	*Raisins*	Grapes
Cacahouète	Peanut	*Marrons*	Chestnuts		
Cassis	Blackcurrants	*Melon*	Melon	**Terms**:	
Cérises	Cherries	*Myrtilles*	Bilberries	*Beignets*	Fritter
Citron	Lemon	*Noisette*	Hazelnut	*Compôte de . . .*	Stewed . . .
Citron vert	Lime	*Noix*	Nuts	*Coulis*	Sauce
Figues	Figs	*Orange*	Orange	*Flambé*	Set aflame in
Fraises (de	Strawberries	*Pamplemousse*	Grapefruit		alcohol
bois)	(wild)	*Pêche (blanche)*	(White) peach	*Frappé*	Iced

Desserts *(Desserts* or *Entremets)* and Pastries *(Pâtisserie)*

Bombe	A moulded ice cream dessert	*Parfait*	Frozen mousse, some-
Brioche	Sweet, high yeast breakfast roll		times ice cream
Charlotte	Custard and fruit in lining of	*Petit Suisse*	A smooth mixture of
	almond fingers		cream and curds
Crème Chantilly	Vanilla-flavoured and sweet-	*Petits fours*	Bite-sized cakes/pastries
	ened whipped cream	*Poires Belle Hélène*	Pears and ice cream in
Crème fraîche	Sour cream		chocolate sauce
Crème pâtissière	Thick eggy pastry-filling	*Yaourt, yogourt*	Yoghurt
Crêpes suzettes	Thin pancakes with orange		
	juice and liqueur	**Terms**:	
Fromage blanc	Cream cheese	*Barquette*	Small boat-shaped flan
Glace	Ice cream	*Bavarois*	Refers to the mould, could
Ile flottante/	Soft meringues floating on		be a mousse or custard
oeufs à la neige	custard	*Coupe*	A serving of ice cream
Macarons	Macaroons	*Crêpes*	Pancakes
Madeleine	Small sponge cake	*Galettes*	Buckwheat pancakes
Marrons Mont	Chestnut purée and cream on a	*Gênoise*	Rich sponge cake
Blanc	rum-soaked sponge cake	*Sablé*	Shortbread biscuit
Mousse au	Chocolate mousse	*Savarin*	A filled, ring-shaped cake
chocolat		*Tarte*	Tart
Palmiers	Caramelized puff pastries	*Tartelette*	Small tart

Cheese *(Fromage)*

There are over 400 types of French cheese, most of them named after their place of origin. *Chèvre* is goat's cheese. Le *plateau de fromages* is the cheeseboard, and bread, but not butter, is served with it. The best-known cheeses from the area covered by this book all come from the Pays d'Auge region of Normandy; *Pont l'Evêque, Livarot,* and, most famous of all, *Camembert,* and are discussed in detail on p.145.

And one final note: always call the waiter or waitress *Monsieur* or *Madame* (*Mademoiselle* if a young woman), never *garçon*, no matter what you've been taught in school.

Normans more often consume it in bars. Most of the many varieties are very dry and very wonderful. *Poiré*, pear cider, is also produced but on a small scale and is not commercially distributed.

The familiar Belgian and German brands account for most of the **beer** you'll find. Draught (*à la pression*, usually *Kronenbourg*) is the cheapest drink you can have next to coffee and wine – ask for *un demi* (defined as 25cl). Bottled beer is exceptionally cheap in supermarkets.

British-style ales and stouts are becoming increasingly popular, with quite a few special beer-drinking establishments appearing in such cities as Rennes and Quimper. There's even a home-grown Breton real ale, *Coreff* – see p.220.

Strong alcohols are drunk from 5am as pre-work fortifiers, right through the day; Bretons have a reputation for commitment to this. Brandies and dozens of *eaux de vie* (spirits) and liqueurs are always available. The most famous of these in Normandy are *Calvados*, brandy distilled from apples and left to mature for anything upwards of ten years, and *Benedictine*, distilled at Fécamp from an obscure mix of ingredients. Measures are generous, but they don't come cheap, especially in restaurants (where Calvados is traditionally drunk as a *trou*, or hole, between courses). The same applies to imported spirits like whisky (*Scotch*).

On the **soft drink** front, you can now buy cartons of unsweetened fruit juice in supermarkets, although in cafés the bottled nectars such as apricot (*jus d'abricot*) and blackcurrant (*cassis*) still hold sway. Some cafés serve tiny glasses of fresh orange and lemon juice (*orange/citron pressé*); otherwise it's the standard fizzy cans. Bottles of **mineral water** (*eau minérale*) and spring water (*eau de source*) – either sparkling (*pétillante*) or still (*eau plate*) – abound, from the best-seller *Perrier* to the obscurest spa product. But there's not much wrong with the tap water (*l'eau du robinet*).

Coffee in Normandy is invariably espresso and very strong; in Brittany, particularly in villages, it is sometimes made in jugs, very weakly. *Un café* or *un express* is black, *un crème* is white, *un café au lait* (served at breakfast) is espresso in a large cup or bowl filled up with hot milk. Most bars will also serve *un déca*, decaffeinated. Ordinary **tea** (*thé*) is Lipton's, nine times out of ten; to have milk with it, ask for *un peu de lait frais*. After overeating, **herb teas** (*infusions*), served in every café, can be soothing. The more common ones are *verveine* (verbena), *tilleul* (lime blossom) and *tisane* (camomile). *Chocolat chaud* – hot chocolate – unlike tea, lives up to the high standards of French food and drink, and can be had in any café.

COMMUNICATIONS: POST, PHONES AND MEDIA

MAIL SERVICES

As a rule, French **post offices** – *postes* or *PTTs* – are open from 9am until noon and 2pm to 5pm (Mon–Fri), and 9am until noon only on Saturday. However, in the larger towns you'll find a main office open through the day, while in Breton and Norman villages, lunch hours and closing times can vary enormously.

You can have letters sent to you **poste restante** at any post office in the country. For whatever town you choose, always specify the main post office (*Poste Centrale*) to avoid possible confusion. The addresses of the two largest in the region covered by this book are:

Poste Restante, Poste Centrale, 76000 ROUEN.

Poste Restante, Poste Centrale, 44000 NANTES.

To collect mail you'll need a passport, and should expect to pay a charge of a couple of francs. If you're expecting mail, it's worth asking the clerk to check under your surname and all possible Christian names as well – filing systems tend to be erratic.

Sending letters, the quickest international service is by *aérogramme*, sold at all post offices. You can buy ordinary stamps (*timbres*) at any *tabac* (tobacconist); postcards (*cartes postales*) go at a cheaper rate than letters (*lettres*). If you're sending **parcels** abroad, remember that small *postes* don't often send foreign mail and may need reminding of, for example, the huge reductions for printed papers and books. **Faxes** can be sent from all main post offices: the official French word is *télécopie*, but everyone understands *fax*.

TELEPHONES

You can make domestic and international phone calls from any call box (or *cabine*), and can receive calls where there's a blue logo of a ringing bell. Most payphones only take **phone cards** (*télecartes*), obtainable from post offices, *PTT* boutiques, train stations and some *tabacs*; the cheapest card is 40F for 50 units. In coin-only boxes, still common in cafés, bars and rural parts, put the money in (50 centimes, 1F, 5F, 10F pieces) after you lift the receiver and before you dial – you can add more once you are connected.

For calls within France – local or long distance – dial all eight digits of the number (which these days includes what used to be the area code – displayed in every *cabine*). The exception is Paris: from Paris to the provinces first dial ☎16, or to call a Paris number from anywhere else, first dial ☎16/1.

An alternative to dialling internationally from *cabines*, if you prefer to avoid wrestling with piles of loose change, is to use the numbered **booths at main post offices**. You apply at the counter to be assigned a number and then dial as above. The disadvantage – odd, given the French obsession with technology – is that you can't tell how much you're spending. It's worth counting your units and checking calculations – mistakes are made.

To speak to the **operator** dial ☎10; the **international operator** ☎19.33.11; the **police** ☎17; **medical emergencies** ☎15.

To avoid payment altogether, you can, of course, make a reverse charge or **collect call** – known in French as "*téléphoner en PCV*". You can

---

INTERNATIONAL CALLS

To place a call **to France** from the UK, North America or virtually anywhere in the world, dial ☎010 331 followed by the eight-digit number.

To make an international call **from France**, dial ☎19, wait for a tone, and then dial the relevant country code, and the number you want minus its initial 0.

INTERNATIONAL DIALLING CODES:

Britain	☎19 44	Australia	☎19 61
Ireland	☎19 353	New Zealand	☎19 64
USA & Canada	☎19 1		

also do this through the operator in the UK, by dialling ☎19.00.44 and asking for a "reverse charge call". To get an English-speaking AT&T operator for North America, dial ☎19.00.11.

MINITEL

In theory at least, every French phone subscriber has a **minitel**, an on-line computer allowing access through the phone lines to all kinds of directories, databases, chat lines, etc. You will also find them in post offices, libraries and so on. Most organizations, from sports federations to government institutions to gay groups, have a code consisting of numbers and letters to call up information, leave messages, make reservations, etc. You dial the number on the phone, wait for a fax-type tone, then type the letters on the keyboard, and finally, press *Connexion Fin* (the same key ends the connection). If you're at all computer-literate and can understand keyboard terms in French (*retour* – return, *envoi* – enter, etc), you shouldn't find them hard to use. Most services cost more than the equivalent phone rates.

NEWSPAPERS AND MAGAZINES

British newspapers and the North American press – at the very least in the form of the *International Herald Tribune* – are intermittently available in Brittany and Normandy. In the larger resorts, and in cities such as Nantes and Rouen, you should find reasonable selections of foreign-language papers. Elsewhere, it's mostly down to the British *Times*, *Daily Mail* or *Sun*.

As for the **French press**, the widest circulations are enjoyed by the **regional dailies**. Throughout Normandy and Brittany, the most

important and influential paper is *Ouest-France*. This is based in Rennes but has numerous local editions – worth picking up for their listings supplements, if nothing else. Of the **national dailies**, *Le Monde* (Tues–Sun) is the most intellectual and respected, with no concessions to entertainment (such as pictures), but a correctly styled French that is probably the easiest to understand. *Libération* (*Libé* for short; Tues–Sun), is moderately left-wing, independent and colloquial with good, selective, coverage; *L'Humanité*, the Communist party newspaper, has a constantly dwindling readership. All the other nationals are firmly on the right.

Weeklies, on the *Newsweek/Time* model, include the wide-ranging left-leaning *Le Nouvel Observateur*, and its rightist counterweight, *L'Express*. The best, and funniest, investigative journalism is in the satirical *Canard Enchaîné*, unfortunately almost incomprehensible to non-native speakers. **Monthlies** include *L'Autre Journal*, which covers culture as well as news, and *Actuel* which is good for current events. *Le Monde* publishes a beautifully designed monthly, *Le Monde des Débats*, and there are, of course, all the French versions of *Vogue*, *Elle* and *Marie-Claire*, as well as the *Paris-Match* for gossip about stars and royalty. In addition, **comics** (*bandes dessinés* – *BD*) occupy a far more prestigious status in the bookshops and newsstands than they do in Britain or America. *Charlie-Hebdo* is one with political targets; *À Suivre* is a showpiece for amazing graphic talents.

TV AND RADIO

French TV broadcasts six channels, three of them public, along with a good many more cable and satellite channels, which include the *BBC World Service*. If you've got a **radio**, you can tune into English-language news on the *BBC World Service* on 648khz or between 6.195 and 12.095MHz shortwave at intervals throughout the day and night. *BBC Radio 4* from 5am to 11.45pm GMT, and the *World Service* from 11.45pm to 5am GMT on 198KHz long wave, are usually quite clear throughout Brittany and Normandy, while the *Voice of America* transmits on 90.5, 98.8 and 102.4FM. *Radio Classique* (FM 101.1) is a classical music station with a minimum of chat and no commercials. For **news** in French, there's the state-run *France Inter* (FM 87.8, 220 longwave), *Europe 1* (FM 104.7, 180 longwave) or round-the-clock news on *France Infos* (FM 105.5).

BUSINESS HOURS AND PUBLIC HOLIDAYS

The basic hours of business in France are 8am until noon and 2pm to 6pm. Almost everything – shops, museums, tourist offices, most banks – closes for a couple of hours at midday.

Food shops often don't reopen until halfway through the afternoon, closing around 7.30 or 8pm just before the evening meal. So if you're looking to buy a picnic lunch, you'll need to get into the habit of buying it before you're ready to think about eating.

The standard **closing days** are Sunday and Monday, and in smaller towns you'll find everything except the odd *boulangerie* (bakery) shut on both days. This includes **banks**. It's all too easy to find yourself dependent on hotels for money-changing – an alternative that invariably means low rates and high commission.

Museums are not very generous with their hours, tending to open at around 10am, close for lunch at noon until 2pm (sometimes 3pm) and then run through until only 5 or 6pm. Summer opening times, usually applicable between mid-May or early June and mid-September, but sometimes only during July and August, often differ from winter times; all variations are indicated in the listings given in this book. The closing days are usually Tuesday or Monday, sometimes both. Admission charges can be very off-putting, though most state-owned museums have one or two days of the week when they're free, and you can get a big reduction at most places by showing a student card (or passport if you're under 26 or over 60).

Churches and **cathedrals** are almost always open all day, with charges only for the crypt, treasuries, or cloister and little fuss about how you're dressed. Where they are closed you may have to go during Mass to take a look, on Sunday morning or at other times which you'll see posted up on the door. In small towns and villages, however, getting the key is not difficult – ask anyone nearby or hunt out the priest, whose house is known as the *presbytère*.

PUBLIC HOLIDAYS

There are thirteen national holidays (*jours fériés*), when most shops and businesses, though not museums or restaurants, are closed:

January 1
Easter Sunday
Easter Monday
Ascension Day (forty days after Easter)
Pentecost (seventh Sunday after Easter, plus the Monday)
May 1 (May Day/Labour Day)
May 8 (VE Day)
July 14 (Bastille Day)
August 15 (Assumption of the Virgin Mary)
November 1 (All Saints' Day)
November 11 (1918 Armistice Day)
Christmas Day

FESTIVALS AND EVENTS

The most interesting Breton events are without doubt the cultural festivals. At the largest of these, the *Lorient Festival Inter-Celtique* (first two weeks of August), music, performance, food and drink of all seven Celtic nations are featured in a completely authentic gathering that pulls in cultural nationalists (and ethnic music fans) from Ireland to Spain. If you can't get to Lorient, there are – smaller and more particularly Breton – alternatives in *Les Printemps de Châteauneuf-du-Faou*, held in the small town near Carhaix (Easter Sunday), Nantes' *Quinzaine Celtique* (June/July) and Quimper's *Festival Cornouaille* (mid to late July).

Look out also for local **club events** put on by individual Celtic folklore groups – *Cercles*, *Bagadou*, or best of the lot, *Fests-Noz*. These are most prolific in Nantes, though wherever you are in the province, listings pages of the *Ouest-France* can be worth scrutiny. The "Breton Music" section at the end of this book has detailed recommendations of clubs and venues to check out in the province.

The religious *pardons*, sometimes promoted as tourist attractions in Brittany, are rather different affairs. These are essentially church processions, organized by a particular community on the local saint's day. Though generally small-scale, some, like that at Sainte-Anne d'Auray, have over

CALENDAR OF EVENTS

Whitsun – **Honfleur** Seamen's Festival

Third Sun in May – **Treguier** *St Yves Pardon*

June 6 – D-DAY Ceremonies on Invasion Beaches

End June/start July – **Nantes** *Quinzaine Celtique*

Early July – **Lamballe** Golden Broom Folk Festival

First ten days of July – **Rennes** *Tombées de la Nuit* theatre and music festival

Second Sun in July – **Locronan** *Troménie Pardon*

July 16 – **La Haye du Routot** *Fête de Ste-Claire*

July 26 – **Ste Anne d'Auray** *Pardon*

July – **St-Brieuc** Festival of Breton Music

Late July – **Huelgoat** Aquatic 2 CVs race

Late July – **Quimper** *Festival de Cornouaille*

Last Sun in July – **Locquirec** Festival of the Sea

First week in Aug – **Vannes** Jazz Festival

First full week in Aug – **Lorient** *Festival InterCeltique*

First fortnight in Aug – **Quimper** *Semaines Musicales*

Early Aug – **Dives** Puppet Festival

Second Sun in Aug – **Lizio** *Festival Artisanal*

Mid-Aug – **Guingamp** *Saint Loup* Breton Dance Festival

Mid-Aug – **Lamballe** Horse Festival

Mid-Aug – **Le Roche-Jagu** Jazz Festival

First Sun in Sept – **Le Pin** Horse Show

First Sun in Sept – **Le Folgoet** *Pardon*

Early Sept – **Douarnenez** Film Festival of International Minorities

Second weekend of Sept – **Lessay** Holy Cross cattle & animal fair

First week in Sept – **Deauville** American Film Festival

Sun nearest 29 Sept – **Mont-St-Michel** Archangel Michael Festival

Last Sun in Sept – **Caudebec** Cider Festival (even-numbered years only)

Late Sept – **Bellême** Mycology Festival

End of Oct – **St-Brieuc** Art Rock festival

Second week in Dec – **Rennes** *Les Transmusicales* international rock festival the centuries taken on more region-wide status as pilgrimages. Rather than being carnivals or fêtes, they are primarily very serious occasions, centred on lengthy and rather gloomy church services. If you're not interested by the religious aspects, only the food and drink stalls, and low-key accompaniments, hold any great appeal.

Normandy lacks any specific cultural traditions to celebrate, doing its best to make up with celebrations of related **historic events** – births and deaths of William the Conqueror, Sainte-Thérèse, etc. The **D-Day** (June 6) landings along the Invasion Beaches are always marked too.

In both Normandy and Brittany, avoid the *Spectacles*, camp and overpriced outdoor shows on some mythical theme or other, held most regularly (and most tackily) at Bagnoles and Elven.

On the more mainstream **cultural side**, the larger cities – Rouen, Rennes and Nantes – have active theatre, opera and classical music seasons, though little happens during the summer. **Cinema** is most interesting in these cities, too, and the region is host to one of the more accessible French film festivals – Deauville's American Film Festival (September). Almost all foreign films will be dubbed into French; *v.o.* in the listings signifies original language.

Both **Rennes** and **Rouen**, have laid recent claim to be "the capital of French **rock**"; Rennes is increasingly the one to watch, with its December *Transmusicales* attracting international stars to share the stage with local groups. St-Brieuc's rival Art Rock festival caters to more specialist tastes. A few large rock concerts also take place during the holiday season, at places such as Brest and Concarneau, with the usual bland multinational billing of fading "rock giants".

TROUBLE AND POLICE

Compared to Paris or the south of France, crime is a low-key problem in Brittany and Normandy. However, you still need to take normal precautions against petty theft – keep your wallet in your front pocket or your handbag under your elbow.

If you should be attacked, hand over the money and start dialling the cancellation numbers for your travellers' cheques and credit cards (see below). For British travellers, *Barclaycard* offers a free "International Rescue" service (☎0181/667 1393), in which a replacement card or cash can be sent to you within 24 hours.

If you need to report a theft, go to the local *gendarmerie* (police station), and do your best to persuade them to give you the requisite piece of paper for a claim; the first thing they'll ask for is your passport. The two main types of French police, the **Police Nationale** and the **Gendarmerie Nationale**, are for all practical purposes indistinguishable; you can go to either.

Drivers are one of the most obviously vulnerable groups, with the ever-present risk of a break-in. Vehicles are rarely stolen, but tape decks as well as luggage left in cars make tempting targets and foreign number plates are easy to spot. Good insurance is the only answer – see p.19 – but whether you have it or not, make sure you don't leave your valuables in sight.

If you have an **accident** while driving, you have to fill in and sign a *constat à l'aimable* (jointly agreed statement); car insurers are

---

---

supposed to give you this with a policy, though in practice few seem to have heard of it.

For non-criminal **driving violations** such as speeding, the police can impose on-the-spot fines. Should you be arrested on any charge, you have the right to contact your nearest consulate. Although the police are not always as cooperative as they might be, it *is* their duty to assist you – likewise in the case of losing your passport or all your money.

As for offences of your own making, treatment by the police is little different from anywhere else in Europe. **Camping** outside authorized sites can bring you into contact with the authorities, though it's more likely to be the landowner who tells you to move off. **Topless sunbathing** is universally acceptable, but **nudity** limited to a few specifically naturist beaches.

Officially, you're supposed to carry **identification documents** at all times, and the police are entitled to stop you and demand it. In practice this doesn't happen much to tourists, at least to whites. If you're black it can be a different matter; the French police have a reputation for racism. In fact, being black can make entering the country difficult, and immigration officers can be obstructive to black holiday-makers.

Sexual harassment is generally no worse than in North America or the UK, but it can be a problem making judgements without the familiar linguistic and cultural signs. **Hitching** is definitely not advisable. Women who need help may prefer to contact women's organizations in the larger cities – *Femmes Batues, Femmes en Détresse* or *SOS Femmes*, all reachable through the Hôtel de Ville – before trying the police, while a consulate is likely to be of most immediate assistance. The **rape crisis organization** *SOS Viol* can be reached on ☎05.05.95.95, but it's not 24hrs (Mon–Fri 10am–6pm).

LOST OR STOLEN CARDS

Before leaving home, check with your bank or credit card company as to what number to call if your credit card is **lost or stolen**; you may have to call your home country. All the French numbers (which will tell you British or US contact numbers if necessary) are in Paris, so dial ☎16.1 first from Brittany or Normandy:
American Express ☎47.77.72.00
American Express travellers' cheques ☎05.90.86.00
Barclaycard ☎47.62.75.00
Diners' Club ☎47.62.75.00
Eurocard/Mastercard ☎45.67.53.53 or 45.67.84.84
Visa ☎54.42.12.12

STAYING ON: WORK AND STUDY

Although EU citizens are in theory free to move to France and find jobs with exactly the same pay, conditions and trade union rights as French nationals, for anyone who isn't a specialist, casual work in Brittany or Normandy is hard to come by. Furthermore, while the French minimum wage (the *SMIC*) is currently around 35F per hour, employers are likely to pay lower wages to temporary foreign workers who don't have easy legal resources.

The region has just one wine harvest (around Nantes), almost wholly automated, and there is small chance of picking up any other kind of short-term employment. Visitors from North America or Australasia without a pre-arranged job offer would be foolish to imagine they have any chance of finding paid employment.

For EU citizens who arrange things in advance, however, there are work possibilities in au-pairing, teaching English as a foreign language, and in the holiday industry. And if you're just looking for an interesting way to fill the summer, assorted archeological schemes, mostly on Brittany's megalithic sites, sometimes have space for foreign volunteers.

FINDING WORK

Whatever you are looking for, it's important to plan well ahead. The best **general sources** for all jobs in France are the publications *Emplois d'été en France* (£7.95; available in Britain from Vacation Work, 9 Park End St, Oxford; ☎0865/241978) and *1000 Pistes de Jobs* (69F; available from *L'Étudiant*, 27 rue du Chemin-Vert, 75011 Paris). *Working Holidays* (£8.89; published by Central Bureau, Seymour Mews House, Seymour Mews, London W1H 9PE) is also useful. In France, Thursday evening's *France Soir* has the best selection of job ads.

TEACHING ENGLISH

Teaching English is one of the easiest ways to find a job in France. Such posts are freqently advertised in Britain; check the *Guardian's* "Education" section (every Tuesday), or the weekly *Times Educational Supplement*. Late summer is usually the best time. You don't need fluent French to get a post, but a *TEFL* (*Teaching English as a Foreign Language*) qualification may well be required. If you apply from home, most schools will fix up the necessary papers for you. It's also quite feasible to find a teaching job when you're in France, but you may have to accept semi-official status and no job security. For the addresses of schools, look under *Écoles de Langues* in the Professions directory of the local phone book. Offering **private lessons** (via university notice boards or classified ads), you'll have lots of competition, and it's hard to reach the people who can afford it, but it's always worth a try. The best places to live and teach are probably St-Malo, Quimper, Rennes and Rouen.

BECOMING AN AU PAIR

Au pair work is usually arranged through one of a dozen agencies, all of which are listed in *Working Holidays*. In Britain, *The Lady* is *the* magazine for classified adverts for such jobs, arranged privately. As initial numbers to ring, try *Euroyouth* (☎01702/341434) or *Scattergoods* (☎01483/63640); either can fill you in on the general terms and conditions (never very generous), and the state of the market. Don't accept less than 1000F a month (on top of board and lodging), and make sure you have an escape route (such as a ticket home) in case you find the conditions intolerable – many people have had bad experiences. *Scattergoods* also runs a summer-holiday scheme, placing people in French families for two or three weeks, where you get free board and lodging in exchange for giving English lessons.

TRAVEL INDUSTRY JOBS

Temporary jobs in the **travel industry** revolve around courier work — supervising and working on bus tours or summer campsites. You'll need good French (and maybe even another language) and should write to as many tour operators as you can, preferably in early Spring. Ads occasionally appear in the *Guardian's* "Media" section (every Monday). Working on a campsite usually involves putting up tents at the start of the season, taking them down again at the end, and general maintenance and trouble-shooting work in the months between; experienced teachers are also in demand to provide child care. *Canvas Holidays* (☎01383/644000), *Eurocamp* (☎01565/626262) and *Sunsites* (☎01565/625555) are worth approaching.

ARCHEOLOGICAL DIGS

Volunteer work on **archeological sites** varies from year to year, according to available grants and priorities. Recently, there have been opportunities to work on a number of Breton Gallo-Roman and megalithic sites — including Locmariaquer — and on neolithic sites in Normandy. Food and campsite or student hall accommodation is generally provided, though there may be a small weekly charge; travel costs are not normally paid. It's best to write a number of letters to potential authorities asking for details of any projects. Excavations are regularly organized by the following:

Laboratoire d'Anthropologie Préhistorique: write c/o Dr Jean Laurent Monnier, Charge de Recherche au CNRS, Université de Rennes I, Campus de Beaulieu, 35042 Rennes.

Ministère de la Culture Circonscription des Antiquités Historiques et Préhistoriques de Bretagne, 6 rue du Chapitre, BP 927, 35011 Rennes Cedex.

Musée d'Histoire Naturelle: write c/o Jean Pierre Watte, Archaeologue Municipal, place du Vieux Marché, 76600 Le Havre.

ORGANIC FARMING

One final offbeat possibility if you want to discover green rural life is being a **working guest** on an organic farm. The period can be anything from a week to a couple of months and the work may involve cheese making, market gardening, bee-keeping, wine producing or building. For details of the scheme and a list of French addresses, write to WWOOF, 19 Bradford Road, Lewes, East Sussex BN7 1RB, UK.

CLAIMING BENEFIT

If you're an EU citizen — and you do the paperwork in advance — you can sign on for **unemployment benefit**. To do so, you must collect form E303 before leaving home, available in Britain from any DSS office. The procedure is first to get registered at an *ANPE* office (*Agence Nationale pour l'Emploi*), then take the form to your local *ASSEDIC* (benefits office) and give them an address, which can be a hostel or a hotel, for the money to be sent. You sign once a month at the *ANPE* and receive dole a month in arrears — theoretically, at least, payments can be delayed in small towns for up to three months. After three months, you must anyway either leave the country or get a *carte de séjour*.

British and other EU **pensioners** can arrange for their pensions to be paid in France, but not unfortunately to receive French state pensions.

STUDYING IN FRANCE

It's relatively easy to be a **student** in France, and many foreign students perfect their fluency in the language while studying. Foreigners pay no more than French nationals to enrol for a course, and the only problem then is to support yourself. Your *carte de séjour* and — if you're an EU citizen — social security will be assured, and you'll be eligible for subsidized accommodation, meals and all the student reductions. In general, French universities are relatively informal; strict entry requirements, including an exam in French, apply only for undergraduate degrees, not for post-graduate courses. For full **details and prospectuses**, contact the Cultural Service of any French embassy or consulate (see p.17).

It's worth noting that if you're a full-time non-EU student in France (see below), you can get a non-EU **work permit** for the following summer so long as your visa is still valid.

Language schools all along the coast provide intensive French courses for foreigners. Many of these are listed in the handout *"Cours de Français pour Étudiants Étrangers"*, also obtainable from embassy or consular cultural sections, with the most popular being those organized each summer at St-Malo by the University of Rennes.

DIRECTORY

BEACHES are public property within five metres of the high tide mark, so you can walk past the private villas, and set foot on islands. Another law, however, forbids you to camp.

BUYING PROPERTY If you're looking to buy a home in Brittany or Normandy, the best source for information and advice is *Buying Residential Property in France*, available from *Chambre de Commerce Française de Grande Bretagne*, Knightsbridge House, 197 Knightsbridge, London SW1 (☎0171/225 5250).

CAMERAS AND FILM Film and videotape is considerably cheaper in North America than France or Britain, so stock up if you're coming by that way. If you bring a camcorder, make sure any tapes you buy in France are compatible.

CHILDREN AND BABIES are generally welcome everywhere, including most bars and restaurants. **Hotels** charge by the room, with a small supplement for an additional bed or cot, and many family-run places will babysit or offer a listening service while you eat or go out. Especially in the seaside towns, most **restaurants** have children's menus or cook simpler food on request. You'll have no difficulty finding disposable nappies (*couches à jeter*), but nearly all baby foods have added sugar and salt, and French milk powders are very rich indeed. *SNCF* charge nothing on **trains and buses** for under-4s, and half-fare for 4–11s (see p.27 for other reductions). Most SIs have details of specific activities for children – in particular, many

resorts supervise "clubs" for children on the beach. And almost every town has a **children's playground** with a good selection of activities. Something to beware of – not that you can do much about it – is the difficulty of negotiating a child's **buggy** over the large cobbles that cover many of the older streets in town centres.

ELECTRICITY is almost always 220V, using plugs with two round pins.

FISHING You get fishing rights by becoming a member of an authorized fishing club – SIs have details. The main areas for river fishing are in Brittany, in the Aulne around Châteaulin and in the Morbihan.

GAY/LESBIAN France is more liberal on homo-sexuality than most European countries. The legal age of consent is 15 and gay communities thrive in Paris and many southern towns, though lesbian life is rather less upfront. Brittany and Normandy, however, have very little conspicuous gay life.

LAUNDRY Launderettes (laundromats) are not all that common in Breton or Norman towns, although some are listed in this guide. The alternative *blanchisserie* or *pressing* services are likely to be expensive, and hotels in particular charge very high rates. If you're staying in hotels, keep quantities small as most officially forbid doing any laundry in your room.

LEFT LUGGAGE Lockers of various sizes are available at all *SNCF* stations, as well as *consigne* for longer periods or larger items.

SWIMMING POOLS (*piscines*) are well sign-posted in most French towns, and reasonably priced. SIs have addresses.

TIME France is one hour ahead of Britain throughout the year, except for a short period during October, when it's the same. It is six hours ahead of Eastern Standard Time, and nine hours ahead of Pacific Standard Time. This also applies during daylight savings seasons, observed in France (as in most of Europe) from the end of March through to the end of September.

VACCINATIONS are neither required nor necessary.

WATER The tap-water is always safe to drink; bottled mineral water, always available, may taste better.

PART TWO

NORMANDY

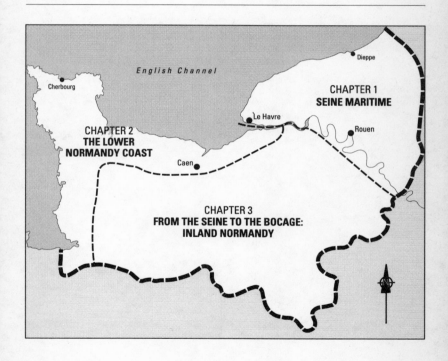

English Channel

Cherbourg

Dieppe

CHAPTER 1
SEINE MARITIME

Le Havre

Rouen

CHAPTER 2
**THE LOWER
NORMANDY COAST**

Caen

CHAPTER 3
**FROM THE SEINE TO THE BOCAGE:
INLAND NORMANDY**

CHAPTER ONE

SEINE MARITIME

he *département* of **Seine Maritime** makes an untypical introduction to Normandy. Though scattered with the characteristic Norman half-timbered houses and small farms, the countryside is stark along the coastline and often dull in the flatlands of the chalk Caux plateau behind. Only along the sheltered ribbon of the **Seine valley** do you find the province's usual greenery and profusion of flowers and fruit.

Which is not to say this is all territory to pass through or ignore. Arriving at **Dieppe** you can take advantage of the low-key resorts along the **Côte d'Albâtre**,

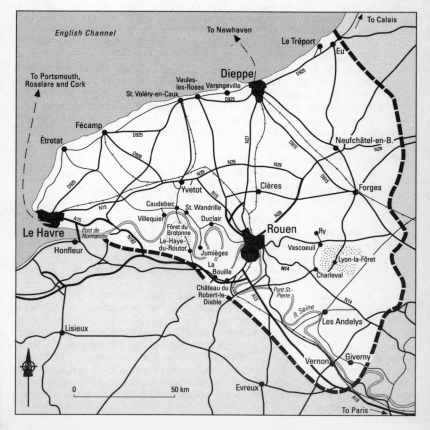

which hold occasional surprises behind their windswept and tide-chased walks. At **Fécamp** is an absurd Hammer House of Horror Benedictine distillery; at **Étretat** spectacular stacks and arches of rock, to either side of one of the nicest little coastal towns in Normandy; at **Varengeville**, architect Edwin Lutyens' wonderful **Bois des Moutiers**. On the Seine estuary, **Le Havre** is less conventionally enticing – but worth attention all the same, for its art collections and, as France's second port after Marseille, for its liveliness.

The extravagant meandering course of the **River Seine**, however, determines most people's travels in this region. **Rouen**, scene of the trial and execution of Joan of Arc, is one of the major provincial capitals of France; the combination of contemporary verve with its heavily but effectively restored medieval centre makes it by far the most interesting Norman city. Along the valley and riverbanks there is plenty to delay your progress: tranquil villages such as **Villequier** and **La Bouille**; the evocatively ruined Romanesque abbeys of **St-Wandrille** and **Jumièges**; the English frontier-stronghold of **Château Gaillard** looming above Les Andelys; and, an unmissable last stop before Paris, **Monet's garden** and waterlilies at **Giverny**.

THE NORTHERN PORTS

There is no confusing the northern ports of Normandy, **Dieppe** and **Le Havre**, with their rivals to the east. Each has managed to retain a distinct individual identity in a way that Calais and Boulogne, which have to cope with ten times the number of passengers, simply do not; if you're using either port, you shouldn't feel obliged to rush on out as soon as you arrive, or dice with time to coincide to the minute with the ferries back.

Both offer the same obvious choice of **routes**: inland towards Rouen, or along the coast. If you're setting off from Dieppe with your own transport, the **coast road** is the most immediately gratifying. Until you get as far south as Rouen, there is little of interest on the plains of the Caux plateau inland, while harbour towns such as **Le Tréport** to the east, and **Étretat** and **Fécamp** to the west, make diverting overnight stops. Both are also within easy reach of Le Havre, although here you are poised at the start of the route along the Seine. As well as the river towns, places such as Honfleur (see p.94) on the lower Norman coast, covered in Chapter Two, only take a few minutes to get to from Le Havre via the huge Seine bridges.

Dieppe

Crowded between high cliff headlands, **DIEPPE** is an enjoyably small-scale port at which to arrive, very French but with a long and intimate association with England. As the nearest harbour to Paris, it has had an eventful history. Its existence is first recorded in 1030, when the abbey of Mont Ste-Catherine-de-Rouen acquired the area for an annual rent of 5000 smoked herrings. The port was regularly used by William the Conqueror when he was King of England, and passed into French hands in 1195 when Phillippe Auguste burnt Richard the Lionheart's fleet in the harbour. It changed ownership several times during the Hundred Years War, before being finally taken for France by the future Louis XI in 1443.

It was from Dieppe, in 1524, that the Italian explorer Giovanni da Verrazano sailed to found the settlement that later became New York. Early emigrants to Canada used the port too, and the strong links established with the French colony there were to continue long after the French lost Canada to the British in 1759.

When the edict of Nantes was revoked in 1685, Dieppe was one of the main escape routes used by fleeing Protestants; during the French Revolution, three Brighton captains of the Channel Packet Service ran a regular – and profitable – service for aristocrats on the run. In 1848, the railway from Paris reached Dieppe, and, from the 1850s, the Newhaven Packet operated a daily service. The town became a fashionable seaside resort, attracting French aristocracy and British royalty. The French would promenade along the seafront, while the English

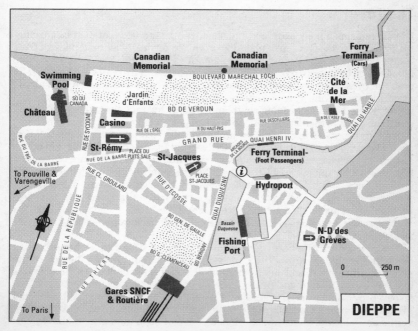

DIEPPE

colony indulged in the peculiar pastime of bathing. Hence the extravagant amount of clear space between the shelving shingle beach and the first buildings, and the "salt water therapy centre", now hemmed in with car parks.

Arrival and Information

Dieppe's **SI** is on the pont Ango, which separates the ferry harbour from the pleasure port; you can't miss it if you're arriving by ferry (May–Sept, Mon–Sat 9am–noon & 2–7pm; Oct–April Mon–Sat 9am–noon & 2–6pm; ☎35.84.11.77). A beach annexe at Rotonde de la Plage is open in summer (July & Aug, Tues–Sun 10am–1pm & 3–8pm; May, June & first two weeks of Sept, Sat & Sun 10am–1pm & 3–8pm; ☎34.84.28.70). The main **post office** is at 2 bd Maréchal-Joffre (Mon–Fri 8am–6pm, Sat 8am–noon; ☎35.04.70.14).

There are between three and four daily *Stena Sealink* **ferries** from Dieppe to Newhaven all year round. The **gare maritime** is on quai Henri IV (foot passengers can buy tickets daily 10am–6pm & 10pm–5am, or call ☎35.06.39.19; the car terminal is open daily around the clock except between 6am & 9am, and vehicle tickets can be reserved on ☎35.06.39.00). Connecting trains for the ferries draw up alongside on the quay, although the town's main **gare SNCF** (☎35.98.50.50) is 500m away on boulevard Clemenceau, 1km from the beach. The **gare routière** (☎35.84.21.97) is right alongside. Dieppe is a small town and local buses only serve three routes. All start at the gare SNCF, pass through the bus station and call at the SI.

The Town

Dieppe remains a busy **port**, and the sheer bustle and verve of the place cannot fail to strike passengers disembarking from the ferries. Vast quantities of **fruit** from all over the world – and forty percent of all **shellfish** eaten in France – are unloaded at its commercial docks, but the quayside **fish stalls** are what really grab the eyes. Every morning the previous night's catch is displayed with all the usual mouthwatering French flair, an appetizing profusion of sole, scallops and turbot. Even if you are heading south immediately by train, the railway tracks run along the *quais* of the fishing port, so you can get a whiff of what you're missing.

Modern Dieppe is laid out along three axes dictated by its eighteenth-century town planners, though now these central streets have become a little run-down, and are in any case left in continual shadow. The **bd de Verdun** runs for over a kilometre along the seafront, from the fifteenth-century castle in the west to the port entrance, and passes the Casino, along with the grandest and oldest hotels. A short way inland, parallel to the seafront, is the **rue de la Barre** and its pedestrianized continuation, the **Grande Rue**. Along the harbour's edge, an extension of the Grande Rue, **quai Henry IV** has a colourful backdrop of cafés, brasseries and restaurants.

The **place du Puits-Salé**, dominated by the huge **Café des Tribunaux**, is at the centre of the old town. The *Café* was built as an inn towards the end of the seventeenth century, and briefly became Dieppe's town hall after the previous one was bombarded by the British in 1694. In the late nineteenth century, it was favoured by painters and writers such as Renoir, Monet, Sickert, Whistler and Pissarro. It's now a cavernous café, with sombre wooden panels and dark brown velveteen walls, the haunt of college students and open until after midnight. For

English visitors, its most evocative association is that the exiled and unhappy Oscar Wilde drank here regularly. He lived (as M. Melmouth) at Berneval, 10km east of Dieppe, which was where he wrote *The Ballad of Reading Gaol*.

From the *Café*, rue Saint Jacques leads to the **church** of the same name, with its fourteenth-century lantern tower. Inside the church, along with the usual chapels to Ste-Thérèse and the Sacred Heart, there's one to the "Canadian Martyrs", dedicated in 1951 but nothing to do with World War II. Instead it's devoted to two Dieppe priests, shown in modern stained glass being hacked to death by "Mohawks" in 1648. Nearby, the **Mur de Trésor** bears intricate and potentially fascinating carvings of Brazilian Indians – but unfortunately high up and all but indecipherable – dating from the seventeenth century.

Northwest of the place du Puits-Salé, **rue Bouchard** heads to the sixteenth-century church of Saint Rémy, which was partly destroyed when, used as an arms dump by the Germans, it was blown up the day before the town was liberated in August 1944. It is now being restored, but has yet to re-open to the public.

The Château

The most obvious and conspicuous sight in Dieppe is the medieval **castle** overlooking the seafront from the west. This is the home of the **Musée de Dieppe** (June –Sept daily 10am–noon & 2–6pm; Oct–May Mon & Wed–Sat 10am–noon & 2–5pm, Sun 10am–noon & 2–6pm; 13F), which in addition to its exhibition on local history – and Dieppe's maritime past means that "local history" can stretch as far as including pre-Columbian pottery from Peru – houses two showpiece collections.

The first is a group of **Dieppe carved ivories** – virtuoso specimens of sawing, filing and chipping of the plundered riches of Africa. The ivory was shipped back to the town by early Dieppe "explorers", in such quantities that during the seventeenth century over three hundred craftsmen-carvers lived here.

The other permanent exhibition is made up of a hundred or so prints by the co-originator of Cubism, **Georges Braque**, who went to school in Le Havre, spent his summers in Dieppe, and is buried just west of the town at Varengeville-sur-Mer (see below). Only a few prints are displayed at any one time, but in theory you can see the rest if you ask.

The Square du Canada

A flight of steps leads down from the castle to the **square du Canada**, originally a commemoration of the role played by sailors from Dieppe in that country's colonization. After the last war, however, it acquired an additional significance, for it was at Dieppe in August 1942 that the Allied **commando raid**, Operation Jubilee, took place. The first large-scale assault on the continent after Dunkerque, the operation claimed over three thousand Canadian casualties in a near-suicidal series of landings and attacks up sheer and well-fortified cliff faces. Many were cut down as soon as they left their landing craft, before they even touched dry land, while some German defenders are reputed not to have bothered with firing their weapons – simply dropping projectiles over the edge.

The Allied Command later justified the carnage as having taught valuable lessons for the 1944 invasion; the Channel ports were seen to be too heavily defended to be vulnerable to frontal attack, and the invasion plan was changed to one which required the amphibious landing armies to bring their own harbour with them (see p.110).

The Cité de la Mer

Dieppe's newest attempt to keep tourists in town for longer than it takes to get to or from the ferry terminal is the **Cité de la Mer**, housed in a featureless white concrete block in the tangle of streets just back from the harbour, at 37 rue de l'Asile-Thomas (April–Sept Mon 2–7pm, Tues–Sun 10am–12.30pm & 2–7pm; Oct–March Mon 2–6pm, Tues–Sun 10am–noon & 2–6pm; 25F). This simultaneously sets out to entertain children and to serve as a centre for scientific research, and succeeds in both without being all that interesting for the casual adult visitor.

Kids are certain to enjoy learning the principles of navigation by operating radio-controlled boats (5F for three minutes). Thereafter, the museum traces the history of sea-going vessels, leading from maps of the great Norman voyages of exploration and conquest, via a Viking *drakkar* under construction following methods depicted in the Bayeux Tapestry, right up to an oddly sketchy account of the insides of a nuclear-powered submarine. Next comes a very detailed geological exhibition covering the formation of the local cliffs, in which we learn how to go about converting shingle into sandpaper. Visits culminate with the large **aquariums**, filled with the marine life of the Channel: flat fish with bulbous eyes and twisted faces, retiring octopuses, battling lobsters, and hermaphrodite scallops (a caption helpfully explains that the white part is male, and the orange female). Thanks to a typical lack of sentimentality, jars of fish soup, whose exact provenance is not made explicit, are on sale at the exit.

Accommodation

You're unlikely to experience much difficulty finding accommodation in Dieppe. There are plenty of **hotels**; on the whole, prices get progressively cheaper as you head further inland from the seafront, which is actually among the quietest areas of town, especially near the castle end, away from the car-ferry traffic. The recently renovated **youth hostel**, still not very convenient, stands atop a hill at 48 rue Louis Fromager, 2km southwest of the gare SNCF in the Quartier Janval (June–Oct; ☎35.84.85.73; 40F). It's on bus routes #1 (get off at La Ferme des Hospices) and #2, direction Val Druel (get off at Château Michel).

The same bus continues to one of Dieppe's two **campsites**, the three-star *Camping Vitamin*, Chemin des Vertus (April–Oct; ☎35.82.11.11). The other, the two-star *Camping du Pré Saint Nicholas* is west along the coast, 3km beyond the château on the route de Pourville (year-round; ☎35.84.11.39).

Hotels

Many of the dearer hotels in Dieppe are at the western end of bd de Verdun facing the sea; they (and others with restaurants) are likely to insist on half-board, or even full-board, in the season, which can make them very expensive.

Hôtel Les Arcades, 1–3 Arcades de la Bourse (☎35.84.14.12). Facing the port; particularly suitable for tired passengers arriving at midnight and not wanting to walk more than 200 yards to find a bed. Restaurant with full, good-value menus from 75F. ③.

Hôtel Epsom, 11 bd de Verdun (☎35.84.10.18). Facing the sea. Refurbished; bright and cheerful, with TV in all rooms. *English Bar* with tartan carpet and pianist. No restaurant. ④.

Grand Duquesne, 15 place Saint Jacques (☎35.84.21.51). Recently refurbished pension, just off place du Puits Salé in view of the main door of the Cathedral,. The simplest menu, at 69F, includes squid or salmon *choucroute*. ②.

Hôtel de la Jetée, 5 rue de l'Asile Thomas (☎35.84.89.98). Very welcoming place overlooking the sea, with plain but spacious rooms. ②.

Hôtel La Plage, 20 bd de Verdun (☎35.84.18.28). Slightly upmarket rooms, all with English (satellite) TV, facing the beach. No restaurant. ⑤.

Hôtel-Restaurant Pontoise, 10 rue Thiers (☎35.84.14.57). Away from the beach, not far from the gare SNCF. ②.

Hôtel Select, 1 rue Toustain (☎35.84.14.66). Very grand red-brick building at the far (western) end of rue de la Baine, opposite the steps up to the château. Serves a "Great British Breakfast" for 59F all day long – to all comers. No restaurant. ③.

Hôtel Tourist, 16 rue de la Halle au Blé (☎35.06.10.10). Very plain rooms in a converted town house, one block back from the beach behind the Casino. No restaurant. ②.

Hôtel Windsor, 18 bd de Verdun (☎35.84.15.23). You pay premium rates for sea-facing rooms in this *logis*, where the panoramic first-floor dining room – *Le Haut Gallion* – has menus from 80F. Lavish buffet breakfasts. ③–⑤.

Eating and Shopping

The most promising area to look for **restaurants** in Dieppe is along the quai Henri IV, but there are alternatives all over the town – and note that many of the hotels reviewed above also have good dining rooms. All show a marked tendency to change name and owner overnight. Competition for ferry passengers keeps prices extremely low; so Dieppe is one of the few towns in Normandy where you can still find a good menu for around 50F.

As well as the daily spectacle of the fish on sale in the **port de péche**, described above, open-air **markets** are held in the place Nationale and Grande Rue on Tuesday and Thursday mornings, and all day on Saturday. Otherwise, the main shopping streets in Dieppe are rue de la Barre and the Grande Rue. The chain store *Printemps*, 7 Grande Rue, incorporates a duty-free shop, and there's a *Shopi* supermarket at 59 rue de la Barre. *L'Épicier Oliver* at 18 rue Saint Jacques has more specialist items. The biggest **hypermarket** in the area is *Mammouth* (Mon–Sat 9am–9pm), out of town at the Val Dunel commercial centre on the route de Rouen (RN 27).

Restaurants

Ankara, 18 rue de la Rade (☎35.84.58.33). Turkish restaurant between quai Henri IV and bd de Verdun. Midday menu from 45F; evening menu from 69F; vegetarian menu from 75F. Closed Weds.

Les Ecamias, 129 quai Henri-IV (☎35.84.67.67). Small, friendly traditional French restaurant, at the quieter, seaward end of the main quay not far from the Cité de la Mer. The 58F menu includes *moules marinières* and stuffed shellfish, and they also serve skate with capers.

Gril de la Mer, 15 rue de la Morinière (☎35.82.14.44). *À la carte* meals from 65F, on the street which connects Grande Rue with the beach.

Marmite Dieppoise, 8 rue Saint Jean (☎35.84.24.26). Between St-Jacques church and arcades de la Bourse. Lunch menu from 80F. Small, rustic and busy, featuring the local speciality *marmite Dieppoise* (seafood pot, with shellfish and white fish). Closed Sun pm and Mon, and also Thurs pm out of season.

Le Mélie, 2 Grande rue Pollet (☎35.84.21.19). One of Dieppe's best fresh-fish restaurants, right where the fishing boats come in. Menus from 100F.

Les P'tits Bateaux, 23 quai Henri IV (☎35.06.14.74). Menus 80F and 110F. Sixteenth-century cellar with live music until late; last orders midnight. The more upmarket *Pergola* is on the ground floor. Out front, there's a lavish display of seafood on ice, and a macaw; the bright yellow plastic tables are sheltered out of season.

Les Tourelles, 43 rue du Commandant Fayolle (☎35.84.15.88). Just behind the Casino, and renowned for its paellas, though it also serves the standard seafood dishes. Menus from 65F.

The Côte d'Albâtre

The high white cliffs that characterize the Norman coast west from Picardy to Le Havre have earned it the name of the **Côte d'Albâtre** – the Alabaster coast. All this shoreline is eroding at a ferocious rate, and it's conceivable that the small resorts here, tucked in at the mouths of a succession of valleys, may not last more than another century or so. For the moment, however, they are quietly prospering, with casinos, sports centres and yacht marinas ensuring a modest but steady summer trade.

Although to arrive at Dieppe and promptly head **east** along the coast towards Calais and Boulogne may not be instinctive behaviour for travellers embarking on a tour of Normandy, doing so gives the opportunity to see a couple of surprising little towns: venerable **Le Tréport**, still an appealing seaside resort, and the village of **Eu** with its thick forest surround, just inland.

Le Tréport

Thirty kilometres east of Dieppe, at the mouth of the River Bresle which serves as the border with Picardy, **LE TRÉPORT** is a seaside resort that has clearly seen better days. It was already something of a bathing station when the railways arrived in 1873, and promoted this as "the prettiest beach in Europe, just three hours from Paris". It remained the capital's favoured resort until the 1950s – and is still served by around five trains daily – but it can't ever have been that pretty, and these days its charms are definitely fading.

Le Tréport divides into three distinct sections: the flat wedge-shaped seafront area, bounded on one side by the Channel, on another by the harbour at the canalized rivermouth, and on the third by imposing 100m-high white chalk cliffs; the old town, higher up the slopes on safer ground; and the modern town further inland. The **seafront** itself is entirely taken up by a hideous pink-and-orange concrete Sixties apartment block, with one or two snack bars but no other sign of life, facing the Casino and a drab grey shingle beach. It's the more sheltered harbourside **Quai Francois 1er** around the corner that holds most of the action, lined with restaurants, souvenir shops and cafes. A venerable little brick fish-market stands across the road by the water, alongside a turn-of-the-century carousel. The assorted stone jetties and wooden piers around the harbour are enjoyable to stroll around, watching the comings and goings of the fishing boats that still keep Le Tréport busy. In its heyday it was possible to ride up the cliffs on a *téléphérique*; the tunnel through which it pierced the cliff face is still open to the air at either end, but the cables have rusted away, and the facilities are abandoned.

Climbing up from the Quai, you come to the heavily nautical **Église St-Jacques**, built in the fifteenth century to replace an eleventh-century original that crumbled into the sea, along with the cliff on which it stood. Nearby, next to the fortified former town hall that is now the local library, successive flights of steps, 365 of them in all, lead up to the top of the cliffs, with views to either side of the decaying mansions of Le Tréport and across to the longer beach of Mers-les-Bains, which being in Picardy falls outside the scope of this book.

Practicalities

Both **trains** and **buses** arrive in Le Tréport on the far side of the harbour, a short walk from the main quai. Turning left as you hit the main drag will bring you to the town's new **SI**, on quai Sadi-Carnot (Easter–Sept daily 10am–noon & 2–6pm; Oct–Easter Mon–Sat 10am–noon & 2–6pm; ☎35.86.05.69).

Of the **hotels** in town, the best in terms of a sea view and good-quality food is the *Riche-Lieu* at 50 quai Francois-1er (☎35.86.26.55; ④), which has modernized rooms with showers on four floors and a wide range of menus starting at 70F for a "bistrot" meal. The other seafood **restaurants** along the quai are too numerous to review in detail, each boasting of its fresh *assiette de fruits de mer* and offering similar meals from around 90F; the one with the highest gourmet reputation is the *Matelote*, 34 quai Francois-1er (☎35.86.01.13).

Eu

Queen Victoria twice visited Le Tréport with Albert. She didn't come to play on the beach, though, but to stay at the château at **EU**, a couple of kilometres inland. When she did so for the first time, she became the first English monarch to visit France since Henry VIII arrived for the Field of the Cloth of Gold.

Today, Eu is something of a backwater, consisting of a few pedestrian streets at the top of a hill, and a straggle of newer districts reaching down the slopes. The **château** that stands at its heart has been heavily restored, and is now a rather routine museum (guided tours April–Oct, daily except Tues 10am–noon & 2–6pm). This castle was constructed in the sixteenth century; of Eu's previous castle, deliberately burned in 1475 to forestall its capture by the English, only the tiny chapel remains, which was the site of William the Conqueror's marriage to Mathilda. Unlikely as it may sound, the town's Gothic church, **Nôtre-Dame et St-Laurent**, is dedicated to St Lawrence O'Toole, an Archbishop of Dublin who died here in 1181 while en route to visit Henry II in Rouen, to intercede on behalf of the Irish. His effigy still lies in the brightly-lit and eerie crypt, along with various fourteenth-century members of the Artois family.

If you find yourself staying in Eu, you can spend an enjoyable afternoon by venturing into the **forest of Eu**, a mysterious and ancient tangled woodland dominated by tall beeches, with a lost Roman city supposedly hidden in its depths. A good way to explore it more thoroughly, though you'll need your own transport, is to follow the **River Bresle** upstream, along the border between Normandy and Picardy.

Practicalities

Eu is on the Lé Treport rail line, with its **gare SNCF** 500m down the hill from the centre, and **SI** up in the pedestrianized section at 41 rue Bignon (Mon–Sat 9.15am–12.15pm & 2–6.30pm; ☎35.86.04.68). The *Hôtel de la Gare* at 20 place de la Gare (☎35.86.16.64; ④) is a slightly delapidated red-brick town house next to the gare SNCF, offering menus from 80F, and there's a **youth hostel** in the former royal kitchens, Centre des Fontaines (☎35.86.05.03). It serves meals, and acts as a general resource for local youngsters. Eu is otherwise short of places to eat.

Pourville sur-mer

Heading **west** from Dieppe along the coastal D75, which starts from rue Faubourg de la Barre, you come after three kilometres to the resort of **POURVILLE-SUR-MER**, an extremely tranquil last- or first-night stop for ferry passengers. It amounts to no more than a very simple curving bay which briefly interrupts the line of cliffs, with a few buildings along the road, most of them **hotels**. Among these is a *logis* confusingly named *Produits de la Mer* (☎35.84.38.34; ④), where all eight rooms have showers or baths, and the plainest seafood menu costs 74F. Next to it is a crazy golf course, and there's a campsite set in the fields further back from the sea.

Varengeville-sur-mer

If the museum in Dieppe has awakened your interest in **Georges Braque**, you may be interested in visiting **VARENGEVILLE-SUR-MER**, 8km west of Dieppe (25min on bus #311 or #312, afternoons only). This small town has long been popular with artists, including at different times Monet, Miró, and the parents of British Prime Minister Anthony Eden, who was born here, but Braque (1882–1963) was its greatest devotee. His **grave** is situated outside a church perched spectacularly above the cliffs a couple of kilometres north of the centre, a smooth marble tomb topped by a sadly decaying mosaic of a white dove in flight. More impressive is his vivid blue *Tree of Jesse* stained-glass window inside the church, through which the sun rises in summer.

Back along the road towards town from the church, the **Bois des Moutiers** was one of architect **Edwin Lutyens**' first commissions, built for Guillaume Mallet, and un-French in almost every respect. The gardens, designed by Mallet, are open from mid-March to mid-November (9am–noon & 2–7pm; closed Sat am; 25F), and the house in July and August (closed Sun am & Tues). Enthusiastic guides lead you through the highly innovative engineering of the house and grounds, replete with quirks and games. The colours of the Burne-Jones tapestry hanging in the stairwell were copied from Renaissance cloth in William Morris' studio; the rhododendrons were chosen from similar samples. Paths lead through vistas based on paintings by Poussin, Lorrain and other eighteenth-century artists; no modern roses, with their anachronistic colours are allowed to spoil the effect.

Of **accommodation** possibilities in Varengeville, the *logis Hôtel de la Terrasse* , on the cliffs west of town (mid-March to mid-Oct; ☎35.85.12.54; ④), stands out from the rest. Fishy menus in its panoramic dining room cost from 80F.

On from Varengeville

The coastal road immediately beyond Varengeville is not very interesting. **QUIBERVILLE**, the main name on the map, makes a popular target for wind-surfers, but in itself is little more than an overgrown caravan park; at Veules, you pass a couple of ludicrous folk-sculptures, including a seashell snowman; **ANGIENS** is a pretty village but with nothing much to linger over.

St-Valéry-en-Caux

The first sizeable community west of Dieppe is **ST-VALÉRY-EN-CAUX**, a rebuilt town which provides the clearest reminder of the fighting – and massive destruc-tion – of the Allied retreat of 1940. To either side of the shingle beach rise crum-bling brown-stained cliffs. A monument on the western heights pays tribute to the French division who faced Rommel's tanks on horseback, brandishing their sabres with hopeless heroism, while beside the ruins of a German artillery emplacement on the opposite cliffs, a second monument commemorates a Scottish division, the 51st Highlanders, rounded up while fighting their way back to the boats home.

There's now a characterless new Casino in the centre of the curve, and an even newer church in the streets a little way behind, which appears to be made almost entirely of stained glass.

Practicalities

Much the most attractive house to survive in St-Valéry is the Renaissance **Maison Henri IV** on the quai d'Aval, with its intricately carved wooden facade. It's now the **SI** (mid-June to mid-Sept daily 10am–12.30pm & 3–7pm, mid-Sept to mid-June Wed–Sat 10am–12.30pm & 2.30–6.30pm, Sun 10am–noon; ☎35.97.00.63).

The *Terrasses*, 22 rue le Parrey (☎35.97.11.22; ④), is the only hotel-restaurant actually facing the sea; the other, much cheaper, *logis* in town, *La Marine*, 113 rue St-Léger (☎35.97.05.09; ①), is tucked away in a backstreet on the west side of the harbour. The *Restaurant du Port*, 18 quai d'Amont (☎35.97.08.93), has a delicious 115F menu, abounding in seafood. St-Valéry has a **market** on Fridays, and summer Sundays, and plays host to a **herring and cider festival** each December.

Fécamp

FÉCAMP, roughly halfway between Dieppe and Le Havre, is, like Dieppe, a serious fishing port, although one with a more frivolous sideline as a holiday resort. It is a striking town, so much surrounded by high cliffs that, approaching from inland, you don't see the sea until you're right upon it. It has kept the railway link which runs right into the small harbour, where fishing boats, yachts and *vedettes* jostle for position. The town's long promenade fronts a uniform steep beach of shingle, framed by crumbling and overhanging cliffs. As ever along this coast, windsurfing is more appealing than bathing. In the absence of any major attraction out to sea, the *vedettes* offer cruises to watch the sun set.

The Benedictine Distillery

Fécamp owes much of its popularity to an utterly bizarre tourist attraction – the **Benedictine Distillery** in rue Alexandre le Grand (amid the narrow streets that run parallel to the port towards the town centre). This mock-Gothic monstrosity may look like a decaying mansion that has survived nightmarish aeons, but was in fact built at the end of last century for the manufacture of the sweet liqueur known as *Benedictine*. To see inside you have to go round on a rather dismal guided tour (daily 9.30–11.30am & 2–5.30pm; 45min; 25F), the first part of which treks through a museum of local antiquities and oddments. Most visitors are frantic to get to the alcohol at the end, but the tour does have its moments. There are headless bishops, serpentine musical instruments, carved wood and ivory, and – a kitsch treat – a stained-glass window in which Alexandre le Grand, former owner of the *Benedictine* company (Alexander the Great; no relation), is being treated to a bottle of his liqueur by a passing angel.

Eventually you pass on to the distillery section (although commercial operations have moved to a new factory outside town), where boxes of exotic herbs are thrown into great copper vats and alembics. There is then a massive surge drink-wards, for the (disappointingly modest) *dégustation* across the road; it must be said it's nice stuff, especially the *B&B*, served either neat or on *crêpes*. Make sure you hang on to your admission ticket to get the free drink.

Église de la Trinité

If your aesthetic sensibilities need soothing after the distillery, head away from the sea to the **Église de la Trinité**. This medieval abbey church is light and almost frail with age, its bare nave echoing to the sound of birds flying free beneath the high roof. The wooden carvings are tremendous, in particular the dusty wooden bas-relief *Dormition of the Virgin*. The abbey also has a fine selection of saintly fingers and sacred hips, authenticated with wax seals, and even a drop of the Precious Blood itself, said to have floated all the way here in a fig tree despatched by Joseph of Arimathea. Until Mont-St-Michel was built, this was the religious centre of Normandy; Edward the Confessor is more reliably known to have made extensive gifts to the abbey and may have lived here at some point before his coronation as King of England.

Opposite the main entrance, the few vestiges that remain of the palace of the early dukes of Normandy – both Richard I and Richard II are buried in the abbey – have been landscaped to create an attractive little public garden. William, bastard son of Duke Robert, was presented here at the age of seven to the assembled lords and bishops of Normandy, when his father left for the Crusades; and returned here as William the Conqueror for Easter 1067.

Practicalities

Fécamp's main **SI** is opposite the distillery at 113 rue Alexandre-le-Grand (mid-June to Aug Mon–Fri 10am–6pm; Sept to mid-June Mon–Sat 9am–12.15pm & 1.45–6pm; ☎35.28.51.01); the peculiar hours are because there's another summer-only office on the seafront (mid-June to Aug daily 11am–1pm & 2.30–8pm). The **gares SNCF** and **routière** are between the port and the town centre on av Gambetta.

Hotels tend to be set back away from the sea on odd side streets. It's a popular place; you need to reserve a room at the *Hôtel de l'Univers*, facing St-Etienne church at 5 place St-Etienne (☎35.28.05.88; ③), or the *Angleterre*, 93 rue de la Plage (☎35.28.01.60; ②). Good-value **fish restaurants** include the *Escalier*, 101 quai Berigny (closed Sun pm & Mon in low season; ☎35.28.26.79), and the *Martin*, 18 place St-Étienne (closed first fortnight in March & Sept, plus Sun pm & Mon; ☎35.28.23.82; ①), which also has a few budget rooms. The **youth hostel** (July to mid-Sept; ☎35.29.75.79; for reservations ☎35.29.36.35) stands high up near the lighthouse on the Côte de la Vierge east of the port, along the route du Commandant Roquigny. A superb **campsite**, the *Camping de Renneville* (☎35.28.20.97), is a short walk out of town on the western cliffs.

On to Étretat

The minor road **D28** runs from Fécamp through a thickly wooded and idyllic valley to Benarville – a good cycling route, even though it manages to lose the river somewhere along the way. The **D150** (covered by buses #261 and #311 from Fécamp) is less pastoral, but leads to the remains of the **Abbaye de Valmont** (10am–noon & 2–6pm; closed Wed &, Oct–April, Sun as well). In its spacious grounds you can feast your eyes on a Renaissance chapel, grass-floored and open to the sky, and an intact Gothic lady chapel.

Étretat

ÉTRETAT, another twenty kilometres west towards Le Havre, is a very different kettle of fish to Fécamp. Here the alabaster cliffs are at their most spectacular – their arches, tunnels and the solitary "needle" out to sea will doubtless be familiar from tourist brochures long before you arrive – and the town itself has grown up simply as a pleasure resort. There isn't even a port of any kind; the seafront consists of a sweeping unbroken curve of concrete above the shingle beach.

Étretat is a very pretty little place, centering on the **place Foch** just back from the sea, where the old wooden market *halles* still stand, the ground floor now converted into souvenir shops but the beams of the balcony and roof bare and ancient.

As soon as you step onto the beach you're confronted by the cliff formations to either side. To the west, on the **Falaise d'Aval**, a straightforward if precarious walk leads up the crumbing side of the cliff, with lush lawns and pastures to the inland side – much of them converted for use as a golf course – and German fortifications on the shore side extending to the point where the turf abruptly stops, occasionally ripped by the latest fall. From the windswept top you can see further rock formations and possibly even glimpse Le Havre, but the views back to the village sheltered in the valley, and the **Falaise d'Amont** on its eastern side – which Maupassant compared to an elephant dipping its trunk into the ocean – are what stick in the memory.

The cliff itself presents an idyllic rural scene, with a gentle footpath winding up the green hillside to the little chapel of Nôtre-Dame. Just beyond that is the futuristic white arch erected to commemorate the French aviators Nungesser and Coli, who set out from Paris in the *Oiseau Blanc* in May 1927, hoping to make the first transatlantic flight, and were last seen over Étretat. What happened to them is not known – there are suggestions that they crashed somewhere in deepest Maine, New England – but a mere 18 days later Charles Lindbergh arrived coming from the opposite direction (see p.123) and went into the history books. In the turf alongside the arch, a life-size aeroplane is set in concrete relief, and there's a museum nearby.

Practicalities

Étretat's **SI** is alongside the main through road in the centre of town, on place M. Guillard (mid-June to mid-Sept daily 10am–7pm; mid-March to mid-June & mid-Sept to mid-Oct, daily 10am–noon & 2–6pm; mid-Oct to mid-March Fri 2–6pm, Sat 10am–noon & 2–6pm, Sun 10am–noon; ☎35.27.05.21).

Four **hotels** crowd onto the corners of place Foch, all significantly cheaper than the grand sea-view places. Much the most picturesque is the *Hôtel la Résidence* (☎35.27.02.87; ③), a dramatic half-timbered old mansion with beautiful wooden carvings decorating its every nook and cranny; the quality of rooms is variable, and you have to pay well over the odds to get one to match the setting. More dependable, and also without a restaurant, is the *Hôtel des Falaises* opposite (☎35.27.02.77; ③) – in fact from its modernized rooms you get a better view of the *Résidence* than if you're actually staying there. *L'Escale*, also on place Foch (closed Dec & Jan; ☎35.27.03.69; ③), has simple but pleasant rooms, and a snack restaurant downstairs specializing in *moules-frites* and *crêpes*. **Campers** will find the *Camping Municipal* (mid-March to mid-Oct; ☎35.27.07.67) 1km out on rue Guy-de-Maupassant.

For an absolute blow-out on seafood, you couldn't do better than *La Huitrière*, in the place de Gaulle at the foot of the steps up the Falaise d'Aval (☎35.27.02.82), which has a panoramic first-floor dining room and an enormous range of seafood platters from 82F up to the four-person triple-decker 920F extravaganza which comes with two lobsters and a scattering of caviar. *Le Clos Lupin*, 37 rue A. Kerr (☎35.29 67.53), is a more intimate wood-panelled fishing-village sort of restaurant with a good 82F menu.

Le Havre

Most ferry passengers head straight out of the port of **LE HAVRE**, at the mouth of the Seine, as quickly as the traffic will allow, to escape a city that guidebooks tend to dismiss as dismal, disastrous and gargantuan. While it is not the most picturesque or tranquil place in Normandy, neither is it the soulless urban sprawl the warnings suggest, even if the port, the second largest in France after Marseille, does take up half the Seine estuary, extending way beyond the town.

The city was originally built on the orders of François I in 1517. Its function was to replace the ancient ports of Harfleur and Honfleur, then already silting up, and its name was soon changed from Franciscopolis to Le Havre – "the Harbour". After serious flooding in 1540 it was redesigned, and rebuilt to a grid pattern, by Girolamo Bellarmato, an exiled Italian engineer, who had experience of working in the unstable soil of Venice. It became the principal trading post of the northern French coast, prospering especially during the American War of Independence and thereafter, importing cotton, sugar and tobacco. In the years before the outbreak of war in 1939, it was the European home of the great luxury liners such as the *Normandie*, *Île de France* and *France*.

Le Havre suffered heavier damage than any other port in Europe during World War II. Following its all but total destruction, it was rebuilt to the specifications of a single architect, **Auguste Perret**, between 1946 and 1964 – which makes it a rather rare entity, and one visibly circumscribed by constraints of time and money. The sheer sense of space can be exhilarating, the showpiece monuments have a dramatic and winning self-confidence, and the few churches and other relics of the old city to survive have been sensitively integrated into the whole. The skyline has been kept deliberately low – there are no tower blocks, and even the new mirrored World Trade Centre only manages five storeys – but the endless mundane residential blocks, which simply had to be erected as economically and swiftly as possible after the war, do get dispiriting after a while However, with the sea visible at the end of almost every street, and open public space and expanses of water at every turn, even those visitors who ultimately fail to agree with Perret's famous dictum that "concrete is beautiful" should enjoy a stroll around his city.

Arrival and Information

Le Havre's **SI** is at the back, on the right, of the main Hôtel de Ville (April–Sept Mon–Sat 8.45am–12.15pm & 1.30–7pm, Sun 10am–1pm; Oct–March Mon–Sat 8.45am–12.15pm & 1.30–6.30pm, Sun 10am–1pm; ☎35.21.22.88), and the **post office** is on rue Jules Siegfried (Mon–Fri 8am–7pm, Sat 8am–noon; ☎35.42.45.67).

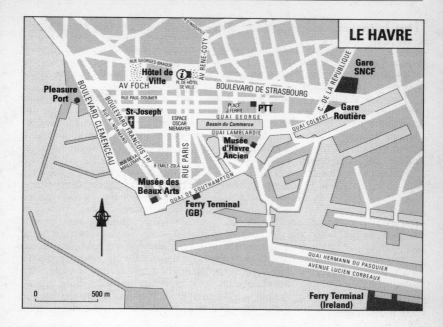

Boats

The cross-Channel **ferries** from Britain and Ireland to Le Havre dock in two separate harbours. The *P & O* **European Ferries Terminal** (☎35.21.36.50), the nearer to the centre of the two, is served by two daily sailings from Portsmouth, while the **Terminal d'Ireland**, a little further east (☎35.53.28.83), is the point of arrival for *Irish Continental* boats from Rosslare, and, in summer, Cork. Both have small tourist information kiosks, open in summer.

Trains and Buses

The **gare SNCF** (☎35.98.50.50) is 1.5km west of the Hôtel de Ville, on Cours de la République, right alongside the **gare routière** (☎35.26.67.23) across bd de Strasbourg. Fast **trains** (though not TGV) timed to connect with the ferries go to Rouen (1hr) and Paris (a further 1hr 15min). If you're travelling west, you have to change at Rouen – a very circuitous route. Local services run regularly to Harfleur in around five minutes.

Shuttle buses from the gare SNCF run to both ferry terminals. All the **buses** that pass the gare SNCF and continue to the Hôtel de Ville. You can pick up time-tables or make enquiries at the bus kiosk there or nearby at *CGTE*, 115 rue Jules Lecesne (☎35.41.72.22), which is where most buses park.

Express **buses** (#20) run by *Bus Verts du Calvados* (☎31.44.77.44) leave from the gare routière to Honfleur, Trouville, Deauville, Cabourg and Caen (two each day start at the quayside, to coincide with arriving boats). Only on Fridays is the journey to Caen non-stop. *Les Autocars Gris* (☎35.28.19.88) run regular services to Fécamp.

The Town

One reason visitors tend to dismiss Le Havre out of hand is that it's easy, whether you're travelling by train, bus, or your own vehicle, to get to and from the city without ever seeing its downtown area, and simply to get an impression of the city as an endless industrial sprawl.

The central **Hôtel de Ville**, a logical first port of call as it houses the tourist office (see below), is a low flat-roofed building that stretches for over one hundred metres, topped by a seventeen-storey concrete tower. Surrounded by pergola walkways, flower beds and flowing water from several strata of fountains, it's an attractive, lively place with a high-tech feel, and is often the venue for imaginative civic-minded exhibitions.

Perret's other major creation, clearly visible some way northwest of the town hall, is the church of **St-Joseph**. Instead of the traditional elongated cross shape, the church is built on a cross of which all four arms are equally short. From the outside it's a very plain mass of speckled concrete, the main doors thrown open to the street to hint at dark interior spaces within that resemble an underground car park. In fact, when you get inside it all makes sense. The altar is right in the centre, with the 100-metre bell tower rising directly above it. Very simple patterns of stained glass, all around the church and right the way up the tower, produce a bright interplay of coloured light, all focussing on the altar to create the effect of a church "in the round". Its plain monolithic exterior has something almost Egyptian in its simplicity. A tight spiral concrete staircase winds its way up one corner of the shaft of the tower – not that visitors can climb it, or indeed would want to.

Le Havre's boldest specimen of modern architecture is considerably more recent – the cultural centre known as the **Volcano**, which stands at the end of the Bassin du Commerce dominating the **Espace Oscar Niemeyer**. The Brazilian architect for whom it is named designed this slightly asymmetrical smooth gleaming white cone, cut off abruptly just above the level of the surrounding buildings, so that its curving planes are undistributed by doors or windows; the entrance is concealed beneath a white walkway in the open plaza below. A large green copper hand emerges from the Volcano just above its base, slightly cupped and pouring out water as a fountain, inscribed with the sentiment that "One day, like this water, the land, beaches and mountains will belong to all". A smaller white building alongside also forms part of the centre.

The **Bassin du Commerce**, which stretches away from the complex, is in fact of minimal commercial significance; kayaks and rowboats can be rented to explore its regular contours, and a couple of larger boats are moored permanently to serve as clubs or restaurants; it's all disconcertingly quiet, serving mainly as an appropriate stretch of water for the graceful white footbridge of the Passarelle du Commerce to cross.

Harfleur is still there, 6km upstream and visibly older than the modern city that engulfs it, but not sufficiently distinctive to be worth visiting.

The Musée des Beaux Arts

The **Musée des Beaux Arts André Malraux**, overlooking the port entrance on bd J.-F.-Kennedy, is one of the best designed art galleries in the country (daily except Tues 10am–noon & 2–6pm; free). The lovely collection of French nineteenth- and twentieth-century paintings includes fifty canvases by Eugene

Boudin, as well as works by Corot, Courbet, Pissarro, Sisley, Gauguin, Léger, Braque and Lurçat. **Raoul Dufy**, a native of Le Havre (1877–1953), has a whole room for his drawings and paintings, in which the windows at the base of the walls show waterlilies in a shallow moat outside. Waterlilies in oil appear along with Westminster and a snowscape sunrise by Monet.

Jean-Paul Sartre's Le Havre

If you have the time, you might like to see what old Le Havre looked like in the pre-war days when **Jean-Paul Sartre** wrote *La Nausée* here. He taught philosophy for five years during the 1930s in a local school, and his almost transcendent disgust with the place cannot obscure the fascination he felt in exploring the seedy dockside quarter of Saint François, in those spare moments when he wasn't visiting Simone de Beauvoir in Rouen.

Little survives of the city Sartre knew, but pictures and bits gathered from the rubble are on display in one of the very few buildings that escaped, the **Musée de l'Ancien Havre**, somewhat incongruous amid the new concrete at 1 rue Jerome Bellarmato, just south of the Bassin du Commerce (Wed–Sun 10am–noon & 2–6pm; free).

Accommodation

It's hard to see why anyone would stay more than a single night in Le Havre. One consequence of the lack of idiosyncratic old buildings in the city is that its **hotels** tend to be faceless in the extreme, hidden away behind indistinguishable concrete facades. There are two main concentrations of hotels: one group faces the gare SNCF, and most of the rest lie within walking distance of the ferry terminal.

The nearest **youth hostels** are at Fécamp (July to mid-Sept; see p.66), and Yvetot (open all year; ☎35.95.37.01). However, it is usually possible to find a dorm room in the YMCA equivalent *Union Chrétienne des Jeunes Gens*, 153 bd de Strasbourg (☎35.42.47.86).

The nearest **camping** is at the *Forêt de Montgeon* site (mid-April to Sept; ☎35.46.52.39), north of the town centre in a 700-acre forest. Take bus #1 from the Hôtel de Ville or gare SNCF, direction *Jacques-Monod*, getting off at *Sainte-Cecile* or *Noisetriers*.

Hotels

Hôtel Britania, 5 cours de la République (☎35.25.42.51). Rather shabby breeze-block building opposite the gare SNCF on a busy street, with its own bar and brasserie. ③.

Hôtel Celtic, 106 rue Voltaire (☎35.42.39.77). Friendly and comfortable option, not too far from the ferry terminal, in the long buildings that flank the Espace Oscar Niemeyer, overlooking the Volcano. No restaurant. ③–④.

Hôtel Foch, 4 rue de Caligny (☎35.42.50.69). Plain cream-coloured cement building, beside the main entrance to the St-Joseph church, offering a good standard of accommodation. ④.

Hôtel Green, 209 bd de Strasbourg (☎35.22.63.10). Double glazing – and easy parking – near the gare SNCF. Ten percent discount on weekends, Sept to March. It doesn't have its own restaurant, but there are plenty nearby. ③.

Hôtel-Restaurant Monaco, 16 rue de Paris (☎35.42.21.01). The closest hotel to the ferry terminal, on quite a busy corner overlooking the quay, with a highly recommended and good-value restaurant (reviewed below). Closed second fortnight in Feb, and Mon from July to Oct. ③.

Grand Hôtel Parisien, 1 cours de la République (☎35.25.23.83). A well appointed place, with congenial management, facing the gare SNCF on the busy corner of the same block as the *Britania*. twenty-five percent reductions on Fri & Sat from Dec to March. ③.

Hôtel Richelieu, 132 rue de Paris (☎35.42.38.71). Efficient and well-kept place, with comfortable rooms, between the Hôtel de Ville and the ferry terminal. No restaurant. ③.

Hôtel Séjour Fleuri, 71 rue Emile-Zola (☎35.41.33.81). On a side road off rue de Paris, close to the ferry terminal; not exactly *"fleuri"*, but cheered up by some bright red shutters. Two hotels knocked into one make for some uneven corridors. No restaurant. ①–③.

Hôtel Yport, 27 cours de la République (☎35.25.21.08). Another option opposite the SNCF station, this time slightly quieter, being set just back from the street, and unusually hospitable. Without restaurant. ②–④.

Eating and Shopping

Few of the **restaurants** in Le Havre are worth making a fuss about, except perhaps for some in the suburb of **Sainte-Adresse**, which is no longer quite as picturesque as you might imagine from Monet's depictions of it (and where the beachside bd Albert I commemorates the fact that this was the seat of the Belgian government in exile during World War I). There are however lots of bars, cafés and brasseries around the gare SNCF, and all sorts of creperies and ethnic alternatives – couscous, South American, Caribbean – in the backstreets of the St-Francis district.

If you're **shopping** for food to take home, possibilities include the central market, just west of place Gambetta and ideal for fresh produce, and two hypermarkets: *Mammouth* at Montivilliers (signposted from the Tancarville road) or the larger *Auchan* at the Mont Gaillard Centre Commercial (follow cours de la République beyond the gare SNCF, through the tunnel, then look for signs). The *Flunch* (☎35.46.59.82) at *Auchan* is a good self-service cafeteria.

Restaurants

La Chope d'Or, 163 rue Victor Hugo (☎35.43.62.15). Off rue de Paris, between the Hôtel de Ville and place Gambetta. *Plat du jour* 40F, *menu economique* 56F. Mon–Fri only, 7.30am–8pm.

L'Huitrière, 12 quai Michel Féré (☎35.21.24.16). Seafood specialists in the St-Francis quarter, facing the rotating bridge between the English and Irish ferry ports. Even the simplest 82F *assiette* includes clams, shrimps and langoustines; the four-person 980F *Abondance* has to be seen to be believed. They also have branches in Étretat and Dieppe.

Lescalle, 39 place de l'Hôtel de Ville (☎35.43.07.93). Good if not desperately inspiring or original food, served in opulent dining room overlooking the huge town hall square. Menu from 97F. Closed Aug, plus Mon & Sun pm.

Hôtel-Restaurant Monaco, 16 rue de Paris (☎35.42.21.01). Hotel near the ferry terminal, (see above), where the downstairs brasserie has outdoor seating. In the more formal restaurant upstairs, menus begin at 115F, with an unusual Livarot salad starter and salmon steaks served with langoustines. Closed second fortnight in Feb, and Mon from July to Oct.

Nice-Havrais, 6 place Frederic Sauvage, Ste-Adresse (☎35.46.14.59). Lovely sea views, excellent cooking, especially fish; moderately expensive. Closed Sun, and Mon pm.

La Petite Auberge, 32 rue de Ste-Adresse (☎35.46.27.32). Traditional French cooking, with few surprises but no disappointments. The 125F menu offers particularly good value. Closed Mon and Sun pm.

Tilbury, 39 rue Jean-de-la-Fontaine (☎35.21.23.50). Attractive and unusual place, with an emphasis on baked dishes, and specializing in low-priced lunches. Closed Mon, Sat am and Sun pm.

Entertainment and Culture

If you're looking to pass an evening or two in Le Havre, the SI will be very happy
to provide information on cultural events in and around town. For all events spon-
sored by the municipality (a wide and impressive range) book at the Théâtre de
l'Hôtel de Ville box office (☎35.41.45.74). The most likely venue has to be *Le
Volcan*, in the Espace Oscar Niemeyer, described above (☎35.21.21.11), though
you may also hear music performed in the cathedral and other churches. Among
several **cinemas** in town are the *Eden* in the Espace Oscar Niemeyer
(☎35.21.70.00), and the *Sirius* at 5 rue Duguesclin (☎35.26.52.15), which usually
programmes *VO* films.

L'Audito, a *FNAC*-style shop selling records, CDs and videos at 104 rue Victor
Hugo (35.42.13.38), is another useful source of information about local activities.

THE SEINE VALLEY

As far back as the Bronze Age, the **Seine** was a crucial part of the "Tin Road" link-
ing Cornwall to Paris. Fortresses and monasteries lined its banks from the time of
the Romans onwards. Now, with the threat of its tidal bore and treacherous sand-
banks very much a thing of the past, heavy ships make their serene way up its
sinuous course to the provincial capital of **Rouen**.

An enormous **new bridge** across the mouth of the Seine opened in January
1995, linking Le Havre with Honfleur and making access between the coasts of
Upper and Lower Normandy much more direct. Further inland, the immense
Tancarville suspension bridge offers another choice of banks and routes.
Scenically, the best way to go is along the **north (right) bank** – fortunately the
route taken by Le Havre–Rouen buses (#191, #192) – which incorporates such
sights as the riverside towns of **Villequier** and **Caudebec**, and the abbey of
Jumièges. If you choose the **south bank** instead, you'll need your own transport
in order to stray out and away from the motorway to Paris.

Between Tancarville and Rouen, just two **bridges** cross the river, both charg-
ing quite hefty tolls. However, there are also intermittent *bacs* (**ferries**) along the
way; cheaper, these tend to leave on the hour (and to have long lunch breaks).

Towards Rouen

Le Havre and Rouen are such vast industrial conglomerates that the countryside
in between the two might not seem to have any obvious promise. The refineries
and cement works of Le Havre in particular feel as if they go on forever.
However, just beyond them is the **Parc Naturel Régional de Brotonne**, an area
that is surprisingly beautiful even if not entirely rural. The park shelters a wide
range of conservation projects and traditional industry initiatives, run by local
people, as well as its more obvious abbey and château sites. Details on all its
aspects can be obtained from the very helpful *Maison de Parc* at 2 Rond Point
Marbec, Le Trait.

If you have your own transport, it's worth taking time to cross the **Pont de
Brotonne** to explore the less frequented **southern side** – the edges of the
Vernier marshes where Camargue horses and Scottish highland cattle graze, and
the deep thick woods of the **Forêt de Brotonne**.

Villequier

The first of the riverbank towns you come to on the **D81 along the north bank**
is quite undeservedly one of the least known – **VILLEQUIER**. As a stop on the
way to or from Le Havre it's ideal, having a quite exceptional **hotel**. The *Grand
Sapin* (☎35.56.78.73; ④) is a gorgeous rambling old building, the rooms equipped
with eccentric brass and enamel period-piece fittings, and rickety balconies over-
looking the river. It's absolutely magical on a misty morning – and not bad in the
evening, when the wood-panelled dining room is in full swing (menus start at
65F). Tables in the riverside garden are laid out under the shade of the epony-
mous *grand sapin* itself.

There's no entertainment whatsoever in Villequier, and the only possible
"sight" is a mournful statue of Victor Hugo, peering out into the Seine, across a
helpfully marked concrete arrow, to the spot where his daughter and her
husband drowned in 1843, just six months after their marriage. The waterfront
promenade, however, is well laid out, with shaky wooden jetties where the estu-
ary and river pilots for the Seine swap responsibilities.

Caudebec-en-Caux and Around

Just over four kilometres on from Villequier, the bigger and more popular
CAUDEBEC-EN-CAUX is an old town which has few traces of its past following
firestorm devastation in the last war. The local tourist authorities extend a rather
sad invitation to visitors to join a "heritage trail" of places that used to be attrac-
tive, while the damage – and previous local history – is recorded in the museum
at the thirteenth-century **Maison des Templiers**, one of the handful of buildings
spared (June–Sept daily 2–6pm, April & May Sat & Sun 2–6pm). As well as enjoy-
ing "one of the most important collections of chimney plaques in France", you
can take a look there at pictures of the Seine's regular tidal swell, which still
threatens at this narrow point to swamp unwary promenaders. The magnificent
flamboyant **Notre Dame church** still dominates the main square, which has
been the site of a **market** every Saturday since 1390.

A little way out of town to the south, a **stone aeroplane** propels itself out of the
cliff face across the water – a memorial to another curious episode of aviation
history, contemporary to that commemorated at Étretat. In 1928, a plane was
being prepared here for an attempt at what would have been the first transatlantic
flight. But shortly before it was due to set off, the Norwegian polar explorer
Amundsen issued a worldwide appeal for help to rescue some Italian sailors who
had been shipwrecked off Spitzbergen in the Arctic. The French government
offered the plane, and its four crewmen left with Amundsen. Two days later they
were lost.

Practicalities

Caudebec's **SI** is slightly south of the centre, in the place Charles de Gaulle
(Mon–Sat 9am–12.15pm & 2–6pm, Sun 2–6pm; ☎35.96.20.65); out of season you
are invited to contact the riverside town hall (☎35.96.11.12).

Two absolutely indistinguishable *logis de France* stand side by side facing the
river on quai Guilbaud, identical buildings with identical balconies and identical
prices – the *Normotel La Marine* at no. 18 (☎35.96.20.11; closed Jan; ③), and the
Normandie at no. 19 (☎35.96.25.11; closed second fortnight of Feb; ③); the restau-

rants in both are closed on Sunday evenings. The slightly cheaper *Cheval Blanc* (☎35.96.21.66; ③) is a little way back from the river, and there's a riverside **camp-site** to the north, the *Barre Y Va* (April to mid-Oct; ☎35.96.11.12). You can **rent bicycles** from *Cycles Velhano* at 10 rue de la Vicomte (☎35.96.24.77).

On the last Sunday in September of every even-numbered year (1992, 1994, etc), Caudebec comes alive with a large **Cider Festival**.

The Pont de Brotonne

Slightly upstream from Caudebec, the magnificent span of the **Pont de Brotonne**, completed in 1977 as the world's highest and steepest humpback bridge (charging a toll for motorists), climbs out above the Seine. It has an unexpectedly appealing colour scheme – the suspension cables are custard yellow, the rails pastel green, the walkway maroon, and the vast concrete columns left bare. If you don't lose both heart and hat to the sickening drop and the seaborne winds, walking across it is one of the big treats of Normandy. From a distance, its stays refract into strange optical effects, while far below small tugs flounder in the wash of mighty cargo carriers.

Abbaye de St-Wandrille

Just beyond the Pont de Brotonne as you continue towards Rouen, the medieval **ABBAYE DE ST-WANDRILLE** was founded, so legend has it, by a seventh-century count who, with his wife, renounced all earthly pleasures on the day of their wedding. The abbey's buildings make an attractive if curious collection: part ruin, part restoration and, in the case of the main buildings, part transplant – a fifteenth-century barn brought in just a few years ago from another Norman village miles away. Benedictine monks are on hand to show visitors around the abbey every afternoon at 3 and 4pm, and also at 11.30am on Sunday (15F); you can hear their **Gregorian chanting** in their new church at morning (Mon–Sat 9.30am, Sun 10am) and evening (Mon–Wed, Fri & Sat 5.30pm; Thurs 6.45pm, Sun & hols 5pm) services.

There's a *crêperie* opposite the abbey, and the more upmarket *Deux Coronnes* restaurant (closed Sun pm & Mon; ☎35.96.11.44), in the place de l'Église, is a seventeenth-century inn where delicious menus start at 120F.

Abbaye de Jumièges

In the next loop of the Seine, twelve kilometres upstream from St-Wandrille, squats the more famous **ABBAYE DE JUMIÈGES**. A haunting ruin, it was destroyed – as a deliberate act of policy – during the Revolution. Its main outline, as far as it can still be discerned, dates from the eleventh century; William the Conqueror himself attended its consecration in 1067. The towers, over 170ft high, are still standing. So too is one arch of the roofless nave, while a one-sided yew tree stands in the centre of what were once the cloisters. How evocative you find these bleached stone ruins will depend on your mood. Visits consist of an unescorted ramble across the lawns and scramble over the walls (daily summer 9am–noon & 2–6pm, winter 10am–noon & 2–4pm; 25F).

The *Auberge des Ruines* in the place de la Mairie (☎35.37.24.05; ③), a grand restaurant where dinner menus start at 165F, has a handful of simple rooms overlooking the abbey.

La Haye du Routot

On the opposite, southern, side of the river near **HAUVILLE** (off the road to Guerande), it's possible to look round a **windmill**, one of six owned by the monks of Jumièges, who farmed and forested all this area in the Middle Ages. Now restored by the *parc*, its outline – based on contemporary castle towers – looks like a kid's drawing (July & Aug daily 2.30–6.30pm; May, June & Sept Sat & Sun 2.30–6.30pm; March, April & Oct to mid-Nov Sun 2.30–6.30pm; 10F).

If you've time, move on from here to the neighbouring village of **LA HAYE DU ROUTOT**. The churchyard is a novelty, featuring a pair of millennium-old yew trees that are still alive but have been sufficiently hollowed out to shelter a chapel and grotto. The feature for which the village is best known (at least in Normandy) is its annual **Fête de Ste-Claire**, held on Saint Claire's feast day, July 16. The centrepiece of this is a towering, conical bonfire, topped by a cross which must survive to ensure a good year. The smouldering logs are taken home to serve as protection against lightning. Should you miss the big day, a video recording of the goings on is featured in the local crafts museum, which also displays a traditional functioning bread oven, adjacent to the church, and a clog-specialist shoemaker opposite (March & mid-Sept to Nov Sun & hols 2–6.30pm; April–May Sat, Sun & hols 2–6.30pm; June to mid-July Sat 2–6.30pm, Sun & hols 10am–6.30pm; mid-July to mid-Sept, daily 10am–6.30pm; 8F).

For **accommodation** south of the river, there's a *gîte d'étape* at Routot (c/o M Verhaeghe, ☎32.57.31.09) and a few rooms available at the *Maison des Métiers* (☎32.57.40.41) in Bourneville, which is also a beautifully presented **museum** of traditional farming and building techniques (July & Aug daily 2–7pm; mid-Feb to June & Sept to mid-Oct Mon & Wed–Sat 2–6.30pm, Sun 2.30–6.30pm; 10F). **LA MAILLERAYE** has a good **campsite** (mid-March to mid-Sept; ☎35.37.12.04).

Duclair

If you want to **cycle** beside the river for any distance, the D982 tends to be forever climbing and descending, and in any event a bit busy. However, the stretch from Le Mesnil (just beyond Jumièges) as far as Duclair is long, quiet, and flat, and has a wonderful view of the lush riverside. **DUCLAIR** itself has a couple of nice **hotels**, with the *Hôtel de la Poste* opposite the landing stage for the town's little *bac*, at 286 quai de la Libération (☎35.37.50.04; ③), and *Le Tartarin* further up at 125 place du Général-de-Gaulle (☎35.37.50.38; ②).

As you continue from here towards Rouen, you get a first panoramic prospect, from beside the church at Canteleu, of the docks, the island and the city. The road onwards coasts endlessly down into the maelstrom. (Don't attempt to cycle *out* of Rouen in this direction – the gradient, and the fumes, are unbearable.)

Rouen

ROUEN, the capital of Upper Normandy, is one of the most ancient and historic cities of France. Standing on the site of Roman Rotomagus, which was the lowest point on the river then capable of being bridged, it was laid out by the Viking Rollo shortly after he became the first Duke of Normandy in 911, and was the venue in 1431 of the trial and execution of Joan of Arc. However, it had to be almost entirely rebuilt after World War II, and now you could spend a whole day wandering around the city without realizing that the Seine ran through its centre. War-time bombs, specifically during the fierce onslaught that coincided with the D-Day landings, destroyed all its bridges, the area between the cathedral and the *quais*, and much of the left bank's industrial quarter. The immediate riverside area has never been adequately restored – it seems to be a permanent construction site, now more than ever thanks to work on a new Metro system – and what you might expect to be the most beautiful part of this venerable city is in fact an abomination.

Enormous sums have, however, been lavished on an upmarket restoration job on the streets a few hundred metres north of the river, which turned the centre into the closest approximation to a medieval city that modern imaginations could come up with. The project was supervised by Louis Arretche, who re-designed post-war Saint Malo so successfully (see p.171). The suggestion that for historical authenticity the houses should be painted in bright, clashing colours was not deemed appropriate by the city authorities, but so far as it goes, the whole of this inner centre can be very seductive, and its churches are extremely impressive by any standards.

Outside the renovated quarters, things are rather different. The city spreads deep into the loop of the Seine to the south, and increasingly into the hills to the north, while the riverbank itself is lined with a fume-filled, multi-laned motorway. As the nearest point that large container ships can get to Paris, the port remains the country's fourth largest – albeit in decline. Rouen's docks and industries stretch endlessly away to the south.

Arrival and Information

Rouen's **SI**, opposite the cathedral at 25 place de la Cathédrale, stands in the early sixteenth-century "House of the Exchequer" (May–Sept, Mon–Sat 9am–7pm, Sun 9.30am–12.30pm & 2.30–6pm; Oct–April, Mon–Sat 9am–12.30pm & 2–6.30pm; ☎35.71.41.77). The **post office** is halfway down rue Jeanne-d'Arc, at no. 45, in the centre of town (Mon–Fri 8am–7pm, Sat 8am–noon; ☎35.08.73.73).

Trains

The main **gare SNCF** (☎35.98.50.50), high up above the river at the top end of rue Jeanne-d'Arc, is referred to as Gare Rive Droite; Gare Rive Gauche on the south bank only handles goods traffic. The passenger station is not immediately conspicuous on most maps, because the train lines run underground, but on the ground you can't miss it. From the outside, its minaret makes it resemble a nineteenth-century confection, intended perhaps for Algiers or Istanbul; in fact it was completed in 1928. The main hall is decorated with garish murals.

Rouen is roughly halfway between Paris and the Channel ports; both **Le Havre** and **Dieppe** are one hour away on different train routes, while the journey to **Paris** takes an hour and a quarter. You can also get trains west to **Lisieux** (1hr 15min) and **Caen** (2hr).

Buses

All town **buses** except #2A from the gare SNCF take five minutes to run down rue Jeanne-d'Arc to the town centre – a walk of perhaps twenty minutes. It makes little difference whether you get off at the third, fourth or fifth stop. The last of these is the *Théâtre des Arts* by the river, with the **gare routière** one block to the west in rue des Charettes (☎35.71.81.71), again not very obvious as it is tucked

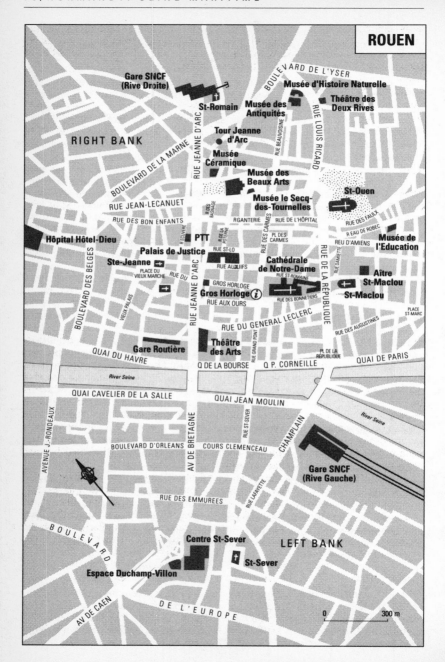

ROUEN

Gare SNCF
(Rive Droite)

St-Romain

Musée d'Histoire Naturelle

Musée des
Antiquités

Théâtre des
Deux Rives

BOULEVARD DE L'YSER

RIGHT BANK

RUE JEANNE D'ARC

Tour Jeanne
d'Arc

RUE BEAUVOISINE

RUE LOUIS RICARD

Musée
Céramique

BOULEVARD DE LA MARNE

Musée des
Beaux Arts

Musée le Secq-
des-Tournelles

St-Ouen

RUE JEAN-LECANUET

RUE DES BON ENFANTS

R DES
BASNAGE

R GANTERIE

RUE DE L'HÔPITAL

RUE DES FAULX

R EAU DE ROBEC

Hôpital Hôtel-Dieu

Palais de Justice

R CROIX DE FER

PTT

R DE LA
PILORIE

PL DES
CARMES

REU D'AMIENS

Musée de
l'Education

BOULEVARD DES BELGES

Ste-Jeanne

RUE ST-LO

RUE DES CARMES

Cathédrale
de Notre-Dame

RUE DE LA RÉPUBLIQUE

RUE GAMBETTA

Aître
St-Maclou

RUE AULOIFS

PLACE DU
VIEUX MARCHE

RUE D'ARC

RUE ST-ROMAINE

St-Maclou

VIEUX PALAIS

GROS HORLOGE

RUE DES BONNETIERS

PLACE
ST-MARC

Gros Horloge (i)

RUE AUX OURS

RUE DU GENERAL LECLERC

RUE DES AUGUSTINES

Gare Routière

QUAI DU HAVRE

Théâtre
des Arts

RUE GRAND PONT

PL DE LA
RÉPUBLIQUE

Q DE LA BOURSE

Q P. CORNEILLE

QUAI DE PARIS

River Seine

QUAI CAVELIER DE LA SALLE

QUAI JEAN MOULIN

River Seine

AVENUE J.-RONDEAUX

BOULEVARD D'ORLEANS

COURS CLEMENCEAU

AV DE BRETAGNE

RUE ST-SEVER

CHAMPLAIN

Gare SNCF
(Rive Gauche)

RUE LAFAYETTE

RUE DES EMMUREES

BOULEVARD

Centre St-Sever

LEFT BANK

St-Sever

Espace Duchamp-Villon

AV DE CAEN

DE L'EUROPE

0   300 m

away behind the riverfront buildings. Out-of-town buses from here include services south to **Evreux** (1hr), #191 and #192 to **Le Havre** along the river via Jumièges and Caudebec, #193 to **Dieppe** via Totes and Bacqueville, #150 to Dieppe and **Le Tréport**, and #261 to **Saint-Valéry**.

Cycle and car rental
You can rent **bicycles** from *Rouen Cycles*, 45 rue St-Éloi (closed Mon; ☎35.71.34.30), as well as at the gare SNCF. Among **car rental** companies are *Avis*, 50 rue Jean-Ango (☎35.07.73.33), *Budget*, 14 rue de Lisbonne (☎35.98.64.38), and *Hertz*, 38 quai Gaston-Boulet (☎35.98.16.57).

The Town

Rouen spends a higher proportion of its budget on **monuments** than any other provincial town, which maddens many a Rouennais. As a tourist, your one complaint may be the lack of time to visit them all. Certainly there are some great sights to be seen – the **Cathédrale de Notre-Dame**, the **Gros Horloge**, the **Aître St-Maclou**, all the delightful twisting streets of timbered houses – and the history too is there to be relished, most notably the links with **Joan of Arc**.

Place du Vieux-Marché
One obvious place to start exploring the city is the **place du Vieux-Marché**, in which a small plaque and a huge cross, 65 feet high, mark the site where Joan was burned to death on May 30, 1431. Louis Arretche was commissioned to design a memorial **church** to the saint in the square in 1969, and the result was dedicated in 1979. It's a wacky, spiky-looking thing, said to represent either an upturned boat or the flames that consumed Joan, but indisputably an architectural triumph, part of an ensemble of buildings that manages to incorporate in similar style a covered food market (more for show than practical shopping). The theme of the church's fish-shaped windows is continued in the scaly tiles that adorn its roof, which is hugely elongated to form a covered walkway across the square. Part of Arretche's brief was to incorporate some sixteenth-century stained glass, removed from the church of St-Vincent that stood on this site before it was destroyed in the war; the outline of the vanished church's foundations is visible on the adjacent lawns. The square itself is surrounded by fine old brown and white half-timbered houses; many of those on the south side now serve as restaurants.

Also on the south side of the *place*, the privately owned **Musée Jeanne d'Arc** draws large crowds to its collection of tawdry waxworks and facsimile manuscripts (daily except Mon, May to mid-Sept 9.30am–6.30pm, mid-Sept to April 10am–noon & 2–6.30pm; 20F). Among the bric-a-brac is a page from the records of the Paris parliament, dated May 10, 1429, which refers to reports reaching Paris that, on the previous Saturday, the French had trounced the British at Orléans. A sketch in the margin, possibly by a bored clerk, depicts a young woman, with her hair tied back, a banner in one hand and a sword in the other: the maid of Orléans, who led the French to victory – and who was then betrayed, outwitted and put to death.

Gros Horloge
From place du Vieux-Marché, rue du Gros-Horloge leads east towards the cathedral. Just across rue Jeanne-d'Arc you come to the **Gros Horloge** itself. A colour-

ful one-handed clock, it used to be on the adjacent Gothic belfry until it was moved down by popular demand in 1529, so that people could see it better. You can climb up rather too many steps to see its workings and, if the sponginess of the lead roofing agrees with your nerves, totter around the top for a marvellous view of the old city, and the startling array of towers and spires around (Easter–Sept Wed 2–5.45pm, Thurs–Mon 10–11.45am & 2–5.45pm; 11F, combined with Beaux Arts and Le Secq). The bell up there, cast in 1260, still rings what's known as the "Conqueror's Curfew" at nine each night. A block to the north are the Renaissance splendours of the former **Palais de Justice**.

Cathédrale de Notre-Dame

The **Cathédrale de Notre-Dame** stands on the site of a Roman place of worship, erected some time in the third century AD at a major crossroads. Despite the addition of all sorts of different towers, spires and vertical extensions, it remains at heart the Gothic masterpiece that was built in the twelfth and thirteenth centuries. Later accretions include the Flamboyant **Tour du Beurre**, named for what was probably the erroneous belief that it was paid for by the granting of dispensations allowing wealthy church-goers to eat butter during Lent, and the nineteenth-century iron spire of the central lantern tower. Cast in the foundries of Conches, it was built to replace a tower that burned down in 1822, and was at the time, at 151 metres, the highest in France. The west facade, which is intricately sculpted like the rest of the exterior, was Monet's subject for over thirty studies of changing light, which now hang in the Musée d'Orsay in Paris. Inside, the carvings of the misericords in the choir depict fifteenth-century life, in secular scenes of work and habits as well as the usual mythical beasts. The ambulatory and crypt hold the assorted tombs of various recumbent royalty, among them the husband of Diane de Poitiers, and the heart itself of Richard the Lionheart; both are closed on Sundays and during services.

Église Saint-Maclou and Aître Saint-Maclou

A short way east of the cathedral, the intricate wooden panelling in the porch of the fifteenth-century church of **Saint-Maclou** is the highlight of what is often cited as the most spectacular example of Gothic Flamboyant architecture in France. The whole building was so badly damaged by bombs on June 4, 1944 that it could only re-open in 1980, although the ornate stone stairway up to the organ inside is as ethereal as ever. That the interior is so light is in part because most of its stained glass was destroyed, and the windows are now clear. Saint Maclou himself – perhaps more familiar as Saint Malo – was a seventh-century missionary from Wales.

Nearby, with its entrance a little hard to find in between 184 and 186 rue Martainville, is the **Aître Saint-Maclou**. This was built between 1526 and 1533, in an era of mass plague deaths, as a cemetery and charnel house. The ground floor was used as an open cloister, and in the rooms above, the bare bones of countless victims were exposed to view. At first sight it looks very picturesque – a tranquil garden courtyard of half-timbered houses – but look closely at the carvings on the beams of the one open lower storey of the surrounding buildings, and you see traces of a macabre **Dance of Death**, while in the case to the right of the entrance is a mummified cat. The buildings are still in use, and still stimulating morbid imaginations, not as a morgue but as Rouen's Fine Arts school. In the square outside are several good antique bookshops and a few art shops.

Saint-Ouen

The last of Rouen's great churches is **Saint-Ouen**, next to the Hôtel de Ville in a large open square to the north. It's larger than the cathedral and has far less decoration, with the result that its Gothic proportions and the purity of its lines have that instant impact with which nothing built since the Middle Ages can compete. Originally, it was an abbey church, founded in the seventh century before the Viking invasion. The present building was begun in 1318 and completed in the fifteenth century.

The Museums

Of all Rouen's **museums**, the most interesting and unusual is the ironmongery museum, **Musée Le Secq des Tournelles** (Wed 2–6pm, Thurs–Mon 10am–noon & 2–6pm; 11F). Housed in the old and barely altered church of St-Laurent on rue Jacques-Villon, it consists of a brilliant collection of wrought-iron objects of all dates and descriptions, mong them nutcrackers and door knockers, spiral staircases that lead nowhere and hideous implements of torture. The museum is right behind the **Beaux Arts** (which has the same hours), and admission is by the same ticket, as are the Gros Horloge belfry and the nearby **Ceramics** museum on rue Faucon. The Beaux Arts itself is not very enthralling but it does include works by the Rouennais Géricault, Sisley and Monet in its Impressionist section. Look out, too, for Dadaist pictures by Marcel Duchamp, and a collection of portraits by Jacques Emile Blanche (1861–1942) of his contemporaries – Cocteau, Stravinsky, Gide, Valéry, Mallarmé and others.

The **Musée des Antiquités** (Mon & Wed–Sat 10am–5.30pm, Sun 10am–noon & 2–6pm; 10F) and the Musée d'Histoire Naturelle, Ethnographie and Prehistoire (Wed–Sat 9.45am–noon & 1.45–5.30pm, Sun 2–7pm; 10F) are both a long way north at the top end of rue Beauvoisine. Antiquités is very good on tapestries, but otherwise neither deserves too much attention.

On the corner of rue Eau de Robec and rue Ruissel there is one of the new breed of intellectually self-conscious French museums – the **Musée National de l'Education** (Tues–Sat 1–6pm; 10F), which covers the upbringing, education, and general influences on children. If you're interested in establishment French ideology, it's illuminating. If not, **rue Eau de Robec** is itself a good example of Rouen restoration, described in an earlier age by one of Flaubert's characters as a "degraded little Venice". Where once a shallow stream flowed beneath the raised doorsteps of venerable half-timbered houses, a thin trickle now makes its way along a stylized cement bed crossed by concrete walkways. It remains an attractive ensemble, if a rather ersatz one, and the houses themselves are now predominantly inhabited by antique dealers, interspersed with the odd café.

To understand more of Flaubert himself, and for an insight into the Rouen that he knew, don't go to the **Pavillon Flaubert** at Croisset-Canteleu. Like Rouen's two other literary museums – the two homes of Pierre Corneille – it only proves the pointlessness of the genre. Visit, instead, the **Musée Flaubert et de l'Histoire de la Médicine**, at the Hôtel-Dieu Hospital (daily except Mon 10am–noon & 2–6pm; ring several times; free). This stands on the corner of rue de Lecat and rue du Contrat-Social, walkable from the centre (or bus #2A), and it's infinitely more relevant to Flaubert's writings than the manuscript copies and personal mementoes in the Pavillon museum. Flaubert's father was chief surgeon and director of the medical school, living with his family in this house within the hospital. Even during the cholera epidemic when Gustave was 11, he and his sister were not stopped from running around the wards or climbing along the garden wall to look into the autopsy lab. Some of the medical exhibits would certainly have been familiar objects to him – a phrenology model, a childbirth demonstrator like a giant rag-doll, and the sets of encyclopedias. There's also one of his stuffed parrots, as featured in Julian Barnes' novel *Flaubert's Parrot*.

Accommodation

There should be no difficulty in finding appropriate accommodation in Rouen, even at the busiest times. Few of the **hotels** have restaurants, chiefly because there's so wide a choice of places to eat all over town. Motorists who just want to spend a day or two looking at the sights of Rouen should seriously consider the possibility of staying at one of the delightful riverside hotels in **La Bouille** (see p.86), or in the woods at **Lyons-la-Forêt** (see p.87).

The city's **youth hostel** is south of the river at 118 bd de l'Europe (☎35.72.06.45; 11pm curfew). From the gare SNCF on the north bank, take bus #12, direction *Parc des Expositions*, as far as the *Diderot* stop. The **Camping Municipal** is 4km northwest on rue Jules-Ferry in **Déville-lès-Rouen** (☎35.74.07.59), reached by taking bus #2 from the Théâtre des Arts, while the significantly less acessible *Camping L'Aubette* is 5km east at 23 Vert Buisson in **Saint-Léger du Bourg-Denis** (☎35.08.47.69).

Hotels

Hôtel-Restaurant le Cache Ribaud, 10 rue du Tambour (☎35.71.04.82). Between the Palais de Justice and the Gros Horloge. The cheapest rooms share toilets in the corridors. Restaurant (closed Sun pm) with *plat du jour* 55F; evening menu from 88F. ③.

Hôtel des Carmes, 33 place des Carmes (☎35.71.92.31). Beautifully decorated old house in quiet central square, a short way north (and uphill) from the cathedral. Guests are not given keys to stay out late. No restaurant, but buffet breakfasts for 35F. ④.

Hôtel de la Cathédrale, 12 rue St-Romain (☎35.71.57.95). One of the very nicest hotels in Rouen. Quiet, central rooms alongside the cathedral and archbishop's palace, with a quaint old courtyard with flowers. Set in a pedestrianized street, lined with fourteenth-century timber-framed houses. No restaurant. ④.

Colin's Hotel, 15 rue de la Pie (☎35.71.00.88). Very modern place, set around a venerable old courtyard, just a toss of a match from the place du Vieux-Marché. A high standard of comfort has quickly made this the most popular upmarket hotel in town. ⑦.

Hôtel des Familles, 4 rue Pouchet (☎35.71.69.61). Very friendly and characterful place near the Gare Rive Droite. Incorporates the old *Hôtel de la Paix*; hence the two entrances. No restaurant. ④.

Hôtel Foch, 6 rue Saint Etienne-des-Tonneliers (☎35.85.11.44). Near the Théâtre des Arts, and popular with actors and dancers – the walls are graced with their signed photographs. No restaurant. ③.

Hôtel de Lisieux, 4 rue de la Savonnerie (☎35.71.87.73; ⑤). At the junction of rue de la Savonnerie and rue du Bec, between the cathedral and the river. Pierre Cauchon, Bishop of Beauvais, who prosecuted Joan of Arc at her trial in 1431, is said to have stayed – and died – here in 1442. If so, it has been considerably modernized since, largely at the expense of any character it may once have had. No restaurant. ③.

Hôtel de Québec, 18–24 rue de Québec (☎35.70.09.38). Near place de la République and pont Corneille, and run by a Parisian couple who are firm Anglophiles. No restaurant. ③.

Hôtel de la Rochefaucauld, 1 rue de la Rochefaucauld (☎35.71.86.58). Basic rooms, near the Gare Rive Droite, but not easy to find; bear left from the station exit, and the hotel is opposite the Saint Romain church. No restaurant. ②.

Hôtel Saint Ouen, 43 rue des Faulx (☎35.71.46.44). Downmarket option near the Hôtel de Ville, reached on bus #2A from the Gare Rive Droite. No restaurant. ①.

Hôtel Sphinx, 130 rue Beauvoisine (☎35.71.35.86). Very basic accommodation, at the north end of the street near the Musée des Antiquités. None of the rooms has a shower; there's a charge of 16F per shower, and having an extra bed in the room costs 60F. No restaurant. ①.

Hôtel-Restaurant l'Union, 11–12 place du Générale-de-Gaulle (☎35.71.46.55). Facing Hôtel de Ville, overlooking Saint-Ouen church; not all that welcoming, but the prices make it worth considering. *Plat du jour* 39F and not very inspiring *à la carte*. ②.

Hostellerie du Vieux Logis, 5 rue de Joyeuse (☎35.71.55.30). Cheap, old-fashioned but very comfortable place, officially considered as offering *pension de famille*, with a good-value restaurant. Guests must arrive before 10pm. ①.

Hôtel Viking, 21 quai du Havre (☎35.70.34.95). Just in front of the gare routière, to the right at the bottom end of rue Jeanne-d'Arc. Overlooking the river – and the main roads, the noise of which is only partly dampened by the double glazing. No restaurant. ③.

Eating

Rouen has a good reputation for **food**, with its most famous dish being *caneton* (duckling). Unlike the hotels, which sometimes have cheaper weekend rates, the city's upmarket restaurants tend to charge more over weekends, when families eat out. The greatest concentration of restaurants is in place du Vieux-Marché, an area in which, perversely, there are few hotels.

There's a daily **food market** in the square, while the area just north is full of Tunisian **take-aways, crêperies** and so forth. There are, too, sumptuous **patisserie** shops everywhere – a stall selling superb cream-laden *gaufres* does business between the post office and the Beaux Arts on the rue Jeanne-d'Arc.

Restaurants

Auberge St-Maclou, 224–226 rue Martainville (☎35.71.06.67). Half-timbered building in the shadow of St-Maclou church, with tables on the street outside and an old-style ambience inside. The pedestrian street gets crowded in summer, but the menus are far from over-priced – the 62F set lunch includes cocktail, wine and coffee. Prices to suit all budgets, and dishes including mussels and duck, as well as excellent desserts. Closed Sun pm and all day Mon.

Des Beaux Arts, 34 rue Damiette (☎35.70.17.15). On pretty pedestrianized street north of Saint-Maclou church. Very good-value Algerian cuisine: *couscous* or *tajine* from 50F, with all kinds of sausages and assorted meats. Closed Wed.

Le Boeuf Couronné, 151 rue Beauvoisine (☎35.88.68.28). Traditional Norman house, offering extremely traditional Norman cooking – the menu makes a theme of "grandmother's specialities". Assorted stews, skate with mustard, and above all *choucroute* of assorted meats. Menus start at 65F and rise to take in double *choucroute* in champagne. Closed Sun.

Flunch, 60 rue des Carmes (☎35.71.81.81). Large and good self-service, with many fresh dishes. On street running north from the cathedral. Daily 11am–10pm.

Jumbo, 11 rue Guillaume le Conquerant (☎35.70.35.88). Off the northeast corner of place du Vieux-Marché. Another good self-service.

Les Maraichers – Le Bistrot d'Adrien, 37 place du Vieux Marché (☎35.71.57.73). Deservedly the most popular of the Vieux-Marché's many restaurants, with a streetside terrace right in front of the ruined outline of the St-Denis church. Styled to resemble a fin-de-siècle Parisian bistro, serving varied set menus until 11pm nightly and *à la carte* until midnight. Menus start at 87F, lots of *andouillettes*, snails and tongues, but plenty of wholesome possibilities too, and great desserts.

Les Nymphéas, 7–9 rue de la Pie (☎35.89.26.69). Just off place du Vieux-Marché. Formerly the *Warin*. Said currently to be the most chic restaurant in Rouen, but a little over the top for most tastes, with set menus at 160F, 180F and 240F. Closed Sun evening and Mon lunchtime.

Le Paris-Rouen, 21 rue du Grand-Pont (☎35.07.76.05). Modern building, just south of the SI and the cathedral, and named in 1994 for the centenary of the first-ever automobile race, from Paris to Rouen. Formal dining, though with menus starting at 78F the prices are reasonable and the quality exceptional. Closed Sun pm & Mon, and first three weeks of Aug. The fish soup is good at the best of times; in autumn and winter there's a magnificent bouillabaisse.

Pascaline, 5 rue de la Poterne (☎35.89.67.44). North of Palais de Justice, near the flower market; classic bistro with purple wooden enclosure attached to the front of a half-timbered house. Somewhat formal, but probably the most reasonable place to sample Rouennais *caneton* (duckling). Menus 55F (with a salad buffet), 75F and 95F. Same owner as *Le Quatre Saisons* (see below).

Le P'tit Bec, 182 rue Eau de Robec (☎35.07.63.33). Friendly lunchtime brasserie which has become Rouen's most popular lunch spot, with a simple 69F menu holding such joys as salmon tagliatelle and chocolate fondants. Lovely outdoor setting on pedestrianized street, beside the running water and next door to a gorgeous blue half-timbered mansion. The only evening it's open is Friday; closed all day Sun.

Le Quatre Saisons, place Bernard Tissot (☎35.71.96.00). The restaurant of the very expensive *Hôtel de Dieppe*, facing the gare Rive Droite; if money is no object, the definitive place to eat duck, perhaps with a basil gazpacho to start. Bar menu from 125F, restaurant menu from 135F, but brunch from 45F.

Le Queen Mary, 1 rue du Cercle (☎35.71.52.09). Off northwest corner of place du Vieux-Marché. Brasserie upstairs: *plat du jour* 38F, *formule express* 50F, and a more expensive restaurant on the ground floor. Closed Mon. Named after the boat, hence the gender; the staff are dressed to sail.

Au Temps des Cerises, 4–6 rue des Basnages (☎35.89.98.00). If you've come to Normandy for the cheeses, this is the place to get it all out of your system. Turkey breast in camembert, goats' cheese crepes, and above all fondues of every description. Lunch menus from 52F, from 78F in the evening. Trendy if slightly over-styled. Closed Mon lunch and all day Sun.

Walsheim, 260 rue Martainville (☎35.98.27.50). Lively Alsacian place alongside St-Maclou church. *Choucroute* specialists; all sorts of meats nestling on a fine shredded cabbage base. Menu from 59F. Ask to see the two old cider presses. Open until midnight Tues–Sat, or 10.30pm Sun & Mon.

Shopping

Most of the classier **shops** in Rouen are in the pedestrian streets near, and slightly north of, the cathedral. If you are looking for fancy foodstuffs, patisseries, chocolates and the like, there are shops on rue Jeanne-d'Arc around and just above rue du Gros-Horloge. For **hypermarkets** and cheap clothes, however – or just a laugh on a rainy day – go south of the river to the modern multi-storey Saint-Sever complex. There's an open-air antiques and bric-a-brac **market** nearby in the place des Emmurées.

For books, maps and guides, largely in French, visit *l'Armitière*, 5 rue des Basnage, or the more specialist *Imprimateur*, 34 Saint-Nicolas. English-language titles, as well as a wide range of CDs, videos and computer paraphernalia, can be found at the all-purpose *FNAC*, 39 rue Ecuyère (Mon 2–7pm, Tues–Sat 10am–7pm), behind the post office near the place du Vieux-Marché, or the *ABC Bookshop*, 9–11 rue des Faulx (Tues–Sat 10am–6pm), near *Hôtel Saint Ouen*.

Nightlife and Entertainment

As you would expect in a conurbation of 400,000, there's always plenty going on in Rouen, from classical concerts in churches to alternative events in community and commercial centres. An annual handbook, *Le P'tit Normand*, available in all newsagents, is helpful with addresses and telephone numbers. For current events, pick up the free *Cette Semaine à Rouen* from the SI. Tickets (and further information) can also be had from *FNAC*, on rue Ecuyère.

Rouen has four **theatres**, which mainly work to winter seasons. The most high-brow and big-spectacle is the **Théâtre des Arts**, 22 place des Arts (☎35.98.50.98), which puts on opera, ballet and concerts. The more adventurous repertory company of the **Théâtre des Deux Rives** (☎35.70.22.82), now based opposite the Antiquités museum at the top end of rue Louis Ricard (happily at the junction with rue de Joyeuse), presents work by playwrights such as Beaumarchais, Shakespeare, Beckett and Gorky.

A long way south of the river are **Théâtre Charles Dullin**, allée des Arcades, Grand Quévilly (☎35.69.51.18), and **Théâtre Maxime Gorki**, rue Paul Doumer, Petit Quévilly (☎35.72.67.55), which specializes in contemporary and traditional music from around Europe.

Concerts and other spectacles are held in *Hangar 23* (☎35.70.04.07), a converted warehouse down by the river, while a wide assortment of one-night performances (jazz, rock, dance, satire) is presented at *Théâtre de la Ville* (☎35.62.31.31) in place de la Verrerie, Saint-Sever, south of the river. The Saint-Sever complex also contains a **cinema**, and there are two multi-screen cinemas just north of the river.

Bars and Music venues

Some of Rouen's most agreeable **bars** are in the maze of streets between rue Jean Lecanuet and place du Vieux-Marché. Incoming sailors used to head straight for this area of the city, and the small bars are still there even if the sailors aren't.

Big Ben Pub, 95 rue du Gros-Horloge (☎35.84.44.50). Right under the big clock – hence the name. A restaurant which incorporates an always-packed bar, strictly speaking entered from a side street – 30 rue des Vergetiers. Usually as crowded inside as is the street outside. Open noon to 2am, closed Sun.

Le Bateau Ivre, 17 rue des Sapins (☎35.70.09.05). Low-key but atmospheric hang-out, with wooden tables, which puts on a mixed cabaret-style programme of music and performance. Open until 2am Tues & Wed, 4am Thurs–Sat. Closed Sun, Mon & all Aug.

La Boite à Bières, 35 rue Cauchoise (☎35.07.76.47). Half-timbered house, on the corner with rue de Fontenelle, near place du Vieux-Marché. "*Cool et pas cher*"; good choice of beers. Open 3pm–2am daily.

Exo 7, 13 place des Chartreux (☎35.72.33.88). The centre of Rouen's **heavy rock** scene, a long way south of the centre. Note the militaristic pun. Open Wed–Sat 10.30pm–4am.

Au Grès d'Alsace, 13 place Saint-Marc (☎35.71.55.88). More of a restaurant but, despite the title and the renowned *strudel d'Alsace*, there are "frequent evenings of Irish music played by expert Bretons". In a run-down area, on southwest corner of place Saint Marc and junction with rue des Augustins.

Le Nickel Chrome, 26 rue Saint-Étienne-des-Tonneliers (☎35.15.37.37). Glamorous late-night drinking spot that spotlights jazz, rock and blues bands after 11pm. Open until 2am Tues–Thurs, 4am Fri & Sat.

Scottish Pub, 21 rue Verte (☎35.71.46.22). Bar and restaurant right next to the station, open until 2am, which puts on jazz groups from time to time. Closed Sat lunchtime and Sun all day.

La Taverne Saint Amand, 11 rue Saint-Amand (☎35.88.51.34). Popular bar with draught Guinness, off rue de la République above the cathedral.

Around Rouen

Though it only takes a few minutes of travelling along the river from Rouen in either direction to reach pleasant small towns well worth an overnight stop – such as Villequier or Les Andelys, both described elsewhere in this chapter – a number of places only just outside the city proper make good day trips while you are based in the city. Some are also worth considering as alternative bases for visits to the metropolis.

The Château du Robert-le-Diable

A long and very badly signposted haul southwest from central Rouen, past the docks and refineries of Petit and Grand Quévilly (where there are at least a few cycle lanes), suddenly climbs from Moulineaux up to the ruined **Château du Robert-le-Diable**. Robert the Devil is a legendary figure who may or may not have been William the Conqueror's father, but certainly didn't build this early Norman castle. It's now privately run, with a crazy golf course, a slightly clumsy reconstruction of a Viking *drakkar*, and tacky waxworks of the Battle of Hastings and other such scenes. But its strengths are the very damp and spooky passages underground, and then the magnificent view from the top of the tower down to the Seine, the port of Rouen and the châteaux on the other side. The only drawback is that the château is right next to an extremely busy motorway.

Just across the motorway is the **Forêt de la Londe**. Although dissected by a number of busy railway lines, it survives in the gaps – and is used by local cyclists to race the pollution of Rouen out of their systems.

La Bouille

More or less immediately below the Château du Robert-le-Diable, 10km southwest from central Rouen along the southern riverbank, the small village of **LA BOUILLE** stands near a magnificent sweeping bend in the Seine. Little more than a couple of narrow twisting lanes lined with gnarled half-timbered houses, pressed hard against the steep hillside, it makes an utter contrast to the noise and bustle of the city, and makes a perfect place to spend a couple of nights for anyone not dependent on public transport. Not far north, a little *bac* (ferry) crosses the river to the small Forêt de Roumare.

Several expensive but exquisite **hotels** line the main road through the village, including the *Bellevue* (☎35.18.05.05; ③), and the luxurious *Saint-Pierre* (☎35.18.01.01; river views ⑥, otherwise ⑤), both of which have superb dining rooms.

Clères

Roughly 16km northeast of Rouen, and reachable on bus #161, the pretty village of **CLÈRES** has a large and popular **zoo** (Easter–Sept Mon–Sat 9am–6.30pm, Sun 9am–7pm; Oct, Nov & March–Easter Mon–Sat 9am–noon & 1.30–5pm, Sun 9am–noon & 1.30–6pm; 30F), set in the grounds of an eleventh-century castle of which few traces remain. The more modern château which replaced it was in turn recently devastated by a fire, but the animals survived. One aviary is even housed in what was the château's main hall. Colette made the impenetrable but presumably complimentary remark that "At Clères, in the zoo park, it is easy to lose the melancholy feeling of inevitability."

The Forêt de Lyons

Around 25km east of Rouen, the **Forêt de Lyons** was a thousand years ago a favoured hunting ground of William the Conqueror and other Dukes of Normandy, and in parts it feels little changed since then – remarkable considering its proximity not only to Rouen but also to Paris. Almost any of the little roads through these dense woods rewards exploration by cyclists or walkers; the oaks and beeches are consistently magnificent, with particularly vast specimens indicated by roadsigns.

Lyons-la-Forêt

At the heart of the forest, the little hill village of **LYONS-LA-FÔRET** was the site of William's now completely indiscernible castle, but has retained a superb ensemble of half-timbered Norman houses dating from around 1610. In the centre of the village stand the plain old wooden *halles*, often used as a film set, while the roads around abound in splendid rural mansions. One such, on rue d'Enfer, was much used by the composer Ravel in the 1920s. Others are now **hotels**, including the brick-fronted *Grand Cerf*, right next to the *halles* on place Benserade (☎32 49.60.44; ④), with a secluded garden tucked away behind the archway, and the *Licorne* nearby (☎32.49.62.02; ⑤). Both have menus from around 75F, and there are also a couple of less expensive restaurants with outdoors seating in the main square.

Abbaye de Mortemer

Half a dozen kilometres south of Lyons, clearly signed off a main road, the ruins of the twelfth-century Cistercian **Abbaye de Mortemer** amount to little more than heaps of rubble scattered across gentle lawns, amid a landscape of rolling parklands (park daily 9am–1pm & 2–6.30pm; museum Mon–Sat 2–6.30pm, Sun 9am–1pm & 2–6.30pm; 20F park, 35F with tour). Plenty of outbuildings survive, however, including a round stone *pigeonnier*, with a spiders-web tangle of wood inside, and little niches for hundreds of pigeons (reared by the monks for food); a cast-iron pigeon stands permanently on top. The highlight of the visit are tours of the museum in the eighteenth-century château that dominates the grounds, where you see models of the abbey as it is now, and an audio-visual show of life as it used to be, complete with plenty of tales of hauntings and bumps in the night.

Beyond the abbey, which was quarried after the Revolution to build the nearby village of Lisors, a couple of marshy lakes are populated by geese and swans and surrounded by woods and lawns that accommodate free-roaming deer.

Charleval

In **CHARLEVAL**, on the edge of the woods 7km west of the abbey, the *Auberge de l'Écurie* at 16 rue Grande (☎32.49.30.73; ①) has some of the forest's least expensive – if rather dilapidated – rooms. It also offers a very atmospheric low-ceilinged dining room, where the 80F menu includes salmon baked in foil, there's an open wood barbecue, and the desserts come flamboyantly decorated with coloured designs on custard.

Vascoeuil and Ry

The small but graceful **Château de Vascoeuil**, on the northwest edge of the forest 12km from Lyons, is renowned for having top-quality temporary art exhibitions in summer (May–Sept daily 11am–7pm; April & Oct daily 2.30–6.30pm). However, the village of **RY**, 4km northwest, is of more dependable interest, as the real-life location of Flaubert's fictionalized Madame Bovary. A monument in its churchyard commemorates Delphine Couturier, who committed suicide in Ry in 1849 having married a local doctor ten years previously at the age of 17.

Ry consists of one main street, with green hills visible rising at either end, and a church to one side with an unusual carved wooden porch. Delphine's husband is buried in the churchyard, and Madame Bovary is immortalized throughout the village, which seems to have had little else to celebrate for a century or so. The local florist is *Emma's*, the video shop is *Bovary*; the chemist's was her real house.

An expensive museum of automata, of appeal largely to young children, though some of its mannequins jerkily act out the less explicit moments of Madame Bovary's career, stands next to a pretty bridge over the Crevon (Easter–Oct, Sat–Mon 11am–noon & 2–7pm; July & Aug also Tues–Fri 3–6pm; 25F). There are no hotels, but the *Rôtisserie Bovary* serves reasonable lunches (☎35.23.61.46) in the town's smartest building, near the church.

Upstream from Rouen

Upstream from Rouen towards Paris, high cliffs on the north bank of the Seine imitate the coast, looking down on waves of green and scattered river islands. By the time you reach **Les Andelys**, 25km out of Rouen, you're within 100km of the capital, meaning that accommodation and eating prices tend to be geared towards affluent weekend- and day-trippers.

Large country estates abound in this agreeable countryside, and public transport too is minimal – it's assumed any visitor has, if not a residence, then at least a car. However, infrequent buses run from Rouen to Les Andelys, and an expensive but enjoyable boat trip from the Poses Dam (bus #130 from Rouen) goes to Les Andelys and on to Vernon – ask at Rouen SI for details. Trains from Rouen call at Vernon.

Pont St-Pierre

The first point south of Rouen at which the Seine begins to be enticing again is **PONT ST-PIERRE**, where it's joined by the River Andelle. Any surplus money you may have could be enjoyably spent on a stay at the half-timbered *Hostellerie la Bonne Marmite* (closed last week of July & first two weeks in Aug; ☎32.49.70.24; ⑤), whose ivy-coated buildings are set around a little courtyard, a little way south of the eponymous bridge on the main road. Duck-and-lobster-loaded menus in the restaurant start at 140F.

At the junction of the two rivers you are confronted with the spectacularly sharp **Côte des Deux Amants**. This sheer escarpment, leading to a plateau high above the Seine, takes its name from a twelfth-century legend, in which a cruel king stipulated that the man who would marry his daughter must first run with her in his arms to the top of this hill. Noble Raoul sprinted up carrying the fair Caliste, but then dropped dead, and, out of sympathy, so did she. That story provides precious little incentive for anyone else to make the climb – but rumour has it that the view from the top does.

Les Andelys

The next town of any size is **LES ANDELYS**, which consists in fact of two towns, overshadowed by the magnificent Château Gaillard. **Petit Andely** lies along the riverfront, and is equipped with a modern marina for pleasure boats. **Grand Andely**, at the end of a mile-long boulevard stretching inland, is the centre for shops, bars, and a **market** on Saturday.

Château Gaillard

The single most dramatic sight anywhere along the Seine short of Paris – especially awesome and magical by night – has to be **Château Gaillard**, perched high above Les Andelys. The castle was constructed in the space of a single year, 1196–97, under the auspices of Richard the Lionheart and the Duke of Normandy, who had to bribe the Pope for permission to do so. Their object was to deny the King of France access to Rouen by establishing total control of traffic along the Seine by road and river. That was successful until after Richard's death, when Philippe-Auguste managed to storm the castle in 1204 (his armies gaining access via the latrines). It might well have survived intact into this century, though, had Henry IV not ordered its destruction in 1603. Even then, it would have taken more recent devices to reduce Château Gaillard to rubble: the substantial outline remains and can be visited between April and October only (daily except Tues 10am–noon & 2–6pm).

On foot, you can climb up to the castle from the path off rue Richard Coeur-de-Lion in Petit Andely. By car you have to follow a long-winded one-way system from opposite the church in Grand Andely. You can then scramble about over green and chalky knolls, and across the ruined moat, to explore Richard's one-year wonder.

Les Andelys Practicalities

The **SI** for Les Andelys is at 24 rue Phillippe-Auguste in Petit Andely (June–Sept daily 9.30am–noon & 2–6pm; Oct–May Mon–Fri 2–6pm; ☎32.54.41.93). The nicest places to **stay** have to be the two attractive Seine-side hotels in Petit Andely; the eighteenth-century *Chaîne d'Or*, 27 rue Grande (☎32.54.00.31; closed Jan, Sun pm & Mon; ④), and the *Normandie* at 1 rue Grande (☎32.54.10.52; closed Wed pm & Thurs; ③). Both have high-quality expensive restaurants; prices for both rooms and food are cheaper at the *Soleil Levant* at 2 rue du Général-de-Gaulle in Grand Andely (☎32.54.23.55; restaurant closed Sun, & Mon in low season; ③), but it's a bit too far to walk back to the river for an evening stroll.

Monet's Gardens at Giverny

At **GIVERNY**, twenty kilometres south of the ancient fortifications of Les Andelys, Claude Monet lived from 1883 until his death in 1926, and laid out the **gardens** which many of his friends considered his masterpiece. Each month is reflected in a dominant colour, as is each room in the house, which remain just as he left them, covered floor to ceiling with his collection of Japanese prints.

At the bottom of the garden, reached by a passage under the road, is the famous **waterlily pond**. May and June, when the rhododendrons flower around the pond, and the wisteria that winds over the Japanese bridge is in bloom, are the best of all times to visit. But any month, from spring to autumn, is overwhelming in the beauty of this arrangement of living shades and shapes.

The gardens are not large, and you'll have to contend with crowds of camera-happy visitors jostling to capture their own impressions of the waterlilies. If you've brought a picnic, it's forbidden to eat in the grounds, and the surrounding countryside is not particularly pleasant. Above all, Monet enthusiasts may be disappointed by the absence of any of his actual paintings; there are just shoddy reproductions on sale, and to see his renditions of the lilies you need to go to the Orangerie and Musée d'Orsay in Paris. But for all that, there's no place like it, and this has to be one of the most pleasurable visits anywhere in Normandy. (Gardens and house are open April–Oct only, Tues–Sun 10am–6pm; 30F for both, 20F for gardens only).

Access

You can rent bikes at the gare SNCF in nearby **Vernon**, or catch the bus to the gardens that leaves from the station at 1.15pm (and returns from the car park opposite the gardens at 3.15pm and 5.15pm; 12F return).

Vernon

VERNON itself straddles the Seine just before it leaves Normandy altogether, with walks laid out along either bank. The central *Hôtel d'Évreux*, 11 place d'Évreux (☎32.21.16.12; ③), has rooms at assorted prices, and a good restaurant, and you can also eat well at the *Restaurant de la Poste*, 26 av Gambetta (☎32.51.10.63; closed Tues pm & Wed), where menus start at 80F. The **youth hostel** can be hard to find; it's a twenty-minute walk out of town, upstream along the river, at 28 av Île de France (April–Sept only, book ahead; ☎32.21.20.51; 40F); there's a **campsite** alongside. Elvis Presley's dad was called Vernon.

travel details

Buses

From Dieppe 5 daily to Paris (2hr 15min); 1 daily to Fécamp (1hr 30min), #311 or #312 via St Valéry.

From Caen 6 daily #20 to Le Havre (2hr 30min, via Honfleur, Trouville, Deauville, and Cabourg; 1hr 40min direct, Fri only); 3 daily to Fécamp (50min).

From Rouen hourly to Le Havre (2hr 45min), #191 or #192 via Jumièges and Caudebec; 2 daily to Dieppe (1hr 45min) #163, and #150 on to Le Tréport, Fécamp (2hr 30min) and Lisieux (2hr 30min). Also to Clères, #161, to Le Neubourg, #337, and to Elbeuf.

Trains

Through trains to Paris connect with all ferries.

From Dieppe 8 daily to Rouen (1hr); 8 daily to Paris-St-Lazare (2hr 15min).

From Le Tréport 5 daily to Paris (2hr 45min) via Eu (4min) and Beauvais (1hr 40min).

From Le Havre 12 daily to Rouen (1hr) and Paris (2hr 15min).

From Rouen 8 daily to Caen (2hr 15min); 12 daily to Paris-St-Lazare (1hr 15min); at least hourly to Fécamp (1hr).

From Fécamp 6 daily to Rouen (45min).

From St-Valéry 4 daily to Rouen (30min) via Motteville.

Ferries

From Dieppe *Stena Sealink* (☎35.06.39.00) 4 daily to Newhaven (4hr).

From Le Havre *P&O* (☎35.21.36.50) 2 daily to Portsmouth (5hr 30min). *Irish Continental* (☎35.26.57.26) daily to Rosslare (21hr) and, in summer, to Cork (21hr).

For more details, see p.3 onwards.

CHAPTER TWO

THE LOWER NORMANDY COAST

T he **coast of Lower Normandy** takes on a succession of very different characters as you move from east to west. Along the **Côte Fleurie**, from Honfleur to Cabourg, it is moneyed and elegant, a would-be northern counterpart to the Côte d'Azur. Then, through the **Côte de Nacre** and into the area known as the **Bessin**, around Caen and Bayeux, it drifts into anonymity: wide stretches of sand, backed by scrubland and still dominated by the memories of 1944 when they served as the landing beaches for the Allied forces. West again, separated from the bulk of the mainland by a series of marshes, is the **Cotentin peninsula**, with low-key harbour villages along its east front, cliffs across the north, and vast dunes and wild beaches to the west. And finally there is the **bay of Mont-St-Michel**, where the island abbey is swept by treacherous tides.

The most enjoyment along the **Côte Fleurie** is to be had from **Honfleur** – a real gem of a harbour town, familiar from the paintings of Eugène Boudin, Monet and other Impressionists. Elsewhere, the prevailing air is one of wealthy sterility. **Trouville**, **Deauville** and **Cabourg** preoccupy themselves with such events as Rolls Royce rallies, forever harking back to a nineteenth-century past of leisured aristocrats – though with futuristic prices.

The **Côte de Nacre** and the **Bessin**, despite the prominence of their war past, are much more likeable; in the small-scale traditional resorts here, the sea may be a little overexposed, but you can at least eat well and wander without crowds. The history of the D-Day landings – and the numerous cemeteries and memorials – draws its own kind of tourists, still with many veterans among them. A tour can be instructive and moving. For sites actually to enjoy, however, **Bayeux** must be

ACCOMMODATION PRICE CODES

All **hotel prices** in this book have been coded using the symbols below. The price shown is for the least expensive double room, which for categories ① and ② usually means a room without shower, bath and toilet. Most hotels in those categories have other rooms with en-suite facilities, which typically cost 30–50F extra.

For a full explanation see p.31.

①	up to 120 F	④	220–300F	⑦	500–600F
②	120–160F	⑤	300–400F	⑧	600–700F
③	160–220F	⑥	400–500F	⑨	700F and over

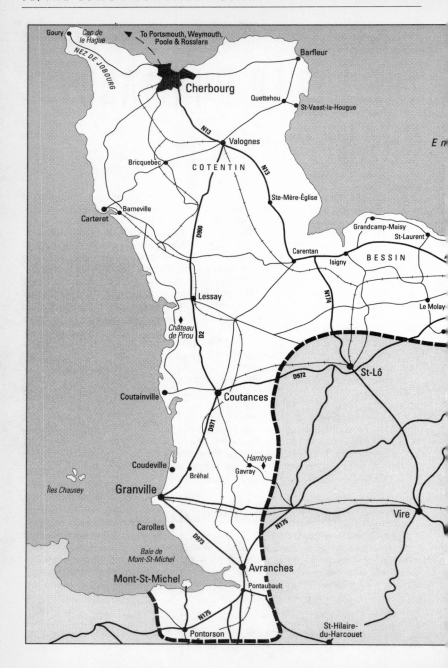

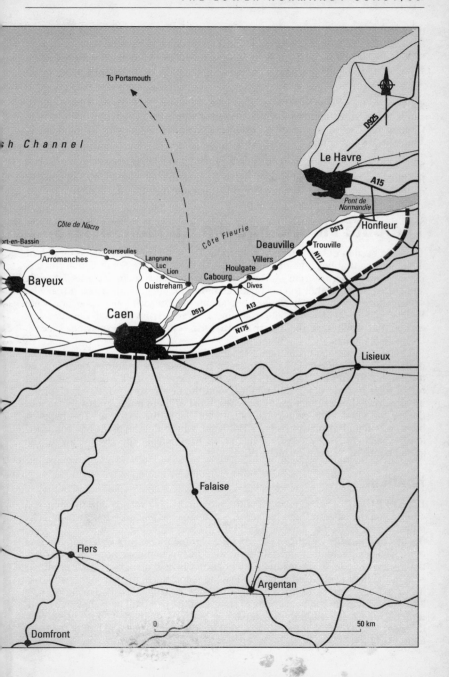

the pre-eminent destination. It holds, of course, the famous **tapestry**, its drama remaining as vivid as its colours, and is a stylish and interesting town in its own right. Considerably more so, in fact, than war-ravaged **Caen**, though the infra-structure of the latter has received a hefty boost over the decade since the open-ing of the cross-channel ferry harbour at **Ouistreham**.

Cherbourg is even less of a ferry port to linger over. But if you arrive here, you're just a short distance from the beaches, dunes and amazing windsurfing along the western coastline of the **Cotentin peninsula**, between Carteret and Coutainville. These serve to delay progress towards the glorious island abbey of **Mont-St-Michel**, France's most visited and most distinctive monument (after Versailles), which, from **Granville** onwards, is visible across the bay. Beaches hereabouts, however, are no temptation – dangerous for the most part and flanked by generally tacky resorts. Having come this far, better to head straight on to the delights of the Breton **Côte d'Émeraude** (see Chapter Four).

The Côte Fleurie and the Norman Riviera

The only section of the Norman coast to have any serious delusions of grandeur is the stretch that lies immediately east of the mouth of the Seine. The forthcom-ing new bridge across from Le Havre threatens to make such places as Trouville and Deauville altogether too hectic for comfort, but only Honfleur could really be said to have much that it would be a shame to lose, with the appealing Côte Fleurie just west of town. The coastline between Trouville and Cabourg has earned the epithet of the **Norman Riviera**, with Trouville playing Nice to Deauville's Cannes.

There's an obvious distinction all along this stretch of the coast between old ports such as Honfleur and Dives, which have over the centuries been pushed further and further back from the sea by heavy deposits of silt from the Seine but retain their historic medieval buildings, and the new resorts which have sprung up alongside the resultant sandy beaches, most of them unimaginatively laid out during the nineteenth century and characterless in the extreme. The happiest balance is found at places such as Houlgate, where development has remained low-key and the rocky coastline has stood firm against the river – giving the added bonus of pleasant corniche drives.

Honfleur

HONFLEUR, the best-preserved of the old ports of Normandy and the first you come to on the eastern Calvados coast, is a near-perfect seaside town which lacks only a beach. It used to have one, but with the accumulation of silt from the Seine the sea has steadily withdrawn, leaving the eighteenth-century waterfront houses of bd Charles V stranded and a little surreal. The ancient port, however, still func-tions – the channel to the beautiful *Vieux Bassin* is kept open by regular dredging – and though only pleasure craft now use the moorings in the harbour basin, fish-ing boats continue to tie up alongside the pier nearby. Fish is usually on sale either directly from the boats or from stands on the pier, still by right run by fish-ermen's wives. It's all highly picturesque, and very upmarket, but not so very different to the town that had such appeal to artists in the second half of the nine-teenth century.

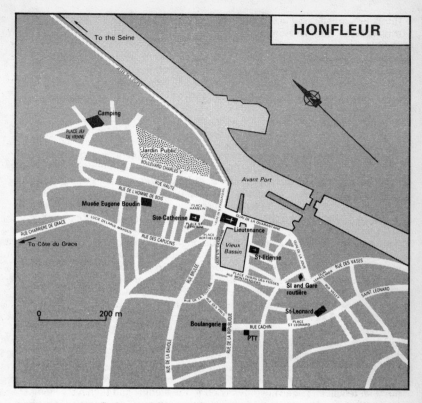

Things may well change following the construction of a vast new bridge across the mouth of the Seine, which opened to traffic in January 1995. Honfleur has become just a few minutes' drive from giant Le Havre, leaving its population divided as to whether they should build connecting roads to encourage new trade, or bypasses to keep the traffic as far away as possible.

Though the town has modern suburbs and developments, it's the old centre, around the *bassin*, to which you'll inevitably gravitate. At the *bassin*, slate-fronted houses, each of them one or two storeys higher than seems possible, harmonize despite their tottering and ill-matched forms into a backdrop that is only excelled by the **Lieutenance** at the harbour entrance. This latter was the dwelling of the King's Lieutenant, and has been the gateway to the inner town from the time that Samuel Champlain sailed from Honfleur to found Québec in 1608. The church of **St-Stephen** nearby is now the **Musée de la Marine**, which, with its accompanying ethnographic collection, is open for rather formal guided tours in high season (April–Sept daily 10.30am–12.30pm & 2.30–6pm; Oct–Dec & mid-Feb to March Mon–Fri 2.30–6pm, Sat & Sun 10.30am–12.30pm & 2.30–6pm; closed Jan to mid-Feb; 25F). Just behind it, two seventeenth-century **salt stores**, used to contain the precious commodity during the days of the much-hated *gabelle*, or salt tax, now stage much more palatable temporary art exhibitions during the summer months.

Honfleur's artistic past – and its present concentration of galleries and painters – owes most to Eugène Boudin, forerunner of Impressionism. He was born and worked in the town, trained the fifteen-year-old Monet, and was joined for various periods by Pissarro, Renoir and Cézanne. At the same time, Baudelaire paid visits to the town, which was also home to the composer Erik Satie. There's a fair selection of Boudin's works in the **Musée Eugène Boudin**, west of the port on place Erik-Satie, and his crayon seascapes in particular are quite appealing here in context, though the Dufys, Marquets, Frieszes and above all the Monets are the most impressive paintings on show (mid-March to Sept daily except Tues 10am–noon & 2–6pm, otherwise Mon & Wed–Fri 2.30–5pm, Sat & Sun 10am–noon & 2.30–5pm, closed Jan to mid-Feb; 16F).

The church of **Ste-Catherine**, with its distinctive detached belfry (one of Monet's favourite subjects), is the town's most remarkable building. It was built almost entirely of wood, during the Hundred Years War; all stone was at that time reserved for military use, and so the town's ship-builders, experienced in working with wood, took responsibility for its construction. All the timbers inside are now exposed to view, having been sheathed in white plaster during the nineteenth century, when an incongruous four-columned porch (long since removed) was added to the front. The changing patterns on its tiles, both along the main body and the belfry, delineate religious symbols. It all makes a change from the great stone Norman churches, and has the added peculiarity of being divided into twin naves, with one balcony running around both. Nearby, along the rue de l'Homme-de-Bois, incongruous views combine the stately backs of what were once ship-builders' houses with the industrial desert of Le Havre's docks in the distance.

A couple of blocks below, past the public gardens by the place Augustin Normand, you can follow the **shipping channel** out towards the mouth of the Seine and the sea. A rusty old pipeline runs alongside, inside which you can hear rats and mice scampering to and from the sea. However, it would not occur even to the most hard-nosed mud-caked sewer rat to swim in the sea once it got there – the shore is a slimy grey wasteland, the water foul and sluggish. Nonetheless, it is possible to slip and squirm your way on to the shingle and then walk along the sea coast, with the beautiful wooded hills of the Côte du Grâce tantalizingly above you. Inland, the grand old houses of ancient aesthetes, and the **Chapelle Notre-Dame de Grâce**, beloved of the Impressionists, nestle dry-footed in the forests.

Arrival and Information

Honfleur's **SI** can be found on place Arthur-Boudin (Mon–Sat 9am–12.30pm & 2–6.30pm, also open Sun Easter–Oct 10am–noon & 3–5pm; ☎31.89.23.30), across from the town hall. For most of the year, the SI organizes two-hour guided tours of the town (July–Sept, Mon, Wed & Fri 3pm, Tues & Thurs 10pm; March–June & Oct, Sat 3pm only; 28F). The **gare routière**, on the place de la Porte-du-Rouen, is served by seven direct **buses** per day from Caen (#20; *Bus Verts* enquiries ☎31.89.28.41); however, the nearest train station is at Pont-l'Evêque (see p.144), connected by the Lisieux bus, #50 (a 20min ride).

Accommodation

It's not quite so easy to live the Bohemian life in Honfleur these days; if finding budget accommodation is one of your main priorities, it probably makes sense not to stay here at all, and simply to visit for the day. Especially on summer weekends, so many visitors come to what is after all a small town, that even the most ordinary hotel can get away with charging rates well above the average for Normandy. No hotels overlook the harbour itself. Motorists face the additional problem that it is all but impossible to park anywhere near a central hotel. There is however a **campsite**, the *Camping du Phare* (April–Sept only; ☎31.89.10.26) at the west end of bd Charles V on place Jean-de-Vienne.

A l'Amiral, 18 rue Brulée (☎31.89.38.26). Very plain building on a quiet side street just 100m inland from Ste-Catherine church. Garage for bikes and motorbikes. Simple but well-furnished rooms. ④.

Hotel des Cascades, 17 place Thiers (☎31.89.05.83). Large hotel/restaurant open onto both place Thiers and the cobbled rue de la Ville behind. (Slightly noisy) rooms upstairs, and a good value if not all that exciting restaurant with outdoor seating on both sides; menus climb upwards from 80F towards the expensive *fruits de mer*. Closed Mon pm, all Tues out of season, and mid-Nov to mid-Feb. ④.

Hotel du Dauphin, 10 place Berthelot (☎31.89.15.53). Grey slate town house just around the corner from Ste-Catherine church, with a wide assortment of rooms. Closed Jan. ③–⑦.

Hotel le Hamelin, 16 place Hamelin (☎31.89.16.25). Five basic rooms, some with showers, in plain building very near the Lieutenance in the liveliest part of town The restaurant downstairs has standard seafood menus from 70F, and manages to squeeze a few tables onto the street. ②–⑤.

Hotel de la Claire, 77 cours Albert-Manuel (☎31.89.05.95). Ordinary rooms in an unattractive sort of half-timbered motel on the main approach road from Lisieux, around 1km out from the centre but potentially convenient for motorists. As a *logis de France*, it has its own restaurant; menus start at 75F. ③.

Tilbury, 30 place Hamelin (☎31.98.83.33). Absolutely central, a stone's throw from the Lieutenance. Well-equipped and comfortable rooms above a *crêperie*. ③–⑥.

Eating

With its abundance of day-trippers and hotel guests, Honfleur supports an astonishing number of **restaurants**, most naturally specializing in seafood and many of them very good at it indeed. Surprisingly few restaurants actually face onto the harbour itself; the narrow buildings around the edge seem to be better suited to being snack bars, *crêperies*, cafés and ice-cream parlours. Few of the town's hotels attempt to compete with the restaurants; the *Cascades* (see above) is probably the best of the few that do.

One local speciality, available mainly in October and November, is *crevettes grises* – tiny shrimp eaten with an unsalty Spanish-style bread, *pain brié*. If you're buying your own food, look out for the excellent *La Panatérie*, a *boulangerie* selling granary and wholemeal breads, on the corner of the rue des Prés and av de la République.

L'Ascot, 76 quai Ste-Catherine (☎31.98.87.91). The only formal restaurant on the more cramped but brighter west side of the harbour, with limited and unadventurous menus starting at 99F.

Auberge de la Lieutenance, 12 place Ste-Catherine (☎31.89.07.52). Not in fact by the Lieutenance, despite the name. Plenty of outdoor seating on the cobbled pedestrian square facing both church and nave. Gourmet dining with a heavy emphasis on oysters; menus start at 96F.

Bistro du Port, 14 quai de la Quarantaine (☎31.89.21.84). The middle of five adjacent and substantially similar restaurants, all with outdoor seating but in a not very picturesque setting beside the main road just east of the harbour. The *Bistro* has a slight competitive edge on prices for its conventional seafood menus, with good 85F and 128F menus.

Le Gars Normand, 8 quai des Passagers (☎31.89.05.28). Right in the thick of things, two small dining rooms crammed into a little house all but next door to the Lieutenance. Menus from 88F, with clams and mussels, but the main courses are very unadventurous.

Au P'tit Mareyeur, 4 rue Haute (☎31.98.84.23). Next door to a fish shop and no distance from the centre, with all seating indoors and no view. Very good fish dishes – red crab soup with garlic – plus plenty of creamy *pays d'Auge* sauces and a superb chocolate and Cointreau dessert. Main menu 119F.

Taverne de la Mer, 35 rue Haute (☎31.89.57.77). Magnificent selection of fresh seafood, in a small converted bar not far from place Hamelin, with no outdoor seating. Starters on the cheapest (118F) menu include deep-fried triangular filo parcels of scallop and salmon served in blackberry vinegar; among main courses is a seafood *marmite* in a sweet cider sauce. Also grilled fish on open wood fire.

Le Vieux Honfleur, 13 quai St-Etienne (☎31.89.15.31). The best of the restaurants around the harbour itself, with spacious alfresco dining on the (usually shady) and pedestrianized eastern side of the harbour. Very simple menus, but the seafood is very good, as befits prices starting at 150F.

Along the Côte Fleurie

For the fifteen kilometres **west along the corniche** from Honfleur to Trouville, green fields and fruit trees line the land's edge, and cliffs rise from sandy beaches. The resorts, **VILLERVILLE** most conspicuously, aren't cheap, but they're relatively undeveloped, and if you want to stop by the seaside this is the place to do it.

Trouville and Deauville

The adjacent towns of Trouville and Deauville lie within a stone's throw of each other to either side of the mouth of the River Touques, sharing many of their amenities, and also their rather exclusive reputations.

TROUVILLE retains at least some semblance of a real town, with a constant population, industries other than tourism and a history that includes Henry V landing on his way to Agincourt. But it is primarily a resort, and has been ever since Napoléon III started bringing his court here for the summer in the 1860s (his Empress, Eugénie, fled France from here in 1870 in the yacht of an English admirer). Spectacular villas line the beach, patterned with complex brickwork and topped by ornate turrets.

One of the Emperor's dukes, looking across the river, saw not marshlands but money, and lots of it, in the form of a **racecourse**. His vision materialized, and villas appeared between the racecourse and the sea to become **DEAUVILLE**. Now you can lose money on the horses, cross five streets to lose more in the Casino, where Winston Churchill spent the summer of 1906 gambling every night until five in the morning, and finally lose yourself in the 200 metres of sports and "cure" facilities, and private bathing huts, that intervene before the *planches*. Beyond this half-kilometre of duckwalk, rows of primary coloured parasols obscure the sea.

Practicalities

Visits to the **SI** on place de la Mairie in Deauville (Mon–Sat 9am–12.30pm & 2–6.30pm, Sun 11am–4pm; ☎31.88.21.43), or the one at 32 quai F-Moureaux in Trouville (April–Nov, Mon–Sat 9am–1pm & 2–7pm, Sun 10am–12.30pm & 2.30–5.30pm; Dec–March Mon–Sat 9am–12.15pm & 2–6pm; ☎31.88.36.19), are repaid with some spectacularly revolting brochures (in English). The towns share their **gare SNCF** (served by trains from Paris via Lisieux) and **gare routière**, in between the two just south of the marina. Each day, seven of the hourly buses from Caen continue along the coast to Honfleur.

As you might imagine, **hotels** are either luxurious or overpriced. The *Café-Hôtel des Sports*, 27 rue Gambetta (☎31.88.22.67; closed Sun; ③), behind Deauville's fish market is the least expensive, while the *Charmettes*, 22 rue de la Chapelle (☎31.88.17.67; ③), is Trouville's closest equivalent. There are also three **campsites**, two in Trouville and one in Deauville. The *Café Chez Marie* at 44 rue Mirabeau in Deauville (☎31.88.34.29) is a top-quality bistro with prices that are high but not outrageous, while the *Bristol* at 1 rue Paul-Besson in Trouville (☎31.88.10.37) is good for fish all day, and especially good value for lunch. *La Petite Auberge*, 7 rue Carnot in Trouville (☎31.88.11.07), is another fine seafood place which gets very crowded at weekends.

If you're tempted to **gamble** in Deauville's Casino, formal attire is compulsory, and you have to pay a temporary membership fee of around 100F to be allowed anywhere near the tables. One more congenial reason to visit is the **American Film Festival** held in Deauville in the first week of September – a festival that's the antithesis of Cannes, with public admission to a wide selection of previews.

Towards Cabourg

The smaller resorts on **towards Cabourg** are equally crowded and equally short of inexpensive hotels. But they're less snobbish, and there are plenty of camp-sites, such as *les Falaises* (☎31.91.09.66) at Gonneville-sur-mer, and *Camping Simar* (☎31.87.52.41) and *Bellevue* (☎31.87.05.21), straddling the Greenwich Meridian at **VILLERS**.

With an eye on the tides, you can also escape the never-ending villas along the promenades, and walk beneath the **Vaches Noires** cliffs from Villers to Houlgate. However, industrial Le Havre is a bit too visible across the water for it to be an especially picturesque stroll.

Cabourg

At **CABOURG**, you are confronted by little more than an exercise in style – a pure creation for a certain aged class, contemporary with Deauville and seem-ingly stuck entirely in the nineteenth century. There's an awful lot of town plan-ning, but not really any town. At the centre of the straightest promenade in

---

PROUST IN CABOURG

As both child and adult, between 1881 and 1914, Marcel Proust stayed repeatedly at the *Grand Hôtel* in Cabourg. The town is the "Balbec" of *Du Côté de Chez Swann*, and the hotel itself now thrives on its Proustian connection. All guests are served with a *madeleine* for breakfast, and Proust's own room is available at a cost of over 1200F per night (not the most expensive in the hotel by any means). The rock star Sting stayed in that very room in 1991, and drank from the same well of inspiration. The main dining room, which has a superb sea view, is now called *Le Balbec*. For the ambivalent Proust it was "the aquarium"; each night locals would press their faces to its window in wonder at the luxurious life within, "as extraordinary to the poor as the life of strange fishes or molluscs".

France, the **Grand Hôtel** looks out towards the sea, while behind it the crescent that defines the formal **Jardins du Casino** is the first of several concentric crescents, spreading out like ripples and lined with large, placid, undistinguished – and usually empty – houses. Notices request that you "avoid noise on the beach", and picnics are forbidden.

Practicalities

Trains run all the way from Paris Gare Ste-Lazare to the **gare SNCF** which Cabourg shares with Dives (see below) every day from the end of June until the start of September, and otherwise at weekends only. Arriving by **bus** in Cabourg – it's on route #20 between Caen and Honfleur – you'll be dropped off at the gardens on av Pasteur; walk through them and turn right down av de la Mer to reach the Jardins du Casino.

The **SI** in the Casino gardens has full details on **hotels** (July & Aug daily 9am–7pm, Sept–June Mon–Sat 9.30am–12.30pm & 2–6.30pm, Sun 10am–12.30pm & 2.30–6pm; ☎31.91.01.09). The *L'Oie qui Fume*, at 18 av de la Brèche-Buhot (closed Sun pm & Mon, and all Jan; ☎31.91.27.79; ③), is 100 metres back from the sea on a quiet road half a dozen streets west of the centre; menus at 119F and 169F both feature goose (*oie*). The half-timbered *Hôtel de Paris*, 39 av de la Mer (☎31.91.31.34; ③), is more central, on Cabourg's only commercial (semi-pedestrianized) street. It has no restaurant, but *La Cremaillère*, two doors down at no. 41 (☎31.91.14.40), has menus at all prices, and there are plenty of pizzerias and snack bars nearby.

Dives

Just across the river from Cabourg is the somewhat more interesting – and much older – town of **DIVES**, the port from which William the Conqueror sailed for Hastings, and, like Honfleur, now pushed well back from the sea. Dives has nothing in common with the aristocratic resort, other than its significance for Proust, whose dream vision "land's end church of Balbec" is the town's **Notre Dame** church.

A lively **Saturday market** focusses around the ancient wooden *halles*, tucked away south of the main through road. The steep tiled roof of the *halles* must be five times the height of its walls, and its venerable weather-beaten timbers are held together by tight metal bands; on market days, it's crammed with mouthwatering delicacies and Norman specialities, while more mundane produce and imported jeans are sold in the square alongside and up and down the narrow streets. The town hosts a **puppet festival** in early August.

Dives has a reasonable **hotel**, the *de la Gare* (☎31.91.24.52; ③), and there's a **campsite** on the way to Cabourg (and two more off the Cabourg–Lisieux road).

Franceville

Continuing along the coast towards Caen, in **FRANCEVILLE** the main road passes a half-timbered *logis*, also called the *Hôtel de la Gare* (☎31.24.23.37; ③), with adequate rooms and good food, and the bizarre *Le Surfer*, a disco concealed in a German bunker.

A little further on, you can turn right, across what used to be Pegasus Bridge (see p.107), for direct access to Ouistreham and the Landing Beaches.

Caen

Appropriately enough for a city that has been fought over throughout its long history, the name of **CAEN**, capital and largest city of Basse Normandie, originally came from a Celtic word meaning "battlefield". This site was first fortified in 1060 by William the Conqueror, who preferred it to Rouen because it was further from the marauding Franks, and the navigable river Orne afforded him safe access to the Channel. During the succeeding centuries, Caen repeatedly changed hands, and was twice sacked by the English: first by Edward III in 1246, and then by Henry V in 1417. In 1432, the English Henry VI founded the university, but Caen has been French since Charles VII took it in 1450.

The modern city began to take shape when a canal to the sea was completed in 1850, running parallel to the heavily silted Orne. At the same time, the Bassin St-Pierre was built, creating a marina in the centre of the city which is now reminiscent of the "port" in Vannes (see p.301). The smaller river Odon was covered over, and the number of bridges across the Orne was doubled. **World War II** however devastated the city. It was the prime target of the Allied invasion in June 1944, and historians still argue as to quite why it took so long to capture. The "Battle of Caen" lasted two full months – even after the Canadians entered the city four weeks after D-Day, the southern bank of the river remained in enemy hands. Three quarters of the town was destroyed before they were finally dislodged.

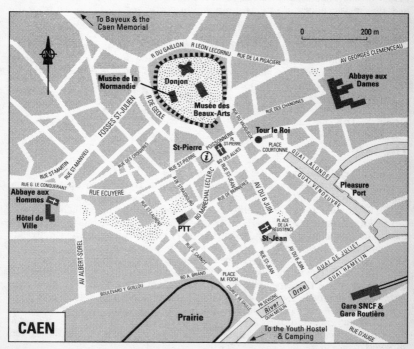

Caen today is not a place where you're likely to spend much time, though in parts it remains highly impressive. The central feature is a ring of ramparts that no longer has a castle to protect, and, though there are the scattered spires and buttresses of two abbeys and eight old churches, roads and roundabouts fill the wide spaces where pre-war houses stood. Approaches are along thunderous dual-carriageways through industrial suburbs – once an economic success story, currently hammered by unemployment.

Arrival and Information

Caen's **SI** is in the central Hôtel d'Escoville, at 14 place St-Pierre (June–Sept, Mon–Sat 9am–7pm, Sun 10am–12.30pm & 3–6pm; Oct–May Mon 10am–noon & 2–7pm, Tues–Sat 9am–noon & 2–7pm, Sun 10am–12.30pm; ☎31.86.27.65). This beautiful sixteenth-century house, across the street from the church of St-Pierre, is typical of the early Renaissance in Caen, with a strong Italian influence evident in its Florentine flourishes. For details of forthcoming events in the city, pick up a copy of their free weekly *Caen Scope*. On summer Sundays, when the banks are closed, the SI's currency exchange service can be a life-saver. The main **post office** is on place Gambetta (Mon–Fri 8am–7pm, Sat 8am–noon; ☎31.39.35.78).

The **gare SNCF** (☎31.83.50.50) is 1km south of the town centre across the river, with the **gare routière** so close at hand that you can walk directly to it from platform one. The *Brittany Ferries* service from Portsmouth, promoted as sailing to Caen, in fact docks at **Ouistreham**, 15km north; see p.107. Buses from the gare routière connect with each sailing.

CTAC, the extensive **local bus** service (☎31.85.42.76), makes a one-way circuit through town between the *Tour le Roi* stop just north of the pleasure port and the gare SNCF, travelling north up avenue du 6 Juin and south down rue St-Jean. Digital displays at the main stops show when the next bus is due, and free timetables are available from *CTAC*, 11 bd Maréchal-Leclerc, and the SI.

Long-distance buses from the gare routière include those run by *Bus Verts* (11 rue des Chanoines; ☎31.44.77.44). Line #32 goes to Vire; #20 to Dives, Deauville, Trouville and Honfleur; #26 to Ouistreham, Riva Bella and Luc-sur-mer.

The City

Around the **château ramparts**, a virtue has been made of the necessity of clearing the rubble of the medieval houses which formerly pressed up against the walls. The resulting open green space means that those walls are now fully visible for the first time in centuries. Within are two **museums**, of which much the best is the **Beaux Arts** (daily except Tues 10am–6pm; 20F, free on Sun), which amid comprehensive displays – from fifteenth-century Italian and Flemish primitives to contemporary French artists – includes masterpieces by Poussin, Géricault, Monet and Bonnard, as well as an exceptional collection of engravings by Dürer and Rembrandt. The other museum, devoted to Norman history, is unmemorable (April–Sept Wed–Fri 10am–12.30pm & 1.30–6pm, Sat–Mon 9.30am–12.30pm & 2–6pm; Oct–March daily except Tues 9.30am–12.30pm & 2–6pm; 6F, free on Sun).

A walk around the castle walls also gives a fine view of the reconstructed fourteenth-century facade of the church of **St-Pierre**. On the ground, take a look at the church's east end, where some magnificent Renaissance stonework has survived intact.

Just to the north of the château lies the complex of **University** buildings, originally founded in 1432 by Henry VI of England. Their latest acquisition is the largest nuclear particle accelerator in Europe. An expensive toy built with EU money, it has done little for the city's economy.

Over to the west is the **Abbaye aux Hommes**, founded by William the Conqueror and designed to hold his tomb. His burial here, in 1087, was hopelessly undignified. The funeral procession first caught fire and was then held to ransom, as various factions squabbled over his rotting corpse for any spoils they could grab. A further interruption came when a man halted the service to object that the grave had been constructed without compensation on the site of his family house, and the assembled nobles had to pay him off before William could finally be laid to rest. During the Revolution the tomb was again ransacked and it now holds at most a solitary thigh-bone rescued from the river. Still, the building itself is a wonderful Romanesque monument, although not enhanced by the latest desecration – "multi-lingual, computerized audio-visual visits". There are also guided tours, every hour, on the hour – except at 1pm – from 9am to 5pm. Look out for the huge wooden clock to the left of the altar.

The **Hôtel de Ville** alongside, which all but obscures the abbey, is housed in what used to be its convent buildings – hence the surprising harmony with which the two blend together.

William's queen, Mathilda, lies across the town in the **Abbaye aux Dames** at the end of rue des Chanoines. She had commissioned the building of the abbey church, La Trinité, well before the Conquest. It's starkly impressive, with a gloomy pillared crypt, superb stained glass behind the altar, and odd sculptural details like the fish curled up in the holy-water stoup. (Guided tours daily at 2.30pm & 4pm; free.)

Most of the centre of Caen is taken up with busy new shopping developments and pedestrian precincts, where the cafés are distinguished by such names as *Fast Food Glamour Vault*, and one sports shop is called *Athlete's Foot*. The **shops** are good, possibly the best in Normandy or Brittany if Parisian style is what you're after. Outlets of the big Parisian department stores – and of the aristocrats' grocers, *Hédiard,* in the Cours des Halles – are here, along with good local rivals. Rue Ecuyère has a fine assortment of shops full of unusual and cheap oddments; antiques, stuff for collectors and jokes.

If you're looking for books, records or tickets for local events, call in at the branch of *FNAC* (☎31.39.41.00) in the Centre Paul-Doumer, on the corner of rue Doumer and rue Bras. The main city **market** takes place on Friday, spreading along both sides of Fosse St-Julien, and there's also a Sunday market in place Courtonne. The **pleasure port,** at the end of the canal which links Caen to the sea, is where most life goes on, at least in summer.

The Caen Memorial – A Museum for Peace

Daily June–Aug 9am–9pm, last entry 8.15pm; Sept–May 9am–7pm, last entry 5.45pm. Closed first fortnight of Jan. Admission 55F, reduced to 46F for students, the young and the over-65s; under-10s and World War II veterans free. ☎31.06.06.44 – note the significance. The museum is just north of Caen, at the end of av Marshal-Montgomery in the Folie Couvrechef area. It's on bus routes #12 (Mon–Fri) and #14 (Sat & Sun) from the *Tour le Roi* stop in the centre of town.

North of Caen, at the end of av Marshal-Montgomery, the relatively new **Caen Memorial** stands on a plateau named after General Eisenhower, which ends on the clifftop beneath which the Germans had their HQ in June and July 1944.

Funds and material for it came from the US, Britain, Canada, Germany, Poland, Czechoslovakia, the USSR and France. It is a war museum with a big and very welcome difference, in that it proclaims itself to be a "Museum for Peace", and for the most part succeeds admirably in that intention.

All visitors have to follow a prescribed route through the ultra-modern building, which, with a slightly heavy-handed literalism, leads you on a downwards spiral from World War I and the Treaty of Versailles towards the maelstrom of World War II. From the start you hear the voice of Hitler booming in the distance; his image recurs with increasing size and frequency on screens beside you as the events of the 1920s and 1930s are recounted.

The war itself is superbly documented, with a greater emphasis on the minutiae of everyday life in occupied France than on military technology. Nothing is glossed over in the attempt to provide a fully rounded picture of the nation under occupation and at war. The collaborationist Vichy government is set in its context without being excused, with such statements as Pierre Laval's "I wish for the victory of Germany, because without it Bolshevism will spread everywhere" on prominent display alongside a book of the "99 most touching answers of French schoolchildren to the question 'Why do you love Maréchal Petain?'". Secret Nazi reports show how Resistance activity in Normandy grew as the war continued, and what reprisals were taken.

Each visit culminates with three films, each one in a separate auditorium. The first is a harrowing account of D-Day itself; the second traces the course of the rest of the war; and the third looks at the winners of the Nobel Peace Prize in arguing for the need to establish lasting peace in the world.

All in all, this museum creates something new in a genre which can occasionally seem morally suspect, and the display cannot be recommended too highly for anyone with a serious interest in the war and its lasting legacy. Allow at least two hours for a visit, as the films alone occupy a whole hour.

Accommodation

Caen has a great number of **hotels**, though as ever in the bomb-damaged cities of Normandy, few could be called attractive; even those that advertise their antiquity tend to have been totally rebuilt. The main concentrations are near the gare SNCF, around the pleasure port, and just west of the castle and SI – the latter being particularly convenient for motorists heading to or or from the ferry. There are also a number of charmless motel-type places on the ring road around town. With plenty of dedicated restaurants in town, few hotels other than those specifically mentioned below bother to provide food.

The summer-only **youth hostel** is in the *Foyer Robert-Remé* at 68 bis rue E-Restout, Grace-de-Dieu (June–Sept; ☎31.52.19.96; 67F), about 500m southwest of the gare SNCF. Take bus #17 from the town centre (*Tour le Roi*) or gare SNCF, direction Grace-de-Dieu, getting off at stop *Lycée Fresnil*. The municipal **campsite** *Camping OMJ* (☎31.72.60.92) is nearby, beside the river Orne, on route de Louvigny (bus #13, direction *Louvigny*, stop *Camping*).

Hotels

Central Hôtel, 23 place J-Letellier (☎31.86.18.52). By Caen standards a budget hotel; not as quiet as it used to be, but very central. Good views of the château from the balconies of the higher rooms. ②.

Hôtel-Restaurant le Dauphin, 29 rue Gémare (☎31.86.22.26). Rather ugly but very central hotel, tucked away behind the SI. Part of it was a priory during the eighteenth century, not that you'd ever guess; the rooms are comfortable without being exciting in any way. Grand restaurant, with a 95F weekday menu; weekend menus 165F and 235F. Closed Sat, and mid-July to early Aug. ⑤.

Hôtel-Restaurant Petite Auberge, 17 rue des Equipes-d'Urgence (☎31.86.43.30). On the way into town, just off av du 6 Juin opposite St-Jean church. Good restaurant, reviewed on p.106. ③.

Hôtel le Quatrans, 17 rue Gémare (☎31.86.25.57). A little way behind the SI, but unmissable thanks to its garish neon-lit exterior. The pastel theme of the facade continues inside; some might find it all a bit cloying, but the service is friendly, and at least everything works. Cheaper rooms are without showers. ③.

Hôtel-Restaurant Rotonde, 4 place de la Gare (☎31.82.24.25). One of several options facing the gare SNCF. Restaurant closed Sat midday and Sun. ②.

Hôtel Rouen, 8 place de la Gare (☎31.34.06.03). Reasonable and convenient accommodation, facing the gare SNCF. No restaurant. ①–④.

Hôtel St-Etienne, 2 rue de l'Académie (☎31.86.35.82). Old stone house, dating back to before the Revolution, in the characterful St-Martin district not far from the Abbaye des Hommes. The cheapest rooms do not have showers. ①.

Hôtel St-Jean, 20 rue des Martyrs (☎31.86.23.35). Simple but well equipped rooms – all have shower or bath – facing St-Jean church near the *Petite Auberge*. No restaurant. ②.

Hôtel St Pierre, 40 bd des Alliés (☎31.86.28.20). In town, immediately opposite the Tour le Roi, alongside the eponymous bus stop and place Courtonne. Cheaper rooms do not have showers. No restaurant. ②.

Hôtel Univers, 12 quai Vendeuvre (☎31.85.46.14). In town, near the port de Plaisance. All rooms have shower or bath. No restaurant. ③.

Eating

The centre of Caen offers two major areas for **eating**. Cosmopolitan restaurants in the attractive pedestrianized **quartier Vaugueux** include the *Kouba*, specializing in couscous, the pasta-fixated *Toscanne*, and even *L'Age du Pierre*, which claims to prepare "stone age" food by cooking slabs of meat on super-heated stones. The streets off **rue de Geôle**, near the western ramparts, particularly rue des Croisiers and rue Gémare, house rather more traditional French restaurants. There are also several restaurants and brasseries facing the gare SNCF, of which many are either in, or connected with, hotels.

Restaurants

L'Alcide, 1 place Courtonne (☎31.44.18.06). Very conspicuous but rather anonymous-looking bistro-style place, which turns out to be surprisingly good, serving classic French dishes cooked with great attention to detail. Menus from 70F up to 130F.

Le Boeuf Ferré, 10 rue des Croisiers (☎31.85.36.40). Standard gourmet restaurant, all indoors, with stone walls and timbered ceiling. Rich and substantial meals; oysters and scallops to start, followed by *rable de lièvre* with fresh pasta. Midday menu 75F, dinners from 99F. Closed Sat am & Sun, also the first fortnight in March and the second fortnight in July.

Le Boeuf Gourmand, 8 rue des Croisiers (☎31.85.13.83). Next door to the *Boeuf Ferré*, with similar food and virtually identical prices; once they were one and the same, now they're estranged. The 100F menu includes snails with wild mushrooms and a plethora of dead ducks. Also closed Sat am & Sun.

Insolite, 16 rue du Vaugueux (☎31.43.83.87). Not the prettiest of this row of half-timbered houses, but some outdoor seating, and a wide assortment of fish dishes. Open until late, with menus at 95F and 160F. Closed Sun pm and Mon.

Le Paquebot, 7 rue des Croisiers (☎31.85.10.10). Very much in vogue at the moment; sophisticated but relatively inexpensive French cooking in the courtyard of the Ancien Abbaye des Croisiers, west of the château. The 60F lunches are a real bargain, but even in the evenings the set menus start at 75F. Closed Sat am & Sun.

Hôtel-Restaurant Petite Auberge, 17 rue des Equipes-d'Urgence (☎31.86.43.30). Plain and simple restaurant, with a nice view of the St-Jean church. Very good-value Norman specialities – a 65F menu which doesn't force you to eat tripe. Closed Sun pm and Mon.

Tongasoa, 7 rue du Vaugueux (☎31.43.87.15). Midday menu 55F; evening menus from 85F. Dishes from Madagascar, Réunion and the Seychelles – especially fish, curried, cooked with ginger and tropical fruits, or just plain. Cocktails galore, in lurid colours. Open every day.

The Invasion Beaches

It is hard now to picture the scene at dawn on **D-Day**, June 6, 1944, when Allied troops landed at points along the Norman coast from the mouth of the Orne to Les Dunes de Varneville on the Cotentin peninsula*. For the most part, these are innocuous beaches backed by gentle dunes, and yet this foothold in Europe was won at the cost of 100,000 lives. That the invasion happened here, and not nearer to Germany, was partly due to the failure of the Canadian raid on Dieppe (see p.59) in 1942. The ensuing **Battle of Normandy** killed thousands of civilians and reduced nearly 600 towns and villages to rubble but, within a week of its eventual conclusion, Paris was liberated.

The **beaches** are still often referred to by their wartime code names. The British and Commonwealth forces landed on **Sword**, **Juno**, and **Gold** beaches between Ouistreham and Arromanches; the Americans further west on **Omaha** and **Utah** beaches. Bits of shrapnel can still be found in the sands, five decades later, but more substantial traces of the fighting are rare. At Arromanches the remains are visible of one of the prefabricated Mulberry harbours that made such large-scale landings possible, and at Pointe du Hoc, the cliff heights are still deeply pitted with German bunkers and shell-holes. Elsewhere, the reminders are **cemeteries** – British and Commonwealth, American and German, each highly distinct in character – and **war museums**, examples of which you'll find in almost every coastal town.

The D-Day events provide a focus for most foreign visitors to this part of the coast; travelling through, you are bound to come across veterans, and their descendants, paying their respects. Taken simply as holiday territory, however, some of the villages and towns can offer rewards. They are traditional seaside resorts, without the inflated prices or flashiness of the Deauville area – old-fashioned seafront villages, with rows of boarding houses and little wooden bathing huts that must have been kept in storage somewhere during the war. And increasingly there is **windsurfing** on offer – better suited to these north-facing resorts than chilly bathing.

In theory *Bus Verts* run all along this coast. **From Bayeux**, bus #74 goes to Arromanches and Corseulles, bus #70 to Port-en-Bessin and Vierville, bus #7 to Isigny. **From Caen**, bus #30 runs directly inland to Isigny via Bayeux, bus #26 to Ouistreham and on to Luc. None of these services, however, except for those linking Caen with the Ouistreham ferries, is all that reliable.

---

* The "D" in "D-Day" stands simply for "day"; hence it is known as "*J-Jour*" in France.

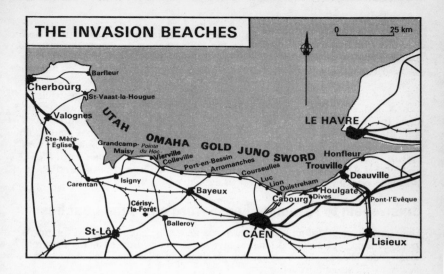

Ouistreham

The small community of **OUISTREHAM RIVA BELLA**, on the coast 15km north of Caen and connected to it by a fast dual carriageway, still gives the impression that it can barely believe its luck at having become a major ferry port. Since *Brittany Ferries* started their ever more regular service here from Portsmouth in 1986, the easternmost of the D-Day resorts has developed an extensive array of reasonable hotels and restaurants.

The town itself is not especially appealing, and most arriving passengers choose to press straight on out – this is one of the Channel's simpler ports to leave, as boats dock just a few hundred metres from the small central square, **place Courbonne**. Ouistreham's road system, at least in summer, is still not quite up to the task of coping with the volume of traffic, and motorists should allow plenty of time to catch their boats. All services are connected by bus with Caen.

If instead of setting off for Caen you head directly west along the coast from the ferry terminal, you come within a few hundred metres to the long straight main drag of **beach** – the "Riva Bella" itself. This is progressively shedding its somewhat run-down image; the large Casino has recently been re-modelled as a 1930s passenger liner, housing an expensive restaurant and cocktail bar, and even the old-fashioned bathing huts have had a fresh lick of paint. Nearby, a War Museum records the local Sword Beach landings.

The main road south passes close by **Pegasus Bridge**, where a museum and memorial mark the landing site of Allied gliders during the night before D-Day; their dangerous (and successful) mission was to secure the bridge a few hours in advance of the landings. Despite protests from veterans, the original bridge was removed in 1994. If you're **cycling**, the dedicated cycle path that follows the canal all the way to the centre of Caen makes a far more pleasant start to a holiday.

Practicalities

The Ouistreham Riva Bella SI is in the place Alfred-Thomas, alongside the casino on the beach (July & Aug daily 10am–7pm, Sept–June daily except Tues 10am–noon & 2–7pm; ☎31.97.18.63). For specific information about *Brittany Ferries* services, call the gare maritime (☎31.36.36.00).

Several cafés and brasseries in the place Courbonne, immediately outside the gare maritime, are eager to liberate passengers from their spare change, while *Le Chanel*, just around the corner at 79 av Michel-Cabieu (☎31.96.51.69; ②), is just about the best value for both eating and sleeping. Menus in the restaurant start with the 52F *menu pecheur*, which includes mussels, while the 85F and 139F options increase in splendour; the guest rooms are in a separate building across the street. Good alternatives near the beach include the *Auberge du Cheval Blanc*, 2 rue de la Mer (☎31.97.18.24; ③), the *Hôtel de la Plage* at 39–41 av Pasteur (☎31.96.85.16; ③), and the *St-Georges*, 51 av Andry (☎31.97.18.79; ④).

Ouistreham to Arromanches: Sword and Juno beaches

The coast along Sword and Juno beaches is generally featureless, but the towns themselves are welcoming. A long promenade curves by the sea all the way from Ouistreham to Lion – it's built-up, though always in a low-key way, and makes a pleasant walk straight from the ferry.

COLLEVILLE-MONTGOMERY, the first village after the port, is one of the few "Montgomeries" in the area really to be named after the British general rather than his Norman ancestors. It's not otherwise distinguished.

Luc-sur-mer

If you're looking for atmosphere – albeit sedate – **LUC-SUR-MER**, 11km from Ouistreham, is probably the best place to stop along here. It's a gentle resort with a small wooden pier, neon-lit *crêpe*-stands, and tearooms along the promenade, with the **hotel** *Beau Rivage*, right on the seafront at 1 rue du Dr-Charcot (☎31.96.49.51; ③), as its most reasonable accommodation. Menus here start at 65F; options on the 135F one include a spectacular salad of smoked fish, langoustines and *foie gras*. *Le Marsouin*, across the road at no. 2 (☎31.97.32.08; ③), is similar in almost every respect.

Langrune and Hermanville

Attractive individual seaside hotels are scattered all along the D-Day coast – typically with simple rooms upstairs above a large glass-fronted sea-view dining room – so ferry passengers have a choice of several *logis* for a first- or last-night stop. *L'Océanide*, 58 rue de Général-Leclerc (☎31.96.32.50; ③), in **LANGRUNE** is definitely one of the best, while the *Hotel de la Brèche*, rue du Dr-Turgis (☎31.97.20.40; ③), in **HERMANVILLE**, which has been weathered virtually to the point of extinction, seems to offer a quite spectacularly soporific time.

Courseulles

COURSEULLES is a bit more of a town, with an enjoyable Friday market in an old square set back from the sea, and, allegedly, the best oysters in Normandy. Briefly during the invasion it served as a crucial British beachhead; within ten days of D-Day it was visited by Winston Churchill and King George VI on morale-boosting excursions.

THE WAR CEMETERIES

The World War II **cemeteries** that dot the Norman countryside are filled with foreigners; most of the French dead are buried in the churchyards of their home towns. After the war, some felt that the soldiers should remain buried in the original makeshift graves dug where they fell. Instead, commissions gathered the remains into purpose-built cemeteries devoted to the separate warring nations. It is both moving and salutary to visit these cemeteries, and to consider how they differ.

The **British** and **Commonwealth** cemeteries are magnificently maintained, and open in every sense. They tend not to be screened off with hedges or walls, or to be forbidding expanses of manicured lawn, but are instead intimate, punctuated with bright flowers. The family of each soldier was invited to suggest an inscription for his tomb, making each grave very personal, and yet part of a common attempt to bring meaning to the carnage. Some epitaphs are questioning – "One day we will understand"; some are accepting – "Our lad at rest"; some matter of fact, simply giving the home address; some patriotic, quoting the "corner of a foreign field that is forever England". And interspersed among them all, is the chilling refrain of the anonymous "A soldier . . . known unto God". Thus the cemetery at **Ryes**, where so many of the graves bear the date of D-Day, and so many of the victims are under twenty, remains immediate and accessible – each grave clearly contains a unique individual. Even the monumental sculpture is subdued, a very British sort of fumbling for the decent thing to say. The understatement of the memorial at **Bayeux**, with its painfully contrived Latin epigram commemorating the return as liberators of "those whom William conquered", conveys an entirely appropriate humility and deep sadness.

An even more eloquent testimony to the futility of war is afforded by the **German** cemeteries, filled with soldiers who served a cause so despicable as to render any talk of "nobility" or "sacrifice" simply obscene. What such cemeteries might have been like had the Nazis won doesn't bear contemplation. As it is, they are sombre places, inconspicuous to minimize the bitterness they must still arouse. At **Orglandes** ten thousand are buried, three to each of the plain headstones set in the long flat lawn, almost hidden behind an anonymous wall. There are no noble slogans and the plain entrance is without a dedicatory monument. At the superb site of **Mont d'Huisnes** near Mont-St-Michel, the circular mausoleum holds another ten thousand, filed away in cold concrete tiers. There is no attempt to defend the indefensible, and yet one feels an overpowering sense of sorrow – that there is nothing to be said in such a place bitterly underlines the sheer waste and stupidity.

The largest **American** cemetery is at **St-Laurent-sur-mer** near the Pointe du Hoc. Here by contrast the atmosphere is one of certainty. The rows of crosses are so neat, so clinical, as to give the appearance of graph paper. At one end, a muscular giant dominates a huge array of battlefield plans and diagrams, covered with surging arrows and pincer movements. Endless rows of impersonal graves stretch away into the distance; there are no individual epitaphs, just gold lettering for a few exceptional warriors. That the place is so much like a balance sheet or corporate report seems something more than a mere difference of emphasis, explicable in terms of national style; the American cemetery is the only one which has placards telling you where to walk, what to wear and how to behave.

Courseulles' main activity these days is as a yachting port, and apart from an excellent crêperie, *du Moulin*, on the outskirts, there's not much choice of hotels and restaurants. The *Crémaillère*, bd de la Plage (☎31.37.46.73; ④), is probably the best option for both eating and sleeping, with menus from just under 100F.

Arromanches

At **ARROMANCHES** an artificial **Mulberry harbour**, "Port Winston", protected the landings of two and a half million men and half a million vehicles during the invasion. Two of these prefab concrete constructions were built in segments in Britain, while "doodlebugs" blitzed overhead, then submerged in rivers away from the prying eyes of German aircraft, and finally towed across the Channel at 4mph as the invasion began. Meanwhile the British 47 Royal Marine Commando were storming Arromanches itself to clear the way.

The seafront **Musée du Débarquement**, in Arromanches' main square (daily May–Aug 9am–6.30pm, Sept–April 9am–11.30am & 2–5.30pm; closed first three weeks of Jan; 30F), recounts the whole story by means of models, machinery, and movies – and the evidence of your own eyes. A huge picture window runs the length of the museum, staring straight out to where the bulky remains of the harbour make a strange intrusion on the beach and shallow sea bed. Its sheer scale is impossible to appreciate at this distance; for the three months after D-Day, this was the largest port in the world. (The other Mulberry, slightly further west on Omaha Beach, broke up within two weeks, but this one was repairable; see below.)

There are war memorials throughout Arromanches, with Jesus and Mary high up on the cliffs above the invasion site and helicopter trips available to overlook the area.

Practicalities

Arromanches somehow manages to be quite a cheerful place to stay, with a lively pedestrian street of bars and brasseries, and a long expanse of sand where you can rent windsurf boards. Two daily *Bus Verts* services (#74) connect it with Bayeux.

Among **hotels**, *La Marine* on quai Canada (mid-Feb to mid-Nov; ☎31.22.34.19; ⑤), is a little expensive but has an excellent restaurant overlooking the sea, serving fishy menus from 85F; further back from the sea is the *Arromanches*, 2 rue du Colonel-Michel (mid-Feb to Dec; ☎31.22.36.26; ③).

West to the Cotentin

PORT-EN-BESSIN, the nearest beach resort to Bayeux (on the #70 bus route), has a thriving fishing industry and – rare on this coast – a sheltered, enclosed site. The fish, caught off Devon and Cornwall, are auctioned three times a week. It's an attractive, unaffected place and a promising stop – try the **hotel** *de la Marine* (Feb–Nov, ☎31.21.70.08; ⑤) on quai Letourner. The squalid *La Prairie* **campsite**, on the other hand, is definitely one to avoid.

At **ST-LAURENT** is the larger of the two **American war cemeteries**; unlike the British and Commonwealth forces, the Americans repatriated most of their dead. It's a disturbing place, described on p.109. Just beyond St-Laurent, **VIERVILLE** was the site for the twin to Arromanches' Mulberry harbour, which lasted just thirteen days before breaking up in an unprecedented storm. There's a **youth hostel** in the Stade Municipal, open June to September (☎31.22.00.33).

Further round the coast, more dramatic American landings took place along the cliff heights of the **POINTE DU HOC**, still today deeply pitted with German bunkers and shell-holes. Standing amid the scarred earth and rusty barbed wire, looking down to the rocks at the base of the cliff, it seems inconceivable that the first US sergeant was at the top five minutes after landing, and the whole complex taken within another quarter of an hour.

Grandcamp-Maisy and Isigny

GRANDCAMP-MAISY, centred on its fishing harbour and market, has a good **campsite**, the *Camping du Juncal* (Easter–Sept; ☎31.22.61.44), and the **hotels** *du Guesclin*, 4 quai Crampon (☎31.22.64.22; closed mid-Jan to mid-Feb; ③), and the *Grandcopaise*, 84 rue A-Briand (☎31.22.63.44; ③).

ISIGNY nearby is renowned for its dairy products, butter in particular; though of no great beauty or interest, it does have a **hotel**, *de France*, 13 rue É-Demagny (☎31.22.00.33; ③), if you're stuck.

Bayeux

BAYEUX, with its perfectly preserved medieval ensemble, magnificent Cathedral and world-famous Tapestry, is 23km west of Caen – a twenty-minute train ride. It's a smaller and much more intimate city, and a far more enjoyable place to visit despite the large crowds of summer tourists.

A mere 10km in from the coast, Bayeux was the first French city to be liberated in 1944, the day after the D-Day landings. It was occupied so quickly – before the Germans had got over their surprise – that it managed to escape any serious damage, and briefly became capital of Free France. A monument now commemorates the spot where General de Gaulle made his first emotional speech after returning to French soil on June 14, 1944. That visit was a day trip undertaken in the face of opposition from the Allied commanders; he was so unexpected that the first two civilians he encountered, two policemen wheeling their bicycles, failed to recognize him.

Arrival and Information

Bayeux's **SI** stands in the very centre of town, in what used to be the fish market on the arched pont St-Jean (Mon–Sat 9am–noon & 2–6pm; also open Sun, July to mid-Sept only, 10am–12.30pm & 3–6.30pm; ☎31.92.16.26). The **post office** is just around the corner on rue Larcher (Mon–Fri 8am–7pm, Sat 8am–noon; ☎31.92.01.00).

The **gare SNCF** (☎31.83.50.50) is fifteen minutes' walk away to the west, just outside the "ring road", while the **gare routière** is on the other side of town on rue du Manche, alongside place St-Patrice (used as a car park, except during Saturday's market), near the fire station. For information on **local buses**, ring *Bus Verts du Calvados* (☎31.92.02.92); tickets are sold at either the gare SNCF or *Librairie 1000 Pages* on place St-Patrice, or on the actual buses.

Travellers without cars who plan to visit the landing beaches and/or the war cemeteries are better advised to join a **minibus trip** with a local operator such as *Bus Fly*, 24 rue Montfiquet (☎31.22.00.08), or *Normandy Tours*, place de la Gare (☎31.92.10.70).

Bicycles can be rented from the *Family Home* (see below), *Pitard*, 29 rue St-Jean (☎31.92.27.85), *Chez Roué*, bd Winston-Churchill (☎31.92.27.75) or, as usual, from the gare SNCF.

The Town

Within the confines of a busy ring road, the core of Bayeux is surprisingly small. It consists largely of one long street, which starts from the place Saint-Patrice in the west (scene of a Saturday market). As the rue St-Malo and rue St-Martin this is lined with the busy little shops of a typical Norman town; it then crosses the attractive canalized River Aure, passing the SI and the old **watermill**, Moulin Crocquevieille, to become the pedestrianized rue St-Jean on the east side, filled with cafés, brasseries, restaurants and souvenir shops (and itself the site of a market on Wednesdays).

Both Bayeux's principal attractions are south of this main thoroughfare. The **Cathedral** is in an attractive tangle of old streets, best reached along rue des Cuisiniers – the fourteenth-century half-timbered house that overhangs the street at 1 rue des Cuisiniers, on the corner with rue St-Malo, was until recently Bayeux's main tourist office. The **Tapestry** is on the other side of the river, housed in an impressive eighteenth-century seminary, re-modelled as the **Centre Guillaume le Conquérant**, and clearly signposted on rue de Nesmond.

The Bayeux Tapestry

Daily May to mid-Sept 9am–7pm; mid-March to April & mid-Sept to mid-Oct 9am–12.30pm & 2–6.30pm; mid-Oct to mid-March 9.30am–12.30pm & 2–6pm. 20F.

The **Bayeux Tapestry** – called by the French the *Tapisserie de la Reine Mathilde* – is a seventy-metre strip of linen that recounts the story of the Norman Conquest of England. Although created over nine centuries ago, the brilliance of its coloured wools has barely faded, and the tale is enlivened throughout with scenes of medieval life, popular fables and mythical beasts. Technically it's not really a tapestry at all, but an embroidery; the skill of its draughtsmanship, and the sheer vigour and detail, are stunning. The work is thought to have been carried out by nuns in England, commissioned by Bishop Oddo, William's half-brother, in time for the inauguration of Bayeux Cathedral in 1077.*

The tapestry looks – and reads – like a modern comic strip. It's generally considered to be historically accurate, albeit presented from a Norman perspective. The villain of the piece is King Harold, with his dastardly little moustache and shifty eyes; he swears an oath to accept William as King of England, and then takes the throne for himself. At this point in the story Harold looks extremely pleased with himself; however, his come-uppance swiftly follows, when William, the noble hero, crosses the Channel and defeats the English armies at Hastings.

Visits are well planned and highly atmospheric, if somewhat exhausting. You can't actually touch or linger over the tapestry itself, which is in any case kept for its preservation under very dim light. However, the display is excellent. First of all, there is a slide show, projected on to billowing sheets of canvas hung as sails; you then pass along a photographic replica of the tapestry, with enlargements and detailed commentaries. Upstairs in the plush theatre, a film (French and English versions alternate) explains the general context and craft of the piece – which you can skip if you feel you know the 1066 story well enough by now. Beyond this – and the souvenirs table – you finally approach the real thing, which has a strong three-dimensional presence you might not expect from all the flat reproductions.

---

* Claims advanced by an English historian in the last few years that the tapestry is of more recent origin are not accepted by most authorities. He argued, among other things, that the "kebabs" grilled in one beach scene show it to be post-Crusades.

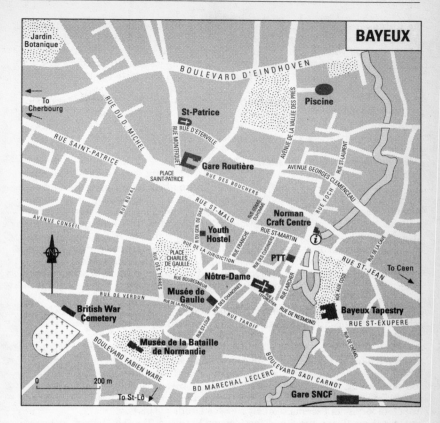

Although the tapestry makes such a bullish and effective piece of propaganda that Napoléon exhibited it in Paris – to show that a successful invasion of England was indeed possible – much of the pleasure of viewing it comes from the incidental vignettes of contemporary life that parallel the main story. The preparation of William's forces is shown in sufficient detail that museums such as those in Dieppe and Douarnanez (see pages 59 and 240) have constructed boats using the same methods, while the depiction of Halley's comet blazing in the sky helped astronomers to establish its orbit. Only the faintest smattering of Latin is required to be able to follow the captions that accompany each major scene.

Cathédrale Notre-Dame

The **Cathédrale Notre-Dame**, the first home of the tapestry, is a short and very obvious walk away from its latest resting place. Despite such eighteenth-century vandalism as the monstrous fungoid baldachin that flanks the pulpit, Bishop Oddo's original Romanesque plan is still intact, for the most part sensitively merged with Gothic additions. The crypt, entirely original, is particularly wonderful with its frescoes of angels playing trumpets and bagpipes, looking exhausted by their eternal performance. Along the nave is some tremendous twelfth-century sculpture, and you shouldn't miss the beautifully carved wooden choir stalls. The tiled floor of the chapterhouse features a fifteenth-century maze depicting the road to Jerusalem. To get access to both crypt and chapterhouse, you may have to seek out the sacristan.

Admission tickets for the tapestry are valid for the **Musée Baron Gerard**, a rather dull jumble of porcelain and lace in place des Tribunaux (daily June to mid-Sept 9am–7pm; mid-Sept to May 10am–12.30pm & 2–6pm; 15F), next to the west front of the cathedral in the shadow of the 200-year-old Liberty Tree.

The Musée de la Bataille de Normandie

Set behind massive guns, next to the ring road on the southwest side of town, Bayeux's **Musée de la Bataille de Normandie** (daily June–Aug 9am–7pm; mid-March to May & Sept to mid-Oct 9.30am–12.30pm & 2–6.30pm; mid-Oct to mid-March 10am–12.30pm & 2–6pm; 24F) is one of the old school of war museums, with its emphasis firmly on hardware rather than humans. Much of its former heavy-handedness seems to have disappeared since the end of the Cold War, and it shows some evocative film footage of the landings, by both sea and air, but nonetheless the obsession with technical minutiae remains a little disconcerting.

By way of contrast, the understated and touching **British War Cemetery** stands immediately across the road (see box on p.109).

The General de Gaulle Memorial Museum

Although Bayeux's newest museum, the **General de Gaulle Memorial** at 10 rue de Bourbesneur, near place de Gaulle (mid-March to mid-Nov, daily 9.30am–12.30pm & 2–6.30pm; 15F), is aimed squarely at French devotees of the great man, it makes an interesting detour for foreign visitors. The sheer obsessiveness of the displays, which focus on the three separate day trips De Gaulle made to Bayeux during the course of his long life, somehow illuminates the extent to which he came to epitomize the very essence of a certain kind of Frenchness – which to foreigners seems scarcely removed from self-parody.

Over three floors, the life of the General is traced from his days as a dashing cadet, first seen in a magnificent plumed hat before he was united with his trademark flat-topped *képi*. He was wounded three times in World War I, including at both the Somme and Verdun. Having argued in vain that France should prepare for the new era of mechanized warfare, he became a general on the battlefield in 1940 just in time to be swept aside by the Nazi Blitzkrieg, and was in London by June 18 to launch his famous (unrecorded) radio appeal; the indecipherable manuscript is on display.

Then come his visits to Bayeux. Number one was the day his exile ended; we see him addressing French sailors on the destroyer *le Combattent*, then landing on French soil at Courseulles, with an incredible haunted look in his eyes, and finally declaiming before a delirious crowd in Bayeux, conducting them in the *Marseillaise*. De Gaulle is hailed throughout the museum as the embodiment of France, not least by the *sous-prefet* who welcomed him in 1944, narrates the closing video and who was still alive to chair the fiftieth anniversary celebrations in 1994. The general returned in 1945 to welcome the first deportees to come home from Germany, and again on June 16, 1946, no longer in power, to proclaim his vision of a new constitution.

Accommodation

As one of Normandy's most important tourist destinations, Bayeux is well equipped with accommodation. On the whole, however, the **hotels** are more expensive than usual; even the "unofficial youth hostel" listed below is far from cheap. The *FUAJ* hostel in the municipal Centre d'Accueil at 21 rue des Marettes (☎31.92.08.19), one and a half kilometres from the gare SNCF near the Musée de la Bataille de Normandie, is open all year.

There's a large **campsite** on bd d'Eindhoven (mid-March to mid-Nov; ☎31.92.08.43), on the northern ring road (RN13) near the river – and the municipal sewage works. In the past, especially in hot weather, the smell could be over-powering, but things seem to be under control now.

Hôtel d'Argouges, 21 rue St-Patrice (☎31.92.88.86). Very stylish eighteenth-century building, with an imposing courtyard entered via an archway on the west side of place St-Patrice, and a well-kept garden around the back. A quiet but expensive place to stay. No restaurant. ⑤.

Family Home, 39 rue Général-Dais (☎31.92.15.22). Central seventeenth-century house which describes itself variously as a *maison d'hôtes* (guesthouse) and an *auberge de jeunesse* (youth hostel). Its prices are over the usual odds (hostel accommodation is around 75F per person) and it's a bit self-consciously jolly – but it has its advocates, and people return again and again. Room prices include breakfasts. Meals are taken communally, Madame Lefèvre presiding at the head of a long table in an old oak-beamed dining room. ②.

Hôtel de la Gare, 26 place de la Gare (☎31.92.10.70). Old but perfectly adequate basic hotel, beside the station, on the ring road 15 minutes' walk from the cathedral. Tours of D-Day beaches arranged. No restaurant. ①.

Hôtel-Restaurant Lion d'Or, 71 rue St-Jean (☎31.92.06.90). Grand old coaching inn set back behind a courtyard, just beyond the east end of the pedestrianized section of the rue St-Jean, outside Les Halles des Grains (now the assembly rooms). Closed mid-Dec to mid-Jan. Menu from 100F. ⑥.

Hôtel Mogador, 20 rue Alain-Chartier (☎31.92.24.58). Recently-renovated hotel, offering quiet rooms and good value. Near place St-Patrice, and entered by an inconspicuous doorway between two shops. Slightly cheaper off-season. No restaurant. ④.

Hôtel-Restaurant Notre Dame, 44 rue des Cuisiniers (☎31.92.87.24). Friendly and very pleasant *logis*, right in front of the Cathedral, with a magnificent view. Menu from 78F. Closed second fortnight of Nov. ②.

Hôtel Reine Mathilde, 23 rue Larcher (☎31.92.08.13). Simple but well equipped rooms – all have showers and TV – backing onto the canal, between the Tapestry and the Cathedral. No restaurant, but a snack-bar downstairs. ④.

Le Relais des Cèdres, 1 bd Sadi-Carnot (☎31.21.98.07). Pretty guesthouse, not far from the station but within sight of the Cathedral. The rooms are fine, and good value, although the atmosphere is not all that welcoming. ②.

Hôtel Sports, 19 rue St-Martin (☎31.92.28.53). Basic rooms not far from the river in the heart of town, with a brasserie downstairs. The management are very reluctant to turn the heating on, so this can be an icebox in winter. ③.

Eating

Several of the hotels, most notably the *Notre Dame*, have good restaurants, while the *Family Home* serves a filling and good-value dinner at 8pm each evening, for around 60F; non-guests should phone ahead to reserve a place. Otherwise, most of Bayeux's restaurants are in the rue St-Jean leading east from the river.

Brasserie de l'Europe, 2 rue St-Malo (☎31.92.09.69). Music until midnight on Tues evenings, and conventional menus from 75F.

La Paillote d'Or, 6 rue Genas-Duhomme (☎31.21.79.33). Chinese and Vietnamese cuisine. Closed Mon & Tues lunchtimes in summer, all day Mon in winter. Menus from 70F.

Le Petit Normand, 35 rue Larcher (☎31.22.88.66). Sixteenth-century house by the cathedral. Good traditional cooking, with seafood specialities and local cider. Closed for lunch on Thurs & Sun. Menus from 65F.

La Rapière, 53 rue St-Jean (☎31.92.94.79). Probably the most popular traditional choice, housed in the fifteenth-century Hôtel du Croissant; however, it's down a side alley and consequently not easy to find. Closed mid-Dec to Jan, as well as Tues pm & Wed out of season. Menus from 75F.

Southwest from Bayeux

Travellers heading **southwest from Bayeux**, towards St-Lô (see p.156), pass close to two remarkable buildings: the Abbaye de Cerisy-la-Forêt and the Château de Balleroy. Neither is easy to get to without transport, but if you have a bike or car they shouldn't be missed.

Cerisy-la-Forêt

CERISY-LA-FORÊT is most pleasurably reached via Le Molay-Littry, which has a **mining museum** and *Raleigh* cycle shop. The eleventh-century Romanesque **abbey** (Easter to mid-Nov daily 9am–6pm; 6F) was founded by William the Conqueror's father on the site of an already venerable monastery. Set on a hill, overlooking an attractive pond just east of the little town, its triple tiers of windows and arches, lapping light into its cream stone, make you sigh in wonder at the skills of medieval Norman masons.

Sitting in its own spacious grounds between town and abbey, the stately *Château de l'Abbaye* (☎33.55.71.73; closed Wed lunch in summer, all day Wed in winter; ⑤) offers luxurious country-house accommodation.

Balleroy

At **BALLEROY**, eight and a half kilometres south of Cerisy across the D572, you switch to an era when architects ruled over craftsmen. The main street of the village leads straight to the **château**, masterpiece of the celebrated seventeenth-century architect François Mansard. It stands like a faultlessly reasoned and dogmatic argument for the power of its owners and their class and, suitably enough, its most recent owner was the late American press magnate Malcolm S. Forbes, pal of presidents Nixon, Ford and Reagan, not to mention Elizabeth Taylor. You can tour the house to see its eclectic furnishings, pieces of modern sculpture and an original *salon* – with superb royal portraits by Mignard.

The focus, however, is on Forbes himself. Forbes was an acquisitor untrammelled by financial restraint – he owned the world's largest collection of Fabergé jewelled eggs (which were almost scrambled by a fire early in 1990), and his palace in Tangier, containing 100,000 lead soldiers, was the scene of a notoriously extravagant seventieth birthday party. At Balleroy, he created a museum to his principal passion, **ballooning**. It's all a bit absurd, beginning with some interesting history, but degenerating into egomania: photos of Malcolm S. Forbes in various Forbes balloons winning various Forbes prizes (as seen, of course, in his own *Forbes Magazine*). Admission is expensive at 40F, and seems a poor substitute for indulging in the real thing, which despite all impressions is more than a hobby for self-publicizing millionaires (both château and museum open April–Oct only, daily except Wed 9am–noon & 2–6pm).

The Cotentin Peninsula

Until *Brittany Ferries* instigated its direct services to Brittany, the **Cotentin Peninsula**, in the far west of Normandy hard against the frontier with Brittany, provided many visitors with their first taste of western France. Now that Caen too has direct sailings, **Cherbourg** sees only a fraction of the traffic it had twenty years ago, but the rest of the largely rural peninsula remains well worth exploring.

Geographically, this is an area of transition. Little ports such as **Barfleur** on the indented northern headland presage the rocky Breton coast, while inland the meadows resemble the farmlands of the Bocage and the Bessin. The long western flank with its flat beaches serves as a prelude to Mont-St-Michel; hill towns such as **Coutances** and **Avranches** contain architectural and historical relics associated with the abbey.

Travelling by bus is not easy in northern Cotentin. Nor is hitching: the local *patois* has a special pejorative word for "stranger", applied indiscriminately to foreigners, Parisians and southern Cotentins alike.

Cherbourg

If the murky metropolis of **CHERBOURG** is your port of arrival, the best advice is probably to head straight out and on; the town itself is almost devoid of interest, and there are some really nice places within a very few kilometres to either side. Napoléon inaugurated the transformation of what had been a rather poor, but perfectly situated, natural harbour into a major transatlantic port, by means of massive artifical breakwaters. An equestrian statue commemorates his boast that in Cherbourg he would "recreate the wonders of Egypt". But there are, as yet, no pyramids nearer than the Louvre in Paris, and if you are waiting for a boat, the best way to fill time is to settle into a café or restaurant or do some last-minute **shopping**, perhaps picking up some **wine** from the extensive selection at the British-run *Maison du Vin*, 71 av Carnot. Don't, however, leave your food shopping for the town. Unless you hit the Tuesday and Thursday markets, held around rue des Halles, the standard fallback is *Le Continent* hypermarket, a real monster on the southeast corner of the Bassin du Commerce.

As for walking off lunch, the only area that really encourages a ramble is over by the Basilique de la Trinité and the town **beach** – an unexpected pleasure, even if you wouldn't dream of swimming from it. Over to the south, you could alternatively climb up to **Roule Fort** for a view of the whole port; the fort itself contains a museum of the war and liberation (April–Sept Wed–Mon 9am–noon & 2–6pm; Oct–March Wed–Mon 9.30am–noon & 2–5.30pm; 12F).

Arrival and Information

Transatlantic services may have dried up, but several cross-Channel ferry companies still sail into Cherbourg. Boats from Portsmouth keep going all year round, operated by *Stena Sealink* and *P & O*, from a terminal on quai de France (☎33.44.20.13). *Brittany Ferries* run their *Truckline* service from Poole between May and September only (☎33.22.38.98) – Cherbourg is twinned with Poole, which explains the British red telephone kiosk on quai de Caligny. *Irish Ferries* also operate, in summer only, from Rosslare (☎33.44.28.96).

Cherbourg's **SI** is at 2 quai Alexandre III (June–Aug, daily 9am–noon & 2–6pm; Sept–May Mon 2–6pm, Tues–Fri 9am–noon & 2–6pm, Sat 9am–noon;

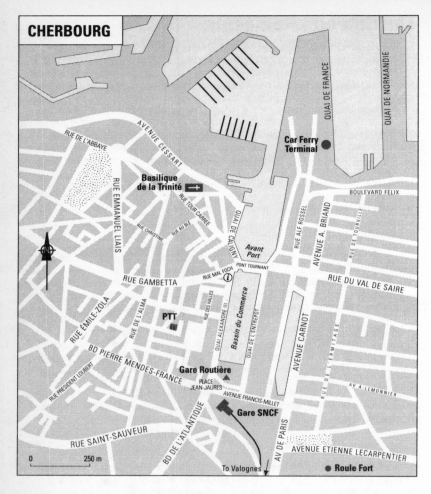

CHERBOURG

☎33.93.52.02). In summer there's also a tourist information kiosk near the *P & O* terminal. The **gare SNCF** (☎33.57.50.50) is on av François-Miller/place Jean-Jaurès; the **gare routière** is opposite, though hidden from view by a building on av François-Miller. The **post office** is on rue d' Ancien Quai (☎33.08.87.01).

Accommodation

By the standards of the rest of Normandy, **room** rates in Cherbourg are very reasonable. There's no great reason for ferry passengers to avoid spending a night here – it's a lively enough place to pass an evening – though the crowds and traffic can get a bit much, and for motorists, the lack of parking space during the day is a real problem. Few of the hotels bother to maintain their own restaurants.

You can't **camp**, but there is a **youth hostel** on av Louis-Lumière, one and a half kilometres east of the gare SNCF (April–Oct only; ☎33.44.26.31; 40F). With prior notice, they will prepare good-value meals for visiting groups. Take bus #1 or #2, direction *Diderot*, and get off at stop *Jean Moulin*.

Hôtel Croix de Malte, 5 rue des Halles (☎33.43.19.16). Simple hotel without restaurant on three upstairs floors, one block back from the harbour and around the corner from the theatre. Clean and recently renovated rooms – the cheapest rates are for the perfectly acceptable attic rooms. ③.

Hôtel de la Gare, 10 place Jean-Jaurès (☎33.43.06.81). Very convenient for the gares SNCF and routière, if not exactly stunning in itself. ②.

Hôtel Moderna, 28 rue de la Marine (☎33.43.05.30). Rooms ranging from basic to lavish, slightly back from the harbour and SI. ②–⑤.

Hôtel La Regence, 42 quai de Caligny (☎33.43.05.16). Small neat rooms with balconies overlooking the harbour, just around the corner from the SI. The restaurant downstairs kicks off with a reasonable 79F menu; it's not the best along the quai, but there's something to be said for eating where you sleep. ④.

Hôtel de la Renaissance, 4 rue de l'Église (☎33.43.23.90). Facing the port in the most appealing quarter of town – the "Église" of the address is the attractive Trinité. ③.

Eating

Restaurant options in Cherbourg divide readily into the glass-fronted seafood places along the quai de Caligny, each with its "copious" *assiette de fruits de mer*, and the more varied, more adventurous and less expensive little places tucked away in the pedestrianized streets and alleyways of the old town.

L'Ancre Dorée, 27 rue de l'Abbaye (☎33.93.98.38). Quite a walk west of the main harbour, but worth it for such superb fish dishes as langoustines cooked in orange sauce. Also mushrooms stuffed with snails. Closed Sat lunch and Mon, menus start 98F.

Le Briqueville, 16 quai de Caligny (☎33.20.11.66). One of the nicer of the quai Caligny seafood specialists, with no outside seating but huge plate-glass windows. The basic 98F menu changes daily, but has very limited choice; once you're prepared to pay 140F you're up to skate in pistachio cream.

Café de Paris, 40 quai de Caligny (☎33.43.12.36). Work your up through the ranks of *assiettes de fruits de mer*, from the 75F *Matelot* to the *Amiral* at 500F for two. Here it's the live lobsters in the fish tanks set into the windows that get the sea views, not you, but the food is excellent.

Café du Théâtre, 8 place de Gaulle (☎33.43.01.49). Attractive set-up adjoining the theatre, with a café behind plate-glass windows on the ground floor and a full-scale brasserie upstairs, arranged on three sides of the central opening. Very varied menus – not just seafood – from 70F, and much more of a sense than usual of participating in the life of the town.

La Fondue, 16 place de la Révolution (☎33.53.76.15). Small but atmospheric restaurant a little way in from the harbour, entirely specializing in fondues and *raclettes*, heavy with Swiss cheeses, from 70F.

Le Grandgousier, 21 rue de l'Abbaye (☎33.53.19.43). The definitive French fish restaurant; the rosy glow starts, but does not end, with the decor. Menus start at 98F, but this is a place to expect to spend a lot and dine well. The waiters share that expectation too – it's amiable enough but they know their worth. Imagine any combination of fish, throw in a bit of caviar and a few crab claws, and you'll find it somewhere on the menu.

La Moulerie, 73 rue au Blé (☎33.01.11.90). For once no set menus – there's no need. Instead, a restaurant solely devoted to the adoration of mussels, served in colossal ceramic bowls with a choice of ten wine-based sauces varying from sauerkraut through mustard to cumin, plus chips galore. All cost around 50F. You could if you want have a mussel salad to start, or even snails for a change, but if you do you'll never finish the main course. Blue checked tablecloths, sailors' costumes, fishing nets . . . an absolute delight.

East from Cherbourg

East from Cherbourg, the **D901**, which switchbacks through a series of pretty valleys, is the most direct route to the old ports of **Barfleur** and **St-Vaast**. Following the D116 along the coast, however, takes you past a succession of stunning viewpoints – particularly at the **pointe du Brulay** – and some really lovely quasi-fortified villages, shielded from the sea winds by stout stone walls.

Barfleur

The pleasant little harbour village of **BARFLEUR**, 25km east of Cherbourg, was the biggest port in Normandy seven centuries ago. The population has since dwindled from nine thousand to six hundred, and fortunes have diminished alongside – most recently through the invasion of a strain of plankton which poisoned all the mussels. It's now a surprisingly low-key place, where the sweeping crescent of the main harbour sees little tourist activity, and the grey granite quayside and formal main street retain an appealing elegance.

Near the town, about a thirty-minute walk, is the **Gatteville lighthouse**, the tallest in France. It guards the rocks on which William, son and heir of Henry I of England (and recently "outed" by historians as being gay), was drowned in 1120, together with 300 of his nobles.

Barfleur has a small **SI** at rond-point Guillaume-le-Conquérant (☎33.54.02.48). Its two best **hotels** are *Le Conquérant*, at 16–18 rue St-Thomas-Becket (☎33.54.00.82; ③), a short distance back from the sea, where the rooms face on to a lovely garden courtyard, and there's a summer-only *crêperie*, and *Le Moderne*, tucked away south of the main road at 1 place de Gaulle (☎33.23.12.44; ①), where some of the rooms are very inexpensive and the restaurant is quite superb. Specialities include a grilled salmon trout stuffed with a salmon soufflé, a traditional blood-rich *coq au vin*, and goats'-cheese *millefeuille*.

St-Vaast

ST-VAAST-LA-HOUGUE, 11km south of Barfleur, is more of a resort, with lots of tiny Channel-crossing yachts moored in the bay where Edward III landed on his way to Crécy. The narrow spit of sand called **La Hougue**, south of the centre, holds various sporting facilities, such as tennis courts and a diving club, although the tip itself is a sealed-off military installation; the fortifications are graceful, courtesy (as ever) of Vauban. The whole area is at its best at high tide; low tide reveals, especially on the sheltered inland side, bleak muddy flats dotted with some of the country's best-loved oyster beds. In 1692 a French and Irish army gathered at St-Vaast and set sail for Britain in an attempt to restore the deposed Stuart King James II to the English throne. The fleet was however destroyed by a combined Anglo-Dutch force, before it could get any further than La Hougue.

That battle took place just off the sandy flat island of **Tatihou**, which now doubles as a bird sanctuary and the location of an ecologically-minded Musée Maritime. A limited number of visitors each day are carried across by amphibious mud-wallowing "ferries" from St-Vaast; the exact schedule is determined by the state of the tides (May–Sept daily 10am–noon & 1.30–5pm; Oct–April Sat & Sun 10am–noon & 1.30–5pm; 45F including admission).

The **hotel** *de France et des Fuchsias*, just back from the sea in St-Vaast at 18 rue de Maréchal Foch (☎33.54.42.26; closed Mon in winter, & mid-Jan to mid-Feb; ③–⑥), with its lovely gardens and good restaurant, is an ideal stopover for ferry passengers – in fact both it and the annexe at the end of the garden are packed throughout the season with British visitors. If you can't get a room there, *La Granitière*, down the road at 64bis rue de Maréchal Foch (☎33.71.57.01; ③), is a very acceptable alternative. It's also possible to stay overnight in some very comfortable rooms on Tatihou island; contact *Accueil Tatihou* (☎33.23.19.92; ④).

Valognes

VALOGNES, around 18km through the woods from St-Vaast on the main road south from Cherbourg, is somewhat ludicrously passed off in tourist handouts as "the Versailles of Normandy". The description might have had some meaning before the war, when the region was full of aristocratic mansions, but now only a scattering of fine old houses remain, along with the very scant ruins of a Gallo-Roman settlement called *Alauna*.

All Valognes has to show for itself are a **cider museum** housed in an old watermill (June–Sept Mon, Tues & Thurs–Sat 10am–noon & 2–6pm, Sun 2–6pm; Easter–May Sat 10am–noon & 2–6pm, Sun 2–6pm; Oct–Easter groups by appointment ☎33.40.22.73; 25F), crammed with bizarre old wooden implements and ancient warped barrels – including a particularly obscene example upstairs – a little public garden, and a big empty square, activated only for the Friday **market**. But it's a quiet, convenient alternative to waiting around in Cherbourg, and the country lanes around are enjoyable.

The rambling ivy-coated *logis*, the *Hôtel du Agriculture* at 16 rue L-Delisle (☎33.95.02.02; ①) is the best of several inexpensive **hotels**, and serves top-quality food.

Ste-Mère-Église

A short way inland from Utah Beach, the westernmost of the main invasion beaches, the church of the market town of **STE-MÈRE-ÉGLISE** featured in the film *The Longest Day* – with an unfortunate US paratrooper dangling from its steeple during the heavy fighting. The film was based on fact, and the man in question, John Steele, used to return occasionally to re-enact and commemorate his ordeal. He's now dead, but a uniformed mannequin is permanently entangled on the roof in his stead. The new stained glass above the main door of the church also depicts American parachutists, surrounding the Virgin with Child.

Just behind and to the right of the church, Ste-Mère's approximately parachute-shaped **Airborne Museum** tells the story of the landings (June to mid-Sept daily 9am–6.45pm; April, May & second half of Sept daily 9am–noon & 2–6.45pm; Feb, March, Oct & first half of Nov daily 10am–noon & 2–6pm; mid-Nov to Dec Sat & Sun 10am–noon & 2–6pm; closed mid-Dec to Jan; 18F).

Discreetly tucked away behind a flashing neon parachutist, the ivy-covered *Auberge John Steele*, slightly north of the square on the main road (no phone; ③) is one of a bunch of similar ordinary hotels in the village. A small café with outdoor seating is just outside the museum entrance, facing the church, and makes a good lunch spot.

West from Cherbourg

The stretch of coast immediately west of Cherbourg is similar to that to the east, although it holds no harbour town to compare with Barfleur or St-Vaast. The old villages of **Omonville-la-Petite** and **Omonville-la-Rogue**, 20km out of

Cherbourg, are lovely places to stroll around, while all the way along you'll find wild and isolated countryside where you can lean against the wind, watch waves smashing against rocks or sunbathe in a spring profusion of wild flowers.

Cap Hague and Goury

The real drawback of this area is that the discharges of "low-level" radioactive wastes from the **Cap Hague nuclear reprocessing plant** may discourage you from swimming. In 1980, the Greenpeace vessel, *Rainbow Warrior*, chased a ship bringing spent Japanese fuel into Cherbourg harbour. The *Rainbow Warrior's* crew were arrested, but all charges were dropped when 3000 Cherbourg dockers threatened to strike in their support. In the spring of 1985 the French secret service finally took their revenge on the *Rainbow Warrior*, killing a member of the crew. The reprocessing plant would be delighted to welcome you to inspect their facilities (April–Sept daily 10am–7pm; Oct–March Sat & Sun 10am–6pm).

The main road, the D901, continues a couple of kilometres beyond the plant to **GOURY**, where the fields finally roll down to a craggy pebble coastline. Almost the only building here, the *Auberge de Goury* (☎33.52.77.01; closed Mon in summer and Sat in winter), is a really excellent **restaurant**, facing the octagonal lifeboat station and looking out towards a slate-grey lighthouse. It specializes in charcoal-grilled fish and meat, with a wide-ranging cheese board that includes the extraordinary *voluptueuse*, and is not surprisingly very popular at lunchtimes.

From the cape of **La Hague** itself, the northern tip of the peninsula, bracken-covered hills and narrow valleys run south to the cliffs of the Nez de Jobourg, claimed in wild local optimism to be the highest in Europe. **South of La Hague** a great curve of sand – some of it military training ground – takes the land's edge to **FLAMANVILLE** and another nuclear installation.

On the other side, facing north, **PORT RACINE** declares itself rather ludicrously to be the smallest port in France – it consists of one little jetty, some way down a hillside from a tiny and extremely tranquil pension-only hotel, *L'Erguillère* (☎33.52.75.31; ⑤).

Barneville- Carteret

The next two sweeps of beach down to Carteret, with sand dunes like miniature mountain ranges, are among the best **beaches** in Normandy if you have transport and want solitude.

CARTERET itself, sheltered by a rocky headland, is the nearest harbour to **Jersey**, just 25km away across seas made somewhat treacherous by the fast Alderney current. The old port area is not especially attractive, but does have several seafront hotels, including a couple of *logis de France*, the *Hôtel de la Marine* at 11 rue de Paris in the little shopping street (mid-Feb to Oct; ☎33.53.83.31; ⑤), and the *Hôtel du Cap* on the quayside route de la Plage further out (March–Nov; ☎33.53.85.59; ②).

Visitors who prefer to be beside a beach should head instead for the twin community of **BARNEVILLE**, directly across the mouth of the bay but a few kilometres away by road. Here an endless (and quite exposed) stretch of clean firm sand is backed by a long row of weatherbeaten villas and the odd hotel, including the *Hôtel les Isles* near the northern end at 9 bd Maritime (mid-Feb to mid-Nov; ☎33.04.90.76; ③), which has a superb sea-view restaurant.

There are two **campsites** in the dunes north of town, at Le Rozel (Easter–Sept; ☎33.52.40.09) and Surtainville (☎33.04.31.04).

Bricquebec

Fifteen kilometres inland from Carteret, halfway to Valognes, the old market town of **BRICQUEBEC** is dominated by the well-preserved castle at its heart. Part of this attractive edifice, centred around a peaceful courtyard, is run as the upmarket *Hôtel-Restaurant du Vieux Château* (☎33.52.24.49; ⑤). At first, the tacky furnishings and slapdash service make it feel like a treasurable piece of kitsch, but unfortunately the restaurant is so bad that there's not much point in staying here.

Lessay

Heading south from Carteret, on the other hand, the road around the headland joins the main D900 at **LESSAY**, where an important Romanesque monastery stands right in the heart of town. Until the war it was one of the few early Norman churches still intact. When it had to be restored from scratch afterwards, guided by photographs, the job was done using not only the original stone but also the original tools and methods.

The square central tower of Lessay is similar to that which collapsed centuries ago on Mont-St-Michel (see p.128). Monks at the abbey sing Gregorian chants each Sunday, and are very much in evidence at the **Holy Cross Fair** in the first half of September, which also celebrates cattle and other animals (more information from the SI on ☎33.46.46.18). The town is served by buses en route between Cherbourg and Coutances.

Lessay's tiny aerodrome, south of town, was where **Charles Lindbergh** landed on completing the first transatlantic flight in 1927; the first beach he crossed is now called plage Lindbergh.

Château de Pirou

Off the main coastal road, the D650, roughly 2km south of the junction for Lessay, turns inland a few hundred metres to reach the **Château de Pirou** (April–Sept daily 10am–noon & 2–6.30pm; 20F). Although you see nothing from the road, once you've passed through its three successive fortified gateways you find yourself confronted by a ravishing little twelfth-century castle.

Considering that it was converted into a farm, and then for centuries forgotten and all but submerged in ivy, it remains remarkably complete. Originally built of wood, on the coast, it was later remodelled in stone and now stands encircled by a broad moat, its towers rising sheer from the water. At your own risk, you can pick your way up to the top of its keep and look out over the surrounding fields. In summer, a tapestry depicting the Norman invasion of Sicily is on display in a barn opposite the drawbridge.

Feugères and Le Mesnilbus

If you have time, it's worth straying east of the main roads towards Coutances, to spend a while on the **D57**, to enjoy the magnificent countryside. The village square of **FEUGÈRES** is completely taken up by an amazing tangle of warped wood, once some sort of cider press and mill. From there on to tiny **LE MESNILBUS** – where the delightfully rural *Auberge des Bonnes Gens* (☎33.07.66.85; closed Sun pm & Mon in low season; ③) offers menus to suit every palate and pocket, as well as arranging **horse-riding** expeditions – the undulating meadows are filled with rich flowers and sleek animals placidly waiting to be eaten.

Coutances

The old hill town of **COUTANCES**, 65km south of Cherbourg, confined by its site to just one main street, has on its summit a landmark for all the surrounding countryside, the **Cathédrale de Notre-Dame**, whose twin towers stand in magnificent silhouette against the sky. Essentially Gothic, it is very Norman in its unconventional blending of architectural traditions. The *sons et lumières*, on Sunday evenings and throughout the summer, are for once a true complement to the light stone building. Also illuminated on summer nights (and left open) are the fountained **Jardins Publiques**, highly formal gardens with smooth rolling lawns, a well of flowers, a fountain of obelisks and an odd ziggurat of hedges. They enclose a small museum (Wed–Mon 10am–noon & 2–6pm), with a rather dull collection of paintings but a nice line in pretentious art exhibitions.

Practicalities

Coutances' gare SNCF (☎33.07.50.77), about a mile southeast of the town centre (at the bottom of the hill), also serves as the stop for buses heading north and south. If you want to stay, the **SI**, in a new wing behind the Hôtel de Ville in place Georges-Léclerc (Mon–Fri 10am–12.30pm & 2–6pm; ☎33.45.17.79), will be happy to find you a room.

The cream-coloured *Hôtel du Normandie*, behind and below the cathedral at 2 place du Gaulle (☎33.45.01.40; ②), has the usual assortment of rooms, and menus that range from the good-value 52F option (not Sun) to an excellent 95F spread. Not far away to the south, the *Hôtel le Champ'bord*, 8 rue de Lycée (☎33.45.01.12; ②), offers simple rooms without showers, over a busy bar near St-Pierre church. A better alternative for motorists is the **hotel** *Relais du Viaduc* (☎33.45.02.68; ③), at 25 av de Verdun – the junction of the D7 and D971, south of town – which can be a little noisy but serves some fine food.

The Manoir de Saussey

Roughly five steep kilometres south of Coutances, up the D7, the **Manoir de Saussey** is a slightly creepy old manor house containing a glass museum and an assortment of venerable furnishings (Easter–Sept daily 2–6.30pm; 12F). Outbuildings serve as antique shops, though not all of their bizarre bric-a-brac is for sale, and that which is tends to be very expensive. Visitors are welcome to walk around the lovely gardens without paying the admission fee.

Coutainville

COUTAINVILLE, the nearest resort to Coutances, is crammed in summer with bronzed and glamorous posers and their turbo-charged status symbols. This is an utterly nondescript stretch of coast, where the open sea batters against an endless, featureless beach. Huge tides expose massive sandflats, while behind the line of dunes dull holiday homes are punctuated by the occasional snack bar, campsite or motel. Coutainville's tiny little centre, out of all proportion to the long strip of coast that comes under its sway, holds the *Hotel Hardy*, place du 28-Juillet (☎33.47.04.11; ④), a pleasant little *logis* with high-priced but very good food.

A long walk south from town, fighting against the wind, brings you to the **Pointe d'Agon** after three or four kilometres, where a lighthouse commands a view of the dune environment at its most ecologically unspoiled.

Abbaye de Hambye

What's left of the **Abbaye de Hambye**, stands in a very sylvan setting 20km southeast of Coutances (and 10km northwest of Villedieu, see p.159), with little lawns laid out in front, an orchard alongside, and cows grazing in the adjacent meadows (Feb to mid-Dec daily 10am–noon & 2–6pm; 15F). The abbey, which is very reminiscent of such Yorkshire abbeys as Rievaulx, was constructed as a Cistercian monastery in the second half of the twelfth century, at a time when builders were trembling on the brink of abandoning the Romanesque tradition in favour of the new Gothic style. Much of the structure was quarried for stone and left in ruins after the Revolution; nineteenth-century prints show the walls drowning in rampant ivy. However, the central tower still stands four-square above the high narrow walls of the nave, and a few delicate buttresses remain in place, the whole ensemble crammed in tight against a wooded hillside and inhabited mostly by crows. There's a little exhibition in the entrance room above the ancient gateway, then visitors are left to wander around and among the ruins, with an optional pause to examine the rather dull displays of vestments in what was once the lay brothers' dormitory.

A luxurious rural hotel, the *Auberge de l'Abbaye*, is located 100 metres from the abbey at the turning off the D51 (☎33.61.42.19; closed Mon; ⑨). There being few alternative ways to pass an evening here, its restaurant is free to serve up extravagant gourmet dinners.

Granville

From Coutances, the D971 runs down to the coast at **GRANVILLE**, the Norman equivalent to Brittany's St-Malo, with a similar history of piracy and a severe citadel, the **haute ville**, guarding the approaches to the bay of Mont-St-Michel across from Cancale. Though the most lively town and popular resort in the area, it simply doesn't match the appeal of its Breton rival, with its nightmarish traffic and hordes of tourists milling around in summer in the vain hope of finding some way of amusing themselves. The great difference between Granville and St-Malo is that here the fortified citadel contains virtually nothing of interest, just three or four long narrow parallel streets of forbidding grey-granite eighteenth-century houses. The views up and down the coast, across to Mont-St-Michel and out to the Îles Chausey, are dramatic, but no more so than in many other towns along the Cotentin coast.

However, if you want to get to the Channel Islands, or to the Îles Chausey whose granite was quarried for the Mont-St-Michel, this is where you embark. Granville had an unexpected brush with destiny on March 9, 1945, when it was overrun for an hour and a half by German commandoes from Jersey, long after the invading Allied forces had swept on to Germany.

Practicalities

Granville's **SI** is down below the citadel at 4 cours Joinville (July & Aug Mon–Sat 9am–7.30pm, Sun 10.30am–12.30pm & 4–6pm; Sept–June Mon–Sat 9am–12.30pm & 2–7pm). Trains between Paris and Cherbourg arrive well to the east at the **gare SNCF** (☎33.57.50.50) on av Maréchal-Leclerc, which also serves as the **gare routière**. Several **ferry** operators – listed on p.132 – carry passengers to Jersey, Guernsey and Sark (all around 300F return), or to the Îles Chausey (see below).

With so many visitors in summer, this is a place where it's well worth booking **accommodation** in advance. There are no hotels in old Granville; most of the possibilities are concentrated in the new town, either beneath the walls near the Casino on the seaward side, or near the station. The *Michelet*, 5 rue Jules-Michelet (☎33.50.06.55; ④), which has no restaurant, is reasonably well equipped but characterless; the *Normandy Chaumière*, 20 rue Paul-Poirier not far from the SI (☎33.50.01.71; ④; closed Tues pm & Wed out of season), has a reasonable restaurant. Options nearer the station include the *Terminus* at 5 place de la Gare (☎33.50.02.05; ③). There's also a **youth hostel** in the *Centre Regional de Nautisme* (☎33.50.18.95), just off bd des Admiraux Granvillois a kilometre south of the station.

Where Granville really does excel is in the selection of waterfront **restaurants**, hard below the citadel walls. The best must be a couple facing the small-boat harbour, towards the end of the peninsula; the *Restaurant du Port*, 19 rue du Port (☎33.50.00.55), has a mouthwatering assortment of very fishy menus, with an unbelievably garlicky fish soup as its speciality; the *Phare*, nearby at no 11 (☎33.50 12.94; closed Tues pm & Wed), has the standard mussels and *panaché de poissons* on its 82F menu, and an extraordinarily copious *assiette des fruits de mer* on the 128F one. In front of the piles of rusting ironmongery of the commercial port, nearer the town proper, the *Hotel de la Mer*, 74 rue du Port (☎33.50.01.86; ③), has a dull 75F menu but gets interesting at 110F; you have to sit upstairs to get a view. Up in the old town, *L'Echauguette*, 24 rue St-Jean (☎33.50.51.87), serves good simple meals, grilled over an open fire.

Bikes can be rented from the station or *Le Coulant* on av de la Libération, and there's a covered **market** opposite the Mairie on Saturday mornings.

The Îles Chausey

Now an uninviting and virtually uninhabited wasteland – though equipped with long beaches of fine sand – the **Îles Chausey** were the site of the quarries which provided the granite that built Mont-St-Michel. They may once have been part of the ancient Forest of Scissy, the rest of which was submerged below the sea twelve centuries ago. There is just one **hotel**, the lonely *Hôtel du Fort et Îles* (☎33.50.25.02; closed Mon; ⑤); they insist on a minimum stay of three nights and are open only during the summer (May–Sept).

Again between May and September, two or three boats daily run out to the islands from Granville, operated by *Emeraude Lines* (☎33.50.16.36) and *Vedettes Blanches* (☎33.50.31.81). The trip takes just under an hour each way, and day returns cost 83F.

Around Granville

If you prefer to be out of town, the coastal countryside is best to the **north**, although the villages tend to be non-events. As well as the ubiquitous wind-surfers, the huge flat sands attract hordes of sand-yachters. Among **accommodation** possibilities, **BRÉVILLE** has the small *Auberge des Quatre Routes* (☎33.50.20.10; ④); **COUDEVILLE** two good campsites on its long beach, the *Phare-Ouest* (Easter–Sept; ☎33.61.67.08) and the *Dunes* (Easter–Sept; ☎33.51.76.07), and a large (and highly unrecommended) hotel in a converted sanatorium, the *Relais des Îles*.

To the south, **JULLOUVILLE** is younger, more upbeat and very tacky, with an endless drag of amusements, fast-food joints and soda bars. **CAROLLES** has a good beach, but little more; its one hotel is uninviting. At **ST-JEAN-LE-THOMAS**, a single street leading up to a beach, the bay becomes so narrow that at low tide it is possible to walk across to Mont-St-Michel. However, this is not a walk to take on a drunken, or any other, impulse; as the notices advise, "It's dangerous to risk you in the bay during the rising tide. This can surprise you at each time". A special telephone line provides details of the times of the tides, on ☎33.50.02.67.

Avranches

AVRANCHES, perched high above the bay on an abrupt granite outcrop, is the nearest large town to Mont-St-Michel. It has always had close connections with the abbey. The Mont's original church was founded by a bishop of Avranches, spurred on by the Archangel Michael who supposedly became so impatient with the lack of progress that he prodded a hole in the bishop's skull (on display in Avranches' St-Gervais basilica). Robert of Torigny, a subsequent abbot of St-Michel, played host in the town on several occasions to Henry II of England, the most memorable being when Henry was obliged, bare-footed and bare-headed, to escape excommunication by doing public penance for the murder of Thomas-à-Becket, on May 22, 1172. The arena for this act of contrition was Avranches Cathedral, designed by Robert himself, though without expertise; it eventually "crumbled and fell for want of proper support", and all that now marks the site of Henry's humbling is a fenced-off platform. A more vivid evocation of the area's medieval splendours comes from the illuminated manuscripts, mostly from the Mont, on display in the town **museum** (Easter–Sept Wed–Mon 9.30am–noon & 2–6pm; 15F).

The ruins of the old **castle** stand high above the SI; the highest point of all is the former keep, which, together with the vestiges of a small section of ramparts, is now landscaped into a small garden. From the very top you get long views over Avranches itself, and the Mont away to the west. The terrace of Avranches' large **Jardins des Plantes**, across town, is another good vantage point for the Mont.

A monument to General George Patton, southeast of the town centre, commemorates the spot where he stayed the night before his crucial Avranches breakthrough, at the end of July 1944. This small plot of land was ceded to the USA, so technically the statue stands on US soil – and literally it does too, earth having been brought across the Atlantic to create a memorial garden.

Practicalities

Avranches is a bit relentless in its cheeriness, with piped music in the streets in summer. Still, it does have a lively Thursday **market** and some reasonable **hotels**, such as *du Jardins des Plantes*, 10 place Carnot (☎33.58.03.68; ③), which has a good-value basic restaurant; the gloriously old-fashioned *Le Croix d'Or*, 83 rue de la Constitution (mid- March to mid-Nov; ☎33.58.04.88; ②), with its gardens and top-notch restaurant; and the *Bellevue*, 2 place du Général-Patton (☎33.58.01.10; ③). The **youth hostel** is at 15 rue du Jardin-des-Plantes (year-round; ☎33.58.06.54).

In high summer, one bus per day runs to Mont-St-Michel from the **SI** on place Géneral-de-Gaulle (July & Aug daily 9am–7pm; Sept–June daily 10am–12.30pm & 2–7pm; ☎33.58.41.30). The **gare SNCF** is a long way below the town centre.

If you're **camping**, a better base for the Mont than Avranches would be the *La Sélune* site (April–Oct; ☎33.60.39.00) at **PONTAUBAULT**, to the south.

Mont-St-Michel

The island at the very frontier of Normandy and Brittany, which for over a millennium has housed – indeed, all but consisted of – the stupendous abbey of **MONT-ST-MICHEL**, was once known as "the Mount in Peril from the Sea". Many were the pilgrims in medieval times drowned or sucked under by quicksand while trying to cross the bay to the eighty-metre-high rocky outcrop. The Archangel Michael was its vigorous protector, the most militant spirit of the Church Militant, with a marked tendency to leap from rock to rock in titanic struggles against Paganism and Evil.

The abbey dates back to the eighth century, when the Archangel appeared to a bishop of Avranches, Aubert, who duly founded a monastery on the island poking out of the Baie du Mont-St-Michel. Since the eleventh century – when work on the sturdy church at the peak commenced – new buildings have been grafted onto the island to produce a fortified hotch-potch of Romanesque and Gothic buildings, piled one on top of the other and clambering to the pinnacle of the graceful church, to form probably the most recognizable silhouette in France after the Eiffel Tower.

Over the course of its long history, the island has many times been besieged. However, unlike all the rest of northern France, it was never captured, not even when the English had a permanent fort on nearby Tombelaine; it took the Revolution to close it down (and convert it into a prison). Although the abbey was home to a large community – a fortress town – there were never more than forty monks, who said mass for pilgrims and ran their own school of art. On its 1000th anniversary, in 1966, the Benedictines were invited to return; today, a handful of nuns and monks maintain a presence.

For many years now, the Mont has no longer, strictly speaking, been an island – the causeway (*digue*) that leads to it is never submerged, and is continuing to silt up to either side. Among plans that have recently been under consideration is a proposal that the causeway should be destroyed; tourist numbers would be far easier to control were the abbey to be accessible only by boat. As it is, access to the Mont itself is unrestricted and free; a thin twisting street curls up the hillside to the abbey.

The Abbey

The abbey, an architectural ensemble which incorporates the high-spired archangel-topped church and the magnificent Gothic buildings known since 1228 as the **Merveille** ("The Marvel") – incorporating the entire north face, with the cloister, Knights' Hall, Refectory, Guest Hall and cellars – is visible from all around the bay, but it becomes if anything more awe-inspiring the closer you approach. In Maupassant's words:

> *I reached the huge pile of rocks which bears the little city dominated by the great church. Climbing the steep narrow street, I entered the most wonderful Gothic building ever made for God on this earth, a building as vast as a town, full of low rooms under oppressive ceilings and lofty galleries supported by frail pillars. I entered that gigantic granite jewel, which is as delicate as a piece of lacework, thronged with towers and slender belfries which thrust into the blue sky of day and the black sky of night their strange heads bristling with chimeras, devils, fantastic beasts and monstrous flowers, and which are linked together by carved arches of intricate design.*

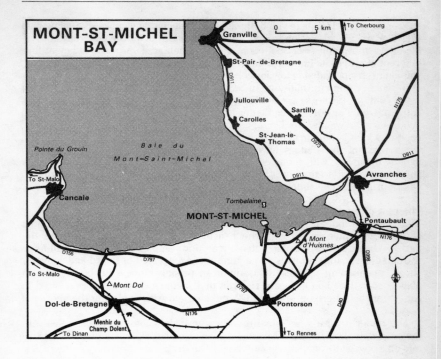

The Mont's rock comes to a sharp point just below what is now the transept of the **church**, a building where the transition from Romanesque to Gothic is only too evident in the vaulting of the nave. In order to lay out the church's ground plan in the traditional shape of the cross, supporting crypts had to built up from the surrounding hillside, and in all construction work the Chausey granite has had to be sculpted to match the exact contours of the hill. Space was always limited, and yet the building has grown through the centuries, with an architectural ingenuity that constantly surprises in its geometry – witness the shock of emerging into the light of the cloisters from the sombre Great Hall.

Not surprisingly, the building of the monastery was no smooth progression; the original church, choir, nave and tower all had to be replaced after collapsing. The style of decoration has varied, too, along with the architecture. That you now walk through halls of plain grey stones is a reflection of modern taste, specifically that of the director of the French Department of Antiquities. In the Middle Ages, the walls of public areas such as the refectory would have been festooned with tapestries and frescoes, while the original coloured tiles of the cloisters have long since been stripped away to reveal bare walls.

Informative and expert official guides run **tours** of the abbey between 9am and 6pm in summer, and otherwise between 9.30am and 11.45am, and 1.45pm and 5pm. One-hour tours in various languages, including English (the exact frequency is listed each day on a timetable at the entrance), cost 36F (student 23F, children 7–17 7F); there are also a number of more detailed two-hour tours, in French only, which take you both higher and deeper and cost 56F. Having paid the standard 36F admission fee, you are also free to wander the generally accessible areas. Intriguing scale models in the reception area show the abbey at four different stages of its historical development. Mass is said at 12.15pm every day, with a nursery provided below for children under eight years old.

In recent summers (mid-June to Sept), the Mont authorities have also opened the Mont to visitors each **night**, an experience they promote as **Les Imaginaires**. For 60F you can enter any time between 10pm and midnight, and you are free to wander until 1am, at your own pace, through twenty-four rooms, each of which is illuminated and has music playing. Particularly after midnight, when most of the visitors have gone, it's an incredibly atmospheric way to explore the abbey, with sound echoing through its ancient chambers and a musty subterranean feel to the lower rooms that conjures up thousand-year-old ghosts. On a stormy night it's unforgettable.

The rest of the island

The base of Mont-St-Michel rests on a primeval slime of sand and mud. Just above that, you pass through the heavily fortified **Porte du Roi** onto the narrow **Grande Rue**, climbing steadily around the base of the rock, and lined with medieval gabled houses and a jumble of over-priced postcard and souvenir shops, maintaining the ancient tradition of prising money out of pilgrims. A plaque near the main staircase records that Jacques Cartier was presented to King François I here on May 8, 1532 and charged with exploring the shores of Canada.

The rather dry **Musée Maritime** offers an insight into the island's ties with the sea, while the Archangel Michael manages in just fifteen minutes to lead visitors on a voyage through space and time in the **Archéoscope**, with the full majestic panoply of multi-media trickery. Further along the Grande Rue and up the steps towards the abbey church, next door to the eleventh-century **church of St-Pierre**, the absurd **Musée Grévin** contains such edifying specimens as a wax model of a woman drowning in a sea of mud. (All open daily Feb to mid-Nov 9am–6pm; 66F for all, or 40F each one.)

Large crowds gather each day at the **North Tower**, to watch the tide sweep in across the bay. During the high tides of the equinoxes (Sept & March), the waters are alleged to rush in like a foaming galloping horse. Seagulls wheel away in alarm, and those foolish enough to be wandering too late on the sands toward Tombelaine have to sprint to safety.

From the **gardens** below the abbey (closed in winter), you can see the giant ramp up the side of the hill, up which prisoners used to haul supplies for the abbey by walking around a treadmill at the top.

Arrival and Information

Mont-St-Michel has its own **SI**, in the lowest gateway (mid-June to mid-Sept daily 9am–7pm, mid-Sept to mid-June Mon, Tues & Thurs–Sat 9am–noon & 2–6pm; ☎33.60.14.30), and **post office**. In addition to the regular **bus** service from the nearest gare SNCF at Pontorson (see below), *Les Courriers Bretons* (☎99.56.79.09) run scheduled services from the gare SNCF in **Rennes** (connecting with the *TGV* from Paris, departing from Rennes Mon–Fri 9.45am, Sat & Sun 10.50am), and from **St-Malo** (summer daily 9.30am, Wed & Sat only in low season). Both cost around 100F return.

If you're visiting by car in summer, it's best to **park** on the mainland well short of the Mont, in order both to enjoy the walk across the causeway and to avoid the 15F parking fees and dense traffic jams. Hotels guests staying on the island itself should park on the causeway, as the tides submerge the car parks on the sands below it.

Accommodation and Eating

The island holds a surprising number of **hotels** and **restaurants**, if nothing like enough to cope with the sheer number of visitors. Most are predictably expensive, though virtually all the hotels seem to keep a few cheaper rooms (presumably there just isn't the space to re-fit and expand them in order to put the prices up); all charge extra if you want to enjoy a view of the sea.

The most famous **hotel**, *La Mère Poulard* (☎33.60.14.04; one room ④, others ⑧–⑨), uses the time-honoured legend of its fluffy omelettes, as enjoyed by Leon Trotsky and Margaret Thatcher (though not, of course, simultaneously), to justify extortionate charges. Higher up, however, prices fall to more realistic levels. The very cheapest options are the *Crêperie la Sirène* (☎33.60.08.60; ③) and the *Du Guesclin* (☎33.60.14.10; ③), where all the rooms have TV but the restaurant, without outdoor seating, is almost unique in Normandy in deserving to be called bad. Both the *Hôtel Croix Blanche* (☎33.60.14.04; ⑤) and the *Mouton Blanc* (☎33.60.14.04; ③) serve much better food, in both cases with basic menus for around 70F and more attractive options for 90F and upwards. All the restaurants on the island seem to serve their own version of the *Mère Poulard* omelette as a budget alternative. The 350-pitch *Camping du Mont-St-Michel* (Feb–Nov; ☎33.60.09.33) is on the mainland a little way short of the causeway, near a cluster of half-a-dozen motel-like hotels such as the *Motel Vert* (☎33.60.09.33; ③).

Pontorson

Most visitors to Mont-St-Michel find themselves lodging either at Avranches or **PONTORSON**, six kilometres inland. The latter has the nearest **gare SNCF** –ı connected to the Mont by an overpriced bus service (25F day-return), but as ever renting out cycles, too. Nothing much about Pontorson itself is worth staying for, although the café attached to the station isn't bad.

The **hotels** are not especially interesting, but both the *Montgomery*, 13 rue du Couesnon (☎33.60.00.09; ④), and the *Le Bretagne*, 59 rue du Couesnon (☎33.60.10.55; ④), along the main road, have very distinguished restaurants. The best budget alternative is the *de France*, 2 rue Rennes (☎33.60.29.17; ②), next to the level crossing beside the station; it has a late, youthful bar, with a pool table. An *IYHF* **youth hostel** stands near the cathedral, a kilometre from the station, in the *Centre Duguesclin* on rue Général-Patton (June–Sept; ☎33.60.18.65).

Along the Bay

The most direct **route from Pontorson to the Mont** runs alongside the river Couesnon, which marks the Normandy–Brittany border. The sands at the mouth of the Couesnon are those from which Harold can be seen rescuing two floundering soldiers in the Bayeux Tapestry, in the days when he and William were still getting on with each other. The sheep that graze on the scrubby pastures of the marshes at the sea's edge provide meat for the local delicacy *mouton pré-salé*.

A more roundabout road to the abbey can take you to the **German war ceme-tery** at **MONT D'HUISNES**, a grim and unforgettable concrete mausoleum on a tiny hill (see p.109).

travel details

Trains
From Trouville-Deauville to Lisieux (30min) and Paris (2hr); about 6 daily out of season and much more frequently in summer; service extends to **Villers**, **Houlgate** and **Dives-Cabourg** (40min from Trouville) on Sundays and holidays throughout the year, and daily in July & Aug .

From Caen at least hourly to Paris-St-Lazare (2hr 15min); 2 daily to Rennes (2hr 20min) via Bayeux (20min), St-Lô (1hr), Coutances (1hr 15min) and Pontorson, near Mont-St-Michel (1hr 40min); 9 daily to Le Mans (2hr) and Tours (2hr 30min), via Argentan (50min) and Alençon (1hr 15min); frequently to Tours (3hr) and Rouen (2hr); hourly to Cherbourg (1hr to 1hr 30min), via Bayeux (20min) and Valognes (1hr).

From Cherbourg 10 daily to Paris (3hr 30min–5hr) via Valognes (25min) and Caen (1hr to 1hr 30min).

From Granville frequently to Paris (3hr 30min) and Cherbourg (45min).

From Coutances 2 daily to Cherbourg (1hr).

Buses
Much the most useful network for travellers in Lower Normandy is operated by **Bus Verts**, *based at 11 rue des Chanoines in Caen (☎31.44.77.44). Contact them for details of the* Carte Plus *and* Carte Liberté *discount passes for regular passengers; however, bear in mind that the frequencies which follow apply to school peri-ods only, and fewer services tend to run in July & August (let alone on Sundays).*

From Caen to Le Havre (3hr); either #20 via Cabourg (40min), Deauville (1hr) and Honfleur (1hr 30min), or #36 via Pont L'Evêque (45min); to Ouistreham (35min), Lion, Courseulles and

Arromanches; bus #30 to Bayeux (4 daily; 50min) and Carentan (2 daily; 1hr 15min); bus #32 to Vire (connections for Brittany; 2–5 daily; 1hr 30min); bus #34 (3–5 daily) to Thury-Harcourt (40min) and Clécy (50min); bus #35 to Falaise (5–6 daily; 50min); to Lisieux.

From Bayeux bus #70 (3 daily) to Port-en-Bessin (25min) and Grandcamp-Maisy (1hr); bus #74 (2 daily) to Arromanches (25min) and Courseulles (50min); to Balleroy (30min) and St-Lô (50min).

Ferries
From Caen (Ouistreham) *Brittany Ferries* 1 or 2 daily to Portsmouth (6hr), ☎31.36.36.00. See details on p.5.

From Cherbourg *Stena Sealink* to Portsmouth (4hr 45min) and Weymouth (4hr 30min), ☎33.44.20.13; *Truckline Ferries* to Poole (4hr 30min), ☎33.22.38.18; *P&O* to Portsmouth (3 daily, 4hr 45min), ☎33.44.20.13; *Irish Continental* to Rosslare (17hr), ☎33.44.28.96. Further details on all these services can be found on p.5.

From Granville to Jersey, Guernsey and the Îles Chausey (daily between April and Oct). *Vedettes Armoricaines*, 12 rue Clémenceau, ☎33.50.77.45, *Emeraude Lines*, ☎33.50.16.36, *Vedettes Blanches*, 1 rue Le Campion, ☎33.50 .31.81, *Jolie France*, gare maritime, ☎33.50.31.81, and *Channiland*, ☎33.51.77.45.

From Carteret to Jersey. *Emeraude Lines*, ☎33.53.52.61.39.

Air
From Cherbourg *Aurigny-Air-Service* to Jersey, Guernsey and Aurigny; *Air Camelot* to Bournemouth, Bristol and Exeter. Both from Maupertus Airport, ☎33.22.91.32.

CHAPTER THREE

FROM THE SEINE TO THE BOCAGE: INLAND NORMANDY

I t is hard to pin down specific highlights in **inland Normandy**. The pleasures lie not so much in sights, or individual towns, as in the feel of the landscapes – the lush meadows, orchards and forests of the Norman countryside. And, of course, in the **food**, always a major motivation in these rich dairy regions. To the French, the **Pays d'Auge**, **Calvados** and the **Suisse Normande** are synonymous with cheeses, creams, apple and pear brandies, and ciders.

However, the territory is not exactly devoid of other sensory pursuits. There are spas, forests, rivers and lakes for lazing or stretching the muscles in, and, everywhere, classic half-timbered houses and farm buildings. If you are staying on the Norman coast, trips inland – even just a dozen or two kilometres – will show rewards, while if you arrive at a Norman port intending to head straight for Brittany or southern France, you may find yourself tempted to linger, or at least to take a circuitous route.

Travelling from **east to west**, you pass through a succession of distinct regions. **South of the Seine**, a natural target from Le Havre, Dieppe or Rouen, are the **river valleys** of the **Eure**, **Risle** and **Charentonne**. These have their industrial side, especially the Charentonne, but for the most part they are lush and rural, with the occasional château, castle ruin or abbey to provide a focus – most memorably at **Bec-Hellouin**, near Brionne, and at the lovely country town

---

ACCOMMODATION PRICE CODES

All **hotel prices** in this book have been coded using the symbols below. The price shown is for the least expensive double room, which for categories ① and ② usually means a room without shower, bath and toilet. Most hotels in those categories have other rooms with en-suite facilities, which typically cost 30–50F extra.

For a full explanation see p.31.

①	up to 120 F	④	220–300F	⑦	500–600F
②	120–160F	⑤	300–400F	⑧	600–700F
③	160–220F	⑥	400–500F	⑨	700F and over

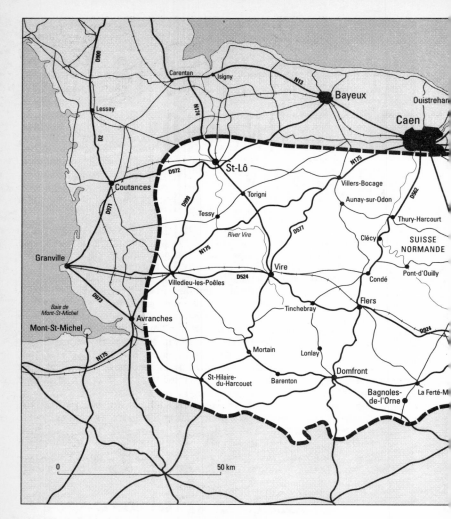

of **Conches**. Further south lie the wooded hills and valleys of **the Perche**, home of the mighty Percheron horse and also of the original Trappists.

Following the rivers northwest, on the other hand, as they head towards the sea near Honfleur or Cabourg, brings you into the classic cheese and cider country of the **Pays d'Auge**, all rolling pastoral hills, grazing meadows and orchards, where **Livarot**, **Pont l'Evêque** and **Camembert are** renowned throughout the world for their cheeses, and **Lisieux**, as the home less than a century ago of Sainte Thérèse, has become one of the major pilgrimage towns of France. To the **south** of the Pays d'Auge extend the forests of the **Parc Naturel Régional de**

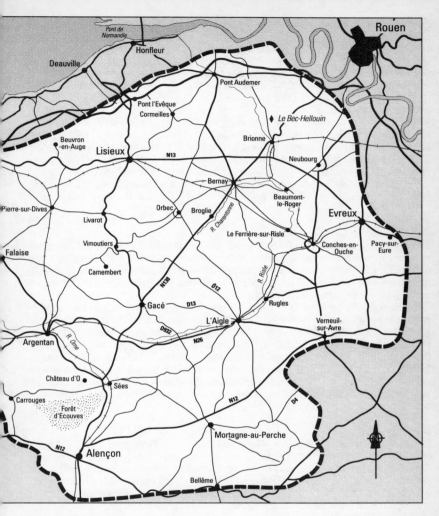

Normandie-Maine, with the sedate and famous spa at **Bagnoles** and the national stud at **Le Pin**.

Further west, on the routes inland from Caen or from Cherbourg and the Cotentin, there is something of a shift. Around Thury-Harcourt and stretching south to Pont d'Ouilly and Putanges is the area dubbed the **Suisse Normande**, for its "alpine" valleys and thick woods; fine walking country if not genuinely mountainous. To its west is the **Bocage**, which begins with grim memories of war around **St-Lô** – this was the main 1944 invasion route – but subsides into a pastoral scene once more, as you hit the gastronomic centres of the **Vire**.

South of the Seine: Évreux and Conches

South across the Seine from Rouen is the long and featureless **Neubourg plain** –
intensive agricultural land where the crumbling barns, Tudor-style houses and
occasional grazing horses look oddly out of place. It's not an area where you can
expect to find hidden charms; far better to press on to **Conches** or **Verneuil**.

Le Neubourg

The only town of any size on the Neubourg plain is **LE NEUBOURG** itself, which
blows any possibility of being charming by festooning its streets with deafening
loudspeakers. It holds little of interest to the traveller, but 4km northwest on the
D83, the seventeenth-century **Château du Champ-de-Bataille**, with its dramatic
entrance arch, is worth a look (daily except Mon 10am–noon & 2–6.15pm).

Le Neubourg is short on interesting hotels; **bed and breakfast** at *La Bergerie*
(☎32.35.86.28; ③), a *chambre d'hôte* 6km away in Marbeuf, is the best option.

Évreux

Twenty kilometres south of Le Neubourg you come to **ÉVREUX**, which is capital
of the Eure *département* despite not being on the Eure river itself. It's an
extremely venerable place that throughout history has suffered violent reversals
of fortune – as early as the fifth century its affluent Gaulish community made an
inviting target for rampaging Vandals.

Bombing raids by both sides during World War II reduced much of the city to
rubble, however, and Evreux today is almost disconcertingly lifeless. Even so, an
afternoon's wander in the vicinity of the cathedral – a minor classic with its flam-
boyant exterior decoration and original fourteenth-century windows – and along
the ramparts by the Iton river bank is pleasant enough. In January 1995, Évreux's
bishop Jacques Gaillot, was dismissed by the Pope for his advocacy of the use of
condoms to prevent AIDS, and his statement that "homosexuals will precede us
into the kingdom of heaven". Demonstrations on his behalf took place around the
world.

Practicalities

Évreux's **SI** is at 1 place de Gaulle (Mon–Sat 9.30am–noon & 2–6.15pm;
☎32.24.04.43). Many of the cheaper hotels are shut during August and in any case
there is no great reason to stay. The attractive old *Biche*, place St-Taurin
(☎32.38.66.00; ②), remains open all summer and is good value, while the *Bretagne*,
3 rue St-Louis (☎32.39.27.38; closed Aug, Mon & Wed pm) is a nice place to eat.

It would be a considerably more enticing prospect, however, to spend the night
at **PACY-SUR-EURE**, 13km east, where the *Hôtel de l'Étape* (☎32.36.12.77; ④)
nestles at the water's edge – or to press on to Conches.

Conches-en-Ouche

Everybody you meet in Normandy seems to recommend **CONCHES-EN-
OUCHE** – both for the town and for the forest around. The town stands above
the Rouloir river on a spur so narrow and abrupt that the railway line is forced to
tunnel right beneath its centre. Arriving, you're barely aware that the place exists
at all; all you see is the cutting, deep into the hill.

On the highest point of the spur, in the middle of a row of medieval houses on the main rue Ste-Foy, is the church of **St-Foy**, its windows a sequence of Renaissance stained glass. Opposite is an interesting ironmongery shop, full of old-style metal jewellery; the town was once renowned for its foundries, which were responsible for casting the iron spire of Rouen Cathedral in 1876. Behind, in the gardens of the **Hôtel de Ville**, a robust, if anatomically odd, stone boar gazes proudly out over a spectacular view, raising its eyes to the horizon far beyond the sewage works.

Next to the town hall, you can scramble up the slippery steps of the ruined twelfth-century **castle**, one of the many haunts of the ubiquitous Bertrand du Guesclin and twice captured by the English during the Hundred Years War. Such sights ensure that Conches remains firmly rooted in the past, but the town is given an added contemporary flavour, too, by the pieces of modern sculpture that you come upon round seemingly every corner.

On the other side of the main road from the castle, you'll find a long and subtly formal **park**, with parallel avenues of trees, a large ornamental lake and fountain.

Practicalities

Full information on Conches' tourist facilities is available in the Hôtel de Ville (☎32.30.23.15). The **hotel** *Grand'Mare*, in a green and quiet location beside the park at 36 rue du Val (☎32.30.23.30; ①), serves up enjoyable dinners in its restaurant, including a good *tartelin*, a flat warm apple tart; the *Bistrot* in the same building is less formal but not necessarily any cheaper.

Other accommodation options include the half-timbered *Donjon*, bulging out of the main street on the castle side, not far from the church (☎32.30.04.75; ②), and the *Cygne* (☎32.30.20.60; ③), set around an appealing little courtyard at the north end of town, but providing distinctly unexciting food. The finest **restaurant** in Conches is commonly acknowledged to be the *Toque Blanche*, near the *Cygne* at 18 place Carnot (☎32.30.01.54), where 98F goes a very long way and they do good-value weekday lunches. There's also a **municipal campsite** (April–Sept; ☎32.30.22.49), and on Thursday the whole town is taken up by a **market**.

The Forêt de Conches

The **Forêt de Conches** is a wild and open woodland. If you feel the need for a direction in your wanderings, head for the village of **LA FERRIÈRE-SUR-RISLE**, where there's an especially beautiful church, with a garish altar but some fine wooden statues, and a restored fourteenth-century covered market hall. Paddocks and meadows lead down to the river, while on the single, very quiet, street you'll find a small and inviting **hotel**, the *Vieux-Marché* (☎32.30.70.69; ③).

Verneuil-sur-Avre

Southwest of Conches, the towns of Rugles and L'Aigle are both industrial and uninteresting. However, 25km due south on the D840, you come to the pretty little hilltop town of **VERNEUIL-SUR-AVRE**. This now marks nothing more significant than the transition from the Ouche to the Perche, but during the Hundred Years War it was a crucial fortified outpost between (English-held) Normandy and France proper. Traces of its former ramparts and deep moat can still be seen along bd Casati on the west side of town, while the three main streets and numerous alleyways are lined with venerable half-timbered houses.

As you approach along the arrow-straight D840 from the north, the solid bell-tower of **La Madeleine** is perfectly framed for several miles' distance by the avenue of trees. The actual church of La Madeleine to which it is somewhat inelegantly attached stands in the main square, completely dwarfed by the belfry. A walk down pedestrian lanes to the south brings you out at the Notre Dame church, built of crude red agglomerate stone in the twelfth century.

Practicalities
Verneuil's **gare SNCF**, five minutes' walk north of the centre, is served by four daily trains from Paris. On the main place de la Madeleine, the *Hôtel Le Saumon* (☎32.32.02.36; ④) is a cream-coloured *logis* where a tankful of live lobsters nervously await patrons of the more expensive menus; in midweek especially the lower-priced menus are very good value. The rooms in the main building are the most luxuriously appointed, and the breakfasts are consistently large. The *Hôtel Le Clos*, at 98 rue de la Ferté-Vidame (Feb–Nov; ☎32.32.21.81; ⑧), is a bizarre little château near the Notre-Dame church which has an even better restaurant and phenomenally expensive rooms.

The **SI**, virtually next door to the *Saumon* facing the church, can provide details of occasional guided tours of the belfry. Nine kilometres southwest of Verneuil is the glass-covered dome of a family holiday complex run by *Center Parcs* (based in Paris: ☎42.18.12.12).

The Perche

All roads south of Verneuil start to undulate alarmingly, as you enter the region known as **the Perche**, which holds some of Normandy's most bucolically appealing countryside, with green valleys nestled between heavily forested hills. Despite its apparent fertility, this has never been a particularly rich area; in the seventeenth century, times were hard enough for a large proportion of the population to emigrate to Canada. It is, however, well known for the mighty **Percheron horses**, the strongest work horses in the world, while its remoteness and seclusion made it an ideal home for the first **Trappist** monks, who took their name from the Forêt de la Trappe.

Mortagne-au-Perche

The largest town of the Perche region stands on a hill set in the heart of the forests. **MORTAGNE-AU-PERCHE** has lost virtually all of its fortifications, but it remains an appealing country town, with a pleasant ensemble of stone town houses. The one part of the ramparts to survive is the **Porte St-Denis**, a fifteenth-century arch topped in the sixteenth century by two ordinary storeys of rooms that now contain an exhibition about Percheron horses.

Mortagne's liveliest square is the **place de Gaulle**, where the nineteenth-century market hall has been imaginatively converted into a cinema, with some post-modern spiral staircases attached to either side, and also holds the local SI. Nearby stands an unusual modern fountain, looking like an open mummy case made of copper, with bright starlight shining in its velvet-painted interior, standing on its end in a pool of turquoise water. From the SI you can cross to the gardens of the Town Hall, for fine views over the Perche hills.

THE TRAPPISTS

The **Abbaye de la Trappe** is set in open rolling fields on the fringes of the Forêt de la Trappe, just beyond a popular fishing lake and 10km north of Mortagne. This was the original home of one of the world's most famous – yet deliberately self-effacing, and consistently misunderstood – Christian monastic orders. Although the abbey was founded in the thirteenth century, and suffered the vicissitudes of the Hundred Years War, it was not until the reforms instigated by the **Abbé Rancé** in 1664 that its monks began to follow the principles for which the Trappists are known today. The Abbé reacted against the excesses of his time by setting out to recreate the lives of the **"Desert Fathers"** of the first few centuries after Christ, who lived in contemplative isolation in the Sinai, and to follow St Benedict's precept that true monks should live by the labour of their own hands.

The monks were driven out by the Revolution, successively to Switzerland, Poland, Russia and as far as the United States, but succeeded in returning to their utterly devastated abbey in 1815, still under the leadership of Dom Augustin l'Estrange –which made them the only order of monks in France not to be wiped out.

The Abbey as it exists today is entirely a nineteenth-century creation The monks live communally –they don't have individual cells – not literally in the absolute silence of popular myth but speaking only for the necessities of work and community life and spending the rest of their time in quiet reflection. Not surprisingly, tourists are not encouraged to disturb them, but anyone with a genuine interest can watch a video in a reception room beside the main entrance. There's also an unusual **shop** (Mon–Sat 10am–noon & 2.30–6.30pm, Sun after 10am mass until 1pm & 2.30–6.30pm) which sells all things monk-made; herbal teas, muesli, metal polish, shampoo, furniture wax, even local *boudin* and coffee grown in Cameroon.

Practicalities

The nicest **hotel** in Mortagne has to be the *Hôtel du Tribunal*, a *logis* on the sleepy little tree-lined place du Palais (☎33.25.04.77; ④), which consists of two or three old stone buildings with a few exposed timbers, crammed together on the corner of an alleyway leading to Porte St-Denis. This is where Yves Montand chose to stay when filming locally; the comfortable bedrooms are in an annex at the back, while the restaurant at the front has a reasonable 66F menu and gets exotic if you pay more, with such dishes as frogs' legs in paprika and barnacles.

The *Genty-Homme*, just off place de la République at 4 rue Notre-Dame (☎33.25.11.53; ③) has a handful of very plush rooms upstairs and a couple of restaurants downstairs; one serving formal menus from 80F, and the less formal *Grillade* alongside. Both serve Mortagne's speciality – the black *boudin noir*, a crumbly black pudding or blood sausage with a healthy dose of fat and tripe thrown in.

Bellême

Tiny **BELLÊME**, 17km due south of Mortagne on the switchback D938, is actually the capital of the Perche despite being very much smaller. In many ways it's more attractive, too, crammed so tightly onto the top of a sharp hill that the views are consistently superb. Here too hardly anything survives of the fortifications that once ringed the very crest of the hill. The one exception is the forbiddingly thick **Porche** – now the home of the local library, but still equipped to take a portcullis if things turn bad – reached by an alleyway leading off from a corner of the Place de la République near the St-Sauveur church.

Practicalities

The grand white facade of the *Relais St-Louis*, 1 bd Bansard-des-Bois (☎33.73.12.11; closed Sun in low season; ④), may be in a slight state of disrepair, but it's elegant enough inside, with its light dining room looking out on one side to a flowery garden and across the town's dimunitive ring road on the other to a small vestige of moat overlooked by an imposing eighteenth-century mansion. The new **SI** is all but next door (as is a miniature golf course), and can provide details of Bellême's annual five-day Mycology Festival, held late each September to celebrate the obscurer mushrooms of the surrounding forests.

The Charentonne and the Risle

Moving **northwest from Conches,** by far the best route is the one taken by the railway, to Beaumont-le-Roger and then on down the **Risle** and **Charentonne** rivers. At **BEAUMONT-LE-ROGER**, shortly before the Charentonne joins the Risle near Serquigny, the ruins of a thirteenth-century priory church are gradually crumbling to the ground, the slow restoration of one or two arches unable to keep pace. Little happens in the village beyond the hourly hammering of the church bell – next door to the abbey – by a nodding musketeer; and with each passing hour, the ruins crumble a little more.

Just across the Risle from here, on the D25 near Le Val-St-Martin, huge stables are spread across an absurdly sylvan setting, and horses are available for rent. At **SERQUIGNY**, where the rail lines and roads converge, in addition to the two rivers, the banks become industrial, clogged with factories and fumes. Best to move on fast, either to Bernay or Brionne.

Bernay

BERNAY, to the west, has a few humpback footbridges and picturesque half-timbered old streets interspersed between the more serious traffic routes, and one of those churches typical of the region with a spire that looks like a stack of inverted octagonal ice-cream cones. Work has been in progress to restore the ancient **abbey church** for years – it should look good when it is finished. The town has few other claims to renown, though one of its bakers has found fame for *running* each stage of the Tour de France during the night before the cyclists race over it.

The nicest place to **stay** in the vicinity is the riverside *Moulin Fouret*, 4km south along D33 (☎32.43.19.95; closed Sun pm & Mon; ③), which is primarily a restaurant (menus from around 100F), but also has a few rooms.

Upstream from Bernay

As you continue up the Charentonne from Bernay, the river loses its industry, and sprawls between its banks on a wide flood plain. It is classic inland Normandy, uneventful and totally scenic; the one flaw in the whole thing is the unseemly preponderance of porcelain donkeys in people's front gardens. At **ST-**

QUENTIN-DES-ISLES, halfway along the valley, old houses are over-shadowed by a derelict sawmill, which looms like a primordial swamp monster from among the riverside willows, in a dripping bulk of red ivy.

Broglie

The last town of any size along the Charentonne is **BROGLIE**, on the brow of whose hill stands an awesomely impressive **château**. This is the ancestral home of the de Broglie family, whose last but one owner, Prince Louis, won the Nobel Physics Prize for demonstrating that matter, like light, has wavelike properties. His work – to "seek the last hiding places of reality", as he put it – formed the foundation of the whole discipline of quantum mechanics. Originally a medieval historian, Louis was supposed to have been attracted to his great theory "purely on the grounds of intellectual beauty".

Brionne

The pleasant little town of Orbec (see p.145) is around 10km west of Broglie. Heading **north**, however, the first stop from Serquigny on the rail line to Rouen is **BRIONNE**, a small town with large regional **markets** on Thursday and Sunday. The fish hall is on the left bank, the rest by the church on the right bank. Above them both, with panoramic views, is a **donjon**.

If you decide to **stay** in Brionne, it holds two good but pretty expensive hotels which also contain excellent restaurants – the *Auberge du Vieux Donjon*, facing the marketplace at 19 rue Soie (☎32.44.80.62; closed Mon, & Sun pm in low season; ④), and the *Logis de Brionne*, 1 place St-Denis (☎32.44.81.73; closed Sun pm & Mon Oct–Easter; ⑤).

The Abbaye de Bec-Hellouin

Following the **Risle** on towards Honfleur and the sea, the **D39** is lined with perfect timbered farmhouses. Four kilometres from Brionne, the size and tranquil setting of the **ABBAYE DE BEC-HELLOUIN** give a monastic feel to the whole valley. Bells echo between the hills and white-robed monks go soberly about their business. From the eleventh century onwards, the abbey was one of the most important centres of intellectual learning in the Christian world; an intimate association with the court of William the Conqueror meant that two of its early abbots, first Lanfranc and then the philosopher Anselm, became archbishops of Canterbury.

Thanks to the Revolution, most of the monastery buildings are recent – the monks only returned in 1948 – but there are some survivals and appealing clusters of stone ruins. Recent archbishops of Canterbury have maintained tradition by coming here on retreat. (June–Sept tours Mon & Wed–Fri at 10am, 11am, 3pm, 4pm & 5pm; Sat at 10am, 11am, 3pm & 4pm; Sun & hols at noon, 3pm, 3.30pm & 4pm; Oct–May tours Mon & Wed–Sat at 11am, 3.15pm & 4.30pm; Sun & hols at noon 3pm, & 4pm; closed Tues; 20F.)

In the rather twee adjacent town of **Bec-Hellouin** is a **vintage car museum** (mid-June to mid-Sept daily 9am–noon & 2–7pm; mid-Sept to mid-June Fri–Tues 9am–noon & 2–7pm; 25F), and a distinctly un-ascetic **restaurant**, the wonderful *Auberge de l'Abbaye* (☎32.44.86.02; closed Mon pm, all day Tues, and mid-Jan to Feb; ⑤), which also has half a dozen expensive rooms. The *Restaurant de la Tour* on place Guillaume-le-Conquérant nearby (☎32.44.86.15) is a more affordable place to eat, with some outdoor tables.

Pont-Audemer

Continuing north, the last major crossing point over the Risle is at **PONT-AUDEMER**, where medieval houses lean out at alarming angles over the criss-crossing roads, rivers and canals. It's an attractive little place, the scene of busy markets on Mondays and Fridays, and the *Auberge du Vieux Puits*, 6 rue Notre-Dame-du-Pré (☎32.41.01.48; closed Mon pm & Tues, first fortnight of July, mid-Dec to mid-Jan; ④), makes an appealing old-fashioned place to stay. A considerably cheaper option is the more basic riverside *Hôtel d l'Agriculture*, 84 rue de la République (☎32.41.01.23; closed Sun pm in winter; ②).

From there you have the choice of making for the sea at Honfleur (see p.94), passing some tottering Giacometti-style barns on the way to St-Georges along the thickly-wooded valleys of the D38, or going on towards the Seine. If you plan to cycle across the Forêt de Brotonne towards Caudebec (see p.74), be warned that, to discourage motorists from spoiling the nicest part of the forest, the roadsigns direct you the long way round via La Mailleraye.

Lisieux

LISIEUX is the main town of the Pays d'Auge, a regional capital successively under the Gauls, the Romans and the Franks. However, it was obliterated by barbarians in 275AD, and again by the Allies in 1944, with the result that what had been a beautiful market town is now for the most part nondescript. Although it still boasts a Norman Gothic cathedral built in 1170, which holds a chapel erected by the judge who sentenced Joan of Arc to death, these days Lisieux's identity is thoroughly wrapped up in the life and death of **Sainte Thérèse** – the most influential French spiritual figure of the last hundred years.

Pilgrims come to Lisieux in considerable numbers, and even a casual visitor will find the Thérèse cult inescapable. The garish and gigantic **Basilique de Ste-Thérèse**, on a slope to the southwest of the town centre, was modelled on the Sacré-Coeur in Paris. Completed in 1954, it was the last major religious building in France to be erected solely by public subscription. Thérèse is in fact buried in

SAINTE THÉRÈSE

Born at Alençon in 1873, **Thérèse Martin** lived for the last nine years of her short life in the Carmelite convent in Lisieux, until she died of TB at 24. She had felt the call to take holy orders when only nine, but it took a pilgrimage to Rome and a special dispensation from the Pope before she was allowed into the convent at the age of fifteen. The prioress said then that "a soul of such quality should not be treated as a child".

Thérèse owes her fame to her book *Story of a Soul*, in which she describes the approach to life she called her "Little Way" – a belief that all personal suffering, all thankless work and quiet faith, is made holy, and made worthwhile, as an offering to God. What to modern sensibilities might appear a meekness and lack of worldliness verging on the selfish proved astonishingly popular after her death, particularly in trying to make sense of the vast suffering of World War I. Thérèse was rapidly beatified and by 1945 was declared France's second patron saint. The recent success of Alain Cavalier's film *Thérèse*, and a visit by Pope John Paul II, suggest that she is still felt to have contemporary relevance.

the chapel of the Carmelite convent, though her presence in the basilica is ensured by selected bones from her right arm (in a reliquary given by Pope Pius XI) and by countless photographs (Thérèse being one of the very few saints to have lived since the invention of the camera). Huge mosaics of her face decorate the nave and every night at 9.30pm, as part of a stunningly tasteless (and expensive) laser show, her beatific smile is simultaneously projected onto every column in the church.

In summer, a white, flag-bedecked funfair "train" runs fifty-minute tours around the holiest sites, chuntering through the open, wide streets and squares, and past the delightful flower-filled park, raised above street level behind the restrained and sober Cathédrale St-Pierre (daily in summer at 10am, 11am, 2pm, 3pm, 4pm & 5pm; 25F).

To get an idea of Lisieux's former glories, take a look at the fading photos preserved in the **Musée du Vieux Lisieux**, 38 bd Pasteur (daily except Tues 2–6pm).

Practicalities

Lisieux is 35 minutes by train from Caen, en route to Paris or Rouen; the **gare SNCF** is on the south side of town, below the Basilica. Turn left out of the station, then right, to reach the **SI**, at 11 rue d'Alençon (June–Sept daily 8.30am–noon & 1.30–7pm; Oct–May Mon–Sat 8.30am–noon & 1.30–6pm; ☎31.62.08.41), which can help with finding accommodation in Lisieux itself, and provides information on the rural areas further inland.

The quantity of pilgrims means that Lisieux is full of good-value places to stay – among its **hotels** are *de la Terrasse*, up on the hill near the Basilica at 25 av Ste-Thérèse (☎31.62.17.65; closed Feb to mid-March, & Mon in winter; ③), the *de l'Avenue*, attached to the *Printania* brasserie lower down at 4 av Ste-Thérèse (☎31.62.08.37; ②), and the *Hôtel des Arts*, backing onto the Bishop's Gardens at 26 rue Condorcet (☎31.62.00.02; ②). There is also a large **campsite**, *de la Vallée* (April–Sept; ☎31.62.00.40), but campers would probably be better off somewhere more rural nearby, such as Livarot or Orbec.

Most of the hotels in town are equipped with tempting restaurants, but if you're just passing through you can get a reasonable 55F lunch at *Au Vieux Normand*, in one of Lisieux's few surviving half-timbered houses at 14 rue H-Chéron (☎31.62.03.35; closed Mon). If Thérèse isn't your prime motivation, Saturday is the best day to visit, for the large **street market** – stacked with Pays d'Auge cheeses.

The Pays d'Auge

South of Lisieux, the rolling hills and green twisting valleys of the **Pays d'Auge** are scattered with magnificent half-timbered manor houses. The sprawling farms often consist of a succession of such "Tudor" (in fact the Norman tradition predates the English) treasures, each family house as it becomes too dilapidated to live in being converted for use as a barn, and replaced by a new one built alongside. The pastures here are the lushest in the province, producing the world-famous cheeses of Camembert, Livarot, and Pont L'Evêque. And beside them are acres of orchards, yielding the best of Norman ciders, both apple and pear (*poiré*), as well as Calvados apple brandy.

The Cheese and Cider routes

The tourist authorities promote two main Pays d'Auge itineraries, the **Route de Fromage** and the **Route du Cidre**. It's not difficult to join either of these well-signposted routes, each of which serves as a welcome opportunity to get off the main highways. For the former, the best starting points are at St-Pierre-sur-Dives and Livarot; for the latter, head for Cambremer, just north of the N13 between Caen and Lisieux. In any event, it doesn't matter much if you stray off the routes; much of the appeal of this area lies in the scope just to wander, rather than to look for any specific sights, and to fill the days sampling the different ciders and cheeses. That said, the manor houses of **Beuvron-en-Auge** on the Cider route, and **Montpinçon** and **Lisores** on the Cheese route, are well worth finding, and at Lisores there's also the **Ferme-musée Fernand Léger** (10am–noon & 2–7pm, closed Wed), with its unlikely mosaics. **Cambremer** has a special crafts market on Sunday morning in July and August.

For fans of really good solid Norman cooking, this is the perfect area to look out for **Fermes Auberges,** working farms which welcome (paying) visitors to share their meals; lists are available from local SIs and from *Calvados Tourisme* (place du Canada, Caen; ☎31.86.53.30). The cider farms are signposted with the words "*Cru de Cambremer*" in green on white.

Beuvron-en-Auge

No village has any right to be as pretty as **BEUVRON-EN-AUGE**, 7km north of N13 halfway between Caen and Lisieux, which consists of an oval central *place*, ringed by a glorious ensemble of multi-coloured half-timbered houses. The largest of these, the yellow and brown sixteenth-century **Vieux Manoir**, stands at the south end of the village, backing onto a stream and open fields. The beams around its first storey bear weather-beaten carvings, including one of a Norman soldier.

Immediately at hand is the eighteenth-century *Auberge de la Boule d'Or* (☎31.79.78.78; closed Sun pm & Mon; ④), where you'd be lucky to find one of the three attractive bedrooms available, while a former farmhouse opposite holds a *chambre d'hôte* (Mme Hamelin; ☎31.39.00.62; ③). The very centre of the *place* is taken up by the *Pavé d'Auge* **restaurant** (☎31.79.26.71; closed Mon pm & Tues), where menus featuring duckling in cider or boned roast pigeon start at 130F.

Pont l'Evêque and Cormeilles

There was little left after the war of the old **PONT L'EVÊQUE**, the northernmost town of the Pays d'Auge. One or two ancient houses remain, most notably along rue St-Michel, but the town as a whole has become such a turmoil of major roads as to be a rather eccentric place to choose to stay. If you do end up in Pont L'Evêque, the *Lion d'Or*, 8 place Calvaire (☎31.65.01.55; ③), offers reasonable rooms and excellent seafood dinners.

The nearby village of **CORMEILLES** makes a more appealing destination for a day out, having been left relatively unscathed by the fighting. Each Friday sees a market in its tiny centre, and there are several half-timbered restaurants scattered around. On the southern edge of town, the *Auberge du President*, 70 rue de l'Abbaye (☎32.57.80.37; ③), is an efficient hybrid, featuring motel-style rooms around the back and a very traditional, formal and good plush-velvet restaurant in the old building facing the street.

Orbec

ORBEC lies just a few miles along a valley from the source of its river, the Orbiquet, and epitomizes the simple pleasures of the Pays d'Auge. It consists of little more than its main road, the Rue Grande, with the huge tower of Notre Dame church at one end and a good, slightly upmarket **hotel**, *de France*, at no. 152 at the other (☎31.32.74.02; closed mid-Dec to mid-Jan; ③).

Along the Rue Grande, you'll see several houses in which the gaps between the timbers are filled with the region's intricate characteristic patterns of coloured tiles and bricks. Debussy composed *Jardin sous la Pluie* in one of these, and the oldest and prettiest of the lot – **Le Vieux Manoir**, a tanner's house which dates back to 1568 – holds a museum of local history. On the whole, though, it's more fun just to walk down behind the church to the river, and its watermill and paddocks.

Livarot

The centre of the cheese country is the old town of **LIVAROT**, with the (not particularly good) **hotel** and restaurant *du Vivier* (☎31.63.50.29; ③), and the enjoyable *Café de la Paix* in its centre.

Livarot's main attraction is the **Conservatoire du Fromage**, a small-scale working cheese factory in which you can see Camembert, Pont L'Evêque and Livarot cheeses at every stage of their production (April–Oct Mon–Fri 9am–noon & 2–6pm, Sat 10am–noon; Nov–March Wed–Fri 9am–noon & 2–6pm, Sat 10am–noon; 15F). There's a **cheese fair** on the first weekend of each August, and you can get a good view of the valley from the thirteenth-century church of St-Michel de Livet, just above the town; to visit you contact a M. Jean Fromage.

THE CHEESES OF THE PAYS D'AUGE

The tradition of cheese-making in the Pays d'Auge is thought to have been started in the monasteries during the Dark Ages; the characteristics of the standard local product seem to have become fairly constant by the eleventh century. At first it was variously known as either *Augelot* or *Angelot*; the *Roman de la Rose* in 1236 referred to *Angelot* cheese, which was identified with a small coin depicting a young angel killing a dragon.

This cheese was the forerunner of the principal modern varieties, which began to emerge in the seventeenth century – **Pont l'Evêque**, which is square, with a washed crust, and is soft but not runny, and **Livarot**, which is round, thick and firm, with a stronger flavour.

Although Marie Herel is generally credited with having invented **Camembert** in the 1790s, a smaller and stodgier version of that cheese had already existed for some time. What seems to have happened is that a priest fleeing the Revolutionary Terror at Meaux (a certain Abbé Gobert) stayed in Mme Harel's farmhouse at Camembert and watched the methods she used for making cheese. He suggested modifications in line with the techniques he'd seen employed to manufacture Brie de Meaux – a slower process, gentler on the curd and with more thorough drainage. The rich full cheese thus created was an instant success in the market at Vimoutiers, and the development of the railways (and the invention of the chipboard cheesebox in 1880) helped to give it a worldwide popularity.

More details on all such matters are to be had from the exhaustive *French Cheese Book*, by Patrick Rance (Macmillan, 1989).

St-Pierre-sur-Dives

The medieval wooden *halles* at **ST-PIERRE-SUR-DIVES**, burned to the ground in 1944, had been rebuilt by 1949. Only traditional techniques were used; there's not a single nail or screw in the place, whose timber frame rests on low stone walls and is held together by chestnut pegs alone. The buildings of the adjacent convent now house the local SI, along with a slightly academic annex to the Livarot cheese museum (April–Oct only, daily except Tues 9.30am–12.30pm & 2–6.30pm; 22F).

The town's other focus of interest is its Gothic-Romanesque church (whose windows depict the history of the town). A large **market** still takes place every Monday in the open space next to the halles.

St-Pierre's best bet for **accommodation** is the *Renaissance*, a *logis de France* at 57 rue du Lisieux (☎31.20.81.23; closed Sun lunch & mid-Oct to mid-Nov; ③), which has a relatively ordinary restaurant.

Ste-Foy de Montgommery

Heading **south from Livarot** towards Vimoutiers, the D579 passes through the village of **STE-FOY DE MONTGOMMERY**, where, outside the *Café La Gosselinais* on the night of July 17, 1944, Field-Marshal Rommel was seriously injured when RAF Typhoons attacked his *Mercedes*. Rommel never returned to the battlefield, and committed suicide three months later. That his nemesis should overtake him in a place called "Holy Faith of Montgommery" became part of the legend surrounding the British field-marshal.

Vimoutiers and Camembert

VIMOUTIERS contains another **cheese museum** (May–Oct Mon 2–6pm, Tues–Sat 9am–noon & 2–6pm, Sun 10am–noon & 2.30–6pm; Nov, Dec, March & April Mon 2–6pm, Tues–Fri 9am–noon & 2–6pm, Sat 9am–noon; 15F), featuring a glorious collection not to be missed by tyrosemiophiles – cheese-label collectors (they do exist) – who will find Camembert stickers ranging from remote Chilean dairies to *Marks & Spencers*. Most of the cheese on display however turns out to be polystyrene.

A statue in the main square honours Marie Harel, who, at the nearby village of **CAMEMBERT** (tiny, hilly and very rural), developed the original cheese early in the nineteenth century, promoting it with a skilful campaign that included sending free samples to Napoléon. There's a photo in the museum of the statue with its head blown off after a US air raid in June 1944; its replacement was donated by the cheese-makers of Ohio.

Vimoutiers is the venue of a **market** on Monday afternoons and Fridays. Its **SI**, at 10 av Génèral-de-Gaulle (June–Sept Mon–Sat 10.30am–12.30pm & 3–6.30pm; April, May & Oct–Dec Mon–Fri 3–6pm; ☎33.39.30.29), has piles of information on local cheese-related attractions. Of its **hotels**, the *Soleil d'Or*, 16 place Mackau (☎33.39.07.15; closed Feb; ②), and the *Couronne*, 9 rue du 8-Mai (☎33.39.03.04; ③), are good, economic places to stay, and there is also a superbly clean and very cheap year-round **campsite**, *La Campière*, 9 rue du 8-Mai (☎33.39.18.86). Nearby is the **Escale du Vitou**, a lake, beautifully sited, with everything you need for windsurfing, swimming, and horseriding. In **Ticheville**, roughly 5km southwest on the D12, *La Maison du Vert* (☎33.36.95.84; ③) is a small British-run hotel, highly unusual for Normandy in serving excellent vegetarian (though not vegan) food.

South to Gacé

The **D26** runs along the **valley of the Vie** south of Vimoutiers – a route that is something of a microcosm of Norman vernacular architecture, lined along the way with ramshackle old barns, outhouses and farm buildings. Faded orange clay crumbles from between the weathered wooden beams of these flower-covered beauties. At the crossroads with the D13 is the **hotel-restaurant** *Relais St-Pierre*. For any sensible kid this should be a principal holiday target – mini 125cc motor-bikes and three-wheelers are for hire to hurtle around a course of bales of hay. There's additional lodging available at a farm a little further north, and several further **hotels** at **GACÉ**.

Four kilometres north of Gacé on the D979, *La Chasterie* (☎33.35.73.42; ④) is a farm which has been converted into a hotel, with its own restaurant in an outbuilding standing in its orchard. **Nonant-le-Pin**, 12 km south of Gacé, was the birthplace in 1824 of Alphonsine Plessis, a celebrated courtesan who served as the inspiration for Dumas' *La Dame aux Camélias* and Verdi's *La Traviata*.

Argentan and around

ARGENTAN centres on a **castle ruin** – the site where Henry II of England received the news on New Year's Day 1171 that his knights had taken him at his word and murdered Thomas-à-Becket. In fact, the entire town was very compre-hensively ruined during General Patton's bid to close the "Falaise pocket" in August 1944, and there's virtually nothing to see; the church of **St-Germain** which dominates all approaches has been under continuing restoration ever since, and remains closed to visitors. The castle ruin and the adjoining market square (active on Tuesday) make Argentan an enjoyable enough halt, and there are boat trips on the River Orne, but the main motivation for anyone to comes here is not monuments but **horses**. Outside the town are numerous equestrian centres, with riding schools, stables, racetracks and studs.

Argentan Practicalities

Trains to Argentan pull in at the **gare SNCF**, across the river Orne a short way southwest of the centre. Full information on the area is available from the **SI** at 1 place du Marché (Mon–Sat 10am–noon & 2–6pm; ☎33.67.12.48). Two **hotels** in town are equipped with excellent restaurants – the modern but antique-furnished *Renaissance*, at 20 av 2ᵉ-Division-Blindée (☎33.36.14.20; closed Sun; ②), and the *France*, 8 bd Carnot (☎33.67.03.65; ②).

There's also a nice *chambre d'hôte* (☎33.67.04.47; ③) at La Gravelle, near Sarceaux a little way south of the town, which rents out bicycles for exploring the surrounding countryside

Le Pin-au-Haras

LE PIN-AU-HARAS, 15km east of Argentan on the N26, is an essential stop for horse lovers – it's the home of the **National Stud** (*Haras National*). The plan for the Stud was originally conceived by Louis XIV's minister, Colbert, and the ground subsequently laid out by Le Nôtre from 1715 to 1730. It can be approached via a number of woodland avenues, but the most impressive is the D304, which climbs slowly from the hippodrome and is lined with jumps and hedges.

While the buildings are magnificent, they're nowhere near as sumptuous as the residents – around eighty of them – incalculable investments that include champions of Epsom and Longchamps, as well as prize specimens of the indigenous Norman Percheron.

Tours of the stud leave every half hour from the main entrance (April to mid-Oct 9.30–11.30am & 2–5.30pm; 25F, arrive one hour before closing). You are escorted by a groom through stables full of stomping, snorting, glistening stallions, rooms of polished harnesses and fine carriages, and great doorways labelled in stone, until eventually you come out to a pastoral vision of the horses grazing in endless sequences of gardens and paddocks. Each tour lasts for around an hour; if you find it hard to follow the rapid French-only commentary, you can amuse yourself by watching the way everybody scrupulously affects not to notice the rampant sexuality – which of course is the *raison d'être* of the whole place.

Displays of horsemanship are held daily at 10.30am, 3pm and 4pm through the summer, with special events on the first Sunday in September, the second Sunday in October, and a few other summer weekends. Between February 15 and July 15, most of the horses are away; and the château itself is never open.

The Château d'O

Just outside Mortrée, 6.5km northwest of Sées on the N158, is the privately owned and postcard-perfect **Château d'O** (daily except Tues, April–Sept 2–6.30pm, Oct–March 2–6pm; mornings by appointment only, ☎33.35.34.69; 10F gardens, 20F house) This turreted château, whose grey slate roof rises to a pencil-case-full of sharp points, is in perfect condition, with a full moat that widens out into a lake. The house dates from the end of the fifteenth century and, unusually, was designed purely as a domestic residence, with no military pretensions, while the lawns of the grounds hold a pitch-and-putt golf course.

Within the grounds, but with its own separate entrance, the *Ferme du Château d'O* (☎33.35.35.27; ③) has plush rooms and quite a gastronomic reputation. Lunch menus start at 95F, including ham cooked in cider, while on the 255F menu you get to sample crayfish *profiteroles*.

Sées

SÉES, midway between Argentan and Alençon, has long had an air of being lost in its own history. A succession of dusty and derelict squares, all with medieval buildings intact, surround the great Gothic, white-ceilinged **Cathedral**, which is the fifth to stand on the site and is magnificently illuminated every summer evening. One of its predecessors was burnt down by its own bishop, attempting to smoke out a gang of thieves – much to the scorn of the Pope.

However, Sées does have a couple of tasteful, long-established and luxurious **hotel/restaurants**, the *Cheval Blanc*, overlooking a pretty little square on the main road south (☎33.27.80.48; closed mid-Oct to mid-Nov, first half of March; also closed Thurs pm in season, Fri pm & Sat all day out of season; ③), and the *Dauphin*, in a quiet location next to the old *halles* (☎33.27.80.07; closed Feb, Sun pm all year, & Mon pm in winter; ④).

En route south from Sées, the *Hotel de la Poste*, 27 place de Gaulle (☎33.27.60.13; closed Sun pm all year, & Mon pm in winter; ①) in **LE-MÊLE-SUR-SARTHE** is another *logis* worth stopping at, with an acceptable 50F menu for guests who happen not to like eating, and a 140F shellfish-packed one for those who do.

Alençon and around

ALENÇON, a fair-sized and busy town, is best known for its traditional – and now pretty much defunct – **lace-making** industry. The **Musée des Beaux Arts et de la Dentelle**, housed in a former Jesuit school (daily except Mon 10am–noon & 2–6pm; 15F), has all the best trappings of a modern museum; but the highly informative history of lace-making upstairs, with examples of numerous different techniques, can be rather deadly for anyone not already fascinated by the subject. The temptation to leave without a visit to the "Minor Lace Exhibition Room" is almost overwhelming; but the room beyond it holds a collection of gruesome Cambodian artefacts, spears and lances, tiger skulls and elephants' feet, gathered by a "militant socialist" French governor at the turn of the century. The paintings in the *Beaux Arts* section downstairs are fairly nondescript, except for a touching *Nativity* by the Norman artist, Latouche, and a few works by Courbet and Géricault.

Stained glass in the **Notre-Dame** church shows the medieval guilds of craftsmen who paid for each specific window, and the baptism of **Ste-Thérèse** is commemorated in the chapel in which it took place. If you haven't already had a surfeit of the saint at Lisieux, you can also wander over to her birthplace, on rue St-Blaise, just in front of the gare routière. The **Château des Ducs**, the old town castle, looks impressive but doesn't encourage visitors – it's a prison. People in Alençon have nightmare memories of its use during the war by the Gestapo.

Thanks to wartime bombardment, little is left of the buildings that once stood on the banks of the River Sarthe. Alençon was the first town in France to be liberated by French forces alone, and a monument right next to the Pont-Neuf honours their leader, the aristocratic **General Leclerc** (whose headmaster at school was General de Gaulle's father). The movements of his army are chronicled through the deserts of north Africa, via Utah Beach, to Alençon, on August 12, 1944. Within two weeks he was in Paris, within a year in Berlin, and by March 1946 he was in Hanoi; he died in a plane crash in north Africa in 1947. Another **lace museum**, with a shop selling samples, stands opposite the monument (Mon–Sat 10–11.30am & 2–5.30pm).

Alençon Practicalities

If you want to stay, Alençon has good shops and cafés in a few well-pedestrianized streets at the heart of its abysmal one-way traffic system. The SI is housed in the dramatic fifteenth-century Maison d'Ozé on place La Magdelaine (May–Sept Mon 9.30am–noon & 2–6.30pm, Tues–Sat 9am–6.30pm; Oct–April Mon 9.30am–noon & 2–6pm, Tues–Sat 9am–noon & 2–6.30pm; ☎33.26.11.36). They also organize daily **guided tours** of town (July & Aug; 2.30pm & 4.30pm).

The **gare routière** and the gare SNCF are both northeast of the centre, with the train station slightly the further out of the two. Its immediate environs hold Alençon's prime concentration of **hotels**. The two *logis, l'Industrie*, 20 place Général-de-Gaulle (☎33.27.19.30; ②), and the *Grand Hôtel de la Gare*, 50 av Wilson (☎33.29.03.93; ②), are decent and have fixed-price menus for around 60F. There's a **youth hostel** out on the D204 towards Colombiers, at 1 rue de la Paix, Damigny (☎33.29.00.48).

If you're interested in **horse riding** – along the banks of the Orne – the *Association Départmentale de Tourisme Équestre et d'Équitation de Loisir de l'Orne* has its headquarters in Alençon at 60 Grand-Rue. They can also tell you about the various local stud farms open to the public.

The Forêt d'Ecouves

The **Forêt d'Ecouves**, reached (under your own steam) from either Alençon or Sées, is the centrepiece of the Parc Régional Normandie-Maine, an amorphous area stretching from Mortain in the west to within a few kilometres of Mortagne-au-Perche in the east. A dense mixture of old spruce, pine, oak and beech, set on high hills a few kilometres north of Alençon, the Ecouves forest is one of the most attractive in Normandy. These commanding heights were bitterly fought over during the war, and a Free French tank still guards the **Croix-de-Médavy** at their very apex.

Unfortunately, the forest is now a favoured spot of the military – and in autumn, of deerhunters too. To avoid risking life and limb, check with the park's offices (see below). You can usually ramble along the cool paths, happening on wild mushrooms and even the odd wild boar. The *gîte d'étape*, on the D26 near Les Ragotières on the edge nearest Alençon, is an ideal spot from which to explore the forest (contact the local *gîte* office at 60 rue St-Blaise in Alençon, ☎33.32.09.00).

Carrouges

One alternative base at the western end of the Forêt d'Ecouves is the hill town of **CARROUGES**, which offers two appealing small hotels – the *Hôtel du Nord* (☎33.27.20.14; closed Fri Sept–June; ③) or the tiny *St-Pierre* (☎33.27.20.02; ③).

Carrouges' **château** (mid-June to Aug 9.30–11.30am & 2–6pm; April to mid-June & Sept 10–11.30am & 2–5.30pm; Oct–March 10–11.30am & 2–4pm; 25F) is a fine old-style castle set in spacious grounds at the foot of the hill. Its two high-lights are a superb restored brick staircase, and a room in which hang portraits of fourteen successive generations of the Le Veneur family, an extraordinary illustration of the processes of heredity. In the **Maison de Métiers**, the former castle chapel, local craftsmen sell their produce.

Heading onwards on the D908 towards Bagnoles, you come after a few kilometres to the delightful village of **JOUÉ-DU-BOIS**, with a diminutive château, lake and a cheap but delicious restaurant, the *Pomme d'Or*, where you can still get a four-course meal for around 50F.

Bagnoles

The spa-town of **BAGNOLES DE L'ORNE** lies at the heart of a long, narrow wood, the **Forêt des Andaines**. Broad avenues radiate into the forest from the centre of the town. As you approach, you begin to encounter pale figures shuffling slowly outwards, blinking as if unused to the light of day, as though silently fleeing some nameless evil. In fact, the forbidding nineteenth-century building from which they emerge contains nothing more fearsome than **thermal baths**. Bagnoles is a mecca for the sick and the invalid from all over France; its springs are such big business that they maintain a booking office next to the Pompidou Centre in Paris.

Although life in the town is conducted at a phenomenally slow pace, it is all surprisingly jolly – redolent with aged flirtations and gallantry. The lakeside gardens are the big scene, with pedalos, horse drawn calèches and an enormous Casino. And with so many visitors to keep entertained, and spending money,

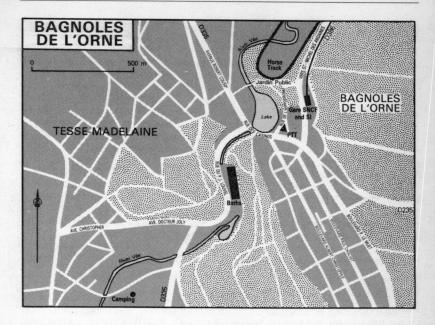

there are innumerable cultural **events**, concerts and stage shows throughout the summer; the ostensible high spot, the annual *Spectacle* in July, is one of the less enthralling.

Away from its main roads, the **Forêt des Andaines** is pleasant, with scattered and unspoilt villages, such as Juvigny and St-Michel, and the secluded, private **Château de Couterne**, a visual delight even from the gates, with its lake and long grass-floored avenue approach.

Bagnoles Practicalities

Whether you'd actually want to spend time in Bagnoles depends on your disposable income as well as your health. Furthermore, the town as a whole operates to a season that lasts roughly from early April to the end of October; arrive in winter, and you may find everything shut. The numerous **hotels** are expensive and sedate places, in which it's possible to be too late for dinner at seven o'clock and locked out altogether at nine, and the **campsite** (April–Oct; ☎33.37.87.45) is rather forlorn.

Contact the **SI** on place République (April–Oct; ☎33.37.85.66) for details on accommodation in Bagnoles and its less exclusive sister town of **TESSE-MADELEINE**. Among the cheaper options in Bagnoles proper are the *Albert 1er* on av Dr-Poulain (☎33.37.80.97; ③) and the *Grand Veneur* on place République (☎33.37.86.79; ③). **Restaurants**, in both towns, tend to be better value; the *de la Terrasse* (☎33.30.80.96) in Bagnoles is well-tried and popular.

If you go in for the traditional activities of **taking the waters**, a "complete cure" of 21 sessions costs around 1400F, with individual baths and showers as little as 30F.

Domfront

The road **through the forest** from Bagnoles, the D335 and then the D908, climbs above the lush woodlands and progressively narrows to a hog's back before entering **DOMFRONT**. Less happens here than at Bagnoles, but it has the edge on countryside. A public park, near the **gare SNCF**, leads up to **castle ruins** on an isolated rock. Eleanor of Aquitaine was born in the castle in October 1162, and Thomas-à-Becket came to stay for Christmas 1166, saying mass in the Notre-Dame-sur-l'Eau church down by the river, which has sadly been ruined by vandals. The views from the gardens surrounding the mangled keep are spectacular, including a very graphic panorama of the ascent you've made to get up. The modern and slightly strange **St-Julien** church, built in the town itself in the 1920s, holds some stimulating mosaics.

Practicalities

Domfront is a useful stopover; the *Hôtel de la Poste* on the hill top (☎33.38.51.00; closed Feb; ②) is very reasonable, and there are others down by the station. Beware though that the **campsite**, *du Champs Passais* (April to mid-Oct; ☎33.37.37.66), is exceptionally small. The **SI** on rue Dr-Barrabé (April–Oct; ☎33.38.53.97) can provide details of local excursions.

Lonlay l'Abbaye and Barenton

The best direction in which to set out from Domfront is northwest, towards the edge of the **Forêt de Lande-Pourrie**. **LONLAY L'ABBAYE**, nine kilometres out on the D22 towards Tinchebray, has a biscuit factory along with various vestiges of its eleventh-century Benedictine past. West from here you can cut across country to the **Fosse d'Arthur**, one of the many unlikely claimants to King Arthur's death scene. A couple of waterfalls disappear into deep limestone caverns, but there's really very little to see.

At nearby **BARENTON**, *Le Relais du Parc* is a good cheap restaurant, and the **Maison de la Pomme et de la Poire** a mildly diverting cider museum (daily March to mid-Nov 9.30am–12.30pm & 2–7pm).

Falaise

William the Conqueror, or William the Bastard as he is more familiarly known to Normans, was born in **FALAISE**, 40km southwest of Lisieux. His mother, Arlette, a laundress, was spotted by his father, Duke Robert of Normandy, at the washing-place below the château. She was a shrewd woman, who scorned secrecy in her eventual assignation by riding publicly through the main entrance to meet him. During her pregnancy, she is said to have dreamed of bearing a mighty tree that cast its shade over Normandy and England.

From a distance, the sheer wall of the **castle keep**, firmly planted on the massive rocks of the cliff (*falaise*) that gave the town its name, and towering over the **Fontaine d'Arlette** down by the river, is one of the most evocative historic sights imaginable. Both were, however, so heavily damaged during the war that they are still often closed for restoration, and are scarcely worth the ten-minute tour when they're not (daily May–Sept; Oct–April Wed–Sat & Sun pm only; 10F).

The whole of Falaise was devastated in the course of the struggle to close the "Falaise Gap" in August 1944 – the climax of the Battle of Normandy, as the Allied armies sought to encircle the Germans and cut off their retreat. By the time the Canadians entered the town on August 17, they could no longer tell where the roads had been and had to bulldoze a new 4-metre strip straight through the middle. Set in almost derelict wilderness right next to the town centre (and opposite the SI) is an isolated survivor, the **Château de la Fresnaye**, housing a rather earnest local museum which is only open during the summer.

Practicalities

The **SI** can be found at 32 rue Georges-Clemenceau (Mon–Sat 10am–12.30pm & 2–6.30pm; also open Sun April–Sept only 10am–12.30pm & 2–5pm, ☎31.90.17.26), the main Caen–Argentan road, which is also the (rather noisy) location of most of Falaise's few **hotels**, such as the *Poste* at no. 38 (☎31.90.13.14; ③). The **campsite**, *Camping du Château* (Easter–Sept; ☎31.90.16.55), next to Arlette's fountain and the municipal swimming pool, is in a much better location.

The Suisse Normande

The area known as the **"Suisse Normande"** lies roughly 25km south of Caen, along the gorge of the River Orne, between Thury-Harcourt and Putanges. The name is a little far-fetched – there are certainly no mountains – but it is quite distinctive with cliffs and crags and wooded hills at every turn. The energetic race along the Orne in canoes and kayaks, their lazier counterparts contenting themselves with pedalos or a bizarre species of inflatable rubber tractor, while high above them climbers dangle from thin ropes and claw desperately at the sheer rockface. For mere walkers the Orne can be frustrating: footpaths along the river are few and far between, whatever maps may say, and often entirely overgrown with brambles. At least one road sign in the area warns of unexploded mines, so tread carefully.

The Suisse Normande is most usually approached from Caen or Falaise, and contrasts dramatically with the prairie-like expanse of wheatfields en route.

Bus Verts #34 can take you to Thury-Harcourt or Clécy on its way to Flers, and SNCF run occasional special summer train excursions from Caen. If you're **cycling**, the least stressful approach is to follow the D212 from Caen, cruising across the flatlands to Thury-Harcourt, although swooping down the D23 from Bretteville, with thick woods to either side of you, is pretty exhilarating. To take the D235 from Caen, follow signs for Falaise, and head straight on through Ifs. Touring the Suisse Normande on a bike, however, is an exhausting business; the minor roads do not follow the gorge floor, but undulate endlessly over the surrounding slopes.

Thury-Harcourt

THURY-HARCOURT is really two separate towns; a little village around a bridge across the Orne, and a larger market town on the hill which overlooks it. The **SI**, 2 place St-Sauveur (Ascension to mid-Sept Tues–Sat 9.30am–noon & 2.30–6.30pm, Sun 10.30am–noon; mid-Sept to Ascension Tues & Thurs 9.30am–noon & 2.30–5pm, Fri 9.30am–noon; ☎31.79.70.45), can suggest walks, rides and

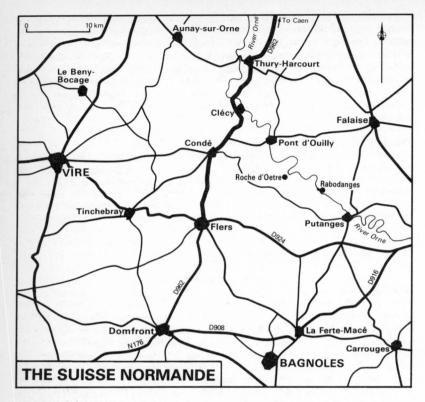

THE SUISSE NORMANDE

gîtes d'étape throughout the Suisse Normande; *SIVOM* at 15 rue de Condé rent out canoes. Between July and September, the grounds of the local manor house are open (for an 18F fee) between 2.30pm and 6.30pm every day, giving access to the immediate riverside.

Hotels in Thury-Harcourt are for the most part quite expensive, though the *Hôtel du Val d'Orne*, 9 route d'Aunay (☎31.79.70.81; closed Sat lunch in summer, Fri pm & all Sat in low season; ②), keeps its room-rates down. For **food**, both that and the other restaurants nearby along the river are good. There are also a couple of three-star **campsites** – *Vallée du Traspy* (mid-April to mid-Oct; ☎31.79.61.80) and *Camping du Bord de l'Orne* (mid-April to Sept; ☎31.79.70.78).

Clécy

The small village of **CLÉCY** stands on a hill about a kilometre up from the actual river at Pont du Vey. On the way down, in the Parc des Loisirs, is a **Musée du Chemin de Fer Miniature** (Easter–Sept daily 10am–noon & 2.15–6.30pm), featuring a gigantic model railway layout certain to appeal to children.

For advice on accommodation and the wide variety of holiday activities available, the **SI** (☎31.69.79.95) is tucked in behind the church. Clécy is a slightly better bet than Thury-Harcourt for finding a room, although its visitors outnumber residents in high season and the whole area can get much too crowded for comfort. The *logis* facing the church, *Au Site Normand*, 1 rue des Châtelets (☎31.69.71.05; closed Tues pm & Wed out of season; ③), consists of an old-fashioned and good-value dining room in the main timber-framed building, and a cluster of newer units opening onto a courtyard around the back. Just down the road, the *Alpes Normands* (☎31.69.45.39; ③), is slightly less expensive.

Down the hill, the *Moulin du Vey* (☎31.69.71.08; closed Dec; ⑤), set in spacious grounds on the far bank of the river, is a luxury hotel that takes its name from the restored watermill right by the bridge, which is itself, confusingly, now a restaurant. The western riverbank continues in a brief splurge of restaurants, takeaways and snack bars as far as the 100-pitch municipal **campsite** (mid-March to Oct; ☎31.69.70.36).

The opposite **east bank** is dominated by the exposed rock face of the giant **Sugarloaf**, looming above the river. Small footpaths, and the tortuous Route des Crêtes, wind up to its flat top, making for some of the most enjoyable walks in Normandy. Picnic sites and parking places along the crest hold orientation maps so weather-beaten as to be almost abstract, but the views down to the flat fields of the Orne valley are stupendous. This is a prime site for **hang-gliders**; disconcertingly, at two points paved concrete ramps lead right to the edge of the precipice, built to facilitate launches.

Pont d'Ouilly

If you're planning on walking, or cycling, one good central spot in which to base yourself is **PONT D'OUILLY**, at the point where the main road from Vire to Falaise crosses the river. It's a small town, with a few basic shops, an old covered market hall and a promenade (with bar) slightly upstream alongside the weir; you can walk along the riverside down to **Le Mesnil Villement**. As well as the **campsite** overlooking the river (Easter to mid-Sept; ☎31.69.80.20), there's an attractive **hotel**, the *du Commerce* (☎31.69.80.16; closed Mon & all Jan; ③). This is the quintessential French village hotel, with a friendly welcome and attentive service. Its **restaurant** is very popular with local families, serving superb, definitive Norman cooking, with plenty of creamy *pays d'Auge* sauces; the dining room is appropriately filled with stuffed animals.

About a kilometre north of Pont d'Ouilly, the more upmarket *Auberge St-Christophe* (☎31.69.81.23; ④) stands in a beautiful setting on the right bank of the Orne, covered with ivy and geraniums and opposite a roofless and now overgrown Art Deco factory. A *Grand Pardon du Ste-Roche* takes place along the river on the third Sunday in August.

The Roche d'Oëtre

A short distance south of Pont d'Ouilly is the **Roche d'Oëtre**, a high rock affording a tremendous view, not over the Orne but into the deep and totally wooded gorge of the Rouvre. The rock itself is private property, though you're under no obligation to visit the café there.

The river widens soon afterwards into the **Lac du Rabodanges**, formed by the many-arched Rabodanges Dam. It's a popular spot, with a multi-facility **campsite**, *Les Retours*, perfectly situated between the dam and the bridge on the D121. There's a play area for kids, and grassy picnic slopes lead down to the water's edge where the occasional bather risks a swim among the waterskiers, speedboats, windsurfers, canoes and kayaks. The imposing Rabodanges château, higher up the hillside, is now a stud farm.

Putanges

Further climbing roads bring you to **PUTANGES**, another possible place to stay, with a small **campsite**, *le Val d'Orne* (Easter–Sept; ☎33.35.89.96). The town lies a bit beyond the main attractions of the region, but nevertheless it's a pleasant stop, with a few bars and pavement cafés, and, just upstream from the bridge, the weirs over which the Orne appears from its source a short way south. The *Lion Verd* (☎33.35.01.86; closed Jan; ①), very near the river, is a well-priced **hotel**.

The Bocage

The region centring on St-Lô, west of Caen and just south of the Cotentin, is known as the **Bocage Normande**. The word *bocage* refers to a type of cultivated countryside common in the west of France, in which fields are cut by tight hedgerows rooted into walls of earth well over a metre high.

An effective form of smallhold farming, at least in pre-industrial days, it also proved to be a perfect system of anti-tank barricades. When the Allied troops tried to advance through the region in 1944 it was almost impenetrable – certainly bearing no resemblance to the East Anglian plains where they had trained. The war here was hand-to-hand, inch-by-inch slaughter; the destruction of villages often wholesale.

St-Lô

The city of **ST-LÔ**, a transport junction 60km south of Cherbourg and 36km southwest of Bayeux which was crucial in the war to the Allied breakout of the Cotentin, is still known as the "Capital of the Ruins". Black and white postcards of the wartime devastation are on sale everywhere and you keep coming on memorial sites as you wander about. In the main square, the gate of the old prison commemorates Resistance members executed by the Nazis, people deported east to the concentration camps and soldiers killed in action. When the bombardment of St-Lô was at its fiercest, the Germans refused to take any measures to protect the prisoners; the gate was all that survived. In similar vein, behind the cathedral, a monument to the dead of the First World War is pitted with shrapnel from the Second. Less depressingly, at the foot of the rock under the castle, you can see the entrance to caves where citizens sheltered from the onslaught, while somewhere far below are great vaults used by the German command. In Studs Terkel's book, *The Good War*, a GI reminisces about the huge party thrown there after the Americans found vast stockpiles of champagne; Thomas Pynchon's *Gravity's Rainbow* has a crazed drinking scene based on the tale. Samuel Beckett was here during the battle and after, working for the Irish Red Cross as interpreter, driver and provision-seeker – for such things as rat poison for the maternity hospitals. He said he took away with him a "time-honoured conception of humanity in ruins".

The newness of so much in St-Lô reveals the scale of fighting. Between the SNCF station and the castle rock, for example, a walk leads along the canalized channel of the Vire – an attractive course but unmistakably an attempt to patch over the ravages. All the trees in the city are the same height, too, all planted to replace the battle's mutilated stumps. But the most visible – and brilliant – reconstruction is the **Cathédrale de Notre Dame**. The main body of this, with its strange southward veering nave, has been conventionally repaired and rebuilt. Between the shattered west front and base of the collapsed north tower, however, a startling sheer wall of icy green stone makes no attempt to mask the destruction.

By way of contrast to such memories, a lighthouse-like 1950s folly spirals to nowhere on the main square; should you feel the urge to climb its stairway, ask at the Mairie opposite. More compelling, around behind the Mairie, is a **Musée des Beaux-Arts** (daily except Tues, April–Oct 10am–noon & 2–6pm; Nov–March 10am–noon; 10F). This is full of treasures: a Boudin sunset; a Lurçat tapestry of his dog Nadir and the Pirates; works by Corot, van Loo, Moreau; a Léger watercolour; a fine series of unfaded sixteenth-century Flemish tapestries on the lives of two peasants; and sad bombardment relics of the town.

Practicalities

St-Lô makes an interesting pause but it's virtually abandoned at night. Full information on what it has to offer can be obtained from the **SI**, just off the central square at 2 rue Havin (☎33.05.02.09); the **gare routière** is on the rue des 80e and 136e, a short way south.

Most of the hotels, restaurants and bars, however, are just across the river, near the **gare SNCF**. Right next to the station, there's the upmarket *logis Hôtel des Voyageurs*, 5–7 av Briovère (☎33.05.08.63; ⑤), with a good 100F menu; up in town, try *des Remparts*, 3 rue des Prés (☎33.57.08.06; ③), which doesn't have its own restaurant, or *La Cremaillère* on rue du Belle (☎33.57.14.68; ②).

The Vire Valley

Once St-Lô was taken in the Battle of Normandy, the armies moved speedily on to their next confrontation. The **Vire Valley**, trailing south from St-Lô, saw little action – and indeed its towns and villages have rarely been touched by any historic or cultural mainstream. The motivation in coming to this landscape of rolling hills and occasional gorges is essentially to consume the region's cider, Calvados and butter-rich fruit pastries.

Although the countryside is filled with orchards of apples and pears, the land is less fertile than elsewhere in Normandy – and has suffered heavily from the recent depression in the fruit market. A booming trade, however, has grown up around illicit Calvados, bolstering the faltering economy of many Vire farmers. Bootleggers smuggle hundreds of thousands of litres throughout France, using the hydraulic suspension of their *Citröen* cars to obscure the heavy loads they are carrying from the eyes of watching taxmen. One much-arrested smuggler has such James Bond accessories as automatically rotating licence-plates, smoke screens and even oil jets for use against pursuing motorcycles.

Between St-Lô and Vire

The best section of the Vire is the valley that comes down from St-Lô through the Roches de Ham to Tessy-sur-Vire. The **Roches de Ham** are a pair of sheer rocky promontories high above the river. They are promoted as a "viewing table", though the pleasure lies as much in the walk up, through lanes lined with black-berries, hazelnuts and rich orchards.

La Chapelle-sur-Vire

Just downstream from the Roches, and a good place to stop over for a night, is **LA CHAPELLE-SUR-VIRE**. Its church, towering majestically above the river, has been an object of pilgrimage since the twelfth century. There's a weir nearby and a scattering of grassy islands. Next to the bridge on the lower road is the *Auberge de la Chapelle* (☎33.56.32.83; ②), a good but rather expensive restaurant, whose walls are adorned with a strange collage of pressed dried leaves, and which also offers a few cheap **rooms**.

Torigni-sur-Vire

An alternative base for the Roches, over to the east, is **TORIGNI-SUR-VIRE**, which was the base of the Grimaldi family before they achieved quasi-royal status upon moving on to the principality of Monaco. A spacious country town, it boasts a few grand buildings and an attractive **campsite**, *Camping du Lac* (mid-March to Oct; ☎33.56.91.74). The *Auberge Orangerie* (☎33.56.70.64; closed Feb, Sun pm & Mon out of season; ③) is a good restaurant with menus starting at 65F and half a dozen rooms.

Tessy-sur-Vire

At **TESSY-SUR-VIRE** there's little to see other than the river itself, banked by rolling meadows that make an ideal venue for a summer's day picnic, though the town again has a luxurious **campsite**, along with a couple of **hotels**, including the *Hôtel de France*, a nice little *logis* on the main street (☎33.56.30.01; closed mid-Jan to mid-Feb; ②) and a Wednesday **market**.

Le Viaduc de la Souleuvre

At the eastern end of the sinuous Vire gorge, 6km west of Le Bény-Bocage, stands the former railway viaduct of **Le Viaduc de la Souleuvre**, designed by Gustave Eiffel. Only the six supporting granite pillars of Eiffel's original struc-ture remain – the railway closed down in 1970 – but in 1990 a wooden board-walk was re-laid across half the span of the bridge, on which visitors can cross to the deepest part of the Gorge. Once there, 61 metres up, they are seriously expected to **jump off** – this is *AJ Hackett's* **bungy-jumping** centre (daily June to mid-Sept; Feb & mid-Dec Sat, Sun & hols, and other times on demand; closed mid-Dec to Jan; reservations essential ☎31.67.37.38). Jumpers have to be aged at least thirteen, and one to three jumps costs 480F; you also have to pay 15F for the privilege of parking in the adjacent field. Less intrepid souls can walk down to the meadows immediately beneath the viaduct and watch the plummeting from there.

Vire

The pride and joy of the people of **VIRE** are their *andouilles*, the blood sausages known in English as chitterlings. If you can avoid these hideous parcels of pigs' intestines, and the assortment of abattoirs that produce them, it's possible to have a good time; in fact Vire is a town worth visiting specifically for its food. The biggest treats are to be found at the *Hôtel des Voyageurs*, 47 av de la Gare

(☎31.68.01.16; ②), down at the bottom by the gare SNCF. For around 72F you can have a sublime and endless meal, in opulent surroundings. There are mouth-watering buffets of both *hors d'oeuvres* and desserts, as well as salmon trout fresh from the river, all duly washed down with local *poiré*. Good **restaurants** are to be found, too, at the more central *Hôtel de France*, 4 rue d'Aignaux (☎31.68.00.35; ③), and *Hôtel du Cheval Blanc*, 2 place du 6-Juin-1944 (☎31.67.19.82; ③).

The only problem is what to do when you're not eating. You can look at the collection of minerals and fossils in the belfry that stands alone in the town centre. You can visit the museum of How to Restore Old Norman Farm-houses. Or you can wander by the little scrap of **canal**, equipped with twee floating houses for the ducks, that lies just below the one stark finger that survives of the castle. The only action is at the Friday **market**, again obsessively dedicated to food.

For some exercise, head six kilometres south along the D76 to **Lac de la Dathée**. Set in open country, the lake is circled by footpaths; in summer it some-times dries up completely, but when it's wet it can also be crossed by rented sail-ing boat or wind-surfer (contact the *Maison des Jeunes et de la Culture*, 1 rue des Halles, Vire; ☎31.68.08.04).

West and South from Vire

Once past Vire, the roads towards Brittany present you with the choice either of heading southwest for the frontier towns of **Fougères** and Vitré (see p.190), or directly to the coast and making the magnificent **Mont-St-Michel** (see p.128) your last port of call in Normandy.

West from Vire, the road to Villedieu passes through SAINT-SEVER, not in itself much to write home about but backed by a dark and magical **forest** in which there's a dolmen, an abbey and a scattering of pukka picnic spots marked by signs showing a champagne bottle in a hamper.

Villedieu-les-Poêles

VILLEDIEU-LES-POÊLES – literally "City of God the Frying Pans" – is a lively though touristified place, 28km west of Vire. Much of this ancient town still retains significant elements of its medieval appearance, especially in its back-streets where perfectly preserved old courtyards are tucked away behind unpre-possessing wooden gateways. Ever since the twelfth century, Villedieu has been a centre for metal-working; copper souvenirs and kitchen utensils gleam from its rows of shops, and the SI can provide lists of dozens of local *ateliers* for more direct purchases. You can see examples illustrating the historical development of Villedieu's copperware in the **museum** on rue Général-Huard (Easter–Oct daily except Tues 10am–noon & 2–6.30pm, Tues 2–6.30pm; 10F).

All of this can seem a bit obsessive, though there is more authentic interest at the **Fonderie de Cloches** at 13 rue du Pont-Chignon, one of the twelve remain-ing bell foundries in Europe. Work here is only part time due to limited demand, but it's open to visits all year round, and you may find the forge lit (July & Aug daily 8am–noon & 2–5.30pm; Sept–June Tues–Sat 8am–noon & 2–5.30pm; 10F). Expert craftsmen will show you the moulds, composed of an unpleasant-looking combination of clay, goats' hair and horse shit.

Practicalities

Villedieu's **SI** is on place des Costils (June–Sept only; ☎33.61.05.69 – for the rest of the year, contact the Mairie, ☎33.61.00.16). If you're charmed into staying, there's a **campsite** by the river, *Le Pré de la Rose* (Easter to mid-Sept; ☎33.61.02.44), and excellent basic food and accommodation at the *Hôtel de Paris* on route de Paris (☎33.61.00.66; ③). The *Fruitier* on place Gostils (☎33.90.51.00; closed Sat in winter; ④) is a slightly more luxurious option, with a good restaurant, while the stylishly refurbished dining room of the very welcoming *logis Hôtel St-Pierre et St-Michel*, 12 place de la République (☎33.61.00.11; closed Jan; ③), makes another pleasant venue for a fine meal. Much the nicest **bar** in town, with a good selection of music and a youngish clientèle is *Le Pussoir Fidèle*, 2 place du Pussoir Fidèle (☎33.51.94.58).

Through the Forests

South from Vire, if you are heading for Fougères or Domfront, you pass through the **Forêt de Mortain** and its continuation, the **Forêt de Lande-Pourrie**. The forests' most interesting sites – the Fosse d'Arthur and the abbey at Lonlay – are easiest approached from Domfront (see p.152). Outside the town of **MORTAIN**, there are **waterfalls** and a tiny chapel on a high rock from which the neighbouring province of Maine spreads before you. On a clear day you can even see Mont-St-Michel.

St-Hilaire-du-Harcoët

The thriving (Wednesday) market town of **ST-HILAIRE-DU-HARCOËT**, 28km north of Fougères, amounts to little more than a crossroads near the big market square. It does however hold a few restaurants and **hotels**, such as *Le Cygne* (☎33.49.11.84; closed Fri pm in winter; ④), a comfortable, newly-modernized *logis* on route de Fougères with an appealing set of somewhat pricey menus, and the cheaper *L'Agriculture* on rue Waldeck-Rousseau (☎33.49.10.60; ①), where the 60F menu includes fresh oysters.

St-Symphorien-des-Monts

As you head south from St-Hilaire towards Brittany, one last Norman stop, just off the N176 seven kilometres out of town, is the **wildlife sanctuary** at **ST-SYMPHORIEN-DES-MONTS**, set in the park of the now non-existent château. Contented-looking beasts, like yaks and bisons and threatened domestic animals, graze in semi-liberty in fields and woods around a lake inhabited by swans and flamingos; wolves lurk somewhere in the undergrowth. Admission (mid-March to mid-Nov, daily 9am–8pm; 30F) is a little more expensive than usual, but worth it.

travel details

Trains

From **Évreux** 5 daily to Conches (15min), Serquigny (30min), Bernay (45min), Lisieux (1hr) and Caen (1hr 30min); also 12 daily to Paris St-Lazare (1hr).

From Lisieux 6 daily to Rouen (1hr 30min) via Bernay (25min) and Serquigny (30min); regular service to Paris (2hr) via Bernay and Évreux (45min); 10 daily to Cherbourg (2hr 40min) via Caen (30min) and Bayeux (50min); to Trouville-

Deauville (25min), about 6 daily out of season and more frequently in summer; service extends to Villers, Houlgate and Dives-Cabourg (40min from Trouville) on Sundays and holidays throughout the year, and daily in July & Aug.

From Alençon 6 daily to Caen (1hr 15min) via Sées, Argentan and St-Pierre; to Tours (2hr) via Le Mans.

From St-Lô 4 daily to Caen (1hr) via Bayeux (30min); 4 daily to Rennes (2hr) via Coutances and Pontorson.

From Vire Regular service to Paris via Argentan (1hr) and L'Aigle (1hr 30min); to Villedieu (20min) and Granville (1hr).

Buses

The main inland bus networks are operated by **Bus Verts**, *based at 11 rue des Chanoines in Caen (☎31.44.77.44), who cover Calvados in particular, and* **STAO** *(Alençon ☎33.26.06.35; Argentan ☎33.67.04.66; Mortagne ☎33.25.19.11), further south in the Orne region.*

From Caen *Bus Verts* #32 and #33 to Vire (1hr 30min) via Villers-Bocage; *Bus Verts* #34 (5 daily, 2 on Sun) to Flers (1hr 20min) via Thury-Harcourt (36min) and Clécy (50min); *Bus Verts* #35 to Falaise (45min); to Lisieux (45min).

From Lisieux *Bus Verts* #50 to Pont l'Evêque (25min) and on to Honfleur (50min) or Deauville (45min); *Bus Verts* #52 to St-Pierre-sur-Dives (35min); *Bus Verts* #53 to Vimoutiers (1hr) via Livarot; *Bus Verts* #56 to Orbec (45min).

From L'Aigle to Gacé (1 daily; 45min); to Vimoutiers (1–2 daily; 1hr 10min).

From Mortagne to Bellême (1–4 daily; 20min).

From Argentan to Carrouges (1–3 daily; 45min); to Domfront (1–3 daily; 1hr 50min) via Bagnoles (1hr).

From Alençon to Bagnoles (30min); to Évreux (1 daily; 2hr) via L'Aigle (1hr 40min); to Vimoutiers (1–3 daily; 1hr 30min) via Sées (30min) and Argentan (1hr 17min); to Mortagne (1–3 daily; 1hr); to Bellême (1–2 daily; 1hr).

From St-Lô to Bayeux (30min); to Cherbourg (1hr 30min); to Coutances (30min).

From Vire *Bus Verts* #81 to Condé-sur-Noireau (30min); to Fougères (1hr 30min); to Avranches (45min).

PART THREE

BRITTANY

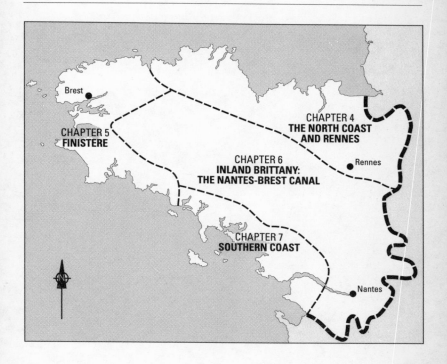

Brest

CHAPTER 4
**THE NORTH COAST
AND RENNES**

CHAPTER 5
FINISTERE

CHAPTER 6
**INLAND BRITTANY:
THE NANTES-BREST CANAL**

Rennes

CHAPTER 7
SOUTHERN COAST

Nantes

CHAPTER FOUR

THE NORTH COAST AND RENNES

Brittany's **northern coast** has its extremes. Long sections, open to the full force of the Atlantic, are spectacular but much too dangerous for swimming; others shelter some of the region's best natural harbours and most peaceful resorts. The old *citadelle* port of **St-Malo** is an attractive point of arrival, from which you are well positioned for exploration, even if your main goals are elsewhere, in the south or in Finistère.

The best of the **resorts** are concentrated along the two strips of coast designated as the Côte d'Emeraude and Côte de Granit Rose. The **Côte d'Émeraude**, as green as its name suggests, remains largely unspoiled, especially the heather-covered wilds of Cap Fréhel. Here the seaside towns are traditionally English-dominated – and perhaps a little too much in the Anglo-Saxon image for their own good. **Le Val-André** and **Erquy** in particular, however, have superb beaches, and everywhere there are secluded campsites for a night or two's stopover.

Further west, beyond the placid **Baie de St-Brieuc** (the town of St-Brieuc itself is for most holiday-makers a nuisance to be avoided) the coastline erupts into an almost garish tangle of pink granite boulders, the famed **Côte de Granit Rose**. This harsher territory was once, at **Paimpol** and elsewhere, the home of cod and whaling fleets which embarked on annual transatlantic expeditions. Today it's more reliant on tourism, most resolutely so at the twin resorts of **Perros-Guirrec** and **Ploumanac'h**. These are attractive nonetheless, and there are plenty of smaller places where you can avoid the crowds, such as **Loguivy** on the mainland, and, just offshore, the **Île de Bréhat** – among the most beautiful of all northern French islands.

ACCOMMODATION PRICE CODES

All **hotel prices** in this book have been coded using the symbols below. The price shown is for the least expensive double room, which for categories ① and ② usually means a room without shower, bath and toilet. Most hotels in those categories have other rooms with en-suite facilities, which typically cost 30–50F extra.

For a full explanation see p.31.

①	up to 120 F	④	220–300F	⑦	500–600F
②	120–160F	⑤	300–400F	⑧	600–700F
③	160–220F	⑥	400–500F	⑨	700F and over

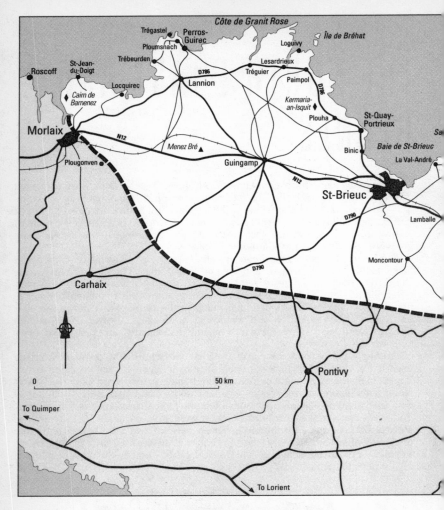

Heading **inland** from St-Malo, the Rance estuary and the road south to Rennes provide most of the interest. On the latter, you are introduced to prehistoric and megalithic sights at **Dol**, and to the characteristic Breton **forests** at **Ville-Cartier** and **Fougères**. Down the Rance, **Dinan**, connected frequently by boat with both St-Malo and Dinard, is the medieval fortress town *par excellence*, the legacy of piratical and trading wealth through the Middle Ages and beyond; **Jugon-les-Lacs**, nearby, is a lakeside retreat.

To the **east**, the redoubtable **citadelles** of **Fougères** and **Vitré** still guard the frontier with Normandy. **Rennes** is less martial, but after centuries of rivalry with Nantes is now firmly established as the Breton capital. By no means the prettiest

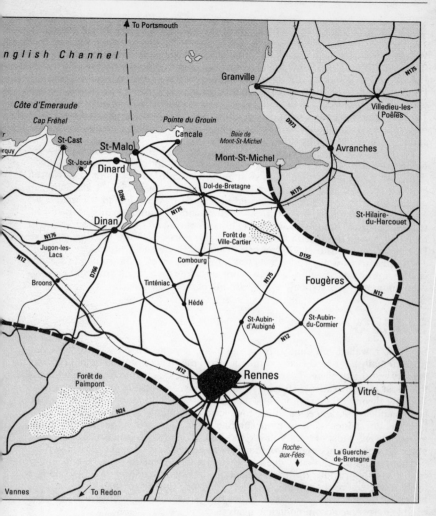

town in the province, it is without doubt the liveliest, hosting a considerable university and most of the Breton political and cultural organizations.

Rennes takes pride of place as far as **festivals** in the region are concerned, playing host in July to the **Tombées de la Nuit**, ten days of theatre and music, and in December to **Les Transmusicales**, which has become one of the major dates in the French rock calendar. Among numerous other annual events, the biggest and most compelling is the **Breton Music** festival, held each July at **St-Brieuc**, where there's also the ominous-sounding **Art Rock** festival at the end of October. The major traditional celebration is the *pardon* of St-Yves in **Tréguier** on the third Sunday in May.

EAST: THE RANCE AND RENNES

Whether you approach across the Channel by ferry from Portsmouth, or along the coast from Mont-St-Michel in Normandy, the wide estuary of the **River Rance** makes a spectacular introduction to Brittany. The towns of **St-Malo** and **Dinard** stand to either side of its mouth, each with its own very distinct ambience, while **Dinan** guards the head of the river itself twenty kilometres upstream. The few crossing places, such as along the top of the **Barrage de la Rance**, the tidal power dam, take in magnificent views of the sheltered banks – rich, fertile, and repeatedly pierced by tributaries.

To the east of the river spreads the **Mont-St-Michel Bay**, dominated by the pinnacle of the Mont itself (see Normandy, p.128), and swept by extraordinary tides that make it unrealistic for swimming. **Cancale**, the bay's most sheltered point in Brittany, is a good viewpoint from which to appreciate it all, filling up meanwhile with the town's famed and acclaimed oysters. Inland, all roads curl eventually to **Rennes**, or out towards Normandy. In addition to the medieval fortress towns of **Fougères** and **Vitré**, lesser known and quieter pleasures are to be found beside the lake in **Combourg**, in the **Forêt de Ville Cartier**, south of Dol, and along the **Ille et Vilaine canal**, around **Hédé** and **Tinténiac**.

Getting around anywhere away from the coast or off main routes to Rennes can be a problem. If you don't have your own transport, keep your sights low – even Fougères is served only by a scattering of market buses.

St-Malo

ST-MALO, walled and built with the same grey granite stone as Mont-St-Michel, was originally a fortified island at the mouth of the Rance, controlling not only the estuary but the open sea beyond. Now inseparably attached to the mainland, it is the most visited place in Brittany – and not just because of its ferry terminal. Walking through the *intra-muros* ("within the walls") streets of its **old citadelle** is a unique experience: at times they can be sombre and grim (particularly beneath grey skies), but in high summer or at sunset they become light and almost unreal. Most of what you see has had to be lovingly and precisely rebuilt, stone by stone; eighty percent of the city was destroyed in August 1944.

Though the old city can, when busy, feel a little claustrophobic – and in any case it hardly provides the most authentically Breton experience – St-Malo is a lively town, where there's always a lot going on. Having to spend a night here before or after a ferry crossing is a positive pleasure – so long as you take the trouble to reserve accommodation in advance.

Although it began as a monastic settlement, founded by Saints Aaron and Brendan early in the sixth century and then from 550 AD onwards identified with the Celtic Saint Maclou (or possibly MacLow), St-Malo later became notorious as the home of a fierce breed of pirate-mariners. Not only did these adventurers force English ships passing up the Channel to pay tribute, but they also brought wealth from further afield. Jacques Cartier, who colonized Canada, lived in and sailed from St-Malo, and the Argentinian name for the Falklands, *Las Malvinas*, derives from the islands' first French colonists, *Les Malouins*. St-Malo was itself an independent republic for four years in the sixteenth century, under the motto *"Ni Français, Ni Bretons, Malouins Suis"*, and the long succession of pirates were

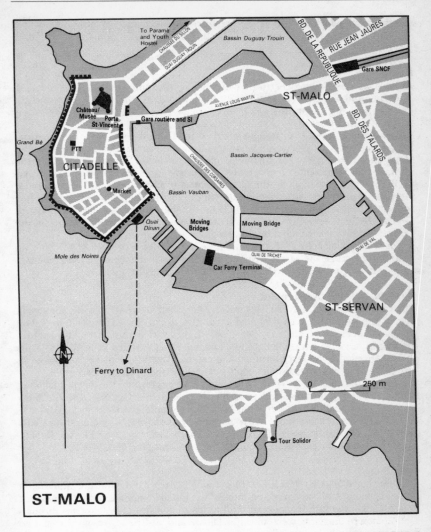

ST-MALO

never quite under anybody's control but their own. Even when the Duke of Marlborough landed 15,000 men just up the coast near Cancale in 1758, and attempted to take the city by land, St-Malo's defences proved too formidable.

Arrival and Public Transport

St-Malo presents its best face to the **sea**; if you don't arrive by *Brittany Ferries* from Portsmouth, you may well want to consider the ten-minute shuttle across the river Rance from Dinard as an alternative. If you come in by **bus** or **train**, the old city is concealed by modern suburbs and dockside industry almost until you're in it.

Boats

As well as the *Brittany Ferries* sailings to Portsmouth (1 daily between mid-March & mid-Nov, leaving at either 10.45am or 10am; otherwise less frequently; journey time 9hr), from the *Gare Maritime du Naye* (☎99.82.41.41), St-Malo is busy with other **boats**.

In summer, regular passenger **ferries to Dinard** operate from the **quai Dinan**, just outside the westernmost point of the ramparts in front of the port (*Émeraude Lines*; ☎99.40.48.40; 20F single, 30F return). The trip across the estuary takes an all-too-short ten minutes. *Émeraude Lines* also conduct excursions up the river to Dinan, along the Brittany coast to Cap Fréhel and Cézembre, to the Îles Chausey and Granville in Normandy. In addition, they connect St-Malo with the **Channel Islands**; you'll find details of their services, along with those of *Condor Hydroglisseurs* (☎99.56.42.29) and *Channiland* (☎99.40.40.90), in the "Travel Details" at the end of this chapter.

For a touch of luxury, in summer *Le Chateaubriand* (☎99.46.44.44) puts on gastronomic cruises in Mont-St-Michel Bay and up the Rance from the gare maritime de la Richardais, at the Dinard end of the Barrage de la Rance.

By road; car and cycle rental

Approaching central St-Malo or the ferry terminal by **road** can be somewhat dismal; the signposts seem designed to confuse, and all the roads seem to end on tramlined docksides. Lost and bewildered cars circle the port like seagulls. Driving in to catch a ferry, keep the Chaussée des Corsaires in mind: this links the old town with the ferry terminal and can be closed for long periods while its moveable bridge is opened to let boats out of the Bassin Jacques-Cartier.

Most of the major **car rental** companies are represented in town, including *Avis* at the ferry terminal and gare SNCF (☎99.81.73.24), *Budget* at the ferry terminal (☎99.82.89.79), and *Hertz* at 48 bd de la République (☎99.56.31.61).

If you prefer to enjoy more active pursuits, you can rent **bicycles** from *Cycles Diazo*, 47 quai Duguay-Trouin (☎99.40.31.63), *Cycles Nicole*, 11 rue Robert-Schumann in Paramé (☎99.56.11.06), or, as usual, from the gare SNCF.

Trains

St-Malo's **gare SNCF** (☎99.65.50.50) is two kilometres out from the *citadelle* on place Hermine, and convenient neither for the old town nor the ferry (take care if you're planning a tight connection). All trains to and from St-Malo pass through Dol. If you're heading west towards Dinan and St-Brieuc, or northeast into Normandy, you will normally need to change trains at Dol – most services continue through to Rennes.

Buses

Officially, the **gare routière** (☎99.40.83.33) – not a building, just an expanse of concrete – is right next to the SI (see above), but most buses, whether local or long distance, coincide also with trains at the gare SNCF (see below).

The *Compagnie de Transport d'Ille et Vilaine* (*TIV*; ☎99.40.83.33) run services to Dinard, Dinan, Cancale, Combourg and Rennes. *Les Courriers Bretons*, 13 rue d'Alsace (☎99.56.79.09), go to Cancale, Mont-St-Michel and Fougères, and also run day trips to Mont-St-Michel (summer daily 9.30am, Wed & Sat only in low season; 100F). Dinan buses are also operated by *CAT* (☎96.39.21.05).

Information

The helpful **SI** (July–Sept Mon–Sat 8.30am–8pm, Sun 10am–7pm; last fortnight of June & first fortnight of Sept Mon–Sat 9am–7pm, Sun 10am–noon & 2–6pm; Easter to mid-June & last fortnight of Sept Mon–Sat 9am–noon & 2–7pm, Sun 10am–noon & 2–6pm; Oct–Easter Mon–Sat 9am–noon & 2–6pm; ☎99.56.64.48) is housed in a single-storey building, right in front of the city walls, beside the Bassin Duguay-Trouin in the **Port des Yachts**. As well as good detailed city maps, they can provide information on annual festivals such as the **Étonnants Voyageurs** ("Amazing Travellers"), dedicated to the film and literature of travel and adventure, which takes place for three days in late May.

The main city **post office** is at 1 bd de la Tour d'Auvergne (July to mid-Sept Mon–Fri 8.30am–6.30pm, Sat 8.30am–12.30pm; otherwise Mon–Fri 8.30am–12.30pm & 1.30–5.30pm, Sat 8.30am–noon; ☎99.56.12.05), but for most travellers the branch office within the walls in the place des Frères Lamennais is more convenient (same hours; ☎99.40.89.90). If you want to arrange to pick up *poste restante* letters, make sure you distinguish between the two – specify either *35401 St-Malo Principal* or *35402 St-Malo intra-muros*.

Several shops and kiosks within the *citadelle* advertise that they handle **foreign exchange** transactions without charging commission; the rates they offer are so abysmal that they don't need to.

The Town

The **citadelle** of St-Malo, very much the prime destination for visitors, was for many years joined to the mainland only by a long, single causeway, before the original line of the coast was hidden forever by the construction of the harbour basin. Although its cobbled streets of restored seventeenth- and eighteenth-century houses can be crowded to the point of absurdity in summer (and the cobbles present quite a challenge to parents pushing buggies), away from the more popular thoroughfares random exploration is fun.

Thanks to the limitations on space on this tiny peninsula, the buildings tend to be a little more high-rise than you might expect. Stern and ancient as they may look, they are almost entirely reconstructed – photographs of the damage suffered in 1944, when General Patton bombarded the city for two weeks before the Germans surrendered, show barely a stone left in place. But you can surface to the sunlight on the **ramparts** – first erected in the fourteenth century, and re-designed by the master builder Vauban (see also p.292) four hundred years later – to enjoy wonderful views all round, especially to the west as the sun sets over the sea.

The main gate of the *citadelle* as you approach by road is the **Porte St-Vincent**. The town **museum** in the castle to the right (June–Sept daily 9.30am–noon & 2–6.30pm; Oct–May daily except Tues 10am–noon & 2–6pm; 19F) is something of a hymn of praise to the "prodigious prosperity" enjoyed by St-Malo during its days of piracy, colonialism and slave-trading. Climbing the 169 steps of the castle keep, you pass a fascinating mixture of maps, diagrams and exhibits –

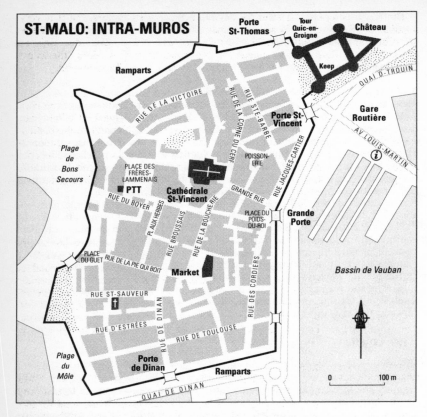

chilling handbills from the Nazi occupation, accounts of the "infernal machine" used by the English to blow up the port in 1693, and savage four-pronged *chausse-trappes*, thrown by pirates onto the decks of ships being boarded to immobilize their crews. At the top a gull's eye prospect takes in the whole *citadelle*.

It is possible to pass under the ramparts at a couple of points and on to the open shore, where a huge beach stretches away beyond the rather featureless resort-suburb of **Paramé**. When the tide is low, the most popular walk is out to the small island of **Grand-Bé** – sometimes you even need to queue to get on to the short causeway. Solemn warnings are posted of the dangers of attempting to return from the island when the tide has risen too far – if you're caught there, there you have to stay. The island "sight" is the tomb of the nineteenth-century writer-politician Chateaubriand (who was born in St-Malo on Sept 4, 1768, and died in 1848). Marx described him as "the most classic incarnation of French *vanité* . . . the false profundity, Byzantine exaggeration, emotional coquetry . . . a never-before-seen mishmash of lies". Suitably enough he features heavily on all the tourist brochures, which – with no apparent irony – extol his "modesty" in choosing so "isolated" a burial spot.

The coast along here is safer for paddlers than for swimmers, but it is very popular for **windsurfing**. Boards are available for rental from *Surf School*, 7 rue de Courtoisville (☎99.40.07.47), or *Centre de Voile*, quai du Bajoyer (☎99.40.84.42); most surfers make for the beaches further along the coast towards Cancale, the **plage du Verger** and the larger **Anse du Guesclin**.

St-Servan

St-Servan, within walking distance along the corniche to the south of the *citadelle*, is actually older than St-Malo itself. It was on the site of the Gallo-Roman city of *Aleth* that Saint Maclou established his church, and the seat of the bishopric only moved onto the impregnable island fortress when danger threatened in 1142. The town curves round several small inlets and beaches to face the tidal power dam across the river. Its **Tour Solidor**, three linked towers built in 1382, is open all year for 90-minute guided visits to a museum of clipper ships (summer daily 10am–noon & 2–6pm; Oct–March daily except Tues 2–6pm).

Accommodation

St-Malo boasts of having over 100 **hotels**, including the traditional seaside boarding houses just off the beach, and also has several **campsites** and a couple of **youth hostels**. In high season it needs every one of them; the demand is phenomenal. Motorists intending to stay the night before catching a summer ferry sailing should make reservations well in advance; if you don't have a reservation, don't demoralize yourself hunting around, and settle for spending the night somewhere else along the coast or nearby. Apart from the obvious alternatives of Dinard and Dinan, it's worth considering peaceful smaller towns such as Combourg, Cancale, Jugon-les-Lacs or Erquy.

Hotels in the *citadelle*

You pay a premium for the privilege of staying within the city walls, since that's where any nightlife takes place, and it's a fair walk in through the docks from any of the surrounding suburbs. Unfortunately, the *intra-muros* hotels tend to take advantage of high summer demand by insisting that you eat in their own restaurants.

Hôtel-Restaurant Aux Vieilles Pierres, 4 rue des Lauriers (☎99.56.46.80). One of the better bargains within the walls, some way from the Grande Porte near place aux Herbes. Open all year. Menus at 75F with fish soup and steak, or 105F for the full spread, in theory totalling six courses but half of those are just intended to keep you ticking over until the next one arrives. ②.

Hôtel Bristol Union, 4 place de la Poissonerie (☎99.40.83.36). Very correct rooms, in a nice little square facing the former fish market, just off the Grande Rue. Closed mid-Nov to Jan, no restaurant. ④.

Hôtel Le Croiseur, 2 place de la Poissonerie (☎99.40.80.40). Clean and relatively modern place, near the Grande Porte. Open all year, no restaurant. ③.

Hôtel du Louvre, 2 rue des Marins (☎99.40.86.62). Pleasant family-run place just off Grande Rue, between the Grande Porte and Cathédrale St-Vincent. Closed mid-Nov to mid-Feb, except Xmas and New Year. ③.

Hôtel-Restaurant Pomme d'Or, 4 place du Poids-du-Roi (☎99.40.90.24). Modernized rooms in a venerable building, just inside the *citadelle* near the ramparts – take a sharp left after entering through the Grande Porte. Conventional menus start around 80F. The *patronne* has an eccentric predilection for animals. ④.

Hôtel-Restaurant Porte St-Pierre, 2 place du Guet (☎99.40.91.27). Comfortable *logis de France*, peeping out to sea over the walls of the *citadelle*, near the small Porte St-Pierre and very handy for the plage de Bon Secours. Menus from 68F to 250F. ④.

Hôtel San Pedro, 1 rue Ste-Anne (☎99.56.82.15). Small refurbished hotel in a nice quiet setting, just inside the walls in the north of the *citadelle*, near the porte des Bés. Rooms on the higher floors enjoy sea views. ④.

Hôtel-Restaurant L'Univers, 10 place Chateaubriand (☎99.40.89.52). One of the grand hotels that face you immediately upon entering the porte St-Vincent. Some good-value rooms, and an excellent 68F menu in the restaurant downstairs, with tables out on the square opposite the château. ④–⑦.

Hotels outside the walls

If cheaper rates are a high priority, a number of lower priced places can be found near the gare SNCF, or in suburban Paramé, but it has to be said that there's not all that much pleasure in staying outside the *citadelle* for the sake of saving a few francs.

Hôtel Arrivée, 52 bd de la République (☎99.56.30.78). Budget hotel on a corner very near the gare SNCF. Open all year, no restaurant. ②.

Hôtel les Charmettes, 64 bd Hébert, Paramé (☎99.56.07.31). One of Paramé's cheaper options, not on the front itself, though a few rooms have sea views, but very near the beach and the imposing *Grand Hôtel*. Closed Jan, no restaurant. ②.

Hôtel de l'Europe, 44 bd de la République (☎99.56.13.42). Year-round cheap rooms in a genuinely friendly hotel, near the gare SNCF. ②.

Hôtel Neptune, 21 rue de l'Industrie (☎99.56.82.15). Cheap rooms – especially good value for groups of three or four – outside the walls, near the gare SNCF. No restaurant, but a bar downstairs. ②.

Hôtel-Restaurant Terminus, 8 bd des Talards (☎99.56.14.38). Reasonable hotel near the station (not to be confused with the other *Hôtel Terminus*, in distant Rothéneuf), with an inexpensive restaurant where menus start at 48F. Open all year. ③.

Hostels

Paramé is also the site of a **youth hostel** – one of the busiest in France, although not formally part of the national network – in the *Centre des Rencontres International*, 37 rue du Père-Umbricht (☎99.40.29.80; 67–78F). This is 2km north-east of the gare SNCF, on Paramé's main street, a short way back from the beach on bus routes #1, #2 or #5. It does not operate a curfew. There's another, cheaper, IYHF hostel just to the south, in the *Maison de l'Hermitage* at 13 rue des Écoles (☎99.56.22.00), half an hour on foot from the station or on bus routes #2 and #4.

Camping

St-Malo's four municipal **campsites** also tend to be full in July and August, and you may have to travel inland to find space; there are several private sites in the locality. If in difficulties, you could try ringing the Camping Department of the Mairie (☎99.40.71.11) for the up-to-date position.

La Cité d'Aleth, St-Servan (☎99.81.60.91). Much the nearest campsite to the *citadelle*, on the headland southwest of St-Malo. Open all year. Reachable in summer on bus #1.

Les Îlôts, av de la Guimorais, Rothéneuf (☎99.56.98.72). June–Sept only. Inland, to the northeast.

Le Nicet, av de la Varde, Rothéneuf (☎99.40.26.32). Easter–Sept only. On the coast by Pointe de Nicet. Reservations essential.

Les Nielles, av John Kennedy, Paramé (☎99.40.26.35). Mid-June to mid-Sept only. On the beach at the plage du Minhic.

Eating

Intra-muros St-Malo boasts even more **restaurants** than hotels, with a long crescent lining the inside of the ramparts between the porte St-Vincent and the Grande Porte. Prices are probably higher than anywhere else in Brittany, however, especially on the open café terraces – the demand is inflated by the numbers of day-trippers, from as far afield as the Channel Islands, and ferry-passengers having last-night blow-outs. Bear in mind that most of the *crêperies* also serve *moules* and similar quasi-snacks. If you just fancy an **ice cream**, call in at *Sanchez Glacier*, 9 rue de la Vieille-Boucherie.

All the restaurants listed below are in the *citadelle*.

Astrolabe, 8 rue des Cordiers (☎99.40.36.82). Quality cuisine, near the Grande Porte. Lunches for 75F, otherwise the cheapest menu is 105F, featuring *soupe de moules* and duck in honey. Serves until late, open all year, but closed all day Mon & Tues lunchtime.

Borgnefesse, 10 rue du Puits aux Braies (☎99.40.05.05). Feels more like the tavern it once was, or a pub, than a restaurant. Heavily pirate-themed dining room with good solid French cooking. 59F lunch with steak, otherwise 95F. Closed Sat lunch & Sun all day.

Brick, 5 rue Jacques-Cartier (☎99.40.18.88). One of the best of the many options here, near the Grande Porte; still maintains its tradition of good-value seafood. Menus from 89F, which feature mussels, stuffed "queen" scallops and ray with capers. Serves until late, open all year but closed Wed.

Le Chalut, 8 rue de la Corne du Cerf (☎99.56.71.58). Quite an exclusive address, a short way in from the porte St-Vincent. A small 90F menu offers the catch of the day, otherwise you pay 175F or 300F for gourmet fish dinners. Reservations preferred, closed Sun pm & Mon.

Le Chasse Marée, 4 rue Groult St-Georges (☎99.40.85.10). Nautical decor and haute cuisine, just round the corner from the post office, with a few tables out on the quiet street. The 82F menu, served until 9pm, has oysters followed by red mullet or squid; the 135F features a scallop and duck salad to start, and a mixed fish grill or fish couscous; on the 185F menu you get half a lobster.

Crêperie Chez Chantal, 2 place aux Herbes (☎99.40.93.97). Sweet and savoury pancakes at very reasonable prices – the seafood fillings are exceptional. Daily noon–11pm.

Delauney, 6 rue Ste-Barbe (☎99.40.92.46). Between Porte St-Vincent and Cathédrale St-Vincent. Formerly owned by Jean-Paul Delauney, it has changed hands (albeit within the family) to Brigette and Didier Delauney, but the traditional French cooking remains to the same high standard. Open all year, closed Sun pm & Mon. Menus from 115F.

Duchesse Anne, 5–7 place Guy-la-Chambre (☎99.40.85.33). Right next to the Porte St-Vincent. The best known of St-Malo's upmarket restaurants, which continues to work hard to keep up its reputation – and its prices. Lunch can cost 80F, but the evening menus *start* at 220F. Closed Wed.

Le St-Laurent, 7 place de la Poissonerie (☎99.40.38.38). Brasserie-cum-*crêperie* with seating on a pleasant little square a little way in from the ramparts. Of most interest as a self-proclaimed *moulerie*, with mussels cooked in all sorts of sauces – their much-vaunted secret ingredient tastes pretty much like garlic, but there's no harm in that – from around 45F. The ideal place for a lunchtime *moules-frites*.

Shopping

For last-minute **shopping** in St-Malo before you catch the ferry home, the *citadelle* contains a few specialists. *Au Poids du Roy*, for example, in the place du Poids-du-Roi, is a superb, if somewhat upmarket, *épicerie*. However, buying in any quantity is best done in *Le Continent* **hypermarket** on the southwest outskirts of the town (follow the signs to the barrage de la Rance if you're driving; thanks to the one-way systems, it's a circuitous route but you do get there).

There are **markets** in both St-Malo (*intra-muros*) and St-Servan on Tuesdays and Fridays, and in Paramé on Wednesdays and Saturdays.

Dinard

The former fishing village of **DINARD** sprawls around the western approaches to the Rance estuary, just across from St-Malo but a good twenty minutes' drive away. It's a town that might not feel out of place on the Côte d'Azur, with its Casino, spacious shaded villas and social calendar of regattas and ballet. Here in Brittany, it's a little incongruous, though pleasant enough – and quite amusing in its uncanny resemblance to an enlarged mini-golf course.

Its nineteenth-century metamorphosis was largely thanks to the tastes of affluent English and Americans, though these days age rather than nationality seems to be the common factor uniting most of its summer influx of tourists. Although Dinard is a hilly town, undulating over a succession of pretty little coastal inlets, it attracts great numbers of older visitors; as a result, prices tend to be high, and pleasures sedate (literally so, with benches scattered in abundance where weary legs can rest while their indefatigable owners admire the views).

Arrival and Information

Full information on Dinard's hotels, restaurants, local tours and transport facilities can be picked up from the **SI**, right in the centre at 2 bd Féart (Mon–Sat 9am–noon & 2–6pm; ☎99.46.94.12).

Many visitors, however, simply come over for the day on one of the regular *Émeraude Lines* **boats** from St-Malo; tickets can be bought in Dinard a couple of hundred metres east of the SI at 27 av George-V, directly above the pleasure port where the ferries actually come in (April–mid-Nov only; ☎99.46.10.45; 20F one-way, 30F round-trip, plus 15F for bicycles). If the ten-minute crossing only serves to whet your appetite, you can also take a trip down the Rance to Dinan.

Local **buses** run regularly between Dinard and St-Malo, across the dam, while long-distance buses go from the old gare SNCF and *Le Gallic* stop (near the SI) to Dinan and Rennes (run by both *TIV*, ☎99.40.82.67 and *TAE*, ☎99.50.64.17), as well as to St-Jacut, Cancale, Dol and Mont-St-Michel (*TIV* only, in summer). Dinan buses are also operated by *CAT* (☎96.39.21.05). The day trips to Mont-St-Michel from St-Malo mentioned on p.171, and run by *Les Courriers Bretons* (☎99.56.79.09) start out from Dinard (summer daily 8.50am, Wed & Sat only in low season; 100F).

Cycles are available for rental from *Cycles Duval*, 53 rue Gardiner (closed Oct; ☎99.46.19.63).

The town

Central Dinard faces north to the open sea, across the curving bay that holds the attractive **plage de l'Écluse**. As so often in Breton resorts, the buildings that line the waterfront are, with the exception of the Casino in the middle, venerable Victorian villas rather than hotels or shops, and so the beach itself has a relatively low-key atmosphere, despite the summer crowds. An unexpected statue of Alfred Hitchcock dominates its main access point; standing on a giant egg, with a ferocious-looking bird perched on each shoulder, he was placed here to commemorate the town's annual festival of English-language films.

Enjoyable **coastal footpaths** lead off in either direction from the principal beach, enlivened by noticeboards holding reproductions of various paintings produced at points along the way. It may well come as a surprise to see that Pablo Picasso's *Deux Femmes Courants sur la Plage* and *Baigneuses sur la Plage*, both of which look quintessentially Mediterranean with their blue skies and golden sands, were in fact painted here in Dinard, during his annual summer visits throughout the 1920s. The path that heads east leads up to the Pointe du Moulinet for views over to St-Malo, and then as the **Promenade du Clair du Lune** continues past the tiny and now-exclusive port, and down to the estuary beach, the plage du Prieuré. Between mid-June and mid-September, it is floodlit each evening. Setting off west, on the other hand, takes you around more rocky outcrops to the secluded strand at neighbouring St-Enogat.

The Barrage de la Rance

The road from St-Malo to Dinard crosses the Rance along the top of the world's first **tidal power dam**. Built in 1966, the Barrage de la Rance alas failed to set a non-nuclear example to the rest of the province, where less than a hundred years ago there were 5000 working windmills. You can see how the whole thing works in a half-hour visit (daily 8am–8pm) from the entrance on the west bank, just downstream from the lock. If you come here on foot or bicycle from St-Malo, try to make your way on the small roads through St-Servan, following the line of the estuary southwards rather than the signposted (circuitous) inland route used by motorists.

Accommodation and Eating

On the whole, Dinard is an expensive place to stay, but it does at least have a wide selection of **hotels** to choose from. If you're looking for a cheaper bed, it also has some unofficial **youth hostels**, of which the best is the *Centre International du Port Blanc*, over a kilometre west of the centre on rue du Sergent-Boulanger near the plage du Port Blanc (April–Oct; ☎99.46.10.32).

Campsites include the "municipal" *Port Blanc*, also near the plage du Port-Blanc on rue de Sergent-Boulanger (April–Oct; ☎99.46.10.74), and *La Ville Mauny* (April to mid-Oct; ☎99.46.94.73), in the woods southwest of the centre.

All the hotels listed below have reasonable **restaurants**. Good alternatives in town include the busy *Brasserie Le Cancaven*, whose outdoor tables take up most of place de la République (☎99.46.15.45); their 58F menu is not all that interesting, but for 104F they offer a real cornucopia of fish and shellfish, from spider crab to squid.

Hôtel-Restaurant Altair, 18 bd Féart (☎99.46.13.58). Central and very English option, a little way inland from the SI. The cheapest menu, at 88F, offers the inevitable *moules marinières* or *soupe de poissons*. Closed mid-Nov to mid-Dec. ④.

Hôtel-Restaurant des Dunes, 5 av Georges-Clémenceau (☎99.46.12.72). Grand old hotel in the finest Dinard tradition, halfway between the port and the main beach, and very handy for either. Meals in the elegant dining room start at 95F. Closed mid-Nov to mid-March. ⑤.

Hôtel-Restaurant du Parc, 20 av Edouard-VII (☎99.46.11.39). Friendly little hotel on a busy street a short way west of the place de la République. Simple restaurant offering menus from 60F. Open all year. ②.

Hôtel-Restaurant Printania, 5 av George-V (☎99.46.43.07). Good-value place around 250m east of the centre, on a relatively quiet seafront street near the Port de Plaisance. Menus in the magnificent terrace restaurant, looking over to St-Malo, start at 90F, featuring stuffed clams and grilled salmon. Closed first two weeks in Nov. ③–⑥.

Hôtel-Restaurant de la Vallée, 6 av George-V (☎99.46.13.58). Attractive *logis de France*, right down at sea level in the pleasure port, but unfortunately facing the wrong way for views of St-Malo. The most basic rooms look straight onto a bare cliff face, but basically this is a nice spot. Menus from 95F, feature grilled sardines and skate. Closed mid-Nov to mid-Dec. ②–⑤.

Dinan

The wonderful citadel of **DINAN** has preserved almost intact its three-kilometre encirclement of protective masonry, along with street upon colourful street of late medieval houses. However, for all its slightly unreal perfection (it would make the ideal film set for *The Three Musketeers*), it's seldom excessively overrun with tourists. There are no very vital museums; the most memorable architecture is vernacular rather than monumental, and time is most easily spent wandering from *crêperie* to café, admiring the overhanging half-timbered houses along the way.

Arrival and Information

Dinan's **SI** is very central, almost opposite the Tour de l'Horloge, in the sixteenth-century Hôtel Kératry at 6 rue de l'Horloge (May–Sept Mon–Sat 9am–7pm, Sun 10am–1pm & 2–7pm; Oct–April Mon–Sat 8.30am–12.30pm & 2–5.45pm; ☎96.39.75.40), where the ground floor is built of stone with pillars, the first floor is lath and plaster, and the extensive garden is complete with a weeping willow. The **post office** is on place Duclos (☎96.39.25.07).

Both the Art Deco **gare SNCF** (☎96.39.22.39) and the **gare routière** (☎96.39.21.05) are in Dinan's modern quarter (a rather gloomy exile from the *enclos*), on place du 11-Novembre, ten minutes' walk west of the main (Grande Rue) entrance of the walled town. *Armor Express* **buses** (☎99.50.64.17) go direct to Dinard and to Rennes, which saves changing trains at Dol.

In summer, **boats** sail from the port downstream to Dinard and St-Malo, taking anything from three and a quarter to five and a half hours, depending on the state of the tides; for details, contact *Émeraude Lines* in Dinard (☎99.46.10.45) or St-Malo (☎99.40.48.40), or the *Agence Boutin* at 7 Grande Rue in Dinan (☎96.39.12.32). To complete a day trip, you can catch a scheduled bus or train back to Dinan.

The town

Like St-Malo, Dinan is best seen when arriving by boat up the Rance. By the time the ferries get to the port du Dinan, down below the thirteenth-century ramparts, the river has narrowed sufficiently to be spanned by a small but majestic old stone bridge. The steep cobbled **rue du Petit-Fort** leads up from the artisans' shops and restaurants along the quay, climbing, with fields and bramble thickets to either side, past ancient flower-festooned edifices and even a half-timbered poodle parlour, to enter the city through the **porte de Jerzual**.

Above that imposing gateway, **St-Sauveur** church sends the skyline even higher. It's a real hotchpotch, with a Romanesque porch and an eighteenth-century steeple. Even its nine Gothic chapels feature five different patterns of vaulting in no symmetrical order; the most complex pair, in the centre, would make any spider proud. A cenotaph contains the heart of Bertrand du Guesclin, the fourteenth-century Breton warrior (and later Constable of France) who

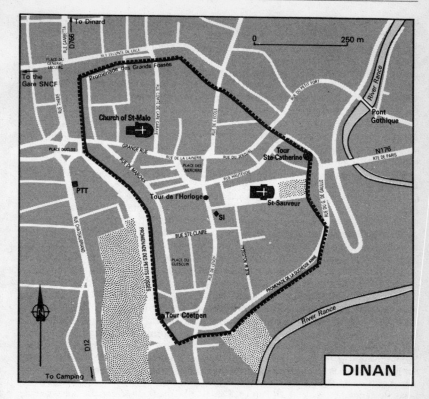

fought and won a single combat with the English knight Thomas of Canterbury, in what is now place du Guesclin to settle the outcome of the siege of Dinan in 1364. Relics of his life and battles are scattered all over Brittany and Normandy; in death, he spread himself between four separate burial places for four different parts of his body (the French kings restricted themselves to three burial sites).

At the heart of town, two small squares, the **place des Merciers** and the **place des Cordeliers**, hold the finest assortment of medieval wood-framed houses, painted in all sorts of lively hues, and with their upper storeys perching precariously on splintering wooden pillars that appear to buckle beneath the weight.

Unfortunately, you can only walk along one small stretch of the **ramparts**, from the Jardin Anglais behind St-Sauveur church to a point just short of Tour Sillon overlooking the river. You can however get a good general overview from the wooden balcony of the central **Tour de l'Horloge**, which dates from the end of the fifteenth century (April–Sept, daily 10am–7pm; 13F). The original mechanism of the clock here was made in Nantes and put in place in 1498; in 1507, the ubiquitous Duchesse Anne presented the monumental bell. A small and not at all interesting shopping mall has recently been created around the foot of the belfry's stout stone walls.

The fourteenth-century keep which once protected the town's southern approach now houses a small local history museum. Together with the ancient **Tour Coëtgen**, this is known as the Château de Duchesse Anne (June to mid-Oct daily 10am–6.30pm mid-Oct to May daily except Tues 1.30–5.30pm; 20F). On the lower floor of the Tour Coëtgen a group of stone fifteenth-century notables looks for all the world like a medieval time capsule, about to de-petrify at any moment.

During the first weekend in September (the date varies – check with the SI) the **Fête des Remparts** is celebrated with medieval-style jousting, banquets, fairs and processions, culminating in an immense fireworks display. There's a **market** every Thursday in the adjoining places du Champ and du Guesclin, which constituted the original fairground but are now for most of the week just a large open-air car park.

Accommodation

Unless you're prepared to pay upwards of 400F for a room, Dinan doesn't really have any of the welcoming good-value hotel-restaurants that characterize so many Breton towns. It's also not a very nice place to try to drive around, or to find a parking space in summer, so motorists might do best to visit only as a day trip. If you're on foot, and don't mind climbing steep hills with heavy bags, there are however plenty of budget options around the old town.

In addition, there is also an attractive year-round **youth hostel**, set amid green fields and trees far below the walls in the Moulin de Méen, Vallée de la Fontaine-des-Eaux (☎96.39.10.83; 46F), two kilometres from the gare SNCF. Unfortunately it's not on any bus route; to walk there, follow the quay downstream from the port on the town side, and after a few hundred metres you'll see a small sign to the left. From there it's another 500 metres. The **Camping Municipal** is at 103 rue Chateaubriand (March–Nov; ☎96.39.11.96), just outside the western ramparts.

Hôtel-Restaurant Duchesse Anne, 10 place du Guesclin (☎96.39.09.43). Comfortable if not luxurious rooms on the quieter side of the square, above a basic restaurant where set menus start at 60F. ③.

Logis de Jerzual, 25 rue du Petit Fort (☎96.39.09.43). *Chambres d'hôte* on the exquisite little lane that leads up from the port, halfway up to the porte du Jerzual. Garden terrace looking down on the street. Inaccessible by car, so deathly quiet in the mornings. ③.

Hôtel-Restaurant le Marguerite, 29 place du Guesclin (☎96.85.23.88). Comfortable and spacious, if not desperately modern or atmospheric, rooms on the busy side of the main square. Conventional restaurant with menus from 85F. Closed mid-Nov to Jan. ④.

Hôtel de l'Océan, 9 place du 11-Novembre (☎96.39.21.51). Extremely convenient and well-run hotel, outside the walls opposite the gare SNCF. No restaurant. ①.

Hôtel le Papillon, 27 rue du Quai, port du Dinan (☎96.39.93.76). Simple hotel in romantic location, right on the waterfront down in the port. A long climb up to town for a bit of night-life, but a lovely place to wake up. No restaurant. March–Nov only. ④.

Hôtel Porte St-Malo, 35 rue St-Malo (☎96.39.19.76). Very comfortable rooms in a tasteful small hotel just outside the walls, beyond Porte St-Malo. No restaurant. ②.

Hôtel du Théâtre, 2 rue Ste-Claire (☎96.39.06.91). Very simple rooms above a bar, right by the SI and Théâtre des Jacobins, and under the same efficient management as the nearby *Restaurant Cantorbery* (see below). ②.

Eating and Drinking

All sorts of specialist **restaurants**, including several ethnic alternatives, are tucked away in the old streets of Dinan. Stroll of an evening through the town and down to the port, and you'll pass at least twenty places to choose from.

Once you've eaten, the area to head for **bars** is the series of tiny parallel alley-ways between the place des Merciers and the rue de la Ferronerie. Along rue de la Cordonnerie, the busiest of the lot, the various hang-outs define themselves by their taste in music; *A la Truye qui File* at no. 14 is a sort of contemporary folky Breton dive, while *Morgan's Tavern*, next door at no. 12, is considerably more raucous.

Cantorbery, 6 rue Ste-Claire (☎96.39.02.52). Reasonable food served in an old stone house, with rafters, a spiral staircase and a real wood fire. Open every day in season. Traditional menus from 65F.

Chez Flochon, 24 rue du Jerzual (☎96.87.91.57). Fine old carved house on the lane up from the port, with a few tables perched on a wooden platform outside so you can watch the world stagger by. Fondues, galettes and crêpes. Closed Sun pm, & Mon in low season.

Crêperie Connetable, 1 rue de l'Apport (☎96.39.02.52). Magnificent old house opposite the *Mère Pourcel* beside the place des Merciers. Sit if you dare at the pavement tables, where all that prevents the upper storeys from crashing down around your ears are a couple of misshapen pillars. Crêpes and snacks in the perfect spot for people-watching.

Mère Pourcel, 3 place des Merciers (☎96.39.03.80). Beautiful half-timbered fifteenth-century house in the central square. Closed Jan, Feb, and Sun pm and Mon out of season. The cheapest menu, at 92F, is pretty minimal, but you're up to gourmet class with the crab and exquisitely simple fish on the 155F one.

Le Relais des Corsaires, 7 rue du Quai, port du Dinan (☎96.39.40.17). Just across the road from the waterfront. Restaurant menu from 115F, offering cockles and mussels followed by scallops or monkfish. The *Grill* menu, in theory served in the adjacent *Petit Corsaire* but in low season served in the same building, costs 69F and is "grill" in name only.

Le Saigon, 12 rue Ste-Claire (☎96.85.21.20). Small, friendly Chinese and Vietnamese place near the *Hôtel du Théâtre* (see above). Open every day of the year. Menus start at 55F.

Les Terrasses, 2 rue du Quai, port du Dinan (☎96.39.09.60). Lovely waterfront setting, with good menus from 95F. Closed Tues out of season.

Around Mont-St-Michel Bay

The **coastal road** D201 runs east from St-Malo to Cancale, past a succession of coves and beaches, where lines of dunes attempt to hang on against the battering from the sea. Look out for the **sculpted rocks** at Rothéneuf, shaped in the 1870s by the hermit priest Abbé Fouré into the forms of sea monsters. At the Pointe du Grouin, the line of cliffs turns sharply back on itself, at one extremity of the **Baie de Mont-St-Michel**. This is a huge flat expanse of mud and sand, over which the tide – as just about every piece of literature on this region will tell you – can race faster than a galloping horse. It is dangerous to wander out too far, quite apart from the risk of quicksands, and, in the Breton part of the bay at least, the beaches have little appeal for bathers.

The course of the **River Couesnon**, which marks the border between Brittany and Normandy, has shifted repeatedly over the centuries. So too has the shore-line of the bay – in which traces of long-drowned villages can be seen when the tide is out. Bretons like to say that it is just an accident that the river now runs west of Mont-St-Michel; be that as it may, the Mont and Pontorson, the nearest town to it, are both in Normandy (see p.128). The pinnacle of *La Merveille*, however, remains clearly visible from every vantage point along the coast. The most spectacular views of all are from the **Pointe du Grouin**, a perilous and windy height which also overlooks the bird sanctuary of the **Îles des Landes**, to the east.

Cancale

Just south of the **Pointe du Grouin**, and less than 15km from St-Malo across the peninsula, **CANCALE** is not so much a one-horse as a one-mollusc town – the whole place is obsessed with the oyster, and with *"ostréiculture"*. Its current population is, at 4600, less than it was a century ago, but the town looks much bigger than that would suggest – and the reason must be the visitors attracted by its edible hinged bivalves.

Oysters may have been a staple, cheap working-class food in the past; these days in Cancale they are clasped to the bosoms and slurped by the lips of elegant *bourgeois* holiday-makers. In the old church of **St-Méen**, at the top of the hill, a small **Musée des Arts et Traditions Populaires** documents this obsession with meticulous precision (July–Aug Mon 2.30–6.30pm, Tues–Sun 10am–noon & 2.30–6.30pm; June & Sept Fri–Sun 2.30–6.30pm, and groups by appointment; closed Oct–May; ☎99.89.79.32; 15F). Cancale oysters have been found in the camps of Julius Caesar; were taken daily to Versailles for Louis XIV; and even accompanied Napoléon on the march to Moscow. The most famous symbol of the town – and its oyster cultivation – is the stark Rocher du Cancale just offshore; the museum lists all the *Rochers du Cancale* restaurants that have ever existed, including ones in Shanghai and Phnom Penh, and one in Moscow which closed in the 1830s.

From the rue des Parcs, next to the jetty of the port, you can see at low tide the **parcs** where the oysters are grown. At one time there was an annual event, *La Caravanne*, when a huge flotilla of sailing vessels dragged nets along the bottom of the sea for wild oysters; now they are farmed like any other crop. The seabed is divided into countless segments of different sizes, each segment having an individual owner who has the right to sell what it produces. The oysters are cultivated from year-old "spat" bought in from elsewhere. Behind, the rocks of the cliff are streaked and shiny like mother-of-pearl; underfoot the beach is littered with countless generations of empty shells.

Practicalities

Cancale's **SI** is at the top of the hill, at 44 rue du Port (☎99.93.00.13). The port area down below is very pretty and very smart, with a long line of upmarket glass-fronted hotels and restaurants. Cancale's **hotels** mostly insist that you eat if you want to stay – no great problem considering that there's nothing much else to do in the town. *Le Phare* (☎99.89.60.24; ④) and the *Émeraude* (☎99.89.61.76; F④) on quai Thomas, both of which are set above their own restaurants, and *La Houle*, 18 quai Gambetta (☎99.89.62.38; ④), are among the best value.

There's no great reason to recommend any one **restaurant** above the rest; all without exception serve enticing seafood spreads, and which of the twenty or so adjacent options you choose will depend on your mood and your particular favourite dish. If you're looking for scallops, *Le Phare* prepares a superb scallop kebab on its 135F menu; as a rule, **oysters** here are no less expensive than on a Paris boulevard, but the daytime-only *Au Pied de Cheval*, 10 quai Gambetta, is an informal place to sample a few, with great baskets of them spread across its wooden quayside tables.

Cancale has a **market** on Sunday in the streets behind the main church, the rue de la Marine and the rue Cocar.

Dol

During the Middle Ages, **DOL-DE-BRETAGNE**, thirty kilometres west of Mont-St-Michel, was an important bishopric. It no longer has a bishop, though its fortified thirteenth-century **Cathédrale Saint-Samson** endures, with its strange, squat, tiled towers and ornate porches. Alongside is the **Musée Historique de Dol** (daily Easter–Sept 9.30am–6pm; Oct 2.30–6.30pm), bloated by the usual array of posed waxworks but with two rooms of astonishing wooden bits and pieces rescued in assorted states of decay from churches, often equally rotting, all over Brittany. These carvings and statues, some still brightly polychromed with their crust of eggy paint, range from the thirteenth to the nineteenth centuries.

Dol still has a few streets packed with venerable buildings, most notably the pretty **Grande-Rue**, where one Romanesque edifice dates back as far as the eleventh century, an assortment of five-hundred-year-old half-timbered houses look down on the bustle of shoppers below, and a launderette claims to have been visited by Victor Hugo in 1836.

Mont Dol

All approaches to Dol from the bay are watched over by the former island of **Mont Dol** – now eight rather marshy kilometres in from the sea. This abrupt granite outcrop, looking mountainous beyond its size on such a flat plain, was the legendary site of a battle between the Archangel Michael and the Devil. Various fancifully-named indentations in the rock, such as *"the Devil's Claw"*, testify to the savagery of their encounter, which was inevitably won by the saint. The site has been occupied since prehistoric times – flint implements have been unearthed alongside the bones of mammoths, sabre-toothed tigers and even rhinoceroses. Later on, it appears to have been used for worship by the druids, before becoming, like Mont-St-Michel, an island monastery.

Traces of the abbey have long vanished, though the mythic battle may recall its foundation, with Christianity driving out the old religion. A plaque proclaims that visiting the small chapel on top earns a Papal Indulgence (presumably on the condition that you don't add to the copious graffiti on its walls). The climb is pleasant, too, a steep footpath winding up among the chestnuts and beeches to a solitary bar.

If you fancy an extended walk, Dol, and Mont Dol, are in fact located on the long-distance **GR34** trail, which leads east to Mont-St-Michel (reckoned as an eight-hour stroll), and west along the coast way beyond St-Malo.

The Menhir du Champ-Dolent

A short way out of Dol to the south, a small picnic area fenced off among the fields contains the **Menhir du Champ Dolent**. According to one legend, this 9.6m standing stone dropped from the sky to separate two brothers who were on the point of mutual fratricide. Another has it that the menhir is inching its way into the soil, and the world will end when it disappears altogether. It has to be said that this would not be a particularly interesting spot on which to experience the end of the world. The unadorned stone, big though it undoubtedly is in its banal setting, has little of the romance or mystery of the megalithic sites of the Morbihan and elsewhere.

Practicalities

There is not a great deal to keep casual visitors in Dol for very long. However, the SI, at 3 Grande-Rue (☎99.48.15.37), can direct you eastwards to a very reasonable hotel, the *Bretagne*, next to the market at 17 place Chateaubriand (☎99.48.02.03; closed Oct; ②–④). Rooms at the back look out across a small vestige of ramparts towards Mont Dol. Among good campsites nearby are the *Vieux Chêne* (May–Sept; ☎99.48.09.55), 5km west towards Baguer-Pican on RN176, and the phenomenally luxurious *Castel-Camping des Ormes* (May to mid-Sept; ☎99.73.49.59), set around a lake in the grounds of a château 6km south towards Combourg on the N795, which arranges horse-riding for its guests.

A couple of nice fish restaurants can be found in the ancient houses on rue Ceinte, as it winds its way from Grande-Rue to the Cathedral: *Le Porche au Pain* at no. 1, and *La Grabotais* at no. 4 (closed Mon; ☎99.48.19.89). After you eat, the *Katédral* bar, between the church and museum (☎99.48.05.40), is worth a brief pause.

The Forêt de Ville-Cartier

The *Circuit Touristique* signposted from Dol continues beyond the menhir and the village of Trans to the Forêt de Ville-Cartier. The pines and beech of the forest sweep thickly down to a lake in which it is possible – in fact almost irresistible – to swim. Keeping to the *circuit*, along the D155, would lead eventually to Fougères (see p.190).

Combourg

As well as being a pleasant little town in its own right, COMBOURG, 17km south of Dol and 24km southeast of Dinan, has two chief attractions. The first is a château, perched on a hill and dominating magnificent landscaped gardens, which was the childhood home of the writer Chateaubriand, now buried at St-Malo (see p.172). The Tour du Chat of the castle may be haunted, by a ghost taking the form of a cat. Chateaubriand himself claimed it was haunted by the ghost of the wooden leg of a former lord – and that the cat was merely an acquaintance of this phantasmal limb. The entrance to the château is not where you expect it to be; turn right at the end of Combourg's main square, instead of continuing straight towards the keep, and it's a short way up on the left (April–Sept daily except Tues, château 2–5.30pm, gardens 9am–noon & 2–6pm; Oct daily except Tues, château 2–4.30pm, gardens 9am–noon & 2–4.30pm; March & Nov by appointment ☎99.73.22.95; 25F).

Down below both château and town, the tranquil cypress-lined lake is, if anything, more appealing than the château itself. Misty and quiet early in the morning, busy only with anglers, it provides a welcome opportunity for leisurely countryside walks, perhaps after a night of indulgence.

Practicalities

Two superb if somewhat expensive (and not very imaginatively named) hotels square off against each other across place Chateaubriand, which squeezes in between château and lake. While the *Hôtel du Château* at no. 1 (☎99.73.00.38; ④) is beyond reproach, the *Hôtel du Lac* at no. 2 (☎99.73.05.65; ④) just has the edge, with lake views from most of the rooms and a 98F menu offering a *cassoulet* of mussels with wild mushrooms, followed by duck with grapes.

Beside the Canal: Hédé and Tinténiac

The main road **south to Rennes**, the N137, crosses a particularly pleasant stretch of the **Canal d'Ille-et-Vilaine**, between the two old towns of **HÉDÉ** and **TINTÉNIAC**. There are excellent places to collapse in the sun between the many locks and lock-keepers' cottages, although the towpath isn't consistent enough to follow for any distance on foot, let alone bike.

Both Hédé, with the *Hostellerie du Vieux Moulin* (☎99.45.45.70; closed Sun pm, Mon & Jan; ④), and Tinténiac, with the *Auberge du Halage* (☎99.68.03.64; ③), have excellent *logis*. St-Aubin d'Aubigné and St-Aubin du Cormier (see p.192) are other possible bases. The **Forêt du Paimpont** (see p.267), too, is well within reach and allows you to bypass Rennes.

Rennes

For a city that has been the capital and power centre of Brittany since the 1532 union with France, Rennes is – outwardly at least – uncharacteristic of the province, with its neoclassical layout and pompous major buildings. What potential it had to be a picturesque tourist spot was destroyed in 1720, when a drunken carpenter managed to set light to virtually the whole city. Only the area known as **Les Lices**, at the junction of the canalized Ille and the river Vilaine, was undamaged. The remodelling of the rest of the city was handed over to Parisian architects, not in deference to the capital but in an attempt to rival it.

It was the successful siege of Rennes by Charles VIII in 1491 that obliged Duchesse Anne to marry him, and led to the union of Brittany and France, which was sealed in 1532 in the Cohue in Vannes (see p.303). From 1561, the Breton parliament met in Rennes and helped to preserve a measure of autonomy for Brittany in the face of growing centralization. To "celebrate" four centuries of the union in 1932, Breton separatists blew up a statue outside the Hôtel de Ville which showed Brittany swearing allegiance to Louis XV. At the same time, an unsuccessful attempt was made to blow up the Cohue in Vannes, while as recently as 1994 separatists staged an arson attack on the parliament buildings here in Rennes.

Arrival and Information

Rennes' **SI** is in the very heart of town, on the Pont de Nemours, where the river briefly disappears (Mon 2–6pm, Tues–Sat 9am–6pm; ☎99.79.01.98); there's also an information office in the gare SNCF further south (Mon–Fri 8am–7pm, Sat & Sun 10am–1pm & 3–6pm; ☎99.53.23.23).

There are **post offices** in the Palais du Commerce in the heart of town on the place de la République (Mon–Fri 8am–7pm, Sat 8am–noon; ☎99.79.50.71), and at 27 bd du Colombier, just west of the gare SNCF (same hours; ☎99.31.42.72).

Trains

The modern **gare SNCF** (☎99.65.50.50) is south of the Vilaine, around fifteen minutes' walk from the SI and considerably more from the medieval quarter. As well as direct TGV trains to and from Paris – which take only just over two hours – it also has connections east to Brest, north to Dol and south towards Nantes.

Buses

The **gare routière**, on bd Magenta (☎99.30.87.80), is a couple of blocks north of the gare SNCF, but most local buses start and finish on or near place de la République, alongside the SI. Rennes is a busy junction, with direct services to St-Malo (*TIV*; ☎99.79.23.44), Dinan and Dinard (*Armor Express*; ☎99.50.64.17), and Nantes (*Société Transports Tourisme de l'Ouest*; ☎40.20.45.20). *Les Courriers Bretons* (☎99.56.79.09) run day trips to **Mont-St-Michel**, timed to connect with the morning *TGV* from Paris (departing Rennes gare SNCF Mon–Fri 9.45am, Sat & Sun 10.50am; 108F return).

The city

Rennes' surviving **medieval quarter**, bordered by the canal to the west and the river to the south, radiates from the **Porte Mordelaise**, the old ceremonial entrance to the city, which, following building work in the last few years, is now more prominently exposed. This is the liveliest part of town and it stays up late, particularly in the area around St-Aubin church and along rue St-Michel and rue de Penhöet.

Today, the **place des Lices** is dominated by two empty market halls, but originally it was, as its name suggests, the venue for tournaments – that is, jousting "lists". It was here, in 1337, that the hitherto unknown Bertrand du Guesclin, then aged seventeen, fought and defeated several older opponents. This set him on his career as a soldier, during which he was later to save Rennes when it was under siege by the English. However, after the Bretons were defeated at Auray in 1364, he fought for the French and twice invaded Brittany. He may be a French hero but, for some Bretons, he is a knave and a traitor. In 1946, Breton separatists destroyed a memorial to him in the Thabor gardens.

The south bank of the river is every bit as busy, if not busier, than the north – should you feel upon arriving that Rennes feels oddly empty, the chances are that everyone's in the giant **Colombier Centre**, just west of the gare SNCF. This vast new mall is Rennes at its most modern, packed with shops of all kinds, plus cafés and snack bars, and featuring an amazing crystal model of itself in its main entrance hall. Slightly nearer the river, **rue Vasselot** has its own array of half-timbered old houses.

The Palais de Justice

The one central building to escape the 1720 fire was symbolically enough the **Palais de Justice** on rue Hoche downtown. It is possible to see round the building, where the Breton *parlement* – a mixture of high court and council with unelected members – fought battles with the French governor from the reign of Louis XIV up until the Revolution. Tours start from the far right-hand corner of the courtyard (daily except Tues 9.45am, 10.30am, 11.15am, 2.15pm, 3pm, 4pm & 4.45pm). Each of the seventeenth-century chambers is more opulently gilded and adorned than the one before, culminating in the debating hall hung with Gobelin tapestries depicting scenes from the history of the duchy and the province. Every centimetre of the walls and ceilings is decorated – the Sun King style, but on a relatively small scale.

Contrary to several official guides, the Palais de Justice was *not* the scene of the retrial of **Captain Alfred Dreyfus** in 1899. He had been wrongly convicted of treason in 1896 and it took three years (and Émile Zola's famous letter *J'accuse*) to

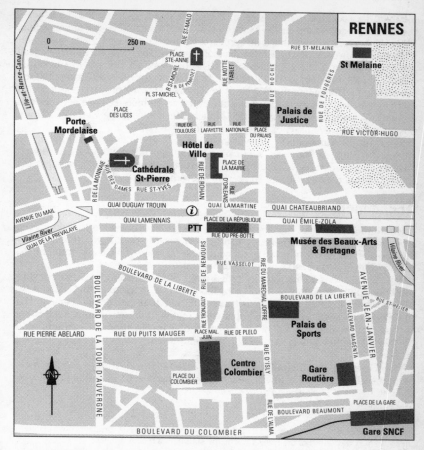

obtain a retrial. In fact, the retrial took place in what is now the **Lycée Emile Zola**, and is marked, on the corner of avenue Janvier and rue Toullier, with a modern steel statue, *La Dégradation de Dreyfus*, by Igael Tumurkin.

The Museums

The **Vilaine** flows through the centre of Rennes, narrowly confined into a steep-sided channel, and even forced underground at one point. Two major **museums** are housed in former university buildings at 20 quai Emile-Zola, on its south bank (both open daily except Tues 10am–noon & 2–6pm; 15F each). The **Musée de Bretagne** gives one of the best possible introductions to the history and culture of Brittany. The prehistoric section is good, and includes the bones of a woolly rhinoceros found at Dol, but the greatest strength of the museum is the audio-visual presentation of the transition from the last century to the present. The **Musée des Beaux Arts** owns some Leonardo drawings in addition to more local exhibits. Its specifically Breton room combines paintings of mythical themes – the Île d'Ys legend (see p.243) by Luminais – and of real life – a woman waiting for the fishermen to come back through stormy seas.

At the **Ecomusée de la Bintinais** (daily except Tues 2–7pm; 22F), south of the centre on the route Chatillon sur Seiche (reached on city bus #14 from the place de la République, getting off at the *Le Gacet* stop, or bus #61 from the gare routière to *La Bintinais*), the Ferme de la Bintinais is being preserved as a monument to the rural history of the area. State-of-the-art techniques have been used to recount the minutiae of five centuries of daily life, showing the vital role Rennes has played in the evolution of Breton agriculture.

The **Musée Automobile** (daily 9am–noon & 2–7pm; 25F), northeast of the city on the route de Fougères, holds over 80 vintage cars. If you don't have your own much-prized vehicle, take bus #3, direction St-Laurent, and get off at the Gayeulles roundabout – where you're still left with quite a walk.

Accommodation

It is an unfortunate fact that there are surprisingly few **hotels** in the old part of Rennes – and those that there are can be very hard to find. If you've arrived by train or bus, it's easier to settle for staying near the gares SNCF and routière. All Rennes' hotels seem to stay open all year round.

The city also has a year-round **youth hostel**, 3km out from the centre, next to the Canal d'Ille et Rance – the *Centre International de Séjour*, 10–12 Canal St-Martin (☎99.33.22.33). Charging between 65F and 105F per person per night, it has a cafeteria and a laundry, and operates a midnight curfew. You can get there on bus routes #20 and #22 from the gare SNCF, direction St-Gregoire, stop Coëtlogon; neither bus runs over the weekend, when you have to catch bus #2 instead.

The **Camping Municipal des Gayeulles** is at rue de Professeur-Maurice-Audin (April–Sept; ☎99.36.91.22), reached by taking bus #3, direction St-Laurent, and getting off at Parc des Bois.

Hotels

Hôtel d'Angleterre, 19 rue du Maréchal-Joffre (☎99.79.38.61). Not brilliant, but relatively cheap, a short way south of the river towards the station. No restaurant. ②.

Central Hôtel, 6 rue Lanjuinais (☎99.30.85.37). Probably the nicest of Rennes' more upmarket hotels, on a quiet little street just around the corner from the SI, less than 50 metres south of the river. No restaurant. ④.

Hôtel des Lices, 7 place des Lices (☎99.79.14.81). Forty rooms, all with TV, in a very comfortable and friendly modern hotel on the edge of the prettiest part of old Rennes. Very convenient for the *place des Lices* parking, and distinguished by a spectacularly garish fluorescent sign outside (depicting a penguin; they briefly called the hotel *Le Pengouin*, but the name didn't stick). No restaurant. ④.

Hôtel le Magenta, 35 bd Magenta (☎99.30.85.37). Roomy but slightly noisy accommodation opposite the gare routière. No restaurant. ②.

Hôtel le Maréchal-Joffre, 6 rue du Maréchal-Joffre (☎99.79.37.74). Small family-run place, south of the river on the way to the station. No restaurant. ①.

Hôtel Riaval, 9 rue de Riaval (99.50.65.58). Friendly hotel with neat budget rooms, well away from the centre, but only a few minutes walk east of the gare SNCF, on a quiet street. No restaurant. ①.

Hôtel-Restaurant Au Rocher de Cancale, 10 rue St-Michel (☎99.79.20.83). Five-room hotel on a lively pedestrian street, between place Ste-Anne and place St-Michel, in the heart of medieval Rennes and ideally positioned for the city's nightlife. Beautifully restored frontage and ground floor, but with modern facilities upstairs. The restaurant, which is closed at weekends, has menus from 58F at lunchtime and 85F in the evening; the 130F exclusively fish menu is excellent. ③.

Hôtel Tour d'Auvergne, 20 bd de la Tour-d'Auvergne (☎99.30.84.16). Rather rudimentary option, ten minutes' walk from the SI, between the gare SNCF and the river. No restaurant. ①.

Eating

Most of Rennes' more interesting **bars**, **restaurants** and nightlife in general are to be found in the streets just south of the place Sainte-Anne, towards the place des Lices. Rues St-Michel and Penhoët, each with a fine assemblage of ancient wooden buildings, are the epicentre at the moment. Interesting ethnic alternatives can be found along rue St-Malo just to the north – such as the African *Le Maquis* and the Tunisian *Byblos*, adjacent at no.13 – which has long been the more or less exclusive preserve of students but is now decaying fast. While you're exploring, take a look around the back of the excellent *crêperie* at 5 place Ste-Anne, through an archway off rue Motte-Fablet, to get an extraordinary glimpse of medieval high-rise housing (and there's also a bootleg CD shop tucked away round there).

Rue Vasselot is the nearest equivalent south of the river, though if you're just looking for a quick snack don't forget the various outlets in the Centre Colombier.

La Boutique Antillaise, 5 place du Bas-des-Lices (☎99.30.54.44). Midday menu 58F, or upwards of 98F in the evening. The Caribbean influence goes a little deeper than the colourful cocktails; you can also get chicken cooked in coconut or court-bouillion, and even kick off with a *boudin antillais*. A small, friendly restaurant – booking advisable.

La Chope, 3 rue de la Chalotais (☎99.79.34.54). A little way below place de la République on the south side of the river. Classic, busy brasserie open until midnight every day except Sunday, serving meals from 70F upwards.

Le Chouin, 12 rue d'Isly (☎99.30.87.86). A fine fish restaurant, not far from the gare SNCF. Menu 99F midday, *à la carte* in the evening. Closed Sun and Mon.

La Ganges, 34 place des Lices (☎99.30.18.37). Quality Indian restaurant with a vegetarian menu at 85F, and meat-based ones from 110F.

La Khalifa, 20 haut de la place des Lices (☎99.30.87.30). Assorted Moroccan dishes: couscous 54F and up, brochettes 63F and tajine 66F, as well as various set menus. Closed Sun in winter.

Le Locomotive, 12 place de la Gare (☎99.30.29.87). Cheap French food right by the station, open all week from 7am until 1am. Menus at 39F, 59F and 79F.

Le Louisiane, 7 place St-Michel (☎99.79.25.94). Cajun-styled place with lots of outdoor seating in the old town – but unfortunately there's nothing very Cajun about the food. Conventional menu from 70F weekday lunch, but from 90F evenings and weekends. Closed Sat lunchtime.

Le Parc à Moules, 8 rue George-Dattin (☎99.31.44.28). On a small street leading north from the river halfway between the SI and the place des Lices. Mussels from Mont-St-Michel Bay cooked in twelve different delicious ways for around 45F, and a weekday lunch menu offering *moules-frites* for 49F, plus various more expensive fishy dishes. Closed Sat lunch & Sun.

Ti-koz, 3 St-Guillaume (☎99.79.33.89). Classic French cooking in a beautiful sixteenth-century house north of the river. Lunches from 70F, dinner menus at 98F, 155F and 250F.

Entertainment and culture

Rennes is seen at its best in the first ten days of July, when the **Festival des Tombées de la Nuit** takes over the whole city to celebrate Breton culture with music, theatre, film, mime and poetry in joyful rejection of the influences of both Paris and Hollywood (advance information from 8 place du Maréchal-Juin, 35000 Rennes; ☎99.30.38.01).

In the second week of December, an annual rock festival, **Les Transmusicales**, attracts big-name acts from all over France and the world at large, though still with a Breton emphasis; over the last decade it has helped to make Rennes an important centre for French rock (information on ☎99.31.55.33).

The varied season of the *Théâtre National de Bretagne*, 1 rue St-Helier (☎99.30.88.88), runs from mid-October to mid-June. All year round, in a different auditorium on the same premises, *Club Ubu* (☎99.31.55.33) puts on large-scale gigs. There's regular live **jazz**, daily except Sundays, at *Déjazey Jazz Club*, 54 rue St-Malo (☎99.38.70.72). The *Barantic* on rue St-Michel is currently one of the city's favourite **bars**, putting on occasional live music for a mixed crowd of Breton nationalists and boisterous students.

The presence of so many students – 35,000 all told – gives Rennes a rather more visible level of political and cultural activity than most places in Brittany (the Czech Milan Kundera wrote *The Book of Laughter and Forgetting* while based at the university, which is on a huge campus to the east).

The friendly co-operative bookshop *Breizh* at 17 rue Penhöet has cassettes of Breton and Celtic music along with books and posters. *L'Arvor* cinema at 29 rue d'Antrain (☎99.38.72.40) shows *v.o.* (original language) films, and there's a large selection of English books in the *FNAC* bookshop in the Colombier shopping centre.

Fougères

FOUGÈRES, which lies fifty kilometres short of Rennes on the main road into Brittany from Caen, has a topography impossible to grasp from a map. Streets that look a few metres long turn out to be precipitous plunges down the escarpments of its split-levelled site, lanes collapse into flights of steps. The only way to get around, needless to say, is on foot.

Perhaps the oddest feature of the site is the positioning of the **castle**, built well below the main part of the town, on a low spit of land that separates, and is towered over by, two mighty rock faces. Massive and stunningly strong, it is protected by great curtain-walls and circled by a hacked-out moat full of weirs and waterfalls. In its heyday it also had the additional protection of the River Nançon. None of this, however, prevented its repeated capture by such medieval adventurers as, of course, du Guesclin.

Within the castle keep, a romantic setting in *Les Chouans* (see opposite), the focus is disappointingly prosaic. Footwear, to this day the main industry of the town, is presented in a **museum** included in the **château tours** (on the hour, mid-June to mid-Sept daily 9am–7pm; April to mid-June 9.30am–noon & 2–5.30pm; Oct–March 10am–noon & 2–4.30pm).

The best approach to the castle is from place **des Arbres** beside St-Léonard's church off the main street of the old fortified town. The formal terraces give way

BALZAC'S FOUGÈRES

The flavour of eighteenth-century Fougères is evoked in Balzac's *Les Chouans*, a bit of a potboiler with its absurd twists but nonetheless an essentially historical account of the events surrounding the *Chouan* rebellion in Brittany, the attempt to restore the monarchy after the Revolution. Balzac makes great play of the town's unusual layout and of the various bloodthirsty survivors of the revolt that he met whilst doing his research: "In 1827, an old man accompanied by his wife was selling cattle at the Fougères market unremarked and unmolested, although he was the killer of more than one hundred persons."

to the water meadows of the River Nançon, which you can cross beside a little cluster of medieval houses still standing on the riverbank – the sculpted doorway at 6 rue de Lusignan is particularly attractive.

If, on the other hand, you take the longer route down rue Nationale, you'll pass, at no. 51, the **Musée de La Villéon**, which commemorates an Impressionist who painted numerous memorable Breton landscapes (mid-June to Aug daily 10.30am–12.30pm & 2.30–5.30pm; Easter to mid-June & first fortnight of Sept Sat & Sun 11am–12.30pm & 2.30–5pm).

Practicalities

Fougères's old gare SNCF, down below the modern town, is now inactive; the buses which use the square beside it are the only form of public transport to pass through. The **SI** at 1 place Aristide-Briand provides copious information on all aspects of the town and local countryside (July & Aug Mon–Sat 9am–7pm, Sun 10am–noon & 2–4pm; Sept–June Mon–Sat 9.30am–12.30pm & 2–6pm, Sun 10am–noon & 2–4pm; ☎99.94.12.20).

The *Grand Hôtel des Voyageurs* at 10 place Gambetta (☎99.99.08.20; closed second fortnight of Aug; ③) is a particularly nice place to stay, with TVs in all rooms. It's just round the corner from the SI, on the main road – ask for a room at the back. Selecting the cheapest, 85F menu in the excellent downstairs restaurant (run by a different management, and closed Sat) gives you the choice of *tournedos de thon*, and grants you access to a well-laden *chariot des desserts*; other menus cost 125F and upwards. *Hôtel Balzac* at no. 15 in the semi-pedestrianized rue Nationale (☎99.99.42.46; open all year; ③) is central and a little less expensive, though the rooms are rather damp and depressing, while the *Buffet* just down the street at no. 53 (closed Wed pm & Sun; ☎99.94.35.76) does more economical meals. Its 54F menu includes wine, and carries the option of gorging yourself on a full buffet of hors d'oeuvres.

The Forêt de Fougères

The **Forêt de Fougères**, a short way out on the D177 towards Vire (see p.158), is one of the most enjoyable in the province. The beech woods are spacious and light, with various megaliths and trails of old stones scattered among the chestnut and spruce. It's quite a contrast to their normal bleak and windswept haunts to see dolmens sporting themselves in such verdant surroundings. If you have time, walk through the forest as far as **Le Chatellier**, a village set high in thick woods. For a **horseback** tour, contact the *Centre d'Initiation aux Activités de Plein Air* in Chennedet (☎99.99.18.98).

St-Aubin-du-Cormier

Halfway between Fougères and Rennes on the N12, **ST-AUBIN-DU-CORMIER** makes a peaceful overnight stop. A bit too peaceful perhaps, the kind of town where the only entertainment in the only bar open at ten o'clock on a Saturday night is to take it in turns to look at a pet white hamster. But the very cheap *Hôtel du Bretagne*, 68 rue de l'Ecu (☎99.39.10.22; ①), has to be recommended, a rambling old building, lumpy lino corridors stretching off in random directions upstairs and good food down.

There is, too, a major sight in St-Aubin – the keep of its old **castle**, which was demolished after the great battle here in 1488 in which the forces of Duke Francis were defeated by the French army. Many Breton soldiers were dressed in the English colours of a black cross on white silk, to scare the French into believing that the Duke had extensive English reinforcements. The victorious French were told to spare all prisoners except the English; and so the hapless Bretons were massacred. Just one sheer wall of the castle survives, with a fire-place visible halfway up. A small monument in a field marks the actual site of the battle.

Immediately below the castle, next to a small lake, is the municipal **campsite** (mid-April to Oct; ☎99.39.10.42). A few kilometres out of town, the **Ville Olivier** on the D102 between St-Ouen and Mezières is a château which organizes riding, canoeing and kayaking, and has its own *gîte d'étape* (☎99.39.34.72).

Vitré

VITRÉ, just north of the Le Mans–Rennes motorway, is a lesser rival to Dinan as the best-preserved medieval town in Brittany. Its walls are not quite complete, but their effect is enhanced by the fact that what lies outside them has changed so little. To the north are stark wooded slopes, while into the western hillside beneath the castle burrow thickets of stone cottages that must once have been Vitré's medieval slums. This little suburb is called **Rachapt**, a corruption of the French for "repurchase", in memory of the time during the Hundred Years War when the castle's defendants finally paid the English army, by whom they'd been besieged for several years, to go away. By 1589, when the castle successfully resisted a siege by the Catholic League, Vitré had become a Huguenot stronghold.

The towers of the **castle** itself have pointed slate-grey roofs in best fairy-tale fashion (they look like freshly-sharpened pencils), though, unfortunately, the municipal offices and museum of shells, birds, bugs and local history inside are not exactly thrilling (July–Sept daily 10am–12.30pm & 2–6.15pm; April–June daily except Tues 10am–noon & 2–5.30pm; Oct–March Wed–Fri 10am–noon & 2–5.30pm, Sat–Mon 2–5.30pm).

Vitré is a market town rather than an industrial centre, with its principal **market** held on Mondays in the square in front of Notre-Dame church. The old city is full of twisting streets of half-timbered houses, a good proportion of which are **bars**. The rue de la Baudrairie is the most picturesque, but the rue d'En Bas, which climbs up from Rachapt to the castle, has the best selection of bars; the *Aston* for example, at no. 7, is a nice place to spend an evening. An unusual visual treat, if you happen to be using the **post office**, is its modern stained-glass window behind the counter.

Practicalities

Vitré's **gare SNCF** is a little way south of the centre, where the ramparts have disappeared and the town imperceptibly blends into its newer sectors. Nearby are the **SI**, on the promenade St-Yves (Mon–Fri 10am–noon & 1.30–6pm, Sat 10am–noon; ☎99.75.04.46), and most of the **hotels** too.

This is a cheap as well as a pleasant place to stay; the *Petit-Billot*, place du Général-Leclerc (☎99.74.68.88; ③), and *Chêne-Vert*, place de la Gare (☎99.75.00.58; closed late Sept to late Oct; 25F car parking charge; ①), are both good value, while rooms on the higher floors of the *Hôtel du Château*, 5 rue Rallon (☎99.74.58.59; closed Sun out of season; ②), on a quiet road just below the castle, have views of the ramparts.

Of the **restaurants**, *Le St-Pierre*, on the corner with the main road at 1 place St-Yves (☎99.75.36.52), serves a different interesting menu each day, while *La Soupe aux Choux*, at the top of rue de la Baudrairie at 32 rue Notre-Dame (☎99.75.10.86; closed Tues), prepares simple but classic French food, with 39F lunches.

Around Vitré

There are several interesting smaller towns in the area. **DOMPIERRE** is attractive in its own right and claims a tiny (and disputed) place in history as the town where Roland, Charlemagne's nephew, might have died, were one to accept that the *Chanson de Roland* got the story entirely wrong.

CHAMPEAUX, eight kilometres west of Vitré, has – is – a central paved square, surrounded by stone houses, with an ornate well in the centre, and a fifteenth-century church containing fine stained glass and carved stalls.

CHATEAUBOURG, halfway to Rennes, has a wonderful but expensive hotel, the *Ar Milin* (☎99.00.30.91; ⑤), straddling the River Vilaine in huge gardens at 30 rue de Paris. Breakfast consists of an enormous buffet of fresh pastries.

The Roche-aux-Fées

About fifteen kilometres to the south, not far from the road just off the D341 near Retiers, the **ROCHE-AUX-FÉES** is the least-visited of the major megalithic monuments of Brittany. The "fairy rock" is a twenty-metre-long covered alleyway of purplish stones, with no apparent funerary purpose or indeed any evidence that it was ever buried. It's set on a high and exposed spot, guarded by just a few venerable trees, and it's thought the slabs had to be dragged a good 45km to get here. There's no admission charge. Tradition has it that engaged couples should come here on the night of a full moon, and separately count the stones; if they agree on the total, things are looking good.

WEST ALONG THE COAST

To the west of the Rance, beyond Dinard, stretches the green of the **Côte d'Émeraude**. While this region has its fair share of developed family resorts, such as **St-Jacut**, **Erquy** and **Le Val-André**, it also offers wonderful camping, at its best around the heather-surrounded beaches near **Cap Fréhel** – for once unencroached upon by the military.

As you move further west, the coast becomes wilder and harsher. Beyond **St-Brieuc** the seaside towns tend to be crammed into narrow rocky inlets or set well back in river estuaries, and only a few beaches manage to break out from the rocks. Past **Paimpol** the shoreline is known as the **Côte de Granit Rose** – no figure of speech, but a literal description of its primeval tangle of vast pink granite boulders. They certainly deserve to be seen, at the very least as a quick detour before catching the ferry at Pointe de l'Arcouest (near Paimpol) for **Bréhat**.

The Côte d'Émeraude

The coast immediately **west of Dinard** is one of Brittany's most traditional family resort areas, with old-fashioned holiday towns, safe sandy beaches and a plethora of well-organized campsites.

St-Jacut-de-la-Mer

ST-JACUT, which takes up most of the tip of a narrow peninsula roughly 16km west of St-Malo, looks today like a classic nineteenth-century bathing resort, but was in fact founded a thousand years earlier by an itinerant Irish monk. Though possibly not the most exciting of places, it has everything young children could want – good sand, rocky pools to clamber about, and woods to scramble in.

St-Jacut also boasts one of Brittany's most distinctive **hotels**; as the *Hôtel le Vieux Moulin* is housed in a fifteenth-century windmill, in the middle of the peninsula, its guest rooms are completely round (☎96.27.71.02; closed Nov–Easter; ③). It also serves good if unadventurous food. The summer-only *Camping Municipal* is beside the plage de la Manchette (☎96.27.70.02).

Much the best **fish restaurant** in the area is the *Restaurant la Presqu'île*, at 164 Grande-Rue (☎96.27.76.47; closed Jan & Feb, & Mon in winter), where the menus start at 120F.

St-Cast-le-Guildo

The pleasant seaside community of **ST-CAST**, on the next promontory along, is a 30-kilometre drive from St-Malo, and connected by SNCF buses with the nearest station, at Lamballe (see below). Most of its commercial activity takes place in the rather uninspiring Bourg, set back from the water, but the port area down below is very nice, and there are good walks along the coast to the headland.

Among medium-price **hotels** in St-Cast are the attractive ivy-covered *Hôtel du Centre et des Plages*, 10 rue Frigate-la-Place (☎96.41.91.13; ③), and the much plainer *Chrisflo*, 19 rue du Port (☎96.41.88.08; closed Nov–Jan, & Tues & Wed out of season; ③), both well back from the sea. The **SI** on place Charles-de-Gaulle (July & Aug daily 9am–7pm; Sept–June Mon–Fri 9am–noon & 2–6pm; ☎96.41.81.52) can provide details of local **campsites**, such as the *Châtelet* beside the bay (Easter to mid-Sept; ☎96.41.96.33).

Cap Fréhel

The only really out-of-the-ordinary place on this stretch, however, is **CAP FRÉHEL**. This high, warm expanse of heath, cliffs and heather is over-visited, but camping is prohibited for five kilometres around the tip and the headland itself, 400m walk from the road, remains unspoilt with no more than a few ruins of old buildings and a small "tearoom" nearby. Offshore, the heather-covered islands are grand to look at, although too tiny to visit; the view from the cape's lighthouse can extend as far as Jersey and the Île de Bréhat.

The **Fort la Latte**, to the east, is used regularly as a film-set. Its tower (containing a cannonball factory) is accessible only over two drawbridges. To visit, you have to take guided tours (June–Sept daily 10am–12.30pm & 2.30–6.30pm; rest of the year Sun and holidays only, 2.30–5.30pm; 15F).

The nearest places to stay to the Cap are the ideal, isolated **campsite** at Pléherel, the *Camping du Pont L'Étang* (May–Sept; ☎96.41.40.45), and a basic summer-only **youth hostel** on the D16 just outside Plévenon en route towards the Cap – full address Kérivet-en-Frehel, La Ville Hardrieux (mid-April to Sept; ☎96.41.48.98).

Erquy

Further round, Erquy and Le Val-André both have huge beaches; the perfect crescent at **ERQUY** curves through more than 180 degrees. At low tide, the sea disappears way beyond the harbour entrance, leaving gentle ripples of paddling sand. Adventurers equipped with suitable boots could walk right across its mouth, from the grassy wooded headland on the left side over to the picturesque little lighthouse at the end of the jetty on the right.

Erquy's **SI** on the bd de la Mer (summer daily 9.30am–12.30pm & 2–7pm, otherwise daily except Mon 9.30am–12.30pm; ☎96.72.30.12) coordinates information for the surrounding area. The *Hôtel Beauséjour*, 21 rue de la Corniche (closed Sun pm & Mon in winter; ☎96.72.30.39; ④), has a good view of the bay, and excellent fish dinners from around 70F, while the more upmarket **restaurant** *l'Escurial* (☎96.72.31.56) by the seafront serves a five-course menu (for 190F) which consists entirely of **scallops**, the town's speciality.

There are several campsites on the promontory (dotted with tiny coves) that leads to the Cap d'Erquy north of town, including the *St-Pabu* (April–Oct; ☎96.72.24.65) right beside the sea.

Le Val-André

The beach in the broader bay of **LE VAL-ANDRÉ** is of finer and somehow sweeter-smelling sand, and the endless pedestrian promenade that stretches along the seafront feels oddly Victorian, consisting solely of huge old houses undisturbed by shops or bars. However, Le Val-André is definitely more of a town than Erquy, and rue A-Charner, running parallel to the sea one street back, is busy with holiday-makers in summer.

Le Val-André's helpful **SI** (☎96.72.20.55) is located in the modern Casino at the very centre of the waterfront. Of its **hotels**, the tastefully refurbished *Hotel de la Mer*, 63 rue A-Charner (☎96.72.20.44; ②), serves food that is utterly magnificent, using a fine muscadet to transport *moules marinières* onto a hitherto undreamed-of plane (available on their 89F menu along with rabbit or quail and a delicious raspberry mousse). However, with the success of the business many guests find themselves having to sleep in the characterless *Nuit et Jour* motel, run by the same management, and one group even reported having to sleep in their car after being locked out of the hotel after an evening drink. The similar-looking but slightly more imposing *Hôtel Regina*, slightly nearer the centre at 45 rue A-Charner (☎96.72.22.63; ③), is a more dependable if perhaps less exciting choice; a couple of its rooms have attractive balconies. The *Restaurant au Biniou*, 121 rue Clémenceau (March–Dec; ☎96.72.24.35), is probably the best of several adjacent seafood specialists just back from the Casino; in additional to the usual choices, its 80F menu features stuffed mussels and oysters.

A few kilometres west – reachable by an enjoyable footpath around the headland – the small lagoon of **DAHOUËT** is more secluded, and has its own **campsite**. In summer, a peculiarly irregular boat service run by *Les Vedettes de Bréhat* (☎96.55.86.99) operates day trips every four or five days from Erquy (☎96.72.30.12; 8.30am; 150F) and/or Dahouët (☎96.72.20.55; 8.30am or 9am; 150F) out to the island of Bréhat (see p.202).

Jugon-les-Lacs

An alternative route west from Dinard and Dinan heads inland along the D768 through the market town of Plancoët (home of a popular brand of mineral water, obtainable here free) to **JUGON-LES-LACS**. This tiny old town lies at one end of its own artificial lake (the *grand étang*). Peculiarly, the central place du Martray – scene of a market each Friday – is well below the water level, and you have to climb uphill to reach the massive cobblestone dyke that shields it from inundation. At the opposite end of town, the main road from Dinan to St-Brieuc crosses high above the valley on a viaduct. Jugon, nestled cosily between the two, has no room to expand even if it wanted to – a subdued place whose few streets are almost deserted in the evenings.

For most of the way around **the lake**, there's no approach road or footpath, only meadows and trees sweeping down to the water. However, at *Le Bocage* **campsite** (☎96.31.60.16), just out of town along the D52 towards Mégrit, there's a small beach from which you can go swimming. It's very much a family campsite, with a heated swimming pool as well, and the rental of boats and **windsurfers** available with tuition from its *École de Voile* (☎96.31.64.58).

Jugon itself has a handful of moderately priced **hotels**, including *La Vallée Verte*, at 11 rue Penthièvre on the main road through town (☎96.31.64.86; ③), which has menus from 70F and a lively bar; *Le Petit Palace*, tucked away on a small alleyway just behind it (☎96.31.65.24; ②); and *La Grande Fontaine*, a couple of hundred metres east of the centre on the road towards Dinan (☎96.31.61.29; ②). The local **SI** is in the Hôtel de Ville on the main square (☎96.31.61.62).

Lamballe

The main N176 westwards from Jugon brings you after twenty kilometres to **LAMBALLE**, an old town crammed into a narrow valley beside a broad river, dominated by a church high up on battlement walls. Its most famous former citizen was the Princess of Lamballe, a lady-in-waiting to Marie Antoinette, who was guillotined in 1792.

In summer, it's possible to visit the branch of the **national stud** (the *haras national*), which all but adjoins Lamballe's picturesque main square, the place du Martray. Though not quite on the same scale as Le Notre's dramatic park near Argentan (see p.147), it will still delight any horse-lover (mid-July to Sept Mon–Sat 2–6.30pm, Sun 10am–noon & 2–6.30pm). It's the focus of a big **horse festival** on the first weekend after August 15.

Central **hotel-restaurants** include the *De La Porte St-Martin*, 12 rue de la Porte St-Martin (☎96.34.71.61; ①), and the *Tour d'Argent*, on 2 rue Dr-Lavergne, which becomes the D102 (☎96.31.01.37; ③), a slightly more upmarket *logis* where menus start at 52F. The **SI** is in the grandest of the half-timbered buildings on place du Martray (Easter hols & June to Sept Mon–Sat 10am–noon & 2.30–6pm; otherwise Tues 10am–noon & 2.30–6pm, Fri 2.30–6pm; ☎96.31.05.38), which also holds a couple of tiny local museums.

Moncontour

The attractive little hill town of **MONCONTOUR**, 18km southeast of Lamballe and 23km southwest of St-Brieuc, was, during the Middle Ages, one of the more prosperous towns of the region, thanks to its hemp industry. Having been under no pressure to grow since then, it remains largely enclosed by its medieval fortifications – not that you get much impression of them once you're actually in the town, as the houses all face inwards onto the narrow streets.

Moncontour centres on the pretty, triangular **place du Penthièvre**, where the Romanesque tower of the church of St-Mathurin was blessed in 1902 by the addition of a delightfully eccentric new belfry, a confection of wooden eaves and grey-slate domes that now constitutes the highest point on the hill. The village can offer day-trippers a couple of quite pleasant restaurants, but the only overnight accommodation is in *chambres d'hôte* scattered around the nearby countryside – pick up details from the **SI** (☎96.73.41.05).

On the final Sunday of August, Moncontour echoes its days of glory by playing host to a hectic and atmospheric "medieval fair".

The Bay of St-Brieuc

Although the town of **St-Brieuc** itself is more of an obstacle to be avoided than an appealing destination, it serves as a gateway to the further series of attractive little resorts that dot its eponymous Bay. It also marks the point at which visitors usually begin to become aware that Brittany really does amount to something more than just another indistinguishable corner of the French coastline, and has its own very distinct culture and traditions.

St-Brieuc

The major city on the Côte d'Émeraude, **ST-BRIEUC** is far too busy being the industrial centre of the north to concern itself with entertaining tourists. It's an odd-looking city, with two very deep wooded valleys spanned by viaducts at its core, and it's almost impossible to bypass, however you're travelling. The streets are hectic, with the town centre cut in two by a virtual motorway, unrelieved by any public parks, and not much distinguished either by a mega-shopping complex. Motorists and cyclists, unfortunately, have little choice but to plough straight through rather than attempting to negotiate the backroads and steep hills around.

Every July, St-Brieuc makes a concession to summer visitors by organizing a **Festival of Breton Music**, while at the end of October comes the **Art Rock festival** (☎96.33.77.50); if you're interested, the SI (see below) can supply relevant information on both. Worth looking in on, too, are the **Comité Départmentale de Tourisme** for the Côtes-du-Nord at 29 rue des Promenades (☎96.62.72.00); throughout the summer they organize one-day tours in the area to visit craft workshops of every variety – taxidermists, bakers, farmers, makers of furniture and cider.

Practicalities

Trains between Paris, Dol and Brest stop at the gare SNCF, around a kilometre south of the centre of St-Brieuc, and regular buses run to the nearby resorts.

There's an information desk at the station in summer, though the official **SI** is in the town centre, right by the cathedral at 7 rue St-Gouéno (daily July & Aug 9am–12.30pm & 1.30–7pm; Sept–June 9am–noon & 2–6.30pm; ☎96.33.22.50).

One ordinary but economical place to **stay** is the *Hôtel du Parc*, 8 rue Jean-Mermoz (☎96.33.51.02; ②); you can get significantly more class and comfort at the central *Champ du Mars*, 13 rue de Général-Leclerc (☎96.33.60.99; ④), which has a good brasserie downstairs. St-Brieuc also has a **youth hostel**, two kilometres out, in the magnificent fifteenth-century Manoir de la Ville-Guyomard (☎96.78.70.70); dorms cost around 50F per night. It's roughly 3km on foot from the place du Champs-de-Mars, which is on bus route #1 from the station, and has bicycles and canoes for rent.

Among **eating** options in town are the traditional French cooking at *Le Madure*, 14 rue Quinquaine (☎96.51.20.17; closed Sun & Mon), where menus start at 78F; the fondues at *Le Chaudron*, 19 rue Fardel (☎96.33.01.72; closed Sun & Wed lunchtime); and the "biological" restaurant at 19 rue de Maréchal-Foch, *Le Grain de Sel* (☎96.33.19.61; closed Jan, Sat pm & Sun), which serves **vegetarian** meals (including fish, for some reason) made with the fresh organic produce it also sells both on the spot and at local markets.

Around the Bay

As you move northwest from St-Brieuc along the edge of the V-shaped bay towards Paimpol, the countryside becomes especially rich – it's called the *Goëlo* – while the coast itself grows wilder and harsher. The seaside towns, few of which are particularly exciting, tend to be crammed into narrow rocky inlets or set well back in river estuaries.

Binic
BINIC is probably the nicest place to stay, all on a very small scale with a narrow port, a sandy beach, a tiny promenade around the town and to either side Devon-like meadows that roll down to the sea. The main industry is the sale of mud from the River Ic for fertilizer.

The good if relatively pricey *Hôtel Benhuyc*, 1 quai Jean-Bart (☎96.73.61.16; ⑤), now offers the only waterfront accommodation in town, but there are several nearby **campsites**, the best of them the secluded *Les Madieres*, back from the sea off the main road south of the centre (☎96.79.02.48). *Les Vedettes de Bréhat* (☎96.73.60.12) run occasional day trips during the summer to the Île de Bréhat (see p.202), costing 160F and setting off at 8am.

St-Quay-Portrieux
ST-QUAY, a little to the north, is considerably more upmarket and a bit soulless, though there's certainly a lot of activity going on in its sister town of **PORTRIEUX**, where a new yachting marina has encouraged what used to be a slightly seedy waterfront – dating back to the days of the Newfoundland fishing fleets (see below) – to smarten itself up.

In St-Quay itself, the *Gerbot d'Avoine*, 2 bd de Littoral (☎96.70.40.09; ③) beside the beach, makes an entertaining *logis* in which to stay; the food is good, and the decor upstairs is quite astonishing. Crimson carpets creeping up the corridor walls make it look hideously like the hotel in *The Shining*, while in the rooms themselves washbasins and even showers are discreetly hidden away in

---

INTO THE BRETON HEARTLAND

At **Plouha**, a short way along the D786 from St-Quay, you cross what was tradition-ally the boundary between the French-speaking and Breton-speaking areas of Brittany. As a general indication, you can tell which language used to be spoken in a particular area by its place names. Thus from here on west there is a preponderance of names beginning with the Breton "PLOU" (meaning parish), "TREZ" (sand or beach), "KER" (town) or "PENN" (head). See *Contexts* for a comprehensive glos-sary of Breton words that you are likely to come across.

---

cupboards. The *Hôtel le Bretagne*, 36 quai de la République (☎96.70.40.91; ③), is an alternative if you'd rather stay by the seafront in Portrieux.

In summer, *Les Vedettes de Bréhat* (☎96.70.40.64) run a few sailings each week, according to an erratic schedule, to the Île de Bréhat (see p.202), for a return fare of 150F (departures 8.30am), while *Émeraude Lines* catamarans connect St-Quay with the Channel Islands, daily between April and September (☎96.70.49.46; day trips cost around 300F).

Kermaria-an-Isquit

You may well get your first exposure to spoken Breton (see box) in smaller villages such as **KERMARIA-AN-ISQUIT**. This is not an easy place to find, espe-cially coming from Lanloup to the north; the best signposted of its approaches is along the D21 from Plouha. It is so much hidden away that rarely more than one or two visitors a day get to see the village's **chapel** and its extraordinary *Dance of Death*, one of the most striking of all French medieval images. Even in the summer, the church is not open regularly – you have to find Mme Hervé Droniou in the house just up the road on the left to let you in.

The **Dance of Death** is no delicate miniature; this huge series of frescoes covers the arcades all round the chapel. Painted in the plague-fearing fifteenth century, they show Ankou, the skeletal death-figure, leading representatives of all social classes in a *Danse Macabre*. Some of the original colours have faded, as a consequence of having once been whitewashed over, and many of the figures are now just silhouettes, but the fresco has lost little of its power to shock. In yellow, on a red background, the skeleton alternates with such living characters as a King, a Knight, a Bishop and a Peasant. Verses below, now mostly illegible though avail-able in transcription, have each person pleading for life and lamenting death while Ankou insists that all must in the end come to him. Elsewhere in the church is a representation of the classic medieval theme of the encounter between the *Trois Vifs*, three finely-apparelled noblemen out hunting, with the *Trois Morts*, three corpses reflecting in a cemetery on the transience of all things human:

> *Nous avons bien este en chance*
> *Autrefoys, comme estes a present*
> *Mais vous viendrez a nostre dance*
> *Comme nous sommes maintenant*

In other words, we were lucky enough once to be like you, but you'll have to come and join our dance in the end.

The chapel was originally the private property of the lords of the manor of Noë Vert, and there is a tunnel, now flooded, linking it with the manor house five kilometres away. A small display case behind the altar contains the skull of one of the lords, and a couple of grotesque heart-shaped boxes hold the hearts of another and his wife. There is also a unique statue of the infant Jesus refusing milk from the Virgin's proferred breast, symbolizing the choice of celestial over terrestrial food. A processional boat, raised on poles, and the ship-like vaulting of the roof, decorated with stylized yellow stars, lend an oddly Egyptian air.

Guingamp

The only town of any size in the centre of this northern peninsula, on the most direct route towards Finistère should you choose to skip the Pink Granite Coast, is the old weaving centre of **GUINGAMP** – its name possibly the source of the striped or checked fabric "gingham". It's an attractive place of cobbled streets, but there's not much to see beyond the main square, where a fountain bedecked in griffins and gargoyles is overlooked by a splendid pair of lopsided old timber-frame houses propping each other up, and the Black Virgin in the thirteenth-century **basilica**. A big *pardon*, featuring a night procession to the basilica, is held on the first Saturday in July.

Practicalities

Guingamp is the next stop on the rail route west of St-Brieuc towards Morlaix; its **gare SNCF** (☎96.94.50.50) is southeast of the place du Vally, where you'll find the **SI** (Mon 2–6pm, Tues–Sat 10am–noon & 2–6pm; ☎96.43.73.89) and the **gare routière**.

Of its **hotels**, *l'Escale*, 26 bd Clémenceau (☎96.43.72.19; ①) is probably the best value, with well-cooked meals from 85F. The best restaurant in town, however, is in the expensive hotel *Le Relais du Roy*, 42 place du Centre (☎96.43.76.62; ⑧), where you can eat in the magnificent dining room for a minimum of 125F.

The Ménéz Bré

On the road out towards Morlaix is the "mountain" of the **Ménéz Bré**, a spectacular height amid these plains. In the mid-nineteenth century the local rector was often observed to climb to the mountain's peak on stormy nights, accompanied only by a donkey laden with books. For all his exemplary piety, his parishioners suspected him of sorcery and witchcraft; he was in fact doing early research into natural electrical forces.

Paimpol

To the north, back on the coast and served by a branch railway line from Guingamp, is **PAIMPOL**. Though still an attractive town, with a tangle of cobbled alleyways lined with fine grey-granite houses, it has lost something in its transition from working fishing port to pleasure harbour. It was once the centre of a cod and whaling fleet that sailed for the fisheries of Iceland each February, sent off with a ceremony marked by a famous *pardon*. From then until August or September the town would be empty of all young men. Within a few years of the first expedition in 1852, the annual exodus consisted of as many as fifty vessels, with twenty-five men in each. A haunting glimpse of the way Paimpol used to look can be seen in the recently re-released silent film of Pierre Loti's book *Pêcheur* *d'Islande*, made on location here by Jacques de Baroncelli in 1924. Loti, and the heroine of his book, lived in the **place du Martray** in the centre of town.

Thanks to naval shipyards and the like, the open sea is not visible from Paimpol; a maze of waterways leads to its two separate harbours. Both are usually filled with the high masts of yachts, but still also used by the fishing boats that keep a fish market and a plethora of *poissonneries* busy. This is doubtless a very pleasant place to arrive by yacht, threading through the rocks, but from close quarters the tiny port area is a little disappointing, very much rebuilt and quite plain. Even so, it is always lively in summer.

Practicalities

Paimpol's **SI** is in the Hôtel de Ville on rue Pierre-Feutren, near the prominent Notre-Dame church (June to mid-Sept Mon–Sat 9am–7.30pm, Sun 9.30am–1pm; otherwise Mon–Sat 9am–noon & 2–5pm; ☎96.20.83.16).

Possible places to **stay** include the luxurious *Repaire de Kerroc'h*, overlooking the small-boat harbour from quai Morand (☎96.20.50.13; ⑤), which serves gourmet meals from 85F up to 350F; the very hospitable *Hôtel Berthelot* at 1 rue du Port (☎96.20.88.66; ③); the plainer *Hôtel Origano*, just back from the front in a semi-pedestrianized area at 7 bis rue du Quai (☎96.22.05.49; ③); and the pink *le Goëlo* on quai Duguay-Truin, the ugly new block that lines the inland side of the fishing harbour (☎96.20.82.74; ③), which has the simple brasserie *La Chaumière* downstairs. A year-round **youth hostel** in the grand old *Château de Kerraoul* (all year; ☎96.20.83.60) offers dorm beds for around 45F, and has facilities for camping.

As for **restaurants**, the menu of the *Restaurant du Port*, 17 quai Morand (☎96.20.82.76; closed Sun pm, Mon, & Jan in winter), may be appealing, but it's spoiled by rude service and meagre portions; the 68F menu is basic in the extreme, and you have to allow at least 95F for a reasonable meal. *La Cotriade*, across on the far side of the harbour on the quai Armand-Dayot (☎96.20.81.08; closed Thurs), is a better bet for authentic fish dishes, with a simple 90F menu including a *veritable Cassoulet Paimpolais* and a 125F menu that features a delicious crab mousse. They positively prefer diners to pay using credit cards. Almost next door is the *Restaurant Gandhi*, 2 rue de l'Yser (☎96.20.70.74), where the usual jolly white-bearded model fisherman in his yellow sou'wester for once advertises a full authentic Indian menu. The 69F set menu is uninspiring, but if you're prepared to pay 100F or more for a full spread, they also cook south Indian-style fish specialities and even *paneer* (cheese) dishes.

Very near the *Origano* hotel, the *Corto Maltese* **bar** serves a fine selection of British and other beers.

Loguivy-sur-mer

If Paimpol is too crowded for you, it's well worth continuing a few kilometres further across the headland to reach the little fishing hamlet of **LOGUIVY**. All of the long river inlets along this northern coast tend to conceal tiny coves; at Loguivy a working harbour manages to squeeze into one such gap in the rocks. There are no hotels, but *chambres d'hôte* (which don't work out any cheaper) are available at **Kéréveur** (M. Chaboud; ☎96.55.82.76; ③) and **Kerloury** (I. Le Goaster; ☎96.20.85.23; ③). Lenin came here for his summer holidays in July 1902.

Both Loguivy and Paimpol are within easy reach of the spectacular **Pointe de l'Arcouest** and Bréhat.

The Île de Bréhat

The **ÎLE DE BRÉHAT** – in reality two islands joined by a slip of a bridge – gives the appearance of spanning great latitudes. On the north side are windswept meadows of hemlock and yarrow, sloping down to chaotic erosions of rock; on the south, you're in the midst of palm trees, mimosa and eucalyptus. All around is a multitude of little islets – some accessible at low tide, others *propriété privée*, most just pink-orange rocks. All in all, this has to be one of the most beautiful places in Brittany.

As you might expect, this island paradise has attracted Parisians, among others looking for holiday homes. Over half the houses now have temporary residents and young Bréhatins leave in ever-increasing numbers for lack of a place of their own, let alone a job. In winter the remaining 300 or so natives have the place to themselves, without even a *gendarme*; the summer sees two imported from the mainland, along with upwards of 3000 tourists. As a visitor, though, you should find the Bréhatins friendly enough – it's the holiday-home owners that they really resent.

The beach to swim from at low tide is the **Grève de Guerzido,** on the east side facing the mainland. Near **Le Bourg** – Bréhat village, which is the centre of

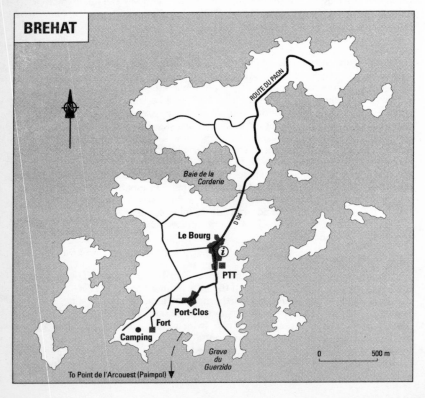

BREHAT

ROUTE DU PAON

Baie de la
Corderie

D 104

Le Bourg

i

PTT

Port-Clos

Fort

Camping

Greve
du
Guerzido

0   500 m

To Point de l'Arcouest (Paimpol) ▼

all activity on the island – the sea tends to be a bit murky, and the east coast generally is less accessible because of private property. But in the north, even when Le Bourg is blocked up with visitors, you can walk and laze about in near solitude. Bréhat no longer has a castle (blown up twice by the English), but it does have a lighthouse and a nineteenth-century **fort**, in the woods near the campsite (see below).

Getting There

Bréhat is connected regularly by **ferry** from the Pointe de l'Arcouest, 6km northwest of Paimpol and served by regular buses in summer from the gare SNCF there. Sailings, with *Vedettes de Bréhat* (☎96.55.86.99), are roughly hourly in high summer, and every two hours for the rest of the year, with the last boat back from Bréhat around 7pm; the round-trip costs 35F. Up to three daily guided boat tours circle the island, for a cost of 65F.

There are also boats from Binic and St-Quay-Portrieux (both p.198), and Erquy (see p.195).

Practicalities

No cars are permitted on the island, and there's barely a road wide enough for its few light farm vehicles. You can rent bikes at the ferry port (or take one with you for 45F; to do so in summer you have to catch a ferry before 10am), but it's easy enough to walk from one end to the other in half an hour.

The **SI**, in the old Mairie in the main square in Le Bourg (daily 10am–1pm & 3–6pm; ☎96.20.04.15), has full details on **accommodation** available on the island. The three hotels are expensive and in any case tend to be permanently booked through the summer, while all close for at least part of the winter. Both the *Vieille Auberge* in Le Bourg (Easter–Sept; ☎96.20.00.24; ⑧) and the *Bellevue* in Port-Clos (☎96.20.00.05; closed Jan; ⑧) insist on *demi-pension* in high season.

Most days there's a small market in Le Bourg; restaurants are neither numerous nor cheap, so buying your own picnic food is the best bet. The SI can also provide **campers** with information on the wonderful campsite in the woods high above the sea west of the port (mid-June to mid-Sept; ☎96.20.00.36); when that's closed you can pitch your tent almost anywhere.

The Côte de Granit Rose

The whole of the northernmost stretch of the Breton coast, from Bréhat to Trégastel, has loosely come to be known as the **Côte de Granit Rose**. There are indeed great granite boulders scattered in the sea around the island of Bréhat, and at the various headlands to the west, but the most memorable stretch of coast lies around **Perros-Guirec**, where the pink granite rocks are eroded into fantastic shapes.

Pink granite is an absolutely gorgeous stone, wearing smooth and soft but also glittering sharply. It's hard to tire of it, despite being given every opportunity to do so, which is just as well, for everything in this area seems to be made of it. The houses are faced with granite blocks, and the streets paved with them; the breakwaters in the sea are granite, and the polished pillars of the banks are granite; the hotels even have overgrown granite mini-golfs with little pink granite megaliths as obstacles; and the markets claim to sell *granit-smith* apples.

Tréguier

The D786 turns west from Paimpol, passing over a green *ria* on the bridge outside Lézardrieux before arriving at **TRÉGUIER**. This is one of the very few hill-towns in Brittany, set at the junction of the Jaudy and Guindy rivers. It was rebuilt on this fortified elevation in 848 AD after an earlier monastery was destroyed by Norman raiders.

The central unmissable feature of Tréguier is the **Cathédrale de St-Tugdual**, whose geometric Gothic spire, dotted with holes, contrasts sharply with its earlier Romanesque "Hastings" tower. Inside, the masonry blocks are appealingly crude, and dripping with damp that has somehow spared the wooden stalls. The cathedral contains the tomb of Saint Yves, a native of the town who died in 1303 and – for his incorruptibility – became the patron saint of lawyers. Attempts to bribe him continue to this day; his tomb is surrounded by marble plaques and an inferno of candles invoking his aid, including one special plea from a group of American lawyers. A *pardon* of Saint Yves is held each year on the third Sunday in May.

The half-timbered houses of the square outside look down on a statue of Ernest Renan, a local writer and philosopher whose work formed part of the great nineteenth-century attempt to reinterpret traditional religious faith in the light of scientific discoveries. Worthy Catholics were so incensed at the erection of this memorial in 1903 that they soon built their own "Calvary of Reparation" on the quayside.

Practicalities

Tréguier's SI is in the Hôtel de Ville, round the back of the cathedral (Mon–Sat 9.30am–12.30pm & 2.30–5.30pm, Sun 9.30am–12.30pm; ☎96.92.30.19). The *Hôtel-Restaurant d'Estuaire* on the waterfront (☎96.92.30.25; ②) is a nice place to stay – the sea views are great – with reasonable menus from 65F; *la Poissonnerie du Trégor*, up in town at 2 rue Renan (☎96.92.30.27), is an excellent fish restaurant which is no more expensive.

The town holds a **market** each Wednesday, with clothes and so on spread out in the square up by the Cathedral, and food and fresh fish further down by the port. The assorted cafés and delis of the main square save their best displays for that day.

Château de la Roche-Jagu

About 10km inland from Tréguier and Lézardrieux, overlooking the Trieux river just where it starts to widen, is the fifteenth-century **Château de la Roche-Jagu**. Its rooms are not especially interesting in themselves, but there are regular temporary exhibitions, and the château is worth visiting for its site alone (July & Aug daily 10am–noon & 2–7pm; Easter–June & Sept–Oct daily 10am–noon & 2–7pm; 30F). In August each year it makes a superb venue for a **jazz festival**.

Perros-Guirec

PERROS-GUIREC is the most popular resort along this coast, though not perhaps the most exciting. It has a reputation that seems to attract the retired – its tourist brochures list "playing *Scrabble*" as an attraction – and an array of shops intended to match: antiques, bric-a-brac and pottery with a big line in granite guillemots and puffins. And Perros is, too, a lot less city-like than it looks on the maps: most of its network of roads turn out to be tree-lined avenues of suburban villas.

However, the commercial streets of the centre (up the hill from the port) hold little of interest, and are often jammed solid with traffic in summer. Much more enjoyable is to take a walk around the headland to see the magnificent view from the Table d'Orientation at the sharp curve of the bd Clémenceau.

The best beach is the **Plage de Trestraou**, on the opposite side of town to the port, a long curve of sand speckled with bars and restaurants (the *Homard Bleu* and *l'Excelsior* are recommended). Between March and October, boats sail from here on three-hour round trips to the bird sanctuary of **Sept-Îles**, circling though not actually landing on the seven craggy islands. Similar excursions, costing in the region of 80F, are run by *Vedettes Blaches* (☎96.91.13.21) and *Vedettes des Sept-Îles* (☎96.91.11.31).

Practicalities

If you don't have your own transport, Perros-Guirec is surprisingly hard to reach; what buses there are arrive at and leave from the **Bassin du Lin Kin** in the port – a few hundred metres down from the town centre. If you arrive this way and plan to stay, a good first move is to rent a **bike**; *Cycles Henry*, near the gendarmerie in the bd Aristide-Briand (☎96.91.03.33), can oblige.

The extremely efficient **SI** is at 21 place de l'Hôtel-de-Ville (July & Aug daily 9am–1pm & 1.30–7.30pm, Sept–June Mon–Sat 9am–1pm & 2–6.30pm; ☎96.23.21.15). If you'd rather stay here than in the smaller community of Ploumanac'h (see below), good **hotels** include the *Hôtel de la Mairie*, also in the place de l'Hôtel-de-Ville (open all year; ☎96.23.22.41; ③), and two with sea-views, the *Gulf Stream*, 26 rue des Sept-Îles (April to mid-Nov; ☎96.23.21.86; ③), and the *Bon Accueil*, rue de Landerval (open all year; ☎96.23.23.45; ⑤), whose gourmet restaurant is the best in town. The nicest place to **camp** has to be the *Camping du Trestraou* (June–Sept; ☎96.23.08.11), right beside the beach.

The Sentier des Douaniers

Perros-Guirec's Trestraou beach is made of ordinary sand; the pink granite coast proper starts just beyond its western end. The long **Sentier des Douaniers** pathway winds round the clifftops to **Ploumanac'h** past an astonishing succession of deformed and water-sculpted rocks. Birds wheel overhead towards the sanctuary, and battered boats shelter in the narrow inlets or bob uncontrollably out on the waves. There are patches and brief causeways of grass, clumps of purple heather and yellow gorse. Occasionally the rocks have crumbled into a sort of granite grit to make up a tiny beach; one boulder is strapped down by bands of ivy that prevent it rolling into the sea.

The rocks, in good French cataloguing fashion, have all been given "names" based on supposed resemblances in their shapes. The more banal ones – such as the great big *Foot* and the *Pancake* – are in a way the best; you can't help wondering, though, what committee it was, and when, that went along labelling the *Torpedo*, the *Armchair*, the *Tortoise* and *Napoleon's Hat*. Backing on to the path near a little beach about halfway round, though directly accessible on the other side by road, is an excellent **campsite** – *Le Ranolien* (Feb–Nov; ☎96.91.43.58).

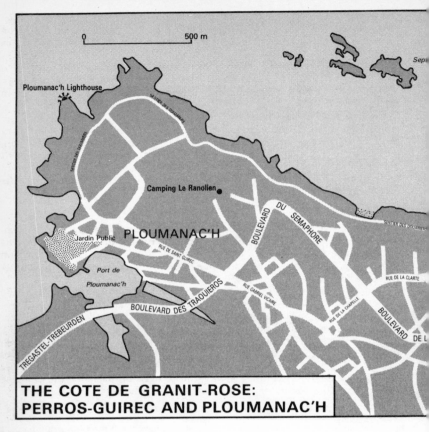

THE COTE DE GRANIT-ROSE:
PERROS-GUIREC AND PLOUMANAC'H

Ploumanac'h

PLOUMANAC'H is a more active resort than Perros-Guirec, though again with a dominant and specific clientele – this time families with youngish children. A pleasantly wild municipal park separates its two halves, the Bourg and the Plage; the tiny **Château du Diable** on one of the many little islands, which frames the horizon above the high tides, was where the novel *Quo Vadis* was written around the turn of the century.

Slightly back from the beach, there's a small lively square of restaurants and snack bars (including the unfortunately named *Coste Mor*). The *Mao-Snack* here is very good value and (like most places in this town) has special cheap menus for children.

The emphasis on children does mean that Ploumanac'h goes to bed early; you can find yourself locked out of a slumbering hotel at 9.30pm. But prices at the *Hôtel du Parc* (April–Sept; ☎96.91.40.80; ③) are at least very reasonable, and it serves good seafood menus from 75F, while *Les Rochers* (Easter–Sept; ☎96.91.44.49; ⑤) verges on the luxurious.

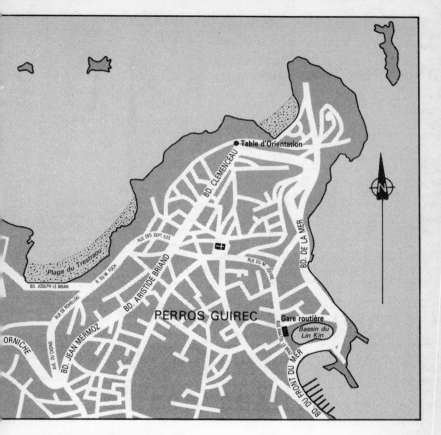

The Traouïéro Valleys

A very short distance west of Ploumanac'h, two dramatic little valleys, which bear a close resemblance to the forest at Huelgoat (see p.260), lead down to the sea. It was the devastation caused by the hurricane of 1987 that led to the **Grand Traouïéro** and the **Petit Traouïéro** becoming accessible to casual visitors – the process of clearing away ancient fallen trees, and disentangling them from centuries of ivy, resulted in the paths being sufficiently opened up so that now either valley makes a gorgeous and undemanding stroll of a few kilometres inland from the coast.

Each of the two is complete with its own gurgling creek, towered over by a huge tumble of pink granite rocks, cascading between old oaks and chestnut trees, with the occasional stand of Monterey cypresses. The Grand Traouïéro in particular is dwarfed beneath mighty boulders, reminiscent of gargantuan Henry Moore sculptures; the Petit Traouïéro is less deep and more delicate. In spring, both are filled with bright bluebells, and the broom is in full blossom.

At the mouth of the Grand Traouïéro, you can visit a 400-year-old tidal mill, one of several in the area. It was in use for grinding flour until the start of this century.

Trégastel and Trébeurden

Of the smaller villages further round the coast to the west, **TRÉGASTEL**, with a **campsite**, and **TRÉBEURDEN**, with a **youth hostel** (*Le Toëno*; open all year; ☎96.23.52.22; 43F), are functional stopovers. Trébeurden has managed to squeeze in an **aquarium** under a massive pile of boulders, and has a couple of huge lumps of pink granite slap in the middle of its fine beach.

The strangest sight along this coast, however, outdoing anything the erosions can manage, is just south of Trégastel on the **route de Calvaire**, where an old stone saint halfway up a high calvary raises his arm to bless or harangue the gleaming white discs and puffball dome of the **Pleumier-Bodou Telecommunications Centre**. A new pink granite "dolmen" commemorates its opening by De Gaulle in 1962, when it was the first receiving station to pick up signals from the American Telstar satellite. The centre is still operating, but is open to visitors on guided tours, along with its Museum of Telecommunications. (Tours daily at 10am, 1.30pm, 5.30pm, 6pm & 7pm in July & Aug, declining in frequency to just 1.30pm & 5.30pm in Feb, March and Oct–Dec; closed Sat before May and after Sept, and closed all Jan.)

The Bay of Lannion

Despite being located significantly back from the sea on the estuary of the River Léguer, **Lannion** gives its name to the next bay west along the Breton coast – and it's the bay rather than the town that is most likely to impress visitors. One enormous beach stretches from **St-Michel-en-Grève**, which is little more than a bend in the road, as far as **Locquirec**; at low tide you can walk hundreds of metres out on the sands.

Lannion

LANNION, set amid plummeting hills and stairways, is an historic city with streets of medieval housing, and a couple of interesting old churches – but it's also a centre for a burgeoning and extremely high-tech telecommunications industry, and as such one of modern Brittany's real success stories. Hence its rather self-satisfied nickname, *ville heureuse* or "happy town".

In addition to admiring the half-timbered houses around the place de Général-Leclerc and along rue des Chapeliers (look out for nos. 3 & 4), it's well worth climbing from the town up the 142 granite steps which lead to the twelfth-century Templar **Église de Brélévenez**. This church was re-modelled three hundred years later to incorporate a granite bell tower, and the views from its terrace are quite stupendous.

Practicalities

Lannion's **gare SNCF** is across the river from the town proper. Arriving passengers make their way into the centre across an attractive little bridge, from which you should spot the **SI**, next to the post office on the quai d'Aguillon on the other side (July to mid-Sept Mon–Sat 9am–7pm, Sun 10.30am–12.30pm; otherwise Mon–Sat 9am–12.30pm & 2–6pm; ☎96.46.41.00).

The *Hôtel le Bretagne* at 32 av de Général-de-Gaulle (☎96.37.00.33; closed Sat & Sun pm out of season; ④), opposite the station is a *logis* with a good restaurant; the *Porte de France*, an eighteenth-century coaching inn at 5 rue Jean-Savidan (☎96.46.54.81; ④), is a more luxurious option with no restaurant. There's also a year-round **youth hostel**, conveniently positioned very near the station and the town centre at 6 rue du 73^e Territorial (☎96.37.91.28; 46F). Its friendly management do not operate a curfew, and they arrange birdwatching and similar expeditions and rent out bikes – not that you'll necessarily relish cycling around Lannion itself, with its ferocious hills.

Locquirec

LOCQUIREC, across the bay from Lannion, manages to have beaches on both sides, without ever quite being thin enough to be a real peninsula. Around the main port, smart houses stand in sloping gardens, looking very southern English with their whitewashed stone panels, grey slate roofs and jutting turreted windows.

On the last Sunday in July, Locquirec holds a combined *pardon de St-Jacques* and Festival of the Sea.

Practicalities

Locquirec veers dangerously close towards being over-twee, and none of its **hotels** is all that cheap either – although the *Grand Hôtel des Bains* (☎98.67.41.02; ③) has so gorgeous a setting that perhaps it doesn't matter. It became widely known in France when it was used as the location for *Hôtel de la Plage*, a coming-of-age movie about youngsters summering in Brittany.

Nearby, the *Hôtel du Port* (☎98.67.42.10; ③) also enjoys a sea view, and the municipal **campsite**, a kilometre south along the corniche (April to mid-Sept; ☎98.67.40.85), is beautifully positioned, too.

St-Jean-du-Doigt

Locquirec is just across the border of the department of Finistère, and by the direct road it is only a few kilometres further to Morlaix (see p.218). Following the coast, however, you come to **ST-JEAN-DU-DOIGT**, where the parish church contains an object held in veneration as the finger of John the Baptist. This sanctified digit is dipped into the Sacred Fountain to produce holy water. It was brought here in 1437 and is the principal object of the *pardon* on June 23 and 24 each year. A more recent tradition of pilgrimage has made St-Jean the site of massive anti-nuclear demonstrations.

Ploumilliau

An alternative inland route – or a detour from Lannion – is to **PLOUMILLIAU** on the D30. Here the parish church contains a unique wooden representation of Ankou, the skeletal symbol of death. The statue, carrying a scythe to catch the living and a spade to bury them, was once carried in local processions.

The Cairn du Barnenez

At the mouth of the Morlaix estuary, 6km north of Plouézoch, the prehistoric stone **CAIRN DU BARNENEZ** surveys the waters from the summit of a hill (daily July & Aug 10am–1pm & 2–6.30pm; April–June & Sept 10am–12.30pm & 2–6.30pm; Oct–March 10am–noon & 2–5pm; free). As on the island of Gavrinis in the Morbihan (see p.307), its ancient masonry has been laid bare by recent excavations, and provides a stunning sense of the architectural prowess of the megalith builders. Radio-carbon testing has shown the work here to date back to around 4500BC, which makes this one of the oldest large monuments in the world. There is evidence that it remained in continuous use for around 2500 years; it was probably used repeatedly as a place of burial, then sealed off and abandoned.

The ensemble consists of two distinct stepped pyramids, the older one constructed of local dolerite stone, and the other of grey granite from the nearby Île de Sterec. Each rises in successive tiers, built of large flat stones chinked with pebbles (but no mortar); the second was added on to the side of the first, and the two are encircled by a series of terraces and ramps. The whole thing measures roughly 70 metres long by 15 to 25 metres wide; the current height of 6 metres is thought to be smaller than that of the original structure. Both were long buried under the same 80-metre-long earthen mound. While the actual cairns are completely exposed to view, most of the passages and chambers that lie within them are sealed off. The two minor corridors that are open simply cut through the edifice from one side to the other, and were exposed by quarrying activities around thirty years ago – which inadvertently provided a good insight into the construction methods. Each is covered with great slabs of rock; in fact most of the familiar dolmens seen all over Brittany and elsewhere are thought to be the vestiges of similarly complex structures. Local tradition has it that one tunnel runs right through this "home of the fairies", and continues out deep under the sea.

travel details

Trains

From St-Malo to Rennes (12 daily; 1hr; connections for Paris on *TGV*); to Caen (8 daily; 3hr 30min); to Dinan (8 daily; 1hr). All trains pass through Dol (25min).

From Rennes 8 daily *TGV* trains to St Brieuc (45min), Morlaix (1hr 40min) and Brest (2hr 10min); 10 daily slower services also stop at Lamballe, Guingamp and Plouaret; 8 daily *TGV* trains to Paris-Montparnasse (2hr 10min), plus 5 ordinary services (3hr 15min); 4 daily to Caen (3hr) via Dol and Pontorson; to Vannes (4 daily; 1hr) and Quimper (2hr 30min); to Nantes (4 daily; 1hr 30min).

From Lannion connecting service with Plouaret, holidays & June–Sept.

From Paimpol connecting service with Guingamp.

Buses

From St-Malo to Dinard (8 daily, 30min); to Dinan (4 daily; 45min); to Mont-St-Michel (4 daily; 1hr 30min); to Cancale (4 daily; 35min); to Fougères via Pontorson (3 daily; 2hr); to Combourg (2 daily; 1hr); to Rennes (3 daily; 2hr).

From Rennes to Fougères (7 daily; 1hr); to Dinan (hourly, 1hr); to Dinard (8 daily; 1hr 40min).

From Fougères to Vitré (4 daily – all early or late in the day, 35min); to Vire (Normandy) (2 daily; 1hr 30min).

From St-Brieuc to Lannion via Guingamp (4 daily; 1hr 40min); to Cap Fréhel via Val André and Erquy (4 daily; 1hr 40min); to Carhaix (1 daily; 3hr), more frequently to Rostrenen (2hr); to Paimpol (8 daily; 1hr 30min); to Dinan (4 daily; 1hr); to Moncontour (4 daily; 1hr).

From Lannion to Trégastel and Perros-Guirrec (6 daily; 1hr); to Locquirec and Morlaix (4 daily; 1hr 20min).

Ferries

From St-Malo *Brittany Ferries* (St-Malo ☎99.82.41.41, Portsmouth ☎01705/827701) to Portsmouth (1 daily mid-March to mid-Nov, otherwise less frequently; 9hr daytime crossing). Regular ferries to Dinard (10min) in season, operated by *Émeraude Lines* (☎99.40.48.40), who also sail to Dinan up the River Rance, and along the Brittany coast to Cap Fréhel, Cézembre and Dinard (May–Sept). They also go to to Jersey (mid-March to mid-Nov) and to Guernsey and Sark (April–Sept), and to Îles Chausey and Granville in Normandy. *Condor Hydroglisseurs* (☎99.56.42.29) run services to Jersey (4 daily April–Sept, 2 daily Oct, 1 daily second half of March and first half of Nov), Guernsey (2 daily April–Oct, 1 daily second half of March and first half of Nov) and Sark (daily April–Oct), and on from the Channel Islands to Weymouth. *Channiland* (☎99.40.40.90) go to Jersey (1–4 daily mid-March to mid-Nov), slightly less frequently to Guernsey and Sark.

Bréhat Island is reached using *Vedettes de Bréhat*, who run regular 10min trips from Pointe de l'Arcouest (☎96.55.86.99), and by longer excursions from Erquy and/or Dahouët

(☎96.55.86.99), Binic (☎96.73.60.12), or St-Quay-Portrieux (☎96.70.40.64). Full details are given in each of the relevant accounts.

From St-Quay-Portrieux. Catamarans *Trident* (☎99.70.49.46) sail to Jersey and Guenrsey (1 daily; April–Sept).

Barges

Boats for use on the River Rance and the Canal d'Ille-et-Vilaine can be rented from the following companies:

Chemins Nautiques Bretons, M et Mme Alan Gaze, **La Vicomté-sur-Rance**, 22690 Pleudihen-sur-Rance (☎96.83.28.71).

Diffusion Nautique R.M., M René Michel, **La Vicomté-sur-Rance**, 22690 Pleudihen-sur-Rance (☎96.83.35.40).

Breiz Marine, 5 Quai de la Donac, 35190 **Tinténiac** (☎99.68.10.15).

Argoat Nautic, B.P. 24 Port de Betton, 35830 **Betton** (☎99.55.70.36).

Base Nautique de Pont-Réan, M le Teinturier, Pont-Réan, 35580 **Guichen** (☎99.42.21.91).

Crown Blue-Line, Port de Plaisance, 35480 **Messac** (☎99.34.60.11).

*For **general information** contact the **Comité de Promotion Touristique des Canaux Bretons**, Office du Tourisme, place du Parlement, 35600 Rennes (☎99.71.06.04).*

CHAPTER FIVE

FINISTÈRE

F inistère – literally, "the End of the World" – has always been isolated from the French, even from the Breton, mainstream. This was the last refuge of the Druids from encroaching Christianity, and its forests and elaborate parish closes are testimony to its role as the province's spiritual heartland. Today, even though the port of Roscoff has re-opened the old maritime links with England, high-speed *TGV* trains mean that Brest is just 4 hours from Paris, and the motorway now makes a complete loop around the end of the peninsula, it remains only sporadically touched by tourism and modern industry. It is here that you'll most often hear the Breton language spoken; here too, especially in the "Bigouden country" in the south, that you will see traditional costumes worn for other than commercial reasons.

Memories of when Brittany was "Petite Bretagne", as opposed to "Grande Bretagne" across the water, linger in the names of Finistère's two main areas. The northern peninsula is **Léon** (once Lyonesse), the southern is **Cornouaille** (the same word as "Cornwall"); both feature prominently in Arthurian legend. The ragged **coastline**, indented with a succession of estuaries each of which shelters its own tiny harbour, is the prime attraction. Rarely are conditions as bleak as you might expect from a land so exposed to the force of the Atlantic; heading west from **Roscoff**, your most likely point of arrival, there are possible stopping places all the way to **Le Conquet**. What can be a treacherous stretch of ocean separates that from **Ouessant** and **Molène**; and yet those two islands have the mildest winter climate of all France.

In the south, Cornouaille has two classic resorts in **Loctudy** and **Bénodet**, either side of the Odet estuary, while if you'd rather stay in a genuine lived-in town, **Quimper** is just upriver – the liveliest place here and one of the most pleasant, and least-sung, in France. A short distance east, **Pont-Aven** was Gauguin's home before he made off to the South Seas, and still maintains its artistic traditions. There are surprises everywhere – take the amazing **Museum of**

ACCOMMODATION PRICE CODES

All **hotel prices** in this book have been coded using the symbols below. The price shown is for the least expensive double room, which for categories ① and ② usually means a room without shower, bath and toilet. Most hotels in those categories have other rooms with en-suite facilities, which typically cost 30–50F extra.

For a full explanation see p.31.

①	up to 120 F	④	220–300F	⑦	500–600F
②	120–160F	⑤	300–400F	⑧	600–700F
③	160–220F	⑥	400–500F	⑨	700F and over

Mechanical Musical Instruments near Combrit, or the perfectly preserved medieval village of **Locronan**, used as a film set for Polanski's *Tess*.

All Finistère offers the enticement of growing but not yet full-blown tourist development – facilities without the crowds. Its most popular region for holiday-makers is the **Crozon peninsula**, jutting into the sea beneath the **Ménez-Hom** mountain as a distinct entity between the two ancient realms. **Morgat** and **Camaret** here are both ideal for long and leisurely seaside stays, and all around there are opportunities for secluded camping.

LÉON

The sequence of estuaries that score the coast in the north – the wildest and most dramatic in Brittany – are known both as *abers* (as they are in Welsh place names) and as *rias* (as they are in Spanish Galicia). In season, the vast beaches

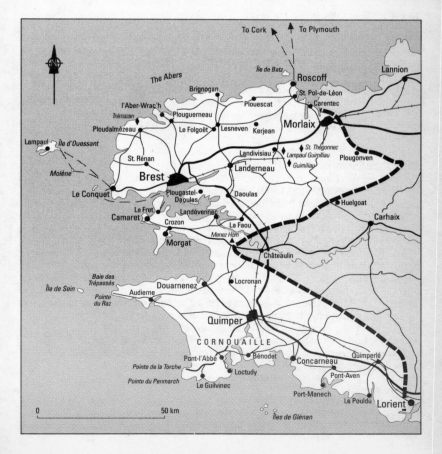

and dunes on the open Atlantic coast, for example around **Porspoder**, can be magnificent, while at any time you can stumble across tiny and deserted coves as the twisting and narrowing estuaries reach inland. One of the choicest spots is at **Trémazan**, where the ruins of an ancient castle look out across a great expanse of sand, while the working fishing village of **Le Conquet** is perhaps best of all. The one coastal place to avoid is the regional capital, and lone big city, of **Brest**, the base of the French Atlantic Fleet.

Inland, the **Parish Closes** lie strung out southwest of **Morlaix**, a sequence of little villages whose ornate churches and associated ensembles still perpetuate their fierce medieval rivalry. Also deserving a detour from the coast are the Renaissance **château of Kerjean** and the **menhir de Kerloas** (the highest still standing).

Roscoff

ROSCOFF has long been a major port – Mary Queen of Scots, for example, landed here in 1548 on her way to Paris to be engaged to the son of Henri II of France, as did Bonnie Prince Charlie in 1746, after his defeat at Culloden – and the opening of its deep-water harbour in 1973 had especial significance in the general revitalization of the Breton economy. The town itself, however, has remained a small resort. It may not look so on the map, but almost all activity is confined to the **rue Gambetta** and the **old port** – the rest of the roads are residential backstreets full of retirement homes and stern institutions. The preservation of its old character is helped by the fact that both the ferry port and gare SNCF are some way from the town centre, which has recently been pedestrianized.

Arrival and Information
Brittany Ferries **boats** from Plymouth (6hr) or Cork (19hr) dock at the new Port de Bloscon (☎98.29.28.28), to the east (and just out of sight) of Roscoff. To get into the town, turn right from the terminal, and follow the signs across a narrow promontory and down into the crescent of Roscoff's original natural harbour. Later than 9.15pm it's difficult to find a restaurant still serving; if you're arriving on an evening ferry it's probably best to eat on the boat.

The helpful **SI** is at 46 rue Gambetta in town (Mon–Fri 9.30am–12.30pm & 2–6pm, Sat 10am–noon; ☎98.61.12.13), next to a *boulangerie* and the **post office** at 19 rue Gambetta (☎98.69.72.90). Regular trains run to Morlaix, with connections beyond from the **gare SNCF** (☎98.69.70.20), a few hundred metres south of the town proper. Most buses also go from here, including a direct service to Brest run by *Les Cars du Kreisker* (☎98.69.00.93). Another service to Morlaix leaves from the fish hall (known locally as *La Criée*) by the old harbour, with connections on Mondays, Fridays and Saturdays to Quimper (*Tourisme Verney*; ☎98.88.56.58).

Bikes can be rented from *Desbordes François*, 13 rue Brizeux (☎98.69.72.44), as well as from the gare SNCF.

The Town
The old **harbour** is the liveliest part of Roscoff, mixing an economy based on fishing with low-key pleasure trips to the Île de Batz. The island looks almost walkable; a narrow pier stretches over four hundred metres towards it before

abruptly plunging into deep rocky waters. The Pointe de Bloscon and the white fisherman's chapel, the Chapelle Ste-Barbe, make a good vantage point, particularly when the tide is in; the tide goes out a long way (and dictates the precise embarkation point for the boat trips). Below the headland are the *viviers*, where you can see trout, salmon, lobsters and crabs being reared for the pot.

In addition to the island ferries, detailed on p.217, *Armein Excursions* (☎98.61.77.75) also operate three-hour cruises from here around the **Bay of Morlaix** (July & Aug Tues, Wed, Fri & Sat at 2.15pm; April–June & Sept–Oct, Wed & Sat at 2.15pm), and excursions to the **Cairn de Barnenez** (see p.210), depending on the demand and the state of the tides.

Until the last couple of centuries, Roscoff made most of its money from piracy, like so many other ports along the Breton coast. There are a few reminders of that wealth along rue Gambetta, which becomes rue Amiral-Réveillère. Two of its ornate grey granite houses, including no. 25 ("the House of Mary Stuart"), claim to be where Mary Queen of Scots spent her first night after eighteen stormy days at sea – despite the fact that both were built after she landed.

The sculpted ships and protruding stone cannons of the Renaissance belfry which tops the sixteenth-century town church, **Notre-Dame de Croas Batz**, also recall the seafaring days. From the side, rows of bells can be seen hanging in galleries, one above the other, like a tall narrow wedding cake created by the young Walt Disney.

A short way past the church, on place Georges-Teissier, the **Charles Perez Aquarium** contains a well displayed and comprehensive collection of marine fauna of the Channel (April–Oct daily 10am–12.30pm & 1.30–7pm; 25F). It's an interesting enough place, if a little disappointing for anyone expecting the exotic, and forms part of the Institute of Oceanology which undertakes oceanographic, and related biological, research.

ALEXIS GOURVANNEC AND BRITTANY FERRIES

Few British holiday-makers sailing to France with Brittany Ferries will realize the significance of ideology in the origins of that company. The ferry services from Roscoff to Plymouth and to Cork were started not simply to bring tourists, but also to revive the traditional trading links between the Celtic nations of Brittany, Ireland, and southwest England – links which were suppressed for centuries as an act of French state policy after the union of Brittany with France in 1532.

Until the 1960s there were no direct ferries crossing the Channel to Brittany, and until Brittany Ferries started up, all the cross-Channel operators were British-owned. Brittany Ferries is the creation of Alexis Gourvennec, who in 1961, at 24, was the militant leader of a Breton farmers' co-operative. Frustrated at the lack of French government support, the farmers decided to start their own shipping line to find new markets for their produce – the immediate region of Roscoff and Morlaix being particularly noted for its artichokes and cauliflowers.

The financial success of the company has been such that it has expanded to run services from Britain to the Norman ports of Cherbourg and Caen, as well as to Spain; but it has also been an important factor in a resurgence of Breton fortunes that has as much cultural as commercial significance. Meanwhile Breton farmers have been campaigning for the expansion of Brest airport (at Guipavas) so that it will be able to handle jumbo-jet loads of artichokes for same-day sale in New York !

See *Contexts* for more details.

Some way beyond the grand buildings of the Institute is the **Thalassotherapy Institute** of Rock Roum, specializing in seawater cures, and a kilometre further on is Roscoff's best **beach**, at Laber, surrounded by expensive hotels and apartments.

In the opposite direction from town, south along the coast from the ferry terminal, are the tropical gardens at **Rock Hievec**. Here cacti, palm trees and flowers of South America and the Pacific flourish in the mild Gulf-Stream climate.

In 1828, Henri Ollivier took **onions** to England from Roscoff, thereby founding a trade which flourished until the 1930s. In the bar of the *Hôtel du Centre* (see below), you can see old photographs of "Johnnies", men in black berets with strings of onions hanging over the handlebars of their bicycles. Older people of the town remember travelling as children with their fathers as far afield as Glasgow.

Accommodation and Eating

For a small town, Roscoff is well equipped with **hotels**, which are well accustomed to late-night arrivals from the ferries. Be warned however that most of them close in winter. There's also a **youth hostel** on the Île de Batz (see below), and two summer **campsites** – the *Municipal de Perharidy*, 2km west, just off the route de Santec (Easter–Sept; ☎98.69.70.86), and the *Manoir de Kerestat*, 2km south towards St-Pol (July & Aug only; ☎98.69.71.92).

Very much the obvious places to **eat** are the dining rooms of the hotels themselves, though it's seldom easy to get a meal much after 9pm. If you'd prefer something lighter, the *à la carte* meals of sweet and savoury pancakes at the central *Crêperie de la Poste*, 12 rue Gambetta (closed Wed; ☎98.69.72.81) work out economical, so long as you don't get carried away by the exotic seafood options.

Hôtel-Restaurant des Arcades, 15 rue Amiral-Réveillère (☎98.69.70.45). Sixteenth-century building with superb views from some rooms and from the restaurant; menus 48F and upwards. Closed Oct–Easter. ②.

Hôtel-Restaurant Bellevue, bd Jeanne d'Arc (☎98.61.23.38). Seafront *Logis de France* , on the opposite side of the pleasure harbour to the town centre and thus somewhat nearer the ferry terminal. It would in theory be quieter, were it not for the lively downstairs bar. Pleasant rooms, and fine views from the dining room, where the 105F menu offers salmon baked in cheese with mustard. Closed mid-Nov to mid-March. ④.

Hôtel du Centre, 5 rue Gambetta (☎98.61.24.25). *Logis de France* facing the beach, very much run as a family hotel. Also known as *Chez Janie*. Menus from 85F. Closed Jan to mid-Feb. ②.

Les Chardons Bleus, 4 rue Amiral-Réveillère (☎98.69.72.03). Very friendly and helpful hotel with a good restaurant (menus from 75F; closed Thurs out of season) but no sea views. Closed Dec and Jan. ④.

Hôtel de la Gare, 2 rue Ropartz-Morvan (☎98.61.21.42). Cheap rooms, very close to the gare SNCF, with a bar and shop but no restaurant. Open all year. ②.

Le Gulf Stream, rue Marquise de Kergariou (☎98.69.73.19). Definitely one of the more expensive options, just south of the Institute of Oceanology, but with a quite superb seafood restaurant (where the cheapest menu is 140F). Closed mid-Oct to mid-March. ⑤.

Inter Hôtel Regina, 1 rue Ropartz-Morvan (☎98.61.23.55). Very comfortable rooms, but relatively expensive considering the location, near the gare SNCF. Menus from 85F upwards, and live jazz in the bar in what might otherwise be the quieter months. Closed Nov to mid-March. ④.

Hôtel les Tamaris, 49 rue É-Corbière (☎98.61.22.99). Renovated, comfortably furnished rooms looking out towards the Île de Batz. Closed mid-Oct to April. ④.

The Île de Batz

The **ÎLE DE BATZ** (pronounced *Ba*), just off the coast at Roscoff and inhabited by just under a thousand hardy farmers and fishers, is a somewhat windswept spot, but well endowed with sandy beaches. For campers looking to have a stretch of coastline to themselves, it could be ideal.

The island's first recorded inhabitant was a "laidly worm", a dragon that infested the place in the sixth century. Such dragons normally symbolize pre-Christian religions, in this case perhaps a Druidic serpent cult. Allegorical or not, when Saint Pol arrived to found a monastery he wrapped a Byzantine stole around the unfortunate creature's neck and cast it into the sea. These days, there are no dragons; there aren't even any trees, just an awful lot of seaweed which is collected and sold for fertilizer.

Practicalities

Several sailings each day from Roscoff, operated by *Armein Excursions* (☎98.61.77.75), arrive at the quayside of the old island town (July to mid-Sept, daily 8am–8pm, every half hour on the half hour; mid-Sept to Oct & mid-March to June, eight trips 8.30am–7pm; Nov to mid-March, eight trips 8.30am–6.30pm; 25F return). In July and August, the same company runs boat tours right around the island (Sun 2.15pm).

Walk uphill from the port – site of the basic *Hôtel-Restaurant Roch Ar Mor* (April–Sept; ☎98.61.78.28; ②) – and you will come to the **youth hostel**, at the evocatively-named Creach ar Bolloc'h (April–Sept; ☎98.61.77.69; 43F). Higher still, on the island's peak (all of 23m above sea-level) is a 44m lighthouse, which welcomes visitors. And beyond that, it's just the sands and seaweed.

St-Pol-de-Léon

The main road **south from Roscoff** passes by fields of the famous Breton artichokes before arriving after six kilometres at **ST-POL-DE-LÉON**. Pleasantly sited amidst rich gardens, this is not an exciting place but – assuming you've your own transport – has two churches that at least merit a pause.

The **Cathedral**, in the main town square, was rebuilt towards the end of the thirteenth century along the lines of Coutances (see p.124) – a quiet classic of unified Norman architecture. The remains of Saint Pol are inside, alongside a large bell, rung over the heads of pilgrims during his *pardon* on March 12 in the unlikely hope of curing headaches and ear diseases.

Just downhill, the **Kreisker Chapel** is notable for its sharp-pointed soaring granite belfry, now coated in yellow moss. It was originally modelled on the Norman spire of St-Pierre at Caen, which was destroyed in the last war (see p.102), but as an elegant improvement on its Norman counterpart was itself much copied. All over rural Brittany are dotted similar "Kreisker" spires. The dramatic view to be seen if you climb this spire (daily 10–11.30am & 2–6pm), out across the **Bay of Morlaix**, should be enough to persuade you to follow the road along the shore.

If you're looking for **accommodation** in St-Pol, you're likely to fetch up at either the *Hôtel Cheval Blanc*, 6 rue au Lin (☎98.69.01.00; ②), or the *Hôtel-Restaurant le Passiflore*, near the station at 28 rue Pen-ar-Pont (☎98.69.00.52; ③), both of which are open all year and have reasonable restaurants.

Carentec

From St-Pol, take the small foliage-covered lane down to join the D58, just in time to cross the **Pont de la Corde** which carries you over to the resort and penin- sula of **CARENTEC**, studded with small coves and secluded beaches. The **Île de Callot**, an enticing hour's walk away from the slightly drab town itself at low tide, is the scene of a *pardon* and blessing of the sea on the Sunday after August 15 – a rather dour occasion, as are most of the serious religious festivals around Finistère.

The D78 runs on from Carentec beside the sea, the estuary narrowing until at Locquenolé it is just the width of the River Morlaix. From then on it is a beautiful deep valley, with promenades and gardens along the stone-reinforced banks, and views across to isolated villages such as Dourduff on the other side.

This stretch of coast comes alive in summer with a scattering of seasonal **campsites**, among them the excellent *Les Mouettes* (May to mid-Sept; ☎98.67.02.46). For rooms in Carentec, the **hotels** *La Falaise* (Easter to mid-Sept; ☎98.67.00.53; ③) and *Porspol* (mid-April to mid-Sept; ☎98.67.00.52; ④) are both good value.

The Château de Taureau

A short way east of Carentec, the fortified **Château de Taureau**, off Pointe de Pen-al-Lann, guards the entrance to Morlaix bay, 12 km north of Morlaix itself. It was built after a succession of skirmishes that began in 1522, when Morlaix pirates raided and looted Bristol. Henry VIII's pride was hurt, and seeking revenge, he sent a sizeable fleet to storm Morlaix. The citizens were absent at a neighbouring festival when the English arrived. When they returned, they found the English drunk in their wine cellars. Once the Bretons had routed their enemies, they built the château to forestall further attacks from the sea. In the seventeenth century, it was used as a prison; now it's a sailing school. Meanwhile, Morlaix adopted the motto which it keeps to this day – "If they bite you, bite them back".

Morlaix

MORLAIX, one of the great old Breton ports, thrived off trade with England – in between wars – during the "Golden Period" of the late Middle Ages. Its sober stone houses were built up the slopes of the steep valley where the Queffleuth and Jarlot rivers join to flow together into Morlaix bay, originally protected by an eleventh-century castle and a circuit of walls. Little is left of either, but the old centre remains in part medieval – cobbled streets and half-timbered houses. Later, the town grew still more prosperous on piracy and the tobacco trade (both legal and illegal), and spread north, down the valley, towards the port.

Arrival and Information

The **SI** in Morlaix is in a solitary but central one-storey building, almost under the viaduct in place des Otages (mid-June to mid-Sept Mon–Sat 9am–12.30pm & 1.30–7.30pm, Sun 10am–12.30pm; otherwise Tues–Sat 9am–noon & 2–6.30pm; ☎98.62.14.94). The **post office** is on rue de Brest (☎98.88.23.03).

The **gare SNCF** (☎98.80.50.60) is on rue Armand-Rousseau, high above the town at the western end of the viaduct. It was originally intended to connect the station with town by means of a funicular railway, but that was never built and you still have to reach it on foot, climbing the steep steps of the Venelle de la Roche. If you can't face the long trek up to the station to buy a ticket, you can make reservations at travel agencies down in the town proper.

All **buses** conveniently depart from place Cornic, right under the viaduct; long-distance routes include those south to Carhaix and on to Rosporden and Concarneau or Lorient (*SCEATA*; ☎98.93.06.98).

Bicycles can be rented from *Henri Le Gall,* 1 rue de Callac (☎98.88.60.47).

The Town

Morlaix is dominated by its pink granite **railway viaduct,** built high above the valley in the 1860s to carry trains en route between Paris and Brest. Despite all Allied attempts during World War II to destroy it with bombs, it still looms almost two hundred feet above the central **place des Otages,** and as you enter the town today by road from the north, your opening view is of shiny yacht masts in the pleasure harbour paralleling its slender pillars. The first level of the viaduct is intermittently open to visitors, usually (but not always) from 11am until 7pm each day.

There are few actual sights in town, but the pleasure anyway is more in roaming the length of the steep stairways that lead up from the places des Otages and Cornic, or in walking up to the viaduct from the top of Venelle aux Prêtres, along an almost rural overgrown path lined with brambles.

On her way from Roscoff to Paris, Mary Queen of Scots passed through Morlaix in 1548, and stayed at the **Jacobin convent** which fronts place des Jacobins. She was at the time just five years old, an aspect which may have contributed to local interest in the spectacle. A contemporary account records that the crush to catch a glimpse of the infant was so great that the inner town's "gates were thrown off their hinges and the chains from all the bridges were broken down".

The **town museum,** in the convent church, contains a reasonably entertaining assortment of Roman wine jars, bits that have fallen off medieval churches, cannons and kitchen utensils, and a few modern paintings (entrance on rue des Vigues; daily 10am–noon & 2–6pm; closed Tues in winter). The only drawback is the powerful stench of fish that seeps up from the market held immediately below on the ground floor of this former church.

The church of **St-Mathieu,** off rue de Paris, contains a sombre and curious statue of the Madonna and Child; Mary's breast was apparently lopped off by a prudish former priest, to leave the babe suckling at nothing. The whole statue opens down the middle to reveal a separate figure of God the Father, clutching a crucifix. In April 1993, the figure of Christ was stolen, but the thief, who preferred to pray at home, repented in October 1994 and returned it anonymously.

Duchess Anne of Brittany, by then Queen of France, visited Morlaix in 1506. She is reputed to have stayed at the **Maison de la Reine Anne,** 33 rue du Mur, which, although much restored, does indeed date from the sixteenth century. Its intricate external carvings, and the lantern roof and splendid Renaissance staircase inside, make it the most beautiful of the town's ancient houses. It is open to the public between April and September (Tues–Sat 9.30am–12.30pm & 2–5.30pm), and at other times by arrangement (☎98.79.63.85).

In the eighteenth century, Morlaix's wealth was sustained by boat building, textiles and tobacco, and the **tobacco factory,** on quai de Léon by the port, remains active. It employs 500 people who produce annually 300 million cigars, 50 tons of chewing tobacco and 15 tons of snuff, and can be visited on Wednesday afternoons (ring ☎98.88.15.32).

Accommodation

In addition to the many (fairly uninspiring) **hotels** dotted around old Morlaix, there's also a **youth hostel** at 3 route de Paris (open all year; ☎98.88.13.63; 43F), 1km out from the town centre; take the *Kernégues* bus as far as either rue de Paris or place Traoulan, and then it's just off to the left. The municipal campsite is now closed.

Hôtel les Arcades, 11 place Cornic (☎98.88.20.03). Not far from the viaduct, opposite the new bus station. No restaurant. ①.

Hôtel Au Roy d'Ys, 8 place des Jacobins (☎98.88.61.19). Central hotel, across the square from the town museum. The cheapest rooms do not have their own showers; guests have to pay 13F extra to use shared showers. No restaurant, but a downstairs bar. Closed Nov. ①.

Hôtel de l'Europe, 1 rue d'Aiguillon (☎98.62.11.99). Slightly eccentric old place, with an odd line in furnishing but a superb restaurant, where menus start at 95F. ③.

Hôtel-Restaurant les Halles, 23 rue du Mur (☎98.88.03.86). Friendly hotel facing the attractive place des Halles, with a garage for motor bikes and bicycles. Closed Sun. Slightly shabby rooms, but they're clean enough, and there's a very good cheap restaurant with menus at 48F and 66F. ①.

Hôtel le Port, 3 quai de Léon (☎98.88.07.54). A new place, overlooking the port from the left bank. It doesn't have a restaurant, but each room has its own kitchenette – presumably for yacht-owners who fancy a night on shore. ③.

Hôtel-Restaurant le St-Mélaine, 75–77 rue Ange-de-Guernisac (☎98.88.08.79). Self-styled family hotel, not easy to find, above place Cornic and all but under the viaduct. Value for money, but dull. The restaurant serves simple menus from 55F. ①.

Eating

The best hunting ground for **restaurants** in Morlaix is to be found between St-Mélaine church and place des Jacobins.

L'Agadir, 24 rue Ange-de-Guernisac (☎98.63.42.02). Despite the name, this is an Algerian restaurant, serving couscous and so on.

Brocéliande, 5 rue des Bouchers (☎98.88.73.78). In the southeast of town, beyond the place des Halles and St-Mathieu church. Elegant evening-only dining in a *fin-de-siècle* atmosphere; a typical main course from the choice menu costs around 70F.

Dolce Vita, 3 rue Ange-de-Guernisac (☎98.63.37.67). Pizzeria, which also serves pasta dishes. Set menus start at 120F, but you can choose *à la carte*.

COREFF – REAL ALE IN BRITTANY

1985 saw the inauguration of an unlikely new product in Morlaix – the first Breton real ale! Two young Frenchmen, Christian Blanchard and Jean-François Malgorn, set up their own brewery, with the ambition of emulating the beers they had enjoyed on visits to Wales.

You should be able to find the resultant brew, *Coreff*, both locally and throughout Brittany in those bars which take pride in all things Breton. It's also possible to visit the brewery, the *Brasserie des Deux-Rivières*, at 1 place de la Madeleine (tours Mon–Wed at 11am, 2pm, 3pm & 4pm; ☎98.63.41.92).

As for the beer itself, it's a sweet, rich and reasonably authentic brown ale which can make a welcome change from the lagers everywhere on offer.

La Marée Bleue, 3 rampe Ste-Mélaine (☎98.63.24.21). Well respected seafood restaurant; the 78F menu isn't at all bad, while 135F ensures you a superb *assiette de fruits de mer*.

Le Marrakech, Venelle du Four St-Mélaine (☎98.88.78.93). This one *is* a Moroccan restaurant, just round the corner from *L'Agadir. tagine*, etc.

Le Passé Simple, 21 bis place Charles-de-Gaulle (☎98.88.81.39). Lush and very pleasant restaurant, with some excellent seafood specialities on menus which start at just over 50F. Closed Sat lunchtime & Mon.

Nightlife and Drinking

Among bars to look out for while you're in Morlaix are *Ty Coz*, at 10 Venelle Au Beurre (closed Thurs), near the youth hostel, which has boisterous Bretons playing darts, and draught Coreff beer, and the lively *Tempo Piano Bar*, facing the port on quai de Tréguier, (☎98.63.29.11), where there are regular jazz and blues concerts. The *Club Coätelan* (☎98.72.50.71) in Plougonven, 12km east of Morlaix, also books a wide assortment of jazz, rock and blues performers.

Onward routes from Morlaix

Moving on from Morlaix, you are strategically poised. To the **west** are the **Parish Closes** – described in the following section – and, beyond them, access to the best of the **Finistère coast** around Le Conquet and the Crozon peninsula. **South**, via the **Forêt de Huelgoat** (see p.260), is the direct route to **Quimper;** and **east** you can take in the remarkable **Cairn du Barnenez** (p.210) en route to the **Côte de Granit Rose**.

The Parish Closes

A few miles west of Morlaix, bounded by the valleys of the Elorn and the Penzé rivers, lies an area remarkable for the wealth and distinction of its **church architecture**. This is where the best-known examples of what the French call *enclos paroissiaux* are to be found. The phrase translates into English as "parish close", and is used to describe a walled churchyard which in addition to the church itself incorporates a trinity of further elements – a cemetery, a calvary and an ossuary.

The **ossuaries** – which now tend to contain nothing more alarming than a few rows of postcards – were previously charnel-houses, used to store the exhumed bones of less recent burials. They are the most striking features of the closes, making explicit a peculiarly Breton proximity and continuity between the living and the dead. Parishioners would go to pray, with the informality of making a family visit, in the ossuary chapels where the dead bones of their families were on display. The relationship may have originated with the builders of the megalithic passage graves, which by this account served as doorways between our world and the netherworld.

The actual **cemeteries** tend to be small, and in many cases have disappeared altogether, while the **calvaries**, which complete the ensemble, are tenuously based on the hill of Calvary. Each is therefore in theory surmounted by a crucifixion, but the definition is loose enough to take in any cluster of religious statuary, not necessarily even limited to Biblical scenes, standing on a single base.

That there are so many and such fine *enclos* in this region is due to a period of intense inter-village rivalry during the sixteenth and seventeenth centuries, when parishes competed to outdo each other in complexity and ornament. It's no coincidence that most such Breton churches date from the two centuries to either side of the union with France in 1532 – Brittany's wealthiest period – and nothing is more telling of the decline in the province's fortunes than the contrast between the riches on show and the relative lack of prosperity of the present-day villages. An additional, more positive, layer is contributed, however, by the current revival of artisan traditions in the parishes. In several of the towns and villages you find stonemasons once more producing sculptures in granite.

A clearly signposted **route** leading past several of the most famous churches – St-Thégonnec, Guimiliau and Lampaul-Guimiliau – can be joined by leaving the N12 between Morlaix and Landivisiau at St-Thégonnec.

St-Thégonnec

At the **ST-THÉGONNEC** *enclos*, the church **pulpit**, carved by two brothers in 1683, is the acknowledged masterpiece, although it is covered so completely in detail – symbolic saints, sybils and arcane figures – that it is almost too ornate to appreciate. The painted oak **entombment** in the crypt under the ossuary, with a stunning life-size figure of Mary Magdalene, has more immediate effect, while the entire east wall of the church is a carved and painted retable, with saints in niches and a hundred different scenes depicted.

The *Hôtel du Commerce* at 1 rue de Paris (☎98.79.61.07; ②), very near the church, is a *Routiers* hotel (and thus closed Sat, Sun & Aug) which serves very good-value basic meals, while the much more upmarket *Auberge de St-Thégonnec* at 6 place de la Mairie (☎98.79.61.18; closed Jan & Feb, Sun pm, Mon pm in summer and all day Mon otherwise; ⑤) has comfortable rooms and an excellent restaurant.

Guimiliau

The showpiece at **GUIMILIAU** is the calvary, an incredible ensemble of over two hundred granite figures, enacting scenes from the life of Christ. A uniquely Breton illustration, just above the Last Supper, depicts the unfortunate Katell Gollet being torn to shreds by demons in punishment for stealing consecrated wafers to give to her lover (who of course turned out to be the Devil).

OTHER BRETON CHURCHES

Breton Catholicism has a very distinctive character, closer to the Celtic past than to Rome. There are hundreds of saints who've never been approved by the Vatican, but whose brightly painted wooden figures adorn every Breton church. Their stories merge imperceptibly with the tales of moving menhirs, ghosts and sorcery. Visions and miracles are still assumed; and death's workmate, *Ankou*, is a familiar figure, even if no one now would dread his manifestation.

In addition to the three most famous *enclos paroissiaux*, several **lesser-known churches** in the vicinity have interesting details – in particular, representations of the skeletal *Ankou*. At **La Martyre**, the oldest of the *enclos*, built in 1460, he clutches a skull; at **La Roche-Maurice** he declares "I kill you all", a remark given extra force by the nearby ruined castle – in which Katell Gollet is supposed to have lived.

If you're inspired by the parish closes to go in search of similar village churches elsewhere in Brittany, other notable closes and chapels include those at **Kermaria-an-Isquit** (p.199), **Ploumilliau** (p.209), **Grouannec** (p.226), **Pleyben** (p.258), **St-Fiacre** (p.259) and **Guéhenno** (p.266).

Inside the church, the gutted shell of the seventeenth-century organ, a lovely tangle of mangled wood, provides welcome contrast to all the neatness around; the 750 villagers are collecting for its restoration, but it seems fine as it is.

Lampaul-Guimiliau

The third of the major parish closes, **LAMPAUL-GUIMILIAU**, is a few miles further on. Here the painted oak baptistry, the dragons on the beams and the appropriately wicked faces of the robbers on the calvary are the key components.

The *Hôtel de l'Enclos* (☎96.68.77.08; ④), 300 metres beyond the church on the left, is a new hotel with good rooms and a very reasonable restaurant.

Landivisiau

LANDIVISIAU, just south of the N12 twenty kilometres west of Morlaix, makes a good alternative to Morlaix as a base from which to tour the nearby parish closes.

There's not much to the town itself, but coach tours operate regularly (from its main square) and you've a choice of several cheap **hotels**, best value of them *Le Terminus*, 94 av Foch (☎98.68.02.00; closed Sat, Sun pm & all Aug; ②), a *Routier* with excellent meals and a few cut-price rooms, and *de l'Avenue* (☎98.68.11.67; ①).

Landerneau

Following the scenic D712 alongside the pretty Elorn river from Landivisiau, you come after 16km to **LANDERNEAU**, at the mouth of the Elorn estuary. This too was once a major port; now it's more of a tourist showpiece. The **pont de Rohan** in the middle of town is said to be, along with the Ponte Vecchio in Florence, the last inhabited bridge in Europe, and is the site of the local **SI** (☎98.85.13.09).

Landerneau offers several **accommodation** possibilities; either of *Le Clos du Pontic*, rue du Pontic (closed Sat lunch, as well as Sun pm & Mon in low season; ☎98.21.50.91; ⑤), or *l'Amandier*, 55 rue de Brest (closed Sun pm & Mon ☎98.85.10.89; ④), would be a real treat, both being comfortable old-style hotels with excellent restaurants.

Kerjean

KERJEAN is little more than fifteen kilometres from Roscoff, and, if not quite the "Versailles of Brittany", as it is promoted, is a surprisingly classic château for this remote corner of France. It's not that easy to find, however – you need to be on the D30, running from Plouescat to Landivisiau, and to turn right shortly after St-Vougay. The nearest stop on the Roscoff–Brest bus route is **Lanhouarneau**.

What you're confronted by when you do arrive is a moated Renaissance **château**, set in its own park. It was built in the sixteenth century by the lords of Kerjean, with the express intention of overshadowing the mansion of their former feudal overlord, the Carman of Lanhouarneau. Under some archaic quirk of fealty the Kerjean lords had been obliged each year to take an egg, in a cart, and to cook it for the Carman (whatever a Carman may have been). The château must have made the memory a whole lot easier to bear.

The building, state property these days, is an odd jumble of the authentic, the restored and the imported. There is one original ceiling, one original floor and one original door; and the guide on the 45-minute tour has one original joke to match. Nevertheless it's an interesting place, and there's a certain amusement to be derived from the odd placing of objects and the lack of explanations. In the scullery are two thirteenth-century choirstalls from St-Pol cathedral, each seat carved with the head of its occupant; a statue of Saint Sebastian "run through with arrows" has not an arrow in sight; and it is unclear quite what Saint Anthony is doing "with the little pig". More standard Breton furnishings are the cupboard-like panelled box-beds which people used to climb inside to sleep – shut in tight for the night.

Tours, which cost 25F, run every day in July and August between 10am and 7pm, and every day except Tuesday in June and September, from 10am until 6pm; at other times the opening hours are erratic – ring ☎98.69.93.69 for details. The castle gates are shut while each tour is in progress.

Lesneven and Le Folgoët

Continuing inland, whether you are headed for Southern Brittany or for Le Conquet and Ouessant island, Le Folgoët is another stop worth planning for. It is more easily accessible than Kerjean, though by bus you'll probably find yourself dropped a couple of kilometres out at the small town of **LESNEVEN**. The main features here are an abbey, on the main square, and some eccentric houses – slate-roofed and convex-panelled – in the narrow lanes. A visit to the **German war cemetery** a short distance southeast of the centre is a sobering experience (see p.109 for a general piece on war cemeteries).

Lesneven does not itself hold any great interest, though its ivy-coated café is an attractive place to break your journey, and the pretty *Hôtel Breizh-Izel*, rue du Four (☎98.83.12.33; ①), provides cheap accommodation.

Le Folgoët

LE FOLGOËT is about half an hour's walk southwest of Lesneven. At first sight no more than a small village, with a well-kept and rather English-looking green, it owes its **Notre-Dame** church – as well as its name, "Fool's Wood" – to a four-teenth-century simpleton called Solomon. After an unappreciated lifetime repeating the four Breton words for "O Lady Virgin Mary", he found fame in death by growing a white lily out of his mouth. The church was erected on the site of his favourite spring, and holds a *pardon* on September 8 or the preceding Sunday. (On the fourth Sunday of July there is also a *pardon* of St Christopher, which involves a blessing of cars that non-motorists may find verging on the blasphe-mous.) In its quieter moments, however, it's a lovely church, colourfully garnished with orange moss and clinging verdure (a sign of the penetrating damp inside), and with a bumpy and stubbly approximation of a "Kreisker" spire. It has been restored bit by bit since the damage of the Revolution, and an unusual amount of statuary has been placed on the many niches low down all around the outside. The most recent expenditure has been to put fresh white plaster noses on the apostles guarding its entrance, who in consequence look like hastily rounded-up and not quite well-scrubbed enough choirboys.

Immediately opposite, a fifteenth-century manor house has arranged in the lush lawns by its front path a selection of decaying sculpture from the church, gargoyles and griffins and an armless Jesus.

The Abers of the Northwest Coast

The coast west from Roscoff is among the most dramatic in Brittany, a jagged series of **abers** – narrow estuaries, if not as deep or steep-sided as the fjords with which they are occasionally compared – in the midst of which are clustered small, isolated resorts. It's a little on the bracing side, especially if you're making use of the numerous **campsites**, but that just has to be counted as part of the appeal. In summer, at least, the temperatures are mild enough, and things get progressively more sheltered as you move around towards Le Conquet and Brest.

Plouescat

PLOUESCAT is the first real resort out of Roscoff. It is not quite on the sea itself but there are **campsites** at each of three adjacent beaches – **Pors-Guen**, **Pors-Meur** (☎98.69.63.16) and **Poul Foën** (☎98.69.80.81). In the town, you'll find a high-roofed old wooden market hall, for picnic provisions, and a statue of a seahorse with a yin and yang symbol in its tail. At the edge of the bay, 1km from the centre, the *Auberge Le Kersabiec* serves good food. Of the **hotels**, best value is the *Baie de Kernic* (☎98.69.63.41; closed Sun pm & Mon out of season, and all Nov; ②–④). Roscoff to Brest buses stop at Plouescat before turning inland.

At the village of **KEREMMA**, inland from the sea on the way between Plouescat and Brignogan, there's another lovely little **campsite** (mid-June to mid-Sept; ☎98.61.62.79), set along a green avenue lined with meadows of purple and yellow flowers.

Brignogan-Plage

BRIGNOGAN-PLAGE, on the next *aber*, has a small natural harbour, once the lair of wreckers, with beaches and weather-beaten rocks to either side, as well as its own menhir. Here once again the tide recedes way out towards the mouth of the bay, leaving surreal clumps of seaweed-coated stone bulging up among the stranded boats. The **plage de Ménéham**, 2km west of town, is a gem of a beach.

The two high-season **campsites** are the central municipal site at Kéravezan (mid-June to mid-Sept; ☎98.83.41.65) and the *du Phare*, east of town (May–Sept; ☎98.83.45.06), while the hotel *Castel Regis* (April–Sept; ☎98.83.40.22; ④) is expensive but beautifully situated among the rocks, right at the headland. *Ar Reder Mor*, (☎98.83.40.09; ③), in the centre of the little town, is a cheaper but fairly nondescript option. There are also schools of both sailing and riding.

Plouguerneau and Grouannec

Moving west again, along the D10, **PLOUGUERNEAU** has the **hotel/restaurant** *Les Abériades* (☎98.04.71.01; closed Sun pm & Mon out of season; ③) to recommend it. This village of just over 5000 inhabitants was the unlikely recipient in 1990 of the **Prix de l'Europe**, awarded each year by the Council of Europe

---

The council of **Plouescat** attained a certain notoriety in July 1987, when its members decided they could no longer live with the embarrassing presence of an exceptionally phallic rock on one of the local beaches and dynamited it to smithereens at dead of night. Local artists responded by creating several much more embarrassing substitutes which you might care to look out for.

to the most exemplary European community, and presented by President Mitterand. Previous winners include Istanbul, Avignon and The Hague; Plouguerneau was chosen largely on the basis of its vigorous and successful twinning with the German town of Edingen-Neckerhausen, near Heidelberg, which has so far produced 20 Franco-German marriages.

Plouguerneau is also near to an unexpected pleasure, the church of **Notre-Dame de Grouannec**, a small but complete parish close ensemble about four kilometres inland. It has been extensively restored, and looks all the better for it, with its fountain, ossuary, mini-cloister and profusion of gargoyles.

L'Aber-Wrac'h

The *aber* between Plouguerneau and the yachting port of **L'ABER-WRAC'H** has a stepping-stone crossing just upstream from the bridge at Lanillis, built in Gallo-Roman times, and its long cut stones still cross the three channels of water (access off the D28 signposted Rascoll), and continue past farm buildings to the right to "Pont du Diable".

L'Aber-Wrac'h itself is a promising place to spend a little time. It's an attractive, modest-sized resort, within easy reach of a whole range of sandy beaches and a couple of worthwhile excursions. Beyond the tiny fishing port, the Baie des Anges stretches away towards the Atlantic, with the only sound the cry of seagulls feasting on the oyster beds. The *Hôtel la Baie des Anges* (Easter–Oct; ☎98.04.90.04; ③), festooned with ivy and purple clematis, commands lovely views out to sea from the start of its endless curve. Among the dunes at the very tip of the headland, the municipal **campsite** *de Penn Enez* (mid-June to mid-Sept; ☎98.04.99.82) has an idyllic setting.

On the far side of the estuary, at **LILIA**, you can take a boat to visit the 78m **Vierge lighthouse**, while near the end of the next peninsula to the west stands the castle of Trémazan.

Trémazan

Once past **PORTSALL**, the coast becomes a glorious succession of dunes and open spaces, with long beaches stretching at low tide way out towards tiny islands. A particularly romantic spot is where the crumbling walls of the *Sleeping Beauty*-style **castle** of **TRÉMAZAN** look down on a magnificent beach. This is where the fleeing Tristan and Iseult are said to have landed in Brittany, and the cracked ivy-covered keep still stands proud, pierced by a large heart-shaped hole. The castle is not formally open to the public; it's totally overgrown, and to reach it you have to scramble your way through the brambles that totally fill its former moat. Once you're there, however, it's a real haven for a summer afternoon.

In the immediate vicinity, the *logis* at **Kersaint Landunvez**, the *Hostelerie du Castel* (☎98.48.63.35; ③), is a good overnight stop. That's a little isolated, though, and you might prefer to stay either in L'Aber-Wrac'h or in Porspoder a few kilometres further on – pausing to look at the exquisite wooden seaside **chapel of St Samson** on the way.

Porspoder

PORSPODER is itself a pretty quiet place, but does serve as a centre for the many campers who set themselves up on the dunes of the **Presqu'île St-Laurent** which faces it. Most of the houses around are empty other than in summer – it must be pretty bleak in winter – but in season it's an attractive place to be, open to the ocean. There's a cheap **hotel**, the *Pen Ar Bed* (March–Sept; ☎98.89.90.38; ②), as well as **rooms** to let (for example from Mme Gautier, ☎98.89.99.72) along the long seafront rue de l'Europe.

Le Conquet

LE CONQUET, the southernmost of the *abers* resorts, at the far western tip of Brittany 24km beyond Brest, makes the best holiday base of all. A wonderful place, scarcely developed, it is flanked by a long beach of clean white sand, protected from the winds by the narrow spit of the Kermorvan peninsula, and has ferry access to the islands of Ouessant and Molène. It is very much a working fishing village, the grey stone houses leading down to the stone jetties of a cramped harbour – which occasionally floods, to the intense amusement of the locals, the waves washing over the cars left by tourists making the trip to Ouessant.

The coast around Le Conquet is low-lying, not the rocky confrontation with a savage sea that one might expect, and Kermorvan, across the estuary, seems to glide into the sea – its shallow cliffs are topped by a strip of turf that looks as if you could peel it right off. Apart from the lighthouse at the end, the peninsula is just grassland, bare of buildings and a lovely place to walk in the evening across the footbridge from Le Conquet.

The most exciting trips out from Le Conquet are to the islands – detailed below. As a variation, though, a good walk five kilometres south brings you to the lighthouse at **Pointe St-Mathieu**, looking out to the islands from its site among the ruins of a Benedictine abbey. The excellent *Restaurant de la Pointe St-Mathieu* is immediately opposite the abbey entrance (closed Tues & Sun pm out of season; ☎98.89.00.19).

Practicalities

The *Hôtel de Bretagne*, in town at 16 rue Lt-Jourden (Easter–Dec; ☎98.89.00.02; closed Fri pm & Sat out of season; ③), offers cheap **rooms** looking out across the peninsula, and reasonable meals from 65F. With the exception of a few unrenovated and land-facing rooms, the larger *Pointe Ste Barbe* (☎98.89.00.26; closed Mon out of season & mid-Nov to mid-Dec; ③–⑧), right next to the ferry harbour, is more expensive, but its menus, starting at 91F, have quite a reputation among gourmets. There are also two well-equipped **campsites**, *Le Théven* (mid-April to mid-Sept; ☎98.89.06.90) and *Quère* (June–Sept; ☎98.89.11.71). **Market** day is Tuesday.

The Islands : Ouessant and Molène

The island of **Ouessant**, Ushant in English, lies thirty kilometres northwest of Le Conquet, and its lighthouse at Creac'h (said to be the strongest in the world) is regarded as the entrance to the English Channel. It's at the end of a chain of smaller islands and half-submerged granite rocks. Most are uninhabited, or like Beniguet, the preserve only of rabbits, but **Molène**, midway, has a village and can be visited. Both Molène and Ouessant are served by at least one ferry each day from Le Conquet and Brest; however, it is not practicable to visit more than one in a single day.

Ouessant

The ride to **OUESSANT** is generally a tranquil affair – though the ferry has to pick its way from buoy to buoy, through a sea which is liable suddenly to blow up and become too dangerous to navigate. There have been many wrecks among the reefs, most famously the *Drummond Castle* which foundered as the finale to a concert celebrating the end of its voyage in June 1896. For all its storms, though, the climate is mild – Ouessant even records the highest mean temperatures in France in January and February.

You arrive on Ouessant at the new **harbour** in the ominous-sounding Baie du Stiff. There are a scattering of houses here, and dotted about the island, but the only town (with the only hotels and restaurants) is four kilometres distant at Lampaul. Everybody from the boat heads there, either by the bus that meets each arriving ferry, on bicycles rented for about 40F per day from one of the many waiting entrepreneurs, or in a long walking procession that straggles along the one road. Bicycle rental is the most convenient option, as the island is really too big to explore on foot.

LAMPAUL, as well as its more mundane facilities, has Ouessant's best beaches sprawled around its bay. There are few specific sights, and the whole place quickly becomes very familiar. But the town cemetery is worth visiting, with its war memorial listing all the ships in which the townsfolk were lost, graves of unknown sailors washed ashore and chapel of wax *proëlla crosses* symbolizing the many islanders who never returned from the sea. So, too, is the **Eco-Musée** – a reconstruction of a traditional island house – at nearby **Niou** (April & May daily except Mon 2–6.30pm, Sun 10.30am–6.30pm; June–Sept daily 10.30am–6.30pm; Oct–March daily except Mon 2–4pm; 15F).

The **Creac'h lighthouse**, though itself closed to the public, is a good point from which to set out along the barren and exposed rocks of the north coast.

From:	Le Conquet	Brest	Ouessant		Molène	
	All year	All year	April–Sept	Oct–March	April–Sept	Oct–March
Mon	9.30am	8.30am	5pm	4.30pm	5.30pm	5pm
Tues	9.30am	8.30am	5pm	4.30pm	5.30pm	5pm
Wed	9.30am	8.30am	5pm	4.30pm	5.30pm	5pm
Thurs	9.30am	8.30am	5pm	4.30pm	5.30pm	5pm
Fri	9.30am	8.30am	10.30am*	4.30pm	11am*	5pm
	6.30pm[1]		5pm		5.30pm	
Sat	9.30am	8.30am	11am*	11am*	11.30am*	11.30am*
	1.30pm		5pm	2.45pm	5.30pm	3.15pm
Sun	9.30am	8.30am	4pm*	4.30pm	4.30pm	5pm
	5pm[1]		6.30pm		7pm	

TIMETABLE OF ISLAND FERRIES

Sailings indicated [1] operate between April and September only.

Ferries from **Le Conquet** go to Molène (122F return) and Ouessant (140F return).
Ferries from **Brest** go to Molène (150F return) and Ouessant (170F return).
All ferries from **Ouessant** and **Molène** go to Brest and Le Conquet, except those marked with an asterisk, which run to Le Conquet only.
Discounted fares: 25 percent for students ; 50 percent for children 4–10; children under 4 free.

For all details, including the weather (liable to affect sailings), call *Penn Ar Bed* ☎98.80.24.68.
Penn Ar Bed also run some summer services from **Camaret** (p.237) and **Douarnenez** (p.237).

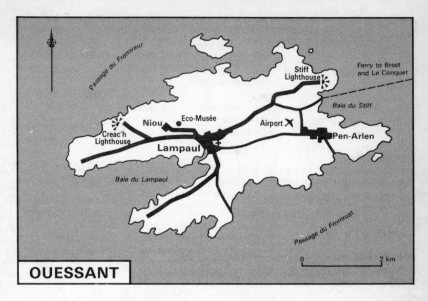

OUESSANT

Particularly in September and other times of migration, this is a remarkable spot for birdwatching; puffins, storm petrels, and cormorants can all be seen. The star-shaped formations of crumbling walls are not extra-terrestrial relics, but built so that the sheep – peculiarly tame here – can shelter from the strong winds.

Practicalities

General information on Ouessant is available from the **SI** in the main square in Lampaul (☎98.48.85.83). **Staying overnight**, you could camp almost anywhere on the island, making arrangements with the nearest farmhouse (which may well let out rooms, too). In Lampaul, the adjacent **hotels** *Océan* (☎98.48.80.03; ②) and *Fromveur* (☎98.48.81.30; ③) both offer a fairly basic standard of accommodation; the *Fromveur* specializes in traditional island cooking, which consists of attempting to render seaweed and mutton as palatable as possible, while the *Océan* also organizes musical evenings. The *Roch Ar Mor*, just down the street (☎98.48.80.19; ②), is a marginally more attractive alternative. There is, too, a small official **campsite**, the *Penn ar Bed* (☎98.48.84.65).

All the hotel **restaurants** serve menus for under 100F, but if you just come for a day, it's a good idea to buy a picnic before you set out – the Lampaul shops have limited and rather pricey supplies.

Molène

MOLÈNE is quite well-populated for a sparse strip of sand. The port itself is better protected than that of Ouessant, and so there are more fishermen based here. The island's inhabitants derive their income from seaweed collection and drying – and to an extent from crabbing and crayfish, which they gather on foot, canoe and even tractor at low tide. The tides are more than usually dramatic, halving or doubling the island's territory at a stroke. Hence the origin of the name Molène, which comes from the Breton for "the bald isle".

As for sights, there is even less of tangible note than on Ouessant. Walking the rocks and the coast is the basic activity. Once again, though, the island cemetery is poignant and interesting, redolent of small community life in its concentration of babies' graves from a typhoid epidemic in the last century; they are marked by silver crosses, repainted each November 1. Equally small-time is the island's main anecdote, told to anyone drinking an evening away, of the evening in 1967 when the whole population gathered to watch the oil tanker *Torrey Canyon* floundering offshore in the passage de Fromveur.

Practicalities

Few visitors do more than look around for an afternoon's excursion from Le Conquet, but it's quite possible to stay on Molène, and to enjoy it. There are rooms – very chilly in winter – at *Kastell An Doal* (☎98.07.39.11; ③), one of the old buildings by the port, and it's also possible to arrange to stay in a private house (☎98.07.39.05 for details).

Brest

BREST is set in a magnificent natural harbour, known as the *Rade de Brest*, and sheltered doubly from the ocean storms – by the bulk of Léon to the north, and by the Crozon peninsula to the south. The Rade (or roadstead) is entered by the narrow deep water channel of the Goulet de Brest, three miles long and one mile wide, with steep banks on both sides.

As one of the finest natural harbours in Europe, Brest has always played an important role in war and in trade whenever peace allowed. Richelieu, Colbert, Vauban and Napoléon were all instrumental in developing the port, which is today the base of the French Atlantic Fleet. Its dry dock can accommodate ships of up to 500,000 tons, and, as a ship repair centre, it ranks sixth in the world.

During World War II, Brest was relentlessly bombed to prevent the Germans from using it as a submarine base. When the Americans liberated it on September 18, 1944, after a six-week siege, they found the town devastated beyond recognition. It was necessary for the city to resume normal life as soon as possible, which meant the rebuilding had to be rushed at the expense of restoration, and the architecture of the post-war town is raw and bleak. There have been attempts, as in Caen, to green the city, but despite the heaviest rainfall in France, the site has proved too windswept to respond fully to these efforts.

From a distance, from across the bay, the city can look appealing. But closer in it takes a real effort of will to decide to stop longer than it takes to change buses or trains. The roads are racetracks; the suburbs remorselessly industrial; and the last war comprehensively destroyed any historic interest that may once have existed. The most rational reason for an outsider to visit would probably be for the bagpipe festival, held here for three days in August.

Arrival and Information

Brest's **SI** on av Clémenceau faces place de la Liberté (June–Sept Mon–Sat 9am–7pm, Sun 10am–noon & 2–4pm; Oct–May Mon–Sat 9.30am–12.30pm & 2–6.30pm;

☎98.44.24.96), while the main **post office** is on place Général-Leclerc (☎98.44.49.58).

The **gare SNCF** (☎98.80.50.50) and **gare routière** (☎98.44.46.73) are together in place du 19ème RI at the bottom of avenue Clémenceau. Brest is very much at the end of the railway system, though now connected to Paris in just four hours thanks to the *TGV* (which follows the northern route, via Morlaix and Rennes; the journey via Quimper takes much longer). Bus services include those to Plouescat and Roscoff (*Les Cars du Kreisker*; ☎98.69.00.93); to the Crozon Peninsula via Landevennec (☎98.27.02.02); and to Le Conquet (*Sarl Saint Mathieu Transport*s; ☎98.98.12.02).

Brest also has an **airport**, at Guipavas, 9km northeast of the centre, which is served by flights to **London** (*Brit Air*; ☎98.62.10.22) and **Ouessant** (*Finist'Air*; 2 daily in season; ☎98.84.64.87), as well as destinations throughout France. Should you need to rent a **car** on arrival, *Avis* have an office at 20bis rue de Siam (☎98.44.63.02).

Boats

As well as the sailings to Ouessant detailed on p.228, in summer (May–Sept; *Vedettes Armoricaines*; ☎98.44.44.04) three **boats** per day make the 45-minute crossing from Brest's Port de Commence to **Le Fret** on the Crozon Peninsula, where they are met by buses for Crozon (15min), Morgat (30min) and Camaret (40min). *Vedettes Armoricaines*, and several other operators including *Société Azenor* (☎98.41.46.23), also do excursions around the harbour and the Rade de Brest (1hr 30min).

The Town

As a tourist centre, Brest has little to offer. Few relics of the past remain. The fifteenth-century **castle** looks impressive on its headland, and offers a superb panorama of the city, but once inside it is not especially interesting. Three of its towers house the **National Maritime Museum** (daily except Tues 9.15am–noon & 2–6pm; 25F).

The fourteenth-century **Tour Tanguy** on the opposite bank of the River Penfeld, with its conical slate roof, serves as the **Museum of Old Brest**. Dioramas convey a vivid impression of just how attractive a city Brest used to be, before World War II (July & Aug daily 10am–noon & 2–7pm; June & Sept daily 2–7pm; Oct–May Wed & Thurs 2–5pm, Sat & Sun 2–6pm; free).

Océanopolis, next to the Port de Plaisance du Moulin-Blanc, incorporates the largest aquarium in Europe (May–Sept daily 9.30am–6pm; Oct–April Mon 2–5pm, Tues–Fri 9.30am–5pm, Sat & Sun 9.30am–6pm; 50F in summer, 47F in winter). Under its white dome, half a million gallons of water contain all kinds of fish, seals, molluscs, seaweed and sea anemones, and there are films and lectures all day. The emphasis is very much on the Breton littoral and Finistère's fishing industry. The **Jardins Botaniques**, a short distance north of Océanopolis in the Parc du Vallon de Strangalard beyond the football stadium, claim to be second in Europe only to Kew Gardens (daily summer 9am–8pm; winter 9am–6pm).

If all this fails to impress or excite you, you can always walk along the **Cours Dajot**, which displays the docklands in all their glory. It holds schools of various naval disciplines, arsenals, the marine records office and the **Pont de Recouvrance**, the largest drawbridge in Europe.

Accommodation

The vast majority of Brest's **hotels** remain open throughout the year; only a few, however, bother to maintain their own restaurants. Several lie within easy walking distance of the stations, in the vicinity of the central place de la Liberté.

The city also has a year-round **youth hostel**, near Océanopolis in a wooded setting on rue de Kerbriant, Port de Plaisance du Moulin-Blanc (☎98.41.90.41; 65F including breakfast). It's 3km east of the gares SNCF and routière, on bus route #7, or the *Bus Albatros*.

The *Camping de Goulet* (☎98.45.86.84) is not easy to find, and not in any case warmly recommended – it's hard to see why campers would choose to stay in Brest. If you need to use it, it is on the outskirts of Brest, across the Pont de Recouvrance and then to the left of the Le Conquet road (D789) in Ste-Anne-Portzic – take bus #71.

Hotels

Hôtel Bellevue, 53 bd Victor-Hugo (☎98.80.51.78). Six-storey sound-proofed building, equipped with a lift. Not easy to find, but not far from the gare SNCF and well on the way to the lively St-Martin area; look for St-Michel church. No restaurant. ③.

Hôtel de la Gare, 4 bd Gambetta (☎98.44.47.01). Facing the stations; renovated in 1989. You pay a little more for an uninterrupted view of the Rade de Brest. No restaurant. ③.

Hôtel du Musée, 1 ru Ducouëdic (☎98.45.70.20). Plain unadorned rooms, just off the rue de Siam down near the Pont de Recouvrance. Closed Sun. No restaurant. ①.

Hôtel le Ponant, 20 rue de la Porte (☎98.45.09.32). A very cheap and basic option, across the Pont de Recouvrance at the bottom of the rue de Siam. No restaurant. ①.

Hôtel le Regent, 22 rue d'Algésiras (☎98.44.29.77). A clean, newish hotel, very near the SI, but without its own restaurant. ④.

Hôtel St-Louis, 6 rue d'Algésiras (☎98.44.23.91). Friendly and reasonably comfortable option, just off the main square near the SI. No restaurant. ③.

Hôtel-Restaurant Vauban, 17 av Clémenceau (☎98.46.06.88). Very near the centre, between the gare SNCF and the Hôtel de Ville. Grand curving white edifice, with a surprisingly homely atmosphere. The simple restaurant, which serves couscous and so on from 50F, is closed Sun pm & all day Mon. ③.

Eating

As well as a concentration of low-priced places in the immediate area of the stations, Brest also offers a wider assortment of **restaurants**. Rue Jean-Jaurès, which climbs up east from the place de la Liberté, holds plenty of bistros and bars, while just off to the north, place Guerin is the centre of the student-dominated quartier St-Martin.

Chez Marie Françoise, 28 rue Navarin. Simple but fashionable bistro on the place Guerin. 45F lunch menu, otherwise everything is *à la carte.*. Stuffed seafood for 30F, frogs' legs 32F, and *crêpes* galore.

Maison de l'Océan, 2 quai de la Douane (☎98.80.44.84). Blue-hued fish restaurant down by the port, open every day and serving wonderful assortments of seafood from 70F.

Le Rapide, rue Comtesse-de-Carbonnières, near place de la Liberté. Modern restaurant with a fast-food tinge and a young following. Conventional, good-value menus at 50F, 60F and 85F, and pizzas *à la carte*. Closed Sat pm & Sun.

Le Ruffé, 1 rue Yves-Collet (☎98.46.07.70). A new and attractive place between the gare SNCF and the SI. Prides itself on good, traditional French seafood dishes, served on menus costing 60F and upwards. Daily except Sun until 11.30pm.

La Taverne St-Martin, 92 rue Jean-Jaurès (☎98.80.48.17). A few hundred metres east (and up) from the SI. Warm and friendly brasserie/restaurant behind a wooden half-timbered facade, open from 8am until 1am daily. Lunch from 60F, dinner from 85F, plus lots of *à la carte* snacks. Steak tartare is the house speciality.

Le Tire Bouchon, 20 rue le l'Observatoire (☎98.44.15.18). Wide-ranging menus from 100F, but a *plat du jour* midday at around 40F. Closed all Aug, plus Sat lunch & all day Sun; otherwise open until 10.45pm. The *Café Record* next door stays open later.

Drinking

Brest is unusual by Breton standards in having plenty of lively **bars.** The basic choice lies between hanging out with the sailors and fishermen down by the port, with the business community around the place de la Liberté, or with the seriously trendy student population in the St-Martin quarter, high up on and around Jean-Jaurès.

Bar l'Amphi, rue Glasgow. Full-scale Goth hang-out; the perfect place to spend an evening trying to work out just what it is about the Cure that appeals to the French so much.

Bar Écossais, 241 rue Jean-Jaurès. An unlikely spectacle, way up at the top of the hill and positively festooned with Scottish memorabilia, which attracts an exuberant Celtic crowd. On November 11 each year (the anniversary of its opening), the owner hides a large Scottish shield in an unnamed pub somewhere in the city, and the regulars, dressed in full Highland costume and making passable attempts at reproducing the drone of the bagpipes by means of holding their noses and grunting, set off in a drunken stupor to try and locate it.

Café de la Plage, 32 rue Massillon (☎98.43.03.30). Classic-looking open-fronted bar, on one corner of place Guerin. Heavy maroon decor and a transient population of citizens of all ages who share a common interest in talking at the tops of their voices.

Café le Triskel, 31 rue Massillon (☎98.44.56.65). Pub-style place with wooden tables, across the square from the *Plage*. Students and Breton activists come to drink and listen to the odd bit of music (literally).

Around Brest

Exploring Léon from a base in Brest, Le Conquet and Ouessant are very much the places to head for – ideally by boat from the Port du Commerce (see p.228 for timetable). Otherwise, the immediate area around Brest is far from bursting with interest.

Take **ST-RÉNAN** for example, 15km northwest of the city on the D5. French towns often set up signs along approach roads to advertise their splendours – "son château", "sa charme" and so on. St-Rénan can only find "son Syndicat d'Initiative" to boast about – but for all that it's quite a pleasant small town and there are two noteworthy prehistoric sites in the immediate area.

Lanrivoaré

Five kilometres northwest of St-Rénan is the **church** of **LANRIVOARÉ**, which has a tiny plot in its graveyard where, alongside eight round stones, the 7777 victims of a fifth-century massacre are supposed to lie buried. Legend records that the stones were transformed from loaves of bread by Saint Hervé – but they're in fact most likely to be "cursing-stones", which exist in several Irish chapels and were used for calling down disease or destruction on an enemy. The person invoking the curse, after a certain number of prayers, turned the stone round seven times.

The Menhir de Kerloas

To find the **Menhir de Kerloas** (also known as Kervéatous or Plouarzel), you need to walk or drive (there's no bus) about five kilometres west of St-Rénan on the *old* Plouarzel road, parallel to the more modern D5. The menhir stands in a small clearing hedged-in by fields, and is the highest point for miles around in these flatlands. Although the tip was knocked off by lightning 200 years ago (and was subsequently used as a cattle-trough), it is at 37ft the tallest menhir still standing in Western Europe.

The stone is probably at its best looming out of a damp and ominous Breton mist, producing, in this isolated spot, a powerful effect on the imagination. A further aid to fantasy are the circular protuberances about four feet from the ground on either side, against which newly married couples (who can only have been rather ill-informed) would rub their naked bodies in the hope of begetting children.

Towards the Crozon Peninsula

Heading south from Brest, cyclists and pedestrians can cut straight over to the Crozon peninsula by **ferry**. A regular service will shuttle you across the bay, for a few francs, to Le Fret (see p.252). The ferry doesn't, however, carry cars, so **drivers** have a longer and more circuitous route, crossing the Elorn river over the vast spans of the **Pont Albert-Louppe** (42m high and almost a kilometre long) and then skirting the estuaries of the **Plougastel peninsula**.

PLOUGASTEL-DAOULAS, just across the bridge, is a possibly rewarding stop on this latter route. It's sited at the edge of the main Parish Closes region and has a particularly nasty calvary depiction of Katell Gollet (see p.222).

Daoulas

A very different, and earlier, image of religion is provided by the **abbey** at DAOULAS, ten kilometres beyond. This has Brittany's only Romanesque cloister – beautiful and isolated at the edge of cool monastery gardens, since its surrounding buildings were destroyed during the Revolution. The abbey is a short walk above the town, and a welcome oasis on a hot summer's day. Since 1984 it has been used as a cultural centre for Finistère, which stages ambitious historical exhibitions lasting for around six months at a time (current information on ☎98.25.84.39).

Le Faou

From Daoulas the motorway and railway cut down to Châteaulin (see p.256) and Quimper. For Crozon, you'll need to veer west at LE FAOU, a tiny medieval port, still with some of its sixteenth-century gabled houses and set on its own individual estuary. A sheltered corniche follows the river to the sea, where there are sailing and wind-surfing facilities. Accommodation is to be found at the **hotels** *Relais de la Place* (☎98.81.91.19; ④) or *La Vieille Renommée* (☎98.81.90.31; closed Mon other than in July & Aug, and all Nov; ③), both of which have top-class restaurants.

From Le Faou, **Crozon** and the **Menez-Hom**, which overlooks the peninsula's eastern reaches, are visible and easily accessible. You cross the River Aulne – outlet for the Nantes–Brest canal – over the **Pont du Térénez**, and, amid forests, you have arrived.

THE CROZON PENINSULA

The **Crozon peninsula** forms part of the **Parc Régional d'Armorique**, a haphazard area stretching from the forest of Huelgoat to the island of Ouessant that is, in principle at least, a protected natural landscape area. What this means in reality is hard to fathom. Doubtless there are firm French bylaws against disturbing the wild flowers. However, for some reason these don't prevent nuclear submarines from lurking in the bay of Brest, nor low-flying helicopters from sporadically sweeping the skies above.

Nevertheless, military installations and operations notwithstanding, Crozon, with its wild beaches and craggy cliffs, is an attractive slice of countryside. A dramatic one too, especially if you make the detour to climb up the **Menez-Hom** for an initial overview.

The Menez-Hom and around

At just 1082ft, the **Menez-Hom** is not really a mountain. But the summit stands sufficiently alone to command tremendous views across Crozon – a chaos of water, with lakes, rivers and bridges wherever you look, and usually a scattering of hang-gliders dangling in the sky. The exposed and windswept viewing table reveals it to be 300 miles from both London and Paris.

A magnificent road sweeps down across the heather on to the Crozon penisula. At the foot of the hill, to the south, **ST-NIC PENTREZ** has excellent beaches – this is the sandy side of the peninsula – and several **campsites**, largest among

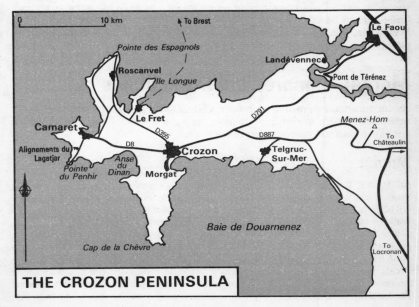

THE CROZON PENINSULA

them the *Menez Bichen* (☎98.26.50.82). There is another good beach and camp-site, *Le Panoramic* (☎98.27.78.41), further round towards Crozon at **TELGRUC-SUR-MER**, and some of the smaller towns inland have **hotels** and **gîtes d'étapes**. Among them are **Plomodiern** with *La Cremaillère* (☎98.81.50.10; closed Oct; ③), and a *gîte* at the nearby Polébret Plage (c/o M. Kervella; ☎98.26.50.14). There's another *gîte* at Kerdiles, 1km from Landévennec (c/o M & Mme Gall; ☎98.27.31.49).

The Musée de l'École Rurale

Still inland from the peninsula, roughly three kilometres north of the Menez-Hom at the intersection of the Argol–Dineault and Trégarven–Menez-Hom roads and unfortunately not on any bus routes, is the village of **TRÉGARVAN**. Its **Musée de l'École Rurale** (Jan–March Mon–Fri 2–5pm; April & May daily 2–6pm; June daily 1.30–7pm; July & Aug daily 10.30am–7pm; Sept daily 1.30–7pm; Oct–Dec daily except Sat 2–5pm; 15F), housed in what used to be the local secondary school, is one of those small, quirky French museums that sound slightly ludi-crous on paper but are distinctly fascinating on the spot.

The school was closed down due to lack of numbers in 1974, then re-opened a decade later as a re-creation of a Breton classroom circa 1920. At that time, all the kids would have spoken Breton at home – but they were forbidden to speak it here. The teacher gave a little wooden cow to the first child to utter a word in the mother tongue, and they could get rid of the *vache* only by squealing on the next offender. The lesson, to parents and pupils alike, was obvious enough: that Breton was backward and a handicap. Breton was suppressed, with considerable efficiency, throughout the province, and only recently have things begun to change. As well as Breton-language nursery and primary schools, there's one secondary school and a fund-raising campaign for a lycée. While a few years back SNCF had to be taken to court before it would accept a cheque made out in Breton, there is now a Breton bank. A battle for a Breton TV channel is also underway.

Morgat, Camaret and the beaches

The first town on the peninsula proper, **CROZON**, is not much more than a one-way traffic system to distribute tourists among the various resorts – though it does keep a market running most of the week.

Morgat

MORGAT, just down the hill from Crozon, makes a more realistic and enticing base. It has a long crescent beach that ends in a pine slope, and a well-sheltered harbour full of pleasure boats raced down from England and Ireland – and the leathery rich telling each other about their spinnakers.

The main plebeian attractions are **boat trips** around the various headlands, such as the Cap de la Chèvre (which is a good clifftop walk if you'd rather make your own way). The most popular is the 45-minute tour of the **Grottes** (May–Sept), multicoloured caves in the cliffs, accessible only by sea but with steep "chimneys" up to the clifftops, where in bygone days saints would lurk to rescue the shipwrecked. Organized by two rival companies on the quay, the trips run every quarter of an hour in high season; they often leave full, however, so it's worth booking a few hours in advance. It's also possible, on Wednesdays and Sundays in July and August, to take a ferry service across to **Douarnenez** (☎98.27.09.54).

Practicalities

The **SI** for the whole peninsula is in what used to be the gare SNCF at Crozon (☎98.26.17.18); an information office for the Crozon-Morgat area stands at the start of Morgat's beach crescent on the bd du France (July & Aug Mon–Sat 9.30am–7pm, Sun 10am–1pm; June & Sept Tues–Sat 9.30am–noon & 2–6pm; ☎98.27.07.92).

All the **hotels** in Morgat are quite expensive. The cheapest, *des Grottes* (☎98.27.15.84; ③), is a long (albeit pleasant) walk from what centre there is, and in any case insists on guests paying for *demi-pension*. Better, if you can afford it, is to splash out on the *Kador*, 42 bd de la Plage (☎98.27.05.68; ④), where you can eat excellent seafood and enjoy the view of the bay, or the similarly grand *Hôtel-Restaurant de la Ville d'Ys* in the port (Easter–Sept; ☎98.27.06.49; ④). The *Julia*, set 400 metres back from the beach at 43 rue de Tréflez (☎98.27.05.89; closed mid-Nov to mid-Feb; ③), is a quiet alternative.

You could always **camp**. With a total of 865 pitches available, campers are spoilt for choice; best perhaps are the three-star sites at *Plage de Goulien* (mid-June to mid-Sept; ☎98.27.17.10) and *les Pins*, towards the pointe de Dinan (June to mid-Sept; ☎98.27.21.95).

Camaret

CAMARET is another sheltered port, at the very tip of the peninsula. Its most distinguishing feature is the pink-orange **château de Vauban**, standing four-square at the end of the long jetty that runs back parallel to the main town water-front. There are two **beaches** nearby – a small one to the north and another, larger and more attractive, in the low-lying (and rather marshy) *Anse de Dinan*.

Camaret also boasts one moment of historical significance. It was here in 1801 that an American, Robert Fulton, tested the first **submarine**. This was a stuffy, leaking, oar-powered wooden craft, whose five-man crew spent some time scut-tling about beneath the waves in the hope of sinking a British frigate. Fulton was denied his glory, though, by the frigate choosing to sail away, ignorant of the heavy-breathing peril that was so frantically seeking it out.

In high season, *Penn Ar Bed* (☎98.70.02.37) operate an irregular **ferry** service from Camaret to the island of **Sein** (see p.242; 162F return), and also to **Ouessant** (see p.228; 162F return); many boats returning from Ouessant continue to Douarnenez, so it's feasible to catch a ride on to there as well.

Practicalities

The town of Camaret is not large, though in season it offers all the shops and supplies you could need. A little walk away from the centre, around the port towards the protective jetty, the quai du Styvel contains a row of excellent **hotels**. Both the *Vauban* (☎98.27.91.36; ②) and *du Styvel* (☎98.27.92.74; ②) are excep-tionally hospitable, though the food in *du Styvel* is marginally better with a 68F menu offering *moules à la crême*, and crabs, oysters and scallops rearing their assorted heads on the 92F menu; both have rooms that look right out across the bay. There are also various **campsites** to fall back on, such as the four-star *Lambézen* (April to mid-Oct; ☎98.27.91.41) and the municipal *Lannic* (June–Sept; ☎98.27.91.31).

Back along the quayside in the centre of town, *La Voilerie*, 7 quai Toudouze (☎98.27.83.87), is an excellent **fish restaurant**; 58F lunches include mussels or *soupe de poissons*, and four-course dinners start at 78F.

From mid-June until September, *Vedettes Sirènes* (☎98.27.91.41) run boat trips that tour the offshore bird sanctuary of the Tas de Pois; their office is next to the SI on quai Toudouze in the port (Easter–Oct, daily 9am–noon & 3–7pm; ☎98.27.93.60).

The Pointe du Penhir

A couple of worthwhile excursions can be made from the towns of the Crozon peninsula. At the **Pointe du Penhir** are sheer cliffs and a little natural amphitheatre to view the Tas de Pois rocks, scattered out in the sea. A monument to the Breton Resistance stands nearby. To one side of the road on the way out to the point, amid the brilliant purples and yellows of the heathland, are the megalithic **Alignements of Lagatjar**. Perhaps, though, you need to imagine that this heath is still blasted and empty, and that there's no "Dolmens" housing estate next to the stones, to appreciate this forlorn, unsignposted prehistoric ruin. The stones are little more than weather-beaten stumps and it's hard to discern a pattern on the ground; the experts responsible for their restoration say there are four distinct lines rather than a circle.

The Pointe des Espagnols

The other popular trip is to the **Pointe des Espagnols**, where a viewing point signals the end of the peninsula. Brest is very close and very visible – without being any the more enticing. Around the cape are several forbidden military installations and abandoned war-time bunkers. You're not allowed to leave the road, and should need no extra dissuasion to avoid straying onto the range. Neither are you encouraged to turn the provided telescope towards Robert Fulton's modern counterparts at the nuclear submarine base on the Île Longue. Nearby **ROSCANVEL** offers a hotel, the *Kreis Ar Mor* (☎98.27.48.93; ③).

Locronan

LOCRONAN, a short way from the sea on the minor road that leads down to Quimper from the Crozon peninsula, is a prime example of a Breton town that has remained frozen in its ancient form by more recent economic decline.

From 1469 through to the seventeenth century, Locronan was a hugely successful centre for woven linen, supplying sails to the French, English and Spanish navies. It was then first rivalled by Vitré and Rennes, before suffering the "agony and ruin" of the nineteenth century so graphically described in its small museum. The consequence of that ruin has been that the rich medieval houses of the town centre have never been superseded or surrounded by modern development. Film directors love its authenticity, even if Roman Polanski, to film *Tess*, deemed it necessary to change all the porches, put new windows on the

Renaissance houses, and bury the main square in several feet of mud to make it all look a bit more English.

Today Locronan is once more prosperous, with its main source of income the tourists who buy wooden statues carved by local artisans, pottery brought up from the Midi, and handbags and leather jackets of less specified provenance. This commercialization shouldn't, however, put you off making at least a passing visit, for the town itself is genuinely remarkable, centred around the focal **Église Saint-Ronan**. The **museum** is worthwhile, and take the time also to walk down the hill of the **rue Moal**, where there's a lovely little stone chapel, with surprising modern stained glass, and a wooden statue of a depressed-looking Jesus, sitting alone cross-legged.

Each year on the second Sunday in July the town hosts a **pardon** at St-Ronan church; the procession, known as the *petit Tromenie*, expands to a week-long festival, the *grand Tromenie*, every sixth year (1995, 2001, and so on). The processions follow a time-hallowed route said by some to be Saint Ronan's favourite Sunday walk, by others to be the outline of a long-vanished Benedictine abbey; it could even follow a pre-Christian circuit of megalithic sites.

Practicalities

If you decide you want to stay in Locronan, it can be an expensive business. One of the artisans suggested to the local authorities that the loft above his studio be converted to a *gîte d'étape* for young visitors, but that was felt not to be in keeping with the town's character – a character affording few opportunities of any kind for the young. As it is, there are a couple of **hotels**, *du Prieuré* (☎98.91.70.89; ④), and the *Fer à Cheval* (☎98.91.70.67; ④), both normally reserved well in advance. In season, and probably out, you'll do a lot better heading on to the bay of Douarnenez.

The latest craze in Locronan is to follow the *Tromenie* route on a **mountain bike**, which you can rent from a garage in rue des Charettes (☎98.91.71.71).

CORNOUAILLE

Once past Locronan, you enter the ancient kingdom of **Cornouaille**. Its capital, **Quimper**, is a city as enticing as any in France, and along the south coast Bénodet, Loctudy and Pont Aven are thriving resorts. Roads radiate from Quimper in all directions, but the **western tip** of Finistère, if you follow the line of the Bay of Douarnenez, still feels isolated. With a few exceptions – most notably its "land's end" capes – it has kept out of the tourist mainstream.

The seaside village of **Ste-Anne-la-Palud**, north of Douarnenez, holds one of the best-known *pardons* in Brittany on the last Sunday in August.

Douarnenez

Sufficient quantities of tuna, sardines and assorted crustaceans are still landed at the port of **DOUARNENEZ**, in the superbly sheltered Baie du Dournenez, south of the Crozon peninsula, to keep the largest fish canneries in Europe busy. However, the catch has been declining ever since 1923, when 800 fishing boats brought in 100 million sardines during the six-month season. Over the last fifteen years or so, Douarnenez has therefore set out – at phenomenal expense, the subject of considerable local controversy – to re-define itself as a living museum of all matters maritime.

The process of transformation culminated in 1993, when the whole area of **Port-Rhû**, on the west side of town, was officially declared open as the remarkable **Port-Musée** (daily June–Sept 10am–7pm; Oct–May 10am–noon & 2–6pm; tickets sold in the Boat Museum, June–Sept 60F, Oct–May 48F). The entire waterfront is taken up with fishing and other vessels gathered from all over northern Europe, which visitors are invited to roam in and out of, up and down ladders and all over the decks, through oily metallic-smelling engine rooms and sleeping quarters divided into separate wooden compartments. Rope- and sail-makers and net-menders work on the jetties, and children can operate a scaled-down eighteenth-century crane by walking inside a wooden treadmill. The far shore has been re-landscaped to reproduce a nineteenth-century environment populated by oyster-catchers and the like (free ferries operate when the tide is high enough, otherwise you walk over a bridge).

Across the street, in the place de l'Enfer, the associated **Boat Museum** doubles as a working boatyard, where visitors can watch or even join in the construction of seagoing vessels, using techniques from all over the world and from all different periods. Once again, the emphasis is on fishing, and the craft on display include a *moliceiro* from Portugal and coracles from Wales and Ireland. With cafés and snack bars on site, there is easily enough here to spend a whole day without seeing it all, though even the most boat-hungry appetite may well be fully slaked after a couple of hours.

Of the three separate harbour areas still in operation in Douarnenez, much the prettiest is the **port de Rosmeur**, on the east side, which is nominally the fishing port used by the smaller local craft. Its quayside, lined with cafés and restaurants, curves between a pristine wooded promontory to the right and the fish canneries to the left, which continue around the north of the headland. You can buy fresh fish at the waterfront, or go on a sea-fishing excursion yourself. The various **beaches** around town look pretty enough, but they are dangerous for swimming.

During the summer, *Penn Ar Bed* (☎98.70.02.37) run occasional **ferries** from the port de Rosmeur out to the **Île de Sein** (see p.242; 140F return), and also to **Ouessant** (see p.228; 170F return) via Camaret.

Practicalities

The **SI** in Douarnenez is at 2 rue du Dr-Mével (daily mid-June to mid-Sept 9am–7pm; otherwise 9am–noon &1.30–6pm; ☎98.92.13.35), a short walk up from the Port-Musée; they can inform you of the current status of plans to open a **youth hostel** in town. In a sense, the holiday trade is as yet just a sideline here, and not all that much accommodation is available. Choose between either of the good-value **hotels** *de la Rade*, 31 quai du Grand-Port (☎98.92.01.81; ②), where behind the blue and white facade there's a bar downstairs and a restaurant on the first floor looking out on the port de Rosmeur, or the *des Halles*, a little higher up alongside the still-busy market *halles* (☎98.92.02.75; closed Sun & all Jan; ②), which has no restaurant.

Close by on the bay, there's a **campsite**, *Croas Men* (☎98.74.00.18), at Tréboul/Les Sables Blancs. Among inexpensive seafood **restaurants** are *La Cotriade*, 48 rue Anatole-France (☎98.92.06.45), at the port de Rosmeur, and the *Pourquoi Pas*, 15 quai de Port-Rhû (☎98.92.76.13), beside the museum, which does fine fishy lunches.

Audierne

Though on the whole the exposed southwestern extremities of Brittany are not areas you'd immediately associate with a classic summer sun-and-sand holiday, **AUDIERNE**, 25km west of Douarnanz on the Bay of Audierne, is something of an exception. An active fishing port, specializing in prawns and crayfish, it spreads along the northern shore of the Goyen estuary a short way back from the Atlantic. From the town centre, the road continues just over 1km to the long, curving, and surprisingly sheltered **beach** of Ste-Evette, at the far end of which – at least another 1km further on – is the departure point for boats to the Île de Sein (see below).

Practicalities

One of the few buildings on the seaward side of the road is the **hotel** *Au Roi Gradlon*, in a superb position at the very mouth of the estuary (closed Sun pm, & also Mon Oct–May; ☎98.70.04.51; ④). Its unusual design means that the road-level dining room – where the 90F menu includes fresh tuna steaks – is in fact on the top storey, with several further floors, concealed from the road, dropping down below it to the beach. Rooms in the newer *L'Horizon*, slightly nearer the town proper at 40 rue J-J-Rousseau (☎98.70.09.91; ②), are half the price, and it serves fish dinners from just 59F.

Plogoff

Most people take in Audierne en route to the Pointe du Raz, which is connected directly to Quimper by bus. Midway, signalled by fading graffiti on its walls and hoardings, is the tiny village of **PLOGOFF**, where ecologists, autonomists and local people fought riot police and paratroopers for six weeks in 1980, attempting to stop the opening move in a nuclear power station project. Although they lost the fight, abandonment of the project was part of François Mitterand's manifesto for the 1980 presidential election – and he kept his promise.

The Pointe du Raz

The **Pointe du Raz** – the Land's End of both Finistère and France – can be a spectacular sight. Not at first view, though; as you arrive the ocean is all but obscured by souvenir shops and breeze-block barracks (it is flanked by another military zone). But once away from the coach park, things are more promising. You can walk out to the plummeting fissures of the *pointe*, filling and draining with a deafening surf-roar, and beyond, high above on precarious paths. (Shoes that can grip are not a bad idea.)

The Baie des Trépassés

The **Baie des Trépassés** (Bay of the Dead), just north of the Pointe du Raz, gets its grim name from the shipwrecked bodies that are washed up there, and is a possible site of sunken Ys (see over page). However, it's actually a very attractive spot; green meadows, too exposed to support trees, end abruptly on the low cliffs to either side, there's a huge expanse of flat sand (in fact little else at low tide), and out in the crashing waves surfers and wind-surfers get thrashed to within an inch of their lives.

Less than half a dozen scattered buildings intrude upon the emptiness, but two of them are **hotels**, both with tremendous views. Right in the middle is the pink

Hôtel de la Baie des Trépassés (closed Jan to mid-Feb; ☎98.70.61.34; one room ③, rest ④), which has menus from 94F. The larger *Relais de la Pointe du Van* is slightly higher up, to the right (April–Sept; ☎98.70.62.79; ④).

The Île de Sein

Just eight kilometres out to sea, off the end of the Pointe du Raz, the little ÎLE DE SEIN was made famous during World War II when the entire male population answered General de Gaulle's call to join him in exile in England. It was reputed also to have been the very last refuge of the Druids in Brittany, a misty and inaccessible spot where they held out long after the rest of the country was Christianized. Roman sources tell of a shrine served by nine virgin priestesses.

A popular saying has it that "Who sees Sein, sees his death"; but that's more because it happens to rhyme in French (*qui voit Sein, voit sa fin*) than because of any particular evil there. The island is featureless enough to have been completely submerged by the sea on occasion, but a few hundred people still live on it, gathering rain water and fishing for scallops, lobster and crayfish.

Practicalities

Sein is hardly bursting with facilities for tourists, but can offer one summer-only **hotel**, the *Armen* (June–Sept; ☎98.70.90.77; ②), and a handful of restaurants. For further information, contact the Mairie (☎98.70.90.35).

The principal departure point for **boats** to Sein is Ste-Evette beach, just outside **Audierne** (see above). Services are operated by *Vedette-Biniou* (June to early July, and first half of Sept, daily at 10am; early July to end of Aug daily at 10am, 1.30pm & 5pm; 105F return, or 85F day-return on Sun only; ☎98.70.20.15), and *Penn Ar Bed* (April–Aug, 1–3 departures daily, first at 9.30am; Sept–March daily except Wed 9.30am; 112F return; ☎98.70.02.37). When weather conditions are bad, *Penn Ar Bed* occasionally use the port at **Douarnenez** instead of Audierne, so it's worth calling ahead to check; in high summer, they also run irregular sailings from both Douarnenez (140F return) and Camaret (162F).

Quimper

QUIMPER, capital of the ancient diocese, kingdom and later duchy of Cornouaille, is the oldest Breton city. According to the only source – legend – the first bishop of Quimper, Saint Corentin, came with the first Bretons across the channel to the place they named Little Britain, some time between the fourth and seventh centuries. He lived by eating a regenerating and immortal fish all his life, and was made bishop by one King Gradlon, whose life he later saved when the seabed city of Ys was destroyed (see box).

Modern Quimper is very relaxed, though active enough to have the bars – and the atmosphere – to make it worth going out café-crawling. Still "the charming little place" known to Flaubert, it takes at most half an hour to cross it on foot. The word "*kemper*" denotes the junction of the two rivers, the Steir and the Odet, around which are the cobbled streets (now mainly pedestrianized) of the medieval quarter, dominated by the cathedral towering nearby. As the Odet curves from east to southwest, it is crossed by numerous low flat bridges, bedecked with geraniums, and chrysanthemums in the autumn. You can stroll along the boule-

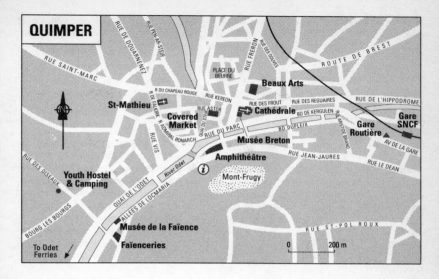

vards on both banks of the river, where several ultra-modern edifices blend in an oddly harmonious way with their ancient – and attractive – surroundings. Overlooking all is **Mont Frugy** (all of 87m above the river), once again green with trees after being denuded by the hurricane of 1987. There is no great pressure in Quimper to rush around monuments or museums, and the most enjoyable option may be to take a boat and drift down "the prettiest river in France" to the open sea at Bénodet.

Arrival, Information and Public Transport

Quimper's **SI**, which seems to move every couple of years, can now be found in a small, single-storey building on the south bank of the Odet at 7 rue de la Déesse, place de la Résistance (July & Aug Mon–Sat 8.30am–8pm, Sun 9.30am–12.30pm & 3–6pm; last fortnight of June and first fortnight of Sept Mon–Sat 9am–noon &

THE DROWNED CITY OF YS

Legend has it that King Gradlon built Ys in the Baie de Douarnenez, protected from the water by gates and locks to which only he and his daughter had keys. She sounds like a pleasant sort, giving pet sea-dragons to all the citizens to do their errands, but Saint Corentin saw decadence and suspected evil. He was proved right: at the urging of the Devil, the princess used her key to open the floodgates, the city was flooded, and Gradlon escaped only by obeying Saint Corentin and throwing his daughter into the sea. Back on dry land, and in need of a new capital, Gradlon founded Quimper. Ys remains on the sea floor – it will rise again when Paris ("*Par-Ys*", equal to Ys) sinks – and, according to tradition, on feast days sailors can still hear church bells and hymns under the water.

2–6pm, Sun 9.30am–12.30pm & 3–6pm; mid-Sept to mid-June Mon–Sat 9am–noon & 2–6pm; ☎98.53.04.05). They organize daily **guided tours** of the city in season (May, June & Sept Mon–Sat 2pm; July & Aug daily 11am & 5pm). The **post office** is at 37 bd de Kérguelen (☎98.64.28.28).

Bicycles can be rented from the gare SNCF, or from *Torch VTT*, 58 rue de la Providence (☎98.53.84.41). The *Fédération Bretonne des Clubs de Windsurfers*, (run by M. Carn, route du Bénodet 29000 Quimper) has information on all aspects of **wind-surfing**.

Trains and Buses

The **gare SNCF** (☎98.90.50.50) and **gare routière** (☎98.90.88.89) are next to each other on avenue de la Gare, 1km east of the centre. Local **buses** #1 and #6 connect with both, but all pass through place de la Résistance near the SI.

Although Quimper is well connected with the rest of Brittany by both train and bus, if you want to use public transport to get to the coast anywhere in the immediate vicinity the **bus** is your only option. Services include those to **Bénodet**, which leave from place de la Résistance (*Compagnie Amoricaine de Transport*, 5 bd de Kérguelen, ☎98.95.02.36); to **Audierne** and Pointe du Raz, from the gare routière or bd de Kérguelen (also *CAT*); to **Pont l'Abbé** and St-Guenolé, from place St-Corentin (*Cariou Castric Lecoeur*, ☎98.47.04.08); and to **Concarneau** and **Pont-Aven**, also from place St-Corentin (*Sarl Transports Caoudal Réné*; ☎98.56.96.72).

Boats

Between May and September you can **sail** from Quimper down the Odet to Bénodet, which takes about 1hr 15min, on *Vedettes de l'Odet* (Bénodet ☎98.57.00.58, Quimper ☎98.52.98.41). Between two and four boats each day leave from the end of quai de l'Odet; times vary with the tides so check with the SI (who also sell tickets).

The Town

The enormous **Cathédrale St-Corentin** is said to be the most complete Gothic cathedral in Brittany, though its neo-Gothic spires date from 1856. When the nave was being added to the old chancel in the fifteenth century, the extension would either have hit existing buildings or the swampy edge of the then unchannelled river. The masons eventually hit on a solution and placed the nave at a slight angle – a peculiarity which, once noticed, makes it hard to concentrate on the other Gothic splendours within.

The exterior, however, gives no hint of the deviation, with King Gradlon now mounted in perfect symmetry between the spires – though whether he would have advised a river bed nave is another question. Before the Revolution, each Saint Cecilia's Day a climber would ascend to give the King a drink, and there was a prize of 100 *écus* for whoever could catch the glass, thrown down afterwards. During the sixteenth century, 1500 refugees died of plague inside the building.

Alongside the cathedral, the **Bishop's Palace** is quirky from the outside, nestling against one of the few remaining fragments of the old city walls, and has a wonderful staircase within, but its Museum of Breton oddments is small and forgettable (June–Sept daily 9am–6pm; Oct–May Tues–Sat 9am–noon & 2–5pm,

Sun 2–5pm). Much more compelling is the **Musée des Beaux-Arts**, alongside the Hôtel de Ville at 40 place St-Corentin (July & Aug daily 10am–7pm, 30F; Sept & April–May daily except Tues 10am–noon & 2–6pm; Oct–March Mon & Wed–Sat 10am–noon & 2–6pm, Sun 2–6pm, 25F), which holds amazing collections of drawings by Cocteau, Gustav Doré and Max Jacob (who was born in Quimper), nineteenth- and twentieth-century paintings of the Pont-Aven school, and Breton scenes by the likes of Eugène Boudin. Only the dull Dutch oils upstairs let the collection down.

The heart of **old Quimper** lies to the west of place St-Corentin, in front of the cathedral. This is where you'll find the liveliest shops and cafés, housed in the old half-timbered buildings, such as the Breton *Keltia-Musique* record shop at 1 place au Beurre, and the Celtic shop, *Ar Bed Keltiek*, nearby at 2 rue du Roi-Gradlon. The old market hall was burned down in 1976, but the light and spacious new **Halles St-Francis**, rue Astor, built to replace it is quite a delight, not just for the food, but for the view past the upturned boat rafters through the roof to the cathedral's twin spires. It's open from Monday to Saturday, with an extra-large market spreading into the surrounding streets on Saturdays.

Pottery has been made in and around Quimper since 1690 and, as you walk through the town, it is impossible to ignore its presence – you are invited to look and to buy on every corner. On weekdays, it's also possible to visit the two major *ateliers*, both to the southwest in the suburb of Locmaria just off the route de Bénodet: *H-B Henriot*, allées de Locmarion (☎98.90.09.36), and the more modern *Keraluc*, 71 rue du President-Sadat (☎98.53.04.50). There's also a pottery museum, the **Musée de la Faïence Jules Verlinque**, not far west of the SI on the south bank at 14 rue Jean-Baptiste-Bosquet (May–Oct Mon–Sat 10am–6pm).

Quimper's latest attraction is the rather uninspiring **Musée de la Crêpe** – pancake museum – 3km from the centre on route de Pont l'Abbe (July & Aug Mon–Fri 10am–6pm; otherwise Mon–Fri 9am–noon & 2–5pm; free), which purports to combine serious history with an element of gluttony.

Accommodation

There are remarkably few **hotels** in the old streets in the centre of Quimper, though more can be found near the station. Rooms can be especially difficult fo find in late July or early August, when reservations are advisable.

There is also a summer-only **youth hostel**, 2km downstream from town at 6 avenue des Oiseaux in Bois de Seminaire (April–Sept; ☎98.55.41.67; 43F), on bus route #1, (direction *Penhars*; stop *Chaptal*). You can **camp** either next to the hostel (enquiries to the Hôtel de Ville, place St-Corentin; ☎98.55.61.09), or at the four-star *Orangerie de Lannion* site on the route de Bénodet (May–Sept; ☎98.90.62.02).

Hotels

Hôtel-Restaurant Celtic, 13 rue de Douarnenez (☎98.55.59.35). Economical rooms, a little way out from the centre. Restaurant closed Sat pm and Sun, except in July & Aug. ①–③.

Hôtel Le Dupleix, 34 bd Dupleix (☎98.90.53.35). Quite expensive and modern hotel, over-looking the Odet with fine views across the river to the cathedral, and run by the same management as the *Transvaal* below. No restaurant. ④.

Hôtel Gradlon, 30 rue du Brest (☎98.95.04.39). Central but quiet, and exceptionally friendly. The rooms are not cheap, but they're very nicely decorated. No restaurant. ⑤.

Hôtel-Restaurant Pascal, 19 av de la Gare (☎98.90.00.81). Run-of-the-mill-rooms, conveniently near the station; the restaurant is not very exciting. ③.

Hôtel-Restaurant La Tour d'Auvergne, 13 rue des Réguaires (☎98.95.08.70). Comfortable rooms in a refurbished hotel tucked away in a quiet street just east of the cathedral. Closed Sun Oct–April. Good menus from 110F. ④.

Hôtel-Restaurant le Transvaal, 57 rue Jean-Jaurès (☎98.90.09.91). Comfortable and central old-fashioned *logis* just south of the Odet, with a good but rather dark restaurant whose menus start at 68F. Garage available. ①–④.

Eating and drinking

Although the pedestrian streets west of the cathedral are unexpectedly short on places to eat, there are quite a few **restaurants** further east on the north side of the river, en route towards the gare SNCF. Rue Aristide-Briand here is a particularly promising area, and also contains a lively **Celtic bar**, the *Ceili* at no 4. For *crêperies*, the place au Beurre, a short walk northwest of the cathedral, is a good bet.

Restaurants

L'Ambroisie, 49 rue Élie-Fréron (☎98.95.00.02). Upmarket French restaurant on the main road north from the Cathedral, with menus from 105F; closed Mon pm, except in summer.

L'Assiette, 5bis rue Jean-Jaurès (☎98.53.03.65). Extremely friendly new restaurant, south of the river, with an imaginative and delicious approach to traditional French cooking. Menus start around 70F.

L'Astragale, 3 rue Aristide-Briand (☎98.90.53.85). Very popular Spanish place. Its excellent seafood paellas range from *La Primera*, 65F, up to the super-abundant *Zarzuela*, 140F. Also a limited selection of other dishes.

Le Capucin Gourmand, 29 rue des Réguaires (☎98.95.43.12). Gourmet French cooking, not far east of the cathedral. Menus start at 160F – for which you can opt for snail ravioli in garlic – and zoom on up to 350F. Closed Sat lunch & Sun.

La Krampouzerie, 9 rue du Sallé on the place au Beurre (☎98.95.13.08). One of the best of Quimper's many crêperies. Closed Sun, & Mon in winter.

Trattoria Mario, 35 rue des Réguaires (☎98.95.42.15). Italian meals of pizza and fresh pasta, behind the post office. Closed Sun lunch.

Entertainment and culture

Quimper's **Festival de Cornouaille** started in 1923 and has gone from strength to strength since. This great jamboree of Breton music, costumes, theatre and dance is held in the week before the fourth Sunday in July, attracting guest performers from the other Celtic countries and a scattering of other, sometimes highly unusual, ethnic-cultural ensembles. The whole thing culminates in an incredible Sunday parade through the town. The official programme does not appear until July, but you can get provisional details in advance from the SI; it's well worth planning a little way ahead, as accommodation is at a premium in Quimper while the festival is on.

Not so widely known are the **Semaines Musicales** which follow in the first two weeks of August. The music is predominantly classical, and tends to favour French composers such as Berlioz, Debussy, Bizet and Poulenc. Founded in 1978, the event serves to bring the rather stuffy nineteenth-century theatre on bd Dupleix alive each year.

Bénodet

Once out of its city channel, the Odet takes on the anarchic shape of most Breton inlets, spreading out to lake proportions then turning narrow corners between gorges. The resort of **BÉNODET** at the mouth of the river (reachable by boat from Quimper – see above) has a long sheltered beach on the ocean side. The town is a little over-developed but the beach is undeniably good, especially for kids, for whom there's a lot laid on – including horse-riding, wind-surfing, and "beach club" crèches. During its less busy periods, such as spring or autumn, Bénodet is a strong contender to be rated as the best spot for a family holiday in the whole of Brittany.

Across the river mouth, the equally attractive **Ste-Marine** is served by regular pedestrian-only ferries. You can also drive there in a matter of minutes over the graceful **Pont de Cornouaille**, 1km upstream, which offers spectacular views of the estuary.

Information and Transport

Bénodet's **SI** is at 51 avenue de la Plage (mid-June to mid-Sept Mon–Sat 9am–7pm, Sun 9.30am–12.30pm; otherwise Mon–Fri 9am–12.30pm & 2–5.30pm, Sat 9am–noon; ☎98.57.00.14). During the school holidays, three **buses** a day run each way between Quimper and Bénodet; in school time, services are more frequent, but tend to run early in the morning. For details contact *CAT* in Quimper (☎98.95.02.36). **Bicycles** can be rented from *Cycletti*, 20 rue Charcot (☎98.57.26.09).

Boat excursions from Bénodet or Quimper to the rather nondescript **Îles de Glénan** are less exciting than the river trips between the two towns. All these services, plus sailings west along the coast to Loctudy and east to Beg-Meil, La Forêt-Fouesnant and Concarneau, are run by *Vedettes de l'Odet*, 2 av de l'Odet (☎98.57.00.58).

Accommodation and Eating

Among the nicest **hotels in** Bénodet are the *Hôtel-Restaurant Le Minaret*, an odd-looking building in a superb position overlooking the sea (April–Sept; ☎98.57.03.13; ④), and the *Hôtel-Restaurant la Poste*, in the centre of the village on av de la Plage (open all year; ☎98.57.01.09; ③). *Hôtel l'Hermitage*, 11 rue Laennec (mid-May to mid-Sept; ☎98.57.00.37; ②), which is a few hundred metres up from the beach, and doesn't have its own restaurant, is a reasonable low-priced alternative.

For a good **meal**, the restaurants of the *Hôtel Gwel-Kaer*, av de la Plage (☎98.57.04.38; ③), and the *Hôtel de Ste-Marine* (☎98.56.34.79; closed Wed in low season, & all Nov; ④), across the river mouth, are also recommended, though neither offers a menu for under 85F, and in summer the Ste-Marine tends to be too full to feed non-guests.

Bénodet also has several large **campsites** – if anything, rather too many of them – such as the *Camping Port du Plaisance* (mid-April to Sept; ☎98.57.02.38), which has its own heated swimming pool, the enormous four-star *du Letty*, southeast of the village next to the plage du Letty on rue du Canvez (mid-June to early Sept; ☎98.57.04.69), and the *de la Pointe St-Gilles* nearby (May–Sept; ☎98.57.05.37).

The Penmarch peninsula

At one time the **Penmarch peninsula** was one of the richest areas of Brittany.
That was before it was plundered by the pirate La Fontenelle, who led three
hundred ships in raids on the local peasantry from his base on the island of La
Tristan in the Bay of Douarnenez; also before the cod, staple of the fishing indus-
try, stopped coming.

Now, in the local tourist literature, the region is known as the **Pays de
Bigouden**, after the elaborate lace *coiffes* you see worn in many of the villages.
Often as much as a foot high, they are sometimes supported by half-tubes of card-
board, sometimes just very stiffly starched. The white of the coiffes swaying in
the wind provides one of the memorable colours of the area, along with the red
fields of poppies and verges of purple foxgloves.

Pont l'Abbé

PONT L'ABBÉ, the principal town of this corner, has a Bigouden museum,
spread over three storeys of the keep of its fourteenth-century château (June–
Sept Mon–Sat 9am–noon & 2–6.30pm) – though you'd need to be quite inspired
by the costumes to find it of great interest. More accessible pleasures lie in a
stroll through the woods along the banks of its estuary.

The *Hôtel de Bretagne*, 24 place de la République (☎98.87.17.22; closed Mon
out of season; ④), is the prettiest hotel in town.

To the west, the world **wind-surfing** championships are often held at **Pointe
de la Torche**, and at any time there are likely to be aficionados of the sport twirl-
ing effortlessly about on the dangerous water.

Le Guilvinec

The coast only becomes swimmable, however, as you round the Pointe de
Penmarch towards Loctudy. The first village you come to, **LE GUILVINEC**, is a
not especially attractive but surprisingly busy fishing port, sheltered in the mouth
of a little river (the boats start to come home around 4pm most afternoons). A
small but very pleasant beach faces onto the open sea.

The *Hôtel du Port*, at 53 av du Port in **Léchiagat**, on the far side of the estuary
(☎98.58.10.10; ③), is thoroughly recommended – especially, of course, for its fish
suppers, which start at 100F with a tasty array of scallops, skate, and all sorts of
dessert, and culminate in a lobster feast for 390F. Don't confuse the *Hôtel du Port*
with the *Auberge du Port*, back in Le Guilvinec itself; if you do choose to stay in
town, the very plain exterior of the *Hôtel du Centre* in rue Penmarch, conceals an
attractive garden within (☎98.58.10.44; ③). The restaurant here isn't bad, so long
as you ignore the 65F menu and go straight for the 95F one.

Loctudy

LOCTUDY is a good target – an equally well-positioned but much less commer-
cial version of Bénodet, which it faces across the mouth of the Odet. There are
several **campsites** along its main beach, including the *Kergall* (April–Sept;
☎98.87.45.93) and the *Kerandro* (July & Aug; ☎98.87.90.91), and some good-value
hotels, such as the *de Bretagne* (☎98.87.40.21; ④).

Boats from Loctudy too sail up the Odet. These should depart daily during the
summer, but you need to make sure they are running on any particular day;
services are cancelled in bad weather or simply if not enough people show up.

The Museum of Mechanical Musical Instruments

If you do find yourself stranded on a rainy and boatless day, don't despair. On the D44 between Pont l'Abbé and Bénodet, just before **COMBRIT**, is a wonderful **Musée des Mechaniques Musiques** (May–Sept daily 2–7pm; Oct–April Sun & public hols 2–7pm, or call ☎98.56.36.03 to make an appointment; 25F).

The museum is the lifetime obsession of one Monsieur Dussour, a rotund old man who cheerfully admits that he's never had the ear to play a musical instrument himself. It's only a small garage behind an antiques warehouse, but each visitor gets a personally guided tour, with M. Dussour miming at innumerable automatic keyboards. These range from barrel organs and claviers, through penny-in-the-slot machines and even a musical lemon, to a huge cabinet with two full size accordions topped with cymbals and drums. You hear all sorts of punch-tape polkas and cylinder Carmens, each recording individually made by a musician playing the same tune over and over again. The twin highpoints are the deafening sound of the restored fairground organ, and the full symphonic sweep of the "Aeolian Orchestrelle".

Along the South Coast

The coast that continues east of Bénodet is rocky and repeatedly cut by deep valleys. It suffered heavily in the hurricane of 1987, but the small resort of **BEG-MEIL** survives, albeit with fewer trees to protect its vast expanse of dunes. These are ideal for **campers**, with several official sites, and just back from the seafront there's also the hotel *Thalamot* (mid-May to Sept; ☎98.94.97.38; ③).

Around **la Forêt-Fouesnant** in particular the hills are much too steep for cyclists to climb, and forbidden to heavy vehicles such as caravans. The la Forêt-Fouesnant minor road may look good, but there are few beaches or places to stop. Motorists would do best to take the more direct D44, a few kilometres inland, followed by the D783, which leads close to the major towns along the route.

Concarneau

The first sizeable town you come to heading east from Bénodet is **CONCARNEAU**, a fishing port that does a reasonable job of passing itself off as a holiday resort. Its greatest asset is its **Ville Clos**, the old walled city situated across a slender causeway on an irregular rocky island in the bay. Its ramparts, like those of the citadelle at Le Palais on Belle-Île, were completed by Vauban in the seventeenth century. The island itself, however, had been inhabited for at least a thousand years before that, and is first recorded as the site of a priory founded by King Gradlon of Quimper. Concarneau boasts that it is a *ville fleurie*, and the flowers are most in evidence inside the walls (which you can walk around between Easter and September, daily 9am–7pm), where climbing roses and clematis swarm all over the various giftshops, restaurants and crêperies.

The **Musée de la Pêche**, immediately inside the Ville Clos (daily mid-June to mid-Sept 9.30am–7pm; otherwise 9.30am–12.30pm & 2–6pm; 30F), provides an insight into the traditional life Concarneau shared with so many other Breton ports. The four rooms around the central quadrangle illuminate the history and practice of four specific aspects of fishing. The whaling room contains model boats and a genuine open boat from the Azores; the tuna room shows boats dragging nets the size of central Paris; there's a herring room, and a model of a sardine cannery – which this building once was. And there are oddities collected by fishermen in the past; the swords of swordfish and the saws of sawfish; a Japanese giant crab; photos of old lifeboatmen with fading beards; cases full of sardine and tuna cans; and a live aquarium where the lobsters little realize they are in no immediate danger of being eaten. In addition, you can buy diagrams and models of ships, and even order a diorama of the stuffed fish of your choice.

Practicalities

Concarneau's **SI** (daily mid-June to mid-Sept 9am–8pm, otherwise 9am–noon & 2–6pm; ☎98.97.01.44) is on the quai d'Aiguillon, not far from the long-distance bus stop; there's no rail service, but SNCF buses connect with Quimper and Rosporden. It's also possible in summer to take **ferries** up the Odet to Quimper or out to the Îles Glénan, with *Vedettes Glénan* (☎98.97.10.31) or *Vedettes de l'Odet* (☎98.50.72.12). The town's main **market** is held in front of the Ville Clos on Friday, with a smaller one on Monday.

The Ville Clos is almost completely devoid of **hotels**, though there are a few expensive rooms in the upmarket restaurant *Le Galion*, 15 rue St-Guénolé (☎98.97.30.16; closed Sun pm, Mon, & all Feb; ⑤), which is otherwise noteworthy only for the meagreness of the portions on its expensive *nouvelle* menus. Most of the rest that Concarneau has to offer skulk in the backstreets of the mainland, and tend to be full most of the time. However, right opposite the entrance to the Ville Clos, the *Hôtel les Voyageurs* at 9 place Jean-Jaurès (☎98.97.08.06; ②) offers cheap basic accommodation, while the *Bonne Auberge*, Le Cabellou (May–Sept; ☎98.97.04.30; ③), is a reasonable *logis*. Probably the best bet of all is the **youth hostel** (open all year; ☎98.97.03.47; 43F), for once very near the city centre but also enjoying magnificent ocean views. It's just around the tip of the headland on the place de la Croix, with a good crêperie opposite and a **windsurfing shop** a little further along.

For a cheap **meal** in the centre, *L'Escale*, at 19 quai Carnot (☎98.97.03.31), is a favourite with local fishermen, with lunch menus for under 50F. *Chez Armande*, 15 av du Dr-Nicholas (☎98.97.0076; closed Wed, & Tues pm in winter, & mid-Nov to mid-Dec) is a bit more expensive, but still very good value, while the *Restaurant du Petit-Château*, at 12 rue Théophile-Louarn (☎98.97.49.98; closed Fri), is a nice quiet spot within the walls.

Pont-Aven

PONT-AVEN, 14km east of Concarneau and just inland from the tip of the Aven estuary, is a small port packed with tourists and art galleries. This was where Gauguin came to paint in the 1880s, before he left for Tahiti in search of a South Seas idyll. By all accounts Gauguin was a rude and arrogant man who lorded it over the local population (who were already well used to posing in "peasant attire" for visiting artists). As a painter and print-maker, however, he produced some of his finest work in Pont-Aven, and his influence was such that the **Pont-Aven School** of fellow artists developed here. He spent some years working closely with these – the best-known of whom was Émile Bernard – and they in turn helped to revitalize his own approach.

For all the local hype, however, the town has no permanent collection of Gauguin's work. The **Musée Municipal** (March–Dec daily 10am–12.30pm & 2–

7pm) in the Mairie holds changing exhibitions of the numerous members of the school, and other artists active in Brittany during the same period, but you can't count on paintings by the man himself.

Gauguin aside, Pont-Aven is pleasant in its own right, with countless galleries making it easy to while away an afternoon, and the small neat pleasure port boasting a watermill and the odd leaping salmon. Just upstream of the little granite bridge at the heart of town, the **promenade Xavier Grall** crisscrosses the tiny river itself on landscaped walkways, offering glimpses of the backs of venerable mansions, dripping with red ivy, and a little "chaos" of rocks in the stream itself. A longer walk – allow an hour – leads into the **Bois d'Amour**, wooded gardens which have long provided inspiration to visiting painters – and a fair tally, too, of poets and musicians.

If you can't afford to take a souvenir canvas home with you, the town's other speciality is more affordable, and tastes better too. Pont-Aven is the home of two manufacturers of **galettes** – which here means butter biscuits rather than pancakes – and their products are on sale everywhere.

Les Vedettes Aven-Belon (☎98.71.14.59) run **cruises** from the pleasure port throughout the summer, down to the sea at Port-Manech and around to Port-Belon near the mouth of the next estuary along. The precise schedule is determined by the state of the tides (July & Aug 1–3 departures daily; April–June & Sept, 1 departure virtually every day).

Practicalities

Pont-Aven's **SI**, 5 place de l'Hôtel de Ville (July & Aug daily 9am–1pm & 2–7pm; Sept–Nov & March–May daily 9am–12.30pm & 2–6.30pm; Dec–Feb Mon–Sat 9am–12.30pm & 2–6.30pm; ☎98.06.04.70), sells an excellent English-language guide-booklet to the town, plus route maps of local walks, for a mere 1F.

Once the day-trippers have gone home, Pont-Aven makes a tranquil place to spend a night. Much the best of its three relatively expensive **hotels** is the central *Hôtel des Ajoncs d'Or*, 1 place de l'Hôtel de Ville (☎98.06.02.06; ④), where the gourmet menus start at 100F. The nicest of the local **campsites** is *Le Spinnaker* (May–Oct; ☎98.06.01.77), set in a large wooded park.

Quimperlé

The final town of any size in Finistère, **QUIMPERLÉ** straddles a hill and two rivers, the Isole and the Elle, cut by a sequence of bridges. It's an atmospheric place, particularly in the medieval muddle of streets around **Ste-Croix** church. This was copied in plan from schema of the Church of the Holy Sepulchre in Jerusalem, brought back by crusaders, and is notable for its original Romanesque apse. There are some good bars nearby and, on Fridays, a market on the square higher up on the hill.

The **hotels** *L'Europe* (☎98.96.00.02; ③) and *Auberge de Toulföen* (☎98.96.00.29; closed Oct; ②) both have reasonable rooms.

Le Pouldu

At the mouth of the River Laïta, which constitutes the eastern limit of Finistère, the community of **LE POULDU** was another of Paul Gauguin's favourite haunts. It is divided into two distinct sections. The tiny **port**, on one bank of the narrow wooded estuary – most of which has not even a road alongside, let alone any buildings – is shielded from the open sea by a curving spit of sand. The **beach**, more developed than in Gauguin's day but still very picturesque, is a couple of kilometres away, with the headland that separates the two indented with a succession of delightful little sandy coves.

The *Hôtel des Bains* (May–Aug; ☎98.39.90.11; ③) drops down to the beach from the main road, with its large glass-fronted rooms commanding superb views, and menus starting at 85F, while the appealingly weather-beaten white *Hôtel de Pouldu* (April–Sept; ☎98.39.90.66; ③) stands next to the port. Le Pouldu would also make an ideal spot to **camp** for a few days; among sites near the beach is the *Vieux Four* (☎98.39.94.34).

travel details

Trains

From Brest 7 daily *TGV* services to Paris-Montparnasse (4hr), via Landerneau (12min), Landivisiau (20min), Morlaix (35min) and Rennes (1hr 10min); also 4 daily cheaper, slower services, taking 6hr. From Brest also to Quimper (6 daily, 1hr 30min), with connecting SNCF buses at **Châteaulin** for Crozon, and inland to Carhaix.

From Roscoff to Morlaix (6 daily; 30min).

From Quimper *TGV* services to Lorient (4 daily; 30min), Vannes (4 daily; 1hr) and Redon (2 daily; 1hr 40min), plus 6 slower services. Most continue to Rennes or Nantes, and on to Paris, Bordeaux or Toulouse.

Buses

From Roscoff to Morlaix (2–4 daily; 50min) and Quimper (1 only, Mon, Fri & Sat; 2hr 30min).

From Morlaix to Roscoff (2–4 daily; 50min); Carantec (4 daily; 20min); Plougasnou and St Jean-le-Doigt (5 daily; 30min); Lannion (2 daily; not Sun; 1hr); Huelgoat (3 daily; 45min) and Carhaix (3 daily; 1hr 30min); Quimper (1 daily; 2hr).

From Brest to Roscoff (5 daily; 1hr 30min), via Plouescat, Lanhouarneau, Lesneven and Gouesnou; to Le Conquet (4 daily; 30min); to Quimper (6 daily; 1hr 30min).

From Châteaulin to Crozon and Camaret (5 daily; 30min/50min); less often to Carhaix.

From Landévennec 3 daily to Camaret (45min) via Roscanvel and Crozon.

From Quimper 5 daily to Locronan (25min), Telgruc (1hr), Crozon (1hr 20min) and Camaret (1hr 30min); 3 daily to Audierne (1hr) and Pointe du Raz

(1hr 15min); 6 daily to Concarneau (30min) and Quimperlé (1hr 30min); 6 daily to Fouesnant (1hr) and Beg-Meil (1hr 10min); 9 daily to the airport at Plugaffan; 8 daily to Bénodet (45min); also to Douarnenez (5 daily; 40min), Lorient (2hr) and Vannes (3hr).

Air

From Brest airport (Guipavas), 2 daily flights to **Ouessant**, subject to good weather; (☎98.84.64.87). Every two days, March–Oct, to **London** (**Brit Air**; in Morlaix ☎98.62.10.22 and in London ☎0171/499 9511).

From **Quimper** airport (Plugaffan), 2 daily flights to **Paris** (☎98.84.73.33). Also connecting flights to **Brest** for London flights, as above.

Ferries

From Roscoff to **Plymouth** (6hr) and **Cork** (13–17hr). Both services *Brittany Ferries*, (Roscoff ☎98.29.28.28, Plymouth ☎01752/21321, Cork ☎215/07666). See p.3 onwards for more details.

From Roscoff to **Île de Batz** (very frequently, 15min), contact ☎98.61.77.75; and in July and August tours of the **Bay of Morlaix**.

From Le Conquet and **Brest** to **Ouessant** and **Molène** (1–2 daily); ☎98.80.24.68. Journey from Le Conquet to Ouessant takes 1hr, from Brest up to 3hr. See timetable on p.228.

From Brest to **Le Fret** on the Crozon peninsula, 3 daily April–Sept, 45 minutes (☎98.44.44.04). Foot passengers and cyclists only, each trip is met by a minibus for **Crozon** and **Camaret**. Trips also run from Brest around the **Rade de Brest**.

From Morgat, trips to caves and headlands. ☎98.27.09.54.

From Douarnenez to **Morgat**, 4hr 30min return trips in July & Aug – which you can also use as a one-way ferry service (☎98.27.09.54); also trips around **Bay of Douarnenez**, and occasional trips to Ouessant, run by *Penn Ar Bed* (☎98.80.24.68).

From Audierne to **Sein** island, 1hr 10min, ☎98.70.02.37 all year (except Weds out of season), or ☎98.70.21.15 summer only.

From Quimper down the Odet to **Bénodet**, and vice versa (May–Sept; ☎98.57.00.58).

You can also **tour the Odet**, daily from **Loctudy** (☎98.57.00.58), daily from **Concarneau** (June 15 –Sept 15; ☎98.97.10.31), and thrice weekly from **Port-la-Forêt** and **Beg-Meil** (☎98.94.97.94). All the Odet companies also do trips (average 1hr) to the **Glénan** islands.

CHAPTER SIX

INLAND BRITTANY: THE NANTES–BREST CANAL

The **Nantes–Brest canal** is a meandering chain of waterways, linking natural rivers with purpose-built stretches of canal, which runs all the way from Finistère down to the Loire. En route it passes through medieval riverside towns, such as **Josselin** and **Malestroit**, that long pre-date its construction; commercial ports and junctions – **Pontivy**, most notably – which

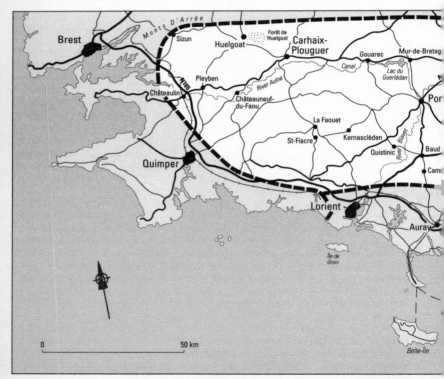

developed along its path during the nineteenth century; the old port of **Redon**, a chequerboard of water, where the canal crosses the River Vilaine; and a succession of scenic splendours, including the string of lakes around the **Barrage de Guerlédan** near Mur-de-Bretagne.

As a focus for exploring **inland Brittany**, perhaps cutting in to the towpaths along the more easily accessible stretches, and then detouring out to the towns and sights around, the canal is ideal. The detours can be picked almost at will – the **sculpture park** at Kerguéhennec, near Josselin, and the village of **La Gacilly** near Malestroit, are among the least known and most enjoyable.

All this area is supposed – in myth at any rate – to have been covered by one vast forest, the *Argoat*. Though vestiges of ancient woodland do remain in several areas, natural and human forces seem to be conspiring to destroy them. The **forest of Huelgoat,** which with its boulder-strewn waterfalls, bubbling streams and grottoes was the most dramatic natural landscape in Brittany, is only now starting to recover from the devastating hurricane of 1987. **Paimpont** – the legendary forest of Brocéliande which concealed the Holy Grail – survived that storm, only to be damaged by a serious fire in the autumn of 1990.

You cannot make the whole journey described in this chapter by literally keeping next to the canal. For much of the way there is no adjacent road, and even

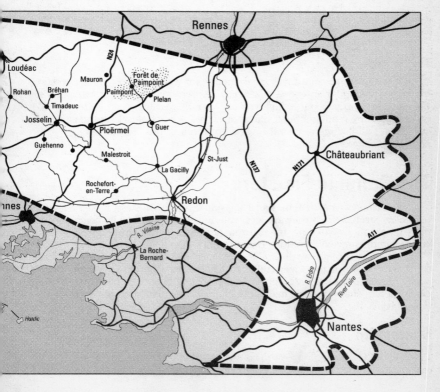

THE CANAL

The idea of joining together the inland waterways of Brittany dates back to 1627 – though as ever nothing was done to implement the scheme until it was seen as a military necessity. That point came during the Napoleonic wars, when English fleets began to threaten shipping circumnavigating the Breton coast. To relieve the virtual blockade of Brest in 1810, Napoleon authorized the construction of a canal network to link it with both Nantes and Lorient.

In the event, economic disasters held up its completion, but by 1836 a navigable path was cut and the canal officially opened. It was not an immediate success. Having cost sixty million francs to construct, the first years of operation, up to 1850, raised a mere 70,000 francs in tariffs. It survived, however, helped by a navy experiment of transporting coal cross-country to its ports. By the turn of the century the canal's business was booming. In the years between 1890 and the outbreak of the First World War, an annual average of 35,000 tons of cargo were carried. In addition to coal, the cargoes were mainly slate, from the quarries near Châteaulin, and fertilizer, which helped to develop agricultural production inland.

After the War, motor transport and more effective roads brought swift decline. The canal had always been used primarily for short journeys at either end – from Brest to Carhaix and Pontivy to Nantes – and in 1928 the building of a dam at Lac Guerlédan cut it forever into two sections, with the stretch from Carhaix to Pontivy becoming navigable only by canoe. Plans for the dam were approved on the basis that either a hydraulic lift, or a side channel, would enable barges to bypass it – but neither was ever built. In 1945 the last barge arrived at Châteaulin, and these days the only industry that has much use for the canal is tourism.

---

though the **towpath** is normally clear enough for walking it's not really practicable to cycle along for any great distance. However, it is certainly worth following the canal in short sections, which you can do quite easily by car, better by bike, or best of all by renting a **boat**, **barge** or even a **houseboat** along the navigable stretches. Full listings of **rental** outlets are given in the "Travel Details" at the end of this chapter.

The Canal in Finistère

The westernmost section of the canal, passing through Finistère, is now one of its least-used stretches. Those travellers who do set out to follow its course are far more likely to do so from the Crozon peninsula or the Menez-Hom – both covered in the previous chapter – than from Brest itself.

However, as recently as the 1920s, steamers made their way across the Rade de Brest and down the River Aulne to Châteaulin. The contemporary *Black's Guide* reckoned the six-hour journey "tedious (in a) boat often overcrowded with cattle"; a judgement that seems a little churlish now that such pleasures are no longer available.

Châteaulin

CHÂTEAULIN is the first real town on the canal route, though in actuality no more than a brief, picturesque waterside strip, overlooked by the pretty little

ACCOMMODATION PRICE CODES

All **hotel prices** in this book have been coded using the symbols below. The price shown is for the least expensive double room, which for categories ① and ② usually means a room without shower, bath and toilet. Most hotels in those categories have other rooms with en-suite facilities, which typically cost 30–50F extra.

For a full explanation see p.31.

①	up to 120 F	④	220–300F	⑦	500–600F
②	120–160F	⑤	300–400F	⑧	600–700F
③	160–220F	⑥	400–500F	⑨	700F and over

chapel of Notre Dame. It's a quiet place, where the main reason to stay is the River Aulne itself. Enticingly rural, it is renowned for its salmon and trout fishing; if you're interested, most bars sell permits (as do angling shops, some of which rent tackle). The only other factor that might draw you is cycling: regional championships are held each September on a circuit that races through the centre and on occasion it's used for the French professional championship, too.

Along **the riverbank**, a statue commemorates Jean Moulin, the Resistance leader of whose murder SS man Klaus Barbie was found guilty in Lyons. Moulin was *sous-prefect* in Châteaulin from 1930 to 1933; the inscription reads "mourir sans parler".

Within a couple of minutes' walk upstream from the statue, and the town centre, you're on towpaths overhung by trees full of birds, with rabbits and squirrels running ahead of you on the path. For the first couple of kilometres, diagrams of corpulent yet energetic figures incite you to join them in unspeakable exercises – if you can resist that temptation, you'll soon find yourself ambling in peace past the locks and weirs that climb towards the Montagnes Noires.

Practicalities

Unless a major cycling event is taking place, you should have little difficulty finding a room in any of Châteaulin's three or four modest **hotels**. The best value of them is *Le Chrismas* at 33 Grande-Rue, a *logis de France* a short walk up the road that climbs east of the town centre towards Pleyben (☎98.86.01.24; ②); meals in its restaurant start at 68F.

The municipal **campsite** – *Rodaven* (June to mid-Sept; ☎98.86.32.93) – is very attractively situated beside the river, but is only open in high summer.

Pont Coblant

If you set out to walk the canal seriously from Châteaulin, **PONT COBLANT** and Pleyben may look just ten kilometres distant on the map, but be warned the meanders make it a hike of several hours (pick your side of the water, too; there are no bridges between Châteaulin and Pont Coblant).

It's possible to rent both **kayaks** and **houseboats** from this small village (contact *Crabing-Loisirs*, M Mercier, 20 rue de Frout, 29000 Quimper; ☎98.95.14.02; or call ☎98.73.34.69). Pont Coblant also has a very basic (and cheap) forty-bed unofficial **youth hostel** (contact the *Moulin de Pont Coblant*, 29190 Pleyben, ☎98.73.34.40 to reserve a bed) and a **campsite** (June–Sept; ☎98.73.31.22).

Pleyben

PLEYBEN, four kilometres north of Pont Coblant, is renowned for its sixteenth-century **parish close** (see p.221). On its four sides the calvary traces the life of Jesus, combining great detail with an appealing naivety. The church of St-Germain itself, twin-towered, with a huge ornate spire dwarfing its domed Renaissance neighbour, features an altarpiece so blackened and buckled by age as to leave only two tiny "windows" decipherable, like an Advent calendar. Pleyben is more openly prosperous than the parish close villages further north; the church is well-scrubbed, and currently undergoing major restoration (not this time due to hurricane damage).

There's an **SI** in the spacious and grandiose main square, the place de Gaulle, and a hotel behind the church, *Le Gai Logis* (☎98.26.63.71; ③). On the N164 in between Châteaulin and Pleyben, the *Run Ar Puns* (☎98.86.27.95) is a **music club** and bar housed in old farm buildings.

Châteauneuf

CHÂTEAUNEUF-DU-FAOU, a little way south of the N164 25km east of Châteaulin, is in a similar sort of vein, sloping down to the tree-lined river. It's a little more developed, though, with a tourist complex, the *Penn ar Pont* (mid-March to mid-Oct; ☎98.81.81.25), which boasts a swimming pool, gîtes and camping as well as cycle and **boat rental**.

The **canal proper** separates off from the Aulne a few kilometres to the east at Pont Triffen, staking its own path on, past Carhaix, and out of Finistère.

Carhaix and onwards

CARHAIX, a further 25km east, is a road junction which dates back to the Romans, with cafés and shops to replenish supplies, but not much to recommend it. The most interesting building in town is the granite Renaissance **Maison de Sénéchal** on rue Brisieux, which houses the **SI** (☎98.93.04.42). The modern *Hôtel Gradlon* at 12 bd de la République (☎98.93.15.22; ④), near the church makes a comfortable if rather pricey place to spend the night, and serves good food with menus starting at 60F.

Beyond Carhaix the canal – as far as Pontivy – is navigable only by canoe. If that's not how you're travelling, it probably makes more sense to loop round to the south, through the **Montagnes Noir**, Le Faouët and Kernascléden, before rejoining the canal at **Lac Guerlédan**. Alternatively, to the north – assuming you resisted the detour from Morlaix – there are the **Forêt de Huelgoat** and the **Monts d'Arrée**. These routes are covered in the next two sections.

South through the Montagnes Noires

The **Montagnes Noires** edge along the borders of Finistère, south of Châteauneuf. Despite the name, they are really no more than escarpments, though bleak and imposing nonetheless in a harsh, exposed landscape at odds with the gentle canal path. Their highest point is the stark slate **Roc de Toullaëron**, on the road between Pont Triffen and Gourin. From its 1043ft peak, you can look west and north over miles of what seems like totally deserted countryside.

Le Faouët and St-Fiacre

If you are driving, the D769 beyond Gourin offers access to the twin churches of St-Fiacre and Kernascléden, built simultaneously, according to legend, with the aid of an angelic bridge. En route is the town of **LE FAOUËT**, a secluded place (served neither by buses nor trains) distinguished mainly by its large wooden market hall, topped by a pinnacle turret. The church at **ST-FIACRE**, just over two kilometres south, is notable for its rood screen, brightly polychromed and carved as intricately as lace. The original purpose of a rood screen was to separate the chancel from the congregation – the decorations of this 1480 masterpiece go rather further than that. They depict scenes from the Old and New Testaments as well as a dramatic series on the wages of sin. Drunkenness is demonstrated by a man somehow vomiting a fox; theft by a peasant stealing apples; and so on.

Practicalities

Two similar and highly recommendable **hotels** in the immediate area of Le Faouët both offer good food – the *Croix d'Or* in town, opposite the old market (☎97.23.07.33; closed mid-Dec to mid-Jan, & Sat in low season; ④), and the *Cheval Blanc* (☎97.34.61.15; ④), a few kilometres east, along the pleasant (but steep) D132, in **PRIZIAC**. Le Faouët also has its own riverside municipal **campsite**, the *Beg-er-Roch* (March to mid-Sept; ☎97.23.15.11).

Kernascléden

At the ornate and gargoyle-coated church at **KERNASCLÉDEN**, fifteen kilometres southeast of Le Faouët along the D782, the focus turns from carving to frescoes. The themes, however, contemporary with St-Fiacre, are equally gruesome. In a Dance of Death, a faded cousin to that at Kermaria (see p.199), the souls of the damned are boiled and minced in Hell.

The Monts d'Arrée

A broad swathe of the more desolate regions of Finistère, stretching east from the Crozon peninsula right to the edge of Finistère, is designated as the *Parc Régional d'Armorique*. The park, in theory at least, is an area of conservation and of rural regeneration along traditional lines; in reality, lack of funding creates rather less impact. The **Monts d'Arrée**, however, which cut northeast across Finistère from the Aulne estuary, are something of a nature sanctuary; kestrels circle high above the bleak hilltops, sharing the skies with pippits, curlews and great black crows.

Over to the east, the ancient woods of the **Forêt de Huelgoat** can offer an atmospheric afternoon's walking, with the lakeside village of Huelgoat itself making an attractive base if you have the time to stay longer.

East across the Monts d'Arrée

The administrative centre of the Parc d'Armorique is at **MENEZ-MEUR**, off the D342 near the Forêt de Cranou – just inland from the Brest–Quimper motorway. Menez is an official **animal reserve**, with wild boar and deer roaming free, and a museum of Breton horses (June–Sept daily 10.30am–7pm; May daily except Sat 1.30–5.30pm; Feb–April & Oct–Dec Wed, Sun & hols 10am–noon & 1–6pm). At the reserve gate you can pick up a wealth of detail on the park and all its various activities (☎98.68.81.71).

Ten kilometres north, at **SIZUN**, a research station, **aquarium** and fishing exhibition set out to increase public awareness of the significance of Brittany's rivers and inland waterways (July & Aug daily 10.30am–7pm; June & Sept Mon–Sat 10.30am–12.30pm & 1.30–5.30pm, Sun 10.30am–12.30pm & 1.30–7pm; March–May & Oct Sun, Wed & hols 2–5.30pm; Nov–Feb Wed 2–5.30pm).

The Moulins de Kerouat

Another three kilometres east of Sizun, along the D764 to Commana, is the abandoned hamlet of **MOULINS DE KEROUAT** (*Milin-Kerroc'h* in Breton – and on the Michelin map), which has been restored as an **Eco-Musée** (July & Aug daily 11am–7pm; mid-May to June daily 2–6pm; mid-March to mid-May & mid-Sept to Oct daily except Sat 2–6pm; otherwise by appointment ☎98.68.87.76). Kerouat's last inhabitant died in 1967 and like many a place in the Breton interior it might have crumbled into indiscernible ruins. However, the idea of eco-museums is big in France at present – they are usually excellent – and one of the hamlet's watermills has been restored to motion, and its houses repaired and refurnished. The largest belonged in the last century to the mayor of Commana, who also controlled the mills, and its furnishings are therefore those of a rich family.

Into the Mountains

The highest point of the Monts d'Arrée is the **ridge** which curves from the **Réservoir de St-Michel** (also known as the Lac de Brennilis) to Menez Kaldor. It is visible as a stark silhouette from the underused **campsite** at **NESTAVEL-BRAZ** on the eastern shore of the lake. From this deceptively tranquil vantage point, the army's antennae near **Roc Trévezel** to the north are obscured, as are those of the navy at Menez-Meur to the west. Right behind you, however, is the Brennilis nuclear power station. In a rare manifestation of separatist terrorism, Breton nationalists attacked this in 1975 with a rocket-launcher; it survived. In 1987, the British SAS conducted an astonishingly offensive exercise in this area, when they were invited by the French government to subdue a simulated Breton uprising, and in the process managed to run over a local inhabitant.

Perhaps appropriately, across the lake where the tree-lined fields around the villages end, is **Yeun Elez**, one of the legendary "holes to hell". You can walk around the lake – gorse and brambles permitting; be very careful not to stray from the paths into the surrounding peat bogs. The ridge itself is followed most of the way by a road but in places it still feels as if miles from any habitation.

The Forêt de Huelgoat

The **FORÊT DE HUELGOAT** spreads out to the north and east of the village of Huelgoat, the halfway point between Morlaix and Carhaix on the minor road D769 and served by the four daily buses that connect the two towns.

While there may be doubt as to whether the *Argoat*, the great forest supposed to have stretched the length of prehistoric inland Brittany, ever existed, the antiquity of Huelgoat cannot be questioned. Until 1987, indeed, this was a staggering, almost impossible landscape, of trees, giant boulders and waterfalls tangled together in primeval chaos. Just how fragile it really was, just how miraculous had been its long survival, was demonstrated by the hurricane of that October, which smashed it to smithereens in the space of fifteen minutes.

After several years of cleaning up, the forest has now returned to a fairly close approximation of its former glories. You might be a little puzzled by some of the hyperbolic descriptions that survive from the old days in the local tourist literature and other sources, but it is once again possible to walk for several kilometres along the various paths that lead into the depths of the woods, and in spring and autumn in particular Huelgoat deserves a substantial detour.

Granite being less delicate than timber, the strange rock formations of Huelgoat have survived better than the trees, and a half-hour stroll in the area close to the village enables you to scramble over, among, and even under a number of inconceivably large specimens. At the **Grotte du Diable**, you can make a somewhat perilous descent, between the rocks, to a subterranean stream. The local story is that a Revolutionary soldier, fleeing from the *chouans*, hid in the cave, lighting a fire to keep warm; when his pursuers saw him by the red glow, brandishing a pitchfork to defend himself, they thought they'd found the Devil. In summer, a "tea house" serves snacks to walkers, a few metres from the disappointingly stable **Roche Tremblante**.

Further into the forest, beside the waterfall known as the **Mare aux Sangliers**, a solitary pine tree used to cling to a massive boulder, its exposed roots wrapped around the stone like tentacles. The hurricane brought it and all its neighbours down; new growth has now replaced it, but it's no longer such a

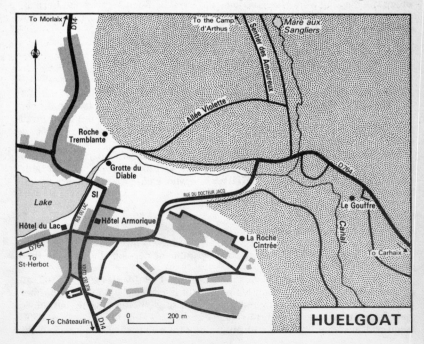

HUELGOAT

compelling sight. The **Camp d'Arthus**, the Gallo-Roman *oppidum*, or hill-fort, large enough to be a settlement for a whole community rather than just a military encampment – and the spitting image of Asterix the Gaul's fictional village – is now barely recognizable.

Practicalities
The village of **HUELGOAT** is still quite a pleasant overnight stop, next to its own small **lake** (on which they hold aquatic Citroën 2CV championships each July – and have the photographs to prove it).

The local **SI**, attached to the Hôtel de Ville, tucked in behind the central place Aristide-Briand (Mon–Fri 2–5pm, Sat 10am–noon; ☎98.99.72.32), supplies walking maps of the forest. One or two of the village's **hotels** were too hard hit by the post-hurricane decline in tourism to survive, but the *Hôtel du Lac*, beside the lake at 12 rue du Général-de-Gaulle (Feb–Oct; ☎98.99.71.14; ②), is still there, offering very basic **rooms** and good food. Also beside the lake, on the road towards Brest, the *Camping du Lac* (June–Sept; ☎98.99.78.80) is complete with swimming-pool. **Bikes** are rented out at the garage at 1 rue du Lac.

Le Gouffre
A walk out from Huelgoat that avoids the heart of the forest is along the **canal** to the east. This stretch – not linked to any of the main Nantes–Brest waterways – was originally built to serve the old lead and silver mines, worked here from Roman times right up to this century. **LE GOUFFRE** is close by (at the junction where the road out from Huelgoat joins the D769 between Morlaix and Carhaix), worth the walk for its deep cave and, more so, for an exceptionally good (and cheap) *Routiers* **restaurant**.

Back to the Canal

Although between Carhaix and Pontivy the **Nantes–Brest canal** is limited to canoeists, it's worth some effort to follow on land, particularly for the scenery along the middle stretch from Gouarec to Mur-de-Bretagne. At the centre trails the artificial **Lac de Guerlédan**, backed to the south by the **Forêt de Quénécan**.

Approaching by road, the canal path is easiest joined at Gouarec, covered by the five daily buses between Carhaix and Loudéac. En route, you pass the rather subdued (and unmemorable) **ROSTRENEN**, whose old facades are given a little life at the Tuesday market.

Gouarec
At **GOUAREC** the River Blavet and the canal meet in a confusing swirl of water that shoots off, edged by footpaths, in the most unlikely directions. The old schist houses of the town are barely disturbed by traffic or development, nor are there great numbers of tourists.

For a comfortable overnight stop, the 2-star **hotel**, *du Blavet* (☎96.24.90.03; ③), is in an ideal waterside position; its restaurant is principally aimed at gourmets prepared to spend several hundred francs on a single bottle of wine, but they're quite happy to serve you with the same excellent food on their cheapest (80F) menu with no wine. If you're **camping**, there's a well-positioned municipal site,

Le Bout du Pont (mid-June to mid-Sept; ☎96.24.90.22), next to the canal and away from the main road.

Lac Guerlédan

For the fifteen kilometres between Gouarec and Mur-de-Bretagne, the **N164** skirts the edge of the **Forêt de Quénécan**, within which is the series of artificial lakes created when the Barrage of Guerlédan was completed in 1928. Though the forest itself suffered severe damage in the hurricane, this remains a beautiful stretch of river, a little over-popular with British camper-caravanners but peaceful enough nonetheless.

The best bases to stay are just off the road, past the villages of **ST-GELVEN** and Caurel. At the former, the ravishing *Hôtellerie de l'Abbaye Bon-Repos* (☎96.24.98.38; closed Tues pm & Wed in low season; ③) nestles beside the water at the end of a venerable avenue of ancient trees, amid the ruins of a twelfth-century Cistercian abbey. Even if you don't stay, it's worth considering pausing for a meal in the magnificent banqueting hall – menus start at 60F.

From just before Caurel, the brief loop of the D111 leads to tiny sandy beaches – a bit too tiny in season – with **campsites** *Les Pins* (☎96.28.52.22) and *Les Pommiers* (☎96.28.52.35). At the spot known, justifiably, as **BEAU RIVAGE** is a complex containing a campsite, hotel, restaurant, snack bar and 140-seat glass-topped cruise-boat.

Mur-de-Bretagne and Loudéac

MUR-DE-BRETAGNE is set back from the eastern end of the lake, a lively place with a wide and colourful pedestrianized zone around its church. It's the nearest town to the barrage – just two kilometres distant – and has a **campsite**, the *Rond-Point du Lac* (mid-June to mid-Sept; ☎96.26.01.90), with facilities for wind-surfing and horse-riding. There's also a pretty little **youth hostel**, a short way further along the N164 at **ST-GUEN** (April–Oct; ☎96.28.54.34; 43F) – take the Loudéac bus and get off at *Bourg de St-Guen*.

LOUDÉAC, useful for changing buses, is in itself unmemorable. Travelling on from Mur-de-Bretagne under your own steam, you'd do better to take the D767 instead and follow the Blavet south.

The Central Canal

Beyond the barrage of Guerlédan, the historic town of **Pontivy** is the central junction of the Nantes–Brest canal, where the course of the canal breaks off once more from the Blavet and you can again take **barges** – all the way to the Loire.

Pontivy

PONTIVY owes much of its appearance, and its size, to the canal. When the waterway opened, the small medieval centre was expanded, re-designed and given broad avenues to fit its new role. It was even re-named Napoléonville for a time, in honour of the instigator of its new prosperity.

These days it is a bright market town, its twisting old streets contrasting with the stately riverside promenades. At the north end of the town, occupying a commanding hillside site, is the **Château de Rohan**, built by the lord of Josselin in the fifteenth century (mid-June to Sept daily 10am–noon & 2–6pm; Oct to mid-June Wed–Sun 10am–noon & 2–5pm; 15F). Used in summer for low-key cultural events and temporary exhibitions, the castle still belongs to the Josselin family, who are slowly restoring it. At the moment, one impressive facade, complete with deep moat and two forbidding towers, looks out over the river – behind that, the structure rather peters out.

Practicalities

If you're looking for a place to stop over, Pontivy has several **hotels**, among them the low-priced *Martin* (☎97.25.02.04; ①) and the *Robic*, 2 rue Jean–Jaurès (☎97.25.11.80; ②), which has a good restaurant with menus from 55F, and there's a very spartan **youth hostel** (☎97.25.58.27; 43F), 2km from the gare SNCF on the Île des Recollets. The **SI** is just below the castle, in a former leprosy hospital on place de Gaulle (☎97.25.04.10).

Rohan and Bréhan

Immediately beyond Pontivy, the **course of the canal** veers north for a while, away from the Blavet. As it curves back, the stretch from St-Maudan to Rohan is wide and smooth-flowing, with picnic and play areas but without a road or towpath you can follow for any distance.

ROHAN looks prominent on the map but it's little more than a strip of houses by the canalside. To the northeast, the attractive village of **LA CHÈZE** has a tiny and private lake, with an equally diminutive **campsite** (☎96.26.70.99). **LA TRINITÉ PORHOËT**, beyond, also has a **campsite**, *Saint-Yves* (☎97.93.92.00), on the long wooded slopes of the valley of the Ninian – otherwise scattered with stone farms and manor houses.

Southeast from Rohan, continuing along the canal towards Josselin, is the Cistercian **Abbaie de Timadeuc**, founded as recently as 1841. You can enter only to attend mass, but it's beautiful anyway from the outside, with its front walls and main gate covered in flowers at the end of an avenue of old pines. The abbey also provides an excuse to stay at **BRÉHAN** a couple of kilometres away, a quiet little village whose **hotel**, the *Cremaillère* (☎97.38.80.93; ①), must be the best value anywhere in the province. A double room with separate luxurious bathroom costs around 100F, and the set menu at around 60F can include a full seafood platter of oysters, crayfish and crabs, with the meringue-in-caramel dessert *îles flottantes*.

West from Pontivy: along the Blavet

If you choose to follow the **River Blavet** west from Pontivy towards Lorient – rather than the canal – take the time to go by the smaller roads along the valley itself. The Blavet connects the canal with the sea, and once linked Lorient to the other two great ports of Brittany, Brest and Nantes.

Quistinic

The D159 to **QUISTINIC** passes through lush green countryside, its hedgerows full of flowers, where by June there's already been one harvest and grass is growing up around the fresh haystacks. The ivy-clad church of **St-Mathurin** in Quistinic is the scene of a *pardon* (in the second week of May) that dates from Roman times. The devotion to the saint is strongly evident on the village's war memorial, too, his name that of almost half the victims. You can **camp** near the river at the *Île de Ménazen* (mid-June to mid-Sept; ☎97.39.70.99).

Baud: The Venus de Quinipily

The main reason to go on to **BAUD**, a major road junction just to the east of the river, is to see the **Venus de Quinipily** – signposted off the Hennebont road, two kilometres out of town. The Venus is a crude statue that at first glance looks Egyptian. Once known as the "Iron Lady", it is of unknown but ancient origin. It stands on, or rather nestles its ample buttocks against, a high plinth above a kind of sarcophagus, commanding the valley in the gardens of what was once a château. Behind its stiff pose and dress, the statue has an odd informality, a half-smile on the impassive face. It used to be the object of "impure rites" and was at least twice thrown into the Blavet by Christian authorities, only to be fished out by locals eager to re-indulge. It may itself have been in some way "improper" before it was re-carved, perhaps literally "dressed", some time in the eighteenth century.

The **gardens** around the statue, despite being next to a dry and dusty quarry, are luxuriantly fertile. To visit, you pay a small fee to a woman at the gatehouse, who matter-of-factly maintains that "pagans" still come to worship.

You can **stay** in Baud at the *Relais de la Forêt* opposite the town hall (☎97.51.01.77; ②), where meals in the wood-panelled dining room start at 65F, and there are rooms to suit all price ranges.

Camors and Locminé

CAMORS, just south of Baud, has a smart square-towered church, with a weathercock on top and a little megalith set in the wall. *The Hôtel-Restaurant Ar Brug* (☎97.39.20.10; ③) opposite the church possesses an excellent restaurant, and the **campsite** *du Petit Bois* (mid-June to mid-Sept; ☎97.39.18.36) stands at one end of the series of forests that grow bleaker and harsher eastward to become the Lanvaux Moors.

Heading east from Baud, to rejoin the canal at Josselin, you pass through **LOCMINÉ**, another one of those towns reduced to piping rock music in its life-less streets on summer afternoons in a desperate attempt to draw visitors.

Josselin and around

The three Rapunzel towers of the **Château de Rohan** at **JOSSELIN**, embedded in a vast sheet of stone above the water, constitute the most impressive sight along the Nantes–Brest canal. However, they turn out in fact to be a facade. The building behind was built in the last century, the bulk of the original castle having been demolished by Richelieu in 1629 in punishment for Henri de Rohan's leadership of the Huguenots. The Rohan family, still in possession, used to own a third of Brittany, though the present incumbent contents himself with the position of local mayor. Tours of the pompous apartments of the ducal residence are not very compelling, even if it does contain the table on which the Edict of Nantes was signed in 1598. But the duchess' collection of **dolls**, housed in the *Musée des Poupées*, behind the castle, is something special. (Château open July–Aug daily 10am–noon & 2–6pm; June & Sept daily 2–6pm; Feb–May & Oct to mid-Nov, Wed, Sun and hols 2–6pm; closed mid-Nov to Jan; hours for the doll museum the same, but open mornings in June & Sept as well).

The **town** is full of medieval splendours, from the gargoyles of the Basilica to the castle ramparts and the half-timbered houses in between. It has a history to match. One of the most famous episodes of late chivalry, the Battle of the Thirty, took place nearby in 1351. Rivalry between the French garrison at Josselin and the English at Ploërmel led to a challenge being issued to settle differences in a combat of thirty unmounted knights from each side. The French won, killing the English leader Bemborough. The actual battle-site is now isolated between the two carriageways of the N24 from Josselin to Ploërmel.

More accessible is the basilica of **Notre-Dame-du-Roncier**, built on the spot where in the ninth century a peasant supposedly found a statue of the Virgin under a bramble bush. The statue was burned during the Revolution but an important *pardon* is held each year on September 8. As ever, the religious procession and open-air services are solemn in the extreme, but there's a lot else going on to keep you entertained.

Practicalities

Josselin's **SI** is in a superb old house on the place de la Congrégation, up in town next to the castle entrance (☎97.22.36.43). Just across from the Basilica, the *Hôtel de France* (☎97.22.23.06; closed Sun pm & Mon between Oct and March; ④) is an ivy-covered *logis* which is amazingly quiet considering its central location, where you can choose on the 77F menu between duck in cider or trout with almonds, while the *Hôtel du Château* (☎97.22.20.11; ②) is a lovely medieval building by the river, facing the castle. There's also a *gîte d'étape* nearby, right below the castle walls, where you can rent **canoes** (☎97.22.21.69). Much the best **restaurant** in town, a short walk east of the Basilica as the road starts to drop towards the river, is the *Frères Blot*, at 9 rue Glatinier (☎97.22.22.08); lunch menus start at 75F. The nearest good **campsite** is at Bas de la Lande, half an hour's walk from the castle, south of the river and west of town.

Guéhenno

At **GUÉHENNO**, south of Josselin on the D123, is one of the largest and best of the Breton calvaries. Built in 1550, the figures include the cock that crowed to expose Peter's denials, Mary Magdalene with the shroud, and a recumbent Christ in the crypt. Its appeal is enhanced by the naivety of its amateur restoration. After damage caused by Revolutionary soldiers in 1794 – who amused themselves by playing *boules* with the heads of the statues – all the sculptors approached for the work demanded exorbitant fees, so the parish priest and his assistant decided to undertake the task themselves.

Kerguéhennec Sculpture Park

Another unusual sculptural endeavour, this time contemporary, is taking place at the **DOMAINE DE KERGUÉHENNEC**, which is signposted a short way off the D11 near St Jean-Brévelay. This innovatory **sculpture park** (April–Nov daily except Mon 10am–6pm; ☎97.60.44.44; 25F) is progressively building up a fascinating permanent international collection. Among the first pieces to be installed, back in 1986, was a massive railway sleeper painstakingly stripped down by Giuseppe Penone to reveal the young sapling within; since then the park has become an increasingly compelling stop. Its setting is the lawns, woods and lake of an early eighteenth-century château; studios and indoor workshops in the outbuildings are used by visiting artists.

Lizio

Over to the east, off the D151, the little village of **LIZIO** has also set itself up as a centre for arts and crafts, with ceramic and weaving workshops its speciality. For most of the year, you might pass along its single curving street of stone cottages without seeing a sign of life; on the second Sunday in August, however, it's the scene of a *Festival Artisanal*, featuring street theatre (and pancakes). Various farmers in the nearby countryside, who welcome visitors, are working to re-create traditional skills such as bee-keeping and cider-making, and one is even rearing wild boars for food. For details of them all, and an overview of long-lost agricultural techniques and implements, call in at the **Eco-musée des Vieux Métiers**, 4km out of Lizio on the D174 towards Ploërmel (daily 10am–noon & 2–7pm).

Lizio has no hotels, but it does have a couple of restaurants. There are also several **gîtes** (information on ☎97.74.92.67) in the immediate area, and a municipal **campsite**, *Le Val Jouin* (mid-May to mid-Oct; also ☎97.74.92.67).

Ploërmel

PLOËRMEL, defeated by Josselin in the fourteenth century, is still not quite a match for its rival. It's not on the canal, although it is on the railway line. Attractions are the artificial **Étang au Duc**, well stocked with fish, two kilometres to the north, and an interesting array of houses: James II is said to have spent a few days of his exile in one on rue Francs-Bourgeois, while the **Maison des Marmosets** on rue Beaumanoir has some elaborate carvings.

Both the **hotels** *St-Marc* (☎97.74.00.01; ②), near the station, and *Cobh*, 10 rue des Forges (☎97.74.00.49; ③), make good bases for venturing further away from the canal, up into Paimpont forest.

The Forêt de Paimpont

The **FORÊT DE PAIMPONT** has a definite magic about it. Though now just forty square kilometres in extent – and in places looking a bit woebegone, while the fire damage from a major blaze in September 1990 grows back – it seems to retain the secrets of a forest once much larger, and everywhere recalls legends of the vanished *Argoat*, the great primeval forest of Brittany. The one French claimant to an Arthurian past that carries any real conviction, it is just as frequently known by its Arthurian name of *Brocéliande*.

The Forest and its Myths

Medieval Breton minstrels, like their Welsh counterparts, set the tales of King Arthur and the Holy Grail both in *Grande Bretagne* and here in *Petite Bretagne*. The particular significance of Brocéliande was as Merlin's forest – some say that he is still here, in "Merlin's stone" where he was imprisoned by the enchantress Viviane.

The stone is next to the **Fontaine de Barenton**, a lonely spot high in the woods that is far from easy to find. Turn off the main road into the forest from Concoret (a village notable for having once had the Devil as its rector) at La Saudrais, and you will come to the village of Folle Pensée. Go past the few farmhouses, rather than up the hill, and you arrive at a small car park. A footpath leads up to the right, running through pine and gorse. At a junction of forest tracks, continue straight ahead for about two hundred metres, then veer left along an unobvious (and unmarked) path which leads into the woods, turning back to the north to the spring – walled in mossy stone in the roots of a mighty tree, and filled with the most delicious water imaginable.

Chrétien de Troyes sang of the fountain in the early Middle Ages:

You will see the spring which bubbles
Though its water is colder than marble.
It is shaded by the most beautiful tree
That Nature ever made,
For its foliage is evergreen
And a basin of iron hangs from it,
By a chain long enough
To reach the spring;
And beside the spring you will find
A slab of stone which you will recognize -
I cannot describe it
For I have never seen one like it.

Legend has it that if after drinking you splash water on to the stone slab, you instantly summon a mighty storm, together with roaring lions and a horseman in black armour. This story dates back at least to the fifth century and is recounted, somewhat sceptically, in Robert Wace's *Romance of the Rose*, written around 1160:

Hunters repair (to the fountain) in sultry weather; and drawing water with their
horns, they sprinkle the stone for the purposes of having rain, which is then wont to
fall, they say, throughout the forest around; but why I know not. There too fairies
are to be seen (if the Bretons tell truth), and many other wonders happen. I went
thither on purpose to see these marvels. I saw the forest and the land, and I sought
for the marvels, but I found none. I went like a fool, and so I came back. I sought
after folly, and found myself a fool for my pains.

The parish priest of Concoret and his congregation are reported nonetheless to have successfully ended a drought by this means in 1835, and a procession endorsed by the church went to the spring as recently as 1925.

Comper and the Val sans Retour

At Barenton, you are at the very spot where Merlin first set eyes on Viviane, although you are not at the Fountain of Eternal Youth, which is hidden somewhere nearby and accessible only to the pure in heart. The enchantress is supposed to have been born at the château at **COMPER**, at the northern edge of the forest near Concoret. Today it serves as the **Centre de l'Imaginaire Arthurien**, which means that each summer it's the venue of different exhibitions and entertainments on Arthurian themes, and also organizes tours of the actual forest (June–Aug daily except Tues 10am–7pm; April, May & Sept daily except Tues & Fri 10am–7pm; 25F).

Viviane's rival, Morgane le Fay, ruled over the **Val sans Retour** (Valley of No Return) on the western edge of the forest. The valley is situated just off the footpath GR37 from Tréhorenteuc to La Guette. Follow the path that leads out from the D141 south of Tréhorenteuc to a steep valley from which exits are barred by thickets of gorse and giant furze on the rocks above. At one point it skirts past an overgrown table of rock, the **Rocher des Faux Amants**, from which the seductress Morgane was wont to entice unwary and faithless youths.

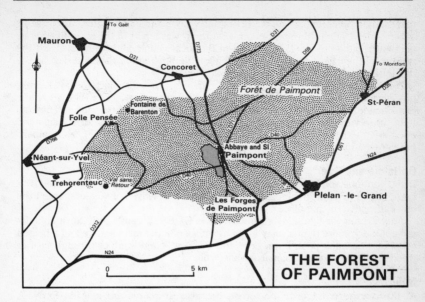

THE FOREST
OF PAIMPONT

Paimpont Village and other forest bases

PAIMPONT village is the most obvious and enjoyable base for exploring the forest. It's right at the centre of the woods, backs on to a marshy lake whose shores are thick with wild mushrooms (*cêpes*), and has some excellent accommodation. At the **hotel** *Relais de Brocéliande* in town (☎99.07.81.07; ③), a real flower-bedecked delight,, you can stuff yourself for 98F in the restaurant under the gaze of stuffed animal heads, and there's a live parrot whose one note sounds like a submarine. There are also a couple of **campsites**, including the municipal one on the edge of the village (March to mid-Nov; ☎97.07.85.25), a *gîte d'étape*-cum-*chambre d'hôte* in tiny Trudeau on the D40 (☎99.07.81.40; B&B ④), and a lovely **youth hostel**, a couple of kilometres out on the Concoret road (May–Sept; ☎97.22.76.75). Information on them all can be picked up from the summer-only SI next to the lakeside abbey (☎99.07.24.83).

Alternative bases include Les Forges and Plélan-le-Grand, at the southern edge of the forest, Mauron at the north, and, further out to the east, Montfort-sur-Meu.

Les Forges

The forges that gave **LES FORGES** its name, and once smelted iron from the surrounding forest, have long since disappeared. Now it's just a rural hamlet, set by a calm lake and disturbed only by the dogs in the hunting kennels. Among the houses coated with red ivy is a *gîte d'étape* (keys held by Mme Farcy; ☎97.06.93.46).

Plélan-le-Grand

The tiny village of **PLÉLAN-LE-GRAND**, at the other end of the lake, has an oddly dramatic history. In the ninth century it was the capital of one of Brittany's early kings, Solomon; its appeal presumably lay in its inaccessibity to Norse or other raiders. Later, in the sixteenth century, it was a part of the short-lived independent republic of Thélin, awarded to the local people after they had paid the ransom of their liege lord. And finally, after the Revolution, Plélan served as the headquarters of Puisaye, the Breton *chouan* leader.

None of which is to say that in itself Plélan is an attractive place to stay. It does, however, have another affordable **hotel** in the *Bruyères* (☎99.06.81.38; ③), while just outside the village is the *Manoir du Tertre* (☎99.07.81.02; closed Tues, all Feb; ⑤), a very grand old country house, preserved with all its furnishings and operating, with high but not outrageous prices (first menu 135F), as a superb hotel/restaurant.

Bellevue and Guer

If you continue south you come to **BELLEVUE-COËTQUIDAN**, dominated by a large military camp; its hotels, full of the anxious relatives of soldiers, aren't the most attractive resting places.

Another four or five kilometres beyond is **GUER**, a gentle little town containing not much more than a rusty ideas box placed in the main square and a heated covered swimming pool. From here, the D776 rolls and tumbles through further woods until it reaches the canal at Malestroit.

Mauron

At the **northern** edge of the forest, the nearest rooms are at **MAURON**. A rambling country town, this has quite a charm – and a reasonable **hotel**, the *Brambily* (☎97.22.61.67; ③) in the town centre. It also has a swimming pool, on the small side but still more than welcome after a hot day in the forest.

East: Montfort-sur-Meu

If you've been seduced by the Paimpont forest, **MONTFORT-SUR-MEU**, east of the forest 25km short of Rennes, has an illuminating **Eco-Musée** which serves to provide some background information (July–Sept daily except Mon 10am–noon & 2–6pm; Oct–June daily except Mon 2–6pm; 15F). Set in the one surviving tower of what in the fourteenth century was a complete walled town, it appears at first the usual small-town museum assortment – costumed dolls and the like. But don't be put off. Upstairs there is a detailed comparison between the forests of Paimpont and Trémelin, proving the somewhat shocking fact that the former is artificially planted (and therefore a poor candidate really to be Brocéliande). And, of more tangible appeal, there's a remarkable display of the area's quarries and stone – exhibited along with modern sculptures exploring their texture or building techniques. From the top of the tower the view takes in some of the still-visible quarries. The museum also runs workshops, where children are taught traditional crafts with materials such as cow-dung, and where sculptors explain their work to casual visitors.

Practicalities

Montfort is on the railway, with a reasonable **hotel**, the *Relais de la Cane* (☎99.09.00.07; ③), close by the **gare SNCF**. Being only a few minutes away from Rennes by train it is a possible point from which to set out if you're coming to Paimpont from the north. You can rent **bikes** at the station, as ever.

Malestroit and Rochefort

Should you choose to follow the course of the canal southwest from Josselin, as opposed to making the detour to the Forêt de Paimpont, the next significant town you come to is the small but appealing **Malestroit**. Beyond that, if you are not actually travelling on the canal, which at this stage is the **River Oust**, the D764 on the south bank, or the D147/149 on the north, will keep you parallel for much of its course towards Redon. Along the way there are two worthwhile detours: south of the canal to **Rochefort-en-Terre**, or north to **La Gacilly**.

Malestroit

Not a lot happens in **MALESTROIT**, which was a thousand years old in 1987. But the town is full of unexpected and enjoyable corners. As you come in to the main square, the **place du Bouffay** in front of the church, the houses are covered with unlikely carvings – an anxious bagpipe-playing hare looking over its shoulder at a dragon's head on one beam, while an oblivious sow in a blue buckled belt threads her distaff on another. The **church** itself is decorated with drunkards and acrobats outside, torturing demons and erupting towers within; each night the display is completed by the sullen parade of metal-festooned youth that weaves in and out of the *Vieille Auberge* bar opposite. The only ancient walls without adornment are the ruins of the **Chapelle de la Madeleine**, where one of the many temporary truces of the Hundred Years War was signed.

Beside the grey canal, the matching grey slate tiles on the turreted rooftops bulge and dip, while on its central island overgrown houses stand next to the stern walls of an old mill.

Practicalities

If you arrive in Malestroit by barge (this is a good stretch to travel), you'll moor very near the town centre. The helpful local **SI** stands on the Bd du Pont-Neuf, right next to the main bridge over the river (daily 10am–noon & 2–6pm; ☎97.75.14.57); they can provide details of **boat rental**. Nearby on the same road is the **gare routière**, served by buses from Vannes and Rennes, while across the river there's a **campsite** down below the bridge, in the Impasse d'Abattoir next to the swimming pool (May–Oct; ☎97.75.13.33), and a **gîte d'étape** up at the canal lock (c/o M Hallier, ☎97.75.11.66). However, what is now the only **hotel** in town is a few hundred metres away on the far side of the old centre. The unexciting *Hôtel St-Michel*, at 1 faubourg St-Michel (☎97.75.13.01; ②), is at the start of the D10 towards Serent, immediately as it leaves the main parking area/market square; it has a bar but no restaurant.

The Musée de la Résistance Bretonne

Two kilometres west of Malestroit (and with no bus connection), the village of **ST-MARCEL** hosts a **Musée de la Résistance Bretonne** (June–Sept daily 10am–7pm; Oct–May daily except Tues 10am–noon & 2–6pm). The museum stands on the site of a June 1944 battle in which the Breton *maquis*, joined by Free French forces parachuted in from England, successfully diverted the local German troops from the main Normandy invasion movements.

The museum's strongest feature is its presentation of the pressures that made so many French collaborate: the reconstructed street corner from which all life has been jerked out by the occupiers; the big colourful propaganda posters offering work in Germany, announcing executions of *maquis*, equating resistance with aiding US and British big business; and against these the low budget, flimsily printed Resistance pamphlets. All the labelling is in French, which non-speakers may find rather frustrating.

Rochefort-en-Terre

ROCHEFORT-EN-TERRE has a commanding site – the high end of a gorge that is followed by the D774 (and at its end by the connecting D777). Its most imposing face is occupied, predictably enough, by a **château**. Less expected, however, is the castle's appearance. Once the property of the American painter Alfred Klots, it is a jigsaw of a building, knocked together early this century from stone pieces of other local houses. Visits feature startling terrace views and a fairly standard collection of furniture, paintings and tapestries (July to mid-Sept daily 10.30am–6.30pm; June & late Sept daily 10.30am–noon & 2–6.30pm; Oct–May Sat, Sun & hols 10.30am–noon & 2–6.30pm).

The rest of the town is a prettified and polished version of Malestroit, something of a tourist trap with little antique shops and expensive restaurants. A curiosity is the Black Virgin in the church of **Notre-Dame de Tronchaye**, which was found hidden from Norman invaders in a hollow tree in the twelfth century, and is the object of a pilgrimage on the first Sunday after August 15. More interesting, though, is the **Lac Bleu**, just south of the town, where there are ancient **slate quarries**, whose deep galleries are the home of blind butterflies and long-eared bats.

Practicalities

Unusually for Brittany, there are no hotels in Rochefort-en-Terre, although the **SI** (☎97.43.33.57 summer, ☎97.43.32.81 otherwise) in the main street displays a list of rather expensive *chambres d'hôte* in the neighbourhood, and operates the municipal **campsite**, *Le Chemin de Bogeais* (April–Sept; ☎97.43.32.81).

At the village of **ST-VINCENT-SUR-OUST**, on the D764 10km northwest of Redon, a **youth hostel**, *Ty Kendalc'h* (☎99.91.28.55; closed mid-Dec to Jan; 45F), serves as a centre for Breton music and dance.

The Parc de Préhistoire de Bretagne

Two kilometres southeast of Rochefort, outside the small community of Malansac, the new and very heavily publicized **Parc de Préhistoire de Bretagne** is a theme park aimed overwhelmingly at children (April to mid-Oct daily 10am–6pm; mid-Oct to Nov Sun 2–6pm; 45F). Separate landscaped areas contain dioramas of gigantic (if stationary) dinosaurs, and human beings at various stages in their evolution; the story ends shortly after a bunch of deformed but enthusiastic Neanderthals hit on the idea of erecting a few megaliths.

La Gacilly

Fourteen kilometres north of the canal, **LA GACILLY** makes a good base for walking trips in search of megaliths, sleepy villages and countryside. The town itself has prospered recently thanks to the creation of a beauty products industry based on the abundantly proliferating flowers in the Aff valley. It is, too, a centre for many active craftsworkers; a walk down the old stone steps of the cobbled street that runs parallel to the main road between town centre and river is both a pleasure in itself, and an opportunity to look in on their workshops. The only real disappointment is that the riverfront is not accessible to walkers, though you can enjoy views of it from a couple of restaurants, and take two-hour **cruises** on it in summer (July & Aug daily 2.30pm & 4.30pm; 48F; ☎99.08.21.42).

Up in the town centre, the *Hôtel de France*, 15 rue Montauban (☎99.08.11.15; ③), is an extremely hospitable *logis*, with quiet and comfortable rooms in what used to be the separate *Hôtel du Square* reached through the long gardens at the back, and a good traditional restaurant. The *patron* is happy to provide detailed information on local walks and attractions for his guests.

Alternatively, the luxurious *chambres d'hôte* (☎99.70.04.79; ⑤) in the nearby château de Trégaret in **Sixt-sur-Aff** provide ideal countryside accommodation.

The megaliths of St-Just

Around 10km east of La Gacilly, in the vicinity of the village of **ST-JUST**, the small windswept **Cojoux** moor is rich in ancient megalithic remains. Only in the last decade or so have they received any great public attention, as a programme of excavations has gradually uncovered all sorts of ancient tombs and sacred sites. During the summer, you should find posters in local villages giving the times of explanatory Sunday **walking tours** of the various sites, many of them led by the archeologists responsible for the digs. In any case, it's a rewarding area to ramble around yourself; the larger menhirs and so on are signposted along dirt tracks and footpaths, and you'll probably stumble upon a few lesser ones by chance.

Redon

Thirty-four kilometres east of Malestroit, at the junction of the rivers Oust and Vilaine, on the Nantes-Brest canal, linked by rail to Rennes, Vannes and Nantes, and at the intersection of six major roads, **REDON** is not a place it's easy to avoid and you shouldn't try to either. A wonderful mess of water and locks – the canal manages to cross the Vilaine at right angles in one of the more complex links – the town has history, charm and life. It's among the best stops along the whole course of the canal.

The city was founded as a religious settlement in 832AD by Saint Conwoïon at the instigation of Nominoë, the first King of Brittany (see p.301), and was a place of pilgrimage until the seventeenth century. Its Benedictine abbey is now the focus of the church of **St-Sauveur** – the rounded angles of the dumpy twelfth-century Romanesque lantern tower are unique in Brittany. All but obscured by later roofs and the high choir, the four-storey belfry is best seen from the adjacent cloisters. The later Gothic tower was entirely separated from the main building by a fire in 1780. Every Friday and Saturday from the end of June to the end of July, Redon puts on a large-scale *son et lumière* re-enactment of ten of the earliest years of its history, 835–845AD.

Inside the church, you will find the tomb of the judge who condemned Gilles de Rais to be hanged in 1440 for satanism and the most infamous orgies. Gilles had fought alongside Joan of Arc, burnt for heresy, witchcraft and sorcery in 1431, and in both cases, the court procedures were irregular to say the least.

Legends of the atrocities of Gilles de Rais served as the source for tales of the monstrous wife-murderer Bluebeard.

Until the First World War, Redon was the seaport for Rennes. Its industrial docks – or what remains of them – are therefore on the Vilaine, while the canal, even in the very centre of town, is almost totally rural, its towpaths shaded avenues. Ship-owners' homes from the seventeenth and eighteenth centuries can be seen in the port area – walk via quai Jean Bart next to the bassin as far as the **Croix des Marins**, returning along quai Duguay-Truin beside the river. A rusted wrought-iron workbridge, equipped with a crane rolling on tracks, still crosses the river, but the main users of the port now are **cruise ships**. These head 40km downstream to the Arzal dam, which is as close as they can get to the sea, past La Roche-Bernard (see below for details).

Flowers abound throughout Redon, which achieves regular success in regional and national contests for the city with the best floral decorations (*villes fleuries*). In 1983, it won the national first prize. As late as October, swathes of chrysanthemums in autumn tints hang from balconies and the numerous iron bridges.

Information and Transport

A very large and sprawling Monday **market** (at which you can buy superb *crêpes*) is centred on the modern *halles*, in the place du Parlement. The **SI** is based there too, for information on the rental of boats and *gîtes* (May–Sept daily 10am–noon & 3–6pm; Oct–April Mon–Sat 10am–noon & 3–6pm; ☎99.71.06.04); in summer they have an additional annex in the port to serve the needs of what the notices in English call the "Pleasure People". There's a **post office** on rue St-Michel, north of the centre (☎99.71.02.30).

Redon's **gare SNCF** (☎99.71.74.10) is in the place de la Gare, five minutes' walk west of the town centre. What long-distance buses serve the town – it takes less than an hour to get to either Rennes, Nantes or Vannes – also operate from here (details from *Redon Transports*, ☎99.71.47.33).

Bicycles can be rented from *Cycles Gicquel* in the place St-Sauveur (☎99.71.02.82), and **canoes** and **barges** from the *Comptoir Nautique* at 2 quai Surcouf (☎99.71.46.03); further details of canal boat rental are given in the "Travel Details" at the end of this chapter.

On Thursday afternoons in July and August, **boat trips** run by *Vedettes Jaunes* (85F; ☎97.45.02.81) head downstream, past la Roche-Bernard to the Arzal dam (2hr 30min); passengers then return by coach via Lantierne, le Guerno, Beganne and Rieux (a further 2hr 30min). Tickets can be reserved at the SI.

Accommodation and Eating

Redon's **hotels** are mostly concentrated in the town and near the gare SNCF rather than in the port area, but it's a small enough place that it makes little difference where you stay. The large white *Hôtel le France* looks down on the canal from 30 rue Duguesclin, at the corner with the quai de Brest (☎99.71.06.11; ②); its recently renovated rooms, all with en-suite bathrooms and TVs, offer a considerable degree of comfort for the price, but it is without a restaurant. Not far from the main square and the SI, the *Hôtel Asther*, 14 rue des Douves (☎99.71.10.91; ③), has its own brasserie, *le Théâtre*. Nearer the station, the *Hôtel Chandouineau*, at 10 av de la Gare (☎99.71.02.04; ⑤) is a luxurious establishment with just seven bedrooms, where the restaurant serves gourmet menus from 120F; its entrance is actually just around the corner at 1 rue Thiers.

La Bogue, 3 rue des États (☎99.71.12.95; closed Sun pm) in place du Parlement, is a friendly and good-value **fish restaurant** where menus start at 75F, while *L'Echo de Sarrasin*, 16 quai de Brest (☎99.72.20.60), is a *crêperie* overlooking the canal. There's live music most nights at *Le Livingstone*, a bar at 14 rue du Plessis, off quai Jean-Bart in the port. Redon also has a new **theatre**, *Le Canal* (☎99.71.09.50), near the main square – the season runs from September to June.

Nantes

NANTES, the former capital of Brittany, is no longer officially part of the province: it was transferred to the Pays de la Loire in 1962 when the modern administrative regions were established. Nonetheless, such bureaucracy is not taken too seriously in the city, and its history is closely bound up with Breton fortunes. A considerable medieval centre, it later achieved great wealth from colonial expeditions, the slave trade and shipbuilding – activities in turn surpassed by more recent industrial growth.

Despite the tower blocks that mask the Loire and motorways that tear past the city, which mean that Nantes is not now an especially attractive place on first acquaintance, it remains to its inhabitants an integral part of Brittany. Although it's not a place to make a great priority on your travels, if you have the time and energy, it holds plenty that is worth seeing – especially the **Château des Ducs** and the **Beaux Arts** museum – while the River Erdre, the vineyards of the Loire and the remarkable Italianate town of Clisson are all within reach.

Arrival and Information

Nantes' **SI**, housed in the colonnaded Palais de la Bourse, in place du Commerce (Mon–Sat 10am–6pm; ☎40.47.04.51), provides a free book-size guide, including an excellent town map, and runs various guided tours of the city. There's a subsidiary office alongside the château at 1 rue du Château (Wed–Sun 10am–1pm & 1.30–6pm). The main **post office** is on place Bretagne (☎40.12.60.60).

The **gare SNCF** (☎40.08.50.50), a little way east of the château, is served by fast trains between Paris and Brittany (three or more *TGV*s daily reach Paris in as little as 2 hours), as well as being the terminus for the local line westwards to St-Nazaire, La Baule and Croisic. The station has two exits; for most facilities (tramway, buses, hotels) use *Accès Nord*.

There are two central **bus** stations. Local buses use the Gare des Bus on cours Franklin, alongside place du Commerce, while the long-distance **gare routière** (☎40.47.62.70) is 400m away on allée Baco, near place Ricordeau. Modern rubber-wheeled **trams** run along the old riverfront, past the gare SNCF and the two bus stations. Flat-fare tickets are valid for one hour, rather than just a single journey, though one-day tickets are also available.

Bicycles can be rented from *Seguir Bernard*, 38 rue des Alouettes (☎40.46.56.32), as well as the gare SNCF.

The City

The **Loire**, the source of Nantes' riches, has dwindled from the centre. As recently as the 1930s the river crossed the city in seven separate channels, but

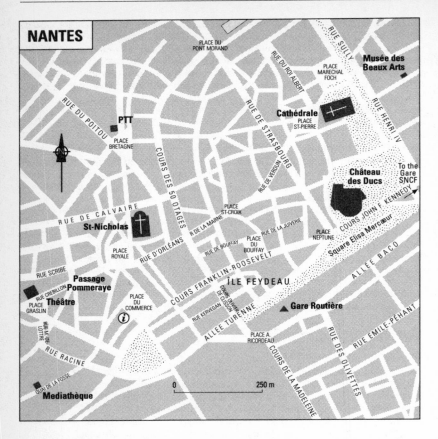

German labour as part of reparations for World War I filled in five of them. What are still called "islands" in the centre are now surrounded and isolated, not by water, but by hectic dual carriageways. These thoroughfares are not easy to cross, but they do at least mean that Nantes is separated into a series of readily discernible districts, each of which can be experienced on its own terms.

The main distinction lies between the older medieval city, concentrated around the Cathedral and with the Château prominent in its southeast corner, and the elegant nineteenth-century town to the west, across the cours de 50-Otages (whose name commemorates a bloody incident during the Nazi occupation in World War II). In a sense, that division has an additional political significance, for Nantes is not solely Breton. As trade along the Loire made the French influence on the city ever more significant, from the end of the eighteenth century onwards, the newer area earned the nickname of "little Paris".

Place Royale was first laid out in the 1790s; damaged by bombing in 1943, it has now been restored. **Place Graslin**, with its theatre, dates from the same period; the theatre's Corinthian portico contrasts with the 1895 Art Nouveau of

La Cigale, embellished with mosaics and mirrors and still a popular brasserie (see p.280).

A spectacular nineteenth-century multi-level indoor shopping centre, the **Passage Pommeraye**, drops down three flights of stairs towards the river on nearby rue Crebillon. The attention to detail lavished upon it by its architects is on a scale undreamed of in modern malls; each of the gas lamps that light the central area is held by an individually crafted marble cherub.

Many of the streets in the two principal regions of the city have been semi-pedestrianized, and they abound in pavement cafés, brasseries and shops. Just south of them both is the elongated **Île Feydeau**, a typical victim of the modern "development" of Nantes. Its eighteenth-century houses, seen at their best in rue Kervegan, retain some of their Baroque charm – but the road is bisected by cours Olivier-de-Clisson and the traffic jams of today.

The Château des Ducs

Though no longer on the waterfront, and subjected to a certain amount of damage over the centuries, the **Château des Ducs** still preserves the form in which it was built by two of the last rulers of independent Brittany, François II, and his daughter Duchess Anne, born here in 1477. The list of famous people who have been guests or prisoners, defenders or belligerents of the castle is impressive. It includes Gilles de Rais (Bluebeard), publicly executed in 1440; John Knox as a galley-slave in 1547–49; and Bonnie Prince Charlie preparing for Culloden in 1745. The most significant act in the castle, from the point of view of European history, was the signing of the **Edict of Nantes** in 1598 by Henri IV (who is said to have exclaimed, on first sight of the castle, "God's teeth, these Dukes of Brittany were no small beer"). The Edict ended the Wars of Religion by granting a certain degree of toleration to the Protestants, but had far more crucial consequences when it was revoked by Louis XIV in 1685. To their credit the people of Nantes took no part in the subsequent general massacres of the Huguenots.

The stout ramparts of the château remain pretty much intact, and most of the encircling moat is filled with water, surrounded by well-tended lawns which make a popular spot for lunchtime picnics. Visitors can walk into the courtyard and up

---

RIVER CRUISES FROM NANTES

To explore the **last section of the Nantes–Brest canal**, you can take a river cruise from the **gare fluviale**, on quai de la Motte-Rouge a little way north of central Nantes. These cruises run up the **Erdre** as far as the point where it is joined by the canal coming from Redon. They thrive mainly because the Loire is not at present navigable by this sort of boat (although there are plans to change that) but the Erdre is itself beautiful and wide, with a fine selection of châteaux alongs its banks, chief among them **La Gascherie**. Boats operate between April and November, on Sundays only in low season but with much greater frequency in mid-summer. Typically, the choice is between a simple 1hr 30min cruise costing around 40F, and setting off at around 3pm, or a three-hour trip on a floating restaurant for lunch (noon) or dinner (7pm), for something in the region of 250F. The SI in town is bursting with brochures and leaflets from rival companies, the best known of which is *Bateaux Nantais* (☎40.14.51.14), who also operate similar trips southwards along the **Sèvre**.

onto the walls for free. Inside, among a rather incongruous pot-pourri of buildings added in differing styles over the years, are a couple of **museums** (daily 10am–noon & 2–6pm, closed Tues out of season; 30F). The first – housed in the old, well-graffitied prison of the Tour de la Boulangerie – is the **Musée des Arts Populaires**, a good introduction to Breton history and folklore, which is depicted in a series of murals and dioramas.

The city's trading history is the subject of the **Musée des Salorges**, which has a good selection of figureheads and model ships. You can also contrast the pitiful trinkets, beads and bracelets traded for West African slaves, and the accounts and diagrams of the voyages, with the pomp of the barge used for Napoléon's ball in Nantes in August 1808 – an occasion when *epée et habit français* were compulsory attire. By the end of the eighteenth century, Nantes was the principal port of France, with huge fortunes being made on the "ebony" (slave) trade – which brought in as much as 200 percent profit per ship. The abolition of slavery coincided with an increased use of domestic French sugar beet as against Caribbean sugar cane, the port began to silt up as it declined in significance, and heavy industry and wine production became more important.

The Cathedral

In 1800 the Spaniards Tower, the castle's arsenal, exploded, shattering the stained glass of the fifteenth-century **Cathédrale de St-Pierre-et-St-Paul** over 200m away. This was just one of many disasters that have befallen the church. It was used as a barn during the Revolution; bombed during World War II; and damaged by a fire in 1971, just when things seemed sorted out again.

Restored and finally re-opened, the building is made to seem especially light and soaring by the clean white stone. It contains the tomb of François II and his wife, Margaret, the parents of Duchess Anne – with somewhat grating symbols of Power, Strength and Justice for him and Fidelity, Prudence and Temperance for her. This imposing monument is illuminated by a superb modern stained-glass window devoted to Breton and Nantais saints.

The Mur des Cheminées

Five centuries of Nantais history can be seen written in stone, brick and mortar on the **Mur des Cheminées**, just off the place du Bouffay in the centre of the old city, where bomb damage during the war left exposed the huge wall of a venerable and much-reconstructed town house. Successive layers of masonry show the development of the building ever since it was erected in 1453; a fascinating diagram of this living cross-section illustrates exactly which pieces belonged to which era.

Other Museums

The **Musée d'Histoire Naturelle** at 12 rue Voltaire (Tues–Sat 10am–noon & 2–6pm, Sun 2–6pm; 30F) centres on a vivarium, whose miserable animals are not for the squeamish (the soft-shelled turtle in particular tugs at the heartstrings). But don't let this put you off the eccentric assortment of oddities of its museum collection: rhinoceros toenails, a coelecanth and an aepyornis egg, and slightly tatty stuffed specimens of virtually every bird and animal imaginable. There is an Egyptian mummy, too, as well as a shrunken Maori head and a complete tanned human skin – taken in 1793 from the body of a soldier whose dying wish was to be made into a drum.

Also in rue Voltaire you'll find the **Palais Dobrée** (daily except Mon 10am–noon & 1.30–5.30pm; 20F), a nineteenth-century mansion given over to two museums, one of which claims to feature Duchess Anne's heart in a box.

The **Musée Jules-Vernes**, on Île Feydeau at 3 rue de l'Hermitage (Mon & Wed–Sat 10am–noon & 2–5pm, Sun 2–5pm; 8F), commemorates the birthplace of the first serious writer of science fiction.

If you have time to kill, take the tram to the **Médiathèque** at 24 quai de la Fosse, where you'll find a superb modern library with bookshops and facilities to watch any of an eclectic selection of videos – Sir Alf Ramsey and the Battle of Iwo Jima side by side (Mon–Fri noon–7pm, Sat 10am–6pm). From there, you can walk along quai de la Fosse to the point where the two remaining branches of the Loire meet up, with a good view of the port.

Accommodation

Although it holds plenty of **hotels** to suit all budgets, Nantes is one of those cities where you won't necessarily stumble upon a suitable place just by walking or driving around at whim. Instead, there are two main concentrations: one, as ever, in the immediate vicinity of the gare SNCF, and one in the narrow streets around the place Greslin. With the exception of the *St-Daniel* (see below), surprisingly few are to be found in the older part of town.

There are also a couple of **youth hostels**. The summer-only one, using student accommodation in a post-modern former tobacco factory at 2 place de la Manu (July & Aug; ☎40.20.57.25; 50–55F per night), has dorms and individual rooms, and is the easiest to reach, being within 100m of the gare SNCF and also accessible by taking tramway #1 towards Malachère and getting off at *Manufacture*.

The other, at 1 rue Porte-Neuve (☎40.20.00.80; 55F), 2km from the gare SNCF on bus routes #36, #40 or #41 (direction place Viarne, stop *Le Marchix*), is open all year, and doesn't require youth hostel membership.

The nearest **campsite** is the well managed and tree-shaded *Val du Cens*, 31 bd du Petit-Port (all year; ☎40.74.47.94).

Hotels

Hôtel Amiral, 26bis rue Scribe (☎40.69.20.21). Well maintained little hotel, suitable for young night-owls, on lively pedestrianized street just north of place Graslin. Room rates for Saturday and Sunday nights are 50F lower, though still within the price category shown here. ④.

Hôtel l'Atlantique, 9 rue Maréchal-de-Lattre-de-Tassigny (☎40.73.85.33). Just below *Hôtel de l'Océan*, and slightly more upmarket – all the rooms have TVs. No restaurant. ②.

Hôtel du Château, 5 place de la Duchesse Anne (☎40.74.17.16). In a slightly noisy location, alongside the Château des Ducs less than 500m from the gare SNCF, with castle views from the best rooms. ③.

Hôtel Fourcroy, 11 rue Fourcroy (☎40.44.68.00). Basic and economical rooms in a backstreet just below place Graslin. ②.

Hôtel Grand, 2 rue Santeuil (☎40.73.46.88). Comfortable rooms, between place Royale and place Graslin. No restaurant of its own, but the expensive *Restaurant Margotte* is on the ground floor. ⑤.

Hôtel Maeva, 3 rue du Marais (☎40.89.60.60). Basic rooms, between the post office and the town hall; take tramway west to place du Bouffay stop, and then take bus #52 or #53 north along cours des 50 Otages to rue de l'Hôtel de Ville. The owner is half-English. No restaurant. Room rates for Saturday and Sunday nights drop by 30F, but are still within the price category shown here. ③.

Hôtel l'Océan, 11 rue Maréchal-de-Lattre-de-Tassigny (☎40.69.73.51). A pleasant hotel, with helpful management, just below place Graslin near the Mediathéque. Parking space is available around the back. No restaurant, though there is a restaurant of the same name on the quai de la Fosse a few metres away at the bottom of the street. Closed last two weeks of Dec. ②.

Hôtel St-Daniel, 4 rue du Bouffay (☎40.74.41.25). These simple but pleasant and well-lit rooms, on a cobbled street just off the place du Bouffay in the very heart of the old city, are much in demand in summer. ②.

Hôtel la Terrasse, 25 bd de Stalingrad (☎40.74.16.48). Down a side street opposite the gare SNCF, and equipped with brasserie and bar. ③.

Hôtel Terminus, 3 allée du Commandant-Charcot (☎40.74.24.51). Very near the gare SNCF, on the way towards the château. All rooms have double beds and TV. A reasonable restaurant, so long as you skip the very limited 50F menu and head for those at 80F and upwards. ③.

Eating

Unlike hotels, restaurants fill the winding lanes of the old city in abundance. It shouldn't take you long to come up with something once you start wandering the pedestrian streets in the centre. Nantes is a big enough city to have all sorts of ethnic alternatives as well, with lots of Algerian, Italian, Chinese, Vietnamese and Indian places in addition to those listed here.

La Cigale, 4 place Graslin (☎40.69.76.41). Famous late nineteenth-century brasserie, offering fine meals in opulent surroundings. Fish is a speciality. Menus 75F and 135F, served until midnight in keeping with the tradition of providing post-performance refreshments for patrons of the adjacent theatre.

Le Gavroche, 139 rue des Hauts-Pavés (☎40.76.22.49). One of Nantes' top gastrononomic haunts, decked out in garish salmon pink. Menus start at 135F, but you get your money's worth. Closed Sun pm, Mon & all Aug

La Mangeoire, 16 rue des Petites-Écuries (☎40.48.70.83). Very good country food. The 60F lunch menu in particular is a real bargain, while the "Gourmet" 128F dinner is a delight; even if you can't stomach the dozen snails, there's a mixed fish grill to sate any appetite. Closed Sun & Mon June–Sept, otherwise closed Sun pm & Mon.

La Palmier, 10 rue des 3-Croissants (☎40.47.97.41). Moroccan food in the maze of pedestrianized streets; *à la carte* in the evening, lunch menu 42F. Prices are higher in mid-summer.

Le Petit Bacchus, 5 rue Beaurigard (☎40.4750.46). Red-painted half-timbered house, with the atmosphere and decor of a World War I *estaminet*, just off rue des 50-Otages in a little alley leading down to the Cours F-Roosevelt. Lovely 75F menu featuring duck *à l'orange* or fish of the day.

Le Prémion, 2 rue Prémion (☎40.35.64.64). Fine restaurant on a cobbled street running along the northern side of the château, with views of the ramparts. Fishy menus, with tuna steak for example, from 97F.

Le Sumo, 4 rue Thurot (☎40.48.57.20). Quite a rarity – a Japanese restaurant, just off the place du Commerce within a few metres of the SI. *Sushi* and *sashimi* menus at 80F, or entire set meals with skewered chicken, beef or salmon plus soup and salad for around 50F. Closed Sun.

Within reach of Nantes

Immediately **upstream from Nantes** you are into the Loire wine-growing country that produces the two classic dry white wines, *Gros-Plant* and *Muscadet*. Any **vineyard** should be happy to give you a *dégustation*. Most operate on a very small scale. The largest, however, the **Chasseloir vineyard** (☎40.54.81.15) at **ST-FIACRE-SUR-MAINE**, is perhaps the most interesting. This occupies the grounds of a former château, with fifty acres of vines – some a century old. The vineyard sells mostly within the catering trade but anyone is welcome to visit their cellars, which are decorated with painted Rabelaisian carvings and candelabra made from vine roots. Like so many of the vineyards in this region, the grapes are now picked and pressed by machines. The old tradition of employing seasonal migrant labour on the harvest is a thing of the past.

Clisson

To the south, at the point where the Sèvre meets the Maine, and the crossroads of the three ancient duchies of Brittany, Anjou and Poitou, is the town of **CLISSON**. This was re-modelled by two French architects in the last century into a close approximation of an Italian hill town. The fact that they already had the raw material of a ruined fortress, a covered market hall and a magnificent situation makes it a sight not to be missed. The best **place to stay** is the *Hôtel de la Gare*, on place de la Gare (☎40.36.16.55; ③).

Trains

No railway line cuts across central Brittany; however, certain towns mentioned in this chapter can be reached by train.

Châteaulin is on the line from Brest to Quimper.

Carhaix is served by 4–6 trains daily from Guingamp (1hr); buses connect with the south coast.

Pontivy and **Loudéac** are served by 3–4 trains daily from St-Brieuc (1hr 30min/1hr), again with connecting buses running south.

Redon is on the main Rennes to Nantes line, and is the junction for trains coming from Brest, Quimper and Vannes.

Nantes connects directly with Paris (10 *TGV* daily, 2hr 15min), Rennes, Quimper, Brest and the south.

Buses

From Carhaix to Châteaulin (5 daily; 30min), Loudéac (5 daily; 1hr), Quimper (4 daily; 1hr) and Morlaix (hourly; 1hr).

From Vannes to Rennes (8 daily; 2hr) via Josselin (1hr) and St-Jean Brévelay (45min); to Pontivy (45 min); and 4 daily to Elven (25min), Malestroit (45 min) and Ploërmel (1hr 25min).

Boats

Barges with accommodation, which can be available with bicycles and even caravans on board, can be rented from the following places :

Châteaulin. *Les Bateaux de l'Aulne* (☎98.86.37.59).

Pont Coblant near Pleyben. Contact *Crabing-Loisirs*, M Mercier, 20 Rue de Frout, 29000 Quimper (☎98.95.14.02).

Châteauneuf du Faou. *Argoat Plaisance*, BP41 Port de Plaisance, 29520 Châteauneuf du Faou (☎98.81.72.11).

Pleyben. *Finistère Canal* (☎98.73.35.20).

Rohan. *Rohan Plaisance*, Écluse de Rohan, BP19 56580 Rohan (☎97.38.98.66).

Baud (on the Blavet). *Au File De L'Eau*, Écluse de la Couard, St-Nicolas-des-Eaux, Plumeliau, 56150 Baud.

Josselin. *Le Ray Loisirs*, 14 rue Caradec, 56120 Josselin (☎97.75.60.98) and at 44000 Nantes (☎40.89.22.42).

Roc St-André. *Plasmor*, M Bourçois, Z.A. 56460 Serent (☎97.75.95.70).

Malestroit. *Heron Cruisers*, M David Chin, La Daufresne, 56140 Malestroit, (☎97.75.19.57).

La Gacilly. *Flotte Vacances* Glenac 56200 La Gacilly.

Redon. *Comptoir Nautique de Redon*, 2 Quai Surcouf 35605 Redon (☎99.71.46.03). *Bretagne Plaisance*, 12 Quai Jean Bart 35600 Redon (☎99.72.15.80).

Plesse. *Gîtes Nautiques Bretons*, La Cour 44630 Plesse (☎40.51.90.77).

Suce-sur-Erdre. *Bretagne Fluvial*, Quai Cricklade, 44240 Suce-sur-Erdre, (☎40.77.79.51).

Nantes. *Le Grand Large*, M Bonami, Quai de Versailles, le Pont-Morand, 44000 Nantes, (☎40.35.44.37) and 254, route de Vannes 447000 Nantes-Orvault (☎40.63.37.87).

*For **general information** contact the* **Comité de Promotion Touristique des Canaux Bretons**, *Office du Tourisme, place du Parlement, 35600 Rennes (☎99.71.06.04).*

CHAPTER SEVEN

THE SOUTH COAST

B rittany's **southern coast** takes in the province's most famous sites and offers its warmest swimming. It is hardly surprising, then, that it is so popular: around the **Gulf of Morbihan** and especially to the south at **La Baule**, you can be hard pushed to find a room in summer – or to escape the crowds.

Not that this should discourage a visit. For the whole coast is a succession of wonders, of both natural and human creation. If you have any interest in prehistory, or even if you just enjoy ruins, then the concentration of **megaliths** around the **Morbihan** should prove irresistible. At **Carnac**, the most important site and possibly Europe's oldest settlement, there are over two thousand menhirs – laid out in alignments that are both dramatic and intriguing. **Locmariaquer**, too, has a gigantic ancient stone, which some theories hold to be the key to a prehistoric astronomical observatory. The most beautifully sited of all is the great tumulus on **Gavrinis**, one of the fifty or so islets scattered in chaos around the Morbihan's inland sea.

As for more hedonistic pastimes, in theory the best of the south's **beaches** are those at **La Baule**. This however is also the one resort in Brittany to be conspicuously affected and overpriced, and it has virtually none of the character of the rest of the region. But there are excellent, lower-keyed alternatives all along the south coast: close by La Baule at **Le Croisic** and **Piriac-sur-mer**; at the megalith centres of **Carnac** and **Locmariaquer**; at **Quiberon**; and out on the **islands** of **Groix** and **Belle-Île**. The largest Breton island, Belle-Île is a perfect microcosm of the province – a beautiful place with grand countryside and a couple of lively towns.

The south coast is also host to Brittany's most compelling **festival**, the ten-day **Inter-Celtic** gathering at Lorient in August. The same month sees a **jazz festival** at the main Morbihan town, Vannes.

ACCOMMODATION PRICE CODES

All **hotel prices** in this book have been coded using the symbols below. The price shown is for the least expensive double room, which for categories ① and ② usually means a room without shower, bath and toilet. Most hotels in those categories have other rooms with en-suite facilities, which typically cost 30–50F extra.

For a full explanation see p.31.

①	up to 120 F	④	220–300F	⑦	500–600F
②	120–160F	⑤	300–400F	⑧	600–700F
③	160–220F	⑥	400–500F	⑨	700F and over

Lorient and its Estuary

LORIENT, Brittany's fourth largest city, is an immense natural harbour –
protected from the ocean by the Île de Groix and strategically located at the junc-
tion of the rivers Scorff, Ter and Blavet. A functional, rather depressing port
today, it was once a key base for French colonialism, founded in the mid-
seventeenth century (in what its charter called a "vague, vain, and useless place")

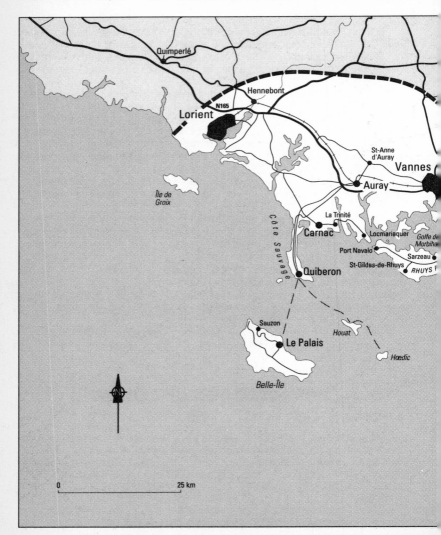

for trading operations by the *Compagnie des Indes*, the French equivalent of the Dutch and English East India Companies. Hence the port's name, originally *L'Orient* ("The East").

Little now remains in the town itself to suggest the plundered wealth that once arrived here. During the last war, Lorient was a major target for the Allies; the Germans held out until May 1945, by which time the city was almost completely destroyed. The only substantial traces to survive were the U-boat pens

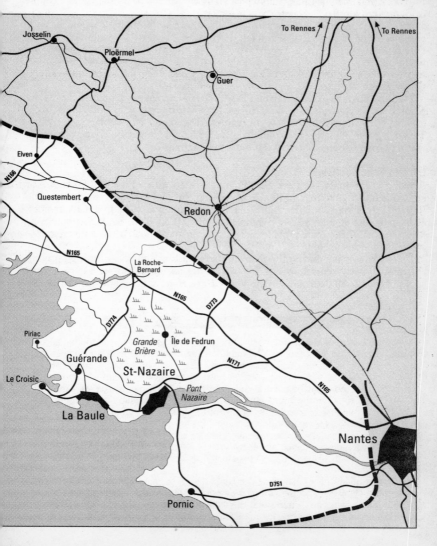

(subsequently greatly expanded by the French for their nuclear submarines). As a result, Lorient is somewhat reminiscent of Le Havre, in that it had to be entirely reconstructed, as rapidly as possible. Here, however, virtually nothing of interest was created; the church of **Nôtre-Dame-de-Victoire** is typical of the drab concrete facades everywhere you look. Most of the waterfront is taken up by off-limits naval bases, and the one splash of colour is the little pleasure port that serves to separate the old town from the new – not that there's any very discernible difference between the two. If you imagine things might pick up if you head to the **fishing port**, a couple of kilometres south of the centre, you're very wrong.

All in all, considering the many joys elsewhere in Brittany, it would be ludicrous to suggest Lorient as a holiday destination. For just about all the year, the only reason you might feel it worthwhile to pause here is to take the boat trip out to the Île de Groix (see below). Briefly each August, however, Lorient is transformed into a vibrant, pulsating maelstrom of Celtic cavorting, during the **Inter-Celtic Festival**.

The one place that does contain a few relics of Lorient's exploitative past is the **Musée de la Compagnie des Indes**, across the estuary in Port Louis (daily except Tues June–Sept 10am–7pm; winter 10am–noon & 2–5pm; closed Nov). This is a good 20km by road, though you may be able to get a ferry across, and it is in any case a somewhat dismal temple to imperialism.

Lorient Practicalities

Arriving in the main-line **gare SNCF**, you're faced with a hike of a kilometre or so south into the centre. Lorient's **SI**, beside the pleasure port on the quai de Rohan (July & Aug Mon–Fri 9am–7pm, Sat 9am–noon & 2–7pm, Sun 10am–noon & 2–5pm; rest of year Mon–Fri 9am–12.30pm & 1.30–6pm, Sat 9am–noon & 2–6pm; ☎97.21.07.84), can provide full details on local boat trips, and organizes some excursions itself.

Unless you arrive during the festival, there's a huge choice of **hotels**. Among reasonable, fairly central options are two on rue Lazare-Carnot as it curves away south of the SI. All the rooms in the *Victor Hugo Hôtel* at no. 36 (☎97.21.16.24; ②–

THE INTER-CELTIC FESTIVAL

Each year, Lorient's shortcomings become quite irrelevant alongside the backdrop of the **Inter-Celtic Festival**, which is held for ten days from the first Friday to the second Sunday in August. This is the biggest Celtic event in Brittany – or anywhere else for that matter – with representation from all seven Celtic countries. In a genuine popular celebration of cultural solidarity, as many as a quarter of a million people come to a hundred and fifty different shows; five languages mingle; and Scotch and Guinness flow with the French and Spanish wines and ciders. There is a certain competitive element, with championships in various categories, but the feeling of mutual enthusiasm and conviviality is more important. Most of the activities – which embrace music, dance and literature – take place around the central place Jules-Ferry, and this is where most people end up sleeping, too, as accommodation is pushed to the limits.

For schedules of the festival, and further details of temporary accommodation, contact the *Office du Tourisme de Pays de Lorient*, place Jules-Ferry, 56100 Lorient (☎97.21.24.29), bearing in mind that the festival programme is not finalized before May. For certain specific events, you need to reserve tickets well in advance.

④) have TV – which, not wishing to labour the point or anything, is something to be thankful for in Lorient – and there's an action-packed 95F menu offering langoustines, wild pheasant pâté and duck *à l'orange*, while the *Hôtel d'Arvor*, at no. 104 (☎97.21.07.55; ②), also has a good-value restaurant.

If you're desperate to find somewhere at festival time, there are a few more hotels along av de la Perrière, the main thoroughfare in the fishing port, such as the *Hôtel-Restaurant Gabriel* at no. 45 (☎97.37.60.76; ②). Assuming you're not such a cheapskate as to get the hard-boiled egg and the intestine-packed *andouillette* on its 50F menu, sensible dinners here cost 68F and upwards. There's also a **youth hostel**, next to the River Ter at 41 rue Victor-Schoelcher, 3km out on bus line C from the gare SNCF (☎97.37.11.65; closed mid-Dec to Jan; 46F), and the *Oeuvres Sociales* hostel at 12 rue Colbert (☎97.21.42.80) was especially designed for the **physically handicapped**.

The *Poisson d'Or* on rue Maître-Esvelin (☎97.21.57.06) is a great **fish restaurant**, with menus from 95F. One of the most congenial **bars** is the *Galway Inn*, near the station at 18 rue Belgique (☎97.64.50.77) – not that Jimmy the guard dog thinks of himself as particularly congenial. Plenty more bars can be found around place Aristide-Briand.

The Île de Groix

The coast immediately around Lorient is unenticing, plagued with thick drifts of weed, but straight out to sea is the eight-kilometre-long steep-sided rock of the **ÎLE DE GROIX**, home to a few thousand nautically-minded souls and a sort of little sister to Belle-Île. It takes forty-five minutes to get there by boat from the south quay of Lorient's new port (*Compagnie Morbihannaise et Nantaise de Navigation*; 4–8 sailings daily depending on the season; 82F return; ☎97.21.03.97).

The island's main interest is to geologists, who come to study its peculiar rock formations, and to birdwatchers, though there are also beaches along the eroded southern shore, and even a few megaliths.

The boat docks at Port-Tudy, about five hundred metres downhill from the eponymous capital of **GROIX**. **Bicycles** are available for rent at the port, well worth it if you want to get away from the crowds. Groix itself does, however, have the island's only facilities. In town, there's the **hotel/restaurant** *de la Marine* (☎97.86.80.05; closed Sun pm, all Jan, Mon in low season; ③), which serves large fish dinners for 70F and upwards, and the much more basic *Moulin d'Or* (☎97.86.82.16; ①). Not far away to the west, next to the sea and a small beach at the Pointe de la Croix, you'll find a summer-only **youth hostel** (April–Oct; ☎97.86.81.38; 39F), with a **campsite** alongside (☎97.86.53.08).

Hennebont

A few kilometres upstream from Lorient, at the point where the River Blavet first starts to widen into the estuary, is the old walled town of **HENNEBONT**. The fortifications, and especially the main gate, the Porte Broerec'h, are imposing, and walking around the top of the ramparts there are wide views of the river below. What you see of the old city within, however, is entirely residential – an assortment of washing-lines, budgies and garden sheds. All its public buildings were destroyed in the war and now not even a bar (or rented room) is to be found in the former centre.

The one time Hennebont comes alive is at the **Thursday market,** held below the ramparts and through the squares by the church. It's one of the largest in the region, with a heady mix of good fresh food, crêpes and Vietnamese delicacies, alongside livestock, flowers, carpets and clothes. On other days, the only places where you'll find any activity are along the **place Maréchal Foch** (in front of the Basilica) and the **quai du Pont Neuf** beside the river.

Practicalities

If you decide to **stay** in Hennebont – and few people do – the *Hôtel de France* at 17 av de la Libération (☎97.36.21.82; ②) is good value near the town centre; the *Toul-Douar* (☎97.36.24.04; ②) – a *logis* which serves good meals from 60F in a grand dining room – takes a bit of finding, on the edge of town nearest Lorient across the river, but is closer to the **gare SNCF.**

The town's **campsite**, *Camping Municipal de St-Caradec* (☎97.36.20.14), has a prime site on the river bank opposite the fortifications, but opens only from June to September. You can rent **bicycles** at 5 av de la République and at 87 rue Maréchal-Joffre, and take **boat trips** either up the Blavet towards the Nantes–Brest canal (see Chapter 6) or out into the estuary around Lorient.

Lochrist

At **LOCHRIST**, just north of Hennebont, the great chimneys of the town's **iron-works** still stand, smokeless and silent, looking down on the Blavet. Strikes and demonstrations failed to prevent the foundry's closure in 1966, and the only work since then has been to convert it into the **Musée Forges d'Hennebont** (summer Mon 2–6pm, Tues–Fri 9am–noon & 2–6pm: otherwise Mon 2–4pm, Tues–Fri 9am–noon & 2–4pm; 25F) which documents its 100-year history from the workers' point of view. Some of the men put on the dole contributed their memories and tools; for others turning their workplace into a museum was adding insult to injury. It is in fact excellent, both in contents and presentation, though in view of the joyful pictures of successful strikes in the 1930s its very existence seems a sad defeat. If it's on your route it's worth a stop: the bus station is just opposite on the other side of the river.

The Quiberon Peninsula

The **Presqu'île de Quiberon** is as close to being an island as any peninsula could conceivably be; the long causeway of sand that links it to the mainland narrows to as little as fifty metres in places. In the past this was always a strategic military location. The English held the peninsula for eight bloody days in 1746; *chouans* and royalists landed here in 1795 in the hope of destroying the Revolution, only to be sealed in and slaughtered; and part of the defoliation that threatens the dunes today is the result of German fortifications constructed during the last war. The peninsula is now, in the summer, packed with tourists. They come not so much to visit the towns, which other than **Quiberon** itself are generally featureless, but to use them as a base for trips out to **Belle-Île** or around the contrasting coastline.

The coast here has two quite distinct characters. The **Côte Sauvage**, facing the Atlantic to the west, is a bleak rocky heathland, lashed by heavy seas. It is the scene of innumerable drownings – the official tourist brochure contains a chilling description of just why it is absolutely impossible for *un imprudent* to swim back to land having once strayed beyond a certain distance. The sheltered eastern side, however, the **Baie de Quiberon**, contains safe sandy beaches, as well as yet another Thalassotherapy Institute.

On to the peninsula

As the D768 curves around the bay outside **PLOUHARNEL**, on its way to the start of the peninsula, you can't fail to notice a reconstructed **Spanish galleon**, standing in something less than three inches of water. This is an obsessive shell museum and shop, with dioramas, created entirely from shells, of eighteenth-century street scenes in Venice and in China, of Donald Duck and his friends, Sioux Indians and flamenco dancers (daily Easter–May 10am–noon & 2–6pm; June–Sept 9.30am–noon & 2–7pm; 15F). Across the road and the railway line, there's a rather uninspiring **waxwork museum** of *Chouannerie* (Easter to mid-Sept daily 10am–noon & 2–6pm; 20F), with displays of the 1795 fighting.

At **PORTIVY**, tucked into the only real shelter along the Côte Sauvage just beyond the slender neck of the *presqu'île*, windsurfers tend to congregate. If you want to join them, you can rent boards in Port Haliguen, near Quiberon town, at 16 rue des Corlis (☎97.50.25.03). There is a **campsite** just outside Portivy, *Camping de Port Blanc* on the Route du Port Blanc (☎97.30.91.30). Others nearby include the *Camping Municipal de Penthièvre* (☎97.52.33.86) and the *Camping Municipal de Kerhostin* (☎97.30.95.25).

Quiberon

The town of **QUIBERON** itself is a lively place, which centres on a miniature golf course surrounded by bars, pizzerias and some surprisingly good clothes and antique shops. The cafés by the long bathing beach are the most enjoyable, along with the old-fashioned *Café du Marché* next to the PTT.

Port-Maria, the fishing harbour and **gare maritime** for the islands of Belle Île, Houat and Hoedic, is the most active part of town and has the best concentration of **hotels** and **fish restaurants**. Port-Maria was once famous for its sardines, canned locally, but those days are long gone.

Port-Haliguen, the other port, is on the eastern coast. Today, it is an active marina, with a little commercial fishing. Boats from the islands occasionally shelter here, and use it for embarkation in rough weather. Captain Alfred Dreyfus disembarked here on his return from Devil's Island in 1899.

Arrival and Information

Between July and September, the special *Tire Bouchon* train links Quiberon's **gare SNCF**, which is a short way above the town proper, with Auray. (The name, which means "corkscrew", refers to the bottleneck at the mouth of the peninsula rather than any circuitousness in the route.) There are also buses right to the gare maritime from Vannes (#23 and #24) and Auray (#24) via Carnac.

The **SI** at 7 rue de Verdun (July & Aug, Mon–Sat 9am–8pm, Sun 10am–noon & 5–7pm; Sept–June Mon–Sat 9am–12.30pm & 2–6.30pm; ☎97.50.07.84), downhill and left from the gare SNCF, has an illuminated map outside which purports to monitor exactly which hotels are full, hour by hour. The **post office** is on rue Gambetta (☎97.50.09.16).

Bicycles can be rented from *Cycl'omar* on place Hoche (☎97.50.26.00), and **horse-riding** can be arranged with the *Centre Équestre l'Eperon*, 38 rue Jean-Pierre-Callock, in Kerne (☎97.50.28.32).

Accommodation

For much the greater part of the year, it's hard to get a room in Quiberon. In July and August, the whole peninsula is packed, while in winter it gets very quiet indeed, with virtually all its facilities closed down. The nicest area in which to stay is along the seafront in Port-Maria, where several good hotels-cum-restaurants face the Belle-Île ferry terminal.

The local **youth hostel** is *Les Filets Bleus*, inland at 45 rue du Roc'h-Priol (May–Sept; ☎97.50.15.54; 42F), 1.5km southeast of the gare SNCF. **Campsites** on the sheltered east coast near Quiberon town include the *Do-Mi-Si-La-Mi*, St-Julien (April–Oct; ☎97.50.22.52), and *les Joncs du Roch*, rue de l'Aérodrome (Easter–Sept; ☎97.50.24.37). The *Côte Sauvage* has only one site, the *Camping Municipal* in the village of Kerne (July & Aug; ☎97.50.05.07).

Pension Au Bon Accueil, 6 quai de Houat (☎97.50.07.92). One of the best value of Port-Maria's seafront hotels. The rooms are basic but inexpensive, and the friendly dining room downstairs, which has something of the atmosphere and decor of a village bar, serves good fish soup and seafood specialities on menus which start at 71F. April–Oct only. ②.

Hôtel-Restaurant de Kermorvan, 45 rue de Kermorvan (☎97.50.11.33). A good fallback in the busier seasons, away from the seafront up near Quiberon's gare SNCF. Reasonable meals, and an attractive garden. April–Oct only. ③.

Le Neptune, 4 quai de Houat (☎97.50.09.62). Alongside *Au Bon Accueil* in Port-Maria, and offering a bit more luxury. Some rooms enjoy seafront balconies, and there are the usual seafood menus, of which the cheapest costs 78F. Closed Jan, & Mon in low season. Seaview rooms ⑤; inland-facing rooms ④.

L'Océan, 7 quai de l'Océan (☎97.50.07.58). Seems to have given up the unequal struggle to keep a restaurant going, but still has reasonably-priced rooms. Easter–Sept only. ②.

Hôtel Au Vieux Logis, St-Julien (☎97.50.07.92). A very attractive flower-draped old stone building opposite the church in St-Julien village, a couple of kilometres north of central Quiberon and a short way east of the main road. Cosy little rooms, and good homely menus from 70F. Hotel closed mid-Oct to mid-March, restaurant closed Oct–April. ③.

Eating

Once again, the most appealing area in which to go browsing the menus looking for a good **meal** is along the waterfront in Port-Maria, with its line of seafood restaurants competing to attract the ferry passengers. Hotel-owners are very insistent on persuading guests to pay for half-board – and at the *Bon Accueil*, for example, that's no great hardship – but there are plenty of alternatives to choose from if you do manage to escape their clutches. To stock up on provisions, try the morning **markets** at Kerhostin on Wednesday, St-Pierre-Quiberon on Thursday and Quiberon on Saturday.

Ancienne Forge, 20 rue Verdun (☎97.50.18.64). Set back from the road that leads down to the port from the gare SNCF, with slightly unadventurous but good-value seafood-heavy menus from 78F. Closed Jan, Wed in low season.

De la Criée, 11 quai de l'Océan (☎97.30.53.09). Changing fish specialities served every day, fresh from the morning's catch at the quayside. The 89F menu includes stuffed mussels, and fish smoked on the premises. Closed Jan, Sun pm, & Mon in low season.

Les Pecheurs, rue de Port-Maria (☎97.50.12.75). Small and not especially attractive place down by the port, where the dependably traditional approach to cooking extends to keeping the portions good and large. Full fishy menus from 70F. Closed Jan, & Mon in low season.

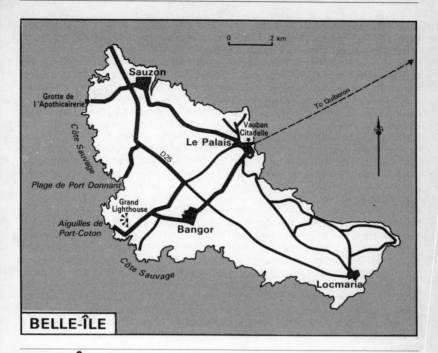

BELLE-ÎLE

Belle-Île

The island of **BELLE-ÎLE**, 15km offshore, due south of Quiberon, mirrors Brittany in its make-up. On the landward side it is rich and fertile, interrupted by deep estuaries with tiny ports; facing the ocean, along its own *Côte Sauvage*, sparse heather-covered cliffs trail rocky crags out into the sea.

You need to be able to cross and re-cross the island to appreciate these contrasts, so some kind of transport is essential – even if you just cross for a day trip. This is no great problem: bicycles are available in profusion at the island port of Le Palais, and small cars are taken over on the ferries for a relatively low charge.

The island once belonged to the monks of Redon; then to the ambitious Nicholas Fouquet, Louis XIV's minister; later to the English, who in 1761 swapped it for Minorca in an unrepeatable bargain deal. Along the way Belle-Île has seen a fair number of distinguished exiles. The citadel prison at Le Palais, closed only in 1961, having numbered amongst its inmates an astonishing succession of state enemies and revolutionary heroes – including the son of Toussaint L'Ouverture of Haiti, Ben Bella of Algeria, and even, for a brief period after 1848, Karl Marx.

Less involuntarily, such celebrated figures as the painters Monet and Matisse, the writers Flaubert and Proust, and the actress Sarah Bernhardt all spent time on the island.

Getting to Belle-Île

Throughout the year, at least five **ferries** each day (ten in high summer) sail from Port-Maria, at the southernmost tip of the Quiberon peninsula, to Belle-Île. They are operated by the *Compagnie Morbihannaise et Nantaise de Navigation* (82F return; Le Palais ☎97.31.80.01; Port-Maria ☎97.50.06.90); the crossing takes 45 minutes. The usual port of call in Belle-Île is **Le Palais**, but in July and August the same company sends a few boats direct to **Sauzon**, which takes about half an hour, and also runs a limited service between Sauzon and **Lorient** (1hr 30min; Lorient ☎97.21.03.97).

Between July and September, and occasionally out of season as well, day trips to the island, organized by *Navix* (165F; ☎97.46.60.00) set out regularly from Vannes, Port-Navalo and La Trinité, and slightly less frequently from Locmariaquer, Auray and Le Bono.

Le Palais

Docking at **LE PALAIS**, the abrupt star-shaped fortifications of the **Citadelle** are the first thing you see. Built along stylish and ordered lines by the great fortress builder Vauban, early in the eighteenth century, it is startling in size – filled with doorways leading to mysterious cellars and underground passages, endless sequences of rooms and dungeons and deserted cells. Though derelict, the structure is quite sound: large signs – *DON'T BE AFRAID* – are scattered about the place, exhorting visitors to explore the abandoned shell. An informative, if over-literary **museum** (daily April–Sept 9.30am–7pm Oct–March 9.30am–noon & 2–5pm) documents the island's history, including its entanglement in Dumas' tales of *The Three Musketeers* (which feature an account of the death of Porthos on the island).

Practicalities

The **SI** for the whole island is next to the gare maritime as you arrive in Le Palais (daily July–Sept 8.30am–12.30pm & 2–7.30pm; Oct–June 9.30am–noon & 2–6pm; ☎97.31.81.93).

Accommodation in Le Palais includes the reasonably priced *Hôtel du Commerce*, place Hôtel-de-Ville (☎97.31.81.71; ③), and the simple *Frégate* at the quayside (April–Oct; ☎97.31.54.16; ②). The newly-refitted *Hôtel-Restaurant de Bretagne* on quai Macé (☎97.31.80.14; ③) is a little more expensive and has an excellent sea-view restaurant.

There's also a municipal **campsite**, *Les Glacis* (April–Sept; ☎97.31.41.76), and a **youth hostel** (open all year; ☎97.31.81.33; 45F), a short way out of town along the clifftops from the Citadelle, at Haute-Boulogne.

Sauzon

SAUZON, Belle-Île's second town, is set at the mouth of a long estuary six kilometres to the west. If you're staying any length of time, and you've got your own transport, it's probably a better place to base yourself.

In addition to a good, inexpensive **hotel** in a magnificent setting, the *du Phare* (☎97.31.60.36; ③) – which insists that guests eat its delicious 90F fish dinners – Sauzon can also offer two **campsites**, *Pen Prad* (April–Sept; ☎97.31.64.82) and *A la Source* (May–Sept; ☎97.31.60.95).

Around the Island

For exploring the island, a coastal footpath runs on bare soil the length of the **Côte Sauvage**. Starting at the **Grand Lighthouse** (open daily in summer 9.30am–12.30pm & 2–6pm), you can see the **Aiguilles de Port-Coton**, where a savage sea foams in the pinnacles of rock, and the delicate beach of **Port-Donnant**, where bathing (despite appearances) is dangerous. At the village of **BANGOR**, nearby, is an incongruous row of huge and very expensive hotels, including the *Castel Clara* (mid-Feb to mid-Nov; ☎97.31.84.21; ⑨), where President Mitterand was a guest in October 1994. Eventually you come to the **Grotte de l'Apothicairerie**, so called because it was once full of the nests of cormorants, arranged like the jars on a chemist's shelves. It's reached by descending a slippery flight of steps cut into the rock: take care, most years at least one person falls – and drowns – from these stairs.

The **D30 inland** from the cave leads along a miniature tree-lined valley sheltered from the Atlantic winds. If you take the **D25** back towards Le Palais you pass the two **menhirs**, Jean and Jeanne, said to be lovers petrified as punishment for wanting to meet before their marriage. Another larger menhir used to lie near these two; it was broken up to help construct the road that separates them.

Houat and Hoëdic

The islands of **HOUAT** and **HOËDIC** can also be reached by ferry from Quiberon-Port Maria (*Compagnie Morbihannaise et Nantaise de Navigation*; ☎97.50.06.90; 82F return). There is at least one sailing every day of the year, except for the first Thursday of each month in winter; the crossing to Houat takes forty minutes, and to Hoëdic another twenty-five. On Tuesdays, Thursdays and Saturdays in July and August, *Navix* run day trips to Houat only from Port-Navalo and La Trinité (105F; ☎97.46.60.00).

You can't take your car (not that there would be any point in doing so) to these two very much smaller versions of Belle-Île. Both have a feeling of being left behind by the passing centuries, although the younger fishermen of Houat have revived the island's fortunes by establishing a successful fishing co-operative. There's a story that in the eighteenth century the rector of Hoëdic lost not only his sense of time but also his calendar, and ended up reducing Lent from forty days down to a more manageable three.

Houat in particular has excellent **beaches** – as ever on its sheltered (eastern) side – that fill up with campers in the summer. Camping is not strictly legal here; Hoëdic on the other hand has a large municipal **campsite** (☎97.30.63.32). There is a small and not particularly cheap **hotel** on each island; on Houat it's the *Hôtel-Restaurant des Îles* (Easter–Sept; ☎97.30.68.02; ④) and on Hoëdic *les Cardinaux* (☎97.52.37.27; closed mid-Jan to mid-Feb; ④). Both accept visitors on a *pension* basis only. It's also possible to rent **gîtes** on Hoëdic – contact ☎97.30.68.32.

Carnac

CARNAC is the most important prehistoric site in Europe – in fact this spot is thought to have been continuously inhabited longer than anywhere else in the world. Its **alignments** of two thousand or so menhirs stretch over four kilometres, with great burial tumuli dotted amidst them. The site, in use since at least 5700 BC, long predates Knossos, the Pyramids, Stonehenge or the great Egyptian temples of the same name at Karnak.

The town of Carnac is split into two distinct halves – the popular seaside resort of Carnac-Plage, and further inland Carnac-Ville near the alignments. It's an amalgam that can verge on the ridiculous with rows of shops named *Supermarché des Druides* and the like; but for all that, Carnac is a relaxed and attractive place, and any commercialization doesn't intrude on the megaliths themselves. Fortunately, the ancient builders had the admirable foresight to construct their monuments well back from the sea.

Arrival and Information

The main **SI** for Carnac is slightly back from the main beach at 74 av des Druides (July & Aug Mon–Sat 9am–7pm, Sun 10am–1pm & 2–6pm; Sept–June Mon–Sat 9am–noon & 2–6pm; ☎97.52.13.52). An annex in the place de l'Église in town is open between Easter and September. Both provide fully comprehensive maps and details.

Buses to Auray, Quiberon and Vannes stop near the SI on av des Druides, and on rue Saint-Cornély in Carnac-Ville. The *Tire Bouchon* **rail** link with Auray and Quiberon runs between July and September; the nearest station to Carnac is at Plouharnel, 4km northwest. Pick up details from the gare SNCF there (☎97.52.11.87), or the SNCF bureau, 74 av des Druides (☎97.52.26.70) alongside the SI. For details of **bicycle** rental, see "Seeing the Stones", below.

The alignments

All sorts of conjectures have been advanced about the **Carnac megaliths**. One of the oldest stories was that they were Roman soldiers turned to stone as they pursued Pope Cornély; one of the most recent, the alleged belief of US soldiers in the last war that they were German anti-tank obstructions. The general consensus today is for a religious significance connected with their use as some sort of astronomical observatory. Professor Thom, whose popular theories have made him the best-known writer on the alignments, sees them – and most of the megaliths of the Morbihan – as part of a unified system for recording such phenomena as the extreme points of the lunar and solar cycles. According to this hypothesis, the Carnac stones provided a grid system – a kind of neolithic graph paper for plotting heavenly movements and hence to determine the siting of other stones (see the further account, together with map, in *Contexts*).

However, it's hard to see any real consistency in the size or the shape of the stones, or enough regularity in the lines to pinpoint their direction. Local tradition has it that new stones were added to the lines, illuminated by fire, each June. An annual ceremony in which willing participants set up one stone does sound more plausible than a vast programme of slave labour to erect them all at once. In any case, the physical aspect and orientation of the stones may have been subsidiary to their metaphysical significance. It's quite possible that no practical purpose was involved nor a precise pattern, and that their importance was entirely symbolic.

The way you see them today cannot be said to be authentic. They were used for generations as a source of ready quarried stone, and then surreptitiously

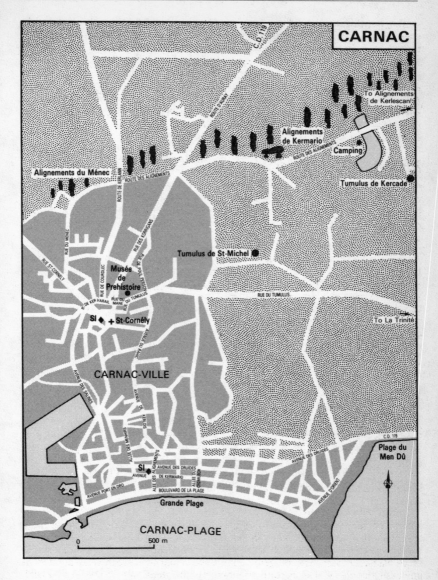

removed by farmers attempting to prevent the influx of academics and tourists damaging precious crops. Not only is it impossible to say how many of the stones have disappeared, but those that remain are not necessarily in their original positions – small holes filled with pink concrete at the base of the stones denote that they have been restored or re-erected.

The **menhirs** range in size from mere stumps to 5-metre-high blocks; they stand alone, in circles known as *cromlechs*, or in approximate lines. In addition there are **dolmens**, groups of standing stones roofed with further stones laid across the top, that are generally assumed to be burial chambers. And there are tumuli – most notably the **Tumulus de St-Michel**, near the town centre, a vast artificial mound containing rudimentary graves. You can scramble through subterranean passages and tunnels beneath the mound to view little stone cairns and piles of charred bones; the tunnels are, however, again not authentic, being the recent creation of archeologists.

Taken all together, the stones make up three distinct major alignments, running roughly in the same northeast–southwest direction but each with a slightly separate orientation. They are the **Alignements de Menec**, "the place of stones" or "place of remembrance", with 1169 stones in eleven rows; the **Alignements de Kermario**, "the place of the dead", with 1029 menhirs in ten rows; and the **Alignements de Kerlescan**, "the place of burning", with 555 menhirs in thirteen lines. All three are sited parallel to the sea alongside the "Route des Alignements", a kilometre or so to the north of Carnac-Ville.

Seeing the stones

Thanks to increasing numbers of visitors (and despite vehement local opposition), the principal Alignements de Menec have recently been fenced off – you are no longer free to wander at will among them, as was possible until just a few years ago. Inevitably, that means some of the magic has been lost. Now you have to settle for seeing the stones from a distance, either from the road or from the roof of the grandly-named **Archéoscope** alongside the site – a vantage point perhaps a dozen feet above ground level. Inside the Archéoscope, a small theatre puts on half-hour audio-visual presentations about the megaliths (mid-Feb to mid-Nov daily 10am–noon & 2–6.30pm; 40F; call for the times of English-language performances ☎97.52.07.49).

If you want to set off on your own, you can rent **bicycles** from several of the town's campsites (see below), or from *Le Randonneur*, 20 av des Druides, Carnac-Plage (☎97.52.02.55), or *Lorcy*, 6 rue de Courdiec, Carnac-Ville (☎97.52.09.73). The *Grande Metairie* site also arranges tours on **horseback**.

Probably the best way of all to see the alignments is from the **air**, which if you split the cost three or four ways, can cost not much more than a good meal. The year-round *Quiberon Air Club* (☎97.50.11.05) and the summer-only *Thalass Air* (☎97.30.40.00) both operate short flights over the Morbihan from the Aérodrome de Quiberon, near the tip of the Quiberon peninsula at Roc'h Priol (☎97.50.11.05).

The Museum of Prehistory

In Carnac-Ville. July & Aug Mon–Fri 10am–6.30pm, Sat & Sun 10am–noon & 2–6.30pm; Sept–June daily except Tues 10am–noon & 2–5pm. 30F.

Carnac's modern **Musée de Préhistoire** documents and examines the various megalithic theories in great and entertaining depth. It's refreshing to find a museum combining serious scholarship with large blow-ups of Asterix cartoons. The history of the area is traced from earliest times, about 450,000 years ago, up to and beyond the Romans. As well as authentic physical relics, such as the original "twisted dolmen" of Luffang, with a carving of an octopus-like divinity guaranteed to chill the blood of any devotee of H. P. Lovecraft, and reproductions and casts of the carvings at Locmariaquer. The museum also attempts to provide some account of the social culture that existed at the time the megaliths were erected – whilst acknowledging that much of this is more or less pure speculation.

The Town and the Beaches

Carnac itself, divided between the original **Carnac-Ville** and the seaside resort of **Carnac-Plage**, is extremely popular and crowded, swarming with holiday-makers in July and August. For most of these, the alignments are, if anything, only a side show. But, as a holiday centre, it has its special charm, especially in late spring and early autumn when it is less crowded – and cheaper. The town and seafront remain well wooded, and the tree-lined avenues and gardens are a delight – the climate is mild enough for the Mediterranean mimosa and ever-green oak to grow alongside the native stone pine and cypress.

Near the museum of prehistory (see above), in the centre of Carnac, the church of **St-Cornély** was built in the seventeenth century in honour of the patron saint of horned animals. Archeological discoveries suggest that the custom of bringing diseased cattle to Carnac to be cured, still honoured at least in theory at the saint's *pardon* on the second Sunday in September, dates back as far as the Romans. The Romans also had heated sea-water baths here; today the **Thalassotherapy Centre** is an ultra-modern building where among other things they treat *maladies de civilisation*.

Carnac's five **beaches** extend for nearly two miles in total, with the largest of them – logically enough, the Grande Plage – running for the full length of the built-up area known as **Carnac-Plage**. For much of the way it's hidden from view by the slightly raised line of dunes that separates it from the Boulevard de la Plage, which is in turn very low-key; the parallel av des Druides, a couple of blocks inland, is much busier with shops and restaurants.

Further west, nearer the yacht club, the small **plage Légenèse** is reputed to be the beach on which the ill-fated *chouan* Royalists landed in 1795. The two most attractive beaches, usually counted together as one of the five, are **plages Men Dû** and **Beaumer**, which lie to the east towards La Trinité beyond Pointe Churchill.

Accommodation and Eating

Hotels in Carnac are at a premium in July and August, when you can expect higher prices and intense pressure to take half-board (*demi-pension*). Carnac-Ville is marginally cheaper than Carnac-Plage, although the distinction is blurred where the two merge.

Hôtel Chez Nous, at 5 place de la Chapelle in **Carnac-Ville** (April–Oct; ☎97.52.07.28; ④), is central and convenient, with a nice garden, but no restaurant; the similar *Hôtel d'Arvor*, 5 rue St-Cornély (April–Oct; ☎97.52.96.90; ④), is run by a couple who speak good English.

In **Carnac-Plage**, the *Hôtel-Restaurant Hoty*, 15 av de Kermario (☎97.52.11.12; closed Dec & Jan; ③), is the best value. The more expensive *Hôtel Le Bateau Ivre*, 71 bd de la Plage (☎97.52.19.55; closed Mon, Jan to mid-Feb; ⑤), is set in large gardens that were formerly owned by Antoine de Saint-Exupery (author of *le Petit Prince*) and Sydney Churchill, a relative of Sir Winston Churchill. Hence the adjacent headland, at the eastern end of Grande Plage, is called Pointe

Churchill, and hence too the name of the hotel's restaurant, *Le Churchill*, comfortably alongside a heated swimming pool.

Most of the **restaurants** worth recommending are in hotels, such as the bright and cheerful *Bistrot du Pêcheur* in the *Hôtel La Marine* at 4 place de la Chapelle (April–Sept; ☎97.52.07.33; ⑤) or the old stone *Hôtel Ratelier* on Chemin de Douet (☎97.52.05.04; closed Sun, Mon, Jan; ④), which has menus from 90F. *Chez Yannick*, 8 rue du Tumulus (☎97.52.08.67; closed Jan), is a worthwhile *crêperie*.

There's a **market** in Carnac on Wednesday and Sunday mornings; in the surrounding area Locmariaquer holds them on Tuesday and Saturday, La Trinité on Tuesday and Friday, and Auray on Monday.

As befits such a family-oriented place, there are as many as eighteen **campsites** in and around Carnac. Among the best are the *Men Dû* (April–Sept; ☎97.52.04.23) near the sea, inland from the plage du Men Dû, and the more expensive *Grande Metairie* (June to mid-Sept; ☎97.52.24.01) near the Kercado tumulus, with tennis, horse-riding and a swimming pool.

La Trinité

An alternative base to Carnac proper is **LA TRINITÉ**, three or four kilometres along the coast to the east, around the sweep of Beaumer bay. The town itself is uninteresting – just an upmarket yacht harbour without a proper beach – but is renowned as the home of yachtsman Eric Tabarley, twice winner of the single-handed transatlantic race in 1964 (*Pen Duick I*) and 1976 (*Pen Duick VI*), and as the birthplace of Jean-Marie Le Pen, founder of the ultra-right National Front. The *Hôtel du Commerce* (April–Sept; ☎97.55.72.36; ②) here is good value.

Auray

Some people find **AURAY**, with its over-restored ancient quarter, slightly dull – but it is a lot less crowded than Vannes, a lot cheaper than Quiberon town, and usefully placed for exploring Carnac, the Quiberon peninsula and the Gulf of Morbihan.

The natural centre of the town today is the **place de la République**, with its eighteenth-century Hôtel de Ville. In a neighbouring square, linked to the place de la République by rue du Lait, is the seventeenth-century church of **St-Gildas**, with its fine Renaissance porch. A **covered market** adjoins the Hôtel de Ville, but on Mondays an open-air market fills the surrounding streets with colour – and stops all traffic for a considerable radius.

However, Auray's showpiece is undoubtedly the ancient quarter of **St-Goustan**, with its delightful fifteenth- and sixteenth-century houses, albeit restored. The bend in the River Loch, an early defended site, was a natural setting for a town – and, with its easy access to the gulf, it soon became one of the busiest ports of Brittany. Today, as you look at it from the Promenade du Loch on the opposite bank, with the diminutive seventeenth-century stone bridge still spanning the river, it is not difficult to imagine it in its heyday. In 1776, Benjamin Franklin landed here on his way to seek the help of Louis XVI in the American War of Independence; Auray is also said to have been the last place Julius Caesar reached in his conquest of Gaul.

Practicalities

Auray's **SI** is on the ground floor of the Hôtel de Ville, place de la République (Mon–Sat 9.30am–noon & 2–6pm; ☎97.24.09.75). A small annex is maintained in July and August at the gare SNCF, twenty minutes' walk from the centre, from where buses run through the centre of Auray and on to La Trinité, Carnac and the gare SNCF at Quiberon. If you're making for the islands, you can pick up comprehensive details at the *Îles du Ponant Promotional Association* at 11 place du Joffre.

The most appealing place to **stay** in Auray is down by the port in the St-Goustan quarter, where the *Hôtel du Marin*, 47 rue de Petit-Port (☎97.24.14.58; ②), offers simple accommodation over a bar. Up in town, *Hôtel le Celtic*, on the way into town at 30 rue Clémenceau (☎97.24.05.37; ②), is also pleasant, and the nearby *Olympic Bar*, 19 rue Clémenceau (☎97.24.06.69), is a friendly restaurant-cum-bar with menus at 58F and 90F. There are also a couple of hotels out near the station, including the *Hôtel Terminus*, place de la Gare (☎97.24.00.09; ②), which has a snack bar and *crêperie*.

North of Auray

A short way north of Auray's train station – and thus quite a long way out from the town, on the B768 towards Baud – is the imposing and evocative **Abbaye de Chartreuse** (daily 10am–noon & 2–5.30pm). This houses a David d'Angers mausoleum of black and white marble, commemorating the failed *chouan* landing at Quiberon in 1795 (see p.288), and viewable, bones and all, 10am until noon and 2pm to 5.30pm. For Bretons the event was something more than an attempt at a Royalist restoration, with strong undertones of a struggle for independence. Another gloomy piece of Counter-Revolutionary history is recalled by the nearby **Champ des Martyrs**, where 350 of the *chouans* were executed. It's located on the right of the D120, going out of town.

Two kilometres further along the D120, towards Brech, you come to the **Eco-Musée St-Degan** (July to mid-Sept daily 2–6pm; 25F), a group of reconstructed farm buildings, representing the local peasant life at the beginning of this century. It's a bit determinedly rustic and charming, but at least it does attempt to escape the glass cases and wax models of most folk museums.

In **BRECH** itself there's a fine parish church with a weather-beaten and faded calvary in its yard; a nice café, *des Bretons*; and a **gîte d'étape** – not a very eventful place to stay, perhaps, but a peaceful one.

Ste-Anne d'Auray

Should you be in the area of Auray around July 26, one of the largest of the Breton *pardons* takes place on that day at **STE-ANNE D'AURAY**. Some 25,000 pilgrims gather for the occasion to hear mass in the church, mount the *scala sancta* on their knees and buy trinkets and snacks from the street stalls.

The origin of this **pardon**, typical of many, was the discovery in 1623 of a statue of Saint Anne (the mother of Mary) by a local peasant, one Nicolazic. He claimed that the saint directed him to the spot where the statue had been buried for over nine hundred years and instructed him to build a church. Twenty years later, on his deathbed, Nicolazic was still being interrogated by the ecclesiastical authorities as to the truth of his story, but the church had been constructed and already become a place of pilgrimage. Nicolazic was an illiterate peasant who spoke no French; it is a testimony to his obduracy that his claims were eventually accepted against the opposition of sceptical clergy and nobility. The continuing campaign for his canonization is polarized along similar lines today. Nicolazic's supporters see him as a representative of the downtrodden classes, and as a symbol of Breton independence – the wealthy Church establishment continue to oppose him.

As a major centre for pilgrimage, Ste-Anne was chosen as the site for the vast **Monument aux Morts** erected by public subscription as a memorial to the 250,000 Breton dead of the Great War. One in fourteen of the population died, the highest proportion of losses of any region involved. The monument, a crypt topped by a dome with a granite altar, is surrounded by a wall that must be 200m long, covered with inscriptions to the dead; and yet even that huge and sombre wall does not contain room to list them all by name, often just cataloguing the horrific death tallies of tiny and obscure villages.

A short distance north on the D102 is a National Necropolis, with dead from all wars since 1870–71.

Practicalities

Ste-Anne is a sad and solemn place. The town, away from the spacious promenades for the pilgrims, is small, low and drab; not really a place for a long stay, although there is no particular shortage of **hotels**. Among the best value are *le Moderne* (☎97.57.66.55; closed mid-Dec to mid-Jan; ③), which has a good restaurant, and the *Croix Blanche*, 25 rue de Vannes (☎97.57.64.44, closed all Feb, Sun pm, & Mon out of season; ③).

Locmariaquer

LOCMARIAQUER, easily accessible from Auray or Carnac, stands right at the mouth of the Gulf of Morbihan – its cape separated by only a few hundred metres from the tip of the Rhuys Peninsula. On the ocean side, it has a long but not very sandy beach, more popular for scavenging shellfish than for bathing; on the Gulf side, a small tidal port.

Boat trips run in all directions, for which tickets are bought in the town centre or at the port, although the boats themselves leave from further down towards the narrow straits. As well as trips around the Gulf and up the River Auray, there is an intermittent ferry service to the island of Gavrinis (see p.307), which is more usually (and more easily) reached from Larmor-Baden. For full details, contact *Navix* (☎97.57.36.78) or *Compagnie des Îles* (☎97.46.18.19).

Menhirs and Dolmens

The **Grand Menhir Brise** at Locmariaquer is supposed to have been the crucial central point of the megalithic observatory of the Morbihan (see *Contexts*). Before being floored by an earthquake in 1722, it was by far the largest known menhir – 66ft high and weighing rather more than a full jumbo jet at 347 tons. It now lies on the ground in four pieces (a possible fifth is missing).

Alongside the Grand Menhir, the **Table des Marchands** is a dolmen which was once exposed but has now been reburied for its protection under a tumulus. It is currently being excavated, though you can still go inside, along a narrow passage, and stand beneath its huge roof, on which carvings seem to depict ploughing. It has recently been discovered that this roof is part of the same stone as that on the tumulus at Gavrinis and on another local dolmen – the carvings match like a jigsaw. This is another mystery for the archeologists, possibly suggesting that the builders did not revere the stones in themselves, as most theories had previously implied.

Both the Grand Menhir and the Table des Marchands are fenced off, and closed for lunch between 12.30pm and 2.30pm. The rest of the megaliths of Locmariaquer are open at all times – open to the weather as well, so watch out for muddy and water-logged underground passages, and be sure to take a torch if you want to explore them thoroughly. The most interesting are the **Dolmen des Pierres Plates**, at the end of the town beach, with an octopus divinity deep in its long chamber, and the **Dolmen de Mané Rethual**, a long covered tunnel leading to a burial chamber capped with a huge rock, reached along a narrow footpath that starts behind the phone boxes next to the Mairie/SI. At a third dolmen, the **Mané-Lud**, a horse's skull was found on top of each stone during excavations.

Locmariaquer accommodation

There are a couple of reasonable small **hotels** in Locmariaquer, the *Lautram* on place de l'Église (April–Sept; ☎97.57.31.32; ③) and *l'Escale* (April–Sept; ☎97.57.32.51; June to mid-Sept; ③); several campsites, too, including the excellent *La Ferme Fleurie* (☎97.57.34.06), one kilometre towards Kerinis and open all year, and the summer-only *Lann Brick* (☎97.57.32.79), 1.5km further on, nearer the beach.

Vannes

It was from **VANNES** that the great Breton hero Nominoë set out to unify Brittany at the start of the ninth century; he beat the hell out of the Franks, and pushed the borders past Nantes and Rennes to where they were to remain up until the French Revolution nearly a millennium later. Here too, the Breton *Etats* assembled in 1532 to ratify the Act of Union with France, in the building known as *La Cohue*; and here also, 22 of the Royalists captured at Quiberon (see p.288) were executed in the Jardins de la Garrène in 1795. Parisian soldiers fired the shots because local regiments refused.

Vieux Vannes, the old centre of chaotic streets crammed around the cathedral and enclosed by ramparts and gardens and a tiny stream, is still there, though now bordered by a new administrative centre. In refreshing contrast to the somewhat insane road system around the modern parts of the city, most of the inner area is pedestrianized.

Arrival and Information

Vannes' SI, which has a well-restored seventeenth-century frontage, is at 1 rue Thiers (July & Aug Mon–Sat 9am–7pm, Sun 10am–noon; Sept–June Mon–Sat 9am–noon & 2–6pm; ☎97.47.24.34), on the corner of rue du Drézen and rue Thiers and near place Gambetta.

The **gare SNCF** (☎97.42.50.50) is 25 minutes' walk north of the town centre. Buses to Auray, Carnac, Quiberon and other destinations leave from the **gare**

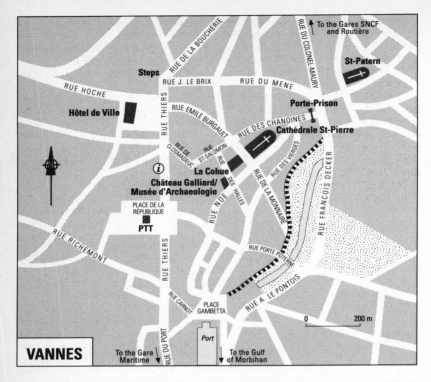

routière alongside; the one to Nantes, run by *Societé Transports Tourisme de l'Ouest* (☎97.47.29.64), avoids the rail journey via Redon, and allows a stopover in La Roche-Bernard.

Boats around the gulf are operated from the **gare maritime**, a little way south of the centre on the parc du Golfe, by *Navix* (☎97.46.60.00) and *Compagnies des Îles* (☎97.46.60.00); see p.306. Pick up all the latest brochures and schedules in the SI.

The Town

The new town centre of Vannes is **place de la République**; the focus was shifted outside the medieval city in the nineteenth-century craze for urbanization. The grandest of the public buildings here, guarded by a pair of sleek and dignified bronze lions, is the **Hôtel de Ville** at the top of rue Thiers.

By day, however, the cobbled streets of the old city, especially in the area around the cathedral, are the chief source of pleasure, as well as being where most of Vannes' busy commercial life takes place. With their skew-windowed and half-timbered houses – most overhanging and witch-hatted, some tumbling down, some newly propped-up and painted – they amply repay time spent wandering.

Place Henri IV in particular, with its charming fifteenth- and sixteenth-century gabled houses, is stunning, as are the views from it down the narrow side streets. The ramparts can be followed for quite a length, above what what used to be the moat but is now for much of the way made into neat and colourful flower beds. Near the **Poste Poterne**, the "back gate", an old slate-roofed wash-house survives.

La Cohue, which fills a block between rue des Halles and place du Cathédrale, has recently become the **Musée de Vannes** (June–Sept daily 10am–noon & 2–6pm; Oct–May Mon & Wed–Sat 10am–noon & 2–6pm, Sun 2–6pm; 15F), having served at various times over the past 750 years as high court and assembly room, prison, revolutionary tribunal, theatre and market-place. Upstairs it still houses the collection of what was the local Beaux-Arts museum, while the main gallery downstairs is the venue for different temporary exhibitions.

The **Cathédrale St-Pierre** is a rather forbidding place, with its stern main altar almost imprisoned by four solemn grey pillars. The light, purple through the new stained glass, spears in to illuminate the finger of the Blessed Pierre Rogue, who was guillotined in the main square on March 3, 1796. Opposite this desiccated digit is the black-lidded sarcophagus that marks the current site of the tomb of the fifteenth-century Spanish Dominican preacher Saint Vincent Ferrier (which has meandered around the Cathedral for centuries). For a small fee, you can in summer examine the assorted **treasure** in the chapterhouse, which includes a twelfth-century wedding-chest, brightly decorated with enigmatic scenes of romantic chivalry.

Housed in the sombre fifteenth-century Château Gaillard on rue Noé, the **Musée Archéologique** is said to have one of the world's finest collections of prehistoric artefacts (Mon–Sat 9.30am–noon & 2–6pm). But unlike the excellent display at Carnac, it's all pretty lifeless – some elegant stone axes, more recent Oceanic exhibits by way of context, but nothing very illuminating. Further collections of fossils, shells and stuffed birds, equally traditional in their display, are on show around the corner in the **Hôtel de Roscannec** at 19 rue des Halles (same hours).

There's a bit more life about the city's excellent **fish market**, active in the covered hall on place de la Poissonnerie every morning between Tuesday and Saturday. A general market spreads slightly higher up on the streets towards the cathedral on Wednesday and Saturday.

The huge **Aquarium**, in the parc du Golfe on the right bank of the port from place Gambetta, claims the best collection of tropical fish in Europe, 400-odd electric eels and a crocodile "discovered in the Paris sewers" (daily June–Aug 9am–7pm; Sept–May 9am–noon & 1.30–6.30pm; 50F).

Accommodation

In peak season Vannes can become quite claustrophobic, but it still offers a better choice of **hotels** than anywhere else around the Golfe de Morbihan. Much the nicest place to stay, if you can get a room, is **place Gambetta** overlooking the port. This is the one part of Vannes that stays busy well into the evening throughout the year, but the traffic noise is not too bad at all.

The nearest **campsite** is *Camping Couleau* at the far end of av du Maréchal-Juin, beyond the Aquarium, and alongside the gulf (April–Sept; ☎97.63.13.88).

Hôtel la Bretagne, 36 rue du Méné (☎97.47.20.21). Just outside the walls, around the corner from the Porte-Prison. Simple rooms above the *Taverne de Maître* brasserie, which specializes in *choucroute* and has a wide assortment of draught lagers. ②.

Hôtel la Marée Bleue, 8 place Bir-Hakeim (☎97.47.24.29). Basic rooms in what is not a very attractive area of town, just outside the walls, but quite a lively one. The restaurant, geared towards local workers rather than tourists, offers very good-value lunches. ①.

Hôtel le Marina, 4 place Gambetta (☎97.47.22.81). Pleasantly refurbished rooms, right in the thick of the things by the port, with sea views and bright sun in the morning. Downstairs there's a bar rather than a restaurant. ③.

Hôtel-Restaurant la Voile d'Or, 1 place Gambetta (☎97.42.71.81). Extremely central, taking up half of the grand crescent at the head of the port, but the actual rooms are neither especially grand nor expensive. Standard menus in the restaurant that spreads out into the square below start at 89F, with the usual *soupe de poissons* and *steack frites*. ③.

Eating and Nightlife

Dining out in old Vannes can be an expensive experience, whether you eat in the intimate little restaurants along the rue des Halles, or down by the port. If you're just looking for a snack, try the area outside the walls in the northeast, extending from the Porte-Prison towards the gare SNCF.

The leading venues for **live music** are *Le Studio*, on place Bir-Hakeim, which puts on jazz, blues, and African bands when they come to town, and *Le Contretemps*, at 22 rue Hoche (☎97.42.40.11), which is more a jazz-buffs' hang-out. During the first week of August, the open-air concerts of the **Vannes Jazz Festival** take place in the Théâtre de Verdure.

Le Cordon Bleu, 13 rue des Halles (☎97.42.74.12). One of the less pricey options on this narrow, cobbled street, but every bit as good as its rivals, with a strong emphasis on Breton dishes and ingredients. Evening menus from 75F. Closed Sun, & Mon lunchtime in low season.

La Jonquière, 9 rue des Halles (☎97.54.08.34). Very central option, part of a popular Brest-based chain with a modern approach and efficient multi-lingual staff. For 60F you can take your pick from the separate buffets of hors d'oeuvres and desserts; set menus start at 73F, and the *Menu Mer* at 149F gets you a full *assiette*, plus, perhaps, pan-fried angler fish with scallops.

Le Lys, 51 rue Maréchal-Leclerc (☎97.42.29.30). Gourmet restaurant, a short way east of the walled city. The *nouvelle*-tinged seafood concoctions get progressivly more inventive as the menus rise from 115F, but the portions are never less than reasonable. Closed Sun pm, & Mon in low season.

Villa Romana, 16 rue des Vierges (☎97.47.88.63). Pizzas baked in a wood-fired oven, most costing just under 50F, plus pasta and fresh fish. Best for lunch, eaten on the outdoor terrace right on the old ramparts, overlooking the formal gardens.

East of Vannes

Though Gavrinis and the other Morbihan islands (see the following section) are the most exciting excursions from Vannes, a number of sights inland, to the east of the city, can fill a good day's round trip. Vannes' **traffic system** will do its damnedest to prevent you leaving the city in any direction, however, so you can't be too choosy about where you end up.

The Château de Largoët

If you follow the **N166** 10km towards Elven, and then turn off to the left about four kilometres short, you come to the ruins of the **CHÂTEAU DE LARGOËT**, perched on an eminence in the small forest. It's still guarded by its old gatehouse, carved all over with granite bunnies.

The castle consists mainly of two stark towers, inside which the wooden floor-ing has long since rotted away to leave the shafts open to the sky. The donjon proper is topped by a finger-like watch tower, one of the highest in the country at over 150ft, where from 1474–76 the Breton Duke Francis imprisoned the future English king, Henry VII. At that time simply Henry Tudor, Duke of Richmond – a title traditionally awarded to royal bastards or English nobility with Breton connections – he had fled to Brittany after the Battle of Tewkesbury, in which Lancastrian ambitions in the Wars of the Roses were defeated. François welcomed Henry as a guest, then realized his value and held him for ransom.

Under its alternative name of *Elven Towers*, the castle also puts on *son-et-lumière* costume spectacles of unsurpassed tackiness, combining Henry's drama with the site's spurious claim to Arthurian authenticity as the home of Sir Lancelot of the Lake. The show takes place on Fridays and Saturdays between mid-June and the end of August, starting at 11pm – far too late at night to be much use to most holiday-makers, certainly those with families.

Le Gorvello and Questembert

There's little point going to **ELVEN** itself, though if you've always wondered where René Descartes grew up you can find the answer en route at the manor house of Kerleau. More rewarding is to head south, to the beautiful village of **LE GORVELLO**, at a crossroads with the D7. Bedecked with potted geraniums and huge azaleas, it has at its centre a perfect roadside cross.

Beyond, the D7 leads on into **QUESTEMBERT**, where the low-roofed wooden market hall from 1675 makes a very classy cycle park. What's reputed to be one of the best restaurants in France is in this little town, the ivy-coated *Hôtel du Bretagne* (☎97.26.11.12; ⑧). Its sumptuous menus start at 150F, while room prices are astro-nomical. The *Hôtel de la Gare* (☎97.26.11.47; ③), in rather nondescript surround-ings well north of town near the gare SNCF, is a *logis* with a good restaurant.

If you continue east or north from Questembert you come to the **Nantes–Brest canal** at Malestroit (see p.271) or Redon (see p.273).

The Morbihan Islands

By popular tradition the scattered islands of the **Golfe de Morbihan** ("little sea" in Breton) used to number the days of the year. For centuries, though, the waters have been rising and there is now about one for each week. Of these, some thirty are owned by film stars and the like; while two – the **Île aux Moines** and **Île d'Arz** – have regular ferry services and permanent populations, and end up extremely crowded in summer. The rest are the best, and a **boat tour** around them, or at least a trip out to **Gavrinis**, near the mouth of the gulf, is one of the most compel-ling attractions of Southern Brittany. As the boats thread their way through the baffling muddle of channels you lose track of which is island and which is main-land; and everywhere there are megalithic ruins, stone circles disappearing beneath the water and solitary menhirs on small hillocks. Flaubert evocatively described Celtic mercenaries far off in Carthage pining for the Morbihan – *"Les Celtes regrettaient trois pierres brutes, sous un ciel plouvieux, dans un golfe remplie d'îlots"* – not that the Celts actually set up the stones in the first place.

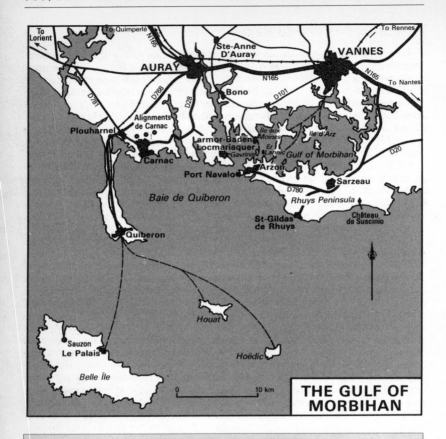

THE GULF OF MORBIHAN

GULF TOURS

In season, dozens of boats leave for **gulf tours** each day from Vannes, Port Navalo, La Trinité-sur-Mer, Auray and Larmor-Baden. Briefly the options are these:

Navix (☎97.46.60.00), who are based in **Vannes**, run deluxe *vedettes* around the gulf, including half-day (70F) and full-day (95F) tours, excursions to the Île-aux-Moines and the Île d'Arz, and gastronomic cruises for lunch (July & Aug, daily except Mon, departs noon) and dinner (July & Aug, Wed, Fri & Sat, departs 8pm). They also go out to the islands of **Belle-Île** and **Houat**. Other *Navix* sailings depart from **Port Navalo** (65–95F, plus some more expensive dinner cruises), and, to no very fixed schedule, from Auray, Le Bono, Locmariaquer and La Trinité.

Compagnie des Îles (☎97.46.18.19), also based in **Vannes**, run gulf tours (70F & 95F) and excursions to the Île-aux-Moines (65F) from there. They also operate similar cruises of varying lengths from **Port Navalo** (65–130F) and **La Trinité** (95–115F) in July & Aug.

Vedettes Blanches Armor (☎97.57.15.27) operate the usual gulf tours and trips to the Île des Moines (mid-June to mid-Sept), as well as a regular shuttle service to Gavrinis from **Larmor-Baden**, connected by a daily bus from Vannes.

Larmor-Baden and Le Bono

Making your own way to Larmor-Baden, the best route is along the main road
down the Auray estuary, the D17. This crosses the River Bono on a high bridge;
visible way below it to the left is a beautiful iron bridge. A side turning before the
river leads across that bridge into **LE BONO**, a harbour village that looks almost
ludicrously idyllic seen from one of the *vedettes* out in the gulf. Simple rooms are
available at the *Vieux-Pont*, a *crêperie* in the heart of the village (☎97.57.87.71; ①),
but for most visitors Le Bono is simply a tempting stopover for a meal or picnic.

   LARMOR-BADEN itself is a subdued little town lying at the bottom of a long
slope of fields of dazzling sunflowers. The port looks out on the tangle of islands
in the Gulf of Morbihan, which at this point is so narrow that Arzon on the Rhuys
peninsula (see p.308) appears to be on just another nearby island. It is not really
an inspiring place to stay – not properly a resort or town – but there's a functional
campsite, the *Ker Eden* (May–Sept; ☎97.57.05.23), and a fair number of hotels
including the *Auberge Parc Fétan* (April–Oct; ☎97.57.04.38; ③) and the *du Centre*
(Feb–Nov; ☎97.57.04.68; ④).

Gavrinis

The reason to visit the island of **GAVRINIS** is its megalithic site. The most
impressive and remarkable in Brittany, it would be memorable just for its loca-
tion. But it really is extraordinary as a structure, standing comparison with
Newgrange in Ireland and – in shape as well as size and age – with the earliest
pyramids of Egypt.

   It is essentially a **tumulus**, an earth mound covering a stone cairn and
"passage grave". However, in 1981 half of the mound was peeled back and, using
the original stones around the entrance as a basis, the side of the cairn that faces
the water was reconstructed to make a facade resembling a step-pyramid. Inside,
every stone of the passageway and chamber is covered in carvings, with a
restricted "alphabet" of fingerprint whorls, axeheads and other conventional
signs, including the spirals familiar in Ireland but seen only here in Brittany. It
has been thought for a long time that the stones were brought at least the few
kilometres from Locmariaquer; and this view received dramatic confirmation
when in 1984 the roof was shown to be made from the self-same piece of carved
stone as covers the Table des Marchands there (see p.300).

   One mystery has consistently eluded explanation; the purpose of the three
holes leading to a recessed niche in one of the walls of the chamber. Some medie-
val monks were buried in the mound, but the cairn itself seems never to have
been a grave.

   Erosion since the site was opened has so rapidly damaged the tumulus that it
may well soon be barred to visitors altogether; it is no longer possible to climb on
the mound itself, and conceivably a replica will be built.

   From Gavrinis, you can look across to the half-submerged stone circle on the
tiny island of **Er Lanic**, which rests on its skirt of mud like an abandoned
hovercraft.

Getting to Gavrinis

The island of Gavrinis is a fifteen-minute **ferry** ride from Larmor-Baden; in
summer, the boat trips include guided tours of the cairn (June–Sept daily, every

half-hour 9.30–11.30am & 1.30–5pm; 52F). Most gulf cruises sail close enough to the island to give a view of the cairn, but do not land.

Southern Morbihan: The Rhuys Peninsula

Though the tip of the **Presqu'île de Rhuys** is just a few hundred metres across the mouth of the Gulf of Morbihan from Locamariaquer, it somehow seems to mark a distinctly southwards shift in climate. The Côte Sauvage is lost and in its wake appear pomegranates, fig trees, camellias, even vineyards (Rhuys produces the only Breton wine), along with cultivated oysters down below in the mud.

There are, unfortunately, fierce currents in the gulf – which all the way along here is very unsafe for swimming. The **ocean beaches**, however, have potential. They break out intermittently to either side of St-Gildas-de-Rhuys, amidst the glittering gold and silver coloured rocks. For details on the whole peninsula, call in at the new information centre just off the main road as you come into Sarzeau.

Arzon

If you're spending any length of time on the peninsula, **ARZON** is probably the best of its towns; stay at the *Hôtel Étoile de la Mer* (☎97.53.84.46; ③) or either of the two big campsites, *Le Tindio* (April–Oct; ☎97.53.75.59) or *Port Sable* (April to mid-Oct; ☎97.53.71.98), and you're well-poised for the less crowded beaches east of St-Gildas.

Not far from the end of the peninsula, clearly visible to the north of the main road, is the **Tumulus de Thumiac**, from the top of which Julius Caesar is supposed to have watched the sea battle in among the islands in which the Romans defeated the Veneti – their only naval victory on the ocean, away from the Mediterranean. **PORT NAVALO**, with a couple of hotels and its ferries to the islands (*Vedettes Thalassa*; ☎97.53.70.25), is on the next cape.

A short way north of the Tumulus, the ivy-covered twelfth-century *Moulin du Pen Castel* is an isolated **restaurant** on a small causeway right on the seashore, where the menus include a vegetarian meal for 100F.

St-Gildas-de-Rhuys

At **ST-GILDAS-DE-RHUYS**, Pierre Abélard, the theologian/lover of Héloïse, was abbot for a period from 1126, having been exiled from Paris. "I live in a wild country where every day brings new perils," he wrote to Héloïse, eventually fleeing after his brother monks – hedonists unimpressed by his stern scholasticism – attempted to poison him.

By the beaches around the village are a handful of **campsites**, among them *Le Menhir* (May to mid-Sept; ☎97.45.22.88) and *Les Govelins* (Easter to mid-Sept; ☎97.45.21.67); there's also an average-priced **hotel**, the *Giquel* (☎97.45.23.12; ③).

Sarzeau and the Château de Suscinio

Near **SARZEAU**, which also has accommodation if you're stuck, is the impressive fourteenth-century **Château de Suscinio**. This completely moated castle, once a hunting-lodge of the Dukes of Brittany, is set in marshland at the edge of a tiny village, and contains a sagging but vivid mosaic floor. You can take a precarious stroll around its high ramparts (April–Sept daily except Wed 9.30am–noon & 2–7pm, Wed 2–7pm; rest of year Tues, Sat, Sun & hols 9.30am–noon & 2–5pm; 20F).

The Grande-Brière

South of the River **Vilaine** at La Roche-Bernard you leave the Morbihan – and technically you leave Brittany as well, entering the *département* of Loire Atlantique. The roads veer firmly east and west – to Nantes and La Baule respectively. Inland between them, as you approach the wide Loire estuary, are the other-worldly marshes of the **Grande-Brière**.

These 20,000 acres of peat bog have for centuries been deemed to be the common property of all who live in them. The scattered population, the *Briéroise*, made and make their living by fishing for eels in the streams, gathering reeds, and – on the nine days permitted each year – cutting the peat. The few villages are known as *îles*, being hard granite outcrops in the boggy wastes. Most of them consist of a circular road around the inside of a ring of thatched cottages, slightly raised above the waters on to which they back. For easy access to the watery flat-lands, filled with lilies and irises and browsed by Shetland ponies, each village is encircled by its own canal, or *curée*. The houses themselves typically consist of two rooms and a stable, with a door on the north side and windows on the south. A few crops are grown in the adjacent ring of fields, which always remain above high water.

This can be quite a captivating region for unhurried exploration, though if you're simply passing through, the waterways are not very visible from the road unless you pause on one of the occasional humpback bridges. Instead, the widely-touted attraction is **renting a punt**, known as a *"chaland"* or a *"blain"*. This activity seems to be promoted with the unstated intention of getting you lost for a few hours with your pole tangled in the rushes.

Much of the Grande-Brière has been designated as a **bird sanctuary**, obviously mostly for waterfowl. The headquarters of the sanctuary (☎40.88.42.72) is in the most authentic surviving village, the **ÎLE DE FEDRUN**, which is filled with traditional dwellings, and also has a small **hotel**, the *Auberge du Parc* (☎40.88.53.01; ④).

The Coast at the mouth of the Loire

There is something very surreal about emerging from the Brière to the coast at **La Baule**. For this is by far Brittany's most upmarket pocket – an imposing, moneyed landscape where the dunes are bonded together no longer with scrub and pines but with massive apartment blocks and luxury hotels. However, in the vicinity of La Baule, **Guérande** is a superb medieval walled town, while **Piriac-sur-mer** and to a lesser extent **Le Croisic** are less frenetic alternatives to the giant resort.

Guérande

On the edge of the marshes of the Grande-Brière, just before you come to the sea, is the absolutely gorgeous walled town of **GUÉRANDE**, which gave its name to this peninsula and derived its fortune from controlling the salt pans that form a chequerboard across the surrounding inlets. This "white country" is composed of bizarre-looking *oeillets*, each 70 to 80 square metres in extent, in which sea water, since Roman times, has been collected and evaporated.

Guérande today, a tiny little place, is still entirely enclosed by its stout fifteenth-century **ramparts**. Although you can't walk along them, a spacious promenade leads right the way around the outside, passing four fortified gateways; for half its length the broad old moat remains filled with water.

Within the walls, pedestrians share the narrow cobbled streets with the odd car, the old houses are bright with window boxes, and there's a market in the centre next to St-Aubin church. Nearby, the pretty *Roc-Maria*, 1 rue des Halles (☎40.24.90.51; closed Wed & Thurs in low season; ④), offers cosy rooms above a *crêperie* in a fifteenth-century town house. Opposite the porte Vannetoise and the most impressive stretch of ramparts, to the north, the *Hôtel de Voyageurs*, 1 place du 8 Mai 1945 (☎40.24.90.13; hotel closed mid-Dec to mid-Jan, Sun pm & Mon in low season; restaurant closed Oct–March; ④), is a *logis* serving good menus from 95F.

Piriac-sur-mer

If you prefer your seaside resorts quiet and peaceful, head west from Guérande to **PIRIAC-SUR-MER**, 13km distant, instead of continuing to La Baule. Although the adjacent headland offers some fine sandy beaches within a couple of minutes' walk from the centre, the pleasant little village itself turns its back on the Atlantic, preferring to face the protective jetty that curls back into the little bay to shield its small fishing fleet. Its twisting narrow lanes see enough tourists in summer to keep half a dozen *crêperies* in business, of which the nicest is the *St-Michel*, whose courtyard tables take up most of the place de la Chope, between the old granite church and the beach.

There are also a handful of **hotels**, with the *Hôtel-Restaurant de la Pointe* (March–Oct; ☎40.23.50.04; closed Wed in low season; ②) looking out over the port, and the *Hôtel de la Poste*, in a large house at 26 rue de la Plage (April–Nov; ☎40.23.50.90; ③), a few streets in from the sea. The shady *Parc du Guibel* (May–Sept; ☎40.23.52.67), further on towards Mesquer, is among the best of several local **campsites**.

La Baule

LA BAULE certainly is a place apart from its rival Breton resorts, almost any of which can seem appealingly rustic and shambolic by comparison. Sited on the long stretch of dunes that link the former island of Le Croisic to the mainland, it owes its existence to a violent storm in 1779 that engulfed the old town of Escoublac in silt from the Loire, and thereby created a wonderful crescent of sandy beach. That has survived, albeit now lined for several kilometres with a Riviera-style spread of palm-tree-fronted hotels and residences.

Neither La Baule's permanence nor its affluence seems in any doubt these days. This is a resort that very firmly imagines itself in the South of France: around the crab-shaped bay, bronzed nymphettes and would-be Clint Eastwoods ride across the sands into the sunset against a backdrop of cruising lifeguards, horse-dung removers and fantastically priced cocktails. It can be fun if you feel like a break from the more subdued Breton attractions – and the beach is undeniably impressive. It's not a place to imagine you're going to enjoy strolling around in search of hidden charms; the backstreets have an oddly rural feel, but hold nothing of any interest.

Practicalities

Full details on staying in La Baule can be had from the **SI**, away from the seafront in a new post-modern office at 8 place de la Victoire (mid-May to mid-Sept daily 9am–7pm; mid-Sept to mid-May Mon–Sat 9.30am–noon & 2–6pm; ☎40.24.34.44). La Baule has two **gare SNCFs**, the barely-used La-Baule-les-Pins, and the main La-Baule-Escoublac near the SI on place Rhin-et-Danube (☎40.66.50.50), where the TGVs from Paris arrive. The **gare routière** is at 4 place de la Victoire (☎40.60.25.58).

Few of the **hotels** are cheap, particularly in the high season, and in the low season more than half of them are closed. The very cheapest year-round options are near the main gare SNCF, less than 1km from the beach; these include *Hôtel Violetta*, 44 av Clémenceau (☎40.60.32.16; ③), and *Hôtel-Restaurant la Coquille*, 10 av Clémenceau (☎40.60.38.47; ②). Right in the centre, set back less than fifty metres from the sea and not far from the SI, is the *Lutetia* at 13 av des Evens (☎40.60.25.81; ⑤), where the *Rossini* restaurant (closed Sun pm & Mon) offers magnificent fish cookery on menus that start at 110F. The best of the **campsites**, 2km back from the beach, is *La Roserie*, 20 av Sohier (April–Sept; ☎40.60.46.66).

Le Croisic and beyond

The small port of **LE CROISIC**, sheltering from the ocean around the corner of the headland, is probably a more realistic (and to many perceptions, more attractive) place to stay than La Baule. These days it's basically a pleasure port, but fishing boats do still sail from its harbour, near the very slender mouth of the bay, and there's a modern **fish market** near the long Tréhic jetty, where you can go to see the day's catch auctioned. The hills on either side of the harbour, Mont Lenigo and Mont Esprit, are not natural; they are formed from the ballast left by the ships of the salt trade. If you are staying, choose between the **hotels** *Les Nids*, 83 bd Général-Leclerc (☎40.23.00.63; ④), or the purple-and-white *Estacade*, near the end of the port at 4 quai de Lénigo (☎40.23.03.77; ④), where the 78F menu includes *soupe de poissons* and fish of the day.

Close by, all around the rocky sea coast known as the **Grande Côte**, are a whole range of **campsites**. Just outside Le Croisic itself is the *Océan* (April–Sept; ☎40.23.07.69); at Batz, another former island, is the *Casse Cailloux* (May–Sept; ☎40.23. 91.71). For equally good beaches and a chance of cheaper **hotel** accommodation, you could alternatively go east from La Baule to **PORNICHET** (though preferably keeping away from the plush marina) or to the tiny **ST-MARC**, where in 1953 Jacques Tati filmed *Monsieur Hulot's Holiday*.

St-Nazaire

The best sandy coves in the region, bizarrely enough, are to be found on the outskirts of **ST-NAZAIRE**: just off to the west, they are linked by wooded paths and almost deserted. But it's a gloomy city, distinguishable from afar by the black silhouettes of its mighty cranes and the soaring arch of the Loire bridge. Bombed to extinction in the last war, its shipyards, in more or less continuous operation since they built Julius Caesar's fleet, are closing all around it.

The one reason you might want to stay is the relative ease of finding inexpensive **hotel** space – so elusive in this area in summer. Options include the *Lapeyre*, 2 rue de la Paix (☎40.22.55.09; ②), and the new *Korali* opposite the station

(☎40.01.89.89; ③). There's also a **hostel**, the *Foyer du Jeune Travailleur*, at 30 rue Soleil-Levant (☎40.22.51.04).

South of the Loire

From St-Nazaire you can cross the mouth of the Loire via an inspired piece of engineering, the **Pont St-Nazaire**. This is a great elongated S-curve of a suspension bridge, its lines only visible at an acute angle at either end. A hefty toll is demanded for the privilege of driving across its 3km length, but bikes go for free.

From this high viewpoint (up to 131m), you can see that **the Loire** is a definite climatic dividing line (a point regularly confirmed by French television weather bulletins). To the north of the river, the houses have steep grey slate roofs against the storms; to the south, in the *Pays de Retz*, the roofs are flat and red tiled. Nonetheless the vast deposits of Loire silt have affected both banks of the huge estuary – they buried the ancient town of Montoise on the southern side just as they did Escoublac to the north.

As you continue **south** along the coast, Brittany begins to slip away. Dolmens stand above the ocean, and the rocky coast is interspersed with bathing beaches, but the climate, the architecture, the countryside and, most obvious of all, the vineyards make it clear that this is the start of the South.

Pornic

The **Pays de Retz** coast is developed for most of its length – an almost unbroken line of holiday flats, *pepsi*, *frites*, and *crêpes* stands. **PORNIC** is the nicest of the resorts, with a still-functional fishing port and one of "Bluebeard" Gilles de Rais' many castles. It is a small place: you can walk beyond the harbour and along the cliffs to a tiny beach where the rock walls glitter from phosphorescent sea water. The **hotels** in town are not cheap, though better value than those of La Baule. The *Relais Saint Gilles* (mid-March to mid-Nov; ☎40.82.02.25; ④), just down the road from the post office, is the most reasonable, with a menu to match.

Inland towards Nantes

As you head away from the coast, towards the metropolis of Nantes, the countryside is once more marshy, although richer than that of the Brière, with some scenic lakes and waterways. The largest of the lakes, the **Grand-Lieu**, contains two drowned villages, Murin and Langon. Along the **estuary** itself, the towns are depressed and depressing, their traditional industries struck hard by unemployment.

For **NANTES** itself, see Chapter 6.

travel details

Trains

Redon–Quimper/Brest 4 times daily *TGV*, stopping at Vannes (25min), Auray (40min) and Lorient (1hr), plus 5 slower services, stopping at Questembert (25min), Vannes (45min), Auray (1hr) and Lorient (1hr 30min).

Auray–Quiberon The *Tire Bouchon* runs 3 times daily between mid-June and mid-Sept (40min), stopping at Plouharnel (20min) with connecting buses to Carnac and La Trinité.

Le Croisic–Paris (3hr 10min), 5 express *TGV* services daily, via **La Baule** (10min), **St-**

Nazaire (20min) and Nantes (1hr 10min); also 5 normal services daily from Le Croisic to **Nantes** (1hr 20min), for connecting trains to Paris and elsewhere.

Buses

From Vannes to Rennes (8 daily; 2hr) via Josselin (1hr); to Nantes via La Roche Bernard (1hr 30min); to Quiberon (1hr 45min) via Auray and Carnac (1hr 15min); and to Larmor-Baden via Arradon: all run by *TTO* (☎97.47.29.64).

From Vannes to Arzon; to Pontivy; and to Elven, Malestroit and Ploërmel: operated by *CTM* from the place de la Gare (☎97.01.22.10).

From Vannes to Port-Blanc (for the Île aux Moines), *Transport Cautru*, 26 rue Hoche (☎97.47.22.86).

From Auray From the *SNCF*: 4 daily to Quiberon (1hr) via Carnac (30min); 4 daily to Vannes (30min); both services operated by *Transports Le Bayon* (☎97.57.31.31).

From Lorient From the *SNCF*: 4 daily to Pontivy (1hr); 2 daily to Carnac (1hr).

Air

From Lorient direct flights to **Paris**, twice daily from Easter–Oct. Contact Lorient (☎97.82.32.93) or Vannes (☎97.60.78.79). To Belle-Île, by arrangement with *Insul'Air* (☎97.31.41.14).

From Quiberon Aérodrome (☎97.31.83.09 or 97.30.40.00), Easter–Oct, trips around Gulf of Morbihan, over Carnac, and to Belle-Île.

Ferries
• Groix
From Lorient: 8 per day July–Aug, 4 per day rest of year; 45min, 82F return (☎97.21.03.97).

From Concarneau: Day trips leave Wed & Sun 8.45am, July & Aug only, 140F (☎98.97.10.31).
• Lorient
Shuttle service to Port-Louis, 20 per day (☎97.33.40.55).
• Belle Île
For details of ferries to Belle-Île from **Quiberon**, **Lorient**, **Vannes**, **La Trinité**, **Port-Navalo**, **Locmariaquer**, **Auray** and **Le Bono**, see p.292.
• Gulf of Morbihan
For details of gulf tours and trips to the islands, from **Vannes**, **Locmariaquer**, **Auray**, **Port-Navalo**, **La Trinité** and **Le Bono**, see p.306 or contact *Navix* (☎97.46.60.00), *Compagnie des Îles* (☎97.46.18.19), or *Vedettes Blanches Armor* (☎97.57.15.27).
• Houat and Hoëdic
From Quiberon, 1hr, 4 daily July–Aug, 1 daily rest of year, 82F (☎97.50.06.90).

From La Trinité and **Port-Navalo**, Houat Tues, Thurs & Sat, July & Aug,105F (☎97.46.60.00).

PART FOUR

THE

CONTEXTS

A BRIEF HISTORY OF BRITTANY AND NORMANDY

Although Brittany and Normandy – the western provinces – have belonged to the French State for over 450 years, they have been distinct entities throughout recorded history and their traditions and interests remain separate.

Brittany, for most of the five millennia during which its past can be traced, drew its cultural links and influences not inland, from the rest of France, but from the Atlantic seaboard. Isolated both by the difficulty of its marsh and moorland terrain, and its sheer distance from the heartland of Europe, it was nonetheless at the centre of a sophisticated prehistoric culture intimately connected with those of Britain and Ireland. It is populated today by the descendants of the Celtic immigrants who arrived from Britain and Ireland at around the time that the Romans were leaving. The "golden age" of Brittany came in the fifteenth century, when it was ruled as an independent Duchy – but it was eventually absorbed into France after centuries of military and dynastic struggles with the English.

The economic decline of the province in recent centuries is attributed by Breton nationalists wholly to the union with France. Other factors, inevitably, were also at play, but it's certainly true to say that the rulers of France often ignored or oppressed their westernmost region, and even now the current revival of Brittany's fortunes is largely due to the conscious attempt to revive the old pan-Celtic trading routes.

Normandy has no equivalent prehistoric remains, and only very briefly did it possess the identity of an independent nation. Its founders were Scandinavian, the Vikings who raided along the Seine in the ninth century. These Northmen gave the region its name, and were the warriors who brought it military glory in the great Norman age of the eleventh century, when William conquered England and his nobles controlled swathes of land as far afield as Sicily and the Near East. They were also responsible for the cathedrals, castles and monasteries that are the most enduring monuments of Normandy's past.

The Normans blended into the general mass of the population, both in France and in England, and Normandy itself was formally surrendered to Louis IX by Henry III of England in 1259. After the fluctuations of the Hundred Years War, the province was firmly integrated into France, and all but disappears from history until the Allied invasion of 1944. Supposedly, a handful of Normans still regard Queen Elizabeth II as the true Duchess of Normandy, a title she does, in fact, bear. The majority of contemporary Normans, however, put their faith in the industrial and agricultural wealth of the province, and take pride in their individualism and conservatism.

THE MEGALITHS OF BRITTANY

Megalithic sites can be found all around the Mediterranean, most notably in Malta and Sardinia, and along the Atlantic seaboard from Spain to Scandinavia. Among the most significant are Newgrange in Ireland, Stonehenge in England and the Ring of Brodgar in the Orkneys. The megalith-building culture is no longer thought to have originated in the Mediterranean and spread out to the "barbarian" outposts of Europe. In fact, the tumuli, alignments and single standing stones of Brittany are of pre-eminent importance. The very words used for the megaliths are Breton: *menhir* (long stone), *dolmen* (flat stone), *cromlech* (stone circle). And, dated at 5700 BC, the tumulus of Kercado at

Carnac, in southern Brittany, appears to be the earliest stone construction in Europe, predating the palace of Knossos on Crete and even the Egyptian pyramids.

Each megalithic centre seems to have had its own distinct styles and traditions. Brittany has relatively few stone circles, and a greater proportion of free-standing stones; fewer burials, and more evidence of ritual fires; different styles of carving; and, uniquely, the sheer complexity of the Carnac alignments, which may be an astronomical observatory. (The fact that so many megalithic remains are on bleak seaside heathland sites may just be because these were the most likely to survive; those at Rétiers and Fougères do not fit the stereotype.)

Little is known of the **people** who erected the megaliths. Only rarely have skeletons been found in the graves, but what few there have been seem to indicate a short, dark, hairy race with a life expectancy of no more than the mid-30s. Legends speak of shambling subhuman giants who served as their slaves, who assisted Merlin in bringing the slabs of

Stonehenge from Wales, and who built the Giant's Causeway on the coast of Antrim. What is certain is that the civilization was a long-lasting one; the earliest and the latest constructions at Carnac are over five thousand years apart.

As for the actual **purpose of the stones**, there are numerous theories and few definite conclusions. Flaubert commented that "those who like mythology see them as the Pillars of Hercules; those who like natural history see here a symbol of the Python ... lovers of astronomy see a zodiac". In the eighteenth century, for example, enthusiasts managed to see snakes in everything, and declared the megalithic sites to be remnants of some Druidic serpent cult. In fact, the stones were already ancient before the Druids appeared. Innumerable theses have wandered off into considerations of "Lost Atlantis", water-divining, mysterious psychic energies and extra-terrestrial assistance.

The **theories** gaining most popular acceptance these days see the megaliths as part of a

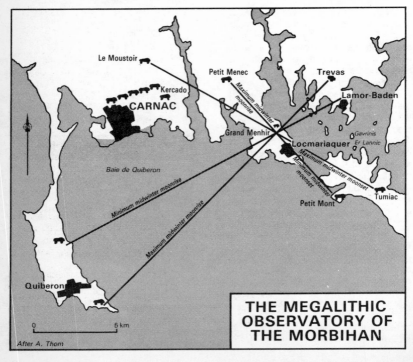

THE MEGALITHIC
OBSERVATORY OF
THE MORBIHAN

vast system of **astronomical measurement**, record-keeping and prediction. Precise measurements of sites all over Europe suggest that they share a standard measure of length, the "megalithic yard" (2.72 modern feet). In Brittany, the argument goes, the now fallen Grand Menhir of Locmariaquer was erected, using this prehistoric calibration, as a "universal lunar foresight". Its alignments with eight other sites are said to correspond to the eight extreme points of the rising and setting of the moon during its 18.61-year cycle. The Golfe de Morbihan was the ideal place for such a marking stone – set on a lagoon surrounded by low peninsulas, the menhir was visible from all directions. Once the need for the Grand Menhir was decided upon, it would then have taken hundreds of years of careful observation of the moon to fix the exact spot for it. It is thought that this was done by lighting fires on the top of high poles at trial points on the crucial nights every nine years. The alignments of Carnac are thus explained as the graph paper, as it were, on which the lunar movements were plotted.

This "megalithic observatory" explanation, researched in great detail by Professor Thom, despite being hindered by occasional "encounters with irate peasants" and most clearly expounded in his *Megalithic Remains in Britain and Brittany* (1978), is certainly appealing. However, **rival experts** have come up with damning counter-evidence. To quote from Aubrey Burl's authoritative *Megalithic Brittany* (1985): "of the eight proposed backsights, three do not exist, and of the five others the Carnac mound at Tumiac is not accurately placed, the Goulvarch menhir, the stone at Kerran, the Carnac mound of Le Moustoir with its menhir, and the passage grave of Petit-Mont, are too dissimilar in architecture and date to be convincing purpose-built Neolithic viewing-stations." Doubts are even cast as to whether the Grand Menhir ever stood, and the measurements are accused of ignoring the difference in sea-level 5000 years ago.

In any case, the stones at Carnac have been so greatly eroded that perhaps it is little more than wishful thinking to imagine that their original size, shape and orientation can be accurately determined. They have been knocked down and pulled out by farmers seeking to cultivate the land; they have been quarried for use in making roads; they have been removed by landowners angry at the trespass of tourists and scientists; nineteenth-century pseudo-scientists have tampered with them, re-erecting some and shifting others; and what may have gone on in much earlier periods is anyone's guess.

An alternative approach is more sociological. This argues that the stones date from the great period of transition when humankind was changing from a predatory role to a producing one, and that they can only have been erected by the co-ordinated efforts of a large and stable **community**. In 1979 an experiment was carried out in which it took 260 people, using rollers, to set up a 32,000 kilogram stone, as well as a large number of others to provide food and shelter. The united physical exertion created very much a festival atmosphere, and the participants described the event as a "bonding" experience. Those who originally and perhaps unwillingly dragged the Carnac stones into place might feel that to be a trifle sentimental. Even so, it does make some sense to imagine the act of setting up a menhir as serving a valuable social purpose, both as an achievement and as a celebration. The annual or occasional setting-up of a new stone is easier to envisage than the vast effort required to erect them all at once. In which case the social significance of constructing these lines, mounds and circles, could have been of greater importance than any physical characteristics of the arrangements themselves.

For all the pervasive legends, the megaliths cannot be attributed to the Celts. Even so, theological parallels have been drawn between ancient and modern **Breton beliefs**. It is argued that there is a uniquely Breton attitude to death, dating back thousands of years, in which the living are in everyday communication with the dead. The phenomenon of the "parish close" is said to mirror the design of the ancient passage graves, with the Christian ossuary serving the same function as the buried passageways of the old tombs – a link between the place of the dead and the place of the living.

True or false, the popular significance of the prehistoric sites was something about which later Christian authorities were somewhat ambivalent. They felt it necessary to place crosses on the top of many menhirs, or even to destroy them altogether. There are reports of the "Indecent Stone" at Reguiny being "cut down and made harmless" in 1825, and of steps being taken to stop naked couples sliding down the Grand Menhir on May Day as a fertility rite, or rubbing against the "protuberances" of the Kerloas menhir.

CELTS AND ROMANS

Both the Bretons and the Normans make their first appearance in recorded history as traders in **tin and copper**. Small trading ports emerged all along the Atlantic coast, and the routes went up the rivers Loire and Seine. Iron Age forts, traces of one of which remain in the forest of Huelgoat, show evidence of large-scale stable communities even far inland. The tin itself was mostly mined in Cornwall, and the Seine became important as the "Tin Road", the most direct means for the metals to be transported towards the heart of Europe.

That was why the **Romans'** top priority, when they came to Gaul centuries later, was to secure control of the Seine valley and tie the province firmly into the network of empire. Brittany, less accessible to the invading armies, was able to put up a more spirited resistance, although sadly there was no such last-ditch rebel stronghold as Asterix's fictional village. The **Breton Gauls**, descendants of a first influx of Celts, were divided into five major tribes, each of which controlled an area roughly corresponding to the modern *départements*.

The most powerful of these tribes were the **Veneti**, based in the Morbihan with what is now Vannes as their capital. The decisive sea battle in which they were defeated in 56 BC took place around the Golfe de Morbihan and was the only major naval battle the Romans ever won outside the Mediterranean. Seafaring was not one of the Romans' strong points – hence their predilection for roads and foot-slogging – but on this occasion their galleys, built somewhere near St-Nazaire, had far superior mobility to the leather-sailed ships of the Veneti. The cost of defeat for the tribes was severe; those who were not killed were sold into slavery, and their children mutilated. Julius Caesar was there to see the battle; he went no further than Auray, but the whole Breton peninsula was swiftly conquered, and incorporated with much of Normandy into the province of Armorica.

Roman Armorica experienced five hundred years of peace, though without the benefit of any great prosperity. While the Roman-built roads were the first efficient means of land communication, they served mainly to channel wealth away towards the centre of their empire. Walled cities were founded, such as Rennes, Vannes, Rouen and Caen, but little was done to change, let alone improve, the lives of the native population.

What civilizing effect the Romans had had disappeared in any case during the **barbarian invasions** as the Empire disintegrated at the start of the fifth century. The one thread of continuity was provided by the Christian church. The first **Christians** had already arrived in Normandy during Roman rule, and at Rouen the bishopric had been established by Saint Mellon as early as AD 300. They were followed in the fifth and sixth centuries by waves of Celtic immigrants crossing from Britain to Brittany. Traditional history considered these to be "Dark Ages" of terror and chaos throughout Europe, with the immigrants as no more than panic-stricken refugees. However, recent evidence of stable diplomatic and trading contact across the Channel suggests that there was a much more ordered process of movement and interchange.

The vigorous Welsh and Irish missionaries named their new lands **Little Britain**, and their Christianity supplanted the old Celtic and Roman gods. The era is characterized by great legendary confrontations of elemental forces – the Devil grappling with the Archangel Michael from Dol to Mont-St-Michel, Saint Pol driving out the "laidley worm" from the Île de Batz – symbolizing the forcible expulsion of paganism. Often the changes were little more than superficial; crosses were erected on top of menhirs, mystical springs and wells became the sites of churches, Christian processions such as *pardons* traced circuits of megalithic sites, and ancient tales of magic and witchcraft were retold as stories of Jesus and the saints. The names of innumerable Celtic religious leaders – Malo, Brieuc, Pol – have survived in place names, even if the Church has never officially recognized them as saints.

The cultural links with Britain and Ireland meant that Brittany played an important role in many of the **Arthurian legends**. Breton minstrels, like their Welsh counterparts, did much to popularize the tales in the Middle Ages. None of the local claimants to Arthur's Camelot carries much conviction, although Tristan who loved Iseult came from Brittany (the lovers may have hidden at Trémazan castle in Finistère – see p.226), as did King Ban and his son Lancelot. Sir Galahad found the Holy Grail somewhere in Broceliande Forest, which was also the home of such diverse residents as Merlin, Morgan le Fay and the Fisher King.

Such legends reflect the fact that for all this time, central Brittany was an almost impenetrable wilderness, and the region as a whole was split into two separate petty monarchies, Dumnonia in the north and Cornubia (the basis of Cornuaille) in the south. Charlemagne amalgamated the two by force under **Frankish control** in 799, after they had consistently failed to pay tribute. When the Frankish Empire began to fall apart, their appointee as governor, **Nominoë**, seized the opportunity to become the first leader of an independent Brittany, by defeating Charles the Bald in the battle of Redon (near modern La Bataille) in 845. He has taken on the status of a prototype independent leader in Breton history.

Without Celtic immigration on anything like the same scale, it took longer for **Normandy** to become fully Christianized. It was only when it too came under the control of Charlemagne's **Merovingian** dynasty that the newly founded monasteries of Jumièges and St-Wandrille became pre-eminent. As the Franks' authority weakened over the succeeding centuries, there were repeated Viking raids along the Seine. Major incursions took place in the second half of the ninth century, interspersed with attempts to conquer England. They came more often and for longer, until in 911 King Charles the Simple acknowledged the inevitable and granted their leader **Rollo** formal title to the **Duchy of Normandy**.

THE NORMANS

In the eleventh century **the Normans** became one of the most significant forces in Europe. Not only did the Dukes of Normandy invade and conquer England, but Norman mercenaries and adventurers fought to gain lands for themselves wherever they found the opportunity. They insinuated themselves into the wars of Italy, individually acquiring control of Aversa, Apulia and Calabria, and most of Sicily, their greatest prize. They took part in the church's wars, too, fighting in campaigns in Greece against Byzantium, and in the First Crusade – which in 1098 saw the Norman leader Bohemond take Antioch.

In their adopted French homeland, the pagan Scandinavians had so rapidly adopted the culture, language and religion of their new subjects that spoken Norse had died out in Rouen by the time of Rollo's grandson, Duke Richard I. Yet they were still seen as a race apart – and not a very pleasant one at that. One authority describes them as without exception physically repellent, cruel and unscrupulous.

Duke William's **invasion of England** is portrayed by the Bayeux Tapestry as a just struggle: the result solely of William's conviction that he was the rightful heir to Edward the Confessor, a succession acknowledged under oath by Harold. Be that as it may, the sheer speed of what proved to be such a permanent conquest indicates the extent of Norman power at the time. Having crossed the Channel to defeat the usurper Harold in September 1066, the Conqueror was crowned King in Westminster Abbey on Christmas Day, and by the next Easter was secure enough to be able to return to Normandy. The Battle of Hastings was a decisive moment in the balance of Europe. Almost paradoxically, the Norsemen from France finally freed England from the threat of invasion from Scandinavia, which had persisted for centuries up until 1070. English attention was thus re-orientated towards the mainland of Europe – a shift that was to have a major impact on history.

The Norman capacity for **organization** was primarily responsible not just for the military triumphs, but also for the consolidation of power and wealth that followed. The Domesday Book, which catalogued the riches of England, was paralleled by a similar undertaking in Sicily, the *Catalogus Baronum*. William's son Henry introduced trial by jury in the King's Courts – justice that had to be paid for. Henry II established the Exchequer to collect royal revenue. **Intellectually**, too, the Normans were dominant; the Abbey of Bec-Helluoin was a renowned centre of learning, inspired first by Lanfranc and then by the theologian Anselm, each of whom moved on to become Archbishop of Canterbury. And **architecturally**, the wealth and technical expertise of the Normans made possible the construction of such lasting monuments as the cathedrals of Bayeux, Coutances and Durham, and the monasteries of Mont-St-Michel, Jumièges and Caen.

The twelfth-century **"Anglo-Normans"** who invaded Ireland were recognizably descended from the army of the Conqueror, and Norman French remained the legal and administrative language of England until 1400. Elsewhere the mark of the conquerors was less distinct. The Norman Kings of Sicily did not style themselves Normans, and ruled over a cosmopolitan society dependent largely on the skills of Moslem craftsmen. Their architecture barely resembles what is thought of today as "Norman", and the Norman bloodline soon vanished into the general population of Sicily.

However, for the duchy and the kingdom on either side of the Channel, the shared rulers made close connections inevitable. The Norman lords in England required luxury items to be imported. Flemish weavers were encouraged to settle in London and East Anglia, and gradually the centre of affluence and importance shifted away from Normandy. By the time Henry II, great-grandson of William the Conqueror, inherited the throne, England was a major power and the seeds of the Hundred Years War had been sown. Fifteen years later Château Gaillard on the Seine was taken by **Phillipe Auguste**, and Normandy for the first time became part of France.

THE HUNDRED YEARS WAR

While Normandy was at the height of its power, the Bretons lived in constant fear of invasion by their belligerent neighbours. Although their own leaders had managed to prevent a parallel Viking takeover of **Brittany**, it was at the price of numerous **warlords** setting up their own private strongholds. Their emergence seriously weakened the authority of Nominoë's successors, and the resultant anarchy devastated the Breton economy. Frequent power bids by the Norman English and the kings of France – the **Hundred Years War** – hardly helped the situation.

Bertrand du Guesclin, born in 1321 in the unprepossessing town of Broons, south of Dinan, was the outstanding military genius of the Middle Ages. After an ignominious start when his father disowned him because of his extraordinary ugliness, he practised his novel tactics as an outlaw chief in the heart of Brittany. With little truck for chivalric conventions, he simplified the chaotic feudal map, and, in a bewildering succession of French and Spanish campaigns, earned the command of the French army. He taught the French to fight dirty – in medieval terms. Nobles were forced to dismount and fight on foot; his soldiers were paid so that they did not alienate the peasantry by plundering. This formidable man was responsible for the development of the use of gunpowder, combined with new assault techniques capable of devastating the strongest fortresses; he eschewed pre-arranged battles in favour of ambush and general guerrilla tactics.

The net result of du Guesclin's strategies was that by 1377 the English had been driven almost completely out of France. Virtually every town and castle in Brittany and Normandy seems to have some du Guesclin connection; not only did he live, besiege or fight almost everywhere, but after his death in 1380, parts of his body were buried in no less than four different cities. Yet despite all his myriad intrigues and battles, Brittany benefited very little from his activities.

The **Hundred Years War** resurfaced after du Guesclin's death, with much of the fighting taking place in Normandy. Henry V recaptured the province step by step, until by 1420 he was in a position to demand recognition of his claim to the French throne. Eight years later, the French were defending their last significant stronghold, Orléans on the Loire. It was here that the extraordinary figure of **Joan of Arc** appeared on the scene and relieved the siege of the city. In a very different way to du Guesclin she ensured that the mass of ordinary, miserable peasants, not to mention the demoralized soldiers of the French army, made the enemy occupation untenable. Within two astonishing years, the Dauphin, not Henry, had been crowned. Joan herself was captured by the Burgundian allies of the occupiers, tried by a French bishop and an English commander, and burnt at the stake as a witch on place

Vieux-Marché in Rouen. But in 1449 her king, Charles VII, was able to make a triumphal entry into the regional capital. Within twelve months this latest thirty-two-year English occupation of Normandy was at an end.

THE DUCHY OF BRITTANY

Breton involvement in the opening stages of the second phase of the Hundred Years War was minimal and from 1399–1442 **Duc Jean V** took a neutral stand, allowing the economy of the province to prosper. Fishing, ship-building and sail manufacture developed, accompanied by a flowering of the arts. It was in this period that the Kreisker chapel and the church of Folgoët were built.

Although involvement in the Anglo-French conflict was inevitable, Jean's heirs for a time continued to rule over a successful and **independent duchy**. Arthur III, duke in the mid-fifteenth century, had fought alongside Joan of Arc but used his connections with the French army to protect Breton autonomy. His successor, however, Duc François II, was less astute. Brittany, the last large region of present-day France to resist agglomeration, was a very desirable prize for King Louis XI. To resist encroachment, François needed allies beyond France; and in looking for those allies he antagonized and alarmed the French. A pretext was eventually found for the royal army to invade Brittany, where the Breton army was defeated at the battle of St-Aubin-du-Cormier in 1488. Duc François was forced to concede to the French King the right to determine his own daughter's marriage, and died of shame, so the story goes, within a few weeks.

François' heiress, **Duchess Anne**, was to be the last ruler of an independent Brittany. Having once been engaged to the Prince of Wales, she then married Maximilian of Austria by proxy, in the hope of a strong alliance against the French. Charles VIII of France (who was himself in theory married to Maximilian's daughter) demanded adherence to the treaty of 1488, captured Nantes, advanced north and west and proposed to Anne.

By and large the population preferred a royal wedding to death by starvation or massacre. Anne bemoaned "Must I thus be so unfortunate and friendless as to have to enter into marriage with a man who has so ill-treated me?" – and

then, to the amazement of all, the couple actually fell in love with each other. Despite the marriage, the Duchy remained independent – but Anne was contractually obliged to marry Charles' successor should he die before they produced an heir. When Charles duly bumped his head and died in 1498, his successor, Louis XII, divorced his wife and married Anne. This time Anne's position was considerably stronger, and in the contract she laid down certain conditions that were to be a source of Breton pride and frustration for many centuries. The three main clauses stipulated that no taxes could be imposed without the consent of the Breton *États*; conscripts were only to fight for the defence of Brittany; and Bretons could only be tried in their own courts. When Anne died, Bretons mourned – all records show that she was a genuinely loved leader.

In 1514, the still independent Duchy passed to Anne's daughter Claude, whom the future François I of France married with every intention of incorporating Brittany into his kingdom. This he did and the permanent **union of Brittany and France** was endorsed by the Breton *États* at Vannes in 1532. In theory, the act confirmed Anne's stipulations that all the rights and privileges of Brittany would be observed and safeguarded as inviolable. But it was rarely honoured and their subsequent violation by successive French kings and governments has been the source of conflict ever since.

THE ANCIEN RÉGIME

As the French crown gradually consolidated its power and began to centralize its economy, the ports of the two western provinces developed, serving the **colonial interests** of the state. In fact as early as 1364 sailors from Dieppe had established the city of Petit Dieppe in what is now Sierra Leone. Le Havre was founded in 1517 to be France's premier Atlantic port and, between intermittent attacks and takeovers by the English, became a centre for the coffee and cotton markets. Sailors from Granville, Dieppe and Cherbourg set up colonies in Brazil, Canada, Florida and Louisiana.

In Brittany, St-Malo and Lorient were the two top trading ports, with the latter benefiting every time the English decided to harass Channel ports and shipping. **Jacques Cartier** of St-Malo sailed up the St Lawrence river and added Canada to the possession of the French crown. Nantes too was an important base for trade with the Americas, India and the Middle East, with **slaves** one of the most profitable "commodities". Though the business of exploitation and battles with rival foreign ships was motivated by private profit, the net result was very much to the advantage of the state.

The early contact with England, and the cosmopolitan nature of its Channel ports, meant that Normandy became one of the main Protestant centres of France, with Caen and its university having very active Huguenot populations. The region was therefore in the front line when the **Wars of Religion** flared up in 1561– 3, and again in 1574–6. When the Edict of Nantes, with its Protestant privileges and immunities, was revoked, large-scale Huguenot emigration took place, seriously damaging the local textile industry.

Brittany, on the other hand, was an area of minimal Protestant presence, and the Wars of Religion were only significant as a cover for a brief attempt to win back independence. Breton linen manufacture had taken advantage of the lack of French tolls and customs dues, and declined much later – when England, post-Industrial Revolution, was flooding the market with mass-produced textiles.

Although the power of the French kings increased over the centuries, practical considerations meant that outlying regions were not always completely under royal control. The rural nobles were persistently lawless, and intermittent **peasant revolts** took place, such as that of the dispossessed *nu-pieds* in 1639. In 1675 came the most serious rebellion against the Crown, when Louis XIV's finance minister put a tax on tobacco, pewter and all legal documents to raise money for the war with Holland. This "Stamped Paper" revolt, which started with riots in Nantes, Rennes and Guingamp, soon spread to the country, with the peasants making demands very similar in their content to those of the revolutionaries over a hundred years later. The aristocracy took great delight in brutally crushing the uprising, pillaging several towns and stringing up insurgents and bystanders from every tree.

The reign of **Louis XIV** saw numerous infringements of Breton liberties, including the uprooting of vines throughout the province on the royal grounds that the people were all drunkards. If the Bretons could not get revenge, they could at least be entertained by court scandals. In 1650 Louis' Superintendent of Finance, **Nicolas Fouquet**, bought the entire island of Belle-Île and fortified it as his own private kingdom. The alarmed King had to send D'Artagnan and the Three Musketeers to arrest him before his ambitious plans went any further.

While taxes on Brittany increased in the early eighteenth century, Normandy found new prosperity from the closeness of Paris for its edible produce. Lace-making became a major regional industry, and several abbeys that had been closed during the Wars of Religion were now in consequence revitalized. However, by 1763 France had lost Canada and given up all pretensions to India. The ports declined and trade fell off as England became the workshop of the world.

THE REVOLUTION

The people of both Brittany and Normandy at first welcomed the **Revolution**. Breton representatives at the *États Généraux* in Paris seized the opportunity to air all Brittany's grievances, and the "Club Breton" they formed was the basis of the **Jacobins**. Caen, meanwhile, became the centre of the bourgeois **Girondist** faction. In August of 1789 it was a Breton *député* who proposed the abolition of privileges. However, under the Convention it became clear that the price to be paid for the elimination of the *ancien régime* was further reductions in local autonomy and the suppression of the Breton language.

Neither province was sympathetic to the execution of the King – in Rouen 30,000 people took to the streets to express their opposition. The Girondins came out worst in the factional infighting at the Convention, having opposed the abolition of the monarchy and supported the disastrous war in the Netherlands. Some Girondist deputies managed to flee the edict of June 2, 1793 which ordered their arrest, but the army they organized to march on Paris was defeated at Pacy-sur-Eure. The final major Norman contribution to Revolutionary history was provided on that same day by **Charlotte**

Corday of Caen, when she stabbed Jean-Paul Marat in his bath.

The concerted attack on religion and the clergy was not happily received, particularly in Brittany where the church was closely bound up with the region's independent identity. The attempt to conscript an army of 300,000 Bretons was deeply resented as an infringement of the Act of Union. The popular image of the Revolution in Brittany, where the riots and disturbances of 1787 had been crucial, was now further damaged by the brief **reign of terror** in 1793 of Carrier, the Convention's representative in Nantes. Under the slogan "all the rich, all the merchants are counter-revolutionaries", he killed perhaps 13,000 people in three months, by such methods as throwing prisoners into the Loire tied together in pairs. This was done without Tribunal sanction or approval, and Carrier was himself guillotined before the end of the year.

All this made Brittany an inevitable focal point for the Royalist **counter-revolution** known as the *Chouannerie*, which also had adherents in a few outlying areas of Normandy. A vast invasion force of exiled and foreign nobility, backed by the English, was supposed to sweep through France rallying all dissenters to the Royalist flag. In the event only 8000 landed at Quiberon in 1795, and were not even capable of escaping from the self-imposed trap of the peninsula. They devastated what little they could before themselves being brutally massacred. Much of the local support was motivated by the age-old desire to win back independence, but the Breton *chouans* ("screech owls") fighting elsewhere ended up being tarred with the same aristocratic brush and then abandoned to years of quixotic and doomed guerrilla warfare.

A rebel army continued to fight sporadically in the Cotentin and the Bocage until 1800, while in Brittany another **royalist revolt** in 1799 was easily crushed. In 1804, Cadoudal, "the last *chouan*", was captured and executed in Paris, where he had gone to kidnap Napoléon – having refused the emperor's offer of a generalship if he surrendered.

The rebel movement lingered on until 1832, when the Duchess of Berry failed to engage anyone's interest in the restoration of the *ancien régime*.

THE NINETEENTH CENTURY

Normandy, at the beginning of the nineteenth century, remained a wealthy region despite the crippling of its ports by the blockade imposed by the European coalition against Napoleon. It had proportionally five times as many people elegible, as property owners, to vote as the impoverished mountain areas of the south. Its agriculture accounted for 11 percent of France's produce on 6 percent of its land, while industry remained relatively unadvanced.

When protectionist tariffs were removed from grain in 1828 and Normandy was forced to compete with other producers, widespread **rural arson and tax riots** ensued. But when the revolution of 1848 offered the prospect of socialism, the deeply conservative Catholic peasantry showed little enthusiasm for change. Even the re-emergence of a rural textile industry in the 1840s, relying on outworkers brutally exploited by the Rouen capitalists, added no radical impetus.

The advent of the **railways** and the patronage of the imperial court encouraged the development of Normandy's resorts, while along the Seine, water mills provided the power for the major spinning centres at Louviers, Evreux and Elbeuf. Serious decline did not come until the 1880s, when **rural depopulation** was brought on by emigration combined with a low birth-rate – and a high death-rate in which excessive drinking played a part.

Nineteenth-century Brittany was no longer an official entity, save as five *départements* of France. The railways were of negative benefit, submitting the province to competition from more heavily industrialized regions, while the Nantes–Brest canal did not achieve the expected success, and **emigration** increased. Culturally, the century witnessed a revival of Breton language, customs and folklore but the initiative came from intellectuals, not the mainly illiterate masses.

Around the turn of the **twentieth century** both provinces experienced a surge of artistic creativity, with painters such as Gauguin in Pont-Aven and Monet in Giverny, and such writers as Proust in Normandy and Pierre Loti in Brittany. As everywhere in Europe, this idyll was shattered by the **Great War**; although removed from the actual battlefields, both

Brittany and Normandy were dramatically affected. Brittany, for its size, suffered the heaviest death toll of anywhere in the world. The vast memorial at Ste-Anne-d'Auray is testimony to the extent of the loss, while a parallel spiritual grief can be seen in the dramatic growth in Normandy of the cult of the recently-dead Thérèse of Lisieux. Symbols of a changing world are the two leading aristocratic families of the regions; the heir to the Rohans of Josselin was killed on the Somme, while Prince Louis de Broglie became the first physicist to question the solidity of matter.

WORLD WAR II AND THE BATTLE OF NORMANDY

That the **beaches of Normandy** were chosen as the site of the Allied invasion of Europe in June 1944 was by no means inevitable. Far from the major disputed areas and communication routes of Europe, Normandy had seen almost no military activity since the Hundred Years War. But in that blazing summer, six armies and millions of men fought bloody battles across the placid Norman countryside. A whole swathe of the province was laid in ruins before Hitler's defensive line was broken and the road to Paris cleared.

France, under **Marshal Pétain**, had surrendered to the Germans in 1940. A year later, the fascist armies turned east to invade the Soviet Union – America and Britain declaring full support for the Soviets but resisting Stalin's demand for a second front. In 1942 the two western powers promised a landing in northern France but all that ensued was an abortive commando raid on Dieppe. By the time the second front materialized the tide of the war had already been turned at Stalingrad.

The Germans had meanwhile fortified the whole northwest seaboard of Europe. They expected the attack to come, however, at the Channel's narrowest point, across the Straits of Dover. The **D-Day invasion** of June 6, 1944, was presaged by months of intensive aerial bombardment across Europe, without concentrating too obviously on the chosen landing sites. In the event, the Nazis vastly overestimated Allied resources – two weeks after D-Day Rommel still thought the Normandy landings might be no more than a preliminary diversion to a larger-scale assault around Calais.

A photographic survey of the whole Norman coast had been prepared in Britain, using every possible source including prewar holiday snaps. The landing forces actually took their own "Mulberry" harbours with them (see p.110). The basic plan was for the British and Commonwealth forces under Montgomery to strike for Caen, the pivot around which the Americans (whose General Eisenhower was in overall command) were to swing following their own landings further west.

Not everything went smoothly. There are appalling stories of armoured cars full of men plunging straight to the bottom of the sea as they rolled off landing craft unable to get near enough to the shore. Many of the early objectives took much longer to capture than was originally envisaged – the British took weeks rather than hours to reach Caen, while American hopes of a rapid seizure of the deepwater port at Cherbourg were thwarted. Most notorious of all, the opportunity of capturing the bulk of the German army, which was all but surrounded in the "Falaise pocket", was lost.

Military historians say that man for man the German Army was the more effective fighting force; but with their sheer weight of resources the Allies achieved a fairly rapid victory. There was never a significant German air presence over Normandy since it was all concentrated on the Eastern Front. Parachutists, reconnaissance flights and air support for ground troops were all able to operate virtually unimpeded, as too were the bombing raids on Norman towns and on every bridge across the Seine west of Paris. Furthermore, the muddled enemy command, in which generals at the front were obliged to follow broad directives from Berlin, caused an American general to comment, "one's imagination boggled at what the German army might have done to us without Hitler working so effectively for our side".

Within a few days of D-Day, **De Gaulle** was able to return to Free France, making an emotional first speech at Bayeux (see p.114), while a seasick Winston Churchill sailed up to Deauville in a destroyer and "took a plug at the Hun". At the end of July, General Patton's Third Army broke out across Brittany from Avranches with the aid of 30,000 **French Resistance** fighters, and on August 25 Allied divisions entered Paris, where the German garrison had already been routed by the Resistance. In the east the Red Army were sweeping back the Axis powers.

Though the war in Europe still had several bloody months to run, with Hitler coming very close to smashing the Western front in December 1944, the road to Berlin was finally opening up.

POSTWAR: THE BRETON RESURGENCE

The war left most of Normandy in ruins; while it remained a relatively prosperous area in terms of its produce, decades of reconstruction were required. The development of private transport also meant that Normandy became ever more filled with the second homes of the rich. This has often been resented – the film actor Jean Gabin, for example, was literally besieged in his new country house by hundreds of peasants insisting that he had "too much land", and was obliged to sell some of it off.

Meanwhile, there was very little happening in **postwar Brittany** save ever-increasing migration from the countryside to the main towns and from there, often, out of the province altogether. By the 1950s some 300,000 Bretons lived in Paris, industry was almost exclusively limited to the Loire estuary, and agriculture was dogged by archaic marketing and distribution.

But since the late 1960s Brittany has experienced considerable economic advance, due in part to the initiatives of **Alexis Gourvennec**. He first came to prominence at the age of 24, in 1961, when he led a group of fellow farmers into Morlaix to occupy the government's regional offices in an effective (if violent) protest at exploitation by middlemen. The act set the pace for his lifetime's concern – to obtain the best possible price for Breton agricultural produce. To this end he lobbied Paris for a deep-water port at Roscoff, and once that was built, his farmers' co-operative set up *Brittany Ferries* to carry Breton artichokes and cabbages to English markets. The company was an explicit move to re-establish the old trading links of the Atlantic seaboard, independent of Paris and central French authority.

Brittany Ferries has prospered, thanks to the British and Irish entry to the EC upon which Gourvennec had gambled. And it has proved

that Brittany's future economic fortunes are more closely linked to its old Celtic connections than to the French state. Yet despite Gourvennec's enthusiasm for his Celtic cousins there have been several instances of ugly right-wing **protectionism** – attacking British lorries importing meat, violently breaking up strikes in Brittany, and forcibly preventing *Townsend Thoresen* from starting a rival ferry service to St-Malo.

In 1973 a semi-decentralized **regional administration** was set up to provide an intermediate level between the *départements* and the state. Normandy, being rich, became two regions – *Basse* and *Maine* – while Brittany, with the Loire-Atlantique *département* around Nantes lopped off, was a single entity. The new boundaries had no impact on people's perception of the provinces, though they did start to have some practical consequence when the socialist government increased regional powers in 1981.

The traditional industrial centres on the Loire estuary, such as the ship-building town of St-Nazaire, no longer come under Breton planning – perhaps just as well given the recession. Fishing and agriculture are still the mainstay of the Breton economy, though the former has never benefited from an equivalent to Gourvennec. The socialist policy of **decentralization** brought certain industries to the region – such as a *Citroën* plant at Rennes and *Renault* in Lorient – but it is still industrially backward compared to most of France. Its isolation has long made it a favourite location for nuclear power stations, despite local opposition which, on occasion (as at Plogoff), has made world headline news.

A decade ago hopes of new riches were raised by drilling for offshore oil in Finistère. If oil is discovered, it would create interesting parallels with the situation in Scotland. As yet, however, these remain pipe dreams and Brittany's experience of oil has been at the receiving end of major disasters – the *Torrey Canyon* in March 1967 and the *Amoco Cadiz* in 1978 both polluting hundreds of miles of coastline.

Towards the end of the 1980s leading Breton economic figures began to prepare themselves for a future in which the provincei may not be able to depend so heavily on its agriculture. They earmarked the development of the city of Brest as being the best way forward. The **Brest Charter**, approved by the French government in February 1988, planned for large-scale investment in the city area, partly on higher education and research facilities, and partly on upgrading the harbour and airport to cope with international traffic. The ultra-fast Paris–Brest *TGV* rail link in particular, inaugurated in 1989, has already made a big difference.

Politically, Bretons consistently provide an above-average proportion of the conservative vote. Almost three-quarters of the population supported De Gaulle in the 1960s, and in 1981 the majority voted against Mitterand. The most traditional, rural, areas are the most conservative of all. Perhaps for that reason the **separatist movement**, as a positive celebration of the Breton nation rather than a reactionary throwback, has never been all that powerful. In 1932 a bomb in Rennes destroyed the monument to Franco-Breton unity, and since 1966 the Front de Libération de Bretagne has intermittently attacked such targets as the nuclear power station in the Monts d'Arrée, and the Hall of Mirrors at the palace of Versailles in 1978. The emphasis for most Breton activists these days, however, is on cultural pride rather than militancy. The idea is to establish a clear and vital sense of national identity – to create, as one leader put it, "the spiritual basis for a new political thrust". Although overall use of the Breton language may be declining, great stress has been placed on its historical and artistic significance, and notable victories have been won on the question of its official status.

Recent years have also been characterized by increasingly bitter inter-European disputes over **agriculture** and **fishing** rights. The economic survival of Breton fishermen in particular has been seriously threatened by a flood of cheap imports from the factory-fishing trawlers of the former Soviet Union. In February 1994, the streets of Rennes were turned into a battlefield when five thousand fishermen rioted during a visit by Prime Minister Edouard Balladur, and a stray flare set light to the roof of the ancient Breton Parliament. The next month, the *GATT* talks on world trade were briefly de-railed by a French blockade on fish flown in from the US; American threats to retaliate by banning imports of Camembert and other French cheeses soon forced a climbdown.

Thirty percent of fish caught by British vessels are exported to Europe through French ports, and throughout the summer of 1994 various Channel ports were blockaded, with hypermarkets being ransacked and Scottish fish landed at Roscoff destroyed by angry mobs. Trawlermen seeking to fish for scallops and spider crabs threatened to blockade the Channel Islands, and a small party of right-wing French Royalists attempted to reclaim the tiny island of Ecrehous of Jersey, ceded to Britain after World War II. Attempting to defuse the crisis, the French government moved to reduce the tax burden on self-employed fishermen, and set minimum prices for cod, haddock, coley and monkfish.

Manoeuvring by rival ferry operators as the opening of the Channel Tunnel approached led to another short-lived crisis. *P&O* abandoned plans to use cheap Chinese labour in the face of union opposition and legal action by *Brittany Ferries*, who charged unfair competition. A blockade of Cherbourg in June 1994 briefly threatened to affect celebrations of the **50th anniversary of D-Day**. However, large-scale commemorations duly took place, attended by the Queen, President Clinton, and 12 other heads of state – though not German Chancellor Kohl.

AN HISTORICAL CHRONOLOGY

BC

c450,000	Evidence of paleolithic activity at St Columban
c5700	Earliest megalithic site – tumulus of Kercado
c4600	Tomb containing antlers and shells, Hoëdic island
up to 1800	Megalithic Age; construction of Carnac alignments
2500 on	Seine becomes the "Tin Road"
6thC	First wave of Celts, the Gauls, arrive
56	Julius Caesar's fleet defeats Veneti

AD

up to 476	Roman occupation of Armorica
497	Franks arrive in Normandy; Clovis occupies Rouen
5th–6th C	Celts fleeing from Britain rename Brittany
6thC	First monasteries founded in Brittany and Normandy
	Saint Pol kills 'laidley-worm' on island of Batz
709	Mont-St-Michel consecrated by bishop of Avranches
799	Charlemagne controls all Brittany
8th–9th C	Forest of Scissy drowns to form Mont-St-Michel Bay
	Viking expeditions against Normandy
845	Battle of Redon, Nominoë first Duke of Brittany
911	Rollo becomes first Duke of Normandy, capital Rouen
9th–10th C	Repeated Norman invasions of Brittany
1035	Birth of William 'The Bastard' at Falaise
1064	Harold and William fight together at Battle of Brittany (Dol)
1066	William invades and conquers England
1067	Abbey of Jumièges consecrated
1077	Bishop Oddo dedicates Bayeux cathedral, complete with Tapestry
11thC	Golden age of Abbey of Bec – Lanfranc and Anselm
1120	William, heir to the English throne, drowns at Barfleur
1136	Pierre Abelard abbot of St Gildas
1162	Eleanor of Aquitaine born at Domfront

12th C	Romanesque cloister of Abbey of Daoulas
1160	Robert Wace visits Broceliande forest "like a fool"
1171	Henry II, in Argentan, hears news of Becket's murder
1172	Henry does public penance at Avranches
1195	Richard the Lionheart builds Château Gaillard
1204	Normandy reunited with French throne
1211–28	Building of *La Merveille* at Mont-St-Michel
1218	Construction of Cathedral at Coutances
1303	Saint Yves dies at Tréguier
1351	"Combat of the Thirty" between Josselin and Ploermel
1359	Du Guesclin fights single combat at Dinan
1375	Building of Kreisker belfry at St-Pol
1420	Henry V of England King of France, after Agincourt
1431	Joan of Arc's trial and execution (May 30) at Rouen
1437	John the Baptist's finger arrives at St-Jean-du-Doigt
1440	"Bluebeard" burnt at stake in Nantes
1450	Normandy finally recovered by France
1450	Frescoes at Kermaria-an-Isquit
1469	Locronan starts its ascendancy in the linen trade
1474–6	Henry Tudor, England's future king, prisoner at Elven
1491	Duchess Anne of Brittany becomes Queen of France
1499	Duchess Anne becomes Queen of France again
1510	Monk, Vincelli, invents Benedictine liqueur
1517	Construction of Le Havre
1526	Aître de St-Maclou, charnel-house, built at Rouen
1532	Vannes Parliament ratifies Brittany-France Union
1548	Mary Queen of Scots at Morlaix
1550–1750	Rival Breton towns build the "parish closes"

1562	Rouen sacked by Protestants	**1883–**	Monet paints waterlilies in his garden at
1598	Henry IV signs Edict of Nantes	**1926**	Giverny
1608	Champlain sails from Honfleur to found Quebec	**1888**	Gauguin at Pont-Aven
1661	Three Musketeers end Fouquet's ownership of Belle-Île	**1896**	*Drummond Castle* goes down off Ouessant
1668	10,000 die of plague in Dieppe	**1899**	Second trial of Dreyfus at Rennes
1675	"Stamped Paper" peasant revolt in Brittany	**1905**	France secularized, although Brittany votes against
1693	English "infernal machine" devastates St-Malo	**1927**	Nungesser and Coli disappear over Étretat attempting first transatlantic flight
1698	Gouin de Beauchère of St-Malo colonizes the Falklands	**1928**	Amundsen's air-rescue flight from Caudebec disappears
1722	Dec 22; Drunken carpenter burns down most of Rennes	**1932**	Bomb destroys Rennes monument to Franco-Breton unity
1745	Bonnie Prince Charlie sails from Nantes	**1930s**	Nauseous Jean-Paul Sartre teaches philosophy in Le Havre
1758	Duke of Marlborough attacks St-Malo with 15,000 men	**1940**	All the men of Sein join de Gaulle in England
1776	Benjamin Franklin lands at Auray (by mistake)	**1942**	March 28; British commando raid on St-Nazaire
1789	Revolution makes no concessions to Breton autonomy	**1942**	August: 1000 Canadians die in commando raid on Dieppe
1793	Carrier kills thousands in "marriages" at Nantes	**1944**	June 6; D-Day – Battle of Normandy
1794	Soldiers play *boules* with heads from Guéhenno Calvary	**1954**	Consecration of Basilica of St Thérèse at Lisieux
1795	Royalist and exile *chouans* land at Quiberon	**1962**	First Telstar transatlantic signals at Pleumeur-Bodou
1801	Robert Fulton tests first submarine at Camaret	**1966**	Tidal power dam built across the Rance estuary
1808	Napoleon arrives by barge for his ball at Nantes	**1967**	*Torrey Canyon* disaster; oil slicks hit Brittany
c1810	Marie Herel invents Camembert	**1972**	Loire-Atlantique no longer officially in Brittany
1821	Flaubert born at Rouen		
1836	Opening of the Nantes–Brest Canal	**1980**	*Rainbow Warrior* pursues nuclear-dumping vessel into Cherbourg; anti-nuclear riots at Plogoff
1843	Victor Hugo's daughter drowns in Seine		
1852	First major Icelandic fishery expedition from Paimpol	**1987**	Oct 15; Hurricane causes extensive damage in Finistère
1866	Composer Erik Satie born in Honfleur	**1988**	Brest Charter on Brittany's economic future approved by French govt.
1873	Thérèse Martin born, Lisieux; died 1897, sainted 1925		
1881	Young Marcel Proust pays his first visit to Combourg	**1994**	World leaders attend commemorations of 50th anniversary of D-Day

BOOKS

Where separate editions exist in the UK and US, publishers are detailed below in the form "British Publisher/American Publisher", unless the publisher is the same in both countries. Where books are published in one country only, this follows the publisher's name. O/P signifies an out-of-print – but still recommended – book. Where necessary for reasons of space, University Press has been abbreviated to UP.

PREHISTORY AND MEGALITHS

Aubrey Burl *Megalithic Brittany* (Thames & Hudson, o/p). Detailed guide to all the prehistoric sites of Brittany, area by area. Very precise on how to find each site, and what you see when you get there, but with little historical or theoretical overview. It is not intended as a practical guide-book for anything other than ancient stones – no details of towns, hotels or anything else.

John Michell *Megalithomania* (Thames & Hudson/Cornell UP). More popular general work about megaliths everywhere, with a lot of entertaining descriptions of how modern visitors have reacted to them.

Mark Patton *Statements in Stone* (Routledge). Sober, scientific account of Brittany's megalithic heritage, re-appraised in the light of recent archeological discoveries.

A. Thom & A. S. Thom *Megalithic Remains in Britain and Brittany* (OUP UK, o/p). A scientific rather than anecdotal account of the Thoms' extensive analysis. The mathematics and astronomy can be a bit over-powering, without necessarily convincing you of anything.

Uderzo and Goscinny *Asterix the Gaul* (Hodder & Stoughton). Breton history mixed together in a magic cauldron.

HISTORY AND POLITICS

Patrick Galliou and Michael Jones *The Bretons* (Basil Blackwell). Accessible and illuminating hardback account of Breton history from the megaliths, through the Romans, as far as the union with France.

David C. Douglas *The Norman Achievement 1050–1100* (Fontana, o/p /University of California Press, o/p). Comprehensive and readable assessment of the Norman Conquerors.

Barbara Tuchman *Distant Mirror* (Papermac/ Ballantine). A history of the fourteenth century as experienced by a French nobleman. Makes sense of the human complexities of the Hundred Years War.

Theodore Zeldin *France 1845–1945* (OUP). Five thematic volumes on French history.

Alfred Cobban *A History of Modern France* (Penguin, three vols). Very complete political history from Louis XIV to de Gaulle.

John Ardagh *France in the 1980s* (Pelican, 1982). Detailed journalistic survey of modern France, with an interesting and relevant section on "Brittany's revival".

Morvan Lebesque *Comment Peut-on Être Breton?* (Editions du Seuil). A classic of Breton separatism, taking a psychological and sociological approach rather than a political one. He argues that awareness of one's cultural identity is vital for participation in the international community.

Kendalc'h *Breiz Hor Bro* (Editions Breiz). Produced by a Breton youth association in French, this militant pamphlet covers history, language, literature and folklore, without ever losing an opportunity to take a swipe at the age-old oppressors of Brittany.

THE NORMANDY LANDINGS

Max Hastings *Overlord* (Papermac/Simon & Schuster). Detailed history of D-Day and its aftermath. Balanced and objective; Hastings distances himself thoroughly from propaganda and myth-making.

Donald Horne *The Great Museum: the Representation of History* (Pluto/Westview). A stimulating analysis of how history is presented to the tourist. Particularly interesting for its treatment of the D-Day landing sites.

John Keegan *Six Armies in Normandy* (Pimlico/Penguin). A fascinating military history, which combines the personal and the public to original effect. Each of the participating armies in the Battle of Normandy is followed during the most crucial phase of its involvement; some of the lesser details of the conflict are missed, but the overall sweep is compelling.

Anthony Kemp *D-Day; The Normandy Landings and the Liberation of Europe* (Thames & Hudson/Abrams). Full-colour pocketbook guide to the D-Day story, with a wealth of fascinating information. Published to mark the fiftieth anniversary of the invasion.

Studs Turkel *The Good War* (Ballantine, US). Excellent collection of interviews with participants of every rank and nation, including civilians, in World War II.

Henry Adams *Mont St-Michel and Chartres* (Penguin). Extraordinary, idiosyncratic account of the two medieval masterpieces, attempting through prayer, song and sheer imagination to understand the society and the people which created them. A tribute to Norman wisdom.

John Ardagh *Writers' France* (Hamish Hamilton, o/p). Entertaining anecdotes about most of the writers mentioned in this book, with colour photos.

Christina Björk *Linnea in Monet's Garden* (Raben & Sjogern/Farrar, Straus & Giroux). A Swedish book for children which tells the story of a young girl achieving her lifetime's dream of visiting Monet's home in Giverny. A well-illustrated introduction to the Impressionists.

Sophie Bowness & others *The Dieppe Connection* (Herbert Press/New Amsterdam Books). Companion volume to a fascinating exhibition in Brighton, exploring Dieppe's nineteenth-century role as a meeting place for artists. Includes colour reproductions of Dieppe scenes by Turner, Whistler, Gauguin and Renoir.

Alfonso Castelao *Les Croix de Pierre en Bretagne* (available by post for 59F from the *Comité Bretagne-Galice*, BP66A, 35031 Rennes) A real collector's item; a pocket-sized collec-

tion of sketches of Breton calvaries made by the Gallego writer and illustrator during a visit in the 1920s. Includes an obsessive series of studies of Christ's ribcage. For more on Castelao, see the *Rough Guide to Spain*.

Claire Joyes *Monet at Giverny* (Matthews Millar Dunbar). Large-format account of Monet's years at Giverny, combining biography with good reproductions of the famous waterlilies.

Honoré de Balzac *The Chouans* (Penguin). A hectic and crazily romantic story of the royalist *chouan* rebellion shortly after the Revolution, set mainly in Fougères.

Alexandre Dumas *The Three Musketeers* (OUP/Penguin). Brilliant swash-buckling romance with peripheral Breton scenes on Belle-Île and elsewhere.

Victor Hugo *Ninety-Three* (Carroll & Graf, US). Rather more restrained but still compelling *chouan* novel.

Jack Kerouac *Satori in Paris* (Paladin/Grove-Atlantic) . . . and in Brittany. Inconsequential anecdotes.

Pierre Loti *Pecheur d'Islande* (Livre de Poche). Much-acclaimed novel (on which the film was based) which focusses on the whaling fleets that sailed from Paimpol. Not available in translation.

Julian Barnes *Flaubert's Parrot* (Picador/Random House). A lightweight novel which rambles around the life of Flaubert, with much of the action taking place in Rouen and along the Seine.

Peter Benson *Odo's Hanging* (Sceptre, UK). Delicate but dramatic fictionalized account of the human stories behind the creation of the Bayeux Tapestry.

Gustave Flaubert *Madame Bovary* (Penguin). "The first modern novel", by the Rouennais writer. Drawn from a real-life story from Ry – see p.88 – it contains little that is specifically Norman, however.

Gustave Flaubert *Bouvard and Pécuchet* (Penguin). Two petty-bourgeois retire to a village between Caen and Falaise and attempt to practise every science of the time. Very funny or dead boring, according to taste.

Marcel Proust *In Remembrance of Things Past* (Penguin/Random House). Dense autobiographical trilogy evocative of almost everything except the places in Normandy and Brittany that his memories take him back to.

Jean-Paul Sartre *Nausea* (Penguin/New Directions). Sartre's relentlessly gloomy description of just how unpleasant it was to drag out one's existence in Le Havre (or "Bouville") in the 1930s.

BRETON MYTH AND FOLKTALES

Pierre-Jakez Hélias *The Horse of Pride* (Yale University Press). A deeply reactionary and sentimental account of a Breton childhood in the Bigouden district earlier this century, which has sold over two million copies in France.

Prof Anatole Le Braz *La Legende du Mort* (Editions Jeanne Laffitte). The definitive French text on Breton myths centred on Ankou and the prescience of death.

F. M. Luzel *Celtic Folk-Tales from Armorica* (Llanerch Enterprises, Lampeter, Wales, UK). A collection of timeless Breton fairy stories translated into English, complete with commentaries.

W. Y. Evans Wentz *The Fairy Faith in Celtic Countries* (Citadel Press/Carol Publishing). Utterly bizarre survey of similarities and differences in folk beliefs and religion between Celtic nations, with extensive details about Brittany.

BRETON MUSIC

Breton music, which draws richly in its themes, style and instrumentation on the common Celtic heritage of the Atlantic seaboard, has remained for centuries a unifying and inspiring part of the culture of the province. Despite the intermittent efforts of a reactionary clergy to stifle its popularity, it survived the union with France and the general suppression of indigenous art and language.

However, attempting to pin even an approximate date on the origins of traditional Breton music is a haphazard business. No literature survives in the native tongue from any period prior to the fifteenth century, although we do know that wandering Breton minstrels, known as *conteurs*, had enjoyed great popularity abroad long before this. Many of the songs they wrote were translated into French, being otherwise unintelligible to audiences outside Brittany, but unfortunately both versions have vanished with time. Only a number of Norse and English translations, probably dating from the twelfth century, escaped destruction. These works tell of romances won and lost, acrimonious relationships between fathers and their sons, and the testing of potential lovers.

The historical record of Breton music really begins with the publication of *Barzaz-Breizh*, a major collection of traditional songs and poems, in 1839. It was compiled by a nobleman, Hersart de la Villemarqué, from his discussions with fishermen, farmers and oyster-and-pancake women, and in view of the scarcity of other literature in the native language has come to be acknowledged as a treasure of Breton folk culture. Though serious doubts have frequently been raised as to its authenticity – many sceptics believe Villemarqué doctored those parts of the material he found distasteful, and even composed portions of it himself – it is unquestionably a work of linguistic brilliance and great beauty, and its appearance triggered the serious study of popular Breton culture.

INSTRUMENTATION

As for the traditional **instruments** on which the music is played, perhaps the most important is the ***bombard*** – an extremely old and shortened version of the oboe which, depending on the condition of your brain on any given day, sounds either like a hypnotic, trance-inducing paean to the gods, or a sackful of weasels being yanked through a mincer. The ***biniou***, the Breton bagpipe, dates in its current form from the nineteenth century, although several types are still in use, distinguished by the length of the chanter.

The harp, ***telenn***, was also a native instrument long ago. Its influence had declined to a barely peripheral level until **Alan Stivell**'s appearance on the scene in the sixties inspired a resurgence. His international hit *Renaissance of the Celtic Harp* introduced Breton, as well as Irish, Welsh and Scottish traditional music, to a worldwide audience, and subsequently stimulated interest in less accessible material.

FESTOU-NOZ

The most rewarding setting in which to witness traditional Breton music is undoubtedly a **Fest-Noz** ("Night Feast") – a night of serious eating, drinking and dancing which can sometimes verge on the orgiastic. During the summer months, such events are very common, attracting hordes of revellers from miles around. Though they are often held in barns and halls in the more isolated parts of the region, discovering their whereabouts shouldn't present any problems, as an avalanche of posters advertising them appears absolutely everywhere. Once the evening gets underway, the dancers, often in their hundreds, whirl around in vast dizzy circles, hour after hour, sometimes frenzied and leaping, sometimes slow and graceful with their little fingers intertwined. It can be a bizarre and exhilarating spectacle – and a very affordable one too, with admission fees rarely amounting to more than a few pounds.

Traditionally, the most common form of *festou noz* music is that of a **couple de sonneurs,** a pair of musicians playing bombard and biniou. They play the same melody line, with a drone from the biniou, and keep up a fast tempo – one player covering for the other when he or she pauses for breath. This is defiantly dance music, with no vocals and no titles for the tunes, although there are countless varieties of rhythms, often highly localized and generally known by the name of the dance. There is a purely vocal counterpart to this, known as **kan ha diskan.** Once again dance music, this is performed by a pair of unaccompanied "call and response" singers. In its basic form the two singers – the *kader* and *diskader* – alternate verses, joining each other at the end of each phrase. As dances were in the past unamplified, the parts were (and are) often doubled up (or more), creating a startling rhythmic sound. The best singers might also give the dancers the odd break with a *gwerz*, or ballad, again sung unaccompanied. Over the past couple of decades, these traditional accompaniments have been supplanted more and more by four- or five-piece **bands**, who add fiddle and accordion, and sometimes electric bass and drums, to the bombard, and less often the biniou. The tunes have been updated with more of a rock sound, while the ballads have given way to folk-style singer-songwriters, with guitar backing. Purists might regret the changes but they have probably ensured the survival of *festou noz*, with the enthusiastic participation of musicians and dancers of pretty much all ages. They have also nurtured successive generations of Breton musicians who move on to the festival and concert circuit.

BARDS AND BANDS

The godfather of the modern Breton music scene, **Alan Stivell**, started the ball rolling in the mid-1960s with one of the first folk-rock bands in Europe. He played harp, bagpipes and Irish flute, alongside **Dan Ar Bras** on electric and acoustic guitar, on a repertoire that drew on wider Celtic traditions. Both artists are still performing and recording, individually. Stivell's efforts are increasingly esoteric, while Ar Bras, who played with Fairport Convention in 1976, is a fixture at that band's Cropredy reunions, and produces mellow acoustic solo albums. The other key figure from Stivell's band was **Gabriel Yucoub,** who led **Malicorne,** the best-known Breton band of the 1970s and '80s, through a series of experiments with folk-rock and electronic music, often using archaic instruments. Latterly, he has played as an acoustic duo, with his wife Marie Matheson.

Folk rock, however, has been just one direction for Breton music in the 1980s and '90s. On the concert circuit, the biggest Breton names tend to be the singers, among whom the most famous is **Andrea Ar Gouilh**. Her recent output includes a return to Breton roots with a recording of old songs taken from the Barzaz-Breizh, though her concert repertoire is as likely to include a rendition of Bob Dylan's *Blowin' in the Wind*, which sounds rather marvellous sung in Breton.

Youenn Gwernig, a Druid and singer, is another name to look out for at festivals. He lived for many years in New York and delivers his own ballads in a deep booming voice, sometimes accompanied by his two daughters who sing Brooklyn English translations.

Equally weird is **Kristen Nikolas**, a wandering poet who makes his own idiosyncratic records, in Breton, in foreign studios, while the most compelling name has to be that of the duo **Bastard Hag e Vab** (Bastard and Son), who have been stalwarts of the live circuit for years.

Other notable Breton singers include **Bernez Tangi**, who for a while fronted a fine band called Storlok; **Yann Fanch Kemener**, well known among Bretons but somewhat inaccessible to others with his unbelievably long traditional *gwerziou;* the singer-songwriter **Gilles Servat**, who sings in both Breton and French, mixing his own protest songs with renderings of Breton poems; and a trio of younger *fest-noz* performers, **Jean Do Robin, Claude An Intanv and Anni Ebrel**, who are slowly gaining recognition and who write some of their own material.

Fest-noz singers are sometimes accompanied by harpists, among whom the best contemporary players are **Ar Breudeur Keffelean**, virtuoso twin brothers who also have a group, **Triskell**. The more mystic '60s

A few Breton discs – mainly of the rock-crossover variety – find their way into international sections of record stores abroad. For the real roots stuff, you'll need to go to Brittany itself, and in particular to **Ar Bed Keltiek**, a record store with branches in Rennes, Quimper and Brest, or, best of all, to **Chant de l'Alouette** (4 rue des États, 35600 Redon, Brittany; ☎99.72.44.94), run by musician Jakez le Soueff – a living Breton encyclopedia on all matters musical, who will track down any recording that exists. These shops are also good for information about forthcoming gigs and events.

Compilations

Various *Celtic La Compile* (Le Cine Jaune, France). An eclectic 18-track compilation of Breton music of just about every style: sentimental balladeers, marching bands, loud rockers, quirky accordions and bagpipes – it's all here.

Various *Dans* (Iguane, France). Traditional dance tunes given new life with superb new arrangements and restrained electrification.

Various *Gwerziou et Chants de Haute-Voix* (Keltia Musique, France). Unaccompanied Breton songs by the region's top artists; the best example of the genre.

Artists/Bands

Dan Ar Bras *Acoustic* (Green Linnet, US). A recent release from the ex-Stivell, Malicorne and Fairport guitarist.

Barzaz *An den Kozh dall* (Keltia Musique, France). A classic 1992 release of mellow, intense acoustic music, with some lovely flute playing.

The Chieftains *Celtic Wedding* (RCA, UK). The Irish band turn their hand to traditional Breton dance tunes. A fresh, and highly accessible, perspective.

Gwerz *Live* (Gwerz, France). Electric and acoustic material from perhaps the best Breton musicians of the last decade, now pursuing individual projects.

Kornog *Première: Music from Brittany* (Green Linnet, US). An excellent live album from this adventurous Breton (and Scots) band, formmed by ex-Gwerz guitanst Soïg Siberil.

Patrick Molard, Jack Molard et Jacques Pellen *Triptyque* (Gwerz, France). An innovative release of jazzy interpretations of Breton traditions.

Pennou Skoulm *Pennou Skoulm* (Slog France). Traditional dance music from a group who regularly appear on the *fest-noz* circuit. Cassette only.

Les Soeurs Goadeg *Moueziou Brudez à Vreiz* (Keltia Musique, France). Alan Stivell produced this disc of old-time Breton singing in 1975. Goadeg, a trio of sisters, were into their seventies at the time, and the album showcases their highly traditional gwerziou (ballads) and *kan ha diskan* singing.

Alan Stivell *Journée à la Maison* (Rounder, US). A good compilation of Stivell's Breton Celtic harp folk-rockery – more accessible than the recent esoteric output.

Visitors to Brittany get the chance to enjoy Breton music at several annual **festivals**. The most famous of these is the pan-Celtic Lorient festival (see p.286); others include Quimper's Festival de Cornouaille (mid-/late July), Rennes' Tombées de la Nuit (early July), and the intimate Printemps de Chateauneuf-du-Faou (Easter Sunday), when Breton singers and musicians take over a small town near Carhaix.

In addition, most Breton towns and villages, even in the middle of nowhere, have **pubs** that offer live music, often of the spontaneous boot-tappin', booze-swillin' variety. Among the best of these are:

Brest: *Café de la Plage*, *Café le Triskel* and the *Bar Écossais*.

Douarnenez: *Le Pourquois Pas* promotes larger bands in the mainstream mould.

Gouarec, near Gourin: *Bar de Daoulas*.

Gwern, near Pontivy: the *Korn Ar Pont* is a highly regarded venue which promotes mostly rock music and attracts punters from miles around for a weekend's bopping and bevvying. Own transport essential.

Île de Bréhat: *La Mary Morgan*.

Lorient: The *Galway Inn* – run by an Irishman – puts on touring bands of an acoustic nature, and has regular Irish folk sessions too.

Plouha: The *Ti Elise*, owned by a Welshman from Merthyr, is the local of Yann Skoarnek, a venerable old character who'll sing you songs about horse-thieving in Breton.

Plouhinec, near Lorient: *Cafe de la Barre*.

Quimper: The *Ceili Bar* specializes in folk music. Very small, very cramped and very drunk.

Quimperlé: The superb hosts at the *OK Pub* arrange occasional summer gigs of a folksy sort – and it serves *Murphys* into the bargain.

Redon: Ask at *Le Chant de l'Allouette* music shop just off the main street for info. They sometimes promote events at a nearby farm.

Rennes: *Barantic* puts on semi-regular gigs in the folk-rock vein as well as less organized affairs at the weekend. Friendly bar-staff, relaxed atmosphere.

side of the tradition is encapsulated by the suitably bearded and misty Merlin-type, Myrzhin, harper of the mysterious.

If you have a more casual interest in Breton sounds, though, you're likely to find some of the bands rather more rewarding. A fine *fest-noz* act to look out for is **Strobinell**, who have a line up of bombard, biniou, violin, flute and guitar, and make occasional forays into a looser, jazzier groove. Another, always visually entertaining group is the mega-ensemble **Klik Ha Farz**, whose members wander around the hall as they play. They use a bass drum in conjunction with traditional instruments, rather in the manner of Gallego and Portuguese groups.

For the electric *festou-noz* sound, complete with full rock drum kit, the best exponents are **Bleizi Ruz** (Red Wolves) and **Sonerien Du** (Black Musicians). Bleizi Ruz, who started out some twenty years ago playing traditional songs, play less at *festou-noz* these days and more on concert stages. They are probably the most successful folk-rock fusion group still on the circuit and have recently added synths and drum machines. Musically, the most adventurous band of the last decade has been **Gwerz**, who made several records of traditional songs and ethereal instrumentals, using bombard,

biniou, uilleann pipes and guitars. Their singer, **Erie Marchand**, has recently been collaborating with Indian musicians to interesting effect. Also making crossovers from a Breton base are **Les Pires**, a zany instrumental quintet comprising violin, accordion, clarinet, double bass and piano, who play essentially middle European dance music. Strangely enough, while these musicians are looking outwards, some of the most interesting new "Breton" sounds have been emerging from bands of mixed nationality. **Etre-Vroadel** (EV), Brittany's most popular rock band, are a mix of Finnish and Breton musicians who use the bombard and cover traditional material. More folk-oriented, and purely acoustic, are Kornog, who feature Scots singer, mandolin and bouzouki player Jamie McMenemy, alongside three Breton instrumentalists, among them Soïg Siberil, who played guitar in Gwerz. They have rearranged Breton material quite radically for guitar, fiddle and bouzouki, slowing down the tempo to highlight solo playing and adding the occasional Scots ballad. At time of writing, they're the Breton band to watch.

Raymond Travers

Reprinted from
The Rough Guide to World Music

LANGUAGE

Although Breton does remain a living language, in both Brittany and Normandy every encounter you are likely to have with the local people will be conducted in French. This is of course a lot more familiar than Breton, sharing numerous words with English, but it's not a particularly easy language to pick up.

The bare essentials of French, though, are not difficult, and make all the difference. Even just saying "Bonjour Madame/Monsieur" when you go into a shop, and then pointing, will usually get you a smile and helpful service. People working in hotels, restaurants and tourist offices almost always speak some English, and tend to use it even if you're trying in French – be grateful, not insulted.

Breton is one of the Celtic family of languages, with an especially strong oral tradition ranging from medieval minstrels to modern singers and musicians. If you have a familiarity with Welsh or Gaelic, you should find yourself understanding, and being understood, in it.

Current estimates put the number of Breton speakers at between 400,000 and 800,000, but you are only likely to find it spoken as a first, day-to-day language either amongst the old, or in the more remote parts of Finistère. For centuries it was discouraged by the State; its use was forbidden for official and legal purposes, and even Breton-speaking parents would seek to enhance their children's prospects by bringing them up to speak French. Although it is now taught in schools once again, learning Breton is not really a viable prospect for visitors who do not already have a grounding in another Celtic language. However, as you travel through the province, it's interesting to note the roots of Breton place names, many of which have a simple meaning in the language. The box below lists some of the most common.

A GLOSSARY OF BRETON PLACE NAMES

Aber	estuary	*Lann*	heath
Avel	wind	*Lech*	flat stone
Bihan	little	*Men*	stone
Bran	hill	*Menz*	mountain
Braz	big	*Mario*	dead
Creach	height	*Menhir*	long stone
Cromlech	stone circle	*Meur*	big
Dol	table	*Mor*	sea
Du	black	*Nevez*	new
Gavre	goat	*Parc*	field
Goat	forest	*Penn*	end, head
Goaz	stream	*Plou*	parish
Guen	white	*Pors*	port, farmyard
Hen	old	*Roch*	stone
Heol	sun	*Ster*	river
Hir	long	*Stivel*	fountain, spring
Inis	island	*Trez*	sand, beach
Ker	town or house	*Trou*	valley
Koz	old	*Ty*	house
Lan	church	*Wrach*	witch

GLOSSARY OF FRENCH TERMS

ABBAYE abbey
ABER estuary
ACCUEIL reception
ARRÊT bus stop
ASSEMBLÉE NATIONALE the French parliament
AUBERGE DE JEUNESSE (AJ) youth hostel
AUTOBUS city bus
BANQUE bank
BEAUX ARTS Fine Arts school (and often museum)
BESSIN harbour basin
BIBLIOTHÈQUE library
BISTRO small restaurant or bar
BOIS wood
BOULANGERIE baker
BRASSERIE café/restaurant
BUREAU DE CHANGE money exchange
CAR coach, bus
CAVE (wine) cellar
CHARCUTERIE delicatessen
CHASSE, CHASSE GARDÉE hunting grounds (beware)
CHÂTEAU castle or mansion
CIMETIÈRE cemetery
CITADELLE fortified city
CLOÎTRE cloister
CODENE French CND
CONSIGNE left luggage
COUVENT monastery
CRÊPERIE pancake restaurant
DÉGUSTATION tasting
DÉPARTEMENT county equivalent
DOLMEN megalithic stone "table"
DONJON castle keep
ÉGLISE church
ENCLOS group of church buildings
ENTRÉE entrance
FERMETURE closing time/period

FORÊT forest
FOUILLES archeological excavations
GARE ROUTIÈRE bus station
GARE SNCF train station
GÎTE D'ÉTAPE countryside hostel
GROTTE cave
HALLES covered market
HLM publicly subsidized housing
HÔPITAL hospital
HÔTEL hotel – but also used for an aristocratic town house or mansion
HÔTEL DE VILLE town hall
ÎLE island
JOURS FERIÉS public holidays
MAIRIE town hall
MAISON literally a house – can also be an office or base of an organization
MARCHÉ market
MENHIR single megalithic stone
OFFICE DU TOURISME (OT) tourist office
OUVERTURE opening time/period
PATISSERIE pastry shop
PHARMACIE chemist
PLACE square
PLAGE beach
PORTE gate
POSTE post office
PRESQU'ÎLE peninsula
PRIVÉ private
PTT post office
QUARTIER quarter of a town
RELAIS ROUTIER truck-stop restaurant
REZ DE CHAUSSÉE ground floor
RN route nationale (main road)
SALON DE THÉ tea room
SI tourist office (see below)
SNCF French railways
SYNDICAT D'INITIATIVE (SI) tourist office
TABAC bar or shop selling stamps, cigarettes, etc.
TOUR tower
VAUBAN seventeenth-century military architect
ZONE BLEUE parking zone
ZONE PIETONNÉ pedestrian zone

A BRIEF GUIDE TO SPEAKING FRENCH

PRONUNCIATION

One easy rule to remember is that **consonants** at the ends of words are usually silent. *Pas plus tard* (not later) is thus pronounced pa-plu-tarr. But when the following word begins with a vowel, you run the two together : *pas après* (not after) becomes pazapre.

Vowels are the hardest sounds to get right. Roughly:

a	as in h**a**t		*i*	as in mach**i**ne
e	as in g**e**t		*o*	as in h**o**t
é	between g**e**t and g**a**te		*o, au*	as in **o**ver
è	between g**e**t and g**u**t		*ou*	as in f**oo**d
eu	like the **u** in h**u**rt		*u*	as in a pursed-lip version of **u**se

More awkward are the **combinations** in/im, en/em, an/am. on/om, un/um at the ends of words, or followed by consonants other than n or m. Again, roughly:

in/im	like the **an** in **an**xious	*on/om*	like the d**on** in D**on**caster said by
an/am, en/em	like the d**on** in D**on**caster when		someone with a heavy cold
	said with a nasal accent	*un/um*	like the **u** in **u**nderstand

Consonants are much as in English, except that: ch is always sh, c is s, h is silent, th is the same as t, ll is like the y in yes, w is v, and r is growled (or rolled).

BASIC WORDS AND PHRASES

French nouns are divided into masculine and feminine. This causes difficulties with adjectives, whose endings have to change to suit the gender of the nouns they qualify. If you know some grammar, you will know what to do. If not, stick to the masculine form, which is the simplest – that's what we have done in this glossary.

today	*aujourd'hui*	that one	*celà*
yesterday	*hier*	open	*ouvert*
tomorrow	*demain*	closed	*fermé*
in the morning	*le matin*	big	*grand*
in the afternoon	*l'après-midi*	small	*petit*
in the evening	*le soir*	more	*plus*
now	*maintenant*	less	*moins*
later	*plus tard*	a little	*un peu*
at one o'clock	*à une heure*	a lot	*beaucoup*
at three o'clock	*à trois heures*	cheap	*bon marché*
at ten-thirty	*à dix heures et demie*	expensive	*cher*
at noon	*à midi*	good	*bon*
man	*un homme*	bad	*mauvais*
woman	*une femme*	hot	*chaud*
here	*ici*	cold	*froid*
there	*là*	with	*avec*
this one	*ceci*	without	*sans*

TALKING TO PEOPLE

When addressing people you should always use *Monsieur* for a man, *Madame* for a woman, *Mademoiselle* for a girl. Plain *bonjour* by itself is not enough. This isn't as formal as it seems, and it has its uses when you've forgotten someone's name or want to attract someone's attention.

Excuse me	*Pardon*	Please	*S'il vous plaît*
Do you speak English ?	*Vous parlez anglais ?*	Thank you	*Merci*
		Hello	*Bonjour*
How do you say it in French ?	*Comment ça se dit en Français ?*	Goodbye	*Au revoir*
What's your name ?	*Comment vous appelez-vous ?*	Good morning/ afternoon	*Bonjour*
My name is . . .	*Je m'appelle . . .*	Good evening	*Bonsoir*
I'm English/ Irish/Scottish Welsh/American/ Australian/ Canadian/ a New Zealander	*Je suis anglais[e]/ irlandais[e]/écossais[e]/ gallois[e]/américain[e]/ australien[ne]/ canadien[ne]/ néo-zélandais[e]*	Good night	*Bonne nuit*
		How are you ?	*Comment allez-vous ?/ Ça va ?*
		Fine, thanks	*Très bien, merci*
		I don't know	*Je ne sais pas*
yes	*Oui*	Let's go	*Allons-y*
no	*Non*	See you tomorrow	*À demain*
I understand	*Je comprends*	See you soon	*À bientôt*
I don't understand	*Je ne comprends pas*	Sorry	*Pardon, Madame/ je m'excuse*
Can you speak slower ?	*S'il vous plaît, parlez moins vite*	Leave me alone (aggressive)	*Fichez-moi la paix!*
OK/agreed	*D'accord*	Please help me	*Aidez-moi, s'il vous plaît*

FINDING THE WAY

bus	*autobus, bus, car*	hitch-hiking	*autostop*
bus station	*gare routière*	on foot	*à pied*
bus stop	*arrêt*	Where are you going ?	*Vous allez où ?*
car	*voiture*		
train/taxi/ferry	*train/taxi/ferry*	I'm going to . . .	*Je vais à . . .*
boat	*bâteau*	I want to get off at . . .	*Je voudrais descendre à . . .*
plane	*avion*		
railway station	*gare*	the road to . . .	*la route pour . . .*
platform	*quai*	near	*près/pas loin*
What time does it leave ?	*Il part à quelle heure ?*	far	*loin*
		left	*à gauche*
What time does it arrive ?	*Il arrive à quelle heure ?*	right	*à droite*
		straight on	*tout droit*
a ticket to . . .	*un billet pour . . .*	on the other side of	*l'autre côté de*
single ticket	*aller simple*	on the corner of	*à l'angle de*
return ticket	*aller retour*	next to	*à côté de*
validate your ticket	*compostez votre billet*	behind	*derrière*
		in front of	*devant*
valid for	*valable pour*	before	*avant*
ticket office	*vente de billets*	after	*après*
how many kilometres ?	*combien de kilomètres ?*	under	*sous*
		to cross	*traverser*
how many hours ?	*combien d'heures ?*	bridge	*pont*

QUESTIONS AND REQUESTS

The simplest way of asking a question is to start with *s'il vous plaît* (please), then name the thing you want in an interrogative tone of voice. For example:

Where is there a bakery ?	*S'il vous plaît, la boulangerie ?*
Which way is it to Caen ?	*S'il vous plaît, la route pour Caen ?*

Similarly with requests:

We'd like a room for two	*S'il vous plaît, une chambre pour deux*
Can I have a kilo of oranges	*S'il vous plaît, un kilo d'oranges*

Question words

Where ?	*où ?*	When ?	*quand ?*
How ?	*comment ?*	Why ?	*pourquoi ?*
How many/	*combien ?*	At what time ?	*à quelle heure ?*
how much ?		What is/which is ?	*quel est ?*

ACCOMMODATION

a room for	*une chambre pour*	do laundry	*faire la lessive*
one/two people	*une/deux personnes*	sheets	*draps*
a double bed	*un lit double*	blankets	*couvertures*
a room with a	*une chambre avec*	quiet	*calme*
shower	*douche*	noisy	*bruyant*
a room with a bath	*une chambre avec*	hot water	*eau chaude*
	salle de bain	cold water	*eau froide*
For one/two/three	*Pour une/deux/trois*	Is breakfast	*Est-ce que le petit*
nights	*nuits*	included ?	*déjeuner est compris ?*
Can I see it ?	*Je peux la voir ?*	I would like	*Je voudrais prendre le*
a room on the	*une chambre sur la*	breakfast	*petit déjeuner*
courtyard	*cour*	I don't want	*Je ne veux pas le petit*
a room over the	*une chambre sur la*	breakfast	*déjeuner*
street	*rue*	Can we camp here ?	*On peut camper ici ?*
first floor	*premier étage*	campsite	*un camping/terrain de*
second floor	*deuxième étage*		*camping*
with a view	*avec vue*	tent	*une tente*
key	*clef*	tent space	*un emplacement*
to iron	*repasser*	youth hostel	*auberge de jeunesse*

NUMBERS

1	*un*	11	*onze*	21	*vingt-et-un*	95	*quatre-vingt-quinze*
2	*deux*	12	*douze*	22	*vingt-deux*	100	*cent*
3	*trois*	13	*treize*	30	*trente*	101	*cent-et-un*
4	*quatre*	14	*quatorze*	40	*quarante*	200	*deux cents*
5	*cinq*	15	*quinze*	50	*cinquante*	300	*trois cents*
6	*six*	16	*seize*	60	*soixante*	500	*cinq cents*
7	*sept*	17	*dix-sept*	70	*soixante-dix*	1000	*mille*
8	*huit*	18	*dix-huit*	75	*soixante-quinze*	2000	*deux milles*
9	*neuf*	19	*dix-neuf*	80	*quatre-vingts*	5000	*cinq milles*
10	*dix*	20	*vingt*	90	*quatre-vingt-dix*	1,000,000	*un million*

HEALTH MATTERS

doctor	*médecin*	stomach ache	*mal à l'estomac*
I don't feel well	*Je ne me sens pas bien*	period	*règles*
medicines	*médicaments*	pain	*douleur*
prescription	*ordonnance*	it hurts	*ça fait mal*
I feel sick	*Je suis malade*	chemist	*pharmacie*
headache	*J'ai mal à la tête*	hospital	*hôpital*

OTHER NEEDS

bakery	*boulangerie*	bank	*banque*
food shop	*alimentation*	money	*argent*
supermarket	*supermarché*	toilets	*toilettes*
to eat	*manger*	police	*police*
to drink	*boire*	telephone	*téléphone*
camping gas	*camping gaz*	cinema	*cinéma*
tobacconist	*tabac*	theatre	*théâtre*
stamps	*timbres*	to reserve/book	*réserver*

DAYS AND DATES

January	*janvier*	November	*novembre*	August 1	*le premier août*
February	*février*	December	*décembre*	September 6	*le six septembre*
March	*mars*			July 14	*le quatorze juillet*
April	*avril*	Sunday	*dimanche*	November 23	*le vingt-trois*
May	*mai*	Monday	*lundi*		*novembre*
June	*juin*	Tuesday	*mardi*		
July	*juillet*	Wednesday	*mercredi*	1995	*dix-neuf-cent-*
August	*août*	Thursday	*jeudi*		*quatre-vingt-quinze*
September	*septembre*	Friday	*vendredi*	1996	*dix-neuf-cent-*
October	*octobre*	Saturday	*samedi*		*quatre-vingt-seize*

DICTIONARIES AND PHRASEBOOKS

Rough Guide French Phrasebook (Rough Guides). Mini dictionary-style phrasebook with both English–French and French–English sections, along with cultural tips for tricky situations and a menu reader.

Mini French Dictionary (Harrap-Chambers). French–English and English–French, plus a brief grammar and pronunciation guide.

Breakthrough French (Pan Macmillan; book and two cassettes). Excellent teach-yourself course.

French and English Slang Dictionary (Harrap-Chambers); ***Dictionary of Modern Colloquial French*** (Routledge). Both volumes are a bit large to carry, but they are the key to all you ever wanted to understand.

À Vous La France; Franc Extra; Franc-Parler (BBC Publications; each has a book and two cassettes). BBC radio courses, running from an introduction for beginners to fairly advanced language.

INDEX

direct orders from

		£	US$	CAN$
Amsterdam	1-85828-086-9	£7.99	US$13.95	CAN$16.99
Andalucia	1-85828-094-X	8.99	14.95	18.99
Australia	1-85828-141-5	12.99	19.95	25.99
Bali	1-85828-134-2	8.99	14.95	19.99
Barcelona	1-85828-106-7	8.99	13.95	17.99
Berlin	1-85828-129-6	8.99	14.95	19.99
Brazil	1-85828-102-4	9.99	15.95	19.99
Britain	1-85828-208-X	12.99	19.95	25.99
Brittany & Normandy	1-85828-126-1	8.99	14.95	19.99
Bulgaria	1-85828-183-0	9.99	16.95	22.99
California	1-85828-181-4	10.99	16.95	22.99
Canada	1-85828-130-X	10.99	14.95	19.99
Corsica	1-85828-089-3	8.99	14.95	18.99
Costa Rica	1-85828-136-9	9.99	15.95	21.99
Crete	1-85828-132-6	8.99	14.95	18.99
Cyprus	1-85828-182-2	9.99	16.95	22.99
Czech & Slovak Republics	1-85828-121-0	9.99	16.95	22.99
Egypt	1-85828-075-3	10.99	17.95	21.99
Europe	1-85828-159-8	14.99	19.95	25.99
England	1-85828-160-1	10.99	17.95	23.99
First Time Europe	1-85828-210-1	7.99	9.95	12.99
Florida	1-85828-074-5	8.99	14.95	18.99
France	1-85828-124-5	10.99	16.95	21.99
Germany	1-85828-128-8	11.99	17.95	23.99
Goa	1-85828-156-3	8.99	14.95	19.99
Greece	1-85828-131-8	9.99	16.95	20.99
Greek Islands	1-85828-163-6	8.99	14.95	19.99
Guatemala	1-85828-045-1	9.99	14.95	19.99
Hawaii: Big Island	1-85828-158-X	8.99	12.95	16.99
Hawaii	1-85828-206-3	10.99	16.95	22.99
Holland, Belgium & Luxembourg	1-85828-087-7	9.99	15.95	20.99
Hong Kong	1-85828-066-4	8.99	13.95	17.99
Hungary	1-85828-123-7	8.99	14.95	19.99
India	1-85828-104-0	13.99	22.95	28.99
Ireland	1-85828-179-2	10.99	17.95	23.99
Italy	1-85828-167-9	12.99	19.95	25.99
Kenya	1-85828-043-5	9.99	15.95	20.99
London	1-85828-117-2	8.99	12.95	16.99
Mallorca & Menorca	1-85828-165-2	8.99	14.95	19.99
Malaysia, Singapore & Brunei	1-85828-103-2	9.99	16.95	20.99
Mexico	1-85828-044-3	10.99	16.95	22.99
Morocco	1-85828-040-0	9.99	16.95	21.99
Moscow	1-85828-118-0	8.99	14.95	19.99
Nepal	1-85828-190-3	10.99	17.95	23.99

In the UK, Rough Guides are available from all good bookstores, but can be obtained from Penguin by contacting: Penguin Direct, Penguin Books Ltd, Bath Road, Harmondsworth, West Drayton, Middlesex UB7 0DA; or telephone the credit line on 0181-899 4036 (9am–5pm) and ask for Penguin Direct. Visa, Access and Amex accepted. Delivery will normally be within 14 working days. Penguin Direct ordering facilities are only available in the UK and the USA. The availability and published prices quoted are correct at the time of going to press but are subject to alteration without prior notice.

New York	1-85828-171-7	9.99	15.95	21.99
Pacific Northwest	1-85828-092-3	9.99	14.95	19.99
Paris	1-85828-125-3	7.99	13.95	16.99
Poland	1-85828-168-7	10.99	17.95	23.99
Portugal	1-85828-180-6	9.99	16.95	22.99
Prague	1-85828-122-9	8.99	14.95	19.99
Provence	1-85828-127-X	9.99	16.95	22.99
Pyrenees	1-85828-093-1	8.99	15.95	19.99
Rhodes& the Dodecanese	1-85828-120-2	8.99	14.95	19.99
Romania	1-85828-097-4	9.99	15.95	21.99
San Francisco	1-85828-185-7	8.99	14.95	19.99
Scandinavia	1-85828-039-7	10.99	16.99	21.99
Scotland	1-85828-166-0	9.99	16.95	22.99
Sicily	1-85828-178-4	9.99	16.95	22.99
Singapore	1-85828-135-0	8.99	14.95	19.99
Spain	1-85828-081-8	9.99	16.95	20.99
St Petersburg	1-85828-133-4	8.99	14.95	19.99
Thailand	1-85828-140-7	10.99	17.95	24.99
Tunisia	1-85828-139-3	10.99	17.95	24.99
Turkey	1-85828-088-5	9.99	16.95	20.99
Tuscany & Umbria	1-85828-091-5	8.99	15.95	19.99
USA	1-85828-161-X	14.99	19.95	25.99
Venice	1-85828-170-9	8.99	14.95	19.99
Wales	1-85828-096-6	8.99	14.95	18.99
West Africa	1-85828-101-6	15.99	24.95	34.99
More Women Travel	1-85828-098-2	9.99	14.95	19.99
Zimbabwe & Botswana	1-85828-041-9	10.99	16.95	21.99

Phrasebooks

Czech	1-85828-148-2	3.50	5.00	7.00
French	1-85828-144-X	3.50	5.00	7.00
German	1-85828-146-6	3.50	5.00	7.00
Greek	1-85828-145-8	3.50	5.00	7.00
Italian	1-85828-143-1	3.50	5.00	7.00
Mexican	1-85828-176-8	3.50	5.00	7.00
Portuguese	1-85828-175-X	3.50	5.00	7.00
Polish	1-85828-174-1	3.50	5.00	7.00
Spanish	1-85828-147-4	3.50	5.00	7.00
Thai	1-85828-177-6	3.50	5.00	7.00
Turkish	1-85828-173-3	3.50	5.00	7.00
Vietnamese	1-85828-172-5	3.50	5.00	7.00

Reference

Classical Music	1-85828-113-X	12.99	19.95	25.99
Internet	1-85828-198-9	5.00	8.00	10.00
World Music	1-85828-017-6	16.99	22.95	29.99
Jazz	1-85828-137-7	16.99	24.95	34.99

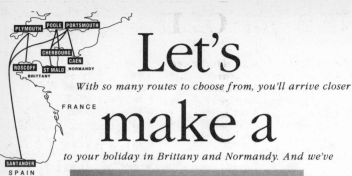

You are
A STUDENT

You travel
THE WORLD

You want
TO SAVE MONEY

Here's
how

The International Student Identity Card

Available at Student Travel Offices Worldwide.

Entitles you to discounts and special services worldwide.